Y0-CAF-637

OUR LIFE IN POETRY

Also by M. L. Rosenthal

POETRY

Blue Boy on Skates

Beyond Power

The View from the Peacock's Tail

She: A Sequence of Poems

Poems 1964–1980

As for Love: Poems and Translations

CRITICISM

A Primer of Ezra Pound

The Modern Poets: A Critical Introduction

The New Poets: American and British Poetry Since World War II

Randall Jarrell

Poetry and the Common Life

Sailing into the Unknown: Yeats, Pound, and Eliot

The Modern Poetic Sequence: The Genius of Modern Poetry
(with Sally M. Gall)

The Poet's Art

EDITIONS

Selected Poems and Three Plays of William Butler Yeats

The William Carlos Williams Reader

The New Modern Poetry: American and British Poetry Since WWII

Poetry in English: An Anthology (general editor)

OUR LIFE IN POETRY

Selected Essays and Reviews

M·L·ROSENTHAL

PERSEA BOOKS

New York

For information, write to the publisher:

Persea Books, Inc.
60 Madison Avenue
New York, New York 10010

Library of Congress Cataloging-in-Publication Data

Rosenthal, M. L. (Macha Louis), 1917–
Our life in poetry : selected essays and reviews / by M. L. Rosenthal.
p. cm.
ISBN 0-89255-149-6
1. American poetry—20th century—History and criticism. 2. English poetry—20th century—History and criticism. 3. Poetry—Book reviews. I. Title.
PS323.5.R62 1990 89-71338

Designed by Vincent Torre
Set in Caledonia by Keystrokes, Lenox, Massachusetts

Printed and bound by Haddon Craftsmen, Scranton, Pennsylvania

FIRST EDITION

❧

Contents

PART I

1944 – 1960

PART II

1961 – 1972

PART III

1973 – 1988

PART IV
PERSONAL CODA 1976 – 1987

Introduction

HERE are selected wanderings, some forty-five years' worth, over the daily streets of our poetry. They begin with a youthful essay on Kenneth Fearing and then, in their wayward progress, map my growing sense of a rich body of work: that of the modern masters and the generations crowding one another in their wake. As they do so, they also reflect the interaction of American, British, and Irish verse, the impact of poetry in other languages (and with it our accelerated passion for translation), and the psychic pressures of our century.

The hospitality of many editors has allowed me space for the essays and reviews that follow. I have been especially lucky in being asked to write about a good number of books as they appeared and about poetic questions generally: first for *Poetry*, the *New York Herald Tribune*, and other publications; then for the *New Republic* and, as poetry editor, for *The Nation;* then for the *New York Times*, the *Reporter, Southern Review*, and, in England, *TLS* and the *Spectator*—to name the best known. Often enough, the review copies that arrived so demurely shut revealed bold new directions, or unexpectedly beautiful qualities, when opened. Ideally a review is an act of recognition, a hazard of accurate response. My longer essays and my books are rooted in the same effort to engage with the life of poems that the reviews present in miniature.

It has seemed best to arrange these selections of greatly varied length, which include two essays originally printed as small books *(A Primer of Ezra Pound* and *Randall Jarrell)*, more or less in order of publication. Thus I can suggest not only the slow progression of my own sensibility but also, and far more to the point, something about the emergence and gradual self-definition of contemporary poetry. The powerful impress of Yeats, Pound, Eliot, Williams, Moore, Stevens, and the other early moderns will be quite evident, marked most clearly perhaps by the essay on Pound just mentioned. It appeared in the same year, 1960, as my *The Modern Poets: A Critical Introduction*. Alongside it, though, rides the evidence of the generations of younger poets already finding their place even while the *Cantos*, and *Paterson*, and *The Auroras of Autumn* were still in the making.

I refer to developments too numerous to recall very quickly. They include the Left poets of Britain associated with Auden and other well-known figures and the parallel American group best represented by Fearing, Muriel Rukeyser, and Horace Gregory; the brilliant Irish cluster of Austin Clarke, Patrick Kavanagh, Thomas Kinsella, and John Montague; Robert Lowell and the American "confessionals"; male and female, whose writing sometimes overlaps with that of Adrienne Rich and other poets of feminist or gay militancy; the Beats; the Black Mountain poets (within whose bosom the subtle, militant African-American poet Amiri Baraka was nurtured); and such diverse English writers as Peter Redgrove, Ted Hughes, Thom Gunn, Charles Tomlinson, and Dannie Abse.

I have noted only a few names, yet enough to summon up the many claims on readers' attention during our century. Accidents of reviewing opportunity, together with constraints of selection, account for the inevitable "omissions" in this volume. I have also spared the reader certain apprentice and journeyman pieces, some of which I still cherish beyond redemption. But surely the works discussed herein do embody much that is centrally indicative. And in my *The New Poets: American and British Poetry since World War II* (1967), as well as in *The Modern Poetic Sequence: The Genius of Modern Poetry* (1983—written in collaboration with Sally M. Gall), the work of the poets I have named and of their peers is explored at length.

My basic critical approach, spelled out most fully in *The Poet's Art* (1987), has been simply to try to grasp what I see and hear in a poem, just by opening myself up to it as best I can. I can say this rather more confidently than I can describe the influence on this process of my own poetry, prose writings, teaching, or editing. More and more I have thought about the shaping energy that makes for memorable poems: what we may call the dynamics of their lyrical structure. This has to do with the shifting states of feeling and awareness, and their degrees of intensity, within a poem's movement. These are subjective states; yet they do not just mirror the poet's private feelings while writing, much less a reader's while reading. Rather, they reside as a sort of independent float of sensibility in the poem's literal phrasing: its tonal resonances as it unfolds within its rhythmic ordering and the tensions it must cope with.

So much current "literary theory" is psycho-socio-linguistic philosophizing, of a sort that can well be provocative and original but is only tangentially related to literary quality, that I'm compelled to insist on the obvious: namely, that works of art remain the chief source of revelation about themselves. As for poems, their lyrical structure is the basic key to what goes on in them and therefore to relevant poetic theory—which may of course concern itself with every possible connection between the life of poems and the rest of reality. Interested readers will find specific illustrations in the pieces that follow, most explicitly in the most recent ones. Several foreshadow *The Modern Poetic Sequence*, a book centered on the form that has, by and large, displaced traditional long poems as our characteristic way of creating extended works of maximum emotive charge and epic import. I do not think my collaborator and I could have recognized the full triumph of this still evolving form, or the dominant presence of the many sequences defining the modern poetic landscape, without the critical method derived from the way poems actually form themselves: a method defined in full and applied in great detail throughout our study. The concept of lyrical structure reflects a shaping process at once impersonal, saturated with private emotion, and expressive of human memory and awareness in action.

I have included pieces on a few writers—for instance, my beloved Dilys Laing and Ramon Guthrie (two poets of passion, wit, and distinction who had no betters in what they did best)—who are too little known or in danger of being forgotten. More than one book might be written about fine poets neglected in this age of swift dismissal and remaindering, and about the ruinous notion that a book not noticed at once has lost the right even to be read, let alone reviewed. Poets once were able to dream that "some day" they would be discovered by readers perhaps yet unborn. They still do, naturally, but the odds seem unfavorable now that old-fashioned book-stalls and used-book shops have all but disappeared.

But . . . enough of that familiar litany of writers' sorrows. To return to the pieces in the present selection, they are so much a part of my own changing experience that all I can say of them is that they speak of "our life in poetry" as I have felt it. Criticism, like poetry, is a rigorous discipline with a human heart and face. Many of the poets whose art I have discussed without knowing them became friends with the passage of time. Others, although we never did meet, nevertheless became people with whom I've been in intimate communion, happy or unhappy. At any rate, some thoughts about the personal side of literary life crop up in a few of the essays, particularly in the five placed at the end in the section (Part IV) called "Personal Coda," all written between 1976 and 1987. At the most serious level, there must always be a tension between severely impersonal standards of art and criticism on the one hand and, on the other, the driving inward preoccupations of the private psyche—which perforce include the pressures of every kind of social and moral circumstance. These worlds of value, so often in conflict, do fuse together in the riskiest poetic and intellectual enterprises. In my prose-ponderings on such dangerous, self-transforming adventures of the spirit, I have ventured furthest in the essay called "The 'Actaeon-Principle': Political Aesthetic of Joyce and the Poets."

Preparing a collection of this sort, ranging from brief, rapid reviews of impressive new work to longer critical and personal essays, means confronting one's former selves in a curious, almost helpless way. One wants, as a clever Greek put it long ago, just one more sentence to set everything straight. And needless to say, I don't always approve of what I once wrote. But the only changes, alas, that I've allowed myself—apart from a few silent corrections of inaccurate quotations and facts, of sentences originally garbled by newspaper and magazine typesetters or copy-editors, and of phrasings that now seem incomprehensible—are typographical ones. So be it.

I am grateful to James Laughlin of New Directions for permission to reprint my essays "Muriel Rukeyser: The Longer Poems" and "William Carlos Williams: More Than Meets the Eye," and to the University of Minnesota Press for permission to reprint my little book called *Randall Jarrell*. The original publication and date are given after each of the following pieces. (A list of books reviewed or otherwise discussed appears on pages 569–572).

Suffern, New York
December 1990

PART I

1944–1960

❧

from *The Meaning of Kenneth Fearing's Poetry*

KENNETH Fearing's first published volumes, *Angel Arms* and *Poems,* were products of the between-wars Marxist literary movement. Although this movement sought primarily to inspire revolutionary feeling and to create a literature of sharply critical realism, it could hardly avoid the thousand experimental and symbolistic influences of the times. In such a context, especially if we keep in mind the swift rise of pure negativism after the Great War, the lines between indignant satire and disintegrating irony are not easy to define. Fearing's work lies precisely within the overlapping area of these two types of bitter and sophisticated criticism, not only in its formal aspects (here only incidentally considered) but even in its very subject matter. . . . The poet sketched in *Angel Arms* a dozen or so big-city types, described by Edward Dahlberg as "an elliptical recollection of the laughing gas of rodents in a dismembered dream." This term, "rodents," is compelled by Fearing's own fixation with the rodent image, a fixation which, at first only suggested by his presentation of thwarted lives, asserts itself a decade later in the semidramatic poem "Payday in the Morgue." Here the main speaker is playing poker desperately with his co-workers in the morgue who are at the same time strangers to him. The outside world, menacingly alive, challenges him by knocks on the door, by cries, by telephone-rings, and by the sounds of music. Afraid to answer the challenge or to turn his back on his competitors (although everything is after all lost already), he remarks finally:

> I'd answer the door, but you know how it is. A fellow with a family.
> Sure.
> It's either them or us, see what I mean?
> Or you could put it like this, either them or some one else.
> Either millions of men with feet like lizards and the heads of rats, or
>   gods made of music bathed in blinding light.

. . . .

The poems of *Angel Arms,* however, are not as irreconcilably pessimistic as the later poems. There is a remote pity, a kind of reverse tenderness, in the early portraits. . . . An example of this not altogether unkind irony is the portrait of Minnie Spohr, the scornful washerwoman, who

> . . . could hide her head in rags and die laughing on the street.
> She could snicker in the broom closet. In the dark of the movies. In bed.

Die, at the way some people talk.
The things they talk about and believe and do.

Minnie finds everything ridiculous: love, philosophy, social protest, idealism of any sort. In a perverted way she represents the poet's own attitude toward the false front of a corrupt society, with its illusions of romantic love, education, and freedom. Her rejection of all ideas, therefore, is identical with Fearing's irony, if only for *ideas* we read *illusions*. But this sympathy of ironists is for the most part suppressed in *Angel Arms*. Most of the portraits are simpler in their implications: gangsters shooting it out with police on St. Agnes' Eve, young men aimlessly and silently walking the streets, and picture after picture of emptiness or false culture or ignorant effrontery. Violent and naive rejection is the theme and substance.

Inconspicuous foreshadowings of the later Fearing, however, are the poems "Green Light" and "Nocturne." The technique of "Green Light" is one of indirection, manifested even in the title. The poet employs predicate sentences, in which the subject is omitted, to achieve this indirection. Thus we have, in the opening lines, a series of half-images:

Bought at the drug store, very cheap; and later pawned.
After a while, heard on the street; seen in the park.
Familiar, but not quite recognized.
Followed and taken home and slept with.
Traded or sold. Or lost.

To what subject do these predicates belong? Certainly the images are of the commercial world—yet they refer also to love and memory. Later, other images, absurd or fantastic or commonplace, are added: the predicates of human existence. The poet makes the point that all the impressions of daily life and of fantasy, inseparable from the self-centered and brooding mind, are "strange, and yet not extraordinary." A tragic pointlessness of truth is suggested, simultaneously defining the universe as zero and raising the pettiest details (for example, the green light on a busy corner) to a level of universal significance. If truth is pointless, then so are the facts of experience, wisdom, morality, love, and death. Those who attach importance to them are posturing without purpose, for they are facts

Bought at the drug store down the street
Where the wind blows, and the motors go by and it is always night, or day;
Bought to use as a last resort,
Bought to impress the statuary in the park.

Are these not, under the protective veiling, Minnie Spohr's views on life? One may suggest that the obscuring of the theme is evidence at once that the poet did not wish to recognize his own pessimism and that his only object was to catch the essence of a mood he could hardly define. Yet he certainly felt, in composing "Green Light," that its harsh view of reality was in a sense irrefutable.

The poem "Nocturne" has similar protective coloring. A fantasy of the city at night at first hides the poet's bafflement. The design, again, is to throw the reader off the track of the poet's personality while imagination and reality are painfully contrasted:

> In the blue, ether night,
> Buildings rise in marble streams that do not end.
> Night does not end.
>
> . . . .
>
> On the floor of night there is no time.
> Men cough and walk away.

To what end this contrast? It can only be to show the inadequacy of men, the impossibility of dream-fulfillment. But these ideas conflict with the themes of revolutionary struggle and of the conquest of matter by man's courage and understanding in Fearing's second volume, *Poems*. Consequently, they are permitted as yet to appear only at unguarded moments. Disillusionment, however, cannot flower without the soil of great hopes. In *Poems*, Fearing provides himself with that soil, in which the seeds of disillusionment can be planted.

The new volume, with its unambiguous, although complex, revolutionary irony, is a remarkable development from the highly personalized *Angel Arms*. Containing only one portrait, it examines life as a whole. The portrait "Dirge" paints a typical American defeat in the jargon of slick magazine and glamorous movie, combined with the language of a dream world of traditional individualism and the unanswerable symbols of economic reality:

> Denouement to denouement, he took a personal pride in the certain, certain way he lived his own, private life,
> But nevertheless, they shut off his gas; nevertheless, the bank foreclosed; nevertheless, the landlord called; nevertheless, the radio broke . . .

The confused, bedeviled "hero" is buried finally, and for the burial scene the tough and callous slang of big-city competitiveness is used:

> With who the hell are you are the corner of his casket, and where the hell're we going on the right-hand silver knob, and who the hell cares walking second from the end with an American Beauty wreath from why the hell not. . . .

Such passages, striking at the economic facts juxtaposed against our culture and institutions, are obviously Marxist in tone. In fact, Fearing is much more concerned in *Poems* with a view of capitalist society as a whole—its mythology, which he treats as shallow and hypocritical, as well as its whole complex of violent competition and mass misery—than with minor political and economic questions, or with isolated moods or characterizations. In " Obituary," for example, he expands upon the "service" slogan of big business—its attitude of concern for the needs of the people. On a busy street, a pedestrian is killed by a ten-ton truck. A policeman takes over: the symbol of official solicitude. He, remarks the poet, is the corpse's "true-blue pal," and so, by extension, are Standard Oil, Will Hays, and a number of other representatives of our economy and culture. The poet suggests that the policeman prove his deep if belated friendship by picking up the corpse, feeding it, and giving it another job. It now becomes clear that the truck and the corpse are symbols of the American scene during the depression years. Conclusion: the only *really* true-blue pal of the dead man is the driver, just because he has brought an end to his victim's thwarted life. . . .

In Fearing, however, his conviction that reality can and must be changed is seldom intimately fused with his stronger conviction of the horror and doom implicit in present reality. It requires an effort for him to assert the force of man's will, an effort sustained only in the one volume *Poems*. Even here, he feels on safer ground, no doubt, in a poem such as "No Credit," in which he asserts that

> Only Steve, the side-show robot, knows content; only Steve, the mechanical man in love with a photo-electric beam, remains aloof; only Steve, who sits and smokes or stands in salute, is secure. . . .

We have mentioned this preoccupation, which eventually sets Fearing apart from the Marxists, with the defeat of the individual. For the time being, it has been subordinated to the broader social criticism and to the vision of a beautiful and romantic future for mankind. But it is still the theme of the early "Green Light," stubbornly persisting despite the poet's revolutionary mood of struggle and change.

Another fixed, if temporarily subordinated, idea is that of a whole people corrupted. The bitterest of Fearing's depression poems," 1933," flays a hypocritical culture manifested in noble gestures, pronouncements and ceremonies, all proclaiming peace and liberty, "repealing" hunger, restoring life to the dead and chastity to the fallen, and rejuvenating a crumbling society. And the poet describes a new, hardened generation:

> The child was nursed on government bonds. Cut its teeth on a hand grenade. Grew fat on shrapnel. Bullets. Barbed wire. Chlorine gas. Laughed at the bayonet through its heart.

This is an indictment of a *system*, to be expected in such a work. But very quietly, at the last, as a sort of afterbeat, Fearing indicts every single one of *us* as well:

> These are the things you saw and heard, these are the things you did, this is your record,
> You.

. . . .

Fearing's third volume, *Dead Reckoning*, shifts from revolutionary irony to one more philosophical and, from a technical standpoint, more polished because more consistent. A painful sense of lost time, of nightmarish crisis and climax, now possesses the poet, whether he is in an introspective mood or is paying satiric attention to the international scene (1935–1938) with its endless stream of old and useless answers to new and burning questions. Here is the essence of Fearing's change. There is no "last word," says Fearing now; there is no specific solution. There are greed, illusion, betrayal, false individualism; and these provide us with answers (all implicit in appeasement) hackneyed and hypocritical, or petty and oversimplified, or impossible and dream-ridden. And we have a series of "pure poems," each dominated by an image of frustration and uncompensated for by any appeal to the will.

Chief among these are four poems: "Memo," "Flophouse," "Requiem," and "Radio Blues." Contrast the conclusion of "Denouement"—with its strong, almost mystic appeal to the idea of continued personality—with the desperate question of "Memo":

> Is there still any shadow there, on the rainwet window of the coffee pot,
> Between the haberdasher's and the pinball arcade,
> There, where we stood one night in the warm, fine rain, and smoked
>   and laughed and talked?

"There has to be," says Fearing, some tangible sign of the reality of shared experience remaining: "no heart could beat if this were not so." Yet his point is that it is *not* so. And this is the point, too, of "Flophouse," with its unconcluded final stanzas:

> Out of so much fantastic knowledge,
> Surgeon, engineer, or clerk,
> From the rags and scraps of dismembered life;
>
> And if now there is nothing, nothing, nothing,
> From even the fatigue sealed deep in the bones,
> From even the chill in the oldest wound.

Again we recall the early "Green Light," whose half-assertion—prelude to a full denial of defeat—now grows into a plaintive question, an all-but-admission. Significant is the return to the incomplete sentence, again to veil a painful conclusion. "Memo" raises a question, but refuses to answer, while "Flophouse" contents itself with a conditional clause: if reality is what it seems to be . . . well, we must draw our own conclusions—the conclusions of the defeated, which lead directly to an intensified preoccupation with death. Of course, death is no new theme to Fearing; even at his most optimistic, he concerns himself over and over with death. In *Angel Arms*, for instance, the poem "Jake" really makes the same point as "Requiem" in *Dead Reckoning:* in both, two men meet, casually discussing the death of a common friend:

> Each feeling, if it were I, instead, would that be all.
> Each wondering, suddenly alone, if that is all, in fact . . .

But in *Dead Reckoning* the tone of desperate resignation illustrated in these lines from "Requiem" is not subordinated any longer, and so the ideas of defeat and death loom much larger than they have done before.

This newly-emphasized tone can be caught most clearly in "Radio Blues," in which Fearing and the reader tinker with a fantastic radio, trying to get "just what you want." At first there are just the usual annoyances, mixed with advertisements and snatches of program. Not satisfied, "you" keep turning the dial to higher and higher numbers, beyond the friendly, purposeful, loving, or bellicose voices to impossible points where you get "the year before last," "the decade after this, with the final results of the final madness and the final killing," "your dead love's grave," and finally—inevitably—"your very own life, gone somewhere far away." For Fearing, the symbols of our civilization lead no longer to anger and action, but to self-tormenting search for some guarantee of permanence and happiness.

Dead Reckoning, then, represents a perfecting of pessimistic irony. We no longer find titles like "Resurrection" or "Denouement," hidden among the "Blues" poems and satiric pieces. Poems which demand new answers while asserting their impossibility, despairing time-poems, and poems which describe a gathering doom of war and fascist victories—all these combine into a wail of complaint which releases the suppressed fear of life of which hitherto we have caught mere glimpses. It is the violence of that life especially, compelling a choice between extinction and brutal triumph, which produces such expressions of absolute hopelessness as "En Route" and "Lunch With the Sole Survivor." No longer concerned with the fusion of satire, idealism, and savage anger, Fearing has returned to the mood apparently most natural to him. . . .

Poetry (July 1944)

Speaking Greatly in an Age of Confusion

THE AGE OF ANXIETY by W. H. Auden

THIS is the first poem, in English at any rate, that speaks boldly, greatly and at length of our sick, desperate confusion in this era of the second world war. It will give sharp reminder to our numerous talented minor poets that there can be strength and responsibility in their art:

All that exists
Matters to man; he minds what happens
And feels he is at fault, a fallen soul
With power to place, to explain every
What in his world but why he is neither
God nor good. . . .

The vigor, even the quality, of the ideas in *The Age of Anxiety* must obviously be tested by their influence on its readers, many of whom will doubtless find Auden's diagnosis, with all its pessimism, infinitely superior to his suggested cure. But no one who takes up this emotionally stunning work is likely to concern himself immediately with whether or not he agrees with the author. Rather, his attention will be absorbed by the various centers of concentration along which the "plot" is strung, each of them one aspect of a continuous, straining effort to get at the heart of the human condition and trace the lines of possible (or impossible) salvation. He will be carried along, too, by the muscular alliterative sweep of the lines, subtly and marvelously varied from the simple basic pattern to fit a number of modes, from sweet lyric to intellectualized argument, from sharp satire to poignant introspection.

Auden calls his poem "a baroque eclogue," because, says the jacket, it adopts the "pastoral convention in which a natural setting is contrasted with an artificial style of diction." (But I fear there is a sad pun in that "baroque," considering the setting of most of the poem!) On All Souls' Night, in a war year, four people—an elderly intellectual, a cynical old failure, who knows a great deal of mythology, an idealistic young sailor who lacks self-confidence, and a day-dreaming Jewish girl whose "experiences" and success as a department store buyer cannot rid her of her feelings of guilt and shame—find themselves in a Third Avenue bar. War news on the radio throws their thoughts in the same channels, and soon they are discussing the terrible moral ambiguities of the war.

From this point on, in three allegorical sequences, the poem explores every man's guilt, in terms of the "seven ages" of Shakespeare and the personal lives of the characters; takes us on a journey in search of that impossible "prehistoric happiness which, by human beings, can only be imagined in terms of a landscape bearing symbolic resemblance to the human body"; and dismisses the great romantic-love-dream as a way out of the trap which man, with helpless yet evil foreknowledge, sets for himself. The world is too much, in different ways, for the youth and the old cynic; but the girl and the intellectual, in burning assertions of their separate faiths, accept suffering and the grim task of reconciling "the clock we are bound to obey. And the miracle we must not despair of."

This poem is so rich, has so many facets, that no brief review can be just to its meaning or technique. It appears, at first reading, to be one of the splendid poems of our language: it convinces, it moves, it dazzles. It is hardly time to quibble with this work, and I doubt that it will ever be. One does not quibble with *The Waste Land*, whatever one's ideas, and this is another such case.

New York Herald Tribune Weekly Book Review (20 July 1947)

A Bearer of Terrible Tidings

SELECTED POEMS by Bertolt Brecht
Translation and introduction by H. R. Hays

AT times Bertolt Brecht's poems sound like the thoughts of the hero of *The Seventh Cross*. Escaping from a Nazi concentration camp with all the forces of the state hot after him, and taking for granted a set of values which are pure poison to the society in which he finds himself, that character is struck by the surface calm which seems to prevail in the world at large—the women with their babies, the workers going to their appointed jobs, everything going on just as if it were not happening in the midst of the Inferno. Just so does Brecht often concentrate a world of bitterness in a few amazed lines:

Ah, what an age it is
When to speak of trees is almost a crime.
For it is a kind of silence about injustice!
And he who walks calmly across the street,
Is he not out of reach of his friends
In trouble?

"He who laughs," writes the poet significantly, "has not yet heard the terrible tidings"—namely, that we live in the dark ages indeed. It is important for Americans to remember that Bertolt Brecht, a vital name in the modern theater, stands for a kind of revolutionary, secular idealism which has caught the imagination of millions. His verse is usually immediate and thoroughly committed to the projection, in simple, dramatic images and rhythmic forms, of this point of view. But the control is a sophisticated one and the satire bites. In the early 1920s he apparently drank deeply of the self-irony, symbolism, and later-naturalism of French literature, making himself at home with the use of shock, of brutal and even morbid detail, and of strongly colloquial idioms. Meanwhile, he identified himself with the movement toward a "proletarian" art, concentrating mainly on basic popular-ballad forms and a flexible free-verse technique. The present volume represents his development over almost a quarter of a century and contains poems from his first book (1927), from such theatrical successes as *Die Dreigroschenoper,* and from his writings since the rise of Hitler.

The very first poem, "Concerning Poor B. B." sets the tone; it is a harsh and pessimistic self-portrait, a little in the manner of Corbière. Then come a number of death poems, the most poignant of which—"Ballad of the Soldier" and "Concerning a Drowned Girl"—have the hopeless anger of Job's outcries to the infinite. Others reveal a rather advanced revolutionary outlook, even in Brecht's earlier period. The songs from theatrical productions will seem rather strange to ears accustomed to the Broadway review. The satire, very serious in its purpose, reaches into unwonted regions of sex and social criticism, and the poetry, as such, is purer (the language and rhythmical effects are more exact and exacting) than that of even our best written stage lyrics. In the final part of the book the language is still more blunt and basic: "A Worker Reads History," "United Front Song," "Thoughts Concerning the Duration of Exile." There are pathetic ballads, hard-bitten jokes, and bits of poetic folk-wisdom. The translation, though uneven, is always clear and often effective. Fortunately, the original German is printed on the opposite page and it is not difficult to catch the tone of these poems. The bleak simplicity creates a special problem, that of not translating a just-caught ironic understatement into a banal and obvious propagandistic phrase.

New York Herald Tribune Weekly Book Review (9 February 1948)

Speak the Whole Mind

OTHER SKIES by John Ciardi
THE KID by Conrad Aiken
THE BEAUTIFUL CHANGES by Richard Wilbur

AT thirty, John Ciardi believes that "to speak the whole mind out is elegy." He is of that generation which, vaguely prepared emotionally and hardly at all intellectually, one fine day found itself mortally involved with catastrophe. The first part of *Other Skies* contains pre-war scenes and moods—a beach scene, a school convocation, a movie whose sound-track jumps—all suggesting an off-center world only dimly responsive to inner necessities. The poet's range of consciousness expands as the war involves him more and more; finally, in "Soldier's Girl," it becomes clear that he is more than just a bright boy using irony as amulet against emotion. Though most of his war-pieces (as combat-flier in Saipan) stress discipline, mechanization, and imminent death, Ciardi's experience deepened his lyric feeling, giving it the tragic quality to be seen, for instance, in "Sea-Burial," a poem which employs the compressed memories of significant feeling in a way far superior to the earlier, slightly satiric "Song." The final section broods over the war's meaning to him; in a series of fine "statements," he reviews the deaths, the illusion of personal efficiency, the fate of man "whose wandering mission is to die," almost for the first time properly subordinating his metrical versatility to the total effect. This is worth much, yet somehow the farther-flung implications of the war have not touched Ciardi as they have others, and he drifts at times toward an easy negativism that is slick death to the poet.

Mr. Aiken, who makes music wherever he goes, does so in *The Kid* mainly to the tune of richly varied tetrameter couplets. They race through delicate catalogues of the American landscape, with its flora, fauna and local associations. They leap through mythical fireworks compounded of native pioneering and individualistic motifs, especially as represented by the contrasting yet mutually attractive figures of the early settler William Blackstone (who preceded the "Lords Brethren" and "Lords Bishops" to Boston but could not bear to remain in the community they established there, and the fascination of whose mystic, intellectual, somewhat ambiguous figure is already familiar to readers of Mr. Aiken's friend Malcolm Lowry) and the later folk-hero Billy the Kid, who gives the poet his opportunity to fuse ballad rhythms and tall-tale themes and characters with the grave lyric introspection which carries the basic theme. And they grow dark and slow when, like T. S. Eliot, he wishes us to consider the relation between death and horror on the one hand and rebirth and new horizons on the other. Meanwhile, in his gentle, subtle fashion, he is having his say on a number of subjects, including the nature of freedom, the dilemmas of conscience it involves, and the interwoven symbolism of our historical, literary, and popular traditions.

"The beautiful," writes Richard Wilbur in his title poem, "changes as a forest is changed / By a chameleon's tuning his skin to it; / As a mantis, arranged / On a green leaf, grows / Into it, makes the leaf leafier, and proves / Any greenness is deeper than any one knows." This is to be Marianne Moore's "literalist of the imagination," and also to be "influenced" without being overwhelmed by the master. Richard Wilbur learns from many, but in the manner of the true original who seeks to master all techniques which will help him say just what he wants to on any level. The art of deliberately juxtaposing images of diverse connotation and clashing rhythms has been carefully studied. It can be used subtly, as in the poem that develops the theme that war "hits childhood more than churches"; or in the one that describes with Imagist precision the first snow of an Alsace winter, yet finds time to note how "this snowfall fills the eyes / Of soldiers dead a little while." It can turn a simple impression of evening in the Place Pigalle, where "the soldiers come, the boys with ancient faces, / Seeking their ancient friends," into one of those romantic outbursts of Pound's which loose a flood of light on past and present. In short, Wilbur is one of those rare poets who not only can think in verse but who are also a pure joy to read. The promise is part of the pleasure, and he should soon strike out on new and independent paths.

New York Herald Tribune Weekly Book Review, (21 March 1948)

❧

Two Modern Poets on Their Art

THREE ACADEMIC PIECES by Wallace Stevens
THE POETIC IMAGE by Cecil Day Lewis

THAT poetry, technically speaking, is essentially compressed and patterned metaphor is the practicing definition of most modern poets of stature. Of course, the phrase "patterned metaphor" contains whole labyrinths of implication which many critics have explored and will explore ever more deeply. But it is always helpful to learn what poets themselves say on their art, particularly when, like both Wallace Stevens and Cecil Day Lewis, they refuse to lose themselves in the labyrinths, but try honestly to keep sight of the relation between what they do and what goes on in the rest of the world of life and thought.

Stevens's little book contains a prose essay ("The Realm of Resemblance") and two poems, all on the subject of metaphor. Poetry, says the essay, has reality as its central reference, for the resemblance between things is one of the "significant components of the structure of reality." In the imagination, as in nature, fortuitous relationships are created by such qualities and concepts as color, sex, time; they bind parts of reality together, suggesting an underlying unity. Stevens has been called hedonist, pluralist and Platonist, and this essay curiously justifies all three labels, especially the last. The points he so beautifully makes about the difference between resemblance and imitation, the poet as pleasure giver and as revealer or transformer of reality, and the true value of ambiguity are basically Platonic; so too are the consideration of what narcissism really is (the ego's search for resemblance in the outside world) and, by way of this consideration, of the relation between metaphor and the ideal.

The first of the two poems that follow is an exact poetic equivalent of the essay. Stevens had suggested a close relation between euphuism and the "school of metaphor." The poem, a long one entitled "Someone Puts a Pineapple Together," does, by its ingenuity and profusion, its attempt to show the total sum of meanings and impressions of a simple object, exemplify this kinship with an overflow of wit that surpasses Cyrano's moon speech. But neither here nor in the next poem, "Of Ideal Time and the Choice," is Stevens content merely to produce an infinite series of imagistic and intellectual variations on a single theme. He explains, in the "Pineapple" poem, that the multiple meanings seen by the imagination, the tangents of himself, are used to "protect him in a privacy," but that nevertheless the "incredible subjects of poetry" have their special function; "the incredible," as he puts is, "gave him a purpose to believe." This idea, together with the concern for resemblance, becomes in the third poem a program for idealists who would free themselves from the limitations of ordinary life:

The orator will say that we ourselves
Stand at the centre of ideal time,
The inhuman making choice of a human self.

While C. Day Lewis's *The Poetic Image* is not a work of art—at least not in the rare sense that *Three Academic Pieces* is—its main theme is strikingly similar: there are even some philosophical ramifications shared by both books. For the alert beginner in poetic criticism, however, Mr. Lewis's clear, charming prose exposition has its advantages. For one thing, he is so very leisurely as he goes about defining the image ("the human mind claiming kinship with everything that lives or has lived, and making good its claims"), its changing uses through the centuries, its dominant qualities of freshness, intenseness, and evocativeness since the early Romantics and its relation to the form of a poem as a whole and to the problem of public indifference to what the poet is doing. For another, Mr. Lewis, though he drops several depth bombs, does not pretend to add any new formulations or revelations to the body of critical theory. Rather, he recapitulates the major points of which all good critics are aware (for instance, in his discussion of the fact that most modern verse is limited to a "semi-lyrical, semi-contemplative medium") and sharply reminds us that a poem is more than a special type of "double acrostic" for the specialist in exegesis—something that poets at times need reminding of. The book employs countless illustrations from English, American and Continental verse and criticism, all brought in with a pleasantly spontaneous air and all highly enlightening. Poets, when they want to, turn out the best critical prose available; and Mr. Lewis, whether describing problems of craftsmanship, or shrewdly expatiating on hints and lines from Coleridge or Auden or, it may be, Christina Rossetti, or discussing the relation of the poem as "total image" to the subconscious and to general truth, does not fail the tradition. *The Poetic Image* seems to me the best review of its subject for the interested "amateur," and perhaps for the hyper-professional "expert," too.

New York Herald Tribune Weekly Book Review, (9 May 1948)

Poetry in Pity

LOSSES by Randall Jarrell

RANDALL Jarrell's *Losses* reminds us of Wilfred Owen's war poetry, and of Owen's belief that poetic meaning was not to be found in the glorifying of war. "The Poetry," Owen wrote, "is in the Pity."

It is the Pity which preoccupies Jarrell, too. Viewed critically, of course, the formulation is a doubtful one. It blurs the edges of distinction and comes close to sentimentality, as Jarrell's poems often do. A pitying statement may or may not be a poem. Sensibility is always close to sentimentality anyway, and that is Jarrell's real subject—his implied sensibility, his fine sympathy, particularly with children. In the third of the "Variations" in *Blood for a Stranger* (an earlier volume), Jarrell gets very near to the heart of suffering innocence. In this volume, too, there are poems like "In the Camp There Was One Alive" and "The Rising Sun," in which the Pity is one element of an immense understanding of how that innocence can be betrayed unbearably, not only by individual men but even by blind patterns of social behavior and objective nature.

At other times, as in "Lady Bates," it is hard to tell. Is the "poor little nigger girl" of this poem a reality at all, in any valuable sense, or is she a special kind of self-indulgence? Sentimentality is not limited to certain standardized modes. It may be that the nagging pathos that rides the bleakness of so much modern poetry is merely an unorthodox version of it, camouflaged by potent images and a philosophical tone:

> Poor black trash.
> The wind has blown you away forever
> By mistake; and they sent the wind to the chain-gang
> And it worked in the governor's kitchen, a trusty for life;
> And it was all written in the Book of Life . . .

And the same thing seems to happen in "Jews at Haifa" and "The Place of Death" and other poems in which, with all due respect to the victims of persecution or war or "life" theoretically under consideration, we spend our major attention on the poet's delicacy and tact and profundity of feeling. Sometimes the confusion between statement, feeling, and what would make for a poem as a whole seems, always surprisingly, to cause the poet to lose perspective and produce something that is as flat, almost banal, as "Money."

Because he is so often brilliant, one feels free to raise these problems—which are really general problems in contemporary verse—in connection with Jarrell's verse. Among others, "A Country Life" shows just how effective he can be with a simple theme and form; how subtly he can interweave subtlety and simplicity; how he can modify the basic movement of his poems and keep the imagery and sound perfectly under control. In a way Jarrell represents, in such poems, an ideal toward which many younger poets are striving. It is for this reason that we cannot help asking whether a New Sentimentality is not arising, even more deadly than that of the nineteenth century because clad in the technical efficiency which is our dazzling legacy from Pound and Eliot.

New York Herald Tribune Weekly Book Review, (28 November 1948)

from *Cloud-Sitwell-Land*

THE CANTICLE OF THE ROSE by Edith Sitwell

IN the preface to her collected poems *(The Canticle of the Rose)*, Edith Sitwell explains one of her images thus:

> The reason I said "The morning light creaks" is this: After rain, the early light seems as if it does not run quite smoothly. Also, it has a quality of great hardness, seems to present a physical obstacle to the shadows—and this gives one the impression of a creaking sound because it is at once hard and uncertain.

Should we quarrel with the demand here made upon our power of sympathetic association? The question carries us to the heart of one of the more interesting problems suggested by Miss Sitwell's admittedly brilliant verse. The poem in question, the early "Aubade," is in one sense merely an exercise in the counterbalancing of two worlds: that of the dead-literal mind and that of the infinitely suggestible imagination. So much is clear in the poem, though the specific train of evocation by which the poet claims to arrive at her image of creaking light is not. The reader may indeed be sympathetic, yet the arbitrariness remains, suggesting a certain detachment from the ordinary, "committed," human frame of reference. The poem, in fact, is addressed rather mockingly, in nursery singsong, to a dull serving girl whose universe is limited by "eternities of kitchen garden." It taunts her with lacking the finer sensibilities. But the form and imagery combine to make this cruelty seem merely incidental, like the cruelty in Alice's wonderland.

Miss Sitwell's own wonderland, ever since she became the grand pioneer—during and after World War I—in the movement to free English verse of its staleness, has been made up of "thick assonances" and "distorted dissonances" and "disembodied sounds" and "lines that rock up and down"—all phrases she has used to denote specific, consciously achieved effects—and of such "facts" as that "thin grass trembling in the wind" resembles "a high whining or whinnying sound." In 1929, her "Gold Coast Customs" showed, as later "The Song of the Cold" and other pieces were to do, the extent to which virtuosity had concealed the typical Western-élite personality at the center of the wonderland. It is a personality, familiar in Pound and Eliot—at times playing the Baudelairean dandy, eager to shock the bourgeoisie and snub the Jew but shudderingly sensitive; at other times gravely moral as it chides mankind for making wars, forgetting Jesus and embracing "cold" science.

Wonderful lines and images and echoes of literary and religious touchstones go into Miss Sitwell's rediscoveries of the Waste Land and her counter-assertions of the "glory of Life." One almost forgets that in "Gold Coast Customs" the Negro is a symbolic counter for everything primitively vicious and anti-human in our blood and that the most representative figure in our modern civilization of blood and betrayal is one Lady Bamburgher. An apologetic footnote "takes care" of the one giveaway; the other is conveniently taken for granted. Yet the poem is magnificent, for the truer spokesmen of a culture thrive on its corruption as well as its power. What they reveal, not what they believe, is what wins our allegiance as a poetic audience.

The New Republic (6 March, 1950)

❧

Fifteen in Transit—An Interim Anthology

MID-CENTURY AMERICAN POETS, edited by John Ciardi

JOHN Ciardi's *Mid-Century American Poets* is an honest, useful book, "its simple principle being to gather together poems reasonably representative of the best work of a generation of poets, and to have each poet preface his poems with a guide to the reader's better understanding of his work and its intent." The generation in question, says Ciardi, is not the one just breaking into print but rather the one that "arrived within the last ten to fifteen years."

The poets are Wilbur, Viereck, Rukeyser, Roethke, Shapiro, Scott, Nims, Mayo, Lowell, Jarrell, Holmes, Eberhart, Bishop, Schwartz, and Ciardi himself. Two of them, Lowell and Viereck, are Pulitzer Prize winners; two more, Rukeyser and Shapiro, have a relatively wide reputation. Yet even these four names are hardly household words to educated people now in their thirties and forties. "Modern poetry," for most of these people, is still identified—if at all—with Eliot, Yeats, Pound, Cummings *et al*. One cannot help wondering if a reason, aside from those commonly advanced, for the separation of poet and public may be the simple fact that it's always hard to listen to someone who's being sorry for himself. As Muriel Rukeyser says in her illuminating little essay, "a way must be found to end the self-pity." You get it, indirectly and beautifully, in Richard Wilbur's "The Death of a Toad." You get it, gasping for attention, in Winfield Townley Scott's absorbing poem "The House"; in the shocked realism of John Frederick Nims's "Apocalypse"; in Randall Jarrell's delicately accurate recordings of the child mind; or in Theodore Roethke's "My Papa's Waltz," which, like so much of his work, excites the reader into a kind of neurasthenic sympathy with the central figure's helpless predicament.

Not all these poets indulge in self-centered pathos, and none of them does so all the time; but the poetry of sensibility has tended to take—most naturally—a self-analytic turn which fits in well with the familiar twentieth-century conception of the artist-intellectual as a suffering soul abroad in a mechanistic nightmare-hell.

The prose contributions, if read merely as a series of essays long and short by poets on their art, seem uneven, often repetitious, only occasionally valuable as criticism. But read in the context of the group of poems which it prefaces, each essay takes on its own glow and relevancy. We forget that most of these writers are trying conscientiously to answer Ciardi's careful, exhaustive list of critical questions and are therefore (as most critics must, anyway) simply presenting the same fundamental observations on the importance of sound-effects, the ideal audience, the function of imagery, and so on. The prose bears in each case a relationship to the verse implicit in the very style—as instanced by, say, Wilbur's cool, almost arrogantly elegant common sense, or Elizabeth Bishop's impatience with "pretentious and deadly" analysis. The editor's questionnaire has in most of these prose-pieces served to discipline the poets' thinking about their work and to give them a relatively objective approach with which to correct a natural tendency to rationalize or, to paraphrase Delmore Schwartz, to be too technical or oracularly pretentious or facetious or "too personal."

Just as style is everything in verse (for in the main any age provides a general stock of ideas which any literate person finds it hard to get away from), so it turns out to be nearly everything in a poet's prose, throwing a great deal of light on the essential speaking personality of the writer. In fact the style *is* the speaking personality, "the very age and body" of the poet. When Karl Shapiro refuses to answer the questions but instead gives us a single poem in all its stages of composition, that (and the particular poem chosen) is a clue and a quality of style; and when Schwartz, like Rukeyser and Bishop, changes the proposed subject of his essay in his own way, that is another indication of some importance. Ciardi is right, in general, in describing the tone of these poets as one of "self-conscious sanity" and as "urbane and cultivated." Their poetry, he writes, "is more nearly a blend of the classical and the metaphysical, a poetry of individual appraisal, tentative, self-questioning, introspective, socially involved, and always reserving for itself the right to meet experience in its humanistic environment." However, he has not sufficiently taken into account the fact that this is the prevailing mode of the day, and that the differences within this mode—as within any stereotype—are what make for the individual achievements of the poets. Their essays, seen in conjunction with the verse, show them strongly aware of the need to work through to meaning. Still, their formal conservatism, their refusal to "take chances," is a block of a sort. Perhaps our poets, like their non-readers, fear the very meanings they need to discover.

We spoke of self-pity, to which must be added a sense of purposeless doom, as being implicit in many of these poems. But there are important exceptions, as in Robert Lowell's piston-powerful, tragedy-ridden "The Quaker Graveyard in Nantucket." And more important are the infinite variations—celebrations of the beauty of woman, counter-assertions of joy, satirical light verses, fantasies, self-questionings—which both deepen the recurrent theme and forbid the reader to oversimplify it. There is little of the boldness and verve of some of the important anthologies of two or three decades ago (such as Pound's *Active Anthology*), and no eccentric "experimentation." At the same time there is far more work of real quality here, and the poems cut deep into what it feels like to be alive at this moment. Ciardi speaks for most of these writers when, in one of his finer pieces, he tells us that

I ritualize my interim and survival.
What was to do is done or simply lost;
What is to do arrives. My surf and shore
Meet in a placid marvel giving back
An unacquisitive distance from this night
I issue from myself in years that keep

An album of myself—a skeleton
X-rayed by hope of love—seen year by year
Posed in the changing fashions of its skin
To match at last the medical negative
Anonymous as catacombs of you,
Your unknown twin in the debris of time.

The New Republic (21 July 1950)

❧

E. E. Cummings' XAIPE: seventy-one poems

THE work of E.E. Cummings has other distinctions than his well-known distrust of conventional capitalization and his lust for parentheses and quotation marks that begin but do not end, or end but do not begin. Because of these other distinctions, no one really hates him for the coy prettiness of some of his posturing—as, for instance, when he imagines "a cheerfulest Elephantangelchild" on a cloud

where his heartlike ears have flown adorable him
self tail and all (and his head's red christmas bow)....

For Cummings, we know by now, is as sentimentally *toujours gai* about life and love in general as he is impatient with all forms of authority and stuffiness. We accept the further fact that he forever strives to shock a long-anesthetized bourgeoisie and forever galvanizes himself instead, because the colloquial impudence and emotional freshness of his style help restore our faith in the importance of our own experience.

Moreover, most of us in some degree share Cummings' "naïve" devotion to the clichés of romantic Bohemianism—the love-swoon, and sex-über-alles, and the mystic superiority of the artist, and down-with-the-brass, and boys and girls o so happy in the great big circus. We want it all to be true, and Cummings reassures us by being so purely and delicately aware, through the sheer sensuousness of his perceptions, of how alive we can be and how much there is to respond to. His broken lines and shuffled sentences and exploded words reveal a world charged with excitement, beauty and comedy. When not too facile, the technique is still a convincing kind of rhetoric. It is the old, attractive Cummings who argues, in his closing poem, that if only we are "innocent" enough, the new moon can teach us its "keen illimitable secret of begin":

> (whying diminutive bright deathlessness
> to these my not themselves believing eyes
> adventuring,enormous nowhere from)

and whose sonnet on Chaucer pictures "honour corruption villainy holiness" all "riding in fragrance of sunlight" together in a poet's-gesture toward eternity:

> down while crylessly drifting through vast most
> nothing's own nothing children go of dust

So his plea for innocence is compelling, because he seems open to all meanings and because he makes his images, his sensations and feelings, seem quite new and spontaneous. But Cummings' satirical poetry, though always amusing and at times sharp and poisonous, has never been as finely or seriously motivated as the purer lyric writing. Hatred of war, for instance, has inspired some of his most telling irony; yet his pacifist satire lacks immediacy and depends mainly on a sort of parody of the jingoist, and a caricaturing of the by-products of militarism, for its successes. Cummings can be shallow, as witness the mountains of sophomoric abuse dumped on respectable elderly ladies and gentlemen, timid virgins, and stupid generals. And as the years have gone by, he has included in the lists of his cant-spewing "enemies" more and more categories—liberals, Communists, trade unions, Roosevelt, and so on—so that in addition to the Bohemian and hedonistic contexts he has provided what seems to be a less "innocent" reactionary-political one.

The dilemma into which this fact sometimes pushes a would-be sympathetic reader is interestingly illustrated in a pair of poems written at different times. The first, poem 135 in the collected volume which appeared in 1938, reads as follows:

IKEY (GOLDBERG)'S WORTH I'M
TOLD $ SEVERAL MILLION
FINKLESTEIN (FRITZ) LIVES
AT THE RITZ WEAR
earl & wilson COLLARS

The second, number 46 in the present volume, is almost equally brief:

A kike is the most dangerous
machine as yet invented
by even yankee ingenu
ity (out of a jew a few
dead dollars and some twisted laws)
it comes both prigged and canted

In the earlier piece, the comedy of the jazzy rhythms, the pictorial handling of upper- and lower-case letters, and the tricky presentation of the theme cannot hide from us the hackneyed anti-Semitic formula. Once we realize that Cummings is capable of this kind of thing, his utterances on related subjects naturally become "suspect." Ordinarily we should take for granted, if it is possible, the basic good will of an author. If we do so with the second poem, we may allow ourselves to brush aside the idea that the poem means just what, on a rapid first reading, it seems to mean: that all Jews are dangerous and phony. Instead, we might paraphrase it thus: "Evil-motivated men have taken the concept of the Jew (a factual term) and by adding certain emotional trimmings have turned it into the concept of the 'kike' (a hate-laden word). That is, they have associated the Jew with unproductive wealth and distorted morality and thus produced an imaginary monster." Now this interpretation is pleasanter and it may indeed be what Cummings intended. But we are not *quite* sure, because we are not sure that what he means by good will and what we mean by it are the same. The possibility remains that to him the fourth and fifth lines are obviously saying that what the Jew (a mere synonym for "kike") produces, exclusively, is "a few dead dollars and some twisted laws." Either way, we must be troubled by doubts concerning the poem's initial assumptions.

Whatever the final answer concerning this particular piece, though, it would take a different sort of mind from Cummings' to ridicule the defects of some of the groups he chooses to satirize without falling into Poundian quagmires (as he tends very clearly to do in his poem on FDR). Doubtless they have their complacencies, jargons, silly taboos, and worse, but Cummings is too fond of his eccentricity to take into account the justifiable sensitivity of other people to certain terms and concepts that have become political dynamite. War and Communism have little to fear, actually, from such a writer; but poems like the bit of whimsy beginning "one day a nigger"—with its key-pun on the word "shine"—do make their little contribution to the cause of human unhappiness. Not that Cummings sees it that way or that we hold with the current worldwide fashion of annihilating those we disagree with. After all, he is still our favorite tough sentimentalist and ponderer of love, sex and death. And he is still, in the main, the winning, undependable acrobat of American verse—and only secondarily the sometimes appalling victim of cultural attitudes which have distorted the work of several other brilliant poets of his generation.

The New Republic (18 September 1950)

❧

Horace Gregory: The Catullus Translations

EARLY in Horace Gregory's literary career, we meet him as translator of Catullus and as a "conservator" in the fashion and spirit of Pound and Eliot. For epigraph to his 1931 volume of translations he used a poem of his own, "In Memoriam M. S. S., Obit 1923." M. S. S.—Moses Slaughter of the University of Wisconsin classics faculty—had been a most valued teacher who, because he divided his time between Wisconsin and the University of Rome, had come to symbolize for the poet the sense of both the American and the European past. It was natural that this poem should employ certain devices familiar to readers of *The Waste Land* and *The Cantos*. M. S. S. became, like Tiresias, the selfconscious and symbolic old man associated both with the whole history of culture and with its supposed present sterility. Another technique used was almost a convention by this time—the unexpected juxtapositions of time and place to give the effect of blending all experience into a unified human consciousness. On these devices was superimposed a third, the pure lyric outburst that transcends intellectual considerations and private memories alike:

> Here in this room, built in the core of Rome,
> sparrows are singing against the fall of rain. . . .

These lines are among numerous hints in this book of Gregory's early interest in and identification with D. H. Lawrence. The initial bird-image is pursued throughout the poem, until in the final stanza it has become a miraculous indication of victory over the fear of death:

> Split the skull of death. I enter him
> while sparrows rise from ancient trees
> sprung from the gardens of the late Valerius Catullus—

sparrows sing
out music from the Vergil-mad Aegean seas.

These sparrows are less like those which so delightfully distracted Catullus' lady-love than like that other bird of "Spring Morning" which recalled to Lawrence and his wife the special revelations to which they had won:

Ah, through the open door
Is there an almond tree
Aflame with blossom!
—Let us fight no more.

Among the pink and blue
Of the sky and the almond flowers
A sparrow flutters.
—We have come through.

The reminiscence of Lawrence is one of many suggestions in this book that Gregory was discovering himself as well as attempting to recover Catullus. His preface, which expresses admiration for Pound's work as an adapter of Latin and medieval French poetry, shows how far he had gone toward assimilating the elder poet's spirit and that of Eliot, described in "Tradition and the Individual Talent." Eliot's essay tells us that "the difference between the present and the past is that the conscious present is an awareness of the past in a way and to an extent which the past's awareness of itself cannot show." And Gregory says, "I have attempted to redefine the symbols of Roman life that have become shopworn in Anglo-classical vocabularies or have dropped into complete obscurity." His models will be Pound, whose adaptations are "among the best examples of what may be done in the way of recreating a literature that has been buried under tons of academic research for many centuries," and Synge, who translated Petrarch into the "vernacular of his own speech." The trouble with most classical translation, he holds, is its remoteness from the forms of pre-Augustan Rome, which were "intertwined," in the sixteenth and seventeenth centuries, with "an Anglo-Christian ethic." Perhaps natural enough in those centuries, the mixture of conventions and the kind of vocabulary then employed have become archaic. The original values of the poetry have been completely lost, and new means are needed to approximate "the music of Catullus' Latin metres." But it is virtually impossible to render Latin metres accurately into English; "such an attempt inverts the order of English speech into absurd artificialities." Therefore Gregory's "compromise" will be to use unrhymed verse while approximating "wherever possible" the original versification, "modified by the speech of our own time." The object will be to make Catullus' self-portrait clear and convincing and to reproduce "the epigrammatic vigour and the rapid transition from lyrical beauty to outspoken grossness that every reader has found in the original text and which are often lost in the process of translation." The explanation is convincing enough on its own terms, but it is easy now to see how eager Gregory was to study in the school of Pound and to apply Symbolist-Imagist techniques to so suitable a body of verse as that of Catullus.

How far he actually succeeded in catching the main spirit of the original through his free verse-forms and use of American vernacular is obviously a matter for scholars (good ones, that is) to decide. Literalists will doubtless object to the rendering of *Salax taberna* as "roadhouse" or *cacata carta* as "toilet paper." The Latin poems have their formal regularity, of course; and this fact can be used to justify their translation into some other conventional form. Thus, Charles Stuart Calverley rendered poem XXXI as a sonnet, apparently because it has fourteen lines:

Gem of all isthmuses and isles that lie,
Fresh or salt water's children, in clear lake
Or ampler ocean: with what joy do I
Approach thee, Sirmio!

Gregory's free, concrete handling of this poem may not be as "even," but it results in poetry with a more vital impact, while Calverley's poem is just another sonnet marching grimly to its death. Taking a cue from Tennyson's "Frater Ave Atque Vale," Gregory, with even greater felicity, wrote:

O my little almost island, little island Sirmio,
this brave eye, this green-bright jewel set in Neptune's fair estate
of lucid waters and broad seas.
And it's good to look upon you. . . .

—which is much closer to the buoyancy and sustained emphasis of

Paene insularum, Sirmio, insularamque
ocelle, quascumque in liquentibus stagnis
marique uasto fert uterque Neptunus. . . .

Calverley, however, is not one of the more important English poets, and we may turn with greater reward perhaps to a comparison of Gregory's and Campion's translations of the famous fifth poem, beginning

Vivamus, mea Lesbia, atque amemus,
rumoresque senum seueriorum
omnes unius aestimemus assis.

Campion's first lines, like his whole translation, are gracefully melodic couplets:

My sweetest Lesbia, let us live and love,
And though the saner sort our deeds reprove,
Let us not weigh them. . . .

Gregory's opening is more abrupt, the language of the second line harsher and closer to the specific original meaning:

Come, Lesbia, let us live and love
nor give a damn what sour old men say.

Campion's lines were midway in a tradition running between Marlowe's "Passionate Shepherd" and the Lucasta poems, and as his translation proceeded it became more and more a smoothly and elegantly artificial creation. Gregory, breaking away from that style—he might have made the first line even brusquer, however—begins like Donne, then shifts into a style like Cummings' "who's most afraid of death?" The whole poem is worth quoting, both because it illustrates his general method and because it calls for some comparison with Ben Jonson, who tried in his own way to "modernize" some of these same lines.

Come, Lesbia, let us live and love,
nor give a damn what sour old men say.
The sun that sets may rise again
but when our light has sunk into the earth,
it is gone forever.
          Give me a thousand kisses,
then a hundred, another thousand,
another hundred
          and in one breath
still kiss another thousand,
another hundred.
          O then with lips and bodies joined
many deep thousands;
          confuse
their number
          so that poor fools and cuckolds (envious
even now) shall never
learn our wealth and curse us
with their
evil eyes.

The downward movement, at once suggesting a deepening of passion and an emotional intensification of argument, seems—with its broken lines, ejaculations, and parenthetical additions—to be a typical poem of the Cummings love-and-death variety. Yet it does exactly match the rapid turns and colloquial impulsiveness of

da mi basia mille, deinde centum,
dein mille altera, dein secunda centum,
deinde usque altera mille, deinde centum.
dein, cum milia multa fecerimus,
conturbabimus illa, ne sciamus,
aut ne quis malus inuidere possit,
cum tantum sciat esse basiorum.

—and the interpolated "poor fools and cuckolds" merely reinforces the contrast between the scorn of the early lines and the "careless rapture" of the lovers. Jonson tried to catch the casual tone by Englishing Lesbia to "Celia" and adding a few English place-names: Romney, Chelsea, Thames. He tried for the casual touch, too, in his opening, altering the meaning at the same time:

Kiss me, sweet; the wary lover
Can your favors keep, and cover,
When the common courting jay
All your bounties will betray.

The short lines and flip diction were partially successful; but, besides changing the literal content of the poem here and in the place-name lines, Jonson shifted the proportions of the poems so that the wit and feeling of the kisses-passage largely disappeared:

First give a hundred,
Then a thousand, then another
Hundred, then unto the other
Add a thousand, and so more. . . .

This, the heart of the poem, is reduced to less than one-fifth its total length, while Gregory—like Catullus—gives it over half his entire space. By escaping the limitations of "Anglo-classical" convention, and by employing newer techniques, Gregory did succeed in coming closer to Catullus' poetic personality than earlier translators. One reason, in addition to his direct, lucid style, is that the "irregular" forms he used enabled him to cut his cloth to fit the originals. Hence his translations have something of the exactness that a running prose translation might have, while the emotional pitch and general sense of patterned and witty statement provide a discipline at least as demanding as formal adherence to the traditional sonnet or the heroic couplet would be. Nor did he always find it necessary to use the roughness, slang, and sudden shifts of movement which he often found helpful. In poem XXXIV, for example, despite the absence of rhyme and the varied line-lengths, he achieved the needed effect of polish, reverence, and mystery in a manner recalling Jonson's brilliantly classical "Hymn to Diana."

Boys and girls, we pledge allegiance
to the moon, virgin Diana,
chastity and innocence,
boys and girls all sing Diana.

Control is the quality most evident here—an excellent support for any sort of unorthodoxy. Whether tenderness, awe, desire, ribaldry, or anger was to be expressed, the poet felt free to use any form which would best convey it. Not the least of his successes is the rendering of the two line poem XCIII, which both in the Latin and the English have the force of a thunderclap of defiance:

Nil nimium studeo, Caesar, tibi uelle placere,
nec scire utrum sis albus an ater homo.

I shall not raise my hand to please you, Caesar,
nor do I care if you are white or black.

It was not only by his freedom of line and image and his use of the element of surprise that Pound influenced these translations, and it was certainly not merely the influence of one translator upon another (which is not to undervalue the importance of translation as a discipline). The incidental parallels help reveal the general mode within which the younger poet was writing. We note, for instance, and take for granted the significance, that Gregory's ease with the particular form of poem I—

> Who shall receive my new-born book,
> my poems, elegant and shy,
> neatly dressed and polished?

—is related to Pound's elegant adaptation of Waller's style in "Envoi." And in the second poem, the reference to "that radiant lady" summons up, as do many of the addresses to Lesbia, Audiart and the heroines of "Ballatetta" ("The broken sunlight for a helm she beareth"), "Apparuit," and "A Virginal." The idiom of Pound's *Cantos* and "Chinese" poems, too, is present in such lines as

> While I was wandering, foot-loose, in the Forum,
> Varus captured me and took me to his lady,
> pretty little piece; at first sight, not bad looking,
> nor did she lack refinement.

The dominant qualities of *Homage to Sextus Propertius* (an unusually difficult experiment in translation-adaptation) were virtuosity, irony, a sometimes bitter sexual exuberance, and a Mauberley-like air of decadence and loss. Gregory's Catullus has the first two of these qualities—although Pound's virtuosity has a special life of its own almost impossible to match—and the others in varying proportions. We must go to Pound's *Lustra*, however, or to scattered passages in the *Cantos* (such as the story of Jim X.), to find a parallel to such scurrility as

> Rufa from Bologna, wife of Menenius,
> spends her time abed
> draining the strength of Rufulus

and the numerous comments by Catullus on homosexual Romans of his day. And we must go to the greater *Cantos* to find the equal of Gregory's translations of the longer narratives and epithalamia (on which, again, Jonson's translations of the same poems had proved influential).

Out of this welter of parallels and influences, we may discern some of Gregory's talents as a lyric poet "in his own right." In a later essay on Landor, he was to give special praise to the *Hellenics*—especially "The Hamadryad" and "Iphigenia," in which "the figures of youthful love and sacrifice are graced with a purity of color and movement." By purity, he wrote, he meant a lucid statement of the simple truth. "I believe that in poetry the presence of simple truth, or the pure expression of it, cannot be called into being by anything less than art, nor can it be conjured out of a vacuum by an act of will." Like Yeats, the later Landor desired "to be a poet only through the demands of an inner being and compulsion, and not through the external circumstances of good fortune or bad, or to be dependent upon the mutations of poetic fame." The result was that for twenty years "he wrote each poem as if it were his last," bringing about a "revival of the elegiac note in English poetry." Authenticity rather than originality was the mark of his work: "The ease of statement and its restraint, the finality of accent, the turn of an excellent conceit—all of which distinguish . . . true style in poetry—are there." In the Catullus translations, we find Gregory striving toward just these ideals which he associates with Yeats and Landor. Indeed, his translation of LX might well have been done by the former of these:

> Were you born of a lioness in the Libyan Mountains,
> or that half-woman monster Scylla,
> screaming in the lowest chambers of her womb,
> sent forth already merciless and hard,
> one who could never hear the cries of a man, even in
> his mortal agony,
> O heart made bitter and cruel beyond all measure.

The elegiac note is here combined with direct statement, if not quite restraint; most of the poems, in fact, provide variants of the same basic combination. For our purposes, it is of no great moment whether or not the effect is mainly due to the Latin original. In the final line just quoted, for example, as in some of the other translations, there is an echo of the *Spoon River Anthology,* but the fact does not counteract the special conditions of translation. For the brief summarizing formulation that concludes most of these poems is characteristic of a tradition easily inclusive enough to hold both Catullus and Masters. The important consideration, for us, is that Gregory feels at home with the style demanded by the convergence of an ancient elegiac tradition and a more "modern" one. So, often, the particular words chosen by Gregory, though they also are a fairly exact rendering of the Latin, may be said to be an equally exact impression of his own poetic personality. Such expressions as "give a damn," "our light has sunk into the earth," "lips and bodies joined," "many deep thousands," and "evil eyes" are both emphatic and impressionistic, conveying a total emotional atmosphere by their opposed kinds of evocativeness. The Latin, too, provides this sort of opposition, yet not in terms suggestive of the love-death association of courtly love as it comes to us by way of Pound and Cummings.

Elegy in the stricter sense we find in other poems, particularly those paying tribute to Catullus' dead brother. One of these, LXV, takes us beautifully through three subtly related but qualitatively distinct moments in a fairly complex poem which challenges all Gregory's skill from the modulation of caesuras to the transition from pervasive melancholy—the dominant mood—to the urbanity of a comic-pathetic final image. This skill, too, carries Gregory through those poems whose effect depends mainly on a turn of wit, a toughness of invective or ridicule, or the shock of what he calls "moral grossness." Here the lessons learned by Eliot and Pound from Browning, especially about the dramatic monologue, and their own experiments in widening the usefulness of this mode, are seen to have been carefully studied by Gregory.

But perhaps the most interesting manifestation of his talent for sympathetic adjustment of modern techniques to classical requirements are to be found in the more subjective lyric poems. In them we see the kinship with the author of "In Memoriam M. S. S." Thus, the four lines of XIV (b) recall the whole Romantic concern with the uncontrollable daemon and its visions of unspeakable depravity:

> If there is anyone
> who reads this foolishness,
> do not fall back in horror, fear to put your hands upon me,
> O you who read these lines. . . .

And again:

> This languid madness destroys you Catullus,
> long day and night shall be desolate, broken,
> as long ago ancient kings and rich cities
> fell into ruin.

There is the desolation of Gerard de Nerval's "El Desdichado" in these lines, travelling back in time to merge with the words of another poet who felt that a crackup, the "death of the world," was upon him. Gregory, elsewhere, has his Catullus say:

> I hate and love.
> And if you ask me why,
> I have no answer, but I discern,
> can feel, my senses rooted in eternal torture

This is not quite "*nescio, sed fieri sentio et excrucior,*" and the difference is perhaps explained by the heightened self-awareness of the Symbolist tradition—"eternal torture" affecting Gregory as various sufferers in Dante's *Inferno* attracted Pound and Eliot. The intensity of suffering implied in our current language of sensibility is hard to avoid, if it were likely the poet wanted to avoid it. Even in the three short passages just quoted we can see that Gregory did not want to do so. One aspect of the heritage of the 1890s is revealed in a vocabulary that resorts a bit too easily to such terms as "horror," "languid madness," "desolate," "ruin," and "eternal torture." A poem like VIII, in which feeling, self-irony, and concreteness are balanced off without loss of control, is more rewarding:

> Poor damned Catullus, here's no time for nonsense,
> open your eyes, O idiot, innocent boy, look at what has happened:
> once there were sunlit days when you followed after
> wherever a girl would go . . .

Something of the thin, sweet pathos of "They flee from me who sometime did me seek" is in these cadenced lines, though the self-pity is much mitigated by the sophistication with which Gregory's Catullus cuts himself down to size.

There is a further relationship between such lines and works as apparently unconnected as Wilder's *The Woman of Andros,* Moody's "The Menagerie," and *The Hamlet* of Laforgue, as well as the more obvious one with that most potent of poetic catalysts, "The Love Song of J. Alfred Prufrock." In Gregory's hands, Catullus becomes one of those nostalgic links to the past that remind modern man of all that he has lost, or rather, has not become. He thus comes to represent more than "the classics" or freedom of sexual expression or the technical apprenticeship of a developing poet. To translate him means to identify oneself with two traditions, that of ancient Rome and that of English neoclassicism; but it means also, in this case, a translation of idioms and implied values out of those traditions into the difficult contemporary world with which the poet must come to terms. Somewhere between these opposed areas of existence waver the sensibilities of the translator-poet. For him, the elegiac mood is what they have in common, apart from the fact that "the cerebral cortex, the nervous system, and the digestive tracts"—Eliot's equivalents for the sheer animal life of men at all times and everywhere—give their own unity to the objective life which the changing intelligence continually reviews. The intelligence that is keenly enough aware of these opposed "truths" is subject to a certain confusion and sense of lost identity. The stamp of death is on a great many of Gregory's poems; their individualism is not Bohemian but is necessitated by an atmosphere of disintegration, the severing of human bonds—loss of contact. Some of Catullus' outcries have the same stamp, and it is particularly with these in mind that we can assert that the translations were invaluable training for one of the most profoundly elegiac American poets of the twentieth century.

Accent (Spring 1950)

Stevens in a Minor Key

THE AURORAS OF AUTUMN by Wallace Stevens

Swatara, Swatara, black river,
Descending, out of the cap of midnight,
Toward the cape at which
You enter the swarthy sea...

HAD we but world enough and time, we would try to prove the assertion that *The Auroras of Autumn* is the most nostalgically philosophical of Wallace Stevens' volumes. The title itself suggests a paradoxical alliance of joy and sorrow, beauty and death (to reduce the unreducible to a crude formula); and the first poem-sequence culminates in much imaginative play around the idea of "an unhappy people in a happy world." This sequence—the key to the book—begins with a poem on the relation of reality to pure idea, and of both to imagination, presenting the elusive, shifting aspects of these associations in the metaphor of a serpent:

> This is form gulping after formlessness,
> Skin flashing to wished-for disappearances . . .

Slippery, dangerous, shedding its old skin with each new insight, reality or meaning appears in many lights. Sometimes it seems to imply the existence, at a higher level, of a "master of the maze," a comfortably Platonic guarantor of ultimate happiness and knowledge; at other times it seems decisively to deny any such possibility. Throughout the sequence, and for the rest of the book, there is a rich and complex poetic treatment of these basic motifs.

Readers familiar with Stevens' verse may gather from all this something of the manner in which he is working the same vein as before, and something of the slightly changed emphasis of this book. The amazing image-making power, the musical skill, the subtle toying with words are as engaging as ever. There are still the offhand precision of phrase ("Wearing hats of angular flick and fleck"), the humorous formulations ("We'll give the week-end to wisdom, to Weisheit, the rabbi"), the self-ironies:

> This day writhes with what? The lecturer
> On This Beautiful World of Ours composes himself
> And hems the planet rose and haws it ripe . . .

But there is now probably more *argument*, with a relative subordination of the other elements. And a harder, darker note runs through the volume, a tragic note like that of the lines quoted at the head of this review. There is a new, less malleable pessimism:

> The day is great and strong—
> But his father was strong, that lies now
> In the poverty of dirt.

There is a bitterness—see "In a Bad Time"—at the sentimental assumption that to imagine an order in nature is to establish it or become part of it. In several pieces, Yeats's early poem "The Lake Isle of Innisfree" is deliberately echoed, quoted, almost parodied as Stevens mercilessly worries at the kind of romantic assumptions it embodies. It is with the savagely passionate older Yeats that Stevens (though his work rarely approaches such intensity) seems to feel most akin.

Like Yeats, for instance, he invents his deity. But Stevens' god, "the spectre of the spheres," is contrived in his own image—a proliferator of resemblances and connoisseur of distinctions in experience and definition that would drive a conscientious Rorschach tester haggard to his final rest. He is a pragmatic sort of god, who has created an expanding, unpredictable, impersonal universe so that its endless possibilities of delight and horror can be a challenge to his probing imagination:

> . . . he meditates a whole,
> The full of fortune and the full of fate,
> As if he lived all lives, that he might know . . .

But in contriving such a god, Stevens is managing to kid his own facile curiosity just a little. Thus, he explains the tragic dilemma of mankind as the poet god's device for balancing off all conceivable meanings so that he can understand them "down to a haggling of wind or weather." Obviously, he could not have gained half so much by arranging "a happy people in a happy world" ("Buffo! a ball, an opera, a bar") or "an unhappy people in an unhappy world" ("too many mirrors for misery"). The old Platonic scale of values was much more dependable than this experimental, fifty-fifty universe. The poet is nostalgic for it, as he is nostalgic for that other frail edifice against things as they really—probably—are: the family of his childhood, with its remembered security, love and innocence:

> Farewell to an idea. . . . The mother's face,
> The purpose of the poem, fills the room.
> They are together, here, and it is warm.

Though a number of these poems have the force of personal memory, none is autobiographical in much detail. Rather, they bring into strong emotional focus the pathos and the bravery of man's desire to read something human into the intractable system of nature, that "color of ice and fire and solitude," by seeing it as a progression of ideas or memories or projections of his own needs. Yet the paradoxes of will and fatality are such (and this is another link with Yeats) that the slightest adjustment of the poet's sights can lead to a reversal of this focus. It suddenly becomes possible to defy the too-scientific god of perhaps and probability:

> The meanings are our own—
> It is a text that we shall be needing,
> To be the footing of noon,
> The pillar of midnight,
>
> That comes from ourselves, neither from knowing
> Nor not knowing, yet free from question,
> Because we wanted it so
> And it had to be.

And it becomes equally possible, in the sad speech of the "angel of reality" that concludes the book, to dissolve once more that mood of courage in the acid of truth's essential "tragic drone." Stevens may not be able to tell us (and we doubt that he ought to try) where to go from here; but what *here* is, and how good and evil and true and untrue it is, he can help us to discover.

The New Republic (7 May 1951)

In the Roar of the Present

PATERSON by William Carlos Williams
THE COLLECTED LATER POEMS by William Carlos Williams

"I'M just the core of the onion—nothing at all," says the hero of one of William Carlos Williams' plays. Good poetry usually finds a center and starting point in some immediacy: a direct statement, a narrative or dramatic moment, a concrete image or emotion. Dr. Williams' immediacies (and he is our master of the spontaneous effect) are so often colored by his unpretentious humanity that he seems almost to be improvising, as if he were not one of the very few really accomplished poets in English today:

> To make a start,
> out of particulars
> and make them general, rolling
> up the sum, by defective means—
> sniffing the trees,
> just another dog
> among a lot of dogs . . .

Well, that is one way to begin an epic poem! And yet, in a sense it is the only way if the poet is to keep himself as free as possible of sentimental and purely literary assumptions while exploring the meanings of his own time and place—"the roar,/the roar of the present, a speech—/is of necessity, my sole concern." *Paterson* is not "strictly" an epic, but a long poem in four parts. (That is its first unpretentiousness.) Structurally, it is loose though not uncontrolled. The poet takes a specific locality in New Jersey and personifies its geography, sociology and history, identifying himself both as just one of the many inhabitants and as the sensibility and consciousness of the area. Readers of his novels and short stories will agree that Williams knows its life. As a local doctor and baby specialist, he has come closer to the people than any other of our poets—far closer than Sandburg, for instance—and the knowledge he must grapple with is simply too intractable to allow of easy triumphs or solutions.

Williams, as has been said often enough, is a pragmatic thinker. ("No ideas," he writes, "but in things.") At the same time and like other pragmatists, he is a mystic—at any rate, a would-be mystic. In *Paterson* we see writ large the kind of human-ecological mysticism that a few scientists have been toying with recently. The entire poem is an attempt to see what meaning, if any, can be read into a given cultural unit, in its way symbolic of life in America and in the modern world as a whole. Can the life force realize itself fully in our society, the poet asks, or do the violent gestures of graceless lust and hatred and self-destruction define irrefutably a "world of corrupt cities" lacking continuity with past tradition or future perspectives? And can the poet himself find a "language" in it comparable to certain achievements in the past and to the vital relationships of primitive societies, a language commensurate with the terrible need of individuals to communicate the nature of their love?

"No ideas but in things." And so private memories, extracts from letters and documents, close-ups of sex and family relations in America, marvelous lyric outbursts and afterbeats, vigorous social comment and satirical vignettes punctuate the poem explosively. In its surface multiplicity it bears a family resemblance to Pound's *Cantos*. It does also in some of its themes and attitudes, but the personality speaking is entirely different. Williams' America is indeed tragic, but at least in part that is seen as the basic human condition; and he holds fast to what is alive and solid in his country, with a firm grasp on the American idiom.

The poem is finally a unit—humane, passionate, self-humbling, assertive of a minimum value: the intellectual and esthetic possibilities arising in counter-dream against the dulling rituals of our society. Not as compressed or "designed" as *The Waste Land,* it nevertheless has a similar dramatic force and is perhaps the product of as rigorous a discipline. (Incidentally, *William Carlos Williams*—Vivienne Koch's detailed study—gives excellent insights into the nature of that discipline.)

It is hard to separate *Paterson* from Williams' other verse of the past decade or so. The over-all meanings converge, and the whole body of later work reveals the sophistication and virtuosity underlying the apparent simplicities even more than did, say, *In the American Grain* (his great prose study of our mythical history) or such a poem as "The Yachts"—both written before the last war. In the *Collected Later Poems* we find the release and surfacing of a compassionate and humorous spirit, particularly in the pieces on Williams' aged mother. More than ever, also, we find a dizzying physical awareness of the body's existence as the central fact of truth and art:

> In Breughel's great picture, The Kermess,
> the dancers go around, they go round and
> around, the squeal and the blare and the
> tweedle of bagpipes, a bugle and fiddles
> tipping their bellies. . . .

And we find, as in Stevens, the whimsical imagination moving from arbitrary association into its deepest sources. There is the exaltation of body and experience despite all weakness of "Choral: The Pink Church." Here, as elsewhere, the moralists and professors get theirs; and the poet looses defiant blasts as of E. E. Cummings. Everywhere is displayed the highly revealing art of juxtaposition, taking us from shock directly into meaning:

> Like a cylindrical tank fresh silvered
> upended on the sidewalk to advertise
> some plumber's shop, a profusion
> of pink roses bending ragged in the rain—
> speaks to me of all gentleness and its
> enduring. . . .

Whether he is arguing in his emphatic, Laurentian way, or being a tough doc or cold observer or singing celebrant, or leading us into the vast relationships the sensibility can discover, Williams is always a committed poet, taking his chances, never resorting to mere irony or the ambiguity that comes of fear or myopia. He is one of the few writers who have gone on from the twenties and thirties without rejecting what once was valid for them but always ready to find new meanings and better ways to state them.

The New Republic (27 August 1951)

❧

Mid-Afternoon Prayers

NONES by W. H. Auden

NONES (which rhymes with *bones*, and *moans*) is—sayeth the venerable Webster—the ninth canonical hour in ancient Roman and Eastern reckoning, or three p.m.; "hence, an office recited" at about this time. And this whole volume, beginning with an apology and ending with a complaint and question, represents an almost ritual effort by the poet to pray and coach himself into the right attitudes for this historical moment between violences. If the day is still too young for revelations and conclusions, yet the blood of recent sacrifice is "already dry on the grass." We are unprepared to meet the demanding silence of this moment-without-resolution, though we feel our responsibility and guilt as well as our helpless common mortality. "What shall we do," the title poem asks, "until nightfall?" Poem after poem, following hard upon the dedicatory piece rejecting Auden's dissident past, states our predicament and prophesies our doom. It is true that the final piece holds that "Only the young and the rich/have the nerve or the figure to strike/the lacrimae rerum note." Nevertheless, at forty-three this is just the note Auden strikes—particularly in his two most beautiful offerings of the present collection, the powerful, musically near-perfect "Prime" and the ironic and savage "Song."

Simultaneously, however, there is one particular counter-note that recurs in this group of poems. In its most flippant form, this note can most clearly be heard in the Harvard Phi Beta Kappa poem "Under Which Lyre a Reactionary Tract for the Times," an attractive if somewhat facile (for Auden) light-verse manifesto against stuffed shirts and heads:

> Read *The New Yorker,* trust in God;
> And take short views.

The notion that keeps recurring is that, for the time being at least, we must content ourselves with minimums. The theme pops up in a surprising number of contexts religious and profane. How consciously the poet employs it may be seen in "The Duet," an equally amusing and exasperating Yeatsian concoction in which a "huge sad lady" sings mournfully of tragic, romantic passion while a "scrunty beggar" with "one glass eye and a hickory leg" praises the world as it is, crying "Nonsense to her large repining"—the said large repining having been sufficiently burlesqued by Auden to make the point clear in any case. So too with the more philosophical "In Praise of Limestone," done in the familiar wry, sly, fly manner; the self-deflating "Serenade"; the tough-minded but poignant "Ischia"; and, among others, the wittily common-sensible "Cattivo Tempo." It is not unlikely, indeed, that Auden recognizes and clings to a sense of kinship with the *bon sens* of seventeenth- and eighteenth-century neo-classicism. There has always been a bold, even a clear, intellectualism in his writing that was never quite Romantic philosophizing and never purely—despite the early experiments in argument through oblique imagery—Metaphysical either.

It is a fact, certainly, that Auden comes closer than any other poet to being a twentieth-century Dryden. In technical versatility he is surpassed only by Pound, but Pound has after all not "specialized" in verse as directly ratiocinative as has Auden, and his work of real distinction has been limited to fewer types. One recalls with amazement the range of moods and lyric, contemplative and narrative forms employed in *The Age of Anxiety,* all disciplined by the basic Anglo-Saxon alliterative verse in which that whole long triumph of poetic virtuosity is written. His combination of humor and seriousness in such a poem as "Footnotes to Dr. Sheldon" and his brief homage to T. S. Eliot on his sixtieth birthday, as well as his delight in formal effects—and in setting them off against a colloquial idiom very often—mark this affinity with Dryden and his more skillful successors.

If we are not, then completely satisfied with these new poems, it is not because of any diminution of Auden's skill. Rather it is because, despite his great skill and ability to delight, he possesses a most un-Drydenesque sense of man's tragic condition, together with a pure emotional insight of a very high order, and these are in constant conflict with his ironic intelligence. What richness there is, for instance, in the beginning of "Prime"! But then the arguments about history and time and guilt—beautifully handled, undoubtedly, but still on a lower plane—tumble in to set the poem in order at the expense of just the highest achievement. As so many of these poems show, it is absolute knowledge which Auden desires and prays for; and that being impossible, he finds he must settle for much less to keep peace with God if not with himself. So it becomes easy for him to satirize his own and our common humanness—our weaknesses, vanity, in fact all our history and limited knowledge. But somewhere along the line, despite our great sympathy and admiration, there has been a failure of power—the original penalty for the original sin.

The New Republic (1 October 1951)

❧

On the "Dissidents" of the Thirties

THE Bollingen Prize controversy—itself now but an "item" for literary histories—curiously echoed certain critical discussions of the 1930s. The head-on collision of moral and esthetic principles that makes it so difficult to evaluate the work of a Pound today was a daily catastrophe in the lives of many writers throughout that "low, dishonest decade." It is true that most of those who were especially identified with Depression-radicalism have moved (or been moved) to new positions at once less political and less optimistic. Yet even a glance as cursory and sweeping as this brief essay can afford must remind us—if we allow ourselves to forget for a moment the absolute categories of political controversy—of certain lines of intellectual continuity temporarily cut off by the war. These were lines of exploration of what it means for the isolated artistic sensibility to commit itself to a given faith or ideology while striving to be true to its own responses.

What we refer to here, then, is not so much the social criticism and urgent demand for total change which we ordinarily associate with the vanished American literary Left and which Kenneth Fearing's "Denouement" so passionately expressed:

> Sky, be blue, and more than blue; wind, be flesh and blood; flesh and blood,
> be deathless;
> walls, streets, be home;
> desire of millions, become more real than warmth and breath and strength
> and bread. . . .

Rather, we are concerned with the general way in which the conscientious creative personality and critical mind functioned within the fairly rigid context of the "revolutionary movement." *"Give me the power,"* wrote Horace Gregory, perhaps the foremost poet of the group, *"to stay in no retreat and not to die."* This was the prayer of a poet with a strong sense of tradition and of his own private identity. It had little of the "heroic" air of doctrinaire propaganda, but was the desperately imperative outcry of a man caught up in a moral dilemma.

Since the Leftist writers have often been justly accused of disregarding precisely this dilemma, one returns to their poetry and criticism of the 1930s with a certain surprise at the degree to which they were concerned about it. So conscious indeed were they of it that, in the important anthology *Proletarian Literature of the United States* (1935), Joseph Freeman's introduction attempted an economic explanation:

> Most men of letters come from the middle classes, which have both the education and incentive for literary production. These classes shared the pangs of the crisis together with the workers and farmers. The un-

> employment, poverty, and insecurity which spread over the country hit the educated classes like a hurricane; writers and artists, among others, were catapulted out of privileged positions; and many of those who remained economically secure experienced a revolution of ideas which reflected the profound changes around them. And at the very moment when our own country, to the surprise of all except the Marxists, was sliding into a social-economic abyss, the new social-economic system of the Russian workers and peasants showed striking gains.

Cosmically inclusive though this explanation was, it did show the subjective spirit of the movement in which such writers as Horace Gregory (and Kenneth Fearing, Muriel Rukeyser, and a good many others) participated. It implied a mood of revelation and, to quote Freeman further, of identification with the working-class "as a motive power of modern history." There was a conviction of personal transformation: "This politicalization of the man of letters was a step toward his transformation *as a poet*." Nevertheless, many "men of letters" resisted the kind of pressures that would make over poets into mere propagandists. At the second American Writers' Congress in 1937, Kenneth Burke summed the whole problem up neatly:

> *Conceptually* one may quickly jump the gap between capitalism and communism. But the poet's way is necessarily more cumbersome. It is the longer way round. It has not got there until it has humanized, personalized.

It is significant that, at the time, a writer like Ralph Bates should have singled out precisely this remark of Burke's as the most important of the Congress. Of course, it was the avowed aim of theoretical Marxist criticism to help writers "lose any sense of remoteness or helplessness and . . . become domesticated in the working-class." So at any rate wrote Granville Hicks in *Proletarian Literature*, with the full pedantic support of William Phillips' and Philip Rahv's directives for revolutionary artists. But in fact the relationship seemed often to work out as a contradiction rather than a reconciliation, and the dilemma of the American writer was not very different from that which C. Day-Lewis had described in 1934 as peculiar to the young British radical poet:

> We have seen him on the one hand rendered more acutely conscious of individuality by the acceptance of current psychological doctrines; and on the other hand, rendered both by poetic intuition and ordinary observation acutely conscious of the present isolation of the individual and the necessity for a social organism which may restore communion. He looks to one side and he sees D. H. Lawrence, the extreme point of individualism in this country's literature . . . , but he has watched him . . . driven ill and mad, a failure. . . . He looks to the other side and he sees Communism, . . . the most wholehearted attempt ever made to raise the individual to his highest power by a conditioning of his environment; yet here too he notices the bully and the spy, and wonders if any system can expel and survive that poison.

Here is the deepgoing, usually conscious cleavage which made itself felt in almost every Marxist literary landmark in the 1930s. Even Michael Gold, infallible oracle of immaculate revolution, seemed to recognize it in his preface to Sol Funaroff's little anthology *We Gather Strength* (1933). Gold complained that "the Babbitt and the Philistine" had won the day in the Party as in the country at large and praised each of the four represented poets for highly individualistic qualities. One was "confused, anarchic, sensitive." Another was a mystic with a "painful sense of cheated beauty." A third had achieved order and design only by yielding to "influences of modern bourgeois poetry, T. S. Eliot, Ezra Pound, William Carlos Williams"—and, though it is hard to find precise meanings in Gold's hasty prose, these were presumably laudable influences as well. Laudable also was the fourth poet's combination of "abstract manifesto and personal lyricism in . . . curious fantasy." The minds of these poets, said Gold approvingly, were "filled with images of death" and alternated between "despair and the wild wonderful dream of our World Revolution." The phrasing, of course, gives the game away, for it suggests a common confusion of ideas, the indiscriminate blending of bohemianism, communism, romanticism, sentimentalism, and anarchist nonconformism that so often is identified with being "artistic" and "radical." One of Gold's poets, Joseph Kalar, exemplified this confusion in his personified vision of "Freedom" as

> . . . a girl with tangled hair
> whose breasts are worthy of caresses,
> whose eyes, imperious with a larger lust,
> vitriol the tissues of the virtuous . . .

No wonder that so many of these writers found themselves involved in a sterner struggle than they had bargained for, and that, like Edwin Rolfe, they sometimes found it necessary to exorcise their dæmons of personalism by a kind of public recantation!

> To welcome multitudes—the miracle of deeds
> performed in unison—the mind
> must first renounce the fiction of the self
> and its vainglory. It must pierce
> the dreamplate of its solitude, the fallacy
> of its omnipotence . . .

Of the poets in *We Gather Strength,* and indeed almost alone among poets of the American Left—with the possible exception of Langston Hughes—Sol Funaroff accepted the idea of class-struggle as an unquestioned fact, and an inspiring one which in no way threatened his integrity of personality. Though he is said to have had, on occasion, the mannerisms of a cartoon commissar, he was at the age of twenty-one the most promising of the four. His work had a bold, experimental, dramatically forceful character even when its imagery was forced into the tendentious patterns of Soviet machine-glorification:

> tigers of our passion concrete leashed
> to expend no energy on parliamentary coquettes.

And he could be very attractive when stung by a mood of romantic-revolutionary nostalgia:

> Look.
>
> There is Karl Marx.
>
> This is your Spring.
>
> There is such a woman.

By the time of his death some nine years later, Funaroff had shown real progress. He had certainly discovered the uses of exuberance and of the lyrical release of energy, and in a later poem had bridged the gulf between private tragedy and the anticipated epic victory of socialism by an image which links him with Hart Crane:

> I am that exile
> from a future time,
> from shores of freedom
> I may never know,
> who hears, sounding in the surf,
> tidings from the lips of waves
> that meet and kiss
> in submarine gardens
> of a new Atlantis . . .

Funaroff's restless, organizing energy, like the early Pound's, enabled him to involve other people in his enterprises, to encourage them, and to get their work published. As Genevieve Taggard has written, his Russian background and sense of actually belonging to the laboring class gave unusual solidity to his revolutionary convictions. Had he lived, it is quite possible that he would have become an American Aragon.

The movement in which Funaroff was so at home reached its peak of enthusiasm in 1935, with the publication of *Proletarian Literature* and the summoning of the first American Writers' Congress. The call to the Congress had been addressed to "revolutionary writers" only, but it elicited a wide response—two-hundred and sixteen writers from twenty-six states, in addition to fraternal representatives from abroad. Such names as John Dos Passos, Nelson Algren, Malcolm Cowley, Theodore Dreiser, James Farrell, Lincoln Steffens, and Lewis Mumford are sufficiently indicative of the range of those writers who felt the Congress met a real need; even William Allen White, though he did not attend, sent a warm message of greeting. The subjects discussed varied from Kenneth Burke's disquisition on antifascist semantics to Waldo Frank's typically mystical attempt to reconcile the ideal of "autonomous" literature with his theory of the "basic social function of art." Yet all these subjects tend to fall into two main classifications: activist politics and the writer's relation as an individual to his political beliefs. Thus we have Aragon's rhetorical assertion: "Because we defend the future of culture we are necessarily among its heirs. Its cause is ours, we stand with the class of workers." And on the other hand we have Dos Passos insisting on the writer as technician and stressing openness, flexibility, independence of authority. The characteristic dichotomy shows up everywhere. Matthew Josephson, after declaring that "Moscow has become an oasis of culture today," took occasion to insist that Russian writers—despite their "audacious, novel attempt to collaborate directly with the political industrial program of the working class"—were not at all regimented. Even Earl Browder found time in the course of a lecture on war and fascism to dismiss as fantastic the natural suspicion that the Communist Party would wish to impose preconceived notions on sympathetic writers.

Only the poet Isidor Schneider attacked the principle of individualism directly, associating it with the rise of capitalism and the decline of all but the more personal sort of lyric poetry. He called for a revival of verse through such mass-media as radio and cinema. Schneider, like Funaroff a poet of considerable but unfulfilled promise, had the year before published a volume in which he mingled sensual-metaphysical themes with such subjects as the Reichstag trials, the death-throes of capitalism, and the greatness of Lenin. The volume, *Comrade: Mister*, also contained a prose argument for total rejection of the bourgeois past which casually mentioned the poet's own "painful" growth away from private poetry. Schneider's extreme anti-individualist position seems to have been part of a violent reaction against something in his own personality, a reaction, in fact, against the sensual hedonism so apparent in his poems and his novel *From the Kingdom of Necessity*. It was counterbalanced at the Congress by Malcolm Cowley's argument that "the movement" would not bring a writer personal salvation or make him a political leader but that it could give him an audience, new subject matter, standards for self-criticism, and a feeling of belonging to a rising rather than a dying culture.

Although the atmosphere in which radical writers of the thirties worked, then, was well symbolized by the excitement, the strong political direction, and the sense of vistas of creativity of the Congress, it was also symbolized by Waldo Frank's fear of "servile art" and of mechanical Marxism. Behind the general agreement that the delegates had met for a common purpose lay a wide, barely concealed arena for the maneuverings of the doubtful, who might move among a number of "prepared positions" without losing a certain glow of participation and ennoblement by a compelling cause. Freeman was hardly accurate in his introduction to *Proletarian Literature* when he wrote that the Congress had become "possible in this country only when in the writer's mind the dichotomy between poetry and politics has vanished, and art and life were fused." This was wishful thinking. The anthology itself, it is true, had, from the Communist point of view, an overall "positive" effect. The fiction and drama sections contained a number of pieces which have not even now lost their social effectiveness—notably Erskine Caldwell's "Daughter," Ben Field's "Cow," Albert Maltz's "Man on a Road," and Clifford Odets's "Waiting for Lefty." The reportage, too, was grimly effective in its portrayal of strike scenes, Chinese Civil War incidents, bonus marchers, and dustbowl victims. And the poetry was carefully selected to strike the most revolutionary note possible, typified by Gold's "A Strange Funeral in Braddock" and Hughes's blues songs about sharecroppers and down-and-outers. Nevertheless the opposite note could not be entirely stifled in these poems. Orrick Johns's "Cleavage" reflected, for instance, the break with family and past which was a familiar, distressing experience for many radicals. Kenneth Fearing's "No Credit," too, reveals the elegiac strain as strongest just where one would least expect it:

> as nevertheless, the flesh grows old, dies, dies, in its only life, is gone;
> the reflection goes from the mirror, as the shadow, of even a communist,
> is gone from the wall . . .

Some of these poems expressed horror rather than militancy. Such a poem was Richard Wright's "Between the World and Me," in which the author recounted his feelings on stumbling upon the skeleton of a lynched Negro—how he suddenly imagined himself in the mob's grip like some mercilessly trapped and beaten animal, being tarred and feathered and finally killed. ("Now I am dry bones and my face a stony skull staring in yellow surprise at the sun.") Genevieve Taggard's "Interior," though less violent in every way, spoke horror of another kind, at the blank lives of so many middleclass women:

> And after you doze brush out your hair
> And walk like a marmoset to and fro
> And look in the mirror at middle-age
> And sit and regard yourself stare and stare
> And hate your life and your tiresome friends . . .

Historians of the 1930s have paid little attention to this "literature of dissidence"—to quote the Beards' apt phrase. Dixon Wecter's *The Age of the Great Depression* dismisses it in a single paragraph devoted mainly to the German-Soviet pact of 1939, and his comment on depression poetry finds no room even for Hart Crane—let alone the contributors to *Proletarian Literature*. The Beards are more generous in *America in Midpassage*. They devote several pages to the arguments at the second American Writers' Congress, held in 1937, and summarize the ideas both of the Marxians there and of those who opposed them. They recognize the wide suggestivenes of Kenneth Burke's "contention that the writer interprets life, that is, history, according to his experience with it, and assumes an attitude either of acceptance or rejection of the forms which life displays." Their chapter on American letters of this period is broadly comprehensive, though it too omits important names, and its historical perspective makes allowances for ideas with which the authors themselves were not wholly in agreement:

> However rough and untravelled the road ahead, the literature of dissidence certainly gave suggestions respecting the way. It expressed and echoed the swelling sentiments that swept every state in the Union in 1936 and shook both the powers and the convictions of those Bourbons who spoke of "restoration." The prose and verse of economic and political sensitiveness were not read by the millions, but they were read and discussed by some men and women, boys and girls, who would help make history in 1950, 1960, 1970.

The best of these writers hardly regarded themselves as "dissidents" merely. Certainly such poets as Gregory, Fearing, Rukeyser did not. Their work seems particularly valuable—apart from its qualities of craftsmanship—because it throws light on the difficulties of the artist who wishes to be true both to his own perceptions and to some "larger" discipline of faith. Such poets wrote not only under the influence of the history of their time, but also within the limits of dominant poetic standards in the twentieth century. They were (we speak in the past tense because they have all changed a good deal since the thirties) disciplined both by the general Romantic tradition as it comes to us by way of Whitman and Lawrence and by the technical standards perfected by Pound, Yeats, and Eliot. The affinity with the latter three is even stronger when we recall such poems as the "Mauberley" sequences, "The Black Tower," and almost the whole body of Eliot's work since "Gerontion." We may, in one sense, think of a great deal of modern poetry as seeking to establish equilibria among sensibility, faith, and objective meaning. Gregory, an elegiac poet for whom Lawrence's personalism and Pound's music and classicism were profoundly formative, for a time used Marxism to achieve such equilibria. As a device for prophecy, it helped him justify his concern with death and personal survival by predicting a magic social rebirth of the self at some future time. To the satirical energies of the individualistic and ironic Fearing, Marxism provided a powerful stimulant in the form of specific, directly communicative symbols of pure evil. As for Muriel Rukeyser, she saw in dialectical materialism a means of reconciling conflicting interests and giving direction to her passion for openness—as well, of course, as of lending force to her humanitarian feelings. Both she and Gregory, like so many other American and British writers, sought new "ancestors" whose creative intelligence might replenish the exhausted stock of heroes in a supposedly deflated national tradition. The search that engrossed these poets was for a new identity that might fit the needs of the modern "displaced personality" without losing touch with actual history and the mass of mankind. That search has hardly been much furthered in the past decade, and it is important for us to recall what these explorers of one avenue of possibility, an integral part of our immediate past, were trying to do and how sincerely they often went about it.

The University of Kansas City Review (1951)

❧

Jubal, Jabal and Moore

COLLECTED POEMS by Marianne Moore

Genesis tells us of Jubal and Jabal.
One handled the harp and one herded the cattle.

HAVING allowed her *Selected Poems* to remain out of print for much too long a time, Marianne Moore's publishers now make amends with a volume including, besides that most important early group, all her later work both collected and hitherto uncollected. This poet of an intricate verse woven around simple experience is very close in spirit to the rest of the poetic generation of which she is a part. Because of her unique realistic and rational yet *spirituelle* idiom, we easily overlook how often her exclamatory outbursts resemble those of Pound and Williams; how many of her subtle threads of argumentation bear a family likeness to those of the second part of *Mauberley;* how her attempts to root her work in concrete observation resemble the attempts of Williams in *Spring and All* or *Paterson;* how much her lyric irony has in common with that of Eliot and Stevens, particularly with the latter.

Readers who have come to know her writing chiefly through the fairly generous representation in anthologies can now discern more clearly, perhaps, her method of understatement for emphasis; because these poems see more truly into the heart of things than does most other more violently and overtly emotional verse. She herself has written that

The deepest feeling always shows itself in silence;
not in silence, but restraint.

And though the general impression, that her urbanity, her Jamesian wit and her subtlety are the special marks of her talent, is in some proportion justified, it nevertheless obstructs recognition of Miss Moore's deeper-going seriousness. The disguise is a deliberate one; Miss Moore will not (to alter a phrase of Yeats's) "break up her lines to weep."

James, of course, wore a similar disguise. In *The Ambassadors*, the "great" scene is the one in which Strether, in the garden, passionately urges on his young friend the value of the elemental meaning of life underlying all things. Miss Moore's vivid emphasis on the details of subhuman organic life—she is the botanist's and the zoologist's poet, as *well* as the poet's poet—makes her poetry swarm with symbolic observation. The pretense is that all this occurs in a hothouse or a zoo, where one watches the flora or the curious beasts with amused and sympathetic detachment, making polite conversation all the while. But how intense the interest really is, how uncompromising the preciseness of detail, how persistent the drive toward universalizing ethical import; how irritated the poet is with softheadedness of any kind! The ostrich "digesteth harde yron" and is therefore superior to all the absurdities of his appearance and, more important, to his ridiculous common mortality. Sometimes her famous "imaginary gardens with real toads in them"—Miss Moore's image for genuine poetic creations—are really not so far from Blake's tiger-haunted forests.

Without, indeed, the underlying seriousness and intensity, it is unlikely that Marianne Moore could be so much the poet of careful distinctions among the possible meanings of experience, the elegant colloquialist who some day, if we *must* seat her with others, will "dine with Landor and with Donne." Without her sense of orderliness and her control, she could not write. Even in the highly emotional "In Distrust of Merits" and "Keeping Their World Large," which are much more direct expressions of feeling than she usually allows herself, her method remains that of refining and correcting an attitude until it fits her perfectly. The most delicately lyrical moments will have their deliberate adjustments of focus, often their little comic turns beginning with the title:

THE MIND IS AN ENCHANTING THING

is an enchanted thing
    like the glaze on a
katydid-wing
        subdivided by sun
        till the nettings are legion.

Such a recognizable method is employed in many idiomatic contexts: sometimes that of a New England Emersonian wisdom, sometimes that of a pure ironic sensibility, sometimes of an anti-philistinism or, it may be, a sort of E. M. Forster liberalism. The type of consciousness at the center does not change; it values its own self-discipline; it seeks grace of bearing; it does not surrender its finely unsentimental if ultimately melioristic morale. Miss Moore never strikes what Auden calls the *lacrimae rerum* note, which is an entirely different note from the tragic consciousness that may underlie gaiety of spirit. We honor such poetry as the poetry of courage and right understanding.

The New Republic (7 April 1952)

❧

Of Pity and Innocence

THE SEVEN-LEAGUE CRUTCHES by Randall Jarrell

RANDALL Jarrell's verse has the "tears of things" in it. It has been linked to Wilfred Owen's poetry of pity, though Owen was simpler and more direct in his nonconformist-pacifist idealism. Jarrell concerns himself less with systematic, patterned injustice in nature or society than with the vulnerable and helpless sensibility of innocence. His best poems often interpret the tragic confusions of children and soldiers in traumatic crises as instances of an unbridgeable contradiction between the operations of the human mind and those of the strange outer world. Myth, hallucination and "realistic" observation converge in these examples to produce a heightened awareness under shock-pressure of the impersonal cruelty of that world, an unoriented awareness that

> Behind everything there is always
> The unknown unwanted life.

In an earlier poem, "The Death of the Ball Turret Gunner," this fusion of subjective responses produced an almost unbearable poignant emotional precision. The reader had no choice: his secret mind was deeply troubled and not directed toward itself, and the recognitions that followed were almost physical ones. So too, in the present volume, the fantasy life and dream imagery of children seek to absorb the painful facts of experience:

> When the swans turned my sister into a swan
> I would go to the lake, at night, from milking;
> The sun would look out through the reeds like a swan,
> A swan's red beak; and the beak would open
> And inside there was darkness, the stars and the moon.

or:

> All the graves of the forest
> Are opened, the scaling face
> Of a woman—the dead mother—
> Is square in the steam of a yard. . . .

Still, Jarrell does try to push past the sense of strangeness, to arrive at meaning in the more objective sense of the term. When he does so, he is not as successful as in the more opaque, self-contained monologues of innocence. His bravest effort outward, "Hohensalzburg: Variations on a Theme of Romantic Character," employs romantic whimsy and imagination in combination with supernatural linkings of love and death to get at a tenuous religious-metaphysical truth behind the strangeness. As in "A Conversation with the Devil" and other poems, the "argument" here is facile, sentimental, and somehow uncommitted and the poem is saved from disaster only by its emotional subtlety; this, and not the poem's overt effort, establishes its value. Jarrell is a romantic idealist, but the fact is not decisive; this mental set is, I think, the only one he has so far found usable to rationalize the ungloved sympathy with vulnerability that is the real key to his finest work. (It is interesting that in a recent essay on Whitman he has disregarded the rhetorical and political associations by which the latter transcends the contradictions of will and fate and has stressed his concrete sense of the strangeness of things, the "magic" way in which he is "faithful to the feel of things, to reality as it seems." The essential difference between the two poets' outlooks may nevertheless be pinned down by comparing Jarrell's lovely, unworldly "A Soul" with Whitman's lusty, affirming 'I believe in you, my soul.')

Despite all qualifications, however, this volume is Jarrell's most solid achievement; there is more full-bodied poetry in it than in the earlier books, and he takes more chances. The translations and adaptations from Corbière and Rilke reveal an outward movement more in accordance with his genius than are the poems that "argue" explicitly. Corbière's "Le Poète Contumace," somewhat softened by Jarrell's italics and idiomatic phrasings, gives a wider range of reference to the concern with isolated, suffering sensibility; his "Rondels pour Après" come through with their heartbreaking "acceptance" heightened, their irony just reduced. In Rilke's, "The Olive Garden," Jarrell has responded to Christ as a lonely one, the type of man's need for a miracle, the German poet's identification of the sign that does not come.

His translating has produced in Jarrell a new mastery that allows him to use a wide variety of forms from the oddly humorous "Nollekens" to the intense essay in humility called "Jonah." *The Seven-League Crutches* is one of the finest books of poems printed in a very fine year.

The New Republic (2 June 1952)

from *Muriel Rukeyser: The Longer Poems*

1.

TO readers nourished on Eliot and Yeats and disciplined by analytical criticism, the faults in Muriel Rukeyser's work may seen more obvious than its merits. Though they do not define her work and are very often absent from it, these faults are real: the unearned triumphant conclusion, the occasional muddy emotionalism that can blur the phrasing almost to a blot, the painful view we are sometimes afforded of the poet desperately trying, under our very eyes, to piece a poem together without quite finding the key (usually, a proper middle part).

But if the faults, which are clearly related to one another, are undoubtedly present, it is also true that they are by-products—though at times more important than the chief fruit of her labor—of equally real achievements in Miss Rukeyser's writing. And in any case, a sufficient number of her poems do earn what they have to tell us, do have organic structure and precision to match their passion. Still in her thirties, Miss Rukeyser has advanced through several stages and deserves, on the scores of talent and commitment and courage, a sympathetic hearing. Because, by and large, most of her verse exists in a different context from that generally given serious critical attention nowadays, it would seem useful to go into the question of what that context is and how it enters into her effort as a poet. It is not a matter so much of the reservations one must bear in mind (just look, after all, at some of Pound's minor pieces and major aberrations—which do not diminish the stature of his poetry but help us to understand it and therefore bear with some of the lapses at least) as of getting at whatever it is of value that a writer has to offer. The longer poem-sequences provide the best clues to her chief directions, and this essay will concern itself with several of them, as well as with the kind of romanticism they breathe, in order to reach a reasonably objective understanding of those directions.

Now current criticism responds well to the poetry of pure and ironic sensibility; less surely, though constrained to recognize its power, to the poetry of incantation. It does by far the least justice, however, to the rhetoric of romantic expression, in which the speaker dares to give the game away because he counts on a relationship of some personal sympathy with the reader. Witness the cheapening of Shelley's accomplishment in Brooks and Warren's otherwise generally excellent *Understanding Poetry*. Yet the romantic element—here seen as the exploitation of the speaking personality to will the actualization of a desired ideal—is almost omnipresent in the arts. . . . The closer a poem comes to being thoroughly romantic in this rhetorical sense, the more devoted it will be to its function of magical transformation; indeed, the spell which the romantic poet seeks to cast over the moral present and future is not far removed from that of the primitive magician in either its purposes or its risks. But the more devoted it thus becomes, the more vulnerable will be its speaking personality. Such vulnerability is readily discovered in Shelley, Whitman, Lawrence, Rukeyser—all, despite differences, exposed spirits, "overstaters" of the case, often denied praise and resisted by those whom they affect most.

Muriel Rukeyser's effort has been to reconcile three sets of assumptions: those of the world-oppressed sensibility which is perhaps our chief modern convention and is by now inseparable from the technique of contemporary poetry, those of the democratic-pragmatic tradition, and those of scientific and revolutionary materialism. The assertion (desire) is that the heart of the poem is the heart of reality, drawing its life from the same sources as a vital culture must: belief in life, an endless reverberation of any heroic act, the dynamic realizations of art and love, strength to absorb the shocks of truth without abandoning its pursuit or denying the joy of thus meeting the meaning of experience:

READING TIME: 1 MINUTE 26 SECONDS

The fear of poetry is the
fear : mystery and fury of a midnight street
of windows whose low voluptuous voice
issues, and after that there is no peace.

That round waiting moment in the
theatre : curtain rises, dies into the ceiling
and here is played the scene with the mother
bandaging a revealed son's hand. The bandage is torn off.
Curtain goes down. And here is the moment of proof.

That climax when the brain acknowledges the world,
all values extended into the blood awake.
Moment of proof. And as they say Brancusi did,
building his bird to extend through soaring air,
as Kafka planned stories that draw to eternity
through time extended. And the climax strikes.

Love touches so, that months after the look of
blue stare of love, the footbeat on the heart
is translated into the pure cry of birds
following air-cries, or poems, the new scene.
Moment of proof. That strikes long after act.

They fear it. They turn away, hand up palm out
fending off moment of proof, the straight look, poem.
The prolonged wound-consciousness after the bullet's shot.
The prolonged love after the look is dead,
the yellow joy after the song of the sun,
aftermath proof, extended radiance.

2.

The main lines of this effort toward a triple reconciliation are evident in Miss Rukeyser's first book, *Theory of Flight* (1935). In the Thirties, the nature of this effort did not appear to need explanation; it was in the air, at least until the fall of Spain and the outbreak of the War. Kenneth Burke's *Attitudes toward History* is derived from similar motivations, and is indeed the best guide to the perspectives of the period. (Burke's review of *Theory of Flight*, incidentally, was easily the most perceptive one I have seen.) The political hope of the day, that the haphazard, easily corruptible, yet creative and idealistic individualism of Western tradition might find enduring common ground with the consciously organized though rigid social disciplines of Marxism, embodied these motivations and gave impetus to the literary movement in which Muriel Rukeyser was one of the younger participants. Of all the poets of any stature involved with that movement, she has been the most consistent adherent of the anagogic faith in possibility implicit in it. No one who reads her poems, early or late, with any attention can doubt the presence of a romantic personality seeking its own fulfillment through identification with its ideals, suffering recurrently depressive agony because of not being able to realize a "coming-through" yet never on that account sacrificing the goal and vision. For an implacably hostile reader, it may be sufficient compensation for her irrevocable commitment to a secular religiosity that Miss Rukeyser is so thoroughly willing to acknowledge the weaknesses that may underlie the commitment and the terrors which it must conjure up. Thus, she tells us candidly that

> The motive of all of it was loneliness,
> All the panic encounters and despair
> Were bred in fear of the lost night, apart,
> Outlined by pain, alone...

And she can speak the language of defeat:

> Who in one lifetime sees all causes lost,
> Herself dismayed and helpless, cities down,
> Love made monotonous fear and the sad-faced
> Inexorable armies and the falling plane,
> Has sickness, sickness...

These passages are from relatively recent poems, but we can easily find parallel passages in the earlier work, passages betraying fear and guilt over the path which the poet, a true Cordelia of the 1930s, is taking by choice as well as by necessity:

> The father and mother sat, and the sister beside her.
> I faced the two women across the table's width,
> speaking, and all the time he looked at me,
> sorrowing, saying nothing, with his hard tired breath.
>
> Their faces said : This is your home;   and I :
> I never come home, I never go away.
> And they all answered : Stay...

As has been observed, the implacably opposed will remain implacable and opposed—rejecting the specific ideas, especially in their threatening psychological associations against the prevailing cultural mode, and regardless of the spirit in which they are held; rejecting too the hysteria at the edge and the open pain at the center of "this sort of thing"; and rejecting finally the autobiographical confession spilling out over the form, not contained and beautifully transformed within it as in Yeats's "Sailing to Byzantium." Against all this must be set the fact that there are poems and passages in Rukeyser which either approach transformation of this kind or, failing that, are too rich even in failure to be dismissed casually. The poetic effort to "become whole," when sufficiently spirited and sensitive to counterbalance for the reader his irritation at being forced to watch the trials and errors of a magician from inside the magician's own brain, has gifts for him at last that much outweigh the inconvenience caused him.

In this essay, therefore, we are particularly to consider certain qualities of two of Miss Rukeyser's earlier long sequences, *Theory of Flight* (the title-poem of her first volume) and *The Book of the Dead*. Together with these we shall consider her *Elegies,* a group of poems written over a period of some ten years; and her most recent long poem, *Orpheus*. Each of these works seeks equilibria among warring factors in the poet's personality and consciousness; and each seeks to render the evil implicit in the fact of conflict nonexistent through its special kind of spell. *Theory of Flight* employs the mechanical and scientific image of an airplane—variously symbolic in its implications, both useful and dangerous in its daily uses, and clearly a token of cultural ideals in its speed, power, and requirement of expert manipulation—to spirit us into the arena of inclusive meaning. *The Book of the Dead,* first published as a unit in 1938, in Miss Rukeyser's second volume *U.S.* 1, has a double system of symbols: the Egyptian salvation-mythology whose sacred writings bear the same name; and the tragic mass-incidence of silicosis in Gauley, West Virginia, subject of national concern and a Congressional investigation in the mid-Thirties. In the first of these two early sequences, the converging of Marxian, personalist, and scientific perspectives is sustained through a combination of prayer similar to that of Crane's "To Brooklyn Bridge" with urgent assertions of wish as law, dramatic projections based on fact and fantasy (such as a scene between an aviator and his pregnant wife, a boardmeeting, a strike episode), and precise imagist impressions. In the second, the pacing is more gradual, the symbolism more convincingly grounded in realistic observation and dramatic structure.

In contrast to both these poems, the *Elegies* are directly "lyric-contemplative." They span the entire range of the poet's interests, beliefs, fears, enthusiasms, and experience from childhood on, recording and making an aesthetic of the major terms in her program of coaching herself into the true prophetic state of the romantic writer acting out his faith. (Similarly, the *Lives,* another group of poems which space prevents our discussing in detail here, considers the same range of subjects in the light of the biographies of other Americans, significant experimenters in their several ways with the idea of possibility and the problem of the communication of vital meanings.) *Orpheus,* in the image of the god made whole again after his dismemberment by the Thracian women, restates without reference to "extraneous" ideas and issues Miss Rukeyser's basic human themes: the indestructability of the creative life, the evil results of inattention to its demands and sources, and the reality of the promise:

> Voices and days, the exile of our music
> and the dividing airs are gathered home.
> The hour of light and birth at last appears
> among the alone, in prisons of scattering.

Reviewers of Miss Rukeyser's early work sometimes overemphasized—partly in deference to current literary fashion—the extent to which a Marxian influence had determined her subject matter, outlook, and emotional tone. There can be no questioning the presence of this motive. I believe, however, that we have in her writing an example, curious or paradoxical only in the altered perspective of the present moment, of a writer in the optimistic activist-idealist tradition of meliorism that runs through American philosophical thought who took literally the hope, not yet after all completely dead, that the best aspects of pragmatism and Marxism might be merged through a kind of social religiosity to the great enrichment of the world at large. A romantic writer, furthermore, and the child of an age of "experimentalism" in the arts as in social organization, she apparently found in the Marxian-Hegelian dialectic (thesis-antithesis-synthesis and the belief in qualitative transformation to follow inevitably after adequate quantitative pressure) and in the drama of political struggle forms comparable to those of lyric and sacred literature that could be used for purposes of poetic magic. It is the magic and the underlying mysticism of the dialectic that have characterized most of her poetry since the Thirties, together with a continuing personalism of thought; the rhetorical structure that so often makes her poems acts of faith in the teeth of her knowledge survives, signalizing an unchanged openness to all ideas of possibility now as before.

3.

The first of the longer structures, *Theory of Flight,* sought like the others to bring together many motifs. Its "Preamble," a secular invocation modeled on that of Crane's *The Bridge,* carries us at once into the wider implications of the idea of flight:

> Earth, bind us close, and time ; nor, sky, deride
> how violate we experiment again.
> In many Januaries, many lips
> have fastened on us while we deified
> the waning flesh : now, fountain, spout for us,
> mother, bear children : lover, yet once more
> in final effort toward your mastery.
> Many Decembers suffered their eclipse
> death, and forgetfulness, and the year bore round ;
> now years, be summed in one access of power.
> Fortresses, strengths, beauties, realities,
> gather together, discover to us our wings
> new special product of mortality.

The "we" here equals humanity conceived of in the most general sense as the human spirit. This spirit is imaged in active sexual terms, "female" in their connotation of readiness to be moved, taught, transformed. The use of such imagery suggests, perhaps more than the sexual freedom of modern thought generally, a feeling by the poet that her scientific-revolutionary frame of reference has justified the putting of poetic meanings from this "new" point of view. The reversal of the "usual" notion of the active element in sex as the masculine one almost exclusively can be defended as a rejection of stale conventional attitudes; and more to the point, doubtless, it can be understood as the "natural" expression of a woman. The search for reconciliation of many warring diversities is thus, at the same time, a search for equilibria within herself. The mind of the race, considered "in female," is accustomed to repeated betrayal—that is, to false starts toward a faith that will clarify, strengthen, and liberate all at once. But though "violate," it is always ready to experiment anew, even in the *coldest* season when traditional attitudes seem reduced to hopeless impotence. Male images are used to focus attention on various aspects of a deeply feminine symbolic structure. In the poem-sequence as a whole, the plane-image brings release to the personality "praying" the poem; the plane's phallic power must bear her away, reveal new vistas, teach her and the reader to "fly" on their own. In the passage just quoted, there is an appeal to the energies of the material universe to provide revelation which will be, as it were, sexually conveyed: by the spouting fountain, by the lover's effort, by the scientific construction of the will and imagination of men. The revelation, like the child who is the fruit of the act of love, will be a "new special product of mortality."

This theme of the self-realization of the female element in the human spirit is not at all a subordinate one, although its "application" in the poem makes it seem so. It is a theme running through all Miss Rukeyser's writing from the start, in such appealing early poems as "Breathing Landscape" and "Cats and a Cock," in the poems of love and growth and self-knowledge called *Night-Music*, and in its fullest and richest expression in the volume *The Green Wave*. The many poems dealing with difficult childhood and difficult growth bear as much relationship at least to this theme as they do to the other "issues" I have mentioned.

Though some critics expressed surprise that the author of the complex *Theory of Flight* should be a girl of twenty-one, the emotional atmosphere is actually quite youthfully ardent and anticipatory, as the following passage, which translates the invocation into self-coaching, demonstrates. It demonstrates too, though not as fully as some other passages might, the immaturity of the style—how the poet tries at times to solve technical problems through the simple device of shouting or groaning or ecstasizing:

> Look! Be : leap ;
> paint trees in flame
> bushes burning
> roar in the broad sky
> know your color : be :
> produce that the widenesses
> be full and burst their wombs . . .
>
> . . .
> lust in a heat of tropic orange
> stamp and writhe ; stamp on a wet floor
> know earth know water know lovers
> know mastery
> FLY

The entire book, in fact, is written in a mood that seems typical of the young intellectual radicals of the 1930s. Day-Lewis, Auden, MacNeice, and Spender had published their first volumes in their early twenties also. In these volumes, as in Miss Rukeyser's, the figures recur of the adventurer, the traveler, the explorer, the aviator, each a symbol of the young speaker breaking the ties of home, authority, and convention and each somewhat ambiguous, despite the pervading Marxian assumptions, as to precise destination. (In a Rukeyser poem, however, the speaker is likely to be awakened *by* a traveler as often as she is likely to *be* one:

> In adolescence I knew travellers
> speakers digressing from the ink-pocked rooms,
> bearing the unequivocal sunny word.

That is to say, she gives us one feminine version of the voyager-image.) The ambiguities are largely the result of a conflict of motives of acceptance and rejection such as one might logically expect in a rapidly maturing and really sensitive young nonconformist personality. There is a new and oppressive consciousness of sympathy with certain aspects of the old rejected life which interferes with the absoluteness of revolutionary conviction. In *Theory of Flight* overt expression of this ambivalence is held to a minimum, yet small indications do appear and the over-all symbol of the airplane is not altogether true to its intended function. A letter from Miss Rukeyser dealing in part with this poem and in part with her own experience in flying school gives other associations:

> Do you know a plane in a stall? A friend of mine says that it is the most neurotic thing demanded of a plane. You go against the plane, and then you have to go against yourself. You pull the nose of the plane up, so that most of the sky is blocked out by the plane, or so it seems; you feel the power spilling from the wings as it noses further up; then it hesitates a moment and plunges. This is the stall; and if you follow your instincts as a land-animal, you try to pull it out by forcing the nose up again. This you must not do, for you will only go into a worse stall. You must give in and let the plane fall; the fall will give it speed, and the speed will level it out again, it is built that way and that is its nature. As for me, I have never got past the stall; and I know that, in falling, I remembered a great many adolescent and infant prohibitions.

An autobiographical statement can be pushed too far as an aid to critical interpretation. I shall simply note here that the plane—whether seen sociologically and historically; or privately, in relation to a family situation—is a somewhat dubious symbol of positive revolutionary action against the reactionary past. The implication is that the force of gravity, the circumstances of daily material existence, is an evil thing against which the organized imagination must be put on guard; and this imagination will always have to operate "in the air" and against the pull of reality. So there is an unacknowledged suggestion that the real thing is there below, that this flight is a temporary escape, a pipe-dream, after which we must come to terms with everything left behind for the moment. The same premise is implied in several of the shorter pieces of this first volume, as well as in the work of other leading leftist writers. For instance, Auden's *Journal of an Airman* contains similar, if more consciously exploited, ambiguities.

A few notes on the structure of *Theory of Flight* may show how it tries to transcend these difficulties and to reconcile many separate value-referents. Much of the poem's ritual quality derives from its modernist and American passion for technical detail. Ideas of beauty, of social dynamics, of war and peace, of occupational hierarchy, of the relation of individuals to systems—all are centered about the mechanics of the airplane. The plane's power partakes of the divine, its flight has sexual mystery, and to master it will be a sign of our mastery over the big mechanism, the world as it is. "These are the axioms: stability, control,/ and equilibrium." The "Preamble" prays to the secular deities—earth, time, sex, space—for a liberating formula of creativity to match the metaphor of the plane, even at the cost of sacrificing real values inherited from the past. It tries, as we have seen, to fuse the idea of flight with orgasmic images of the loss of self in the active realization of the most intense, sensual kinds of experience. It praises the creativity of the human mind which can blueprint a machine that flies, thus bringing the will to triumph over fatality and demonstrating that the liberating formula lies in the dialectical process that returns man to the deepest meanings of nature through his struggles to impose his own stamp on it. The plane is the instrument of the process, and a guarantor of a social if not an individual rebirth:

> We bear the seeds of our return forever,
> the flowers of our leaving, fruit of flight,
> perfect for present, fertile for its roots
> in past in future in motility.

After "The Preamble," an objective equivalent is advanced for the dialectical struggle for order—the stabilizing factor in history—in "The Gyroscope." There is a governing mechanism in physical and social evolution as in the flying plane, a secret will in matter. In man this will becomes conscious power to transform the rest of being as well as himself. This metaphorical argument provides a highly charged transition to the next section, which has to do with what has actually happened to all this human possibility. "The Lynchings of Jesus" catapults us from the adoration of will and plan into the shocked observation of the violence and suffering that have marked our history, from the sacrifice of Jesus (and all its ancient analogues) to the trial of the Scottsboro boys and the deprivations of ordinary people in our own day. "The Tunnel" next brings us a Depression view of an American mining town, with the miners moving toward new perspectives: a strike movement. Their reaction against the waste of their lives suggests the "contact in desire," arising from need also, of lovers.

It is a very old "romantic" insight, this connection between love and death; the poet uses it here much as writers in the past used the ancient concepts of microcosm-and-macrocosm and the great chain of being—to establish a universal analogy, just as she had done with her image of the gyroscope as a symbol of a "secret" governing force in nature and history. The miners find unity and brotherhood facing the guns of company thugs; the young aviator risks his life out of love for his family and devotion to his "mission"; the young woman finds herself in the risks and discoveries of physical passion which destroy her former nature. The fifth section, "The Structure of the Plane," reasserts the universal analogy. The "message" is intended to be one of reassurance: that there is meaning, echoing through every phase of existence. But behind the urgent prophetic voice the cries of disaster, fear, waste rise too loud, and they are increased in volume by "Night Flight: New York," with its background of terror—a mock air raid's deceptive beauty that only heightens its true meaning—

> a burr of dissonance, a swoop of bare
> fatal battalions black against the air.

Despite the "triumphant" tendentious concluding section and the earnest search throughout the poem for true sources of courage, the sense of intransigent evil had taken over the poem by the end.

I have summarized *Theory of Flight* in this manner to indicate the typical thematic structure of a Rukeyser poem. By breaking it down to its basic ingredients, we can easily discover the fact that slogans of the moment and identifications of the hour have been only superimposed on some characteristic concerns and attitudes of modern verse. The influence of *The Waste Land* and of Lawrence, together with that of the British radical poets who had been subjected to the same two powerful influences (and to the *expository* method of MacDiarmid), has led to the conviction of bleakness in the cultural landscape and the need to shore whatever fragments the spirit may possess as a refuge and a weapon against that bleakness. But the leading political motifs of *Theory of Flight* have obscured for many readers the strong bond between Miss Rukeyser and the other poets of the age; that is, the rhetorical method has confused the nature of the insights, or rather can easily lead the reader to oversimplify them. . . .

4.

In *The Book of the Dead* the dramatic, documentary, and rhetorical vocabulary and rhythms are better integrated than they were in *Theory of Flight*. The earlier poem had employed desperate tactics to achieve progression; the poet had arbitrarily invented characters and interpolated moments of lyrical intensity to buoy up her own spirits against the overwhelming sense of pity and terror. The tactics could not quite succeed because the effort was too strenuous at every point and because the major symbol was too obviously "wishful" and in fact, to a certain extent at least, evoked too clearly the opposite of what it was intended to evoke. There is a fairy-tale element in the whole poem too, despite its serious purpose, just as there is in some of Lawrence's fantasies of womanly liberation. The strength of *Theory of Flight* lies in individual passages which break through the self-consciousness and the artificial perspectives, and achieve the driving force of a speaker transported by his own oratory. *The Book of the Dead* is certainly as ambitious a work, with an equally complex symbolic organization, but its structural emphasis remains on the social conditions which it documents.

In this poem, for instance, the traveler-image is more literally "down-to-earth." The poet sets out to "extend the document" by closing in historically and geographically on the scene of action, Gauley Bridge in West Virginia. In her *Selected Poems,* Miss Rukeyser notes that

> The twenty poems of *The Book of Dead* present a valley in West Virginia—a steep river-gorge where a tunnel and dam had been built. Silica, almost pure, had been encountered in the rock. The men who worked there, under threat of illness and death because of the silica, and unprotected, were dying now; they were being fought over in the courts, by the doctors, and in Congress; the women and children in the valley had come into this primitive state of war, among the fierce colored landscape and the precise buildings of the dam and power plant.

The past of the region includes heroism and triumph—early explorations and economic growth, the story of John Brown, the Civil War; its human heritage seems mirrored in "the power flying deep" of the river and falls. And whatever befalls the people there is a sign of the forces at work throughout America:

> Here is your road, tying
>
> you to its meanings : gorge, boulder, precipice.
> Telescoped down, the hard and stone-green river
> cutting fast and direct into the town.

We are introduced to the inhabitants by means similar to the documentary-film director's. A social worker describes their predicament at a Congressional hearing; the bleak town itself comes into view; there is a closeup of one of the victims of silicosis—and we are all the way into Gauley Bridge with the poet. *The Book of the Dead* wisely begins at a middle pitch, expository and colloquial in tone, urgent too but not straining beyond what the raw facts will allow. The pace is varied, giving us enough time to grasp the situation but keeping us moving along the clear plot-lines. Dramatic monologues give us full-length portraits of real people: a Negro miner, a rich girl who has joined the local committee to fight for proper safeguards and compensation, the local undertaker who has gone Frazer's *personae* one better by converting cornfields to cemeteries to bury those dead of silicosis at so much per head from the company, the engineer who designed the power plant, and the others. When, after more testimony, characterizations, and other "documentation" (all based on original research), we reach the climactic group of symbolic poems—"Alloy," "Power," and "The Dam"—we find we have been thoroughly prepared for their more concentrated, imagistic statement.

Using methods borrowed from the cinema, from the Living Newspaper of the Federal Theater Projects, from the symbolistic technics of modern verse, Miss Rukeyser invented a new poetic form based on recently developed devices for concrete dramatic presentation. Without abandoning real poetic values as our age understands them, she had met the challenge of centering a poem on a large social problem. We close in on the site of the problem, we meet the people, the action develops, there are moments of intenser realization, and finally we reach both a specific denouement and a projection of widening perspectives. Rereading the whole poem today, we may well ask why so little attention has been paid its methods.

One of the more interesting experiments in this poem is with the rhythms of the document. Miss Rukeyser seems to have been the first poet to block out a long passage from, say, an actual committee hearing, telescoping and altering its language mainly for reasons of poetic economy. Of course, the use of a long passage of prose, or prosy exposition, has ample precedent—in the *Cantos,* for instance—and has often been successful in providing a contrast and frame for more precise and purer lyric passages. The aim here is a little different, to incorporate a portion of the rhythm of the real situation into the structure of the poem that interprets it. Moreover, the form helps achieve a deliberate emotional restraint in the first half of the poem. It creates interest, has its own inner balance, but does not force unbearable demands for response upon us:

—What was their salary?
—It started at 40¢ and dropped to 25¢ an hour.
—You have met these people personally?
—I have talked to people ; yes.
According to estimates of contractors
2000 men were
employed there . . .

This restraint is supported by the generally expository and antisentimental language of the first part of the sequence. Thus, the camera-eye view gives us detail without comment:

Camera at the crossing sees the city
a street of wooden halls and empty windows,
the doors shut handless in the empty street,
and the deserted Negro standing on the corner.

And in case we are tempted to display a too-easy sympathy, the poet snarls sarcastically—doubtless at herself as much as at the reader—

What do you want—a cliff over a city?
A foreland, sloped to sea and overgrown with roses?
These people live here.

What we have at first, then, is a modified poetic form, just enough heightened in tone to keep us in the realm of incantation rather than of journalism. (Thus, there is a fair amount of precise, connotative language: "in the sudden weather, wet outbreak of spring.") The intensity is released only gradually. At the end of the second poem in the sequence, there is a moment of essential poetic insight; hardly a passionate outburst, however. In the third poem, only some altered syntax and condensation of a committee hearing, together with a scattered repetition of such nonemotive terms as "SiO_2" and "Union Carbide and Carbon Co.," contributes to this release. Not until the fifth poem does the poet allow herself the "license" of lyrical exclamation: "O the gay snow the white dropped water, down" and "O proud O white O water rolling down." And it is still later in the sequence before she feels free to speak prophetically in her own right, commenting in religious symbols on the monologue we have been reading by a mother whose husband and sons have been struck down by silicosis:

I open out a way, they have covered my sky with crystal
I come forth by day, I am born a second time,
I force a way through, and I know the gate
I shall journey over the earth among the living.

She has waited until the reader's grasp of the assumptions of the poem is beyond question, and his sympathies are gained for the people she has been depicting. The mother's determination to make her youngest child's death count for something, to have him live again in her own work of struggle for a better life, is linked with the rebirth-motifs of the great religions, and specifically of Egyptian religion, motifs not unrelated to man's will to overcome the laws of fatality:

I have gained mastery over my heart
I have gained mastery over my two hands
I have gained mastery over the waters
I have gained mastery over the river.

Thus the "social" thesis of the rebirth of humanity through struggle is subsumed under an older mysticism and used to give it a contemporary anchorage.

It is, incidentally, as the prophet of Isis, not Osiris, that the poet utters these "magic" lines. This is another example of the translation "into feminine" of revolutionary and heroic themes. The translation is aided by the echoes of a whole tradition of female protagonists from the great mythological earth-mothers through the heroines of Euripides to the modern self-discovering women of Lawrence and the working-class mothers of such novels as Gorky's *Mother,* Steinbeck's *The Grapes of Wrath,* and Wright's *Native Son.* Later, in a poetic portrait of Ann Burlak, the Communist labor organizer, Miss Rukeyser was to write:

She speaks to the ten greatest American women:
The anonymous farmer's wife, the anonymous clubbed picket,
the anonymous Negro woman who held off the guns,
the anonymous prisoner, anonymous cotton-picker
trailing her robe of sack in a proud train . . .

The triad of symbolic poems, as I have implied, brings the sequence to its emotional heights, translating both plot and larger symbolism into the concentrated poetic statement that the form by now demands—a denouement whose realizations are outgrowths of the silicon-covered countryside, the dam, and the power plant. "Alloy" pays homage to the terrible beauty of that landscape:

Crystalline hill : a blinded field of white
murdering snow, seamed by converging tracks . . .

In this view of the "disintegrated angel on these hills," we have one of the strongest images of perverted industrial mastery of nature in American poetry—comparable perhaps to the imagery in Crane's "The Tunnel." The theme of thwarted possibility is taken up again in "Power." Here the vital force which, uncorrupted, would make nature, human love, and the machine mirrors of one another is first seen in images of sexual potency:

> A day of heat shed on the gorge, a brilliant
> day when love sees the sun behind its man
> and the disguised marvel under familiar skin.
>
> . . .
> The power-house stands skin-white at the transmitters' side
> over the rapids the brilliance the blind foam

But between this promise and the idealistic visions of the Milton-quoting engineer on the one hand and the facts on the other is the familiar, dreary barrier:

> Down the reverberate channels of the hills
> the suns declare midnight, go down, cannot ascend,
> no ladder back ; see this, your eyes can ride through steel,
> this is the river Death, diversion of power . . .

But "The Dam," like the final section of *The Book of the Dead*, and of *Theory of Flight* before it, tries to direct the current of negation back the other way again. Despite the "white brilliant function of the land's disease," it declares, "All power is saved, having no end."

> It breaks the hills, cracking the riches wide,
> runs through electric wires ;
> it comes, warning the night,
> running among these rigid hills,
> a single force to waken our eyes.

The great difference, however, which makes this sequence rhetorically so much more satisfactory than the earlier one, lies in its having refrained from jamming an unaccountable optimism down our throats. The great redemption myths have risen as gestures and projections against adversity, and this poem frankly allies itself with a similar motivation. As for the metaphorical argument that man and water alike have the power ultimately to renew themselves, the long-range viewpoint is hard to disagree with; it is in full accord with the religious analogy, which is equally uncontrived and unhurried:

> Effects of friction: to fight and pass again,
> learning its power, conquering boundaries,
> able to rise blind in revolts of tide,
> broken and sacrificed to flow resumed.

5.

The general intellectual bearings of *Theory of Flight* and *The Book of the Dead* are more difficult, upon analysis, to define than the disparate elements. . . . The basic problem of these poems is one of self-integration, and the main terms are those employed at the beginning of "Ninth Elegy: the Antagonists":

> Pieces of animals, pieces of all my friends
> prepare assassinations while I sleep.
> They shape my being, a gallery of lives
> fighting within me, and all unreconciled.
> Before them move my waking dreams, and ways
> of the spirit, and simple action.   Among these
> I can be well and holy.   Torn by them I am wild,
> smile and revenge myself among my friends
> and find myself among my enemies.
> But all these forms of incompleteness pass
> out of their broken power to a place
> where dream and dream meet and resolve in grace.

In this passage, as the poet tells us in her critical book *The Life of Poetry,* is embodied one of the chief meanings of her most recent longer work, *Orpheus*. The ambiguity of the plane image and the Laurentian overtones of *Theory of Flight,* and the turning to Egyptian mythology in *The Book of the Dead,* had been tokens of a groping toward such a clearer, more personal formulation, and of a holding-off from commitment to any abstraction that might block it off. The early shorter poems, too, had often held off in this sense, or in the sense that they were the work of a person with "other" concerns too—the concern simply to be a recording sensibility, for one thing, and the concern to discover herself and be honest about it. Reality itself was something torn to pieces, and one must explore the various ways of putting it together again, remaking it in the image of graceful resolution: the dream.

The sources of renewal lay for this poet not merely in some overtly plausible social program but in the touching of certain kinds of courage within oneself, certain potentials of will and imagination which could, despite the apparent subjectivity of the whole procedure, bring one directly into the sense of reality—provide an epiphany of the flesh and thereby a grasp of the meaning of wholeness. The *Elegies* are an open record of the search for these sources. . . .

The first five poems in the *Elegies* appeared in the 1939 volume *A Turning Wind*. In the context of that volume and of *U.S.* 1 (published the year before), their effect as a unit was considerably more bitter than that of the entire group of ten elegies printed as a separate book a decade later. *U.S.* 1 and *A Turning Wind* spoke for the young revolutionary poet struggling to keep an optimistic vision intact despite her own state of deep depression growing in part at least out of her experience in Spain and the tailspinning of the cultural movement with which she has been associated. "We were too earnest. We had to lose," she had written earlier than all this, with a slightly different emphasis from the present one in the poem "Eel," a reconstruction of the process of coming of age in America. She had sent herself a reassuring memorandum concerning the value of her poetry in "Homage to Literature"—with its echoing beginning:

> When you imagine trumpet-faced musicians
> blowing again inimitable jazz
> no art can accuse nor cannonadings hurt...

And she had written, in *U.S. 1,* a whole series of poems dealing with guilt, fear of self-betrayal, frustrated love. "Night-Music" is full of revealing ambiguities of the sort which show that a writer's most cherished assumptions are still being subjected to a continuous testing against observation and self-analysis. Now, in *A Turning Wind,* there were poems like "Nuns in the Wind" that smelt out coming disaster:

> That was the year of the five-day fall of cities.
> First day, no writers. Second, no telephones. Third, no venereal diseases.
> Fourth, no income tax. And on the fifth, at noon.
> The nuns blocked the intersections, reading...

In this poem and others there are questionings of the worth of her own character as well as of the ultimate success of her beliefs:

> All that year, the classical declaration of war was lacking.
> There was a lot of lechery and disorder.
> And I am queen on that island.

and:

> It was long before the troops entered the city
> that I looked up and saw the Floating Man.
> Explain yourself I cried at the last. I am
> the angel waste, your need which is your guilt,
> answered, affliction and a fascist death.

A Turning Wind, in its angry knowledge of world-betrayal and in its ability to maintain a feeling of relationship, both to the causes of defeat and to the projection of possibility, is easily Miss Rukeyser's most moving single volume. The group called *Correspondences* takes cues from the observations of Kenneth Burke on the effects on the revolutionary philosopher of his own thinking:

> Democritus laughed when he
> saw his whole universe
> combined of atoms, and
> the gods destroyed...

The irony of his situation carries over to the poet's own; and further cues are taken from the wryly tough work of Bertolt Brecht in a second poem of the group, and from the passionate simplicities of Yeats's refrains in a third. The world is in an ugly state, it must be confessed, despite the "joys" afforded by knowledge and the Yeatsian "gaiety" of artistic realization; the fall of Barcelona was a key, and in the future, perhaps,

> If some long unborn friend
> looks at photos in pity,
> we say, sure we were happy,
> but it was not in the wind.

It is a time when the ritual and politics of war are more powerful than human will, when "humor, saliva of terror, will not save the day," and when

> Laughter takes up the slack
> changes the fact, narrowing it to nothing,
> hardly a thing but silence on a stage.

Against this there is only the understanding of the reverse of these tragic ironies of history, the "joke" of the universe, namely the fact that history is without meaning to objective nature and must remain so until men can prevent the perversion of their own humanity.

> Violent electric night! and the age spiralling past
> and the sky turning over, and the wind turning the stars.

It would have been hard indeed to cast a completely cold eye at the need so acutely and sincerely defined in these poems. *A Turning Wind* begins with the five *Elegies*, which set the tone of hope maintained through nerve and faith alone despite many misgivings and moments of hysteria and despair that sink very near to the bottom. This *dark* element is therefore much more characteristic of these five poems as a group in this volume than of the ten-poem sequence as it now stands.

In their own terms, the *Elegies* are a long report on the perilous journey of the poet's "unfinished spirit" through loneliness, through the disapproval of her parents and others in authority, and through education in the world's brutality. She learns to distinguish between Magicians and Prophets. The former stand only for "inward pleasure," the "trance of doom" that is the magnetic effect of power on its votaries; the latter, less lurid and forceful in their impact, stand for the "unity of light" but can never win a permanent victory:

> The prophet lives by faith and not by sight,
> Being a visionary, he is divided . . .

The allegorical contrast is established in a few violent, concentrated passages which make the second elegy the most successful, perhaps, of the group. The initial personal statement in the *first* poem, however, might lay some claim to precedence:

As I went down to Rotten Lake I remembered
The wrecked season, haunted by plans of salvage,
snow, the closed door, footsteps and resurrections,
        machinery of sorrows.

The warm grass gave to the feet and the stilltide water
was floor of evening and magnetic light and
reflection of wish, the black-haired beast with my eyes
        walking beside me,

The green and yellow lights, the street of water standing
point to the image of that house whose destruction
I weep when I weep you. My door (no), poems, rest,
        (don't say it!) untamable need.

. . . .

However this may be, the poet argues that the Prophet would inevitably triumph over the Magician were it not for the "fear of meaning," presented in the third *Elegy* as inseparable from "fear of form." (The first poem quoted in this essay deals with the same subject from the same point of view.) One underlying theme is that the vital sources of artistic form are to be found in the oppressed but resilient mind of the people. In the fifth *Elegy*, "A Turning Wind," hope is expressed for the defeat of evil through a merging of these sources with the strength for good of science. . . . And the light of history, rightly understood, can help us pierce the present darkness:

the lights winding themselves into a single beacon,
big whooping riders of night, a wind that whirls
all of our motives into a single stroke . . .

This was the culmination of the *Elegies* as they first appeared, and in the context I have described. What their removal from that context, and the addition of five more poems to the group, has done is to shift the whole focus from a struggle for faith to the positive assertion that the faith will become reality. The elegies, now, begin in deep depression and end in triumphant joy, though all are built around similar oppositions and move in the same direction. Or rather, we may say that in outward form the sequence has this pattern, intended to be the earned result of a bitter effort to deal with harsh reality:

Does this life permit its living to wear strength?
Who gives it, protects it.   It is food.
Who refuses it, it eats in time as food.
It is the world and it eats the world.

But the tendency of the sixth to tenth elegies is to oppose just a little too glibly—though often most magnetically—the sense of betrayal in these latter years against the certainty of final victory on all emotional fronts. . . . Some irony, and more commitment to the demands of the poem as a poem are needed if one is to stay on the "right side" of the boundary between self-analysis and the spiritual begetting of Byzantium.

Miss Rukeyser herself must realize these necessities more than anyone else as she strives to maintain a unity despite a constant scattering of forces in her poems. Not only has she developed a good deal of skill in what might be called the moment-by-moment tactics of rhetorical intensity, but she has also, in her recent work, paid more attention than before to the more purely musical aspects of her writing. . . . and her most recent longer poem, *Orpheus,* is organized in accordance with this development. More important, she is experimenting in it—as she had not done since *The Book of the Dead,* written over a decade ago—with the classical discipline of attempting to rewrite a myth while staying within the limits of association of the original version. Instead of "pieces of animals, pieces of all my friends," we now begin with the most unassuming "objective" imagery, the data of the myth of Orpheus' murder by the Thracian women:

> The mountaintop stands in silence a minute after the murder.
> The women are furies racing down the slope; far down,
> copper and black of hair, the white heel running . . .

while Orpheus lies

> Scattered, there lit, in black and golden blood :
> his hand, a foot, a flat breast, phallus, a foot,
> shoulder and sloping back and lyre and murdered head.

"I knew," writes Miss Rukeyser of this poem in *The Life of Poetry,* "what would follow. The pieces of the body would begin to talk, each according to its own nature, but they would be lost, they would be nothing, being no longer together. Like those in love, apart, I thought. No, not like anything. Like pieces of the body, knowing there had been pain, but not able to remember that pain—knowing they had loved, but not remembering whom. They knew there must be some surpassing effort, some risk. The hand moves, finds the lyre, and throws it upward with a fierce gesture . . . through the black air to become the constellations . . . the four strings sing *Eurydice*. And then the pieces begin to remember; they begin to come together; he turns into the god. He is music and poetry; he is Orpheus."

So Orpheus is reborn because without his rebirth there would be no response to the principle of love in man, and because the separated parts of him *need* to be reunited. The structure, even thus described by the poet herself, bears no inner necessity within it, or conviction of heroic challenge. For here again we have the demand for synthesis existing independently of any real link with the reader except his awareness of the poet's desire for it. In *Orpheus* as before in Miss Rukeyser's work the greatest impact is made by those portions of the poem which portray calamity and distress. The long opening stanza, associating the landscape, the shock, and the results of the act of primitive murder, focuses with full dramatic effect on the colors and rhythms of the moment of catastrophe—the speaking voice impersonal yet most seriously engaged in understanding the ritual horror of the moment. In a sense this effect contains the most vital elements of the whole poem, and the succeeding lines in the first movement for the most part simply elaborate while blurring a bit the initial impetus. The second movement begins the exploration of the meaning of loss of contact with a wry comment on the "sideshow of parts, the freaks of Orpheus":

> Scattered. The fool of things. For here is Orpheus,
> without his origin : the body, mother of self,
> the earliest self, the mother of permanence . . .

. . . .

At last the effort is made, the resurrection takes place, and the whole poem is resolved into the god's final, brief, lovely song of possibility, of "creation not yet come." The object, as before, remains to make desire become reality in the course of a single poem despite the shadow; and, as before, the demand on the reader is too great for this purpose, although as a statement of need, and in particular passages, there is no question of the poem's power. My own feeling is that this poem, like *Ajanta*, is a sign that at thirty-five Miss Rukeyser still felt herself under the obligation to prove the truth of every motif she had ever been inspired by, but that she was growing into a surer sense, finally, of the demands of what has been referred to as lyric-contemplative poetry. . . .

New Directions 14 (1953)

Sources in Myth and Magic

THE COLLECTED POEMS OF W. B. YEATS
A VISION by W. B. Yeats

THE simultaneous publication of Yeats's *Collected Poems* (Definitive Edition) and reissuing of his *A Vision* give us nothing significantly new, yet remind us of everything in his work that remains marvelously the same. Both, we are told, contain "the author's final revisions," yet their pagination is identical with the 1951 *Collected Poems* and the 1938 *A Vision*, the latter long out of print. Of course, a comma here and a semicolon there can make a great difference, and we reserve the right (learned journals please note) to descant on those fine bibliographical points in another season. Meanwhile, we are given two happy excuses to think once more about a great poet's work.

One of the first thoughts is the astounding *relevance* of his work to the critical issues of twentieth-century consciousness—astounding partly because the more one reads Yeats the more absorbed and fascinated one becomes by the idiosyncrasies of his technical achievement, his symbols, his many-sided intellectual biography and his system of images. But the simplicities are what count first: the natural yet varied music of his verse, the full vigor and candor of his way of statement, the wit and wide applicability of his insights. You may not like what he has to say in his short poem "Parnell," but you are bound to feel its force:

> Parnell came down the road, he said to a cheering man:
> "Ireland shall get her freedom and you still break stone."

The poem speaks to the modern world, bringing to the fore one of its great fears—of an ultimate futility of politics. So does "The Great Day.":

> Hurrah for revolution and more cannon-shot!
> A beggar upon horseback lashes a beggar on foot.
> Hurrah for revolution and cannon come again!
> The beggars have changed places, but the lash goes on.

To begin with these examples may be to present an unfamiliar, acerbated Yeats, but it will show also his distrust of that callous demagoguery which feeds on mankind's greatest hopes and ideals. A third unfamiliar poem, "Church and State," will recall too the fearless cast of his mind, his ability to appreciate mutually contradictory possibilities at the same time, giving each its weight in the emotional scheme of things. It is a political poem which, like Blake's "London," is not tendentious but deeply responsive to the state of man:

> Here is fresh matter, poet,
> Matter for old age meet;
> Might of the Church and the State,
> Their mobs put under their feet.
> O but heart's wine shall run pure,
> Mind's bread grow sweet.
>
> That were a cowardly song,
> Wander in dreams no more;
> What if the Church and the State
> Are the mob that howls at the door!
> Wine shall run thick to the end,
> Bread taste sour.

But the relevance is not mainly political at all. Even Yeats's superficially political poems—those like "Easter, 1916," for instance—are not really so. This poem sings the glory of the men whose lives were lost in the Easter Rebellion, and the "terrible beauty" born in Ireland as a result of that sacrifice. At the same time, it grants that the rebels may have been mistaken, that England may yet abide by her promise to grant Ireland her independence. The poem is characteristically honest, and all the more convincing because it refuses, as Yeats always did refuse, to be dogmatic. What saves it from dogmatism is the way it turns on a single image (of hearts "enchanted to a stone") which, followed through with strict poetic integrity, forces the poet to shift the ground of his thought and include the possibility that his heroes may have been wrong. And so the truer relevance of the poem lies in the way it allows for a play of opposites against each other. This play, or dialogue, of opposites in his work almost always transcends the warring issues themselves.

The audacity of "Church and State" is characteristic of Yeats's spokesmanship for the contemporary mind and sensibility. In the deepest sense he believed in nothing yet spoke for belief; and speaking for it, he yet detested the thought of vain causes and idealisms that could make a man false to himself. He was interested in folklore, in theories of the occult from Rosicrucianism to spiritualism and mystical idealism of every sort including the doctrines of Plato and Plotinus. His attraction to these cults and doctrines had many motivations, but one was overriding: his belief that they provided symbolic clues to the unconscious life of mind and spirit as well as to the subjective world of image, emotion and creative imagination. He sought a kind of anti-scientific science of symbolic realization, derived from mythical and esthetic sources: a science that would therefore—from a poet's standpoint, at least—go beyond both the materialistic thought-systems that prevailed in his youth and the vague bodiless religiosity that shuddered away from those systems.

A list of his most famous poems brings into the mind a series of vibrant, archetypal pictures, surrounded by passionate song: the rape of Leda; a Sphinx-like beast "moving its slow thighs" over the desert as the annunciation of a new, terrible recording of human destiny; an old whore shrieking beautiful obscene profundities at a doctrinaire priest; an Earthly Paradise where the great sages and heroes of tradition take their whimsical ease while the Innocents of the New Testament "re-live their death" again and again and "nymphs and satyrs copulate in the foam."

Through this symbolic "science" he succeeded in constructing a poetic world in which there was simultaneously room for the most bleak and candid recognitions and the most exalted visionary transformations:

> Those masterful images because complete
> Grew in pure mind, but out of what began?
> A mound of refuse or the sweepings of a street,
> Old kettles, old bottles, and a broken can,
> Old iron, old bones, old rags, that raving slut
> Who keeps the till. Now that my ladder's gone,
> I must lie down where all the ladders start,
> In the foul rag-and-bone shop of the heart.

The organizing system for this poetic world of actively related opposites (which is perhaps most fully realized dramatically in the two Byzantium poems, in the play *The Resurrection* and one or two others, and in 'A Dialogue of Self and Soul') is provided in that surprising, delightful, partly makeshift book *A*

Vision. Behind *A Vision* lies the parallel occultist experience, reading, and thinking of both Yeats and his wife. Her efforts at automatic writing shortly after their marriage in 1917 were what led to the conscious formulation and emergence in images of the themes and diagrams around which the book is built: the cycles of history and of individual personality; the relations between the wheel of time and timelessness, between physical universe and pure spirit; the opposition of Christian and pagan-Renaissance values; the "dreaming-back" by the soul after death of its worldly experience; the new applications of the ancient concept of the "Great Year"—the two-thousand-year cycle within which a dominant mode of civilization is born, flourishes and dies; and the basic symbol of the interpenetrating gyres, or vortexes, forever at war and forever passing through regular phases in their relation to one another.[1]

How many of these ideas Yeats believed in unreservedly is open to question, especially since it is impossible to be sure that he believed unreservedly in *anything*. It is interesting that he begins his introduction to the book with the observation that, as a result of the "incredible experience" it represents, "my poetry has gained in self-possession and power." Also he tells us (*possibly* without intentional humor) that when he offered to spend the rest of his life interpreting the messages received through his wife's automatic writing, the spirits replied: "No, we have come to give you metaphors for poetry." (These spirits, incidentally, were demanding, pedantic, even petulant. For instance, "they asked me not to read philosophy until their exposition was complete," and sent flashes of light or struck chairs violently when they disapproved of the Yeatses' behavior. On the other hand, they quite sentimentally filled the house with the smell of roses when a son was born there.) And he ends his introduction with these words:

> . . . . if sometimes, overwhelmed by miracle as all men must be when in the midst of it, I have taken such periods [the Great Years] literally, my reason has soon recovered; and now that the system stands out clearly in my imagination I regard them as stylistic arrangements of experience comparable to the cubes in the drawing of Wyndham Lewis and to the voids in the sculpture of Brancusi. They have helped me to hold in a single thought reality and justice.

The combination of whimsical writing (the book contains a letter to Ezra Pound that begins: "My Dear Ezra, Do not be elected to the Senate of your country"—although here again Yeats may not have realized the lovely absurdity of this plea), textbookish precision and organization, passages of poetry, and personal speculation of a quite elegant order makes *A Vision* rewarding in many ways. It is surprising that it has no real *literary* reputation in its own right, and is generally thought merely schematic, even if fantastically so. It is full of passages that are not only interesting in themselves but also illuminating for readers of Yeats's poetry:

1. The best book on Yeats's thought, including, of course, *A Vision*, and on its relation to the development of his poetry is Richard Ellmann's *The Identity of Yeats* (Oxford University Press: 1954)—a distinguished study that has been unaccountably neglected.

> A civilization is a struggle to keep self-control, and in this it is like some great tragic person, some Niobe who must display an almost superhuman will or the cry will not touch our sympathy. The loss of control over thought comes towards the end; first a sinking in upon the moral being, then the last surrender, the irrational cry, revelation—the scream of Juno's peacock.

Out of the organized subjectivisms of *A Vision* and his brooding over their implications came the rich art of the later Yeats. He had developed a mode of symbolic thinking that was free and hypothetical, yet emphatic and concrete, and he was enabled thereby to encompass the great issues without being swamped in partisanship. ("I never bade you go," he wrote, "to Moscow or to Rome.") *A Vision* brought to fruition his lifelong search for a supernaturalism and a set of intellectual points of reference that could not commit him to any established religion or philosophical school. It provided the necessary exotic themes and images—he calls them his "circus animals"—which, because largely and primarily esthetic, allowed him the greatest latitude of thought and statement without risk of public outrage or censorship. (Even his espousal of an aristocratic ideal, though "real," is basically esthetic in conception.) His humor too was enriched by this liberating effort— so that we have many effects like that in "Crazy Jane on the Mountain" in which, amidst the painful realization of the loss of heroic meanings in the modern world, there is suddenly called up the vision of the mythical warrior-king Cuchulain and his queen "great-bladdered Emer" (an allusion to a contest in which Emer clearly demonstrated her superiority to certain other mythical ladies). The whole of "John Kinsella's Lament for Mrs. Mary Moore" has this kind of tragic-hilarious quality.

Yeats did achieve the definitive success of transforming his whole consciousness of himself, mind and body, into the objectified and dramatized symbolic counters of his art. And because he *used* the system but was rarely its creature, he could always change the counters, re-explore their implications, try out this solution and that, and if need be discount them entirely:

> But hush, for I have lost the theme,
> Its joy or night seem but a dream;
> Up there some hawk or owl has struck,
> Dropping out of sky or rock,
> A stricken rabbit is crying out,
> And its cry distracts my thought.

The Nation (23 June 1956)

from *Tradition and Transition*

THINGS OF THIS WORLD by Richard Wilbur
ONE FOOT IN EDEN by Edwin Muir

TO liberate oneself from "influences" that not only guide but bully, it is sometimes necessary to reach back behind them, to their own sources. Many contemporary poets, in their several ways and with varying clearsightedness, are now making this effort—an effort to get in touch anew with the root-motivations animating the Romantics, the French Symbolists, the experimentalists of thirty *and* of sixty or seventy years ago, and their other literary ancestors. The currently renewed fascination with sacred and mythological themes indicates even more the effort at self-rediscovery.

The transitions are not easy, especially when there is only dim consciousness of what is happening, and the distress signals are everywhere, and everywhere different. Thus, in *Things of This World* Richard Wilbur seems beset by a sort of ennui, the result of a conceptual dependence which bedevils him with an especially treasonous subtlety. Though he is still one of our better poets, the things his poetry says and lives by are so much of the essence of the modern Anglo-American heritage that others have already preëmpted the original and audacious modes of expression he might otherwise use. Compare his "An Event" with Stevens' "Thirteen Ways of Looking at a Blackbird," for instance. The younger poet has been almost forced into a blander, more discursive tack, for which even his highly developed grace and skill of rhetoric cannot fully compensate. Rhetoric, incidentally, is put to sharper use in the one political piece here: "Speech for the Repeal of the McCarran Act." Genuine poetic energy and concreteness quicken the effect of this piece, which augurs the revival of a genre recently much neglected. But this poet's main chance does not lie in a political direction.

Wilbur's own medicine for his disease is, for him, a good one: translation, and a turn of emphasis toward French sources that goes with it. His dominating vision has always been the aesthetic-secular one of the post-Romantic tradition:

> I take this world for better or for worse,
> But seeing rose carafes conceive the sun
> My thirst conceives a fierier universe.

Still, Wilbur finds it difficult, in his usual voice, to present this vision as truth; he rather argues for it as an ideal. Everything changes, however, when he takes on a different voice or mask by translating from the French. Then, particularly in rendering Baudelaire's *"L'Invitation au Voyage"* and Valéry's "Helen," he is at once far within the vision. Again, with Jammes' "A Prayer to Go to Paradise with the Donkeys," he is from the start at a pitch of pure elation for which he strives in vain elsewhere. Moreover, of the successful poems here that are *not* translations, the best are those most closely approaching the dream-atmosphere of the French Symbolist tradition (as opposed to the Emersonian or morally melioristic streak in contemporary American poetry, which has at times overborne Wilbur's sense of himself). Such poems are "Merlin Enthralled" and "Marginalia," the latter of which tells us that

> Descending into sleep (as when the night-lift
> Falls past a brilliant floor), we glimpse a sublime
> Décor and hear, perhaps, a complete music...

ALMOST seventy now, Edwin Muir has seen his reputation grow considerably in the past decade or so. Partly we may attribute this increased recognition to what might be called his explorations in religious orthodoxy, of which *One Foot in Eden* now marks a culmination. No other poetry that I have recently seen so beautifully embodies the convergence of Judaic, Christian, and Grecian (mythological) ideals with those of the humane secularism that now colors so much of modern thought. Whether one resists or welcomes—from whatever viewpoint—this convergence is irrelevant; Muir's writing shows its deep subjective anchoring and some of the ways it satisfies needs both elementary and complex.

Although these poems are often devout in tone, they are not to be identified with the externalized religious "revival" now packing the churches and synagogues with its vague promise of "a sense of belonging." Muir brings us directly back to the recognition of mysteries such as Eliot's "Gerontion" calls for: "Signs are taken for wonders. 'We would see a sign!'" We sometimes forget that French Symbolist poetry aimed, as C. M. Bowra puts it, to secure through art "the ecstasies which religion claims for the devout through prayer and contemplation." Muir's connection with the Symbolists is clear, and in addition he returns very emphatically in *One Foot in Eden* to the symbols both of Biblical and mythical traditions and of common experience. "The Annunciation" gives us storied mystery as fact:

> The angel and the girl are met.
> Earth was the only meeting place.
> For the embodied never yet
> Travelled beyond the shore of space.
> The eternal spirits in freedom go.

And, at the other end of the scale, "The Island" chants the mystery of what is known through physical experience:

> Men are made of what is made,
> The meat, the drink, the life, the corn,
> Laid up by them, in them reborn.

Yet the poems are never "merely" religious in a stock sense. Thus, there is more compassion and awe than doctrine in "The Animals," squarely based though it is on the Old Testament; similarly, while in "Outside Eden" the forlorn but unquestioning piety of the true believer takes on heroic dimensions, the *truth* of what he believes so truly is not brought into consideration. Muir once wrote that "There is a vast area of life which science leaves in its original mystery; and this is the area with which poetry deals, or should deal." In the present volume he deals with just this area, and if one added "dogmatic theology" to "science" one would doubtless not be distorting his meaning. The ambiguities of faith are part of his subject, and in this and other respects he approaches the complex skepticism of Yeats.

If I have suggested that *One Foot in Eden* is interesting mainly because of the way it handles the problem of belief, I have fallen into a trap of my own making. In its own right it is poetry of a rich though quiet intensity and of enormous emotional concentration. This visionary Orkney Islander, another of our modern semi-metaphysicals, feels—so sharply that he can touch it—the reciprocal elusiveness of experience and of thought; hence the ease of his movement between "real" observation and insight on the one hand and abstractions on the other. The beautiful imagistic poems "Double Absence," "The Late Swallow," and "The Late Wasp" are also philosophic poems without at all straining to be so, while "Nothing But Faith" and "The Grave of Prometheus" bring theoretical conceptions to tangible realization. A few poems, such as "Effigies" and "The Horses," encompass all these considerations through their prophetic scope and, without hubris or ranting, are informed by a transcendent disinterestedness, pity, unsqueamishness of psychological probing, and proffering of hope (but with no *promises*) for the future.

The Nation (10 November 1956)

Poet of the New Violence

HOWL AND OTHER POEMS by Allen Ginsberg

THE two most striking pieces in Allen Ginsberg's pamphlet *Howl and Other Poems*—the long title-piece itself and "America"—are sustained shrieks of frantic defiance. The themes are struck off clearly in the opening lines of each:

> I saw the best minds of my generation destroyed by madness, starving hysterical naked . . .

and

America I've given you all and now I'm nothing.

Isolated quotation, however, will not convey the real tone of these poems, though their drift is not hard to define. We have had smoking attacks on the civilization before, ironic or murderous or suicidal. We have *not* had this particular variety of anguished anathema-hurling in which the poet's revulsion is expressed with the single-minded frenzy of a raving madman.

Ginsberg hurls, not only curses, but *everything*—his own paranoid memories of a confused, squalid, humiliating existence in the "underground" of American life and culture, mock political and sexual "confessions" (together with the childishly aggressive vocabulary of obscenity which in this country is being increasingly substituted for anti-Semitism as the "socialism of fools"), literary allusions and echoes, and the folk-idiom of impatience and disgust. The "best minds" of his generation as Ginsberg, age 30, remembers them "howled on their knees in the subway and were dragged off the roof waving genitals and manuscripts." They "scribbled all night rocking and rolling over lofty incantations which in the yellow morning were stanzas of gibberish."

Would you inquire? discuss? rebuke? "I don't feel good don't bother me."

That is to say, this poetry is not "rational discourse," such as we find in almost all other American literature of dissidence. Nor is it that flaccid sort of negation, too easy and too glib, that so often reduces the charge in the writing of Patchen and others, though it does occasionally lapse into mere rant and scabrous exhibitionism. It is the fury of the soul-injured lover or child, and its dynamic lies in the way it spews up undigested the elementary need for freedom of sympathy, for generous exploration of thought, for the open response of man to man so long repressed by the smooth machinery of intellectual distortion. It is further evidence, the most telling yet, perhaps, of the Céline-ization of nonconformist attitudes in America, or should we say their Metesky-ization? Homogenize the dominant culture enough, destroy the channels of communication blandly enough, and you will have little Mad Bombers everywhere.

Though his style is effectively, sometimes brilliantly, his own, Ginsberg shows the impact of such poets as Whitman, Williams and Fearing in his adaptations of cadence to rhetorical and colloquial rhythms; once in a while he falls entirely into the cadence and voice of one or another of these writers, on occasion—as in "A Supermarket in California"—deliberately. But he does break through as these poets, who are among the men who have most earnestly sought to be true native voices in their several ways, have prepared him to do. Is Ginsberg of the same calibre? Despite his many faults and despite the danger that he will screech himself mute any moment now, is he the real thing?

What we can say, I think, is that he has brought a terrible psychological reality to the surface with enough originality to blast American verse a hair's-breadth forward in the process. And he has sent up a rocket-flare to locate for his readers the particular inferno of his "lost battalion of platonic conversationalists jumping down the stoops off fire escapes off windowsills off Empire State out of the moon," all of them "yacketayacking screaming vomiting whispering facts and memories and anecdotes and eyeball kicks and shocks of hospital jails and wars."

And very simply, this is poetry of genuine suffering. The "early" pieces at the back of the little book have a heavy Yiddish melancholy—

The weight of the world
    is love.
Under the burden
    of solitude,
under the burden
    of dissatisfaction

    the weight,
the weight we carry
    is love.

The more recent poems, as William Carlos Williams writes in his introduction, present "our own country, our own fondest purlieus," as a "Golgotha," a "charnel house, similar in every way to that of the Jews in the past war." Seen from above the water, Ginsberg may be wrong; his writing may certainly have many false notes and postures. For the sake of self-respect and of hope let us take the position that this is all too destructive and therefore mistaken, and that a total assault may be even worse than mere acquiescence. But that is all beside the point. The agony, in any case, is real; so are the threats for the future that it signals.

The Nation (23 February 1957)

Ladies' Day on Parnassus

VILLA NARCISSE by Katherine Hoskins
THE COLLECTED POEMS OF KATHLEEN RAINE
LIKE A BULWARK by Marianne Moore

WHILE all other poets should study simplicity, Katherine Hoskins is at her best moving with gaily elegant artificiality among sad paradoxes. Not that she pretends to be a lady-Pagliacci, but she does get at *reality* better that way, as the high points of *Villa Narcisse*—the few poems like "Excursion," "At Night It's Like a Different Planet," and "To the Patron," this last so much like Marvell yet so beautifully and personally Mrs. Hoskins' own—all show. When she deals with simplicities, we too often find ourselves pondering the obvious, learning how the busy, lecherous bee doth ravish the garish petunia, or how the girl who once lay so happily on her lover's chest, "belly on bone, knee on knee," finds herself, after marriage, a "disappointed housekeeper," or how generous the poor are and how irrecoverable or cruel is childhood. Give her some fine outlandish conceit, however, full of strained and morbid farfetchings, such as that the mind is a dull, habitually terrified rabbit on a wintry landscape, and she goes flying into the empyrean with a zeal that would be pure delight if her empyrean were a trifle sunnier.

> An axle-pole revolves down sealèd
> bearings and the climate of pain
> swings in. Mind's hutch dissolves,
> the carrots long and rose, viridian
> lettuces, the water, silver meshed
> and roofed secure. Mind, reluctant,
> unresistant, pricked and lured
> lopes away. . . .

Such delicate felicity of phrase and line goes with a mind not only fanciful and capable of subtle, sustained elaboration of a thought but also very much engaged in life. A chief objection to these poems is that Mrs. Hoskins is less rigorous with herself than she should be. "A Dream," for instance, promises a great deal. It is charged with a guilty eroticism derived from contemplating a viciously depressing dream the speaker has endured, but is sealed off with a too facile turn at the end. "M's Story," which strikes notes as witty yet poignant as anything of Ransom's, and "The Sisters" are among the other partial successes, in which one feels the necessary last effort has not quite been made. Yet there is something durable and appealing in all these poems, and in the book as a whole: an authoritative feeling for the toughness and resilience of the materials the poet has to master. In Melville's language, may she find the "time, strength, cash, and patience" which the mastery will require.

MYSTERIOUS Kathleen Raine! She is . . . what Anne Lindbergh in another life might have become, perhaps. A kind of intellectual primitive, she is forever seeking to close in on the "still point," the radiant source and center of things. She is a mystic this side revelation, as it seems to me, with a power of concentrated incantation that very nearly overbears her essential coldness. She wants to be taken out of her own skin, and at least once, in her "Invocation" for the making of a poem, has rendered that desire in the imagery of masochistic violence:

> Let my body sweat
> let snakes torment my breast
> my eyes be blind, ears deaf, hands distraught
> mouth parched, uterus cut out,
> belly slashed, back lashed,
> tongue slivered into thongs of leather
> rain stones inserted in my breasts,
> head severed,
>
> if only the lips may speak,
> if only the god will come.

The frenzy here is rare for this poet. More characteristic is her "In the Beck," which catches the strangeness of the life-principle in a figure at once elusive and perfectly lucid:

> There is a fish, that quivers in the pool,
> itself a shadow, but its shadow, clear.
> Catch it again and again, it still is there.

There is charm and spontaneity enough in this conception to thaw its chill somewhat. Not so with "The Crystal Skull," whose calculated structuring has the aim of pulverizing our sense of individuality in a vision of destruction of the humanly meaningful world by "the perfection of light."

> At the focus of thought there is no face,
> the focus of the sun is in crystal with no shadow.
> Death of the victim is the power of the god.

If the pain in Raine stays mainly in the brain, it is probably out of choice—because her feeling is all too strong, not too weak. "Woman to Lover" is couched objectively, in a series of metaphors rippling out into ever wider connotations. A poem on grief, "Introspection," purges its emotions by considering the indifference into which all things die away. The poet finds it necessary to displace private emotion by such means and by striving to invoke the "peace that passeth understanding." She displaces it also through her curious nostalgia, not merely for her own irrevocable past but for the whole past, seen in evolutionary perspective.

> I am what is not what I was.
> Seas, trees, and bird, alas!
> Sea, tree, and bird was I!

The infinity of perspective, the need to escape the here and pierce the "intense inane," carry their own risks: flatness, vapidity, a curious callousness that at times resembles insensitive inspirationalism, a variety of pedantry even. Miss Raine does not always avoid the pitfalls, but when she does come through it is with an indescribable grace and lightness and with the music, as she says, of

> Harmonious shells that whisper for ever in our ears,
> "The world that you inhabit has not yet been created."

NOTHING is easier (*vide* the recent *New Yorker* profile which pictured her as the most delightful animated toy, barring the Dodgers, in Brooklyn) than to take a gourmet's view of Marianne Moore. She is "sprightly" and "spriggy"; if you like to savor plain fare exquisitely garnished and served, she will shred your radishes deftly and add a grain of pepper:

> Look at Jonah embarking from Joppa, deterred by
> the whale; hard going for a statesman whom nothing could detain. . . .

In a shrewd, almost folksy, way she is a fellow of infinite jest, though the jests have an indomitable innocence to them, like the private jokes of families. By now, of course, it is no longer necessary to prove that there is a "good deal more" to Miss Moore's work than fastidious and innocent audacity of wit and association. William Carlos Williams once wrote of her special modernity:

> Unlike the painters the poet has not resorted to distortions or the abstract in form. Miss Moore accomplishes a like result by rapidity of movement. . . . It gives the impression of a passage through.

That was in *1931*! The century has aged considerably since then, but not Miss Moore. Her "Logic and 'The Magic Flute'" might have been written to illustrate the method described by Williams; it begins with the experience of going up into the "small audience-room" of the NBC Opera Theatre to watch a colorcast performance of *The Magic Flute:*

> Up winding stair,
> here, where, in what theatre lost?
> was I seeing a ghost—
> a reminder at least
> of a sunbeam or moonbeam
> that has not a waist?
> By hasty hop
> or accomplished mishap,
> the magic flute and harp
> somehow confused themselves
> with China's precious wentletrap.

The wentletrap is an elegant marine shell whose name derives from the German for winding staircase. The speaker is keenly aware of the analogy she has made between this beautiful creation of an unconscious organism working without anxiety or any sense of being burdened by special "fetters" and the creations of human beings under the circumstances of modern life. "You need not shoulder, need not shove," she writes—even though the performance is being given within the very precincts of the essence of modern pressure,

> Near Life and Time
> in their peculiar catacomb.

Outdoors the "interlacing pairs" of skaters in the Rockefeller Center ice-rink are weaving another formal pattern, again unconscious. Marianne Moore remains as alert to such resemblances within resemblances as ever, and as insistent on her own stubborn, morally tough and challenging meliorism. Woe's us, she chooses Mr. Eisenhower as the parallel symbol in our political life of the most creative pragmatic tradition—and of "Diversity, controversy; tolerance":

blessed is the author
who favors what the supercilious do not favor—
who will not comply. Blessed, the unaccommodating man.

Ah, well, she may yet be right, and it may be that her hero's "illumined eye has seen the shaft that gilds the sultan's tower." If she errs in this matter, and if most Americans err with her, it is not for lack of faith in the qualities thought to inhere in the President. At least she is not too proud to be with the majority, and—as she says of Jonah—she is after all "one who would not rather die than repent." *Like a Bulwark,* indeed, is as a whole a praise of the durable in life, the richly common. Miss Moore's characterization of the rosemary may in this sense stand for the whole. This shrub, she says,

is not too legendary

to flower both as symbol and as pungency.
Springing from stones beside the sea,
the height of Christ when thirty-three—
not higher. . . .

Not higher? Then we'll have to settle for the miraculous best we actually have. And looked at rightly, that's her whole point.

The Nation (16 March 1957)

Mr. Auden and Clio

THE CRITERION BOOK OF MODERN AMERICAN VERSE
edited by W. H. Auden
THE OLD MAN'S ROAD by W. H. Auden

WITH his customary quick omniscience, W. H. Auden has put together an unpredictable and original, if not altogether distinguished, anthology of modern American verse, very different from his and Norman Holmes Pearson's authoritative *Poets of the English Language*. He gives a place to some neglected poems and figures and to *vers de société,* but makes some unfortunate omissions and some rather arbitrary inclusions. There is a Wodehousian breeziness in the misspelling of names,[1] the slightly mishmash quality of the pieces, and the absence of declared principles of selection. The introduction, an essay first printed in *The Anchor Review* in 1955, is barely relevant and begins with a dazzling inaccuracy: "One often hears it said that only in this century have the writers of the United States learned to stand on their feet and be truly American, that, previously, they were slavish imitators of British literature." One *never*, as a matter of fact, hears it said any more, and Mr. Auden's ensuing demonstration that we did too have a truly American literature before this century is a triumphant recapitulation of the utterly familiar. But our poetry—Lord bless it and keep it—generally rises superior to anthological impediments and roadblocks. After its lopsided fashion *The Criterion Book*, no exception to this rule, contains much that is pleasant and some things that are exciting, and is an unusual example of lighthearted editing in a heavy-hearted age.

MR. AUDEN brings us also a small new pamphlet of verse. The seven poems of *The Old Man's Road*, says its jacket, are "a series of reflections on the nature and process of history." We cannot quite resist asking whence cometh the intimacy, which Mr. Auden has always exhibited, with Clio, "Muse of the unique historical fact"? Did *you*, for instance, know that she "looks like any ordinary girl one has not noticed"—"approachable" but not as if she "ever read" the poets?

Perhaps such questions are irrelevant, and perhaps it is equally irrelevant to say that the *thought* in these poems is really very tired. The book opens on a note of sentimentalized and pragmatized piety. True religious history ("the Old Man's Road"), we are told, is not a matter of creeds or theories but runs

> Across the Great Schism, through our whole landscape,
> Ignoring God's Vicar and God's Ape. . . .
>
> The Old Man leaves his road to those
> Who love it no less since it lost purpose. . . .

Among the messages that follow in succeeding poems are these: it may be more admirable for cultured folk at the fag-ends of civilizations to indulge themselves in their hyper-sophisticated pursuits to the end than to engage in vain histrionics (the half-ironies of this poem make it possible to argue that the poet is actually taking the opposite position); Clio loves not the supposed "great" men of an era but the makers of concrete, useful things; wonderful things have been accomplished purely by mistake; absolute and extreme vows and commitments are dangerous; and time, which is so great a healer, is also the reconciler of man to his sufferings.

Ordinarily we ought to disdain the reduction of poems to their bare thematic bones. It should be self-evident that poets do not in general pretend to be

1. For example, "Trumble" Stickney, John Crowe "Ranson," "Ivor" Winters, Richard "Eberhardt."

great primary thinkers, but use ideas as they use other elements of composition—as important but subordinate aspects of the poems they make. Mr. Auden, however, is so clearly bent on teaching us, his aim is so essentially didactic, that it is particularly important to take note of just what he wishes us to learn. Even if we add that the poems are of course not *merely* didactic, that they are variously wry, sardonic, and "sincere" in an informal but determined sort of way, we can see that his rhetorical devices for intriguing us (and himself) are part of the message. We (and he) are to accept the validity of religious faith and Mr. Auden's allied attitudes in part because we are able to look at history in a humorous, knowledgeable, wittily condescending way; entranced by fairy lore and the logic of childhood, we are smilingly to accept the limitations of human intelligence and foresight, and so on. This is the subtlest kind of forensic art.

Still there remains a residue of unfairness, perhaps. Never to judge a book by its tendencies remains a good rule. As this poet himself says, even "banalities can be beautiful." The question then remains whether the sheer intrinsic appeal of the poetry as something created does not outweigh the tendentiousness. Despite the odds, we expect, and receive, a good showing from Auden. No notable advance in technique, no heights of intensity, and always that self-echoing of his that is apparently inescapable. But "C. 500 A.D." is perfect light verse—a greeting to the future from "the last Romano-Briton, / Taking the last hot bath." Similarly, "The Epigoni" summons up at once, and with the gentlest sarcasm, a recurrent predicament and mood of doomed civilizations:

No use invoking Apollo in a case like theirs;
The pleasure-loving gods had died in their chairs
And would not get up again, not one of them, ever,
Though guttural tribes had crossed the Great River,
Roasting their dead and with no name for the yew. . . .

Exceptionally seductive is the music of "Homage to Clio," and its subtle mixture of sensuous and ratiocinative:

Our hill has made its submission and the green
Swept on into the north; around me,
From morning to night, flowers duel incessantly,
Colour against colour, in combats

Which they all win. . . .

The seductiveness is not just a matter of fine passages. Auden remains the virtuoso who can keep a poem going in a great many ways, through sound-modulations, changes of tone and voice, breadth of association:

. . . Artemis,

Aphrodite, are Major Powers and all wise
Castellans will mind their p's and q's,

But it is you, who have never spoken up,
  Madonna of silences, to whom we turn

When we have lost control, your eyes, Clio, into which
  We look for recognition after
We have been found out. . . .

The reader of poetry is forbidden by the rules to be a prude. When there is any seductiveness at all about, seduced he must let himself be. If it all depended on *The Old Man's Road,* though, we doubt the affair would last. It's not Clio's fault, poor little historian's-Muse that she is. The real fault lies in that curious didactic forcing which is not quite concealed by the most knowing insinuations and the sweetest flutings this very clever poet can manage.

The Nation (23 March 1957)

from *The Virtue of Translation*

POETIC translation is one of the great vital means, perhaps the greatest one, of communication between eras and cultures. "Something there is that doesn't love a wall." At whatever level, with whatever makeshifts, we do want to know what "the others" are saying, and they do want us to hear it. Even the crudest translation can put us in touch with what otherwise we might never have experienced at all; even the dreadful translations of Pushkin that appear from time to time suggest a way of seeing and saying things, a world of felt truths, as authentic and valuable as it is "strange" to us. This principle holds especially where the poet is virtually unknown in our tradition, and where all we have is the earnest work of a translator with more dedication than talent.

The case of the Polish poet, Adam Mickiewicz, like that of Pushkin but even more tantalizingly, is an apt example. *Faute de mieux,* I was willing to plow through the impossibly tedious and tritely phrased translations of his work in the edition of his *Selected Poetry and Prose* issued by the Polish Government two years ago. I especially wanted to read the selections from *Pan Tadeusz,* reputed to be the masterpiece of Poland's "national poet," taken from the 1885 translation by Maude Ashurst Biggs. And it is true enough; one does see something of the power of this nineteenth-century Romantic patriot and lover of freedom, and of his tremendous ground sense of his native land; all this despite the Biggs version, which begins "Litva! My country, like art thou to health. . . ." and bounces on forever in like ancient bumpiness to the last recorded decasyllabic line. Enough passion, enough concentration of complex elements in simple, vivid moments of action and description, manifested themselves in spite of everything to sustain my faith that there must be more to Mickiewicz than glazed my eye on most of these pages. The publication, a year later, of the *Selected Poems,* excellently edited by Clark Mills, confirmed that faith. Though *Pan Tadeusz* is not there included, the translations by Auden and other poets of real competence bring out the values one could only guess at before.

Good translation, of course, goes further than just introducing us to an alien body of writing and then leaving us to speculate what it is really like under the ready-made, undistinguished cloak that some half-poet has draped over it. It must have an identification of spirit realized through the most sensitive response of style. We are most demanding when the original is a classic over which many fine poets have toiled. Why Gilbert Highet should offer his own pitiful verse-translations of the Latin poets in *Poets in a Landscape,* or why Frank Copley should print his only slightly less earless versions in *Catullus: The Complete Poetry,* when so many more accomplished versions were available, is one of the great mysteries. *"Vivamus, mea Lesbia,"* writes Catullus—

Vivamus, mea Lesbia, atque amemus,
rumoresque senum severiorum
omnes unius aestimemus assis—

which Horace Gregory's *The Poems of Catullus,* with beautiful economy and accuracy, renders:

Come, Lesbia, let us live and love,
nor give a damn what sour old men say.

Highet, horribly, says:

Life, my Lesbia, life and love forever!
All that gossip of grave and reverend elders—
close your ears to it! it's not worth a penny.

And Copley, who has something of a buck-and-wing touch:

I said to her, darling, I said
let's LIVE and
let's LOVE and
what do we care what those old
purveyors of joylessness say?
(they can go to hell, all of them)

A good translator may make mistakes or deliberate changes in the literal reading, yet he will transcend them by the way in which he carries the whole poem forward in the spirit of its own conception. Almost all such translators disclaim any effort at scholarly exactness. "I have not," writes Dudley Fitts in his introduction to *Poems from the Greek Anthology*, "really undertaken translation at all—translation, that is to say, as it is understood in the schools. I have simply tried to restate in my own idiom what the Greek verses have meant for me." And in introducing *One Hundred Poems from The Chinese*, Kenneth Rexroth says: "I make no claim for the book as a piece of Oriental scholarship. Just some poems." After the translator has swerved from his customary orbit into that of his original, he needs somehow to bring himself back into his own orbit again; in the process the original text becomes less his pattern for copying than his *subject*, and the poem does become his own. Compare Fitts's translation of the "Elegy on Herakleitos" by Kallimachos with that of William Cory (perhaps the most famous translation in the *Anthology* hitherto). Cory, who used Latinized spelling of Greek names, begins:

They told me, Heraclitus, they told me you were dead,
They brought me bitter news to hear and bitter tears to shed.

Fitts, much closer to the heart of the poem, avoids both the non-stop pace and the superimposed adjectives of Cory, and also avoids the awkwardness of his "They brought me . . . tears to shed."

One brought me the news of your death, O Herakleitos my friend,
And I wept for you. . . .

Poets like Fitts and Rexroth (not that there are so many that they make up any large class) are completely free of either servile literalism or pretentiousness in their translations. Fitts, especially, imposes his own discipline on his materials—the discipline of the best, organically balanced, free verse. The familiar takes on new character and feeling in his hands:

The best of all things it were, never to be born,
Never to know the light of the strong sharp sun;
But being born,
The best of all is to pass as soon as may be
To Hadês' gate,
there to lie dead,
Lost, locked close beneath the world's huge weight.

(Theognis, "Gnomic Verses")

Diophantos went to bed
& dreamed of Dr. Hermogenês,

Although he was wearing a Lucky Piece,
he never woke up again.

(Lucilius, "On Hermogenês the Physician")

The challenge of these elegiac and satirical pieces, so many of them exquisitely controlled and chiseled to a deceptive brevity, has stimulated Fitts—always an interesting poet—to his finest work in this book. Rexroth, working less precisely to get just the right *weight* in his poems, presents less formal variety. As in his own original poetry, so in his Chinese translations he strives less for design and concentration than for a central rightness—the tone simple and natural, sometimes humorous, sometimes (usually) wry and nostalgic; and though "objective" and fatalistic, he is not reluctant to introduce a generalization occasionally. The first part of his book, the translations from Tu Fu, is taken from work "I have had . . . by me since adolescence and over the years have come to know these poems better than most of my own." The second consists of translations, many of them freer, from poets of the Sung Dynasty—Su Tung P'o, Li Ch'ing Chao and others. All have the Rexroth touch, though no doubt they are in direct relation to their sources. The heavy melancholy of Tu Fu's "Snow Storm," or his "To Wei Pa," or his "Night in the House by the River" is exactly matched by that of Mei Yao Ch'en's "On the Death of a New Born Child" or of Chu Shu Chen's "Hysteria"; and the poems of other moods follow parallel patterns no matter who their authors. Yet these are all idiosyncratic and convincing, because the translator has found common ground with his ancient Chinese poets, and has in a real sense become one of them himself.

Translation is anything but the sterile exercise it sometimes may seem to be—an exercise in the impossible, most people are tempted to call it. "How in the world can you translate *poetry?* It just can't be done!" At the very least it is a bridge, however unreliable, to the unknown. At its best, it is a voyage of self-discovery as well as of exploration of new-found lands. Incidentally, there is a special use and pleasure, I should think apparent to everyone, in those volumes which print originals and translations side by side—volumes such as Jackson Mathews' edition of René Char's *Hypnos Waking* or Louise Varèse's of the *Éloges and Other Poems* of St.-John Perse. Char's poems, and his poetic prose, are rendered by various hands, and it is especially absorbing to see how his style dominates that of so many able poets who write in our tongue, yet seldom seems to violate their own centers of gravity. What! Is this William Carlos Williams who writes: "Reality, noble, does not refuse herself to the one who comes to prize her, not to insult or take her prisoner"? Yes, of course, it is exactly Williams' "message," though marvelously disguised in Char's more abstract language. Is this W. S. Merwin being so unabashedly sensuous in a love poem?—"Is there a carved throat more radiant than yours? To ask is to die!" Yes, why not? And besides, the poem, "The Room in Space," closes in on itself in the true Merwinian manner, till it reaches a final paradox that is the whole clue to the lovers' relationship. But in addition, it is endlessly instructive to contemplate the differences and similarities between a line of English such as I have just quoted and the French it is based on: "*Est-il gorge menuisée plus radieuse que la tienne? Demander c'est mourir!*" In Char's language, as in his thought, the sensuous and the moral, the immediately present and the mystically implied, the detached and the committed are simultaneously revealed. Char shows us how the fusion of such categories of opposed values in a poetry that is profound without affectation can be as easy as breathing.

St.-John Perse, in Louise Varèse's uneven translation, is another matter. Here we are reminded (and the French across the page makes the reminder infinitely stronger) that the poetry of pure evocation, "every rift more loaded with ore" than Keats himself dreamed of—every petal of association pressed for the evocative attars within it—is no more dead than Symbolism itself.

Each of these translations brings us new faces—and not merely masks but naked faces—for man. Each takes us into a truth we might not have noticed, or at least remembered. Each reinforces our knowledge that essential truth is always a unique realization with its own idiom and mode of revealing itself. Each recalls to us the way in which kindred sensibilities exist where we would not have thought of seeking them. "The others"—the people of past and foreign experience—are something better than pathetically distorted images of ourselves; they are our possibilities, our alternatives in life and in vision, writ large. Ezra Pound strengthened his own vision immeasurably through his summoning up of Propertius in his famous *Homage to Sextus Propertius*. This translation-adaptation, intended "to bring a dead man to life, to present a living figure," enabled him to help revivify the language of poetry by bringing the candid sensibility of the Roman poet to bear on the cant of our century. Inevitably, the effort of our best poets to reconstruct the work of other fine poets who have written in other languages must have a similar effect and thus be an endlessly germinating enterprise.

The Nation (16 November 1957)

Metamorphoses of Yeats

THE VARIORUM EDITION OF THE POEMS OF W. B. YEATS
Edited by Peter Allt and Russell K. Alspach

THE Variorum Yeats! I was going to start by saying what pure pleasure it is to see—and to have—this large and beautiful, yet workmanlike, volume whose editors have tried "to note all the changes Yeats made in his poems in the course of their successive printings."

And yet a certain melancholy grips the vitals. Yeats, like Joyce, had the artistic cunning of the serpent; we see its workings in his endless revisions in book after book during his creative lifetime—and he published poems in more than a hundred books of various kinds. But the triumph of his cunning lay in the Definitive Edition of his *Collected Poems*, the proofs of which he had corrected shortly before his death in 1939. (Owing to the war, this edition did not appear in England until a decade later; the American printing came only two years ago.) Here we received the whole of his poetry as he had come to conceive it and in the order in which he wished it arranged. Half a century ago, indeed, he wrote that when he remade his poems it was "myself that I remake," and in the same year he wove a half-playful incantation against all who might tamper with the remaking:

Accursed who brings to light of day
The writings I have cast away!
But blessed he who stirs them not
And lets the kind worm take the lot!

Beneath the facetiousness lies a poet's inevitable unease at being viewed in any light save that which he himself projects in the living present. Now the *Variorum* reprints more than sixty poems omitted from the definitive *Collected Poems* and recalls the earlier versions of poems drastically remolded over the years. We still have the definitive text on these new pages, but it is surrounded by the old serpent's cast-off husks of skin, preserved in bibliographical formaldehyde. Their presence—who could ever have foreseen this?—has the embalmer-staunched atmosphere of death about it. Poor Yeats is now not only the great poet of this century; he is an Official, Dead, Great Poet—an Industry, a Vested Interest, apart from his intrinsic merits. One can almost, alas, foresee the revolt of the young against the "oppressive" idioms of his phrasing and rhythm, against his aesthetic tenets and his embodiments of a world in revolutionary torment, and against his search for what he called an image of the modern world's self-discovery. It becomes possible to visualize the J. Donald Adamses of the future "defending" him against his true but temporarily alienated heirs and quoting, as we should all perhaps now quote, those vulgarly elegant lines of Auden's—

Earth, receive an honoured guest:
William Yeats is laid to rest. . . .

But these are unjust thoughts. The best writers survive their own institutionalization and the inevitable literary reactions against them. Nor are scholarship and criticism to blame that their aims cannot be identical with those of the creative figures they study. The *Variorum Edition*, product of a long collaboration between Russell Alspach and the late Peter Allt, enables us to see the poems in a setting, as it were, of their own history, illuminating a body of writing which—so subtly, often, did Yeats structure it—sometimes appears to change radically in its implications with every new reading. It provides, moreover, collated versions of Yeats's notes, prefaces and dedications, bringing together almost all the materials necessary to textual study except the manuscript-forms of the poems, publication of which "must await their coming to light through the years." We betray the poet and his vision only if we allow preoccupation with the mechanics of such an edition to obscure what they are intended to illuminate.

Given this starting point, there is much in this particular volume to fill a young poet with courage. Often (though this is deceptive) it does not seem *too* impossible to think of rivaling the early Yeats. We find him publishing, at the age of twenty-four, a long poem that begins:

Oisin, tell me the famous story
Why thou outlivest, blind and hoary,
The bad old days. Thou wert, men sing,
Trapped of an amorous demon. . . .

A later redaction, the one included in the Definitive Edition, alters things drastically, slowing down the jingling movement, sloughing off the archaisms, choosing words of stronger affect:

You who are bent, and bald, and blind,
With a heavy heart and a wandering mind,
Have known three centuries, poets sing,
Of dalliance with a demon thing.

The possibilities for improvement in this poem (*The Wanderings of Oisin*, first printed in 1889) were limited, but Yeats did what he could when the opportunity arose. Following up hundreds of such changes, we can trace his development from an almost unconscious imitator of the modes prevailing in his youth to the most effective craftsman of our day. For the early poems, the definitive version is at many points a sophistication of something basically naive: our modern absorption in complex, paradoxical poetic statement, and in concrete and compressed presentation, does some violence to one tradition of limpid lyricism in English verse. Yeats, who was crucially instrumental in setting up the ideal of a mature, vigorous verse that is intellectually as well as emotionally challenging, did usually improve his early writing in the revision, but sometimes destroyed a delicate fabric whose original simplicity he could not quite recapture. An unfortunate incidental result of his continual efforts at "remaking" has been an almost total discounting by criticism of his work before about 1910, work which includes such lovely variations on folk-materials as "The Stolen Child" and such exquisite arrangements of intellectual, dramatic and symbolic elements as "Adam's Curse." Nevertheless, his need to rework what was already in print, together with his responsiveness to criticism and to the technique of younger poets, was one of the most powerful reasons behind his growth in stature.

Many of the changes show not only stylistic tightening but also self-liberation from the clichés of poetic movements. The sinister faeries of "The Stolen Child" sang, in what we might call a composite early version, that

In pools among the rushes,
That scarce could bathe a star,
We seek for slumbering trout,
And whispering in their ears
We give them evil dreams. . . .

Revising the passage, Yeats omitted the commas closing lines one and three, and altered the fifth line to read: "Give them unquiet dreams." The open punctuation helps the eerie flow of suggestive melody, as does the omission of "we" in the last line and the substitution of the less pretentious but more active "unquiet" for "evil." In addition, though, "evil" is too *easy* a word, a short-cut to Blakean and proto-Symbolist effects. By deleting it Yeats removed an identifying label that was a little too pat by the early 1890s when this change was made. The poems underwent numerous virtually invisible but highly significant alterations of this sort throughout his career.

More exciting, to the general reader certainly, are the revisions one discovers were made in some of the most famous later poems—in "Leda and the Swan," for instance, which originally began:

A rush, a sudden wheel, and hovering still
The bird descends, and her frail thighs are pressed
By the webbed toes, and that all-powerful bill
Has laid her helpless face upon his breast.

These lines, after their first few printings, became:

A sudden blow: the great wings beating still
Above the staggering girl, her thighs caressed
By the dark webs, her nape caught in his bill,
He holds her helpless breast upon his breast.

The action becomes more sudden and powerful, the dramatic onslaught more sensuously felt and visualized; the more mysterious "dark webs" replaces the faintly absurd "webbed toes"; the trite "all-powerful" is dropped, in such a way as to enhance the sharpness of the picture; and an anticlimactic effect in the fourth line is turned brilliantly into a symbolic moment of mysterious sexual confrontation.

Among the hitherto uncollected pieces, incidentally, we find what might be considered a startling variation on the Leda motif in some lines on George Moore:

Moore once had visits from the muse
But fearing that she would refuse
An ancient lecher took to geese
He now gets novels at his ease.

"Made long ago," Yeats comments disingenuously in a 1909 diary entry, "but written now because it comes up into memory, and it may amuse me in some moment of exasperation with that artless man." The more decorous amongst us may think such invective unbecoming an Official, Dead, Great Poet. But he is *not* dead—he lives, and always has lived. Think, too, how alive, and still relevant, is the casual couplet he tossed off almost thirty years ago "on reading poems by certain young writers in an American magazine of verse"—

The heart well worn upon the sleeve may be the best of sights,
But never, never dangling leave the liver and the lights.

Some of the notes and prefaces add much to the richness of this edition. Thus, Yeats's note on "Leda and the Swan," written in 1924 for *The Dial* but never reprinted in any of the collected editions, shows fascinatingly how his imagination worked. It shows, especially, how his political attitudes entered into poems whose conception one would think was as far as possible removed from the issues of the forum. Perhaps Yeats preferred not to publish it again just because it was so revealing in this fashion, or perhaps—one can only guess—he felt it was too much a kind of posing, or was not quite right stylistically, or made the poem out to be less seriously motivated than it should be. But, despite its eccentric identifications, it is saturated with a type of awareness that is an essential clue to the relevance of his poetry to the major questions of his time:

> I wrote "Leda and the Swan" because the editor of a political review asked me for a poem. I thought, "After the individualist, demagogic movement, founded by Hobbes and popularized by the Encyclopaedists and the French Revolution, we have a soil so exhausted that it cannot grow that crop again for centuries." Then I thought, "Nothing is now possible but some movement from above preceded by some violent annunciation." My fancy began to play with Leda and the Swan for metaphor, and I began this poem; but as I wrote, bird and lady took such possession of the scene that all politics went out of it, and my friend tells me that his "conservative readers would misunderstand the poem."

The "conservatism" of the readers here referred to was obviously of literary rather than political attitudes. Yeats's own "conservatism" was of another kind—the kind that kindles vast revolutions of thought: a shifting of perspective toward neglected points of value of such a nature that it hardly mattered what parties he might vote for, or not vote for. This note is but one of the many items we may ponder with delight and passion, and sometimes with bitterness, in this volume; there is no end to the book's instructiveness, nor to our indebtedness to its devoted and distinguished editors.

The Nation (5 April 1958)

Salvo for William Carlos Williams

so much depends
upon

a red wheel
barrow

glazed with rain
water

beside the white
chickens.

—"The Red Wheelbarrow"

THIS year William Carlos Williams becomes seventy-five. The event will be heralded by the appearance of *Paterson V*, from which we are privileged to publish, on the following pages, a few sections in advance. We seize the occasion to make this issue a small Williams-*fiesta*. Nothing very formal, but we are happy to have a poet of his kind writing in the United States today.

Perhaps any sort of literary occasion plays this poet false. Writing about Williams, one always wants to do things *his* way, with that same deceptive ordinariness, those wildly unaffected exclamations—

The trees—being trees
thrash and scream
guffaw and curse—
wholly abandoned
damning the race of men—

Christ, the bastards
haven't even sense enough
to stay out in the rain—

Wha ha ha ha
Wheeeeee. . . .

Williams' own talk, like his writing, is natural and simple, almost diffident though always frank.[1] But it gets where it wants to get; it moves without transition into profundities whenever he so intends. One suddenly grows aware of something precise emerging from the casual exchange, discovering itself, it may be, through a metaphor of green plants in running water or through some sharp, cold projection of thought thrusting above the kindly amenities. In his poetry there is a *mystique* of the physical, but here too one must qualify; austerity is behind it—the quiet irony and self-discipline of the sensitive medical man, reinforced by the artist-moralist's preoccupations. Even the Williams residence partakes of this austerity. The compact, old-fashioned doctor's-house is set right in the midst of Rutherford, with the "downtown" stores almost across the street and the traffic all around and the shabby crisscross of New Jersey's railroads and highways not far off. It has a right relation to everything that holds clear of pretentiousness, whether out of choice or out of necessity.

So it's not quite "good old Bill" or "good old Doc." Apart from his magnificent ear, there is essential to this poet's achievement not only his generosity of spirit but a faith so intense and stern it all but becomes despair. It is a faith in the meaning of experienced reality and in the power of art to reveal it and, as he says, "to right all wrongs." "The Red Wheelbarrow," quoted at the head of these remarks, expresses this faith, quietly but with absolute authority. In each little stanza the opening line, with its two stressed syllables, prepares for a flight of thought and imagination, while the second weighs the tiny unit down with a turn of idiom or the name of a familiar concrete object. The poem's design is a striving for value, for significant realization, against the resistant drag of the merely habitual. Everything "depends" on the way we see color, shape, relationships; the scope of our understanding of life depends on it, the freedom of our consciousness, the way we transcend limitations and communicate with one another as human beings.

Williams' remarkable alertness to the subtler life of the senses—how it feels to be a growing thing of any kind, or to come into birth; how the freshness of the morning or the feel of a particular moment in a particular season impresses itself upon us; what impact the people glimpsed or encountered in a myriad transitory situations make upon us at the moment of the event—gives him a keener and more adventurous insight into the aesthetic potentialities of that life. The general population's insensitivity to those potentialities is one of his concerns. He links this problem to another: the absence of a "language" that will enable Americans to cultivate, direct and shape their crude and, at present, suicidal energies. "The pure products of America," he has written, "go crazy." They have lost contact with European tradition, and left to themselves they run to emptiness and depravity. His *In the American Grain* is an attempt to sum up the materials of an informing American myth; it is one of the truly germinative American prose-works of this century, a perfect complement to his fiction with its close-ups of the splintering violences

1. For many engaging examples of the poet's conversation, see his *I Want to Write a Poem*, reported and edited by Edith Heal—a scholarly bibliography combined with extended comments by the poet on each of his books.

and innumerable undeveloped sources of strength in American culture. The waste of possibility—it is in dealing with this crucial theme in poems like "To Elsie" and "The Raper from Passenack" that Williams comes closest to despair.

His greatest effort to deal with it is in the *Paterson* sequence. In this long poem he chose to base his structure on the movement of the river he has elsewhere called the "filthy Passaic." He sought an *open* structure like that of Pound's *Cantos*. "I decided there would be four books following the course of the river whose life seemed more and more to resemble my own . . . . above the Falls, the catastrophe of the Falls itself, . . . below the Falls and the entrance at the end to the great sea." At the beginning the city of Paterson (an epitome of the American scene, with the poet—sometimes called "Dr. Paterson"—its unrecognized prophet) is seen as a sleeping stone-giant. The people, automatons whom he *might* give more vital existence to, walk "unroused" and "incommunicado." They do not know the organic relatedness that gives unconscious meaning to every moment in the lives of primitive peoples. Grossness, destructiveness, daredeviltry and divorce—and the constant dullness and blocking-off of self-discovery and communication—are the outward signs of our condition. Everywhere the sexual life is thwarted and distorted; we are the victims of a sexual confusion inseparable from our cultural confusions—Williams shares this theme with Lawrence, but gives it a peculiarly American emphasis. The first four books of *Paterson*, completed in 1951, were intended to be the whole work. They constitute a devastating comment on every phase of our life, though a comment relieved by momentary oases of perceived or envisioned beauty, and they "end" modestly and familiarly, as they began, in the midst of things, in the midst of predicament.

Now in his fifth book of *Paterson*, Dr. Williams reopens the issues. Or rather, he refocuses them. The transforming and saving power of the aesthetic imagination is played like a brilliant light over old archetypal motifs and symbols—sexuality versus chaste love, reality versus the ideal, the Virgin and the Whore, the hunted-down Unicorn pictured, in a famous tapestry now at The Cloisters in New York, amid a setting both natural and courtly. Such themes and images do the refocusing, placing the poet's perspectives in sharper relation to the bedeviled perspectives of the culture at large.

The four passages from *Paterson V* presented in this issue can each be viewed as a self-contained poem. I see no diminution of the characteristic skill and excitement of their author's work in them, but rather a mellowing without loss of energy—*Paterson*'s "roar of the present" removed just enough to give the poem another, a much needed dimension. The section we have titled "A Woman" shows how wonderfully human and personal is Williams' conception of the sexual confusion and the need for communication, and what a mysterious gift he has for making poetry out of almost purely private feeling. "The Satyrs" is one of his most concentrated poetic statements of what has been the main subject of the present essay—his view of the artist's relation to a world of distorted possibility, suffering and brutality, but at the same time one of heroism and love. In "A Brueghel Nativity" he shows, as he has before, the kinship of spirit he feels with the elder Brueghel. And in "The Measure" (these titles are all ours) he presents one of his most moving assertions of the function of art, "the measured dance," in the ordering of the poet's own life now, at the age of seventy-four.

The Nation (31 May 1958)

The Naked and the Clad

SELECTED POEMS 1928–1958 by Stanley Kunitz
A LAUGHTER IN THE MIND by Irving Layton
A CONEY ISLAND OF THE MIND by Lawrence Ferlinghetti

STANLEY Kunitz has a rich lyrical style; sometimes, a redundancy of it. Rock-faults of feeling, however, thrust their way up through the smooth surface; and, as he confesses, he looses "a gang of personal devils" and makes them "clank their jigging bones as public evils." The devils are brought to heel formally—Kunitz does not let them run away with his poems—but they are in evidence: the oppressions of love and marriage turned awry, the pain of one generation's inability to communicate with the other (a pain compounded in immigrant families), the private impact of war and race-terrorism, and the everpresent letch for "*Mobility*—and damn the cost!" The one translation in this volume is of the preface to *Les Fleurs du Mal*. It might well stand as epigraph, for though the heavy Baudelairean sense of secular damnation and all-pervasive ennui does not altogether dominate Kunitz's work it has marked it indelibly. An instance among many is the infinitely sad "Father and Son," with its account of the dreaming speaker's terrible plea for a reconciliation that will heal the break of years, while the imago of the old Jewish father, unresponsive, strides relentlessly toward a swamp at whose edge he at last turns to the son "the white ignorant hollow of his face."

Kunitz belongs to a group of distinguished American poets whose devoted craftsmanship is conventional but not rigidly so. He can, if he chooses, write in "free" forms:

> The dialogue of lovers,
> And the conversation of two worms
> In the beam of a house,
> Their mouths filled with sawdust.

For Kunitz, though, the traditional forms liberate more than they confine. Thus, by slight modulations within and away from blank verse in "Father and Son" and "Reflection by a Mailbox," he gets the emotional freedom he needs while retaining the great advantages of a recognizable line that need not be wearyingly "regular":

> . . . . the hunters of man-skins in the warrens of Europe,
> The impossible creatures of an hysteriac's dream
> Advancing with hatchets sunk into their skulls
> To rip the god out of the machine.

The jacket quotes Robert Lowell as calling Kunitz's work "savage," and Theodore Roethke as calling it the products of "a bold dramatic imagination." The attributions are truer of Mr. Lowell and Mr. Roethke than of the poet they are praising. One does not see Mr. Kunitz, as one does them, as stung by the fury of his vision and pushing against the limits of form despite the dizzying risks that lie outside. With all its passion, his writing is more rationally contained and oriented than theirs. They see him, rightly, as a kindred sensibility and therefore have read themselves into him; but there is another side to Kunitz, a world of restraint which is enormously expressive. A poem like "The Waltzer in the House" is almost entirely of that world in its lightness and dry toughness and elegance. It sings of "a sweet, a delicate white mouse . . . among the crackers and the cheese."

O the swaying of his legs!
O the bobbing of his head!
The lady, beautiful and kind,
The blue-eyed mistress, lately wed,
Has almost laughed away her wits
To see the pretty mouse that sits
On his tiny pink behind
And swaying, bobbing, begs. . . .

As in a dream, as in a trance,
She loves his rhythmic elegance,
She loves to see his bobbing dance.

The poem has the sunny ambiguities of Chaucer's description of the Prioress. It is gaily what it is, and also it is "about" the relations of the sexes. A good deal of poetry about sex has come to us lately—a kind of priapic politicalizing in chant-form: endlessly reiterated sloganizing to the effect that if everyone stripped and jumped into bed with everyone else of the opposite sex the resulting melee would be the millennium. A poem like this one allows us to make our own departures from what it offers. It is wry, sly, bawdy, and—who knows?—even bitter. Yet it is clean-lined and luminous in its own way, as so much fine poetry has always been, and unpretentiously holds its many kinds of meaning as it were innocently within its depths. In a recent poem, "The Class Will Come to Order," Kunitz sums up the case for restraint and silence:

Decorum is a face the brave can wear
In their desire to be invisible and so
To hear a music not prescribed, a tendril-tune
That climbs the porches of the ear. . . .

AND on the other hand, the Canadian poet Irving Layton sounds a barbaric yawp and very nearly gets away with it. The interest of his work lies in its myopically observant acidity, its considered nastiness. It is doubtful that he would understand Kunitz's meaning of decorum as "a face the brave can wear." Mr. Layton pretends to a proud scorn ("Nietzsche and Marx," he has written, "have been my teachers; and I worship D. H. Lawrence") for those who do not share his vision. He delights in the models of Lenin's heroic contempt for the "chatterer" Kautsky, of Pound spitting at his critics and annotators, of Joyce and Rimbaud and Crane—

> fanatics without remorse whose pen
> scraped their own and their age's pus—

mocking "the distinguished & amiable men-of-letters." But Layton presumes too much. God knows one can sympathize with his resentment against the various kinds of superciliousness he must have run up against in his career, but this game of haughty contumely—no matter who plays it—is really one form that such superciliousness takes. Joyce was rude to Yeats, Lawrence to Pound, Harriet Monroe to Crane, and many a sibling to his rival any morning. Proving? Only that the spitting and snarling of the "great" are generally more interesting than those of "lesser" figures. One had better be a Lenin or a Pound or a Lawrence first if one wants credit (such as it's worth) for spitting in the faces of one's fellow-men.

Layton's insistence on advance certification of his right to revile would be more suitable for a novitiate bohemian than for an artist of forty-six. It is of a piece with his constant, self-flattering assumption of the satyr's mask (though one must admit he relishes the mask so well it almost fits him):

> When breathing hard spring arrived
> My face stared down at you lecherous
> And like a famished goat. . . .

or

> At my approach
> the ladies, unsubtle and ugly,
> rush their adolescent daughters upstairs. . . .

Even in these passages, which breathe so vividly the speaker's desire to be what he says he is, we feel a certain malice for its own sake, an unworthy urge to assert power and give pain: in Layton's own phrase, "the passionate will to hurt." That will reveals itself throughout the book; perhaps it is what the poet's "Nietzscheanism" really amounts to. In "Cain" he tells of shooting a frog, and of how he "couldn't help sneer" at the way it looked in death, and of how the sight built up in him an urge to kill "anything with the stir of life in it." Here, as in "Cat Dying in Autumn," there is a marriage of the morbid and the sentimental. The two moods, of course, go notoriously together in the superman-dream. Pieces like these two ostensibly take their cues from Lawrence, but the Laurentian trauma at the ruthlessness of things is something different from Layton's self-intoxication with it.

As I have suggested, it is his struggle to bring a not-quite-related malice out into the open that makes this writer interesting. There is a whole movement of this sort in the air, a movement of disgust and, inevitably, self-loathing, that values hot feeling above wisdom, form, or even syntax and has the authority of its own conviction. Sexual exhibitionism is one manifestation; the mere mention of the sex organs is felt to be a splendid triumph. And this desire to wound the self and others: It is startling to see how often Layton refers to castration.

No wonder, one might say, that one of these poems, "On the Jones Biography of Sigmund Freud," is devoted to an attack on the assumptions of psychoanalysis! And yet, out of these compulsions and rejections come some pure notes of suffering at the awareness of life gone sour that are comparable in effect if not in finish to those of Mr. Kunitz. And there are sharp moments of perception and comparison amid the careless posturing. And wit. A clear case of "the poet in spite of himself."

LAWRENCE Ferlinghetti is certainly one of those advocates of universal nakedness, etc., I have alluded to, but he differs from most of the others in his high-flying joyousness of spirit and in his stylistic sophistication. He knows he is not the first man to take a peek at Darien and he has learned some useful things, and gladly, from various European and American experimenters. The religion of sex-and-anarchy, like other religions and creeds, starts off with certain simplicities but does not require its communicants to reiterate them monotonously and mechanically. Ferlinghetti can preach a little tiresomely; he proves he can in the seven "Oral Messages," written "specifically for jazz accompaniment," in which he tries to rival the worst of Ginsberg, Corso, et al. He doesn't quite succeed, for he is too bright and literate and many of his wisecracks and sideswipes are worth hearing, but finally he does become dull. The "great audiences" Whitman called for are not the improvised audiences of night clubs who must have their poetry ranting and obvious if they are to "get" anything at all.

Apart from the "Oral Messages," however, and from a few other preachy pieces, Ferlinghetti is a deft, rapid-paced, whirling performer. He has a wonderful eye for meaning in the commonplace, as in the lovely, sensual snapshot of a woman hanging clothes on a San Francisco rooftop, or in the memory of a New York candy store where

Jellybeans glowed in the semi-gloom
of that september afternoon
A cat upon the counter moved among
the licorice sticks
and tootsie rolls
and Oh Boy Gum

He has a fine imaginative eye, too, as the bawdy description of a contest with "the widder Fogliani" painting mustaches on the statues in the Borghese gardens shows. Even better—far better, because here he conquers his almost indomitable over-whimsicality—is the contrasting picture of laborers putting up a statue of Saint Francis ("no birds sang" despite the presence of a priest, reporters, and many onlookers) while, unnoticed in the crowd, there passes to and fro

a very tall and very purely naked
young virgin
with very long and very straight
straw hair
and wearing only a very small
bird's nest
in a very existential place. . . .

These quotations will indicate Ferlinghetti's obvious debt to the stanzaic and rhythmic technique of William Carlos Williams and the other "modernist" masters, and his equally obvious independence of idiom. I have mentioned his whimsy and his tendentiousness—I think they are related to his failure as yet to find a really adequate form for the intellectual and idiomatic range of which he gives such encouraging glimpses. There are poems in this volume (for instance, "The wounded wilderness of Morris Graves" and "In Paris in a loud dark winter") which demand something more than the light music into which Ferlinghetti's characteristic line virtually forces him. The nakedness-symbolism is another kind of straitjacket. "Take it off!"—or even "*Vive la différence!*"—is a fine old war-cry. But Ferlinghetti is far too gifted to let himself be mesmerized by it, or by his somewhat too-easy mastery of one kind of metrical pyrotechnics.

The Nation (11 October 1958)

In Exquisite Chaos

A new world of poets and poems is issuing forth in exquisite chaos, and it is absorbing to speculate about what its major bearings are likely to be. Scribner's has now printed its fifth volume of *Poets of Today,* each containing the work of three people never before published between book covers. Meridian, to the jeers of the California Renascents and other disestablishmentarians, has given us *The New Poets of England and America*. And Ballantine Books continues to present the New Poems series, under the editorship of Rolfe Humphries. The first of these enterprises reflects the very cultivated but quite conservative taste of John Hall Wheelock. The second and third lean toward work that is interesting or polished without being very adventurous. New Poems, in addition, presents pieces by older, established poets: not a bad idea in itself—the worship of the young is as pernicious in the arts as in ordinary life—but it does becloud the question of what shape our future poetry will probably take.

The Renascents (Allen Ginsberg, Gregory Corso, and others) have struck a false note from the start of their phosphorescent little history. Theirs was a cry, not of the heart, but of the groin—a revulsion from official repression that expressed itself in belches, obscenities, incoherent manifestoes, and great shrieks of "*Libertad!*" The movement had a moment of promise, but between over-publicizing and a spate of bad poetry it lost its impetus. Yet there was, and there remains, something valid in it. It appealed to an instinct in the young everywhere to lash out with blind energy against almost everything, good or bad, that "authority" has constructed. Empty as much of this poetry has been, it has cleared a little place for itself that may be permanent.

But also emerging now is a little-known, ultimately more serious and mature body of non-traditional verse. It is represented by the work of Charles Olson, Denise Levertov, Paul Blackburn, Robert Duncan and Robert Creeley. Their poetry shows the same intensified intransigence as does that of Ginsberg and Co., the same fundamental assumption that the crack-up of values prophesied by an older generation has completed itself. Indeed, these qualities are at the heart of almost all the more impressive new work, traditional or not. Relatively conventional poets like David Galler and Donald Finkel are alert to cultural breakdown, and they have the advantage of being able to display it in a stanza and metric which recall older, sharply contrasting modes of sensibility. By the same token, though, they cannot summon the sense of absolute immediacy and spontaneity that is the great strength of Olson and the others like him. In the Olson group, a renewed emphasis on the feel of specific moments of awareness—as if they were totally detachable from the rest of life—is indispensable to the reordering of sensibility.

Denise Levertov and Paul Blackburn are the most "open" and sensuous writers in this group. Neither is content with sharp physical awareness alone, but both have a freshness that engages you even when what they present seems abstract. Miss Levertov may begin a poem ("The Flight") with a quite sophisticated proposition:

> 'The will is given us that
> we may know the
> delights of surrender.' Blake with
> tense mouth, crouched small (great forehead,
> somber eye) amid a crowd's tallness in a narrow room.

But that is just the bending of the bow. When the conception here stated in so cramped and paradoxical a way is embodied in an anecdote about a trapped bird, the poem flies as an arrow of insight into an important subjective reality. "The Hands" does the same sort of thing in reverse, beginning almost sensually:

> Don't forget the crablike
> hands, slithering
> among the keys.
> Eyes shut, the downstream
> play of sound lifts away from
> the present, drifts you
> off your feet: too easily let off.

The dreaming movement into ecstasy is then translated into abstract aesthetic dimensions, a pattern of tensions like that set up by actors rehearsing "on a bare stage." In such pieces the immediacy is psychological, inward, yet much involved in the senses. Miss Levertov gives us a world of awakened, contemplative selfhood, in which sympathy with other selves may appear, but completely independent of social expectations. Even the poems which come closest to explicit statement of the toughened intransigence I have mentioned—poems like "The Dogwood" and "Something"—seem to regard the civilization against which they react as a sort of cobweb brushing the face, something alien and strangely cold, yet almost unreal.

Blackburn too, gives this impression, but more humorously and evasively than Miss Levertov. His poem "The Assistance" riddles out a ridiculous but real big-city predicament almost casually. The subject is trivial and embarrassing, but Blackburn conjures up a personal universe through his treatment of it. You would think, for the moment (as in actual life you might), that this was the whole of things:

> On the farm it never mattered;
> behind the barn, in any grass, against
> any convenient tree,
>   the woodshed in winter, in a corner
> if it came to that.
>
> But in a city of eight million, one
> stands on the defensive. . . .

Sunken into Existential reality, without pride, definitive, Blackburn's poems seem at times to reduce themselves to an uncritical savoring of consciousness. Whatever is, is; and what you give a damn about is not what it means but what it feels like. The poet's spirit floats and absorbs whatever is there: in "Suerte," he speaks of sitting in the Spanish sunlight and

>   watching
>   weeds grow out of the drainpipes
>   or burros and the shadows of burros
>   come up the street bringing sand
>   the first one of the line with a
> bell
> always. . . .

There is another, darker brooding beneath this surface acceptance; but it too is fatalistic rather than critical in its presentation:

> Another bell sounds the hours of your sun
>   limits
>   sounding below human voices,
> counts the hours of weeds, rain, darkness, all
>   with a bell.

I do not say that what these two poets do is in the key of the future—and yet this is the way that intellectual universes *are* shattered. Not through head-on assault but through indifference, or the refusal to take the present seriously on its own terms. No bang, no whimper, just a new way of looking at things.

Not all the new voices do their re-creating so unobtrusively. Charles Olson states the major cultural issues as loudly and explicitly as ever Pound or Williams did. Almost any page of *In Cold Hell, In Thicket* or of *The Maximus Poems* will recall the older poets' driving involvement. For instance, except that they state as known principles what Pound has exclaimed over with shocked horror, these lines of Olson's in "The Kingfisher" might well have been written for *Mauberley* or the *Cantos:*

with what violence benevolence is bought
what cost in gesture justice brings
what wrongs domestic rights involve
what stalks
this silence

what pudor pejorocracy affronts
how awe, night-rest and neighborhood can rot

No debate is here possible—it is all over with. Similarly, when Olson employs the typical Williams metric—sliding, improvisatory, played by ear—he weighs it down. Williams' freshness and exuberance are emotional assertions Olson cannot make. Something has come to a standstill; another machinery than the one we are familiar with will be needed to get personality going again.

people

don't change. They only stand more
revealed. I,
likewise.
("Maximus, to Gloucester: Letter 2")

Olson has theorized in prose more than the others. In *Mayan Letters,* he derives a slogan from his studies of ancient Yucatan: "I keep thinking, it comes to this: culture displacing the state." Pound, whom he much admires, overvalues the history of the state, and the history of the West as well; and so does Williams, though he developed "an emotional system" in his poetry "which is capable of extensions and comprehensions [that Pound's] egosystem . . . is not." The problem is to get back to sources of meaning anterior to those of our own state-ridden civilization and so to recover the sense of personality and of place which it has all but throttled.

Olson's verse has less natural ease than does most of the poetry I have mentioned, but he has the power of hammering conviction—something like Lawrence's but with more brutal insistence behind it. It is a dogmatic, irritable, passionate voice, of the sort that the modern world—to its sorrow, very often—is forever seeking out; not a clear voice, but one troubled by its own confusions which it carries into the attack:

To begin again. Lightning
is an axe, transfer
of force subject to object is
order: destroy!

To destroy
is to start again. is a factor of
sun. . . .
("La Torre")

Robert Creeley, the friend to whom Olson wrote his letters from Yucatan, has cultivated an oddly balked poetry, of minimal, staccato movements and interrupted fluidities:

What one knows, then, not
simple, convulsed, and feeling
(this night)
petulance of all conditions, not
wondered, not even
felt.
("For Rainer Gerhardt")

His awareness of separateness, of being incommunicado and fearful of his own desire for easy sympathies, makes Creeley's writing so dry as to be almost inhibited. His depressed and prickly little patterns point to withdrawal rather than realization, though there is a kind of honor and courage in producing a body of poems that claims so little for their maker. A new world, Maya reborn, would indeed be needed for the triumphant re-emergence of *this* personality, which seems a perfect expression of the modern failure of communication deplored again and again in our literature. A richer voice and spirit are probably needed to bridge the world of the past and the world to come—a voice and spirit with the luminosity and buoyancy of Robert Duncan at his best—

Whitman was right. Our names are left
like leaves of grass,
likeness and liking, the human greenness

tough as grass that survives cruelest seasons.
("The Dance")

Names of the poets! I have not tried to make this essay an exhaustive list of the newer names, or even of the newer schools. Most of these poets will drift along their own currents, in the very nature of things, and the schools are not as firm and distinct as the Fugitives, or the British Marxian poets of the 1930s, or even the Imagists once seemed to be. They have not really found their own positions so decisively, though new magazines like *Measure* and *The Fifties* may help them to do so. (The dearth of places to publish where one can count on being *read* has militated strongly against such self-definition.) I have mentioned two of the other names, outside the "groups": the Kafkaesque but very American and urbane David Galler and the extraordinarily precise and bitter Donald Finkel. A myriad of others come to mind—the elegantly classical yet intimately modern Ellen Kay, the publication of whose *A Local Habitation* is one of the genuine triumphs of Alan Swallow's New Poetry Series; the extremely casual Joel Oppenheimer, whose slight but astringent poems bring him close to Levertov and Blackburn in spirit if not in poetic authority; the witty and lyrically exciting Jay MacPherson, a Canadian poet whose use of traditional forms and dependence on mythical allusion belie her daring frankness and play of mind; Marie Ponsot, whose religious poetry also expresses a passionate personalism; and many more. It may be that the "new" tendencies will be drowned out by younger poets working in older modes and simply adapting them to their own experiences and perspectives. Some of these younger poets show a brilliant promise, and their immediate predecessors—figures such as Lowell and Nemerov—have been able to work significantly within traditional limits. At the moment, however, it is probably the Olson "group," moving directly out of and away from the experimental work of the poets of Pound's generation, that foreshadows the more dynamic directions of the future.

The Nation (1 November 1958)

from *Three Windows on Cummings*

95 POEMS by E. E. Cummings

WHEN E. E. Cummings' collected volume *Poems 1923–1954* appeared five years ago, its effect was like eating a whole cheesecake at one sitting. Cummings was not put on this earth to publish *Gesammelte Werke*, but to issue forth little sheaves containing a few poems of sensuous life-awareness, some intransigent jeers and shockers, and various visual aids to verbal explosion.

His work has not changed essentially since his early successes, except that quieter, more somber tones can occasionally be detected and that his weaknesses (sentimentality and an insistent presumption of his own superior sensitivity) loom larger than before. His hand is now not always on top of the work, and the old tricks are not generally brought as masterfully into play. There is nothing in this latest book to match poems like "who's most afraid of death? thou" and "(ponder,darling,these busted statues"—lyrical monologues which for a moment can make the earth fall away from under us, even though we all too soon discern behind them the "magic-maker" and his manipulations. Writing of this kind, intensely evocative of the pity of our common mortality and often charged with a nostalgic eroticism, represents the height of Cummings at his most serious—unless we include the best of his angrily satirical poems (e.g., "i sing of Olaf") and of the frankly sexual ones:

i like my body when it is with your
body. It is so quite new a thing. . . .

Out of such moods have come his main triumphs as a performer. If we add the pieces that are pure prestidigitation, and those generally akin to the spirit of Herriman's old comic-strip *Krazy Kat* (whose virtues Cummings has often extolled) or to old-time burlesque, we have the main range of this poet's limited, really two-dimensional art.

95 Poems, thus, adds little to the body of Cummings' brittle best. He has always tottered on the edge of a disastrous banality; indeed, he has slipped over it and been all but killed a number of times. Now, however, he seems less aware that an effort is needed in the structuring of particular poems to save himself; we get too many lines like "the courage to receive time's mightiest dream," and quite often in a limp context. The implication intended in these instances is that the poet's central thought—that he loves someone, or feels that he is an individual separate from other people, or thinks that man must justify himself to God rather than vice versa—is so luminously revelatory that he is required to give no more than a *hint* of poetic form.

Yet often the old bag of tricks is still much in evidence—the broken or delayed word, the grammatical shiftings (adverbs used as adjectives, etc.), the syntactic juggling, the vaguely romantic mysticism implied through the use of certain abstract words and symbolic trademarks. The wonderful thing about it originally was that it enabled Cummings to blow open otherwise trite and bathetic motifs through a dynamic rediscovery of the energies sealed up in conventional usages. But now it is usually presented as if it were an end in itself. And what a task it would be to separate one "enormous" or "dream" or "always" or "death" or "life" or "fragrance" or "universe" from another. The following passage (admittedly out of context—I am not talking about its intelligibility but about its vocabulary and syntax) is indistinguishable from a hundred others in Cummings, and because of that fact alone cannot be read for its intrinsic qualities—

enormous this how

patient creature (who's
never by never robbed of
day) puts always on by always

dream. . . .

In the few pieces where the old tricks do still work wonderfully, the disciplining factor is the fineness of the conception, which compels the poet to make a special effort to get everything down just right. Few other poets could catch an *aperçu* so beautifully and sculpturally on the wing as Cummings does in Poem 40:

silence

.is
a
looking

bird:the

turn
ing;edge,of
life

(inquiry before snow

"Silence is a looking bird; the turning edge of life; inquiry before snow." The images, interesting in themselves, accumulate a range of connotation belied by the poem's physical brevity. Punctuation and line-arrangement control the pace at which the connotations come into view. First, there is the isolated *silence*, emphasized by the space below it and then the period, which is not final but musically transitional: Silence (pause) *is*. Then the "is" becomes a bridge in its turn: Silence is a *looking*. The gerund changes to participle as we move on: a looking *bird*—and perhaps, by association, a *mocking bird* as well? By the poem's end we have crossed many boundaries between subjective awareness and objective universe; silence seems a confrontation of two states whose terms of meaning are always changing. With the concluding (but unclosed) parenthesis the whole mysterious, freshly felt experience of silence has become a relationship between the clear-eyed, awed, but uncowed observer and the imponderable, relentless nature of things. This is Cummings, now, at his best. What a difference between poem 40 and the feeble daubs of half-finished verse that mar so much of this book.

The Nation (10 January 1959)

❧

from *Closing in on the Self*

WORDS FOR THE WIND: THE COLLECTED VERSE OF THEODORE ROETHKE

PICK up one of Theodore Roethke's longer poems and you are confronted with a stunning mishmash of agonized gibber, described by the poet himself in an essay written some years ago as "the muck and welter, the dark, the *dreck*" of his verse. The same essay ("Open Letter," published in Ciardi's *Mid-Century American Poets*) asserts that he nevertheless counts himself "among the happy poets." And indeed, Roethke at his best throws all kinds of dissimilar effects into the great, ceaseless mixer of his sensibility, stirring together notes of driving misery and hysterical ecstasy, of Rabelaisian sensuality and warm, wet regressiveness:

Believe me, knot of gristle, I bleed like a tree;
I dream of nothing but boards;
I could love a duck.

Such music in a skin!
A bird sings in the bush of your bones.
Tufty, the water's loose.
Bring me a finger. . . .
("Give Way, Ye Gates")

Some of the allusion here is a little too private. ("Tufty, the water's loose," for example, has all sorts of obvious physiological connotations but probably has something to do with Roethke's boyhood experiences helping out in his father's greenhouse. And it would take more than a feather to knock me over if I were suddenly to learn that "Tufty" was a family nickname for Theodore.) But the passage as a whole, which begins the poem, is a wildly bawdy outcry of desire, thinly and wittily veiled in euphemism.

Later in the poem all this exhilaration withers up and is replaced by language of frustration and suffering, and then of a sort of minimal self-consolation. The over-excitement of the first part, in which the pain of the need behind desire was muted or hidden in humor, is balanced off by a gross, almost infantile desolateness. The images now are of impotence and shame:

Touch and arouse. Suck and sob. Curse and mourn.
It's a cold scrape in a low place.
The dead crow dries on a pole.
Shapes in the shade
Watch.

This projection without comment of opposed psychological states is characteristic of Roethke's most interesting work. A desperate exuberance that seems at one moment unrepressed joy of life, at the next the pathetic hilarity of the unbearably burdened, makes the manic-depressive mood-spectrum the law of life. Each opposite is implicit in the other, and that is the only necessary logic at work here. The universe of Roethke's poems is a completely subjective one—not what source of meaning the speaker has outside himself but how he feels within is the key to everything. The private sensibility is a mad microcosm; the speaker responds violently to everything that touches it; and he struggles frenetically to win through to a moment of calm realization in the sunlight of "wholeness." The ebullient anguish of poems like "My Papa's Waltz," "Child on Top of a Greenhouse," and "The Shape of the Fire" is a triumphant realization of the aesthetic of hypersensitivity. Consider the opening stanzas of "The Shape of the Fire."

> What's this? A dish for fat lips.
> Who says? A nameless stranger.
> Is he a bird or a tree? Not everyone can tell.
>
> Water recedes to the crying of spiders.
> An old scow bumps over black rocks.
> A cracked pod calls.
>
> Mother me out of here. What more will the bones allow?
> Will the sea give the wind suck? A toad folds into a stone.
> These flowers are all fangs. Comfort me, fury. . . .

The reader will come somewhere near the poet's intention, I think, if he imagines the speaker to be giving a voice to the fire and responding to it. It crackles and whispers—what is the secret of its voice? There is a horror in that devouring sound that considers the wood or coals (or anything else) "a dish for fat lips"; the second stanza gives further images for that dry, merciless sound and its terror—the receding of waters before the "crying of spiders" perhaps the most nightmarish of them. The third stanza shows the speaker overwhelmed with the sheer dread of mutability and annihilation that has been accumulated through all these impressions. The whole process is not so much conceptual as it is self-hypnotic. This is the shaping sensibility in operation, and in this sort of thing Roethke is brilliantly successful.

But it is not his only sort of thing, for in addition he often does try to conceptualize, and he tries to give his poems a further implication of victory over the frenzy through a Freudian rebirth of the self. These efforts are not, by and large, very convincing. Thus, the last two movements of "The Shape of the Fire" are attempts to soar and transcend in the old sense—like the ending of "Lycidas": "To-morrow to fresh woods, and pastures new." But Milton had a vision of "the blest kingdoms meek of joy and love," and the mourner of his poem speaks to a completely different scale of values—that of the macrocosm ruled over by "the dear might of Him that walk'd the waves." That is not the universe of Roethke's poems, and so his ending is contrived, though in its way lovely and delicate.

Something similar happens in "The Lost Son," whose title suggests the psychoanalytical, inward turning of the poet's eye. Roethke's essay "Open Letter" says of this poem that it is at first "a terrified running away—with alternate periods of hallucinatory waiting . . .; the protagonist so geared-up, so over-alive that he is hunting, like a primitive, for some animistic suggestion, some clue to existence from the sub-human." So be it—this panicky hunt for pre-intellectual sources of the sense of being truly alive is without doubt one of the real, if uneasy, enterprises of the modern mind. But the poet is not ruthless enough to carry the hunt through—any more than he was able to remain true to the realizations at the beginning of "The Shape of the Fire." He finds another clue to salvation, an easier one, than the frenzied beginning would imply was possible. It is the "lost son's" psychological re-entry into the world of his most vivid childhood memories—the world of the "long greenhouse" which he has called "my symbol for the whole of life, a womb, a heaven-on-earth."

Re-entry into this paradisal womb, one gathers, is the necessary preliminary for a rebirth of the Self. The true "coming-through" into mature, calm reconciliation has not yet occurred, but faith is expressed that it will do so—

> A lively understandable spirit
> Once entertained you.
> It will come again.

The promise is too pat and wishful—of a Freudian romance with a happy ending. As in most of Roethke's longer work, the dénouement does not live up to the poem's initial demands. Shorter poems like "The Return," "The Minimal," and "The Exorcism" are really better in the way they sustain a sometimes Dantean close-up of minutely detailed, realistic horror on the terms with which they began. I would add also the beautiful "The Visitant," the guilt-filled "The Song," the deeply sad and very original "Dolor," the dreamlike "Night Crow," and the sweatily, feverishly, embarrassedly alive greenhouse poems from Roethke's 1948 volume *The Lost Son and Other Poems*. Together with certain passages in the longer poems, such pieces constitute Roethke's more lasting achievements.

The Nation (21 March 1959)

Poetry as Confession

LIFE STUDIES by Robert Lowell

EMILY Dickinson once called publication "the auction of the mind." Robert Lowell seems to regard it more as soul's therapy. The use of poetry for the most naked kind of confession grows apace in our day. We are now far from the great Romantics who, it is true, spoke directly of their emotions but did not give the game away even to themselves. They found, instead, cosmic equations and symbols, transcendental reconciliations with "this limetree bower my prison," titanic melancholia in the course of which, merging his sense of tragic fatality with the evocations of the nightingale's song, the poet lost his personal complaint in the music of universal forlornness. Later, Whitman took American poetry to the very edge of the confessional in his *Calamus* poems and in the quivering avowal of his helplessness before the seductions of "blind loving wrestling touch, sheath'd hooded sharp-tooth'd touch." More recently, under the influence of the Symbolists, Eliot and Pound brought us into the forbidden realm itself, yet even in their work a certain indirection masks the poet's actual face and psyche from greedy eyes.

Lowell removes the mask. His speaker is unequivocally himself, and it is hard not to think of *Life Studies* as a series of personal confidences, rather shameful, that one is honor-bound not to reveal. About half the book, the prose section called "91 Revere Street," is essentially a public discrediting of his father's manliness and character, as well as of the family and social milieu of his childhood. Another section, the concluding sequence of poems grouped under the heading "Life Studies," reinforces and even repeats these motifs, bringing them to bear on the poet's psychological problems as an adult. The father, naval officer *manqué* and then businessman and speculator *manqué*, becomes a humiliating symbol of the failure of a class and of a kind of personality. Lowell's contempt for him is at last mitigated by adult compassion, though I wonder if a man can allow himself this kind of ghoulish operation on his father without doing his own spirit incalculable damage. But the damage has clearly been in the making a long time, and Lowell knows very well that he is doing violence to himself most of all:

. . . . I hear
my ill-spirit sob in each blood cell,
as if my hand were at its throat. . . .

He does not spare himself in these poems, at least two of which have to do with sojourns in mental hospitals and his return home from them. We have grotesque glimpses into his marital life. "Man and Wife," for instance, begins: "Tamed by *Miltown*, we lie on Mother's bed." It later tells how

All night I've held your hand,
as if you had
a fourth time faced the kingdom of the mad—
its hackneyed speech, its homicidal eye—
and dragged me home alive. . . .

"My mind's not right," says the speaker in "Skunk Hour," the poem which ends the book. It is partly Lowell's apology for what he has been saying in these pieces like Gerontion's mumbling that he is only "an old man, a dull head among windy spaces." And it is partly his assertion that he cannot breathe without these confessions, however rank they may be, and that the things he has been talking about are too stubbornly alive to be ignored:

I stand on top
of our back steps and breathe the rich air—
a mother skunk with her column of kittens swills the garbage pail.
She jabs her wedge-head in a cup
of sour cream, drops her ostrich tail,
and will not scare.

It will be clear that my first impression while reading *Life Studies* was that it is impure art, magnificently stated but unpleasantly egocentric—somehow resembling the triumph of the skunks over the garbage cans. Since its self-therapeutic motive is so obvious and persistent, something of this impression sticks all the way. But as the whole work floods into view the balance shifts decisively. Lowell is still the wonderful poet of "The Quaker Graveyard in Nantucket," the poet of power and passion whose driving aesthetic of anguish belies the "frizzled, stale and small" condition he attributes to himself. He may be wrong in believing that what has happened to New England's elite is necessarily an embodiment of the state of American culture, the whole maggoty character of which he feels he carries about in his own person. But he is not wrong in looking at the culture through the window of psychological breakdown. Too many other American poets, no matter what their social class and family history, have reached the same point in recent years. Lowell is foremost among them in the energy of his uncompromising honesty.

Furthermore, *Life Studies* is not merely a collection of small moment-by-moment victories over hysteria and self-concealment. It is also a beautifully articulated poetic sequence. I say "articulated," but the impact of the sequence is of four intensifying waves of movement that smash at the reader's feelings and break repeatedly over his mind. The poems that make up the opening movement are not personal in the sense of the rest of the book. They are poems of violent contradiction, a historical overture to define the disintegration of a world. In the first a train journeys from Rome to Paris at mid-century. The "querulous hush-hush" of its wheels passes over the Alps and beyond them, but nowhere in the altitudes to which it rises does it touch the sanely brilliant heights of ancient myth and thought. For its riders there are, at one terminal, the hysteria of *bella Roma,* where "the crowds at San Pietro screamed *Papa*" at the pronouncement of the dogma of Mary's assumption and where "the Duce's lynched, bare, booted skull still spoke"; and at the other terminal, the self-destructive freedom of "Paris, our black classic." The next poem reaches far enough back in time to reveal the welter of grossly sensual, mindlessly grasping egotism that attended the birth of the modern age. Marie de Medici, "the banker's daughter," soliloquizes about "blood and pastime," the struggle between monarchy and the "pilfering, pillaging democracies," the assassination of her husband. The third poem returns from modern Europe and its bloody beginnings to our own American moment. All that turbulence of recent centuries now seems frozen into intellectual and moral death:

> Ice, ice. Our wheels no longer move.
> Look, the fixed stars, all just alike
> as lack-land atoms, split apart,
> and the Republic summons Ike,
> the mausoleum in her heart.

But then the fourth poem hurls at us the monologue of a mad Negro soldier confined at Munich. Here the wit, the audacious intimacy, the acutely bizarre tragic sense of Lowell's language take on jet-speed. In this monologue the breakdown of traditional meanings and cultural distinctions is dramatized in the frenzy of one contemporary figure. Thus Lowell begins to zero in on his main target, himself as the damned speaking-sensibility of his world. The humiliated, homicidal fury of the Negro soldier throws its premonitory shadow over the disturbed "comedy" of "91 Revere Street" which follows. It helps us to see, beneath the "Jamesian" nuances of relationship in a society of ritual pretensions but no center of gravity, how anguished is this prose section's murderous dissection of the poet's parents and its complaint against a childhood gone awry. In this way it prepares us for the personal horrors with which the book closes.

But before that long, devastating final wave of poems, there is a smaller one, corresponding in gathering force to the first group. This third wave is again made up of four poems, each of them about a modern writer with whom Lowell feels kinship as an embattled and alienated spirit. Following hard upon the prose, these poems clearly say: "This is what the predatory centuries, and the soul-devouring world in which I walked the maze of my childhood, have done to man's creativity." Lowell first portrays Ford Madox Ford, the "mammoth mumbler" cheated out of his earned rewards, standing up to Lloyd George and, later, scratching along in America, sick and "gagged for air." Then, dear to Lowell's heart, the self-exiled Santayana looms before us—"free-thinking Catholic infidel." The third poem recreates with sentimental bitterness a winter Lowell and Delmore Schwartz spent at Harvard in 1946. Nothing could be more pathetically open about Lowell's state of mind concerning himself and his art than the parts of their conversation he chooses to record and even to italicize:

> . . . . "Let Joyce and Freud,
> the Masters of Joy,
> be our guests here," you said. The room was filled
> with cigarette smoke circling the paranoid,
> inert gaze of Coleridge, back

from Malta—his eyes lost in flesh, lips baked and black. . . .
You said:
"We poets in our youth begin in sadness;
thereof in the end come despondency and madness;
Stalin has had two cerebral hemorrhages!"

The ironic facetiousness that so often marks Schwartz's writing and conversation is here absorbed by Lowell into a vision of unrelieved breakdown centered on the image of Coleridge's "paranoid gaze" in the picture. That image, together with the mocking allusion to Stalin as one of "we poets" who come at last to madness, brings past and present, and all political and psychological realities, into a single focus of defeat. Then in the fourth poem, "Words for Hart Crane," the group comes to a climax paralleling that of "A Mad Negro Soldier" in the first group. Crane's brief, self-destructive career is seen as the demand of the creative spirit, deliberately wearing the most loathsome mask it can find, for unquestioning love from the culture that has rejected it. Here, just before he plunges back into his major theme, the "life studies" of himself and his family, Lowell again—at the most savagely committed pitch he can command—presents the monologue of a dramatically suffering figure whose predicament has crucial bearing on his own.

In large part, the fourteen poems of the final section echo the prose of "91 Revere Street." But they echo it as a storm echoes the foreboding sultriness of a threatening spell of weather before it. Apart from the obvious differences that verse makes, they break out of the cocoon of childhood-mentality that somehow envelops "91 Revere Street" despite its more sophisticated aspects. Lowell, like Yeats and Thomas, casts over his autobiographical prose a certain whimsy (though often morbid) and childlike half-awareness. But the poems are overborne by sadness first and then by the crash of disaster. Side by side Lowell places memories of his confinement in mental hospitals and a denigration of his great act of defiance as a conscientious objector in World War II which led to his imprisonment for a year:

I was a fire-breathing Catholic C.O.,
and made my manic statement,
telling off the state and president. . . .
("Memories of West Street and Lepke")

The only poem of this group in which he does not talk in his own person, "'To Speak of Woe That Is in Marriage,'" is a monologue by the wife of a lecherous, "hopped-up" drunkard. It is placed strategically just before the last poem, "Skunk Hour," and after "Man and Wife," in which Lowell makes certain we know he is discussing his own marriage, and it is a deliberate plunge into the depths of the theme of degradation at all but the last moment. Finally, "Skunk Hour," full of indirections and nuances that bring the sickness of our world as a whole back into the scene to restore a more universal vision, reaches a climax of self-contempt and of pure symbol-making. This is Lowell's fantastic, terrifying skunk-image for the secret self's inescapable drive to assure itself of continued life—

I myself am hell;
nobody's here—

only skunks, that search
in the moonlight for a bite to eat.
They march on their soles up Main Street:
white stripes, moonstruck eyes' red fire
under the chalk-dry and spar spire
of the Trinitarian Church.

Life Studies brings to culmination one line of development in our poetry of the utmost importance. Technically, it is an experiment in the form of the poetic sequence comparable to *Mauberley* and *The Bridge*. To build a great poem out of the predicament and horror of the lost Self has been the recurrent effort of the most ambitious poetry of the last century. It is too early to say whether *Life Studies* is great art. Enough, for the moment, to realize that it is inescapably encompassing art.

The Nation (10 September 1959)

❧

Notes from the Future: Two Poets

HEART'S NEEDLE by W. D. Snodgrass
SELECTED POEMS by Robert Duncan
LETTERS by Robert Duncan

"SNODGRASS," I recently heard a distinguished older poet say, "is frankly bourgeois. The rest of us try to hide our bourgeois nature from ourselves, but he is plainly and openly what he is." I suppose his calling Snodgrass bourgeois had something to do with this young writer's acceptance of simple, normal marital and domestic relationships as possible, and desirable, in themselves. In this sense he is uncritically "bourgeois"; he apparently has no bohemian suspicion that a good marriage in which husband, wife, and children are both affectionate and responsible to one another is necessarily death to the free, creative life.

Not that these are happy poems, as the pieces in John Ciardi's *I Marry You* are. In point of fact, the long title-sequence presents the poet in a state of deep soul-sickness because of his divorce and because of the dangers which a new marriage presents to his relationship with his baby daughter. Snodgrass, though much less violent, is a confessional poet like Robert Lowell, and he is writing about a stubborn if almost abject father-love hanging on to its object with animal persistence. The quietly satisfying bourgeois family is for him an ideal as genuine peace is an ideal for a world ravaged by actual and by cold war. The figure is one on which he depends repeatedly:

> Child of my winter, born
> When the new fallen soldiers froze
> In Asia's steep ravines and fouled the snows,
> When I was torn
>
> By love I could not still,
> By fear that silenced my cramped mind
> To that cold war where, lost, I could not find
> My peace in my will. . . .

The ten-part sequence takes us from the child's birth to the divorce, the second marriage, and the muted triumph that a second winter of separation should have been survived—"and you are still my daughter." Snodgrass has built a moving poem out of something we treat far too casually: early divorce, in which it is the love between children and their parents that receives the deepest wounds. The undramatic misery of the troubled father anxious to create common memories—pushing his child on a playground swing, learning to make omelettes and pancakes so he can feed her at home when she visits him, and so on—has great authority. Snodgrass gains it through a gift of understatement that is yet saturated with feeling:

> The window's turning white.
> The world moves like a diseased heart
> packed with ice and snow.
> Three months now we have been apart
> less than a mile. I cannot fight
> or let you go.

Perhaps another "bourgeois" aspect of this poet's work lies in the kind of psychological problems he admits to having generally. In "April Inventory" he recites some of the lessons he has learned—that is, has *had* to learn—over the past year:

> I taught myself to name my name,
> To bark back, loosen love and crying;
> To ease my woman so she came,
> To ease an old man who was dying.
> I have not learned how often I
> Can win, can love, but choose to die.

Earlier in this same poem he mentions "my analyst," and perhaps that phrase too is peculiar to one kind of bourgeois life adjustment. But I think the older poet's real objection (I'm somehow sure it was really an objection, though it has a certain admiration in it too) was to the absence of hatred in the poems of *Heart's Needle*. Snodgrass pays token service to the usual creed of sophisticated aversion to Philistinism and commercialism, sounding something like a paler Cummings. But he accepts, always. The explosive anger of Lowell is nowhere to be found, and the truly striking notes are of a winning sensitivity and candor, and an ability to endure the rigors of experience with pathetic courage and a nostalgia paid in advance. These observations are not meant as moral judgments, but as a definition of the kind of energy his poems possess. I should add that he has a disciplined skill that is pure delight in the delicately modulated "The Operation," a poem detailing with the most vivid impressionism the successive physical sensations and shifts of awareness before and after surgery, and in the restrained sexuality of "Winter Bouquet"—two examples among several outstanding pieces. He is able to use description and imagery so suggestively that he can postpone explicit statement of feeling; when it is needed at all, to brief, strategic moments, usually at the very end of a poem. He uses this ability so tactfully in the "Heart's Needle" sequence that he sustains without faltering a theme that otherwise, over so long a haul, must have bogged him down in sentimentality. The poem remains true to its germinating feeling of quiet suffering, and to its author's special talents.

FEW poets could be less alike than Snodgrass and Robert Duncan. Where Snodgrass is one kind of modern Classicist, master of a carefully defined range of sensibility, Duncan is a Romantic par excellence, reaching out in every direction for the secret of all realizations. Moreover, he resists Snodgrass' kind of surrender to life's common expectations and predicaments. He resists even the nonconformist tradition to which he himself belongs. For instance, he is tremendously indebted to William Carlos Williams' thought-mannerisms and cadenced style; but, unable to liberate himself from this and other such influences, he indulges his willful, didactic personality in such a way as to make his triumphs almost a conquest *over* style. "I attempt the discontinuities of poetry," he writes in *Letters,* and sets himself the program: "To interrupt all sure course of my inspiration."

> the addition of the un
> planned for interruption:
> a flavor stinking coffee
> (how to brew another cup
> in that Marianne Moore-
> E. P.-Williams-H. D.-Stein-
> Zukofsky-Stevens-Perse-
> surrealist-dada-staind
> pot)   by yrs. R. D.

The result is an unusual richness and springiness of texture when Duncan is at his best. (For a poet of his powers, he is surprisingly inconsistent. Although he is forty years old—some seven years older than Snodgrass—he is only just now, in poems not yet printed in book form, coming into secure control of his work.) Duncan's "natural" lyric voice is a little thin. The effort, therefore, to give an emphatic personal stamp to his work—and because it is naturally so "transparent" he has been most susceptible to the cutting in of other voices than his own, from Dante's to Denise Levertov's—has led Duncan to a private *mystique* and theory. He has cultivated a profound faith that he is running along paths of fire traced out for him by the Masters; he must fulfill their work and, at the same time, achieve a break-through premised on all he has learned from them. "As we struggle towards life, it is thru our inventions that we offend the dead: as they in their time offended." *Letters* is a voyage of exploration into this aesthetic program and its implications for the whole of life. In verse and in prose, Duncan insists and intellectualizes, superimposing on his basic, uncomplicated melodic sense of style the mystical purpose implied in this voyage:

> . . . . Hollows
> of underfeelings reveald in all arrangements.
> The design, the drawing draws from us
> the secret of a dark from our darkness.

These lines are from "Metamorphosis," which, together with the poems on "the theme of Adam" and with "An Owl Is an Only Bird of Poetry," is the most compelling and least derivative section of *Letters*. Duncan's progress in recent years may be seen by comparing this book with the *Selected Poems*, which is much spottier. A few pieces in the latter book stand out sharply from the rest—notably the excited erotic tableau of "The Mirror," the brilliantly pathetic opening part of the "Coda" to "The Venice Poem," and the unusually compressed "Processionals II." However, the usual yardsticks will not measure Duncan. For one thing, his poems in any one period are more or less interlocking, both in the actual continuity between one poem and the next and in the symbolic identifications toward which all direct themselves. For another, the mysticism is not merely a matter of general attitude, as it is, say, in Kathleen Raine, but of certain literal, Blakean intensities. "The vowels," writes Duncan, "are physical corridors of the imagination emitting passionately breaths of flame. In a poem the vowels appear like the flutterings of an owl caught in a web and give awful intimations of eternal life." The casual grossness of language in a poem like "Distant Counsels of Artaud," the unselfconscious sexual frankness of other poems, the blaspheming that again recalls Blake (whose references to "old Nobodaddy" were merely a function of his familiarity with the Eternal) are essential expressions of an indomitably mystic will.

Duncan moves all but blindly in his own orbit, yet insists that he sees all and sometimes does so indeed. At such moments we are in a realm of apperception a hundred times more meaningful than Snodgrass's, though its atmosphere is always endangered by the clouds of rhetoric and of syntactic forcing. What with the pain the one poet so lucidly and objectively reports on from his experience of the well-known world, and the longing the other expresses to break out of the encompassing assumptions of that world—even its most revolutionary and "experimentalist" assumptions—it becomes clear that "acceptance" and "rejection" as frames of thought have become obsolete.

THE two writers curiously complement each other. They are each other's correctives, as it were. Together, they suggest the main preoccupations of the future for bourgeois and anti-bourgeois alike: the true relation of private sensibility to the realities of day-to-day life, and the need to establish a new symbolism to match the expanding creative potentialities of man.

The Nation (24 October 1959)

❧

Edwin Muir: 1887–1959

BRITISH morale is even lower than ours, to judge by the poets. The woods of our Arcady are still crowded with revolutionists and comedians, but their mood is what Philip Larkin calls "an adhesive sense of betrayal." Their past, its very landscape and architecture, is being stolen away. The poems are named "Slough," "Dejection," Despair." History, progress, are "jam-traps."

The recent death of Edwin Muir leads one to brood over his work[1] and thus to see this dwindling of morale in larger perspective. Muir, born in 1887, embodied in his career much of the development and motivation of advanced thought in his time. He belonged to a Scottish farming family that was uprooted and brutally proletarianized. The destructiveness of this ordeal, described in his autobiography, led him to socialism. Later, he tried to heal the wounds of early traumatic experience through psychoanalysis. He became absorbed, too, in Continental romantic, existential and mystical thought. Increasingly he came to feel that our century has all but beaten the humanity out of modern man:

> It was not time that brought these things upon us,
> But these two wars that trampled on us twice,
> Advancing and withdrawing, like a herd
> Of clumsy-footed beasts on a stupid errand
> Unknown to them or us. . . .
>
> ("The Good Town")

We Americans too have been through these wars, but not in this European sense. We do not believe that we and whatever we build must again and again be literally trampled down. We still think that any morning we can rearrange the rules and start everything all over again in a completely new

1. See *Collected Poems 1921–1951* (Grove Press).

way; we even think that any one of us, if he really puts his mind to it and does the proper exercises, can remake the world in the divine image. If we feel guilty, it is because we cannot find the time to bring about this necessary reform. But when a European like Muir feels guilty, it is because he seems to himself part of an inexorable fatality for which he is irrationally responsible as Agamemnon and Oedipus were responsible for the deeds of their ancestors. For Muir the vision of Kafka, which influenced him deeply, was an expression of actual experience, while for Americans it merely adds a sobering dimension to a world of confusing possibilities. Muir's poems—like Kafka's stories—are not difficult, but very often their heavy oppression of tone half-paralyzes the reader as if he were enmeshed in a slow-motion nightmare.

> At the dead centre of the boundless plain
> Does our way end? Our horses pace and pace. . . .
>
> Time has such curious stretches, we are told,
> And generation after generation
> May travel them, sad stationary journey,
> Of what device, what meaning?
> ("Variations on a Time Theme")

Or:

> There is a road that turning always
> Cuts off the country of Again.
> Archers stand there on every side
> And as it runs time's deer is slain,
> And lies where it has lain.
> ("The Road")

The baffling question in such poems as these is, what lies behind the agony of men lost within "the stationary journey" of existence? In any one lifetime, generation, historical cycle we can see only so far: a succession of individual deaths, exhaustions of inspiration, recurrent defeats of the humane ideal. Eternity seems almost a principle of erosion of hope and meaning within time. There are heroic journeys and quests in Muir's poetry, and he wants them to come out right and experiments with a kind of aestheticism in which through pure imagination, man returns to a state of innocence like Adam's or like the poet's own remembered childhood. Also, in certain poems, he experiments with a suspension of skepticism and of reason generally—an as-if projection of pure faith. Characteristically, though, the language and tone belie the "happy" projection. Muir has a way of providing a vision of beauty and joyous acceptance but surrounding it and as it were outnumbering it with notes of sorrow and horror that break down its integrity. Thus, in "Oedipus," he shows the Sophoclean hero accepting his lot as necessary and good, but in words so shot through with tragic knowledge that the acceptance becomes a defeated acquiescence in a principle of evil the gods themselves cannot escape. "All," says Oedipus,

> must bear a portion of the wrong
> That is driven deep into our fathomless hearts
> Past sight or thought; that bearing it we may ease
> The immortal burden of the gods. . . .

Muir's poetry is tortured with the sense of history and personal life as an inescapable, pitifully exhausting compulsion to follow a pointless maze of roads that "run and run and never reach an end." In one poem the victorious Greeks, returning from Troy to their longed-for homes and families, find only disappointment and triviality; if they could they would turn back to that dread wall against which they battered their prime years—the mystery of destiny is rendered unheroic by its banality, and ironic by men's utter ignorance of where they really are and what really awaits them. But neither an Oedipus nor an Odysseus has any choice; heroic or not, man is whipped along whatever road he travels. He cannot rest, cannot retrace his way to the irrevocable through the "sweet and terrible labyrinth of longing," cannot take any sure bearings for the future.

The thing that makes this poetry so difficult to contemplate for very long at a time is its infinite sadness, and the repressed hysteria that underlies it. The horror of "Then" and "The Combat," poems in which the essential discovery of life's cruelty is at once abstracted and condensed into the most elementary dramatic imagery, cuts at us like a sword-slash at the face. The shock of "Troy" or "The Interrogation" or "The Good Town" is rooted in contemporary political experience—the experience of heartless torture and of human beings become scavengers among the ruins of civilization, of the systematic displacement of peoples, of a restless evil eating away at all we consider meaningful. "The Usurpers" stares into the blank face of a world "liberated" from every old concern and value and finds no answer but "black in its blackness"—

> There is no answer, We do here what we will
> And there is no answer. . . .

But the most heartbreaking poems are the ones that picture or seek to evoke the primal innocence of man—"Horses," "The Animals," "The Myth" and others. In Muir we have a great spokesman for the foiled humanistic ideal of European man, and for the era in which that ideal began to lower its flag in utter discouragement. The paltry lugubriosity of so much contemporary British writing is transcended by the vastness of what Muir implies—that once again the stars have "thrown down their spears" and "watered heaven with their tears."

The Nation (25 April 1959)

On Yeats and the Cultural Symbolism of Modern Poetry

WHEN we speak of the cultural implications of modern poetry, and of Yeats's symbolic spokesmanship for them, we are almost compelled to begin with the fact that this poetry is predominantly tragic in its assumptions and forebodings. I mean to use the word "tragic" literally: the major poetic "scene" is the sacrificial struggle of what Stephen Spender has called a heroic sensibility for the maintenance of cherished values and for concerned communication among human beings. And the most pervasive tragic implication of our poetry—in the more general sense of the term "tragic"—is that of a cultural dead end, in which a myriad values at cross-purposes, with modern political values the most virulent of all, are choking one another to death. The despair it reveals concerning the promise of civilization is comparable to that of F. O. Matthiessen's suicide note: ". . . as a Christian and a socialist believing in international peace, I find myself terribly oppressed by the present tensions."

Though I mention it only in passing, I do not mean to invoke the name of Matthiesen frivolously. It bears a special and self-evident relevance to a poetry oppressed by the warring values of contemporary society, including those of aesthetics, politics, and religion. Our best twentieth-century poetry naturally constitutes, as a whole, the embodiment of the most profound tendencies of modern sensibility, and we must acknowledge this sensibility to be largely preoccupied if not obsessed with the actual death, or at least with the death-wish, of a civilization. Moreover, its "positive" projections generally derive from an anguished desire for the utter transformation of the very premises of our social and cultural existence. It is a sensibility alienated from its moral environment, and—even more—from its political one. Whether the politics is revolutionary, moderate, or reactionary matters relatively little. It is true that politics continually thrusts itself upon our poetry, but its terms of reference are constantly resisted and supplanted by prior values. To reread the early poems of Auden, or such a work as *The Ascent of F-6*, is to discover with something of a shock that political symbolism is secondary in them to familial, tribal, and religious symbolism, and that the attempt at forced grafting usually resulted in a glittering, sometimes momentarily very moving, but finally unstable if not shoddy product. It was Yeats, fastening as he did on the sexual act and the mystery of sexuality as his ultimate points of reference and never forgetting their relation to the ritual nature and origins of his art, who dealt most powerfully with the political questions of the age—by holding them in aesthetic perspective. When, overwhelmed by the horrors of Naziism, Thomas Mann—surely the expert *par excellence* on the death-wish of our civilization—wrote that in our day "the destiny of man presents its meanings in political terms," Yeats set down what was, in context, a brutal, contemptuous reply in his little poem "Politics":

How can I, that girl standing there,
My attention fix
On Roman or on Russian
Or on Spanish politics?

As we are all aware, this apparently facetious and insulting reply to Mann hardly gives us the whole of Yeats's view of the subject. To any reader of Yeats it will suggest not simple-souled lechery, but absorption in the sexual mystery of annunciation symbolized in "Leda and the Swan," "The Second Coming," and many other poems and plays. In Yeats's writings *this* "mystery," and not politics, is the well-spring which has everything to do with man's destiny, with the cycles of his civilizations, and with the character of his fated behavior in any era, and which, as the poem "Byzantium" beautifully implies, is at the heart of human creativity itself. And it is profoundly related to his repossession of the subjective symbols of religious and magical tradition in a form usable by a pragmatic age.

In any case, the man in the street and his elected representatives, I believe, would be shocked and dazed if they realized the extent to which the *unacknowledged* legislators reject the motives by which the social order maintains itself. I need not outline the familiar history of poetic alienation since the eighteenth century, with its concomitant theories of aesthetic impersonality (so effectively restated in Eliot's earlier criticism) and its still powerful, indeed increasingly powerful, ideology of the Religion of Art and the Apotheosis of the Symbol. There *have* been valiant attempts to rewed the political and the aesthetic, most often through the symbol of the poet voyager as well as sufferer: the alienated sensibility in search of its true ancestry, home, and meanings. But as Hugh MacDiarmid has cruelly yet accurately written concerning what he calls the "leftish" British poetry of the thirties: "You cannot light a match upon a crumbling wall." And there is the case of Pound. Despite his great energy and power, he has committed what can most charitably be called the romantic error of trying to politicalize an aesthetic slogan, the slogan that it is the poet who protects the "whole machinery of social and individual thought and order" against catastrophe through his heroic tribal role as purifier of the language—its clarity, precision, and vigor. Related to this romantic error is the underlying analogy between the methods of art and those of economic organization which has become Pound's chief obsession. In his work, and I mean in some of his finest as well as in his weaker efforts, we see the poet as citizen refusing to accept the alienation thrust upon him as an artist. The craftsman meets the challenge of cultural crisis by trying to teach the world the secrets of craftsmanship and its ideals of integrity. Here is the key, perhaps, to the two Mauberleys as well as to the two Pounds: the Mauberley of Part I gets his head broken as would-be epic hero, while the Mauberley of Part II becomes the master-ironist and spokesman for the subjective realm. The poet first fights to recreate society in his own image; then, under pressure of the unequal struggle and his own self-knowledge, he splits in two psychologically.

But Pound seldom allows his created symbol of the speaking self to take over a poem as fully as in "Mauberley." Consequently, he rarely achieves the kind of self-transcendence within a short space which is the mark of Yeats's greater genius as a dramatic lyricist. He does not so masterfully and economically move from the particulars of his own condition and outlook to the more universal, encompassing symbolic transformations that enable speaker and reader to get a clearer, more honest view than the particulars themselves provide. This is not to deny his special glories as a poet or to overstress his tendentiousness in the *Cantos*. Nor is it to deny that Pound's "periplum" (what Mr. Hugh Kenner describes as "the image of successive discoveries breaking upon the consciousness of the voyager"), his close-ups of the modern Inferno, and his contrasting pagan visions of the Earthly Paradise all constitute poetic symbolism of a very high order. "Canto XXXIX," for instance, whose sexually charged interpretation of the spell cast over Odysseus and his men on Circe's isle is surely one of Pound's purest successes, is comparable in modern verse only with Yeats's "News for the Delphic Oracle." Vivienne Koch, in her incisive comment on Yeats's last poems, speaks of the "radiant constellation of that sexual universe which so attracted Yeats to the very end." For both poets this "radiant constellation" represents values antedating and superior to those of current civilization and the modern state, and both reach their heights in visualizing it.

In Yeats, however, we find not only the more consistent achievement, but also the more convincing fusion of the two kinds of symbolic referent: that of man's day-to-day predicament and that of envisioned transformation. His great impersonal, archetypal symbols could not have been so passionately conceived and so movingly employed were genuine humane concern and a love of ultimate truthfulness lacking in him. In 1936 he wrote to Ethel Mannin:

> ... as my sense of reality deepens, and I think it does with age, my horror at the cruelty of governments grows greater, and ... to hold one form of government more responsible than any other ... would betray my convictions. Communist, Fascist, nationalist, clerical, anti-clerical, all are responsible according to the number of their victims. ... If you have my poems by you, look up a poem called "The Second Coming." It was written some sixteen or seventeen years ago and foretold what is happening. ... I am not callous, every nerve trembles at what is happening in Europe, 'the ceremony of innocence is drowned.'

Yeats, we know, could not and did not maintain independence of the political maelstrom in his earlier years. Indeed, these words expressing the conviction of his old age gain authority from the fact that they were uttered by a man who had once plunged deeply into political life, personally testing most of the tendencies of his day from left to right. He had deliberately cultivated Irish themes and traditions, yet had fought—and had placed himself in a position to fight—against political tendentiousness in his work and that of others, feeling from the beginning the terrible weight laid upon the sensibilities by such tendentiousness. We need discover no specific Mallarmé influence to realize that Yeats knew in his own nature that "one throw of the dice can never abolish hazard itself"—that no rational system or program can destroy the character of fatality. Nor did he have to learn from Baudelaire that sense of the weariness of the defeated spirit, the eternal negation of the human will, which was in the atmosphere into which Yeats was born as a poet. He accepted, resolutely and courageously, the challenge implicit in the moral situation as it loomed in Symbolist tradition. The challenge lay in what

Laforgue, describing Baudelaire's contribution to poetry, called his recognition of "the boredom implicit in sensuality," his consciousness of "neurosis," his feeling of "damnation on this earth."

Yeats did not deny these realizations, but he did not stop with them either. They are related to the confession of personal helplessness which we find in the main post-Romantic English tradition also, in such poems as "Two in the Campagna" and "Dover Beach." Compare, for instance, the ending of the latter poem with the next-to-last stanza of Yeats's "A Dialogue of Self and Soul." Yeats's stanza reads like a close revision of Arnold's, so near to one another are the situations, imagery, and even metrical patterns of the two passages. But the curious fact is that "A Dialogue" is both darker *and* happier than "Dover Beach." Arnold's simile "as on a darkling plain . . . / Where ignorant armies clash by night" does not strike so deep as Yeats's sharper metaphor "the frog-spawn of a blind man's ditch, / A blind man battering blind men." And Arnold's "Ah, love, let us be true / To one another!" is almost complacent next to the image of

> . . . that most fecund ditch of all,
> The folly that man does
> Or must suffer, if he woos
> A proud woman not kindred of his soul.

And further, the squalor-ridden bitterness Yeats gives these symbols of lost meaning and of desire prepares us for a leap Arnold could never have contemplated. It is the leap *out of the nineteenth century,* truly, into a uniquely modern kind of redemption through self-acceptance. In his closing stanza, Yeats dazzlingly turns to account the Baudelairean oppression with being one of the "daily damned," the fear of nothingness that holds secularism in check, and the whole predicament of the modern consciousness. He does so by shrewdly making the speaking Self his crucial symbol after having thrown out a deliberately false lead by allowing the Soul to dominate the first part of the poem. Enmeshed in its suffering, pride, and sexual need, the Self projects out of the bleak limitations of its existence all that the Soul had threatened would be lost without worldly renunciation. Like the aged protagonist of "Sailing to Byzantium," it builds a universe of meaning out of predicament. It thereby appropriates the uncommunicable values of the Soul, lying outside of life and therefore unattainable to human consciousness, to the living present—and then "everything we look upon is blest."

Of course, it has often been noted that Yeats used aspects of his own experience and personality symbolically, nearly in the way he used figures and abstract schemata out of the storehouse of tradition, mythology, and occultism—the storehouse that he called *Spiritus Mundi*. "I seek an image," he wrote, "of the modern mind's discovery of itself." The "modern mind" is shaped, inevitably, not only by what it has inherited from the past but also by the new pragmatic science and by an awareness of violences well-understood but uncontrollable. It is also, just as inevitably, one's own mind: Yeats's as well as yours or mine. No one of us can very well speak of "the modern mind" and not—however we qualify—to some extent at least conceive of it as his own mind. When Yeats tried to systematize this search in *A Vision,* he could not keep his own special interests and idiosyncrasies out of the system—did not wish to do so—and the result is that we have something that both purports to be an objective universal scheme and confesses to having a certain arbitrary and pragmatic character as a source of metaphor and guide to the structure of poems. In *A Vision* as in the poetry, each of these opposites—the universally encompassing symbolic structure and the arbitrary, sometimes whimsical, personal and idiosyncratic element—implies the other. But it is the image of the speaking self which finally dominates all the others, as we can see in poem after poem in which Yeats broods over the process by which images are begotten and then *seem* to become sources in themselves. The priority is stated, in the guise of a confession of weariness and failure, in the single stanza which forms the opening section of "The Circus Animals' Desertion":

> I sought a theme and sought for it in vain,
> I sought it daily for six weeks or so.
> Maybe at last, being but a broken man,
> I must be satisfied with my heart, although
> Winter and summer till old age began
> My circus animals were all on show,
> Those stilted boys, that burnished chariot,
> Lion and woman and the Lord knows what.

When he was younger, the poet says, the great archetypal images were always there to give him his themes. Now he must perhaps be satisfied only with what he has left when they no longer are present for him—his own heart. He is thrown back on himself, in the *here;* that is all the theme remaining to him.

But in the second section of the poem he seems to forget what he has just said and suddenly offers another alternative: "What can I do but enumerate *old* themes?" The three stanzas of this section allude specifically to three of his earlier works: *The Wanderings of Oisin, The Countess Cathleen,* and *On Baile's Strand.* With each of these works, he says, the original motive out of which it had grown was lost to sight so that "It was the dream itself enchanted me." Each was a dream of "the embittered heart," but as it grew into full realization

> Players and painted stage took all my love,
> And not those things that they were emblems of.

The "things that they were emblems of" were the love-starved, miracle-starved, "embittered" sensibilities of the living self. Yeats chooses, by his language here, to present these things of the heart itself as a composite referent to which his "circus animals" or symbols "on show" all point ultimately.

Now this argument is thoroughly deceptive, for two reasons. In the first place, it is deceptive because of the nature of these works which he has singled out to represent his symbolic method. *The Wanderings of Oisin* is, like such early poems as "The Stolen Child," "The Lake Isle of Innisfree," "The Man Who Dreamed of Faeryland," and "Who Goes with Fergus?" a complaint against the destructiveness of the romantic dream. The realm of the *there,* in each instance, is conceived either as a source of torment because of its unattainability or as a region in which the sufferings of the *here* are only recapitulated and intensified. The late play *Purgatory* expands and brings into terrible focus the latter conception. The mingling of two worlds gives each the qualities of the other; they interpenetrate and there is no pure release from the here, any more than there can be inescapable relegation to it alone. Stanza two of the second section of "The Circus Animals' Desertion" makes the same point about *The Countess Cathleen*. Its source, says Yeats (going out of his way to account for its theme autobiographically), lay in the fact that

> I thought my dear must her own soul destroy,
> So did fanaticism and hate enslave it . . . .

And this, he says, brought forth the "counter-truth" of the vision of "pity-crazed" Cathleen, who would have given her soul away to save her people had she not been prevented by "masterful heaven." *On Baile's Strand* brings the two worlds even closer together. Cuchulain, the free, untrammeled warrior whose services have always been given spontaneously and generously, out of love, is persuaded to betray his own nature by swearing unquestioning allegiance to the king, Conchubar. The result is tragedy without end; he slays his own son, unknowingly, though every instinct forbids him to do so. Thirty-four years after this play, Yeats's poem "Lapis Lazuli" (1938) maintains stubbornly the independence of art and the priority of its concerns to those of the state. None of these works soared out of sight of the Self's concerns and needs, the "heart-mysteries" of which Yeats speaks; though each presents them in a complex symbolic relationship to the search for order and meaning, the primary place of the uncommitted sensibility is maintained throughout Yeats's career. There is a straight line of association between the companions of Oisin, Cuchulain in *On Baile's Strand* and *The Death of Cuchulain,* and even the Cuchulain who learns his final lesson in "Cuchulain Comforted."

But apart from the intrinsic character of the works mentioned in "The Circus Animals' Desertion," the argument of the second section is deceptive in its implication that the self bereft of its usual emblematic satellites is merely a literal referent—not a symbol in itself. As I have suggested, this supposedly literal self is always very much present within Yeatsian symbolism, and not only as a logical referent. Yeats has been charged with intellectual naiveté, but he well understood the elusive problem with which we are now concerned: "I seek an image of the modern mind's discovery of itself." The speaking self, the voice of the heart, are both equivalents, and both symbols of the modern mind and of the predicament of modern man. The third and final section of the poem, like the first section comprising but one stanza, returns to the proposition advanced at the beginning but then seemingly forgotten. Again now the speaker repeats that he has nothing left but the literal *I*—

> Those masterful images because complete
> Grew in pure mind, but out of what began?
> A mound of refuse or the sweepings of a street,
> Old kettles, old bottles, and a broken can,

Old iron, old bones, old rags, that raving slut
Who keeps the till. Now that my ladder's gone,
I must lie down where all the ladders start,
In the foul rag-and-bone shop of the heart.

This climax of supposed despair rings out triumphantly despite what is apparently being said. It is a clear reprise of the kind of acceptance and affirmation of the known life, with all its tragic lacerations and deprivations, which we have in "A Dialogue"—only even more affirmative because it denies itself any proclamation of joy. It is an ecstasy of self-denigration, but the self emerges more vigorous than ever, and more the source of all meaning than ever. We shall perhaps remember Crazy Jane's cry that "Love has pitched his mansion in/ The place of excrement" and the powerful tribute in "An Acre of Grass" to

. . . Timon and Lear
Or that William Blake
Who beat upon the wall
Till truth obeyed his call.

In an important sense, all our best poetry—by which I mean that poetry which in one way or another stands at the frontiers of the art—seeks such an image of the self discovering its own meanings. At any time, but especially in a critical and self-analytical one, the whole poem, considered as a cultural symbol embodying basic identifications, documents its culture by testing its attitudes. It subjects "approved" social attitudes to a simultaneous testing against observed reality and against the poet's inner sense of truth or balance. This balance is decisive finally, for it encompasses the poet's subjective awareness of tradition and of the intellectual landscape of his day as well as his literal feelings and moral bent. If the aesthetic structure has integrity, the implied cultural evaluations will also. A simple example, which I have treated more fully elsewhere, is Yeats's "Easter, 1916." This poem at first sets out to be, apparently, a patriotic tribute to the memory of the martyred heroes of the Rebellion. A "terrible beauty," says the poet, has been born in his countrymen as a result of this experience. He had thought them all drab fellows or fools, but now it seems that they have come under an enchantment and been glorified:

Hearts with one purpose alone
Through summer and winter seem
Enchanted to a stone . . . .

The image of the stone transforms the poem, too, however. It takes over its direction, and soon we are considering whether those hearts had not become *too* stony, unable to grasp the fact that England may be honest in her motives after all, impervious to the tragic waste of life brought about by an inflexible political ideal cherished to the exclusion of all else. At the end, though Yeats still speaks of the Irish rebels with love, the poem has transcended its initial nationalistic bias. Thus, a seemingly incidental figure of speech, the image of the "hearts enchanted to a stone," has become the poem's ruling symbol and enabled the poet's "modern mind" to discover its own bearings despite the pressures of politics and narrowly local loyalties.

In the same way—to recall "The Circus Animals' Desertion" once more—the image of the "foul rag-and-bone shop of the heart" is a comment on the conventional assumption, ironically echoed (but only so that it may be dropped with a heavier thud) throughout most of the poem, that the projections of "pure mind" are prior to and superior to their physical and psychological source in the Here. Yeats deals masterfully with this assumption as it appears in conventional ethical and religious thought in such poems as "John Kinsella's Lament for Mrs. Mary Moore" and "A Dialogue of Self and Soul"; in these the speaking self, by various devices of rhetoric as well as of symbolic transposition, takes over priority in the most moving manner possible. Both are tragic assertions, in that they represent the moment which is the most moving of all in pure tragedy: the moment of self-assessment and the reordering of motives in the immediate wake of defeat. They are but two instances among a good many of the subordination in Yeats of religious to aesthetic motives. The plays *Calvary* and *The Resurrection* bring this result about even more audaciously, as do the poems "The Dolls" and "News for the Delphic Oracle."

But the subordination of religion (or of other great frames of value) does not mean that it is simply discounted. The aesthetic motive in Yeats as in other great poets is a distillation from the whole province of the sensibility—a distillation into formal elements which, when successfully structured, constitutes a *moral* ordering of enormous authority, one that strikes as perception, knowledge, experienced truth. Yeats's free-wheeling use of sacred and mythological and occult symbols is secondary to this effect, but it is essential if his uniquely *tactful* aesthetic secularization of traditional attitudes, which does correspond to the whole drift of modern sensibility, is not to lose touch with mankind's richest resources of faith and psychological power. Hence the recurring patterns of opposition and transcendence that allow for his ambiguous manipulations of the tokens of cultural meaning and cultural crisis. We still are too little concerned about the possibilities of the poetic symbol—its openness, its susceptibility to analysis and to reexamination by each poet in the light of his own cultural experience—as one of our great latent resources for genuine, concerned human communication of every sort. As Richard McKeon puts it, "the development of human conscience and sensitivity to values is precisely the history of the operation of symbols which in their fullest statement in art, philosophy, and religion are subject to repeated and divergent interpretation." I have tried to explore some of the ways in which one great modern poet, at least, has made his contribution to the success of symbolic communication.

The Yale Review (June 1960)

A Primer of Ezra Pound

1
The Early Poetry

EZRA Pound's career is so interlaced with the whole of modern letters and politics that one might devote many pages to it and never touch on his poetry. For a time at least this man of genuine learning and humanity put his great talents to the service of Mussolini and his Fascist party. Yet long before, even while being attracted to ideas which finally led him to this service, he had established himself as a prophet of the open spirit. "My province," he might have declared, "is all creative thought," for he began early to cultivate an eclecticism disciplined by rich understanding of a number of living traditions. His mind and sensibilities darted everywhere, and he encouraged many other writers of promise, whether Communist, Bohemian, proto-Nazi, or whatever, to do the best that was in them. His intelligence, indeed, has been a flowering of Western self-awareness, with life-bestowing and poisonous blossoms intermingled, as if all the beautiful vitality and all the brilliant rottenness of our heritage in its luxuriant variety were both at once made manifest in it.

Therefore, despite the considerable attention paid him by critics and scholars, relatively little has been said to distinguish Pound the poet from Pound the thinker, propagandist, and literary man of action. It is obvious, we must grant, that poet and man are in the long run inseparable. Nevertheless, the artist's reputation has suffered from the activist-thinker's vagaries and even from his achievements. In the *Cantos* especially, that great and complex enterprise of the last several decades, the two Pounds have interfered with each other. The interference, perhaps inevitable, has understandably confused all but the most devoted and professionally informed readers—and them also often enough. Hence their laudable concern to explain his unorthodox principles and his subtleties of method and allusion.

And yet this concern *can* be pushed too far. A normal reader who undertook, simply and innocently, to read *Personae: The Collected Poems*[1] from the beginning could go quite a distance without having to scream for the police or whistle for the experts. Here, among the poems written before Pound was twenty-five, one finds many direct, musical, lively pieces of fresh excellence still. The first of them, "The Tree," opens the book with a curious yet lucid imaginative projection, one incidentally which augurs the poet's later fascination with the motif of metamorphosis, so vital to the *Cantos:*

1. New York: Horace Liveright, 1926; New Directions, 1949. All verse quotations, except from the *Cantos*, are from the 1949 edition.

I stood still and was a tree amid the wood,
Knowing the truth of things unseen before;
Of Daphne and the laurel bow
And that god-feasting couple old
That grew elm-oak amid the wold.

The early poems, too, give frank evidence of his study of the Provençal troubadours, and of Browning and his vigorous, idiomatic roughnesses as well. Thus, "Na Audiart" begins as pure song and word-play:

Though thou well dost wish me ill
                    Audiart, Audiart . . .

But later in the same poem, we hear the unmistakable ring of old R. B.:

Just a word in thy praise, girl,
Just for the swirl
Thy satins make upon the stair. . . .

Even these brief snatches, with their melodic variations of line-length, their skillful play on certain vowels and consonants, their certainty of phrasing, will show how precocious a student of his masters Pound was. At this point he was still in the grip of the late-Romantic tradition as it had come to him by way of the British nineties. The themes are all familiar: the sentimental egocentrism of the artist in "Famam Librosque Cano"; the yearning for spiritual freedom and the company of kindred sensibilities of "In Durance" ("But I am homesick after mine own kind"); the mingled pathos, romance, and comedy of "Marvoil." Even when he is most derivative and imitative, however, Pound's style is charged with a certain essential, idiosyncratic energy. Witness the boisterously insulting epithets of "Marvoil":

All for one half-bald, knock-knee'd king of the Aragonese,
Alfonso, Quattro, poke-nose.

The best known of the earlier pieces, probably, are "Sestina: Altaforte" and "Ballad of the Goodly Fere." In "Altaforte," a work of pure exuberant bombast in a tricky Provençal pattern, Bertrans de Born raves gorgeously of war's delights and the swinishness of peace-lovers. "For the death of such sluts I go rejoicing," he shouts, and Pound's introduction to the poem has equal gusto: "Dante Alighieri put this man in hell for that he was a stirrer up of strife. Eccovi! Judge ye! Have I dug him up again?" The poem is a brilliant, intentionally one-dimensional composition, studded with clanging monosyllables that hammer out the obsession of a blood-drunk brute. Bertrans' outcries are spectacularly spondaic and alliterative. "Damn it all!" he bellows; "all this our South stinks peace." His black piety is uncompromising: "May God damn for ever all who cry 'Peace!'" He "prays" indiscriminately to Heaven and to Hell, and with onomatopoeic fervor: "Hell grant soon we hear again the swords clash!" Pound is said to have roared out the "Sestina" in a Soho restaurant when it was first written, shocking the genteel bourgeois patrons of the place.

Its self-evident technical virtuosity, praised highly by T. S. Eliot among others, thus contributed incidentally and in a small way to the disconcertment of British philistinism: one of the poet's minor aims at least.

The much-anthologized, virile-posturing "Ballad of the Goodly Fere" presents Jesus as "No capon priest" but a "man o' men" especially fond of other "brawny men" and of "ships and the open sea," a scornfully laughing Nietzschean Robin Hood (with dashes of Whitman and Kipling) who drives out the money-changers "Wi' a bundle o' cords swung free." He resembles the risen Dionysus rather more than the gentle Christ. Alien to gentility, he is of the implacable, pre-Classical host of divinities:

> I ha' seen him eat o' the honey-comb
> Sin' they nailed him to the tree.

Though forced and overextended, the ballad illustrates Pound's extraordinary ease with traditional forms and his never-ending search for ways to bring these forms, and traditional themes as well, into renewed if unexpected life. He turns them to his own use, making a triumph of what might otherwise be a mere exercise and creating, as the critic Ronald Duncan has said of "Altaforte," "a boisterous vitality within the confines of the form."[2]

Pound gives his game away more vulnerably in "The Flame," which reveals the depth and implications of his commitment to medieval Provençal values as he found them in Arnaut Daniel and others.[3] In the greatness of Provence he found a reinforcement of the revived Romantic idealism he shared with Yeats and Joyce, among many other writers. Indeed, "The Flame" begins as though composed by Yeats, Joyce, and Pound in committee:

> 'Tis not a game that plays at mates and mating,
> Provence knew;
> 'Tis not a game of barter, lands, and houses,
> Provence knew;
> We who are wise beyond your dream of wisdom,
> Drink our immortal moments; we "pass through."
> We have gone forth beyond your bonds and borders,
> Provence knew;
> And all the tales of Oisin say but this:
> That man doth pass the net of days and hours. . . .

While each of these three writers has a strain of unrelenting materialism in his make-up, each has also this softer idealism in his work, especially in his earlier writings. All have shown enormous faith in the symbol-making power of art as a gift enabling us to "pass through" toward the ineffable. If eventually theirs is a secular way of thought, it remains a secular *religiosity* which substitutes aesthetic creativity for godhead. "Provence knew" that there is more to love than its sensual and its socially practical aspects; the added

2. "Poet's Poet," in *Ezra Pound*, ed. Peter Russell (London: Peter Nevill Ltd., 1950), p. 160.
3. See Ezra Pound, *Literary Essays* (Norfolk, Conn.: New Directions, 1954), pp. 91–200.

dimension, the "more," was the creation of the poetic imagination. It was the troubadours who had made religious vision of the profane, blasphemous rituals of the Court of Love:

> Search not my lips, O Love, let go my hands,
> This thing that moves as man is no more mortal.

Certain passages in "The Flame" glow beyond the rest of this uneven poem, with its sentimental spiritualities in awkward places. (The passage just quoted is one illustration of such bogging-down). On the whole, though, it remains a program-poem—that is, one written primarily to clarify the writer's perspectives to himself. Pound's craftsmanship comes off better in the graceful "Ballatetta": a vision of the Beloved in the best troubadour tradition, and without the overreaching preachments of "The Flame." First we see her as a living being, surrounded by an aureole that "doth melt us into song." And thereupon the song itself takes over the poem:

> The broken sunlight for a healm she beareth
> Who hath my heart in jurisdiction. . . .

"Ballatetta" gives us one of the earliest of the shining moments of exultant vision, suffused with imagery of light, in Pound's poetry. Its success in adapting formal achievements outside the English tradition to the needs of our language is directly related to his never-ending involvement with problems of translation and his boldness in dealing with them.

Perhaps, though, we should not speak of Provençal or any other European poetry as "outside the English tradition." To Pound as to Eliot "the tradition" is something antedating and transcending any one national or linguistic segment of it. At one time, after all, he had been a student of great promise in the Romance languages, a graduate fellow and instructor at the University of Pennsylvania. His purpose in first going abroad in 1906 had been to gather materials for a doctoral dissertation on Lope de Vega. It was natural for him, as natural as for any person of effective education, to think of tradition not as narrow conventionalism but as a driving force in the modern spirit: "a beauty which we preserve and not a set of fetters to bind us," he wrote in 1913.[4] But it took rare understanding to see just how this force can leap across the barriers of language and in what sense, exactly, the melic poets of seventh and sixth century Greece (B.C.) and the Provençal poets might be considered the founders of the two great lyric traditions of the West. "From the first arose practically all the poetry of the 'ancient world,' from the second practically all that of the modern."[5] In both these great sources "the arts of music and verse were most closely knit together" and "each thing done by the poet had some definite musical urge or necessity bound up within it."

Thus, Pound's interest in such poets as Sappho, Arnaut Daniel, Cavalcanti, and Dante (the full list goes beyond Greek and Provençal poetry; an entire

4. *Ibid.*, p. 91.
5. *Ibid.*

curriculum of reading is outlined in *The ABC of Reading* and elsewhere) grows out of a need for models of organic composition. That is, he sought poetry in which sound, sense, and image must be functions of one another. Like Picasso with his thorough classical grounding, Pound has made his knowledge of tradition count toward the originality of his own artistry. One of the great experimentalists of our century is thus, almost inevitably, in another sense the foremost traditionalist of our day. Pound's essay on Cavalcanti (which he developed and modified from 1910 to 1931, maintaining a constant goal while his writing was undergoing its most important changes) defines the kind of poetic vision he has always been after:

> We appear to have lost the radiant world where one thought cuts through another with clean edge, a world of moving energies . . . , magnetisms that take form, that are seen, or that border the visible, the matter of Dante's *paradiso*, the glass under water, the form that seems a form seen in a mirror. . . . Not the pagan worship of strength, nor the Greek perception of visual non-animate plastic, or plastic in which the being animate was not the main and principal quality, but this 'harmony in the sentience' or harmony of the sentient, . . . where stupid men have not reduced all 'energy' to unbounded undistinguished abstraction.
>
> For the modern scientist energy has no borders, it is a shapeless 'mass' of force; even his capacity to differentiate it to a degree never dreamed by the ancients has not led him to think of its shape or even its loci. The rose that his magnet makes in the iron filings, does not lead him to think of the force in botanic terms, or wish to visualize that force as floral and extant. . . .
>
> A medieval 'natural philosopher' would find this modern world full of enchantments, not only the light in the electric bulb, but the thought of the current hidden in air and in wire would give him a mind full of forms. . . . The medieval philosopher would probably have been unable to think the electric world, and *not* think of it as a world of forms. . . . Or possibly this will fall under the eye of a contemporary scientist of genius who will answer: But, damn you, that is exactly what we do feel; or under the eye of a painter who will answer: Confound you, you *ought* to find just that in my painting.[6]

Now all these ideas about past and present, about science and Provence and the neglected universe of forms, converge for Pound in certain crucial attitudes toward craftsmanship. The poet's created world is, ideally, that of Dante: a "radiant" world in which "one thought cuts through another with clean edge, a world of moving energies." Whatever the feelings and ideas he expresses, they must be embodied in a form precise in outline but crackling with the living conception which has given them birth. As these attitudes develop, Pound begins to lay enormous emphasis on the single image, insisting that properly understood it "is an intellectual and emotional complex in an instant of time" and becoming the dynamic instigator of the Imagist movement.

6. *Ibid.*, pp. 154–155.

The classic example of Imagism is generally held to be H. D.'s "Oread," but Pound's own "In a Station of the Metro" is a richer, more compressed example:

> The apparition of these faces in the crowd;
> Petals on a wet, black bough.

The effect of this pure, direct image of fragile, destroyed beauty against its dark background—the aftermath of a rainstorm, perhaps—is compounded of a fusion of numerous nearly invisible "hints": first, a combined affection, helpless "appreciation," and dismay at all these glimpses of faces ("apparitions") in their subway-world of semidarkness; at the same time, a related, elusive suggestion of shades of the damned in Avernus; and along with these impressions, an implied criticism of modern civilization.

Here in miniature is the visualization of "force in botanic terms," the provision of "borders" to define the "shape" and "loci" of contemporary experience. Another example, completely removed this time from a particular urban setting yet bearing much the same meaning, is the poem "April":

> Three spirits came to me
> And drew me apart
> To where the olive boughs
> Lay stripped upon the ground:
> Pale carnage beneath bright mist.

As in the "Metro" poem, the final line brings the whole to a sharp point of pregnant concentration. (In both poems, incidentally, Pound uses the consonants *p* and *b* to help prepare us for, and then to plunge us into, this intensification at the end.) The "stripped" boughs beneath the blossom-laden tree arouse the same kind of compassion that the blown petals stuck on the slick black bough do in "Metro." The "spirits" resemble the faces in the "apparition" there, and the "bright mist" of flowers suggests something infinitely delicate and desirable, now lost forever. Contemplating both poems, we will perhaps recall Homer's description of the multitudinous dead in the *Odyssey,* an abbreviated translation of which Pound was to provide in the first of the *Cantos:*

> Souls out of Erebus, cadaverous dead, of brides
> Of youths and of the old who had borne much;
> Souls stained with recent tears, girls tender . . .[7]

In "April" itself Pound underlines the tragic juxtaposition of "pale carnage" with bright loveliness by his Latin epigraph: "*Nympharum membra disjecta*" (scattered limbs of the nymphs).

"April" and "In a Station of the Metro" are from the volume *Lustra*, containing poems written between 1912 and 1915. Pound's mastery, by his late twen-

7. *The Cantos of Ezra Pound* (New York: New Directions, 1948), p. 3. All quotations from *Cantos 1–84* are from this edition.

ties, of poetic line and metaphor is well illustrated by the two poems just examined. In the volume as a whole, he tries many modes of writing—Catullan satire, light impressionist pieces, rhetorical forays (including an address to Walt Whitman as his "pig-headed father" with whom he is now ready to make a "pact"), witticisms and manifestoes of various sorts. Here is the arresting "Coitus," its startling initial figure one instance among many of the sexual and phallic motifs central to much of Pound's most serious work:

> The gilded phalloi of the crocuses
>   are thrusting at the spring air.

Here is "The Coming of War: Actaeon," with its restless, ominous movement:

> A sea
> Harsher than granite,
>   unstill, never ceasing . . .

And here is the perfect classicism of "The Spring," introducing its nostalgic theme of lost love with a Sapphic sureness:

> Cydonian Spring with her attendant train,
> Maelids and water-girls,
> Stepping beneath a boisterous wind from Thrace . . .

After this start the poem speeds through its description of how Spring "spreads the bright tips" of newness everywhere. Then suddenly the personification is dropped in a rush of bitter memory:

>   And wild desire
> Falls like black lightning.
> O bewildered heart,
> Though every branch have back what last year lost,
> She, who moved here amid the cyclamen,
> Moves only now a clinging tenuous ghost.

The difference between a poem like this one and a poem like "The Flame" does not lie in any absence of *feeling* in the former. But the feeling of "The Spring" is rooted in the poem's physical, sensuous imagery rather than in abstract Romanticism. A few years later, in 1917, Pound was to proclaim, a little stridently, that the genuine poetry of this century would "move against poppycock":

> it will be harder and saner, it will be . . . 'nearer the bone.' It will be as much like granite as it can be, its force will lie in its truth, its interpretative power (of course, poetic force does always rest there). . . . We will have fewer painted adjectives impeding the shock and stroke of it. At least for myself, I want it so, austere, direct, free from emotional slither.[8]

8. *Literary Essays*, p. 12.

It was this rejection of "emotional slither" that led to Pound's parody of Housman:

> O woe, woe,
> People are born and die,
> We also shall be dead pretty soon
> Therefore let us act as if we were
> dead already.

It helps account, too, for the appeal to him of Heine, like Pound a rebel armoring his sensitivity in the ironic mail of a lively intelligence. Thus, Pound's translation from *Die Heimkehr:*

> The mutilated choir boys
> When I begin to sing
> Complain about the awful noise
> And call my voice too thick a thing.

And it throws light on Pound's ambivalent feelings toward Whitman. If it be true that many sons spend their lives revising, in their own behavior, the images of their fathers, we may say, allowing ourselves the license of Pound's own simile in "A Pact," that he took over Walt's vision of the poet-prophet and poet-teacher and recast it in a more sophisticated and Europeanized, a more formally demanding mold. Yet, though we can glance at the question only in passing here, there remains a closer kinship between these two than at first would appear likely. The largeness of their concerns, the sprawling epic character of their major efforts, their attempts to encompass a multitude of contradictory elements through main force, and the revolutionary quality of their careers lock them into undeniable kinship.

Still, Pound's interest in "hardness," in "the tradition," and in the poetry of pure vision does conceal this kinship very efficiently. His growth toward realization of this combined interest had been perfectly evident even before *Lustra*, certainly at least as early as the 1912 *Ripostes*. By this time he had undergone an arduous apprenticeship in translation, and it now bore fruit in one of his best known successes, the rendering of the Anglo-Saxon "The Seafarer" into modern English. Though it contains more Wardour Street English than it should, the poem is vastly successful in its opening section, and in isolated later portions. The success is due in part to Pound's marvelous ear, in part to the fact that Old English metric and alliteration are unusually congenial to his special talents. The Anglo-Saxon kenning may be seen as a frozen Imagist metaphor, and the plaintive melancholy of the monologue, crammed with detail but held to a single emotional pitch, is not far removed from the characteristic modern lyric-contemplative poem. The failure of the translation to sustain interest at every point is not altogether Pound's fault; the original was always, in our temerarious view, too long for its own good. In *Ripostes* also we find the mysterious "Portrait d'une Femme," a compassionate yet satirical characterization which is at the same time a remarkable example of what skillful accenting and the bravura manipulation of a few sounds (especially the pivotal *yū*-sound here) can accomplish. "The Return," one of Pound's most beautiful and economical poems, is a triumph of accentual variation in its wavering opening notes, its gathering of full-blooded speed and strength, and then its hesitant falling-off again. Finally, "The Alchemist," a "chant for the transmutation of metals," is one of our great incantatory poems. As in "The Return," where the hero-gods of the past are through an effort of poetic conjuring brought up into the foreground of consciousness, the vision emerges with the strange clarity of aesthetic transformation fully realized:

> As you move among the bright trees;
> As your voices, under the larches of Paradise
> Make a clear sound....

The Pound we have been reviewing is the ardent and committed young poet who believed in the life of art as few men have ever believed in it. He is the man of whom Carl Sandburg could once say that he was "the best man writing poetry today" while T.S. Eliot, whose direction was so thoroughly different from Sandburg's, could echo Dante's praise of Arnaut Daniel by calling Pound "*il miglior fabbro*," the finest craftsman. Of Pound's poem "The Return" Yeats wrote that "it gives me better words than my own." The work of the later Pound, author of *Hugh Selwyn Mauberley* and the *Cantos*, is solidly based on what he had done by 1915, when he became thirty years old.

2
Basic Frames of Thought

EZRA Pound's commitment to his art is the rationale of that art. Out of it comes the impulse to the longer works, in large degree, and to his larger theoretical interests. It is the key to his fundamental belief in the importance of literature to the state:

> Has literature a function in the state...? It has.... It has to do with the clarity and vigour of 'any and every' thought and opinion. It has to do with maintaining the very cleanliness of the tools, the health of the very matter of thought itself.... The individual cannot think and communicate his thought, the governor and legislator cannot act effectively or frame his laws, without words, and the solidity and validity of these words is in the care of the damned and despised *litterati*. When their work goes rotten—by that I do not mean when they express indecorous thoughts—but when their very medium, the very essence of their work, the application of word to thing goes rotten, i.e. becomes slushy and inexact, or excessive or bloated, the whole machinery of social and of individual thought and order goes to pot. This is a lesson of history....[9]

Now whether Pound was right in saying that the health of individual and state depends on the soundness of the language, which it is the writer's sacred

9. *Ibid.*, p. 21.

task to maintain, or whether perhaps the relationship is just the reverse, or whether, finally, both literature and the state depend on unfathomable, or only partly fathomable, sources we need not try to determine here and now. Whatever the ultimate truth of the matter, there should certainly be general assent to the proposition that the status and integrity of letters is vitally related to the condition of society. Simply to begin thinking about this relationship is to raise the poet out of the musical-doll category to which he is usually relegated.

Pound has always been sharply conscious of the way in which poetry bespeaks the values of whole peoples, bringing to the surface not only their more cheerful wisdom but also their deeply, often secretly and inarticulately felt unorthodoxies of real sentiment. Moreover, he believes literally that the loyalty of genuine poets to sound workmanship and to the meanings of tradition is a kind of guardianship of principled standards in the republic at large, whether in general communication, in the economic life, or in the functioning of government.

We must bear these attitudes in mind most especially when we come to *Mauberley* and the *Cantos*. The first portion of the *Mauberley* sequence is in large part a denunciation of our society's denial to the dedicated poet of his rightful place. Academic and editorial stuffiness and venality, it argues, shoddiness in every phase of human activity, and that final criminal betrayal, the World War, have made for a "botched civilization." At the war's end, the poet-speaker sizes up what is left of this civilization, noting above all the triumph of insensitivity and mass-production tinniness over responsibility and true craftsmanship. The bureaucratic expropriation of literature by businesslike "operators" is, he sees, marked also, and quite logically, by the serious poet's loss of most means of livelihood, literary patronage having in any case passed out of the picture some while back. The speaker considers retreat or self-exile, but summons up his own courage for the time being at least. Against "liars in public places" and the triumphs of "usury age-old" he sets the memory of "Young blood and high blood" sacrificed in the War:

> Charm, smiling at the good mouth,
> Quick eyes gone under earth's lid....

Against the new type of professional who gives him practical tips on the literary game—

> And give up verse, my boy,
> There's nothing in it—

he sets the poets of the nineties, Yeats's friends Dowson and Johnson, who stuck by their poetic guns at all costs (and the costs *were* cruel), and the whole great literary tradition from Homer and Bion through Villon, Shakespeare, and Waller to such moderns as Flaubert, Gautier, and Henry James.[10]

10. John Espey, *Ezra Pound's* Mauberley (Berkeley and Los Angeles: University of California Press, 1955), traces the literary ancestry informing *Mauberley* painstakingly and convincingly. This volume also contains a superior text of the sequence, although our quotations are taken from *Personae* for the reader's convenience.

His own role he defines as that of a contemporary Odysseus who has either mistaken his heroic mission or undertaken it in the wrong century:

> For three years, out of key with his time,
> He strove to resuscitate the dead art
> Of poetry; to maintain "the sublime"
> In the old sense. . . .

But we shall have a fuller look at *Mauberley* and its ironies shortly. If we turn now to the *Cantos*, Pound's chief work-in-progress for a great many years, we find the function of literature and the other arts in the state a central point of focus in it again and again, a critical element in the entire problem of cultural stability. Canto 13 shows Kung (Confucius) saying to his disciples:

> . . . "When the prince has gathered about him
> "All the savants and artists, his riches will be fully employed."

A corollary of this principle is Kung's warning to the lute-player Tian:

> . . . "Without character you will
> be unable to play on that instrument
> Or to execute the music fit for the Odes. . . ."

In shocking, purposeful contrast to the ordered Confucian reasonableness of such pronouncements, the next canto, with Swiftian violence, explodes a nightmare picture of our modern inferno of corruption and profiteering, dominion of that deadliest evil, Usury. Integral to the scene are the howling, stinking "betrayers of language," those "perverts, who have set money-lust before the pleasure of the senses":

> The slough of unamiable liars,
> bog of stupidities,
> malevolent stupidities, and stupidities,
> the soil living pus, full of vermin,
> dead maggots begetting live maggots,
> slum owners,
> usurers squeezing crab-lice, pandars to authority,
> pets-de-loup, sitting on piles of stone books,
> obscuring the texts with philology,
> hiding them under their persons,
> the air without refuge of silence,
> the drift of lice, teething . . . .

Here is the very opposite of the voices heard "under the larches of Paradise" in "The Alchemist" and also, again, elsewhere in the *Cantos*. Subtle in detail, the rhythm is obvious enough in its general pattern, which has two basic characteristics. First, there is a line of rising force, often mounting to a hovering accent (a succession of two or more stressed syllables giving the effect of unremitting emphasis) toward the middle and then shifting to a falling rhythm at the very end (líars, vérmin, and so on). Second, there is a series, with exceptions and variations, of alternating longer and shorter phrases. Alliteration and the repetition of key words, a profusion of spitting sibilants and stop-sounds, and the echoing of vowels and of the dyings-off of line-endings support this pattern. Together these effects help create an atmosphere of absolute revulsion and contempt for the "usurers" and their hangers-on.

"Usury" is the black particular enemy in this war-chant of hate, as it is throughout the *Cantos*. In an essay which sums up Pound's economic theories fairly clearly and altogether sympathetically, Max Wykes-Joyce writes:

> . . . it is a fact that our banking systems are based on usury, no matter by what sweeter name we call it to salve our troubled consciences, or to shrive ourselves of some atavistic condemnation. Hence Pound's first modification of the commonly held view of the function of banks. The levying of interest whether at two per cent. or twenty per cent. is usurious, and usury stands condemned as strongly in this American's view as it did in the teaching of the medieval Fathers.
>
> In all his economic writings, he makes the basic distinction between banks founded for the good of their shareholders and regardless of the wellbeing of any and everyone else, which means almost all banks as we now know them; and banks founded primarily for the good of the whole people. . . .[11]

To illustrate, Wykes-Joyce calls our attention to Canto 71, in which John Adams is quoted in a passage Pound himself marks by a bold vertical line along the margin:

> Every bank of discount is downright corruption
> taxing the public for private individuals' gain.
> and if I say this in my will
> the American people wd/ pronounce I died crazy.

Pound's thinking on economics is thus not without very respectable antecedents. Though strongly influenced by C. H. Douglas, it is like all his thinking even more strongly individual than derivative. In a sense, the viewpoint is an aesthetic one: If economic relationships are bound within limiting, non-organic forms, change the forms. "Make it new!" The conception is primarily of a functional adaptation of currency and credit procedures to the realities of a people's needs and potential productivity in such a way that irresponsible, destructive money-speculation becomes impossible. The program is certainly attractive, but obviously it presents very great difficulties and allows room for as much cynical jargonizing and rhetorical manipulation as the market will bear—and more. Hence its attractiveness to the theorists and apologists of the Fascist state. But though it would take an expert economist *and* student of semantics to pursue this question to its ultimate implications beyond all

11. Max Wykes-Joyce, "Some Considerations Arising from Ezra Pound's Conception of the Bank," in *Ezra Pound*, p. 218.

the crackpotism, double talk, and vaguenesses, clearly it does open up certain real possibilites of social reform and justice and derives from an idealistic and honorable tradition.

It is impossible to say that Pound's record in these matters is without stain. His specific commitments to Mussolini's methods and his anti-Semitism (see Canto 52, for instance), which not even admirers as intelligent and well informed as Wykes-Joyce, Hugh Kenner, and Brian Soper can very convincingly discount or explain away, remain the terrible aberrations of a man of genius. Yet in the face of these imponderables and of his own insufferable dogmatism, we are compelled to recognize, in his poetry at its best, the humane motives and the moral and intellectual power of his essential outlook. It is then, we feel, that he is a child of the Enlightenment after all, of Voltaire and the Encyclopaedists, and that his satires and harangues are quite something else than special pleading for a vicious system of thought and behavior. There is in them the hard ironic honesty and anger against chicanery of Swift's "A Modest Proposal" or, in their less ferocious moments, of Thomas Love Peacock's *Crotchet Castle,* in which we read: "I have always understood . . . that promises to pay ought not to be kept; the essence of a safe and economical currency being an interminable series of broken promises." (See, in this connection, the closing section of Canto 88.)

Moreover, we must remember that Pound's fundamental criticism of modern society has the profound assent, admittedly with every conceivable variation of ideological shading, of almost the whole contemporary artistic community. An instance is the comment of his old friend William Carlos Williams, generally aware as he was of Pound's shortcomings, on a conversation with him during a visit in St. Elizabeth's Hospital (Washington, D.C.). Pound was confined there as a paranoiac after World War II until 1958, and it was only because of this commitment that he was not tried for treason because of his wartime propaganda broadcasts from Italy to American troops. Williams writes:

> Do we have to be idiots dreaming in the semi-obscurities of a twilight mood to be poets? The culmination of our human achievement, all that we desire, can't be achieved by closing our eyes to a veritable wall barring our path. The theme of the poem must at such a point be the removal of the block to everything we might achieve once that barrier is removed. If we are to be taxed out of existence to feed private loans, the revenue from which is used by an international gang to perpetuate armed conflicts, at private profit—to further enrich the same gang—that, the inferno of the *Cantos,* must be one of the poet's nearest concerns.
>
> So we talked, of who is in the know, as against the self-interested mob of "legislators," the pitiful but grossly ignorant big-shots who play in with the criminals—in city, state and nations; of our first duty as artists, the only semi-informed men of the community, whose sweep is the whole field of knowledge. It is our duty at all costs to speak; at all costs, even imprisonment in such isolation, such quarantine, from the spread of information as a St. Elizabeth's affords.[12]

12. *The Autobiography of William Carlos Williams* (New York: Random House, 1951), pp. 337–338.

"Usury," to return now to our consideration of Pound's leading ideas, is in Pound's thought *the* sin around which all others cluster. Sometimes he prefers the Latin form *Usura,* because of its medieval connotations. "With *Usura,*" Canto 45 tells us,

> no picture is made to endure nor to live with
> but it is made to sell and sell quickly
> with usura, sin against nature,
> is thy bread ever more of stale rags
> is thy bread dry as paper,
> with no mountain wheat, no strong flour
> with usura the line grows thick
> with usura is no clear demarcation . . . .

The incantatory, rhetorical, insistent beat of the argument and the parallelisms rises and rises in intensity until, by another path but with equal overbearing concentration of passion, it comes at the very end to a climax like that of Blake's "London." The similarity to Blake is in fact so striking as to throw a blazing light upon Pound's Canto 16 also, as we shall soon see. Blake's catalogue of the evils rotting away the city of London because of the triumph of property exploitation ("chartering") over love and fraternity culminates in one final staggering accusation:

> But most thro' midnight streets I hear
> How the youthful Harlot's curse
> Blasts the new born Infant's tear,
> And blights with plagues the Marriage hearse.

And Pound's Canto 45 concludes:

> Usura slayeth the child in the womb
> It stayeth the young man's courting
> It hath brought palsey to bed, lyeth
> between the young bride and her bridegroom
> CONTRA NATURAM
> They have brought whores for Eleusis
> Corpses are set to banquet
> at behest of usura.

That is to say: The sacred mysteries of love and sex, the cycles of nature, and the rituals of pagan tradition derived from these mysteries and cycles, all inherited in altered form by us together with the most hallowed taboos preserving the untouchableness of human privacy, are now violated in the name of money-power. Such is the final effect of the destruction of meaning and communication. Pound uses all his great skill successfully here in bringing together his feeling for these neglected sources of value and his location of their betrayal in a false principle of social order.

Against the hell of the usurers' dominions the poet repeatedly opposes his vision of the Earthly Paradise. It is a composite vision, drawn from Biblical, Grecian, Provençal, and Dantean imagery and from a wide acquaintance with mythologies and literatures. But its outstanding features are purity and clarity of color and light, together with the classically calm dignity of the figures that move upon its eternally luminous landscape:

Then light air, under saplings,
the blue banded lake under æther,
an oasis, the stones, the calm field. . . .
(Canto 16)

Grove hath its altar
under elms, in that temple, in silence
a lone nymph by the pool.
(Canto 90)

The light now, not of the sun.
Chrysophrase,
And the water green clear, and blue clear. . . .

Zagreus, feeding his panthers,
the turf clear as on hills under light.
And under the almond-trees, gods,
with them, *choros nympharum*. Gods. . . .
(Canto 17)

The dream of repose and quiet projected in this enchanted light no doubt reflects a deeply psychological need on the poet's part. But it is much more than his private "escape" through self-indulgent revery. Pound's visions are conceived as completely serious and relevant to life's most pressing meanings; they even have "scientific" validity in the sense advanced in his Cavalcanti essay, the sense of the "radiant" and significant "world of forms" or of "moving energies" which creates those meanings. The secular and aesthetic religiosity they express is built around the "life-force," to use a term now somewhat hackneyed but still much to the point. At the heart of all the values, therefore, which "Usura" seeks to slay is that same life-force. Its patron-divinity is Zagreus (Dionysus, Bacchus), seen "feeding his panthers" in the passage just quoted from Canto 17. Son of Zeus and Ceres, he is the god of fertility and of allied mysteries, and is celebrated directly or by implication in Yeats's *The Resurrection*, in Lawrence's *The Man Who Died*, and in many other works of this century, becoming a recurrent symbol of the sustained modern attempts to repaganize religious tradition. In his original mythical career, he suffers dismemberment, is made whole and reincarnated and then received with love by the shades in Hades, and is reborn in the spring as Dionysus, favored son of Zeus. Pound's Elysium is Zagreus' also, a haven of pure, unabashed sexuality as in Cantos 39 and 47. Elysium in the *Cantos*, however, is somewhat more cosmopolitan than Homer ever imagined. It has room for gods, heroes, and nymphs from all cultures, for a Renaissance figure like Sigismundo Malatesta whom Pound presents as having fought a losing but unflagging battle against the rise of the modern usury-dominated state, and for thinkers like Confucius and the founding fathers of the American Constitution. (See, for example, the great incantatory paean in Canto 106.)

The poet himself appears in the *Cantos* as a wandering sensibility, seeking like Zagreus to reunite the essential self. Even more, he is an Odysseus of the spirit, here as in *Mauberley* seeking his true home and his true cultural mission and finding his bearings, amid the welter of historical and ethical fragmentation, only by keeping forever in the foreground of his consciousness the difference between life-generating tradition and the death-dealing blight of Usura. Canto 1, as we have noted, is a condensed translation of *The Book of the Dead:* Book XI of the *Odyssey*. Here at the start Pound identifies himself symbolically with Odysseus at the point where the worlds of the living and the dead come together (and by an easy enough association with Zagreus also and with Dante on the verge of his explorations into the horrors of his own day, projected in the *Inferno*).

Throughout the remaining cantos, the poet's moral sense, as acute as and indeed of the same order as his other senses, encompasses the whole of being, both experienced and imagined: life and death, mortals and immortals, heaven and hell and earth, past and present. In Canto 16 we have a concentrated Dantean view of the human condition, between Hell on the one hand and Purgatory and Paradise on the other:

> And before hell mouth; dry plain
>   and two mountains;
> On the one mountain, a running form,
>   and another
> In the turn of the hill; in hard steel
> The road like a slow screw's thread,
> The angle almost imperceptible,
>   so that the circuit seemed hardly to rise.

Four figures of poets are discerned on this symbolic landscape; they are the Provençal troubadours Peire Cardinal and Sordello of Mantua (Dante's admired guide for part of the *Purgatorio*), Dante himself, and Blake. All are in their several ways possessed by the inclusive meaning, awesome in its implications for mankind, of the scene. But it is Blake, the one modern among them and perhaps *the* poet before Pound most deeply engaged by these awesome implications, whose form we first see and who is described in most detail:

> And the running form, naked, Blake,
> Shouting, whirling his arms, the swift limbs,
> Howling against the evil,
>   his eyes rolling,
> Whirling like flaming cart-wheels,
>   and his head held backward to gaze on the evil
> As he ran from it,
>   to be hid by the steel mountain,
> And when he showed again from the north side;
>   his eyes blazing toward hell mouth,
> His neck forward....

Despite this moral purview, Pound does little talking about "humanity" in general. The *Cantos* has been accused of various aesthetic and intellectual derelictions but never of "emotional slither." Its impersonality of method forestalls such criticism. The intricately designed play of its voices and the shifts of space, time, and personae (speaking-characters) make it a dynamic presentation, closer to a motion picture expertly and unsentimentally directed than to a simple cry of the heart. By impersonality we do not mean absence of feeling and viewpoint, but their objective presentation; modern literature has long been concerned to find ways to use the raw materials of experience and imagination without becoming merely confessional, whimsical, or arbitrary. Perhaps the best known statements of this aim are Yeats's poem "Sailing to Byzantium" and Eliot's essay "Hamlet and His Problems," which deals with the expression of emotion in poetry and advances the famous definition of the "objective correlative" as a guide to such expression. But Pound is equally with the other two poets an exponent and exemplar of the deliberate transformation of personal motives into objectified projections that go beyond their psychological origins.

His method is clear enough, and can be understood and enjoyed by the reader long before the literal sense of many passages is grasped. Pound achieves dramatic impersonality as the playwright or the film director does, by letting his characters, his settings, his rhythms do the talking while, strictly speaking, he himself usually "stays out of it." He employs many spokesmen, as we have already suggested—Odysseus, Malatesta, Kung, Adams, and the others—to set up a composite, actively moving consciousness that emerges in varied forms and circumstances. Also, he sets *styles* against one another, each evocative of a whole complex of meanings: lyrical passages against satirical ones, rhetoric against anecdeote, coarseness against elegance. Now he speaks in the idiom of Divus' fifteenth-century Latin translation from Homer, now in that of Ovid or Cavalcanti, and now in the drawl of a shrewd Yankee engineer or the bawdy brogue of an old Irish sailor. Again, the poem may shift into boisterous parody of Browning ("Oh to be in England now that Winston's out") or veer sharply into an echo of the speech in Eleanor of Aquitaine's court. The poem is *kept moving* by an alert, witty mind stocked with allusions and cross references, a mind so interesting that it holds attention even at its least appealing. As Yeats writes of the characters of Shakespearean tragedy, Pound never "breaks up his lines to weep." There are horror and terror, yes but *sentimentality* is held to be a fraudulence of communication, the stylistic counterpart of usury. A striking instance of this viewpoint is Artemis' song against "pity" in Canto 30. Pity is a latter-day softmindedness, she cries, which "spareth so many an evil thing" that "all things are made foul in this season" of a liberal humanitarianism incapable of clear-cut moral distinctions or of root-solutions to the problems of suffering and evil:

> This is the reason, none may seek purity
> Having for foulnesse pity
> And things growne awry;
> No more do my shaftes fly
> To slay. Nothing is now clean slayne
> But rotteth away. . . .

Artemis' "compleynt" epitomizes one of Pound's major themes, but the poet does not state that theme directly. It is enough that the goddess is an embodiment of the ancient Grecian values, and the form of her song an embodiment of the medieval values, which we know he cherishes. She does his work for him, far more reverberatingly than his own haranguing could do it, and typifies the success of his presentational, or objective method.

3
The Mauberley *Sequence*

WE have labeled the *Mauberley* poems and the *Cantos* "sequences," and it may help the general reader to be reminded of the implications of this label. Long poem-sequences are as familiar as, and much older than, the Elizabethan sonnet cycles, or as that cumbersomely unfolded series of allegorical narratives *The Faerie Queene*. In more recent times, to skip over innumerable other instances, we have Whitman's sequences, most notably his *Song of Myself;* and we must bear in mind Whitman's conception of the *whole* of his poetry as organically unified, the Self writ large: "Who touches these poems touches a man." A number of modern poets have turned to the sequence as a rough equivalent for the most ambitious traditional forms, and for the epic particularly. It may well have been Whitman who called this turn most decisively. At any rate, one has only to look at the song cycles of Yeats and the sequences of Eliot, Hart Crane, and a large number of other writers besides Pound to confirm this development.

The sequence is not a fixed form, and through this fact alone becomes very different from the classical elegy, ode, or epic. But we can say of it that in the work of the moderns from Whitman on it consists of a larger structure made up of more or less self-sufficient units, each contributing both conceptually and stylistically to the organic life of the whole. Some units, poems like the "Envoi" of *Mauberley* and Canto 13, are able to stand alone. Others are relatively more dependent on the rest, though they may be essential to the sequence. While the order of parts is as *necessary* as the poet can make it, the principle of the design may not make itself felt at first; on the other hand, though in theory *any* work of art will rearrange itself, so to speak, around whatever in it initially seizes upon our attention, the sequence (like the mural painting) seems to give us more freedom than other poetic forms to start from any point within it that we find convenient. With Pound especially the reader ought to take advantage of this characteristic. For instance, most of us would find the first part of *Mauberley* more quickly available than the second to our understanding, and within it we would find the second, fourth, and fifth poems, and probably the "Envoi," less demanding than the rest. Similarly 13 and 45 are certainly among the most readily intelligible of the *Cantos*. These six poems, therefore, are poems we can fruitfully read first in their respective sequences, together with whatever passages elsewhere along the line take our fancies.

Looking at the first section of *Mauberley* from this standpoint, we shall quickly light upon some salient characteristics. Poem II begins with a little battery of nervous rhymes contrasting the machine age's "aesthetic" with that of classicism:

> The age demanded an image
> Of its accelerated grimace,
> Something for the modern stage,
> Not, at any rate, an Attic grace....

The nervous effect is created partly by the staccato machine-rhythm of line 2, partly by the rhyming of stressed and unstressed syllables in lines 1 and 3. The distorted picture called up by "accelerated grimace" shows the speaker's contempt for what the "age demanded." Pound underlines his contempt in the next two stanzas, coining a slogan for the age:

> Better mendacities
> Than the classics in paraphrase!

Our epoch, he says, "assuredly" prefers plaster to alabaster, a mass-produced art to "the 'sculpture' of rhyme."

Poem II is therefore an assault on the age. Moving on to Poem IV we find an even more typical piece of Poundian rhetorical verse. This poem must be read aloud if the full value of its cumulative compassion and anger is to be felt, but as a poem of profound disillusionment, one of the early literary reactions against the War and a forerunner of the many postwar novels expressing the same responses, what it has to say is perfectly clear. The young, whatever their motives for going to war, are the victims of "wastage as never before." Those who survive must return

> home to old lies and new infamy;
> usury age-old and age-thick
> and liars in public places....

Though the mood here is a continuation of that in Poem II, bitterness and irony are progressively deepened right up to the final, climactic line: "laughter out of dead bellies." The next poem, the fifth, then makes another turn on the same subject: the War. The contrast between the young in all their quickness and fresh zest (described in two lines that have the restrained pathos of a Greek epitaph) and the civilization for which they have died is restated with superb poetic economy. Much of the work of contrast is done through an alliterative device, the linking of words beginning in *b*. First there is the word "best," to suggest the youthful dead themselves, and then in angry machine-gun bursts the words for a rotten society—"an old *b*itch gone in the teeth," "a *b*otched civilization"—and for its neglected heritage recalled only as a cynical pretext for inspiring the young in war: "two gross of *b*roken statues" and "a few thousand *b*attered *b*ooks."

"Envoi," which brings the 1919 section of *Mauberley* to a close, is not an assault on the times but an affirmation of artistic principle. Modeled on Edmund Waller's seventeenth-century poem "Go lovely rose," which was set to music by his contemporary Henry Lawes, it expresses the poet's desire to catch in an eternal moment one essence of both life and art in the image of a loved woman who sings out "that song of Lawes." There is an echo of Shakespeare when the speaker says he would bid "her graces" live

As roses might, in magic amber laid,
Red overwrought with orange and all made
One substance and one colour
Braving time.

And there is a carry-over from the aestheticism of the nineties in the thought with which the poem concludes, that immortality is to be gained only through artistic means which

Might, in new ages, gain her worshippers,
When our two dusts with Waller's shall be laid,
Siftings on siftings in oblivion,
Till change hath broken down
All things save Beauty alone.

These four less difficult poems in the sequence throw enough light on the others to lead us directly to the perspective of the whole: We have moved into an age in which cheap standards of workmanship, anti-aestheticism, and the betrayal of beauty and tradition are the order of the day; but the poet does not accept this order. Rather, he lashes out against it, seeing in the destructiveness of the War its true, annihilating meaning. Through the perfection of his own craftsmanship in these poems, as well as through what he says, he affirms the superiority of his own vision.

Here, then, is the essence of the first section of *Mauberley*. But the sequence consists not merely of a few poems whose attitudes support and complement one another. It also takes the form of a kind of literary (but not literal) autobiography, in which the poet sizes up the state of the world of letters and his own place in it after three years of attempting to make himself and his viewpoint felt. In another sense, it takes the form of a voyage of literary exploration in contemporary England, with attention also to the condition of society at large and to the past circumstances out of which the present situation, at the end of the Great War, has developed. "The sequence," writes Pound, is "distinctly a farewell to London." It is also a crucial statement of the relation between poetry and Anglo-American culture as he sees it, and in the final balance it would seem to be a farewell to the illusion that there is any hope for poetry in that culture.

Going back to the beginning, we can see that although the protagonist of the sequence is the fictitious "Hugh Selwyn Mauberley" the first poem is titled "E. P. Ode pour l'Election de Son Sepulchre." Translated, this is "Ezra Pound, Ode on the Occasion of Choosing His Burial Place." (The self-ironic title is borrowed from a poem by Ronsard.) So Mauberley is Pound's conception of himself at one remove and in whatever dimensions these poems provide. Now who is Mauberley-Pound in this first poem? He is a man, the first two stanzas tell us, who has fought in vain against the drift of the times to "resuscitate the dead art/Of poetry." But England has regarded him as hopelessly "out of key" with the age, especially as he has come from the United States, "a half savage country." Like Capaneus, who defied Zeus and was destroyed by lightning, he is a would-be hero victimized by his own hubris. The reference (to a figure in Aeschylus' play *The Seven Against Thebes*) leads to another classical allusion, this time to Book XII of the *Odyssey*, where the Sirens are shown singing their seductively compassionate song to Odysseus. The comparison between E. P. and Odysseus is developed over two stanzas, establishing an identification like that of the *Cantos*. He has lingered in the dangerous, choppy seas of the "rocks" of English culture; presumably he had cherished hopes that the superficial classical sophistication of the British literary and academic world was the real thing, and that he would find his true home, his Ithaca and Penelope, there. But his "true Penelope" was not the pretentious show-classicism of England but the dedicated, stylistically precise, unsqueamishly truthful art of Flaubert—the true classicism of the modern world. This point established, the last stanza returns to the mock-humble tone of the first with an echo from Villon's Grand Testament in which the poet talks of his own "passing away" in "the thirtieth year of his age" and with a final pompous comment on that event, in the voice of the chairman of some imaginary committee of literary stuffed shirts:

> . . . the case presents
> No adjunct to the Muses' diadem.

On the surface, this supremely ironic opening poem concedes defeat; actually, in various subtle ways, it asserts the continuing value of the poet's frustrated mission. Almost every line, by virtue of its very phrasing, proclaims the glory of "the tradition"; and the Homeric quotation near its center becomes, not only through what it says literally—"for we know all the things that are in Troy"—but also because of its cultural connotation *as* a Homeric quotation, a symbol in its own right. Even untranslated, it would serve as a symbol of the mystery behind the tradition, undefined though apparently related to the associations connected with Capaneus and Odysseus. Hence it should not surprise us that in the next four poems the speaker breaks loose from the pretense that he has been wrong to make his great effort. Rather, he has been entranced by the Siren-song, and after locating himself more accurately he can shift into the specifics of his complaint against the world his art has been unable to affect. Poem II is transitional, but Poem III is a *complete* list of grievances, against the decadence of fashionable women's clothing and popular musical taste as well as against the loss of mystery in modern religion and the supposed emptiness of modern democracy. Lines 15–16 tell us once more that nowadays we see The Beautiful "decreed in the market place," and the poem ends with a mock-despairing cry to Apollo which includes a quotation from Pindar translated for us in the next line. (The "tin" of the last line is a flip pun on the interrogative repeated three times in the Greek quotation.)

The reader will notice somewhere along the line that most of the *Mauberley* poems are written in approximately the same kind of stanza, a quatrain with alternating rhymes, sometimes in the second and fourth lines only. There are inconsistencies of line-length and rhyme-arrangement, but the basic pattern holds even in Poem IV; "Envoi," it is true, departs more than the others from it, but "Go lovely rose," on the form of which "Envoi" is a free variation, comes very close to it. The "inconsistencies," of course, are deliberate modulations to serve particular purposes, as when in Poem IV the shortened lines and piled-up, almost doggerel rhymes help to build up a quick emotional charge and an incantatory rhythm, whereupon rhyme is dropped except for repetitions and the stanzas are broken up into rhetorical units. In "E. P. Ode," on the other hand, the lines are of uniform length and the rhymes, though occasionally polylingual, are all exact. The tone of elegant, subtle, literate intellectual control here demands such exactness. "Envoi," in which the poet bursts into a song whose mood counteracts the cutting, critical drive of the sequence as a whole, is quite properly furthest from the norm set up by the opening "Ode."

After the elegiac and savage climax of the fifth poem, the sequence shifts to some close-ups of the nineties and before. Here we see the beginnings of the modern predicament of the poet—the stuffiness of the late nineteenth century, the attack on the "fleshly school of poetry" by Robert Buchanan in 1871, the "stillbirth" twelve years before that of the English *Rubaiyat*, the abuse of Rossetti and Swinburne, and the relegation of the Muse to prostitute-status. The "Yeux Glauques" of the sixth poem refers to the "thin, clear gaze" of the Muse, here identified with the model for the Burne-Jones paintings alluded to in the third stanza, and also, by a shift of association, with the girl so compassionately presented in Rossetti's poem "Jenny." (Mrs. Rossetti was Burne-Jones's model.) In this period the dedicated artist not only saw his work disregarded, we are told; he also saw himself condemned as immoral. And so in the seventh poem, whose title alludes to the pathetic outcry in the *Purgatorio* of La Pia, we see, through the eyes of M. Verog (actually Victor Plarr, Dowson's biographer), how Dowson and Johnson met the hostile indifference to poetry in the nineties. In these poems Pound employs a number of allusions at first bewilderingly unfamiliar in order to recall the exact atmosphere of the times. But what stands out is the imagery connoting the defeat of art in England:

> Fœtid Buchanan lifted up his voice
> When that faun's head of hers
> Became a pastime for
> Painters and adulterers.

Even the incidental background descriptions carry this connotation of defeat:

> Among the pickled fœtuses and bottled bones . . . .

And here too we have echoes of the poet's ironic "confession" of error in Poem I:

> M. Verog, out of step with the decade,
> Detached from his contemporaries,
> Neglected by the young,
> Because of these reveries.

The portrait of "Brennbaum," a modern assimilated Jew who has all but forgotten his Hebraic heritage in his stiff, uncommunicatively British gentility, gives us yet another view of a society every phase of which reflects loss of meaning. Like Mr. Nixon, the literary businessman, and like the "conservatrix of Milésien" (in Poem XI) who lacks taste and the appreciation of tradition despite her pretensions, he symbolizes a condition which has made retreat or escape virtually a physical necessity for "the stylist" of Poem X. Nor can a poet find literary patronage of the sort which came to an end in Dr. Johnson's day. As Poem XII shows, "The Lady Valentine" may use him to enhance her own social prestige, or to stimulate some incidental sexual excitement in her life, or, "in the case of revolution," as "a possible friend and comforter." But her "well-gowned approbation" will bring him no more real support than the world of professional letters will bring him now that, in Fleet Street,

> The sale of half-hose has
> Long since superseded the cultivation
> Of Pierian roses.

In the second portion of the *Mauberley* sequence (1920), all the themes we have noted are recapitulated, but with a difference. Whereas the speaker in the 1919 group had concentrated attention on specific points of attack in the "outside world" of society and of the cultural situation, bluntly challenging it with his own aesthetic values, his attention is now directed almost wholly inward. *Mauberley* (1919) is externalized, objective; *Mauberley* (1920) gives us the subjective dimension. Here the speaker is sure of his sensitivity but not of his strength as an artist; he discounts himself and withdraws, communicating his uncertainties and fear of failure. The epigraph, modified from Ovid's Latin, gives us an image of pure frustration: "mouths snapping at empty air." Poem I in this section, though it parallels its counterpart in the first movement, is developed in a series of elliptical sentences except for stanza two, in which the antecedent poem is quoted directly:

> "His true Penelope
> Was Flaubert,"
> And his tool
> The engraver's.

Whereas the first part of the sequence had spoken out for a virile, classically precise art in the great tradition, here the poet describes himself as having turned from delicate etching in the nineteenth century manner of Jaquemart to the skill of Roman and Renaissance medalists. That is, though he has turned from more effeminately ornamental minor artistry to a method informed by classical criteria, he is still working in a minor mode. He may approach the successes of a Pisanello, but he feels, or fears, he cannot approach the robust success of the great Greek masterpieces, cannot "forge Achaia" in the image of his Homeric visions. These thoughts come through as half-statements, expressing syntactically a dread of ultimate failure not unlike that of Browning's Andrea del Sarto or Eliot's Prufrock.

The speaker's fears are carried over subtly and somewhat ambiguously into

Poem II. However, the French epigraph, actually Pound's own composition, extends the theme by introducing a new consideration: the relation between aesthetic sensitivity and the ability to know love in terms suggesting both delicate idealism and sensuality. The poem itself, introspective and elusive, employs a partly stream-of-consciousness method to describe and account for the failure of Mauberley's mission during the three lost years. He has been moving among phantasmagoria, among fantastic, illusory images of the night ("NUKTIS 'AGALMA"), finding his bearings and closing in on the "orchid" of his vision of ideal beauty. But given his limited kind of talent, a talent for making, in poetry, "curious heads in medallion," it is to be doubted whether he can in any case realize his ideal. And between the phantasmagoria on the one hand and this newly recognized predicament on the other, he has somehow let go by the opportunity for love in its most full-blown sense.

> He had passed, inconscient, full gaze,
> The wide-banded irides
> And botticellian sprays implied
> In their diastasis. . . .

Both a failure of sexual awareness (and perhaps performance) and a failure to see deeply enough into the orchid's "botticellian" meaning (the reference is to the famous painting of the birth of Venus) to give it richly sensuous embodiment seem to be implied in this phrasing. The psychological components of his failure to impress the public and of his dismissal by his "self-styled 'his betters'" are a stale sensation of having missed out on the main chance and a distrust of his own powers. In this poem Pound adds greatly to the authority of his sequence, by giving Mauberley introspective depth and body. It will be clear that the shadings and qualifications that so profoundly modify our understanding of the speaker's whole nature here could not have been given before we had come to grips with the "outer" Mauberley-Pound of the first part. We have seen him dressed for the forum; now we see him naked and alone. "Envoi," which presents the ideal he would live by, bridges the gap between the two Mauberleys revealed with such moving and startling faithfulness. But after the confession of Poem II and the revisions of the Odysseus-image that follow in the next two parts ("'The Age Demanded'" and Poem IV), "Meadllion"—the closing poem—throws a new light on the speaker's relation to the tradition as it was bravely proclaimed in "Envoi."

But we are moving too quickly perhaps. To go back now and follow through in order, "'The Age Demanded'" takes its title, as the author's note reminds us, from the opening line in Poem II of *Mauberley* 1919. However, it focuses less on "the age" than on what the earlier piece, in its half-mimicry of Philistine criticism, calls "the obscure reveries of the inward gaze." Retreat to the world of these reveries is the poet's response to the age's demand for cheap, time-serving workmanship. As unfit for such drudgery as the doves that draw Aphrodite's chariot would be for a "chain bit," he has put on an "armour/Against utter consternation": the armour of imperviousness, impassive regression, and isolation. What Mauberley says of himself is of course true generally for the drift of modern poetry. Things, though, are not what they seem, for we know that the motives and meaning in which he deals, and in which the poets (like

Pound) for whom he speaks deal, are anything but irrelevant. His fears are real but not finally decisive in his self-evaluation, a fact we need to remember as we see this psychological poetic *novella* in action and watch Mauberley's heroically active image of himself dwindle into that of the merest passive resistance and private self-delighting with "imaginary/Audition of the phantasmal sea-surge." Poem IV carries the dwindling of the image to its logical conclusion short of zero:

> "I was
> And I no more exist;
> Here drifted
> An hedonist."

Finally, "Medallion" portrays the singing lady of "Envoi" in a similarly shrunken imagery. The lovely singer at the piano is still conceived in terms of the service of Aphrodite. But the goddess herself (as Poem II showed) is not revealed in the full "diastasis" of Botticelli's conception; instead, she is seen through the medium of a lesser art, a Luini painting or the illustration in an archaeological study:

> As Anadyomene in the opening
> Pages of Reinach.

The Muse of "Yeux Glauques," though degraded and bewildered, had been more immediately womanly. Now, protected by glaze or a "suave bounding-line," she has a frozen quality, is all unrealized potentiality in "metal, or intractable amber."

But the potentiality remains; the strong and the weak Mauberley are after all one and the same: a single *persona* seen in opposing yet interactive lights.[13] Just as the *method* of the Initial "Ode" counteracts its surface confession of failure, so also does the extraordinary felicity of color, sound, and nuance in the 1920 movement correct, if it does not belie them entirely, the speaker's self-abnegations. Mauberley's confessions are really a charge of cultural failure from the standpoint of the culture's own most cultivated sensibilities, and his psychological crisis becomes an expression of despair for the future of social imagination and integrity. It is not, finally, himself and his art that he denies but the promise of his civilization. *Mauberley* (1920) is thus the purest example we have of Pound's irony.

13. Espey differs considerably from us on this point, although we would certainly both agree that, as he says, "in the person of Mauberley Pound was rejecting—though . . . this is altogether outside the limits of the poem . . .—a mask of what he feared to become as an artist by remaining in England." (p. 83) The greatest irony of *Mauberley* is the strength it gains from confessing vulnerability. The bawdy suggestiveness of Mauberley-Pound's language, to which Espey calls our attention repeatedly, is one more instance of his audacity and defiance in the midst of *apparent* confused retreat.

4
The Cantos

SPACE forbids our going into the *Cantos* in even as much detail as we have into *Mauberley*. We have already, however, noted some of the leading ideas behind this more involved and ambitious work, and though we cannot here trace their handling throughout its winding, Gargantuan progress, a few suggestions concerning its character as a poetic sequence may be useful. First of all, we may take as our point of departure the fact that in motivation and outlook the *Cantos* are a vast proliferation from the same conceptions which underlie *Mauberley*. The difference lies partly in the multiplicity of "voices" and "cross-sections," partly in the vastly greater inclusiveness of historical and cultural scope, and partly in the unique formal quality of the longer sequence; it is by the very nature of its growth over the years a work-in-progress. Even when the author at last brings it to conclusion, reorganizing it, supplying the withheld Cantos 72 and 73, completing his revisions, and even giving his book a definitive title, it will remain such a work. Each group of cantos will be what it is now—a new *phase* of the poem, like each of the annual rings of a living tree. The poet has put his whole creative effort into a mobilization of all levels of his consciousness into the service of the *Cantos;* there has been a driving central continuity, and around it new clusters of knowledge and association linked with the others by interweavings, repetitions, and over-all perspective. Pound has staked most of his adult career as a poet on this most daring of poetic enterprises; literary history gives us few other examples of comparable commitment.

The *Cantos* has been called Pound's "intellectual diary since 1915," and so it is. But the materials of this diary have been so arranged as to subserve the aims of the poem itself. Passage by passage there *is* the fascination of listening in on a learned, passionate, now rowdy, now delicate intelligence, an intelligence peopled by the figures of living tradition but not so possessed by them that it cannot order their appearances and relationships. Beyond the fascination of the surface snatches of song, dialogue, and description, always stimulating and rhythmically suggestive though not always intelligible upon first reading, there is the essential overriding drive of the poem, and the large pattern of its overlapping layers of thought. The way in which the elements of this pattern swim into the reader's line of vision is well suggested by Hugh Kenner, one of Pound's most able and enthusiastic interpreters:

> The word 'periplum,' which recurs continually throughout the *Pisan Cantos* [74–84], is glossed in Canto LIX:
>
> periplum, not as land looks on a map
> but as sea bord seen by men sailing.
>
> Victor Brerard discovered that the geography of the *Odyssey*, grotesque when referred to a map, was minutely accurate according to the Phoeni-

> cian voyagers' *periploi*. The image of successive discoveries breaking upon the consciousness of the voyager is one of Pound's central themes. . . . The voyage of Odysseus to hell is the matter of Canto I. The first half of Canto XL is a periplum through the financial press; 'out of which things seeking an exit,' we take up in the second half of the Canto the narrative of the Carthagenian Hanno's voyage of discovery. Atlantic flights in the same way raise the world of epileptic maggots in Canto XXVIII into a sphere of swift firm-hearted discovery. . . . The periplum, the voyage of discovery among facts, . . . is everywhere contrasted with the conventions and artificialities of the bird's eye view afforded by the map. . . .[14]

Thus, the successive cantos and layers of cantos must be viewed not so much schematically as experientially. Here we see how the early Pound's developing idealization of the concrete image, the precise phrase, the organically accurate rhythm are now brought to bear on this vast later task. The many voices, varied scenes and *personae*, and echoes of other languages and literatures than English reflect this emphasis on experience itself: something mysterious, untranslatable, the embodied meaning of life which we generalize only at peril of losing touch with it. So also with Pound's emphatic use of Chinese ideograms, whose picture-origins still are visible enough, he believes, so that to "read" them is to think in images rather than in abstractions. His use of them is accounted for by the same desire to present "successive discoveries breaking upon the consciousness of the voyager." The first effect of all these successive, varied breakings is not intended to be total intellectual understanding, any more than in real experience we "understand" situations upon first coming into them. But by and by the pattern shapes up and the relationships clarify themselves, though always there remains an unresolved residue of potentiality for change, intractable and baffling.

Pound's "voyager," upon whose consciousness the discoveries break, is, we have several times observed, a composite figure derived first of all from the poet-speaker's identification with Odysseus. A hero of myth and epic, he is yet very much of this world. He is both the result of creative imagination and its embodiment. He explores the worlds of the living, of the dead, and of the mythic beings of Hades and Paradise. Lover of mortal women as of female deities, he is like Zagreus a symbol of the life-bringing male force whose mission does not end even with his return to his homeland. Gradually he becomes all poets and all heroes who have somehow vigorously impregnated the culture. He undergoes (as do the female partners of his procreation and the *personae* and locales in time and space of the whole sequence) many metamorphoses. Hence the importance of the Ovidian metamorphosis involving the god Dionysus, the sea (the female element and symbol of change), and the intermingling of contemporary colloquial idiom and the high style of ancient poetry in Canto 2. The first canto had ended with a burst of praise

14. Hugh Kenner, *The Poetry of Ezra Pound* (Norfolk, Conn.: New Directions, 1951), pp. 102–103. Kenner's use of Roman numerals follows Pound, but the latest groups of cantos *(Rock-Drill* and *Thrones)*, published after Kenner's book, change to Arabic numerals. For consistency's sake we have followed the latter usage throughout.

for Aphrodite, goddess of love and beauty, and in language suggesting the multiple allusiveness of the sequence: to the Latin and Renaissance traditions, as well as the Grecian-Homeric, and to the cross-cultural implications suggested by the phrase "golden bough." The second canto takes us swiftly backward in the poetic tradition, through Browning, then Sordello and the other troubadours, and then to the classical poets and the Chinese tradition. All poets are one, as Helen and Eleanor of Aquitaine and Tyro (beloved of Poseidon) and all femininity are one and all heroes are one.

In the first two cantos, then, the "periplum" of the sequence emerges into view. Three main value-referents are established: a sexually and aesthetically creative world-view, in which artistic and mythical tradition provides the main axes; the worship of Bacchus-Dionysus-Zagreus as the best symbol of creativity in action; and the multiple hero—poet, voyager, prophet, observer, thinker. The next four cantos expand the range of allusiveness, introducing for instance the figure of the Cid, a chivalric hero, to add his dimension to the voyager-protagonist's consciousness. Also, various tragic tales are brought to mind, extending the initial horror of Odysseus' vision of the dead and thus contributing to the larger scheme of the poet in the modern wasteland. In absolute contrast, pagan beatitudes are clearly projected in Canto 2 in the pictures of Poseidon and Tyro:

> Twisted arms of the sea-god,
> Lithe sinews of water, gripping her, cross-hold,
> And the blue-gray glass of the wave tents them . . . .

and, at the scene's close, in the phallic "tower like a one-eyed great goose" craning up above the olive grove while the fauns are heard "chiding Proteus" and the frogs "singing against the fauns." This pagan ideal comes in again and again, sharp and stabbing against bleak backgrounds like the "petals on the wet, black bough" of the "Metro" poem. Thus, in Canto 3:

> Gods float in the azure air,
> Bright gods and Tuscan, back before dew was shed.

In Canto 4:

> Choros nympharum, goat-foot, with the pale foot alternate;
> Crescent of blue-shot waters, green-gold in the shallows,
> A black cock crows in the sea-foam . . . .

In 4 and 5 both there are deliberate echoes of such poets as have a kindred vision (Catallus, Sappho, and others), set against the notes of evil and damnation. The lines from Sordello in 6 serve the same purpose:

> "Winter and Summer I sing of her grace,
> As the rose is fair, so fair is her face,
> Both Summer and Winter I sing of her,
> The snow makyth me to remember her."

The Lady of the troubadours, whose "grace" is a secularized transposition from that of Deity, is another manifestation of "the body of nymphs, of nymphs, and Diana" which Actaeon saw, as well as of what Catullus meant: "'Nuces!' praise, and Hymenaeus 'brings the girl to her man. . . .'"

After these archetypal and literary points of reference have been established, Cantos 8–19 move swiftly into a close-up of the origins of the modern world in the Renaissance, and of the victory of the anticreative over the active, humanistic values represented by Sigismundo Malatesta and a few others. (Canto 7 is transitional; in any case we can note only the larger groupings here.) The relation between the "Renaissance Cantos" (8–11) and the "Hell Cantos" (14–16), with their scatological picturings of the contemporary Inferno, is organic: the beginning and the end of the same process of social corruption. The beautiful dialogue on order in 13 provides a calm, contrasting center for this portion of the sequence, and is supported by the paradisic glow and serenity of Elysium, revealed in 16 and 17. The earlier cantos had given momentary attention to Oriental poetry and myth and, as we have seen, Elysian glimpses also. Now these motifs are expanded and related to a new context, bringing the sequence into revised focus but carrying all its earlier associations along. This leaping, reshuffling, and reordering is the organizational principle behind the growth, the "annual rings," of the *Cantos*.

The next ten cantos interweave the motifs of these first two groups and prepare us for the next leap (in Cantos 30–41) of perspective. There are various preparations for this leap, even as early as Canto 20, in which there is a moment of comment from the "outside" as if to take stock before hurtling onward. From their remote "shelf," "aerial, cut in the aether," the disdainful lotus-eaters question all purposeful effort:

> "What gain with Odysseus,
> "They that died in the whirlpool
> "And after many vain labours,
> "Living by stolen meat, chained to the rowingbench,
> "That he should have a great fame
> "And lie by night with the goddess? . . ."

Is the question wisdom or cynicism? No matter. The poem, given the human condition and the epic tasks that grow out of it, is held in check but an instant before again plunging ahead. The *Cantos* accepts the moral meaning and the moral responsibility of human consciousness. The heroic ideal remains, as on the other hand the evil of our days remains even after the goddess's song against pity is heard at the beginning of 30.

The new group (30–41) is, like the later Adams cantos (62–71), in the main a vigorous attempt to present the fundamental social and economic principles of the Founding Fathers as identical with Pound's own. Adams and Jefferson are his particular heroes, and there is an effort to show that Mussolini's program is intended to carry these basic principles, imbedded in the Constitution but perverted by banking interests, into action. Pound works letters and other documents, as well as conversations real and imagined, into his blocks of verse, usually fragmentarily, and gives modern close-ups of business manipulations. The method has the effect of a powerful exposé, particularly of the glimpsed operations of munitions-profiteers. The cantos of the early 1930s have, indeed, a direct connection with the interest in social and historical documentation and rhetoric that marks much other work of the same period, and at the end of Canto 41 (in which Mussolini is seen) we should not be surprised to find an oratorical climax similar in effect to that of Poem IV in *Mauberley* (1919). As in the earlier groups, however, we are again given contrasting centers of value, especially in Canto 36 (which renders Cavalcanti's *A lady asks me*) and in Canto 39, whose sexually charged interpretation of the spell cast over Odysseus and his men on Circe's isle is one of Pound's purest successes.

The Chinese cantos (53–61) and the Pisan group (74–84) are the two most important remaining unified clusters within the larger scheme. Again, the practical idealism of Confucianism, like that of Jefferson and Adams, becomes an analogue for Pound's own ideas of order and of secular aestheticism. Canto 13 was a clear precursor, setting the poetic stage for this later extension. "Order" and "brotherly deference" are key words in Confucius' teachings; both princes and ordinary men must have order *within* them, each in his own way, if dominion and family alike are to thrive. These thoughts are not clichés as Pound presents them. We hear a colloquy that has passion, humor, and depth, and what our society would certainly consider unorthodoxy. Kung "said nothing of the 'life after death,'" he considered loyalty to family and friends a prior claim to that of the law, he showed no respect for the aged when they were ignorant through their own fault, and he advocated a return to the times "when the historians left blanks in their writings, /I mean for things they didn't know." The Chinese cantos view Chinese history in the light of these principles of ordered intelligence in action, with the ideogram *ching ming* (name things accurately) at the heart of the identity between Confucian and Poundian attitudes. "The great virtue of the Chinese language," writes Hugh Gordon Porteus, "inheres in its written characters, which so often contrive to suggest by their graphic gestures (as English does by its phonetic gestures) the very essence of what is to be conveyed."[15] The development of Pound's interest in Chinese poetry and thought, as well as his varied translations from the Chinese, is in itself an important subject. This interest, like every other to which he has seriously turned his attention, he has brought directly to bear on his own poetic practice and on his highly activistic thinking in general.

With the *Pisan Cantos* and *Rock-Drill*[16] we are brought, first, into the immediately contemporary world of the poet himself, in Fascist Italy toward the close of World War II, in a concentration camp at Pisa, during the last days of Mussolini; and second, into a great, summarizing recapitulation of root-attitudes developed in all the preceding cantos: in particular the view of the banking system as a scavenger and breeder of corruption, and of ancient Chinese history as an illuminating, often wholesomely contrasting analogue to that of the post-medieval West. Even more than before, we see now how

15. "Ezra Pound and the Chinese Character: A Radical Examination," in *Ezra Pound*, p. 215.

16. *Section: Rock-Drill: 85–95 de los cantares* (New York: New Directions, 1956). This was the first group of cantos to be published separately since the *Cantos* appeared in 1948.

the *Cantos* descend, with some bastardies along the line, from the Enlightenment. They conceive of a world creatively ordered to serve human needs, a largely rationalist conception. Hence the stress on the sanity of Chinese thought, the immediacy of the Chinese ideogram, and the hardheaded realism of a certain strain of economic theory. The *Pisan Cantos* show Pound's vivid responsiveness as he approached and passed his sixtieth birthday: his aliveness to people, his Rabelaisian humor, his compassion. The Lotus-Eaters of Canto 20, aloof and disdainful, have missed out on the main chances. Canto 81 contains the famous "Pull down thy vanity" passage in which the poet, though rebuking his own egotism, yet staunchly insists on the meaningfulness of his accomplishment and ideals. As the sequence approaches conclusion, the fragments are shored together for the moral summing-up. In the *Rock-Drill* section, Cantos 85–95, the stocktaking continues and we are promised, particularly in Canto 90, an even fuller revelation than has yet been vouchsafed us of the Earthly Paradise.

Cantos 96–109[17] begin to carry out this promise, though after so many complexities, overlappings, and interlocking voices it must be nearly impossible to bring the work to an end. It is essentially a self-renewing process rather than a classical structure, and there is no limit to the aspects of history and thought the poet has wished to bring to bear on the poem. Canto 96, for instance, touches on certain developments after the fall of Rome, especially two decrees in the Eastern Empire by Justinian and Leo VI concerning standards of trade, workmanship, and coinage. The special emphasis in this canto on Byzantine civilization is particularly appropriate because of Byzantium's historical and geographical uniting of East and West as well as its mystical associations pointing to a new and dramatic paradisic vision. Although the memory of earlier glimpses of "paradise" and the recapitulative, self-interrupting method militate against an effect of a revelation overwhelmingly new, the pacing of the whole sequence has made this difficulty at the end inevitable. Pound's conclusion must be introduced as emergent from the midst of things, still struggling from all in life and consciousness that makes for disorder.

A Primer of Ezra Pound (New York: Macmillan, 1960)

17. *Thrones: 96–109 de los cantares* (New York: New Directions, 1959).

PART II

1961–1972

❧

Kenneth Fearing (1902–1961)

AT about the time Hemingway committed suicide, the New York poet Kenneth Fearing lay dying of cancer. Fearing was nearly as old as Hemingway, had been born in the same suburb of Chicago, and in his own way was just as fine a writer. But he was the least self-publicizing of authors, and had the poverty to prove it. He kept his lanky body and ironic soul together through sheer stubborn refusal to starve: America's one adult poet-in-a garret.

Fearing's reputation suffered greatly because he had been a leading Left poet of the thirties. Unlike their English counterparts, the poets of his group never quite recovered from the anti-Communist intellectual reaction that followed the Spanish Civil War and the Nazi-Soviet pact. Certain writers have been "forgotten," or half-forgotten, in the Freudian sense. Others appear to have forgotten themselves—for instance, the writer of some interest before the last war who was reborn, after it, as the author of a "first" novel. The will to suppress the memory of a phase of American sensibility that affected many gifted people is a powerful psychic force. Fearing, no more doctrinaire than, say, Auden or Spender, was one of its victims. He did not go unpublished; he was merely neglected.

The pity was the greater because he was one of our purest stylists in an age of brilliant American poetry. His ear for the vernacular of our big cities was dead right. All Americans, as Saroyan has noted, are "in the big movie"—and, we may add, in the big vaudeville show and comic strip as well. Fearing loved all this. He put his wonderful ear for it to the service of his elegiac, nostalgic turn of spirit and made a uniquely touching poetry. His is the wise-cracking, brooding world of the everyday metropolis: "SAY THE LAST WORD, YOU LONG STRAIGHT STREETS. . ." It is the world of the terrible emptiness too, where if you're not quite strong enough nothing means anything: "Where the wind blows and the motors go by and it is always night, or day."

The main stream of American poetry today belongs to writers like Eliot, Crane, and Lowell who have drawn on extraordinary resources of energy. The world of each of these men exists unto itself. Enter at your peril; you may never be sure of your own bearings again. Fearing is unlike them in that, like Hemingway's, his voice is but a stronger, sadder, more knowing modulation of the voice of ordinary men. Yet just this tone makes him indestructible, a slender classic. The speaker in Fearing's poems is a connoisseur of the anonymous spirits who scribble graffiti on underground posters, penciling beards on pretty ladies' pictures and crying their amorous joy: "'Myrtle loves Harry.'" He tries to preserve an "important hour in a tremendous year" when friends "stood one night in the warm, fine rain, and smoked and laughed and talked"—it *must* remain. He presents an imaginary radio with an infinite series of numbers; perhaps you can tune in on "your very own life, gone somewhere far away." The emotion in his love-poetry is quietly powerful: "You will remember the kisses, real or imagined." The beloved "sleeps, dreaming that she sleeps and dreams." His satire is equally direct: "the voice of the bought magistrate quivering in horror through the courtroom above prostitute and pimp."

In recent years, Fearing became absorbed in the theme of the anti-humanity of an over-organized society, run in all countries by "racketeers" controlling the communications media and therefore the major supply of wealth and power. But his basic note remained the elegiac one, which reached its perfection in the volume *Dead Reckoning* and in an amazing passage in his novel *The Hospital* describing an East River tugboat's removal of the pauper dead to Potter's Field. He faced the elemental horror of things as candidly and precisely, if more humorously, than did Hemingway. A pity that his unique voice has not reached these shores.

New Statesman (18 August 1961)

No Nook to Hide In

THE BEDBUG AND SELECTED POETRY by Vladimir Mayakovsky
Edited by Patricia Blake; translated by Max Hayward and George Reavey

ALMOST everything, good or bad, I have ever read by Vladimir Mayakovsky—or heard about him—has suggested that vibrant order of human presence without which ideas and faiths are but abstractions and art is but ritual or affectation. I associate his poetry, somewhat arbitrarily, with the memory of certain Yiddish poets and actors I heard declaiming in my childhood; it has the same gloriously rhetorical manner unknown to most English-speaking poets today. At its best, this manner is not bombast but the acting out of a role to its hilt, like the rhetoric of *King Lear*. In someone like Mayakovsky it is the realization, through passion, of feeling so intense it seems to break the shell of art within which it came to birth and to go on to a life of its own:

> I feel
> my "I"
> is much too small for me.
> Stubbornly a body pushes out of me.

Hello!
Who's speaking?
Mamma?
Mamma!
Your son is gloriously ill!
Mamma!
His heart is on fire.
Tell his sisters, Lyuda and Olya,
he has no nook to hide in. . . .
("The Cloud in Trousers")

A poet who writes like this has gone beyond his formal technique, like a scientist who, having solved his problems, is no longer concerned with the laboratory equipment. He has got to where he was going. That may be why some poets burn up the resources of their art at such an early age, abandoning it as Rimbaud did or, at the saddest extreme, committing suicide as Hart Crane and Mayakovsky both did in their thirties, and as Dylan Thomas did less deliberately. Whatever poetry at so intense a pitch of projection may say to the reader, to the poet it is an irrevocable commitment, an end in itself, an achieved state that leaves him naked in the wind. Mayakovsky's suicide in 1930 at thirty-six may well have been caused as much by this fact as by the political pressures so acutely described in Patricia Blake's introduction to her selections from his work. The vital anguish of the original Russian makes itself felt even in these translations. It is the same anguish that dominates his last note: "This is not a way out (I do not recommend it to others), but I have none other . . . . Seriously—there was nothing else I could do. Greetings."

Greetings! It is as from Jesus on the cross, if we imagine a Jesus completely absorbed in the compulsion to sacrifice himself and in the sensation of crucifixion rather than in spiritual indoctrination. (But there is also an elusive but inescapable "spiritual" side to Mayakovsky, particularly in his pursuit of the meaning of love in so many poems. In this respect, he is not far from the paradoxical Christianity of William Blake.) And indeed, in "The Cloud in Trousers" Mayakovsky had written:

I am where pain is—everywhere;
on each drop of the tear-flow
I have nailed myself on the cross. . . .

An earlier poem, "I," written before he was twenty, brings out the anguish of realization in a hard, ironic imagery of cruelty. The poet in a personal way, the Russian people in their revolutionary break from the past, are seen awaking to the death of their previous, childlike innocence and to the horrors behind the awakening:

I love to watch children dying.
Do you note, behind protruding nostalgia,
the shadowy billow of laughter's surf?
But I—
in the reading room of the streets—
have leafed so often through the volume of the coffin.

Hart Crane is the only American poet who could have written these terrifying lines. They strike with an unforgettable authority that is the key to Mayakovsky. "Behind his manner," writes Pasternak, "something like decision took one by surprise, decision when it is already put into action and its consequences can no longer be averted. His genius was such a decision and a meeting with it had once so amazed him that it became his theme's prescription for all times, for the incarnation of which he gave himself without pity or vacillation."

It was Mayakovsky's fate to be dramatically "present," in a way that Pasternak, with his tangential subtleties and fastidiousness of personality, could not have been. Given his background as a Communist in early youth, expelled from school, imprisoned; and given his need to dominate the occasion, he had to become *the* spokesman of that electric Russian moment in which his exuberant and tragic youth realized itself. It was he who made his poetry a bridge between the devout past and the Bolshevist future of Russia:

> I have seen Christ escape from an icon,
> and the slush tearfully kiss
> the wind-swept fringe of his tunic. . . .

and

> the year 1916 cometh
> in the thorny crown of revolutions. . . .

Then, just as war converts individual men with opinions into uniformed soldiers, the Soviet State partially converted the *poète maudit* and prophet into a civil servant, a slogan-coiner and jingle-maker and official bard. Since he was one of those people who must be noticed, must be heard, whether "right" or "wrong" and under whatever system they live, he allowed himself to be used this way and even pitched himself into it with great enthusiasm. Yet he realized clearly that he was sacrificing himself in this work, and tried in the poem "An Extraordinary Adventure Which Befell Vladimir Mayakovsky in a Summer Cottage" to construct an image of heroic expenditure of energies for the common good that would justify the stupendous waste of talent:

> Suddenly—I
> shone in all my might,
> and morning rang its round.
> Always to shine,
> to shine everywhere,
> to the very deeps of the last days,
> to shine—
> and to hell with everything else!
> That is my motto—
> and the sun's!

This vision of sacrificial service seemed appropriate enough for the poet who had once expressed the wish to glorify "men as crumpled as hospital beds" and "women as battered as proverbs." Mayakovsky was sure he could reconcile it with his own extravagant, original personality, and it took a dozen hectic years to wear his morale down to the point at which he could no longer find reassurance in the meaning of the world he had helped create. Probably, too, as with Hart Crane at the end, his poetry was no longer a source of strength to him; the battery had gone dead. What wore him down, Miss Blake thinks, was not so much hostile criticism as a growing sense of the coming terror of the Stalin period. But until these two kinds of breakdown, personal and political, combined to destroy him. Mayakovsky handled himself confidently.

Moreover, despite propagandistic poems like "150,000,000" (categorized by Pasternak as "uncreative"), he continued to write in the old intransigent brooding way. The 1922 sequence "I Love" is not political but psychological, self-analytical. It traces his pursuit of an ultimate, essential experience of a love made spiritual to the bitter deprivations of childhood when his "little heart" had had to content itself with nothing human but only the sun, the river, and a "hundred mile stretch of rock." In Paris the poet became entangled with the most un-proletarian of creatures, the elegant White Russian émigrée who is the subject of "Letter from Paris to Comrad Kostrov on the Nature of Love." The poem is brilliant in its evocation of the sensuousness and turmoil of this love, and explicit in its defiance:

> . . . the stalled motor
>   of the heart
> has started to work
>   again.
> You
>   have broken the thread
>   to Moscow. . . .
>
> Who
>   can
>   control this?
> Can you?
>   Try it . . .

In the year of his death Mayakovsky summoned up all his indignation and disdain in the merciless, unfinished "At the Top of My Voice." He contrasts himself with the sycophantic operators, phonies and effete half-poets of the new order (attacking them by name). He chooses a deliberately unglamorous but extremely sardonic figure (when we consider that the Revolution had originally meant *freedom* to its finest proponents) for the meaning of his own career:

> My verse
>   by labor
>   will break the mountain chain of years,
> and will present itself
>   ponderous,
>   crude,
>   tangible,

as an aqueduct,
by slaves of Rome
constructed. . . .

Then came the crackup. Until that moment he was one of those people of such stature, with voices so ringingly and hypnotically sure, that they survive and make themselves felt long after weaker mortals have lost both courage and perspective. Look at his *The Bedbug,* the only play included in this volume. It is a kind of miracle, but it really was produced. In the first act its protagonist, Prisypkin, is a comic villain, a formerly militant worker who abandons his class-consciousness and his true love to make himself a comfortable marriage and gain all the vulgar, bourgeois satisfactions. Amid the clowning and the marvelous incidental satire he shows up as a pretty contemptible fellow. A drunken quarrel at the wedding leads to a fire in which everyone except Prisypkin is killed. He is preserved in the ice formed from water the firemen's hoses have poured into the zero-cold cellar and is found fifty years later. The second part of the play concerns the unfreezing of Prisypkin in the Utopian world of the future, a world completely if benevolently regimented—scientific, hygienic, banal, and free of art, romance, or, indeed, any kind of purely personal meaning. Now Prisypkin, that same drunken, self-centered, unclean, unpredictable lout, becomes a tragic hero. Before he can infect too many others with his "diseases," he is isolated in the zoo, while the bedbug preserved with him from an earlier era is hunted down and put away as a rare and valuable specimen. At the end we see him pleading with his fellow citizens of the advanced Socialist society to become "unfrozen" and rejoin him in his suffering ordinary humanity.

First produced in 1928, the play was no great success. In 1955, however, it was revived and became, according to Miss Blake, a "smash hit." Actually, the play was first produced before the most reactionary era had set in, so that—as Miss Blake suggests—few people gave it very serious attention. But the very fact that it had been produced probably created a certain "tolerance" for it (though Meyerhold, its first producer, is said to have died in a concentration camp after 1939). In any case, it seems hard to doubt that the play means what it seems to mean, and that it reveals the two sides of Mayakovsky—his devotion to the Soviet cause and his hatred and fear of the mediocrity and the taming of the soul that cause nourished in its bosom. If this is true, then his Prisypkin is the poor, crucified Everyman of *Ulysses* and of *Waiting for Godot,* as well as of the beveled-and-leveled future envisioned by the publicists and planners of East and West alike.

The Nation (30 September 1961)

Found in Translation

IMITATIONS by Robert Lowell

"IMITATIONS" is Robert Lowell's modestly accurate term for his attempts to translate a number of poems by some eighteen Europeans from Homer to Pasternak into "alive English," as though they had been written "now and in America." It is a risky business, and doubtless Mr. Lowell will come in for some of the same kind of criticism Pound once received for his "adaptations" from Propertius and others. He shares Pound's view that a translation should be neither an unalphabetized lexicon nor a formal strait jacket. The poet-translator, as opposed to the pedantic one, has as his motive an idiomatic and emotional tone which has compelled him in the original and which he has brought somehow into harmony with his own poetic voice. He will be faithful to the spirit of the original and adhere closely to it if he can, yet must be making a new poem in his own language at the same time. At any rate, that is his somewhat mystical ideal. "My licenses," Mr. Lowell cheerfully confides, "have been many. I have dropped lines, moved lines, moved stanzas, changed images and altered meter and intent."

So then, if you want a trot (for Sappho especially, I might add), *don't* turn to this book. Not only does Mr. Lowell omit or add sections, not only does he put together passages from different poems, but he makes vigorous extensions into effects and thoughts purely his own. Thus, he changes Giacomo Leopardi's "*A Silvia*" into something more violently passionate, partly by adding a characteristically Lowellian imagery:

> . . . my life was burning out,
> and the heat
> of my writings made the letters wriggle and melt
> under drops of sweat.

He does the same kind of thing even with Baudelaire's "*Au Lecteur*" and "*Voyage à Cythère*," poems exceptionally bitter and writhing to start with. He gives them a contemporary American thrust by occasional injections of language more frankly sexual or scatological than Baudelaire's. With poets like Annensky and Pasternak he has had to work as Pound did with the English versions of Chinese poetry (in *Japanese* translation) he received from Ernest Fenollosa's papers. That is, since he knows no Russian, he has taken his leads from literal prose renderings and from other poets' translations. All these tackings-about and problems make for distortions that will dismay one kind of scholarly mind. In practice, from the viewpoint toward translation that considers it as ideally a meeting of kindred sensibilities, they present no real obstacle. (The purist must always go back to the original anyway.) The real importance of what Lowell does must be seen in the light of the whole drift of poetry today.

One reason I say this is simply that he has been the most forceful poet to emerge in our country since the last war. The authors and pieces he selects, and his handling of them, are deeply interesting for the way they illuminate his thinking and modern poetic thinking generally. For instance, he shows us how deeply rooted our most impressive work still is in the French Symbolists of the last century; over a third of these pieces are from Baudelaire and Rimbaud, with whom he actually competes—indeed, it is his way throughout *Imitations* to vie with his poets in their realizations of themselves. In the Rimbaud pieces especially, he brings out that poet's sense of the sticky vulnerability of childhood with unusual emphasis, a result of Lowell's fierce private identification with Rimbaud's sensibility.

Eliot and Pound have loved to talk about "the tradition"—that is, the vital consciousness of the past that goes on informing our own day and is continually being remade by the most original writers. It is interesting to see to which of those two poets' acknowledged masters Lowell—their most likely heir—pays homage in *Imitations*. Those he includes (no doubt there are others, such as Dante, whom he would insist on, although they are not represented here) are Homer, Sappho, Villon, Heine, Baudelaire, Rimbaud, Mallarmé, and Valéry. His approach to these writers is less pedagogical than Pound's, less stylistically absorbed than Eliot's. He uses them in two opposed ways: first, to discover resemblances in them to himself; second, to provide himself with new departures. The bit of Homer he gives us is a blazingly rapid and pity-laden picture of Achilles' remorseless slaying of Lykaon, which sounds as though a typical Lowell poem had been translated into classical Greek. His Heine is an infinitely sharpened variant of the swaggering ironist in whom Pound saw himself mirrored—a far subtler, more passionately mordant Heine driven to extremities of bitterness and to a language approaching that of the Symbolists as he awaits his death. Rimbaud is seen not only in the way I have already mentioned but also in an unusual aspect, as a poet of the pity of war and of social and political disillusionment, as well as a sensualist who could paint a scene realistically in rich, bold colors. In turning his attention to such work, as in his Villon translations, Lowell deliberately, if only temporarily, abandons his own tremendous inwardness and his agonized use of his literal self as his chief subject, which he perhaps carried to their furthest limits in his 1959 volume, *Life Studies*.

To the Eliot-Pound list of "masters" this volume would add a number of others: Rilke, Montale, and Pasternak especially. With all these men we can see Lowell pursuing the same double aim of finding some kinship and at the same time teaching himself new tones, rhythms, and perspectives that will help him, it may be, to remake himself as a poet—that is, to use his gifts in quite altered ways in the future. Thus, among the Rilke poems included, two are very much in the vein of the familiar Lowell: the poet's sad contemplation of a youthful portrait of his father, and his self-distrustful yet ultimately assertive look at himself. The most effective poem in this group, though, is a reinterpretation of the legend of Orpheus and Eurydice, which requires a tremendous adaptability on the translator's part if he is to catch Rilke's mysteriously quiet but powerful projection of imagination. We see the myth from Eurydice's standpoint; she has gone beyond earthly love, beyond caring for Orpheus or even being aware of him:

> She was drowned in herself, as in a higher hope,
> and she didn't give the man in front of her a thought,
> nor the road climbing to life.
> She was in herself. Being dead
> fulfilled her beyond fulfillment.
> Like an apple full of sugar and darkness,
> she was full of her decisive death,
> so green she couldn't bite into it.
> She was still in her marble maidenhood,
> untouchable. Her sex had closed house,
> like a young flower rebuking the night air.

Lowell's ten translations of Montale may be the single most significant section of this book. Montale (the Italian poet who, many claim, is at least equally deserving with Quasimodo of the Nobel Prize) has been neglected in English-speaking countries until very recently, and it is clear that we must absorb his writing into our consciousness. His work seems to me almost the ultimate in quiet, depressed, but savage statement of the paradoxes of modern man's awareness, a statement that has its glowing moments in such a poem as *"l'Anguilla"* but is perhaps most self-consistent in *"La Casa dei doganieri."* The former poem has the dauntlessness of Yeats's "Lapis Lazuli" in its enormous empathy with the eel, "the North Sea siren," that makes its way further and further inland through estuaries and rivers and "delicate capillaries of slime" to its destined mating places. It is "love's arrow on earth" and points to the meaning of human love in its twin extremes of grossness and beauty, and beyond that to the meaning of the whole human condition. The second of these poems is not so much this kind of difficult, tortuous effort at affirmation (ending in a rainbow burst that is still but a question) as it is a bitter poem of resistance to the thought of the constant erosion of memory and meaning that makes even the most significant human experience so transient. It is difficult to give a proper impression of Montale without citing whole poems and even showing their relation to the original Italian—a remark that might imply that translation itself is useless were it not for the simple fact that the contrary is true. There is something mysterious in even the worst translations. One gets—except in the notorious instance of Pushkin, whose genius no non-Russian-speaking reader can ever be convinced of—some breath of life of the original that gives at least a ghostly impression of wonderful ranges of language still to be explored. In these highly sensitive if idiosyncratic translations by Lowell much more is achieved, a reaching out from one world of associations to another that is in its way an essential communication.

What Lowell feels in common with Rilke and Montale, and with Pasternak too, is an ultimate heaviness of spirit that goes hand in hand with a dazzling keenness of response to sense impression, with the most varied moods, and with a very pure sense of potential joy and perfection. You can get it all, perhaps, in the simple opening lines of Montale's "Arsenio":

Roof-high, winds worrying winds
rake up the dust, clog the chimney-ventilators,
drum through the bald, distracted little squares,
where a few senile, straw-hatted horses wheeze
by the El Dorado of the rooming houses' windows in the sun.

Pasternak, of course, can be much gayer, as gay as his lovers in "Wild Vines":

Beneath a willow entwined with ivy,
we look for shelter from the bad weather;
one raincoat covers both our shoulders—
my fingers rustle like the wild vine around your breasts. . . .

Usually, though, he is juggling more elements, more facets of mood and perception, as in "The Seasons":

Spring! I leave the street of astonished pines,
alarmed distances,
the awkward classical wooden house, apprehending its downfall—
the air blue as piles of faded sky-blue denim
lugged by the prisoners from their wards!

The age is breaking—pagan Rome,
thumbs down on clowns. . . .
The overpaid gladiator must die in earnest.

But each of these poets is a world unto himself, and there is no use in my trying to sum up even my own limited knowledge of such disparate figures. Besides, I quite agree with Mr. Lowell's introductory comment that "this book is partly self-sufficient and separate from its sources, and should be first read as a sequence, one voice running through many personalities, contrasts and repetitions." As such it is an extraordinary enterprise. Despite the fact that we live in an age of fine translation, we usually get our really good interpretations one short poem at a time, in scattered volumes, or else in long, sustained treatments of a single author—the two most notable such works in recent times being, probably, Horace Gregory's *Metamorphoses* and Robert Fitzgerald's *Odyssey*. But *Imitations* is remarkable in its gathering together of so much exciting work by so many different authors within the same covers and interpreted by the same hand, and that hand so strong and disciplined. Mr. Lowell has discovered for himself and his readers so many new points of sympathy that this book must inevitably be a bridge for him to the most interesting new future directions. More scholarly and literal treatments, such as we find in Stanley Burnshaw's endlessly informative *The Poem Itself*, are unquestionably essential for the reader who wishes to penetrate the original accomplishments of foreign poets in their own languages. But Mr. Lowell's book is likely to prove one of the germinative works of its kind for the coming poetic age.

The Reporter (21 December 1961)

The Two Frosts

IN THE CLEARING by Robert Frost

EVERYONE knows there are at least two Robert Frosts. Each of them does some talking in the new book. One of them is a natural, sometimes broodingly bitter or fearful lyric poet and storyteller. He has a fine ear for traditional English metric and combines it beautifully with the tones of native American speech. This, most of us would say, is the "real" Frost. His home is in rural New England, his spirit shy and elusive. It may be true that he became eighty-eight just a week or two ago, but he has always had the delighted eye and voice of ageless youth. He was forty when he published "The Pasture," which begins:

I'm going out to clean the pasture spring;
I'll only stop to rake the leaves away
(And wait to watch the water clear, I may):
I sha'n't be gone long.—You come too.

He uses the third line of this stanza for his present epigraph, I think to suggest that he has now actually seen what he long ago set out to see, and that we readers have "come too" and seen it with him. How delicately accurate, and how absorbed in pure observation, he can still be we may discover from the opening poem of the new volume, "Pod of the Milkweed":

Its flowers' distilled honey is so sweet
It makes the butterflies intemperate.
There is no slumber in its juice for them.
One knocks another off from where he clings.
They knock the dyestuff off each other's wings—
With thirst on hunger to the point of lust.
They raise in their intemperance a cloud
Of mingled butterfly and flower dust
That hangs perceptibly above the scene.

Often this first, truest Robert Frost has the gloom of a great Russian writer. One of his early poems expresses the desire to disappear into a dark forest, "fearless of ever finding open land." Another presents him convincingly as one "acquainted with the night." And altogether, we are constantly surprised by what sad, grim poems he has planted in his books among the happier visions of "these flowery waters and these watery flowers" of spring and the humorous pictures of provincial life. Leaf through the *Collected Poems* (1949) and you will find a long series of forever memorable close-ups of grief, of neurotic agony, of irremediable suffering. Among American poets not even Robinson has matched the horror-filled awareness of woman's vulnerability in poems like "Home Burial," "The Lovely Shall Be Choosers," and "A Servant to Servants," to name only a few. Faulkner himself has not managed to show such vistas of grossness and pain as that last poem provides without any eccentricity or waste motion. Doubtless Frost is talking about more than a plant when he writes, in "Pod of the Milkweed" again:

> And yes, although it is a flower that flows
> With milk and honey, it is bitter milk,
> As anyone who ever broke its stem
> And dared to taste the wound a little knows.

Sometimes the feeling is not so much shock at the grotesque brutality that marks the common life as it is a deeply nostalgic and ambiguous melancholy. The extraordinary poem "Directive" in the 1947 volume *Steeple Bush* was of this order, a tracing back toward buried meanings in the traumatically destroyed and irrevocably eroded past. The little poem "Ends" in the new book, though very much slighter, is of this order in its impulse at least:

> Loud talk in the overlighted house
> That made us stumble past.
> Oh, there had once been night the first,
> But this was night the last.
>
> Of all the things he might have said,
> Sincere or insincere,
> He never said she wasn't young,
> And hadn't been his dear.
>
> Oh, some as soon would throw it all
> As throw a part away.
> And some will say all sorts of things,
> But some mean what they say.

This reminds me on the one hand of the deliberately sterile little marriage poems of the very contemporary Robert Creeley, not in form but in ultimate manner—the dry casting away of all sensational detail in a sort of minimal approach to catastrophe. And, in quite another way, it is like some late minor piece by Yeats, "Quarrel in Old Age," say, or one of his little but heartfelt political outbursts. It is poetry that doesn't give a damn about anything except to make an accurate, telling foray *toward* the truth. As ancient Hebraic lore hath it, "It is upon us to begin the work; it is not upon us to complete the work." Two other somewhat ambiguous poems, "The Draft Horse" and "Closed for Good" (reprinted from *Collected Poems* without its original opening and closing stanzas), add to the sadness of *In the Clearing* a note of dauntless acceptance of fatality. They are like the very touching, deliberately doggerel "Away!" in their valedictory tone, although "Away!" is altogether out in the open and ends with the cockiest of threats:

And I may return
If dissatisfied
With what I learn
From having died.

But there is of course a second Robert Frost, and we hardly know what to do about *him*. He is the handsomely craggy-faced sage and official bard who was chosen to compose a poem for the inauguration of President Kennedy and whose birthday this year was celebrated at a formal affair sponsored by the Secretary of the Interior. For two decades now he has frequently donned this sage's mask and costume, as of a Good Grey Walt Whitman without beard or other taint, and treated us to verse-sermons on sundry topics: science, religion, socialism, capitalism, his own brand of twinkling-eyed pragmatic idealism right out of the cracker barrel, and almost anything else. Except in stray patches, it is as if when he begins sermonizing he loses all his poetic strength and capacity for self-irony and becomes merely the "smiling public man" Yeats once, but how wryly, called himself. Take two of the poems in the new volume, "For John F. Kennedy His Inauguration" and the even longer "Kitty Hawk." Both blandly affirm the technological values of American society today. The inaugural poem suggests as well that we are at the beginning of a new "Augustan" era of splendor and progress under the aegis of the Kennedy administration. Now we cannot reasonably say these are bad poems because of their ideas. On the contrary, we must all hope they prove themselves valid—and besides it is thrilling to see the "mad" absorption of certain great artists, in their later years, in transcendent ideas that so often prove saner than mean common sense can ever understand. But that is just the trouble. It is not "madness" but the descent into literal ordinariness, into Panglossian optimism, and—more to the point—into a style to go with them that makes the second Frost so dismayingly unreal:

Come fresh from an election like the last,
The greatest vote a people ever cast,
So close yet sure to be abided by,
It is no miracle our mood is high. . . .
There is a call to life a little sterner,
And braver for the earner, learner, yearner.
Less criticism of the field and court
And more preoccupation with the sport. . . .

Where are we, anyway? Thinking of these unhappy matters and rather baffled by them—there is still so much of the "true" Frost with us too—I cannot help remembering Kenneth Rexroth's somewhat melodramatic lament for the alienated American poets of Frost's generation:

What happened to Robinson,
Who used to stagger down Eighth Street,
Dizzy with solitary gin?
Where is Masters, who crouched in
His law office for ruinous decades?

Where is Leonard who thought he was
A locomotive? And Lindsay,
Wise as a dove, innocent
As a serpent, where is he?
  Timor mortis conturbat me.

I do not know what it is that has made the difference among the present members of that great generation. Of them all, at least those still resident in this country, perhaps only William Carlos Williams and E. E. Cummings stand with the perpetual opposition. (Marianne Moore and Carl Sandburg liked Ike.) Say what you will against him, Mr. Cummings will never be anybody's official anything; and though somewhat more amenable, Dr. Williams will have to wait until the ideal anarcho-Bohemian-socialist-fraternitarian society of the future to march to the rostrum with his honor guard of loving young poets around him. But they have had a certain salutary neglect by comparison with Frost. They have not had to respond to a public at once interested in hearing them speak prophetically and less concerned with the content than with the air of their wisdom.

But I was going to say that Frost's case is more hopeful, and more complex, than all this may imply. Actually, the "real" Frost is interested in "issues" of all kinds too, though always in small doses and at great intervals. When *he* speaks, he does not shrink so far within a sage-disguise that his own natural voice is lost. His voice is then irrepressible:

Forgive, O Lord, my little jokes on Thee
And I'll forgive Thy great big one on me.

That pops up in *In the Clearing*. It reminds me of a little poem in *Steeple Bush* that shows how capable our poet is of satire in the great tradition, the quick, spontaneous thought of a free mind with the twin gifts of wit and discipline. The poem is "U.S. 1946 King's X." It has the kick of personality and the ability to jeer at oneself lacking in the Kennedy poem:

Having invented a new Holocaust,
And been the first with it to win a war,
How they make haste to cry with fingers crossed,
King's X—no fairs to use it any more!

In the Clearing, too, gives us the truly thoughtful little poem "Our Doom to Bloom," which stands out coolly against the more ponderous and characterless "wisdom" pieces. Asked for a right definition of Progress, the Cumaean Sibyl replies:

. . . if it's not a mere illusion
All there is to it is diffusion—
Of coats, oats, votes, to all mankind.
In the Surviving Book we find
That liberal, or conservative,
The state's one function is to give.

The bud must bloom till blowsy blown
Its petals loosen and are strown;
And that's a fate it can't evade
Unless 'twould rather wilt than fade.

The sadness of this poem is like that of Jeffers's "Shine, Perishing Republic," from which in fact its epigraph is taken. It contains a quiet but sobering recognition that a country like ours must lose its uniqueness as it helps other peoples advance; and it makes its point without too much expansiveness and, finally, through a most appropriate figure. If we look back over Frost's work we shall find that his social and political comments are always best made in this way, for instance the thoughts on war in "Snow," "To E. T.," "The Bonfire," and "Not to Keep," or the thoughts on organized society and its economics in "A Lone Striker." In the long run we shall not be terribly troubled by the second, or false, Frost and the almost innocent garrulity with which he too often beguiles himself and his trusting public. We shall mostly forget the work of that sort, and move among the frightening depths and bright or shadowed surfaces of his characterizations and impressions of places and of significant moments. What we shall remember most, very likely, is his intense repossession of psychological states, whether the near-nightmare richness of "After Apple-Picking," the deep, drowsy acceptance of weakness and death's nearness in "An Old Man's Winter Night," the hilarious though grisly matter-of-factness of "The Witch of Coös," or the coarse and savage erotic strangeness of "The Pauper Witch of Grafton." And the music!—

Ah, when to the heart of man
  Was it ever less than a treason
To go with the drift of things,
  To yield with a grace to reason,
And bow and accept the end
  Of a love or a season?
("Reluctance")

The Reporter (12 April 1962)

from *The American Influence on the Coots of Hampstead Heath, 1960–1961*

AN American in England last year could easily miss his cultural signals, particularly in that rainiest of years when for a time the entire southern part of the island threatened to wash away into the sea. The greatest distraction, besides the waters overflowing Devon and the golf matches under umbrellas and the dauntless BBC weather forecasts promising "bright patches," was the flood of foreign art of every kind. Nigerian sculpture, Irish actors giving the most convincing performance of *The Playboy of the Western World* I am ever likely to see in this world, the immense Picasso exhibition at the Tate Gallery, the Leningrad Symphony Orchestra (trained so superbly that some local critics *complained* of their perfection), these were but a few of last year's cosmopolitan delights of London. One might have been forgiven for mistaking what they had to offer for the essential English note itself—in which case England would have become very American indeed, and in a very short time.

Yet the English *response* to these events, at whatever height of brow, was somehow suggestive: large crowds, relatively muted enthusiasm. Even the Leningrad, with Shostakovitch himself attending some of the performances, was received more calmly than one might expect by the Royal Festival Hall audiences. And the Picasso show was a curiously revealing experience. The mobs stampeding through at all times were like a New York subway crush. With all that overwhelming, prolific, varied display in room after room, one had the choice of either standing stubbornly before a picture and blocking traffic, like someone in the Times Square station trying to decide between a local and an express, or circling the rooms tirelessly like one of the damned in Hell. I spent many hours in an injudicious mixture of both alternatives, and in the course of my travail discovered that most of the people storming through disliked what they saw. (Many had babies in their arms, or dragged stolid, sniffling little creatures behind them; these were definitely family outings.) I think they were especially displeased to see how great a representational artist Picasso can be when he so chooses. Many had come because of the famous name but also feeling that they might be amused at Picasso's expense—and here he was painting some perfectly outrageous subjects, and some extremely appealing ones, beautifully. There were murmurs of "Don't like *that*!" and "Doesn't she look awful?" and so on. In its way this kind of provincial recoil was rather like the critics' (including Kenneth Tynan's) objections to the authentic Irishness of speech and rhythm in *The Playboy*.

The reason Londoners are reluctant to rejoice in what the outside world pours into their city is probably that at this moment the English are looking for something uniquely their own—a new voice, harsh, cantankerous, inward, even cruel, for the new era into which England had now entered. They want to remain a people famous for their "civilization," international-minded, and all that; but they also seek a voice for the renewed sense of the difficulties of self-identification. Perhaps that is one reason why Mr. Michael Foot, the left wing M.P. from Bevan's old constituency, is so widely admired and arouses so much interest, despite the fact that he represents a decided minority position and is by general agreement not the most effective sort of politician. In a deep sense, too, the English are much more political than we are. The War is more than a raw memory for them; it is a traumatic state not yet over. And the political issues of the 1930s have a continuing life that strikes an American with peculiar force. That is why Arnold Wesker's plays—which are Clifford Odets Anglicized and modernized and given a new historical perspective—are hailed and why the Theatre Workshop of Joan Littlewood was so successful, despite the fact that it presented mainly diluted Brecht and bawdier (and cheaper) *Street Scene*, over and over again. These are attempts to give utterance to all that subjective life which has hitherto gone on—and suffered hardly knowing it was suffering—in the lower strata of this society. An immensely popular television comedy program, called *Bootsie and Snudge*, is about two members of the unskilled and uneducated class who have highly insecure jobs as servants in a club. Bootsie and Snudge are partly Charlie Chaplinesque, but both are entirely unscrupulous: they leap at the chance to rub each other's noses into the dirt, and they emulate (when allowed the chance) the airs and callousness toward inferiors of people—i.e., everyone else in the world—who outrank them. In its own fashion this program really beats the Theatre Workshop at its own game and is much more toughminded and closer to the truth of popular consciousness than is Wesker's work, and for the same reason. How Snudge yearns to be a snob! How hypocritically, and with what engaging plainness of soul, Bootsie accepts and then squirms out of all tasks and ideas handed down to him from above! He is one pure embodiment of the great, amoral, apolitical, pleasure-seeking, dirt-eating common folk. Just wait, you fast-talking Beats and Beatsies, until Bootsie comes into his own. Brute nature, colored by imperturbable sentimentality, will put to self-conscious shame your pretensions to elemental directness.

Snudge and Bootsie are "lovable," however. They have a sweet innocence within their squalid spirits, and somehow they reassure us: All's still right with the world; *the lowly are still in their proper place*. Not so the characters of Harold Pinter's *The Caretaker*. This play is the most meaningful expression of the new, emergent England we shall have for a long time. Not that it sets out to be such an expression. Pinter is just a natural inventor of fables; but as the fables develop, all kinds of possible, quite relevant implications cluster around them. It would be easy to argue that—like Wesker's *Roots*, but much more sensitive—*The Caretaker* cannot really be transplanted. Its stinging little cruelties and the panic behind them are just local enough in their psychological idiom to be in danger of becoming blurred in foreign production (which is just what happened in London to *The Connection*). It displays a brutality of class relations and at the same time a paralyzed dismay at their dissolution that are peculiarly English. Dreadful old Davies, the protagonist, a whining, vicious, thieving ne'er-do-well, is a kind of combined Bootsie-and-Snudge in his indomitable selfishness and irresistible urge to lord it over someone else. He even has some of their comic charm, but a great deal more comic treachery and low-mindedness. As the world has tormented him, in reality and in fancy, so he torments the gentle Aston who befriends him, while he himself is kept in a painful state of insecurity and bewilderment by Aston's sadistic brother, Mick. It is excruciating bullying all around, and often excruciatingly funny at the same time. On its home grounds, the play has a bizarre horror and fascination as painful as they are irresistible.

Yet this fear of the play's being purely local would be unwarranted. The shabbiness of the set and of the drab West London world of the play, the pathos of Aston's goodness and gentility, the hopelessly neurotic motivation behind both brothers' ambitions and the caged, useless wildness of Davies' spirit speak for themselves. They are intrinsically absorbing and need no symbolic interpretation. Nevertheless, they also bespeak some terrifying moral problems. Davies offers an impossible challenge to a society already sick and shaken, and the play is endlessly suggestive of the need for self-discovery, and a new language of self-identification, in this new England that is coming to birth. Perhaps that is a special reason, apart from its sheer achievement, that it quickens Americans' hearts so and sends a thrill of recognition through us. The edges of this play are very sharp; Pinter cuts mercilessly at the issues it embodies. Yet, as with most drama of power and authority, the characters are deep-sunk into their private selves and their immediate predicaments. They are unaware of any world outside their own, are stirred in their deep, womblike dream only by the arrival into it of some new, unannounced element. It is this very inwardness, a wonderful entrancement achieved by Pinter's art, that makes them begin to fulfil the demands of a new era and give form to the forebodings expressed in a recent poem of A. S. J. Tessimond's—"The British":

> We are afraid of, one day on a sunny morning,
> Meeting ourselves or another without the usual,
> Outer sheath, the comfortable conversation,
> And saying all, all, all we did not mean to,
> All, all, all we did not know we meant.

In the British Museum Reading Room there is a vast notebook in which scholars inscribe petulant little notes like "Why has not Pzlzfsky's *Archives of Maori Culture: A Tibetan Checklist* been acquired? I have requested this *indispensable* work *four* times since 1911." In the margin, or just below the note or just above it if room has been left between one such missive and another, we find the patient answer: "We have written to the publisher in Tannu Tuva for this book, but cannot decipher his reply." Sometimes the rejoinder is *very* patient: "This work is listed in the catalogue. See catalogue." One inquiry the librarians found beneath contempt and left to languish in its own devices:

> I see the Ind. Imp. Gazetteer
> Is removed from its usual sphere.
> I hope and I trust it
> Is only to dust it,
> And that it will soon reappear.

Like so many English places and people, the Museum is more intimate, or cozier, and at the same time more remote than its American counterparts—say, the Library of Congress or the New York Public Library. Certainly it is more relaxed; it has a *mystique* of relaxation, and you have to remember the turbulent ghosts of such as Karl Marx to realize what this pleasant drowsiness conceals. To look up books published before 1955 one must go to great, cumbersome old bound catalogue volumes, with hand-pasted entries in a slightly unpredictable order. After 1955, the catalogue-card system familiar to Americans was introduced, though vital bits of information, such as the names of publishers, are still usually omitted. An amiable vagueness pervades the library staff, and it takes an hour or so before books are brought up. The library itself remains open only two evenings a week. All of which gives one the comfortably deceptive feeling that practically no one there is actually getting any work done, except one or two American professors who bring along their own books and make notes in them belligerently while everyone else bumbles happily around, old gentlemen boom instructions to their secretaries, and the rapt eccentrics—the bearded walrus, the bony lady in the track suit, and the Laughing Man—perform in their several rings.

I don't—I couldn't—mean the Museum is *noisy*. It has a floating population of people who don't know how to whisper, and the telephones ring in the rafters every few minutes, but there is an air of discretion about the place that is stiller than literal silence. It is like the genteel, or "saloon bar," side of a pub. It calls for, it believes in, silence; for the English are not at all like the Athenians, who knew what virtue is but did not intend to practice it. To be virtuous here means, indeed, not to make a noise about whatever you're doing. When, a year or so ago, Bertrand Russell led several thousand people to sit for two and a half hours outside the Ministry of Defence, one might legitimately have asked whether they had marched for their stated purpose—to protest against the Polaris Base missile agreement—or to honor quietude. "You are asked," said the printed instructions to participants, "not to chant slogans during the demonstration. We would like to emphasize once again that the march from Trafalgar Square to the Ministry of Defence will be held in silence." The *Observer* praised the affair as "the quietest, most orderly, most impressive mass demonstration senior police officers could recall." An unimpeachable source of commendation, that, considering that Lord Russell had called the march "the first step in a campaign of non-violent civil disobedience" against "the nuclear tyrants of East and West" who "threaten the entire human race with extinction."

Not to detract from the seriousness or worthiness of this planned pavement-sitting, there is little doubt it would have seemed less tolerable to the law-abiding English had it not appealed to their profound love of reticence. Even the fiery Scots poet, Hugh MacDiarmid, who had descended reluctantly to the despised Thames Valley to flash his red kilt in the faces of the English police, was sobered to the core by all this non-Gaelic calm. Its most endearing expression perhaps, was in the affixing of the protest declaration to the front door of the Ministry in Storey's Gate, St. James Park. The occasion called for dramatic flourish, as on a famous day in the life of Martin Luther. Here is the *Observer*'s account:

> Bertrand Russell had gone to the door with a hammer and nails, but it was suggested to him that perhaps it would be as well to use less damaging ways of fixing the notice. He said he did not think that was a matter of principle and he used sticky tape. Immediately he turned his back the notice was removed by a Ministry official.

Such absolute composure at the center of things may yet save Western civilization, if only the English can teach it to the rest of us. They do not like themselves when they break it—witness the shamefacedness of the Labour members of Parliament during their days of obstructionism over the new Tory plans for the National Health Service. It is notable that what Robert Bolt stresses in his very successful play, *A Man for All Seasons*, about Sir Thomas More, is the hero's absolute refusal to make a fuss on his own behalf or to let anyone else make one. Silence was More's weapon against the King's and Thomas Cromwell's attempt to force him to support the King's divorce and his reconstitution of the English Church. The first half of the play, in which More does as much talking as the next man, moves rather slowly and coldly. Then, once More gets his passions aroused and therefore grows quieter and quieter, one can feel the audience becoming more and more excitedly sympathetic. It was this theme that really set Mr. Bolt's arteries pulsating; More wasn't talkin' and the play was really rockin'. This is not to be confused with the problem of inarticulateness in a moral crisis, as in Pinter's *The Caretaker*, or with saying interesting things dully, as in Eliot's *The Elder Statesman*. No, the attraction here is that of having everything to say and deciding to keep it under control. How different is Mr. Bolt's hero from Brecht's Galileo, who, faced with comparable alternatives, exhausts himself and his audience in an endless soliloquy which only the greatest actor can sustain.

The Antioch Review (Summer 1962)

New Singers and Songs

THE recent deaths of Robert Frost and William Carlos Williams remind us forcibly of the slipping away of a wonderful series of generations of American poets. They flourished in the three decades after 1910. In the 1930s, when Edwin Arlington Robinson died and Hart Crane and Vachel Lindsay committed suicide, the new poetic impulse they represented was in full flood still. Even as late as Edgar Lee Masters' death in 1950 and that of Wallace Stevens in 1955, many of the familiar, famous names continued to be with us. A number, happily, remain present and active. But now, suddenly, in the past two years alone, we have lost not only Frost and Williams but H.D. (Hilda Doolittle), Robinson Jeffers, E.E. Cummings and Kenneth Fearing. A complex of later groups is taking up their "space."

Before looking at the successors, I want to linger a moment over the older group. What was it that these poets, so intransigently individualistic, nevertheless accomplished together for their art and for their country? First, of course, they gave us a body of splendid poems the best of which, for the most part, are to this day unknown even to the educated public. They liberated technique from narrow formalism and imitativeness, while they heightened the sense of relevant tradition and of the need for rigorous artistic self-discipline. They followed Whitman's lead in exploring native motifs and idioms, and on the other hand they opened our poetry to a host of foreign influences. They cultivated psychological and culturally critical frankness, creating a fearless poetry that faced the tragic meanings of the age with candor if sometimes with boisterous mockery. We may quarrel with certain excesses, but that too is a sign of a living, daring body of work. We have an American poetry now, though only the poets and too small a number of readers know it.

Who are the Frosts, the Williamses, the H. D.'s of the future? Impossible to tell when we are dealing with such unique personalities. Longevity, as various wits have remarked, makes something of a difference, and so may the early adversity and neglect that a number of outstanding writers have known. I can conceive of Howard Nemerov's becoming a sort of Frost—or perhaps more accurately, a sort of Frost-plus-Auden—of the future. He has the copiousness, ability to tell a story, wit, wide curiosity and poetic cunning to carry it off, although he is quite unlike Frost in his quick urban intelligence and, especially, in his long, subjectively symbolic sequences. Or we can call Denise Levertov a kind of feminine Williams, spontaneous, personal, open, yet rich in the deployments of her art. Or perhaps Galway Kinnell, with his glad eye for the particular and his way of looking at himself looking at the world, will be our latter-day Williams. But such speculation is tiresome, unjust to all the parties concerned.

Literature is full of meaningful echoes, but no real writer is merely the echo of another. The unexpected and the uncategorizable are the usual thing in poetry. The latest turn in the work of Conrad Aiken, the quiet strengthening over the years (largely unnoticed) in the work of the 65-year-old Horace Gregory, may well mean much more for poetry's future than the easy audacities of last year's vacuum-packed sensation who swept up all the prizes.

My mind staggers when I think of this aspect of my subject: how little attention is paid to the development of poets after their first impact, for instance, and how much excellence without fanfare is destined to be ignored or to be recognized only by near-accident. We have a better soil than climate for poetry. If I should list a few poets in their fifties, or just becoming 50 this year, who have done a considerable amount of work and have won critical praise and interest, how many would most readers of this piece feel they knew at all well? Here are the names: Richard Eberhart, Karl Shapiro, Theodore Roethke, Winfield Townley Scott, Elizabeth Bishop, Delmore Schwartz, Josephine Miles, Robert Penn Warren, Brother Antoninus, Charles Olson, Stanley Kunitz. It would be easy to triple the list, and in the process to add some names that should be at least as recognizable as those mentioned.

The steadfast effort to sustain moral perspective on Eberhart's part, the intense search for identity of Shapiro, and his trying-on-for-size of many guises in the course of it, the wry astringency of Miles's observations—to select but a few dominant characteristics—are phenomena of revealing importance to us. Scott, whose nostalgic poetry is beautiful and yet abrasive; Brother Antoninus, who shows us what it is to be a religious poet while struggling with daily realities of American life; Olson, who has been trying to crack through the assumptions and expectations both of our modern values and of our modern verse; Kunitz, who has gathered for us in too small a body of writing some of the most wounding motifs of the age—these are all sensibilities at once unique and representative. We ignore them at our own expense, given the fact that each has a language, a style, a way of making poems that is absorbingly suggestive in itself.

The single poet of outstanding power and virtuosity to emerge since the last war is the 46-year-old Robert Lowell. He seems the likeliest heir, in the quality of his genius, to the mantle of Eliot. Our leading "confessional" poet, between his early *Land of Unlikeness* and his 1959 volume *Life Studies* he turned more and more to the exploitation of his own private experiences, family background and psychological predicaments as the controlling center of his work. It is a direction indicated not only by his own growth as a poet, but by the whole tendency of serious poetry since the great Romantics and especially since the later Yeats.

Private humiliation and disorientation become in this perspective (as in certain French poets whom Mr. Lowell has studied and translated) the clue to the general human condition. One is tempted to discount the tendency, sometimes, as a type of nasty exhibitionism leading to an esthetic dead end, particularly as it *is* little more than that in the hands of half-poets. But that is to ignore and to dismiss out of a too-ready squeamishness the profound reorientation of sensibility taking place in our social and personal relationships and reflected in fiction and drama as well as in poetry. In any case, the art of Mr. Lowell is extraordinary in its passion and energy; past the self-degradation, unpoisoned by it and indeed redeeming it, something beautiful comes to birth.

Among the poets we may loosely group with Lowell on the score of either a certain confessional strain or a wildly nervous energy with a self-lacerating backlash to it are Theodore Roethke, Delmore Schwartz, W. D. Snodgrass and Anne Sexton. All have written moving poems based on private anguish. Some of Roethke's relatively early poems based on childhood memories of his father's greenhouse are amazingly vivid evocations. His attempts in other work to get deep into the primal psyche are often forced and sub-Joycean (rather than sub-conscious, as intended), but they do catch the pathos of a compulsion to regress and at the same time, curiously, often carry a roaring bawdy humor as well.

Indeed, almost all the dark and depressive poetry I am alluding to now has its paradoxically high-spirited side, sometimes "manic" and hysterical, perhaps, but also expressive of a highly intelligent and humane irony behind what appears the authors' self-indulgence. Roethke's work, again, can be quite simple; he has written some of the most elementally sad poems we have. Recently, he has received a good deal of recognition in England, where among others he has influenced the gifted poet Ted Hughes and his American wife, the late Sylvia Plath. Miss Plath's very last poems, as represented in a recent issue of the Sunday *Observer,* were morbid but brilliant. In the absolute authority of their statement they went beyond Roethke into something like the pure realization of a latter-day Emily Dickinson.

The reader who is unfamiliar with current poetry may feel that he is better off without having to come to terms with such intractable melancholy as I have been describing. And it is true that, take it by and large, our best poetry is often savagely, bitterly, alienated, or at least driven to some extreme of neurotic exacerbation. (See Frost's "A Servant to Servants," among many forerunners that might be named.) Thus, Snodgrass' most successful poem, "Heart's Needle," concerns the suffering he and his small daughter underwent during the ordeal of his divorce and remarriage. As is characteristic of poets writing in this mode, he associated private with public suffering and built into the poem an imagery of cold weather that suggests the wintry state of the human spirit and even the cold war. Anne Sexton's poems deal often with her own mental illness and Delmore Schwartz's with an oppressed psychic condition that is felt as very much a function of the times. (Here I am speaking more of Schwartz's earlier work than his more relaxed recent poetry.)

If proof were needed, then, that this is an age of vast and painful psychological pressures and dislocations, in which the private self feels engulfed by impersonal forces, especially by the recurrence of war and violence and the equally recurrent threat of more, and worse, to come, then our poetry would certainly provide it. The war poems of Randall Jarrell, and his concern generally with the vulnerability and pity of innocence, the search for reconstruction of the fragmented self in Muriel Rukeyser's poetry, Eberhart's struggle to subdue the active death-consciousness of his work, the sense of pervasive vileness that permeates Allen Ginsberg's wailing autobiographical indictments—these and many other examples amply illustrate the point. One would think our poets were en masse obsessed with the thought at the beginning of James Wright's "Saint Judas":

> When I went out to kill myself, I caught
> A pack of hoodlums beating up a man. . . .

To counteract the clear suggestion of unrelieved depression, anxiety and hostility, we need to recall certain basic principles. A poem that is well-earned through its mastery of its own language, voice and structure, is implicitly an assertion of human value no matter what its explicit theme or viewpoint may be. Their understanding of this principle is one of the things that is so heartening about the poets whose names are usually associated with Charles Olson's—Miss Levertov, Robert Duncan, Robert Creeley and Paul Blackburn.

The actual writing of each of these poets is quite unlike that of the others; but like Lowell they all understand—as Whitman long ago taught—that looking hard at one's own realities is the primary act of courage as well as of sensuous response. They have (Creeley especially) cultivated a way of presenting emotion-laden scenes and situations flatly; Creeley so much so that often he shaves the poetic part of his poem away entirely. Levertov and Blackburn have too intrinsically lyrical a feeling for their phrasing and for the presentative life of the poetic image to go to this extreme.

The feeling that there is more to a successful poem than "mere poetry" is a dangerous one, but some great poets have had it; in practice it means that such a pitch of realization has been reached, or such a desire to break out of given molds, that the poet has a fierce revulsion against any assumption that what he does is an esthetic *performance* instead of an exploration of the possibilities of imaginative projection and emotional discovery. Robert Duncan's work, particularly, reflects this attitude. Despite great unevenness, he seems potentially the most challenging poet on our scene to take up a truly revolutionary artistic direction.

Because of the tendencies I have been emphasizing, I have neglected a number of fine poets whom we might call, if rather misleadingly, "moderates." Richard Wilbur's poems, sometimes of incomparable richness and deftness, stand by themselves in their own modest perfection. He shares the concerns of the age, of course, as his poem against the McCarran Act and his "Advice to a Prophet"—concerning the right way to shock ourselves awake to the horror of the Bomb—show clearly. A very pure, vivid intimacy with language and the possibilities of traditional form have made him a poet of almost Classical cast.

One may quarrel, as I have, with this self-limiting quality against which poets like Duncan strain; and yet, in another mood, I am sure the quarrel is presumptuous, for one should be grateful to have what Wallace Stevens called the "noble accents" and the "lucid, inescapable rhythms" of the true "bawds of euphony." A neglected poet, James Schevill, has been constructing an interesting body of poetry out of a scholarly sensibility—a unique ability to catch the special qualities of historical moments, biographical data, particular scenes fraught with contemporary and traditional significance.

Poets like William Stafford, Gary Snyder and Robert Bly, very close to the life of their local regions, have been cultivating a descriptive precision and economy that still allows room for the play of a sense of strangeness and for a colloquial bite in their language. The spiraling intensities of W. S. Merwin, closing in on his own location in a spinning or fog-laden world; the gay, knotty, complexly centrifugal flights of Theodore Weiss; the self-discounting, witty, offhand, yet penetrating poetic wisdom of Reed Whittemore—these will suggest how many thriving poets we have, each working in his own way and only tentatively and momentarily, if at all, classifiable.

Do I think them all equally successful and promising for the future? Of course not. But I have tried here less to take sides than to indicate the large number of poets worthy of respect and of far more attention than they presently receive who are now at work. They are the descendants of the great generation that preceded them, who made it possible for serious poetry to thrive on the American scene, and their poetry holds many keys to the subjective meaning of contemporary American life.

New York Times Book Review (30 June 1963)

Robert Penn Warren's Poetry

REREADING Robert Penn Warren's poetry, and often admiring it, I am nevertheless struck by its unevenness, really unusual for a poet of such gifts. That is one obvious characteristic, worth some contemplation. Related to it somehow is a second, that the poetry has a discernible pattern of development, has "come through" in a way, and yet its impact decreases for the most part as its clarity sharpens. The third salient characteristic of Mr. Warren's poetry is one that I suppose we should have expected. Although he can on occasion be a fine lyric poet in the elegiac vein, and even sometimes in a brighter mood, he is most often at his best when the poems are narrative in character, and narrative of a special kind. The four or five poems and passages that stand out in this respect all focus on situations involving intransigent or sadistic cruelty. The most morbidly traumatizing of these situations is the butchering of the slave George in *Brother to Dragons* (1953). One finds it foreshadowed, however, in the poems of Mr. Warren's twenties and thirties. Among the earlier pieces of *Selected Poems 1923–1943*, for instance, "Pondy Woods" stands out both for its formal distinctiveness and for its delineation of the terrified anticipation of murderous violence. In the same volume, among the poems written in his thirties, is "The Ballad of Billie Potts," the one poem of Mr. Warren's anthologized by F. O. Matthiessen in *The Oxford Book of American Verse*. Together with these poems, I should mention at least one fairly recent one—"Court-martial," which appears in the 1957 volume *Promises*. These titles stand out with a certain brilliance. The progression they represent embodies the growth of Mr. Warren's talent. Their single obsession with a pervasive brutality at the heart of human nature suggests to me that the poet has waited too much upon this theme and depended too much on the excitement—not exactly artificial but too readily induced in himself—of its realization in action.

To return, though, to the first of these characteristics, the unevenness of Mr. Warren's art. He has natural gifts, the genuine poetic eye and ear, from the start—

> The buzzards over Pondy Woods
> Achieve the blue tense altitudes. . . .

Still, he is not completely the "natural" poet in the sense that these gifts are powerful shaping elements in the vision and unfolding of whole poems, as—to take a supreme example—is the case with Yeats, or in another way, through the proliferation of metaphorical association, with Hart Crane or Dylan Thomas. Nor is the dominating voice so intrinsically powerful as to provide this shaping structure, as for instance Keats's voice does through its lyrical absorption in the human situation felt as a predicament of private sensibility, or even as Auden's does through a glittering play of intellectuality that seeks to hold off subjectivity by wit alone, as it were. A dramatic or narrative structure is almost always necessary to enable Mr. Warren to realize his poem; and yet even the works I have mentioned, "Pondy Woods," "The Ballad of Billie Potts," the murder-scene of *Brother to Dragons*, and "Court-martial," fail to depend on that structure entirely. The realization that Mr. Warren is after is not quite of the sort that Robert Bridges was after in "Screaming Tarn," or Ambrose Bierce in any number of his stories. It is not simple, unexpounded realization of an ironic grimness in the curve of life, the shock of the impact of impersonal nature or fate upon human need and desire. No, he wants something more than that, something like "the union of deep feeling with profound thought" that Coleridge speaks of as present in Wordsworth's poetry. (The phrase is in a passage quoted by Mr. Warren in his excellent essay on "The Rime of the Ancient Mariner," an essay that clearly reveals his admiration for the kind of proliferation of meaning so beautifully embodied in that poem.)

I say this because none of these poems is quite content to present its situation or story without comment. In "Pondy Woods," the young Warren invented a talking buzzard "with a Tennessee accent" to comment on the condition of Big Jim Todd, the Negro who has committed some unspecified crime and is being hunted down by a posse. The Latin-quoting buzzard compares Jim with Christ on the Cross and has him epitomizing the nameless guilt and unearned doom of all humanity. Fortunately the diction of the two stanzas in which this thought is unwound is sufficiently delphic to conceal its forced near-vulgarity, so that our chief impression is of the palpable horror of Jim's time there in the marshes and of the grotesque appropriateness of his having to endure an address from a buzzard who is clearly an American relative of the twa corbies. It is in the concrete evocation of scene and atmosphere that Mr. Warren excels here as elsewhere. In "The Ballad of Billie Potts," the attempt to suggest a significance beyond what the plot itself holds gets quite out of hand. In its bare essence the plot is of that marvelous tragic-ironic order familiar in *Oedipus Tyrannos* or *The Pardoner's Tale,* but lacks the mythical context of the one, as well as the well-ordered dramatic tradition with its room for the chorus and for relevant argumentation, and the implicit allegorical character of the other. I make such comparisons not to snub the poet vicariously—like the medievalist who asked me, long ago when I had first read Kenneth Fearing and expressed my pleasure in his work: "Is he as good as Chaucer?"—but because of the ambitious scope of the poem itself. It has stanzas of varying length, with a loosely rhyming structure vaguely related to the ballad stanza; their length, though, suggests something of greater weight or scope than a mere tale in verse, and so does the fact that there are two basic speaking voices, one of them randy and colloquial—going the folk one better—and the other intellectual, sensitive, portentous. The first voice (I select my example delicately) speaks with extroverted boldness:

> His shoulders were wide and his gut stuck out
> Like a croker of nubbins and his holler and shout
> Made the bob-cat shiver and the black-jack leaves shake. . . .

The second voice, which is presumably that of the poet's most inward sensibility, though it might just possibly be that of T. S. Eliot at his special kind of poetic prayer, is far different:

> There was a beginning but you cannot see it.
> There will be an end but you cannot see it.
> They will not turn their faces to you though you call,
> Who pace a logic merciless as light. . . .

The relationship of the two voices is clear enough. The first voice is that of the storyteller pure and simple, identifying himself with the level of speech and thought of the people in his tale and letting it go at that. In the tale, based on local history, Billie Potts is an innkeeper of the between-rivers region of Western Kentucky who has developed an efficient system for murdering his more promising-looking guests. His son, young Billie, tries to do one of the killings himself, blunders and is wounded by the crafty would-be victim, and is sent out west by his father to avoid any possible further pursuit. Not being "much of a hand with a pen-staff," he never writes to his parents during the ten years or so he is away making his fortune. When he does return, bearded and unrecognizable, he pretends to be a stranger stopping at the inn and is murdered by his father before he can identify himself. All this is in the first voice. The second voice, meanwhile, is parenthetically interspersed throughout the poem. The protagonist of the ballad proper is old Billie Potts himself; the protagonist of the second voice's segment of the poem is an undefined "you" who identifies himself symbolically but not literally with Little Billie. This "you," with his heritage of guilt and fear, is returning to his own sources, whch exercise an irresistible fascination despite his foreboding. The sources are familial, regional, historical. In this sort of thing a little bit of suggestion goes a long way, but "The Ballad of Billie Potts" divides its space just about equally between the two voices, and the consequence is that its force is all but rotted out by the impression of garrulous lugubriousness thereby created. Perhaps that is an overstatement, for there is a good deal of skilful writing, much of it evocative as Mr. Warren intended it to be, in the passages for the second voice. Nevertheless the destructive element is present. If one asks why the poet should have indulged himself in this over-extensive symbolic elaboration, perhaps the answer lies partly in an attempt to outweigh some of the too easy effect of folk diction, including the reveling in facile comic grossness. More important, the poem never does quite close in on the precise character of what the returning "you" is burdened with or seeking out. One can almost feel the influence of Eliot's essay on *Hamlet* in the search for that inexpressible something which is felt to be symbolized in the grotesque horror of the story. Even the use of "you" when the poet really means "I" suggests a fear of closing in on the protagonist's identity and an attempt to elude the issue by universalizing the not quite clarified motivations behind the poem. But suppose the rest of us decline the pronominal gambit?

We find the same ambiguous pronoun throughout the *Selected Poems*. The poem "Terror," for instance, uses it to involve us all in the speaker's sense that the political and technological violence of our era seduces us toward the expiation (or rediscovery) of our secret guilt. "Original Sin: A Short Story" (notice how much of a piece many of these titles are; "Crime" is another; "Letter from a Coward to a Hero" another) suggests a Calvinist correlative to what is seen to be the inevitable wound of the primal psyche, the "nightmare" that wanders distractedly through the soul "like a mother who rises at night to seek a childhood picture" or that, kept at bay, "goes to the backyard and stands like an old horse cold in the pasture." There is a strange appeal, one is almost flattered, to be included in the company of the subtly suffering merely for being one of this poet's readers, and these poems all have passages of bleakness that do indeed evoke the starkness and the finality (a form of commitment) of the antihuman:

Envy the mad killer who lies in the ditch and grieves . . .
("Crime")

. . . . lunar wolf-waste or the arboreal
Malignancy, with the privy breath, which watches
And humps in the dark . . .
("Terror")

These are fine lines, but the intended overlay of significance is unearned, because the speaker refuses to give the game away concretely about himself, preferring merely to hint at moral anguish rooted in familial matters. Hence there is a certain degree of sentimentality in most of the poems before 1943. Only one of these poems, "Bearded Oaks," carries us in fact to a perfectly well-earned resolution. Here the mystical sense of place that is invoked, like that in Donne's "The Ecstasy," leads to a remarkable self-transcendence and to a final state of insight blessedly free of any insistence on our assent to unstated propositions. One can but wish that Mr. Warren could have developed as a lyric poet along the lines indicated in this poem. The influence of Donne and Marvell may well have been decisive for its formal movement, but is well assimilated into a finally rich and original structure. Elsewhere in *Selected Poems*, various other influences, mainly modern, such as Hardy, Auden, Stevens, Ransom, and Eliot are as clearly visible but not as well assimilated because the poems themselves, as I have been trying to show, are but tentatively resolved.

A full decade later we have the long dramatic narrative poem *Brother to Dragons*. Much of the murkiness and unfocused subjectivity has now been externalized away, apparently as a result of the author's experience as a writer of fiction. However, he is still attempting the great transference implied in his earlier use of "you" for "I." He reads the dark, sadistic perversion of spirit of his protagonist, Lilburn Lewis, nephew of Thomas Jefferson, into society at large and into the Jeffersonian meaning in particular. Perhaps the most absurd and touching aspect of all this is the poet's setting himself up in this poem as Jefferson's peer, discussing the meaning of Lilburn's crimes with him and actually getting him, both through what Jefferson explicitly says and through structural implication, to deny his own premises and political faith. The disappointment and suicide of Meriwether Lewis, Jefferson's cousin who opened up the Louisiana Territory with Clark and later became governor of the Territory, are employed to the same rhetorical purpose. The whole poem is marked by clarity and by its dramatic insight into the relations of Lilburn with his wife, his brother, and his slaves. In these scenes, the poet keys himself up most intensely in presenting Lilburn's vileness both in its own right and as a clue to the pessimistic view of human corruptibility with which Jeffersonian optimism is to be confounded. In a strictly poetic sense, the poem lacks much interest except as an illustration that a long poem, fairly straightforward in its presentation and banking on a conventional five-stress line, can still win our attention and respect. As a psycho-political essay it carries considerable interest, as much for what it reveals about Southern white attitudes toward the Negro as for its intellectual wrestling match with Jefferson.

Coming down to the two recent volumes of poetry, *Promises* (1957) and *You, Emperors, and Others* (1960), both of which return to the shorter lyric poem as their main form, we find very few traces of the earlier confusions of style. The new clarity is signaled by an unabashed use of the first person singular, by poems of uncomplicated nostalgia, and by efforts at affirmation. "Court-martial" is perhaps the best poem of Mr. Warren's that fastens its attention on physical terror. This time the poet recalls a conversation with his grandfather, once a Confederate soldier. The grandfather explains who bushwackers were in the Civil War and justifies the summary way in which they were hanged when caught. The horrified boy has a vision of the old man as a young soldier and of his (and the world's) victims:

Calmly then, out of the sky,
Blotting the sun's blazing eye,
He rode. He was large in the sky.
Behind, shadow massed, slow, and grew
Like cloud on the sky's summer blue.
Out of that shade-mass he drew.
To the great saddle's sway, he swung,
Not old now, not old now, but young,
Great cavalry boots to the thigh,
No speculation in eye.
Then clotting behind him, and dim,
Clot by clot, from the shadow behind him,
They took shape, enormous in air.
Behind him, enormous, they hung there. . . .

It is enough, but there is still another stanza, to describe the faces of the hanged, as they appeared in the mind's eye of the boy; and then another stanza, in which the horseman is seen riding "blank-eyed" toward the boy "through the darkening air." A slight belaboring of the point, to show how the imagined youthful grandfather has become the intractable, overwhelming objective world. And then, to fasten the point absolutely, a final, one-line stanza:

The world is real. It is there.

These easily sustained couplets and triplets, these rather Yeatsian four-stress lines with their fairly straightforward phrasing and syntax, may be favorably compared with the sort of writing to be found in most of *Selected Poems:*

Never met you in the lyric arsenical meadow
When children call and your heart goes stone in the bosom—
At the orchard anguish never, nor ovoid horror,
Which is furred like a peach or avid like the delicious plum.
It takes no part in your classic prudence or fondled axiom.
("Original Sin: A Short Story")

Stylistically, Mr. Warren has "come through" to a certain extent, but it has involved accepting the limitations of his poetic vision. He still tries to impose a profundity of a kind by adding something to the initial "givens" of the poem, as at the end of "Court-martial" he provides his final turns to show that the boy will be one of the victims of the world, that the cruel abstracted soldier who comes riding toward him is evidence of the actual existence of objective reality (which thus becomes an ineluctably hostile fact). Contrariwise, in poems like "Gull's Cry" and "Brightness of Distance," he adds a note of insistent hopefulness with which we are reluctant to quarrel for fear of hurting his, and our own, feelings, especially after the plain human sympathy that each of these poems establishes. Some of the recent poems are equally, and beautifully, plain in their nostalgia for the world of the poet's childhood—"Country Burying," "Hands Are Paid"; and the elegiac note, especially in the "Mortmain" sequence, about the death of the poet's father, is of the same order. Yet the new purity is not quite dependable. There are emptily lugubrious pieces, and pieces that derive a cheap energy from a manically antic tone (like an alcoholic diabetic), and pieces that have no vital energy at all.

Robert Penn Warren, then, is a poet of real interest who set himself a greater task initially than he has quite been able to carry out. Despite his lyric and elegiac talents, he has not usually been able to summon up the necessary resources to bring the larger body of his poetry to the pitch of realization. In ridding himself of the knotty ambiguities and anguished struggle for expression of his earlier work, he has lost as well as gained. The divine pathos of "Bearded Oaks," a poem that promised some higher reconciliation of metaphysical and lyric aims and that reached a point of articulate originality of phrasing and of metaphorical extensions that no other poet could have reached in the same way, has received no further cultivation, and indeed it is remarkable that a poet who could write this poem could also let himself down so often. There is little question that in general he shows himself most effective in narrative poetry that exposes man's most vicious possibilities, but the naked implications of this unhappy vision have been too drastic for him to let them stand by themselves. The result is that he has not been able to push consistently in the direction of grim exploration his special talent points to, nor has he been able to abandon it and explore fruitfully the richer indications of his metaphysical bent, as in "Bearded Oaks." Too often, in any case, he stands between us and the poem, commenting, leaping frenziedly through buffooneries of speech and characterization, promoting insights that are unearned by the poems themselves. For all this, he remains poet enough—to the ear, to the visual imagination, to the emotions and sensibility—to make one feel rueful at doing anything but reading him with as much sympathy as he allows.

The South Atlantic Quarterly (Autumn 1963)

from *Surrender to Despair*

THE BURNING PERCH by Louis MacNeice

I FIND it impossible to read the last poems of Louis MacNeice, who died in September at the age of 55, without a special sense of something premonitory in them. There is plenty of the old vigor, sharp observation and riddling wit, but the essential morale is turning morbid. About five of the poems are specifically preoccupied with death; the most imaginative of these, "The Grey Ones"—about the Fates—has the ultimate depression that comes with a frustrated conviction of the tautology of human meanings. This depression, which perhaps it would be wrong to attribute to a weakening of the poet's life-energies, is prevented from coming to a dead halt of weary realization only by the tried weapons of his fine variety of style.

It comes perilously close to such a halt, however, in the interesting sequence of self-contained five-line stanzas called "As in Their Time." Here we are very near total letdown, were it not for the poet's dauntless feeling for the spirited handling of language. He does not quite hold off spiritual surrender, but he does surrender to his despair with almost triumphant style. The vital, unsentimental phrasing is what he pays out to us to allow him to keep his sickened vision almost private. As Charon says in the most explicit of the death poems, "If you want to die you will have to pay for it."

Usually the death sense in these poems carries beyond the speaking self to the age as well. A tainted age, a spoiled world—the argument is fully set out in the long "Memoranda to Horace," a poem in which MacNeice exactly approaches the bitter spirit of Pound's "Hugh Selwyn Mauberley." "Funerary urns from the Supermarket" betoken our day, and for posterity the bleak, plain prospect is of "one's life restricted to standing room only" in a society for which the poetry of the past will be a monument "weaker and of less note" than "a quick blurb for yesterday's detergent." A fierce disgust blazes forth in other poems along the same lines, such as the elegiac "Goodbye to London" and the suicidal "In Lieu."

With all this harshness and pain, MacNeice's last poems display undiminished his keen eye and the humorous, sometimes pawkily whimsical imagination that have always marked his style. These qualities brighten such delightful pieces as "October in Bloomsbury" and "The Taxis" and lend the darker poems a surprisingly livelier surface than one would expect. After the death of a poet, of course, we begin as it were to hear his voice for the first time in all its essential, lonely bravery. Whatever the reason, *The Burning Perch* seems to me now the most moving and most keenly vivid of MacNeice's later volumes.

New York Times Book Review (22 December 1963)

Prospect of Delight

COLLECTED POEMS by Horace Gregory

"DO I have to prove I can sell anything?" cries the indignant speaker in Horace Gregory's "Four Monologues from *The Passion of M'Phail.*" The speaker is very different from Horace Gregory himself, yet the rhetorical question might be rephrased to apply to the peculiar course of this poet's own career. I have long admired his work and wondered at its uncertain reputation, which glows from time to time and then seems to fade away. You would not think he had to prove anything—shouldn't anyone capable of simple delight in language find many of Gregory's lines unforgettable? The ones, for instance, about

> seeing a girl step, white and glittering as a fountain,
> into cool evening air,
> knowing you could not touch her,
> nor dare to still the floating, flawless motion
> of that pale dress above its glancing knees. . . .

Gregory's work is certainly acknowledged; see almost any good anthology, from Harriet Monroe's *The New Poetry* to the present day. Yet no poet of comparable distinction is less known to the general reader. The reasons are doubtless the self-evident ones. He belongs to no school or clique. His career both as writer and as teacher has involved a dauntless, even heroic struggle against ill health, and he has had no time, if he were so inclined, for those public readings by which reputations are sometimes enhanced. Amid all the noise of literary politics, he has worked quietly ahead, hardly noticed even when, from time to time, he does receive some award or honor.

His work is not in the least sensational or exhibitionistic. And now that he has brought out his *Collected Poems* at the age of sixty-six, we can see more clearly than before that many of his best poems have been intense, concentrated, and very self-contained; enduring, yet slight and hard to keep in view; quick trout in cold, almost silent streams. Sensuality and violence are often present in these poems, yet are used not as weapons against the reader but as the raw material of the poet's sensibility. After all, "classical restraint" does imply something to be restrained. The protagonist of "McAlpin Garfinkel, Poet," an early piece, explains:

> It is enough for me to tremble,
> my vital organs directed toward the sun,
> toward the stars,
> trembling.

It is better for me to stand at street corners
staring at women, seeing their bodies flowering
like new continents, hills warm in sunshine and
long deep rivers,
(even as I am,
trembling)
than to be nothing, to fade away in grass and stone.

Another aspect of Gregory's elusive yet passionate presence lies in his talent for assimilating the methods of other poets without losing his own voice in the process. Far more than most young poets of high promise, he showed this talent in his important first book, *Chelsea Rooming House* (1930). Thus, the passage just quoted is a curious derivation from both Masters and Lawrence. Another poem recalls "Prufrock," another, those wryly whimsical pieces of Sandburg's built around bits of casual slang. Only a hint remains, after all the winnowing and rearrangement, of the uncertainties and unevenness of the original 1930 volume. Its best poem, "Longface Mahoney Discusses Heaven," now leads off the entire collection. Nothing could show more beautifully how Gregory accepted the poet's task of being both spontaneous and "academic"—of absorbing experience and the living idiom freshly into his work while learning what he can from the whole poetic tradition. The monologue of Longface presents a derelict's reveries and gives us, simultaneously, the pathetic clichés of vulgar imagination and a subtle rendering of the speaker's inmost feeling:

If someone said, Escape,
let's get away from here,
you'd see snow mountains. . . .

Throughout the poem, Longface himself is banal in his sub-Romantic dream of paradise. First he imagines the freedom of high mountains, then the joys of the tropics, with "a row of girls dancing on a beach," and at last a room of his own with a brass bed and a girl of his own. He lingers over this minimal vision of a paradise "where marriage nights are kept," and then his thought goes full circle like Keats's in the nightingale poem. The last stanza is a peculiarly urban, deadbeat version of Romantic despair:

If you've done something
and the cops get you afterwards, you
can't remember the place again. . . .

"Longface Mahoney" illustrates Gregory's gift for coloring the objective element unifying one of his poems (a dramatic speaker, a transcendent symbol, a physical scene) with his own essentially elegiac pigments. The objective presentation—for instance, that of the bum in this poem dreaming pessimistically of escape—will have its own life, but within it the poet's inwardly rooted feeling shapes a more private realization. Often the speaker is an alienated or rejected character—beggar, salesman *manqué,* carrier of lost traditions. The poet identifies himself with him and yet keeps himself apart, as if to preserve intact his own sensibility, containing it rather than expressing it. His instinct to hold apart some vital private meaning was possibly encouraged by his struggle, in the late 1920s and in the 1930s, to resist the strong pressures toward political tendentiousness, and by the parallel need, oddly, to resist also the overwhelming effects of his interest in Latin poetry. (His early translation of Catullus and his recent work with Ovid have clearly left their impress on his own writing.)

It is interesting to see how, in the poems included from the early 1930s, the intrusively tendentious elements are overborne as it were—though not often completely assimilated—by a powerful advance in ability to handle pure sound, learned from the whole lyrical tradition. In "*The Meek Shall Disinherit the Earth*," the dominant voice is that of a half-forgotten older poet whom a younger man has come to visit. There are some stylistic echoes from "Portrait of a Lady," but instead of Eliot's abrupt transitions and preoccupation with a specific and difficult relationship between the two figures in the poem, the progression is direct and more musical than dramatic or psychological. Even the most objective moments of self-characterization unfold quite simply:

> "I sometimes feel that I have lived forever in this room:
> the rent unpaid, yet I am fed and watered
> like a geranium on that window sill—
> by landlady, charwoman, or foolish girl
> who disappears at noon
> leaving her alms behind. . . .
>
> No, I'm not bitter: I am always friendly.
> I always threaten meekness everywhere,
> my face the preternaturally calm
> forgiving smile. . . ."

In these lines the rhythmic play of rhetoric, which had been expansive, is momentarily minimized, but later it expands again to end the poem, not with a dramatic gesture or psychological nuance but with the music, paradoxically triumphant, of cosmic melancholy:

> "Last night I saw a flame
> pour out of darkness over eastern heavens:
> the earth had perished on the farther shore,
> an ocean wilderness on either hand . . .
> the sound of the sea shall be my requiem."

The poet seems to have discovered the voice of his full maturity with what are now the first and fourth poems of the *Passion of M'Phail* sequence, originally published in *Poems 1930–1940*. These poems still stand as the embodiment of the very idiosyncratic Gregorian method. Witty, sad, incredibly vigorous, sardonic at odd moments, they are the work of a blazing intelligence. Of their kind, they are surpassed only by "The Beggar on the Beach," in *Selected Poems* (1951). I should pause for a moment, too, over "Opera, Opera!"

which appeared in the same 1951 volume and is among our finest examples of Gregory's artistry. Written a half dozen years or so before his magnificent translation of Ovid's *Metamorphoses*, it foreshadows that work in its freely varied imagery as it rings the changes on the theme of appearance, reality, and imagination in their relations to one another. The poem is centered on a clear-seeming focal symbol, a pair of archetypal opera glasses, through which patrons see far more than what goes on before the usual audience at a performance. Through them, a whole series of related symbols and associations is concretely deployed. Sets and backdrops, singers in and out of their roles, the mythical parts they play and the myths behind those parts, and finally, by a daring yet casual redirection of the lenses, the constellations, all of history, and the universe are brought into tragic perspective:

> In the Green Room he saw
> The woman who was once Eurydice,
> Naked as Eve with Adam at her side,
> Kiss the reflection of her lips within a mirror.
> It was then he noticed that the house was empty,
> That the galleries were dark and all the faces gone.
> It was as though he had fallen into a cave,
> And he felt the invisible shadow of Anubis
> Walk through the aisles. . . .

I feel somewhat ridiculous about attempting to introduce this well-established poet to readers. In doing so, I realize, I have neglected his most recent work. The important thing is that a fine, sensitive, original voice, a spirit at once generous and fastidious, sophisticated and energetic, has long been among us, and that we now have the opportunity to read in a single volume one of the most interesting bodies of poems to be made available to us in some years.

The Reporter (10 September 1964)

Poets of Academe

AT a wild symposium some time ago in New York's Poetry Center, a young Beat writer looked at the sensitive, mobile features of one of our most sophisticatedly experimentalist poets and shouted that he could not possibly be a poet—he just did not *look* like one. It was hard to tell just what in the older man had produced this outburst. His good manners? his cleanliness? his *glasses?* Surely not his poems, which would be the only dependable indication of whether he looks like a poet or not. My guess is that it was the fact that he was a professor that offended his accuser, who took the opportunity later on to suggest that the entire professoriat had latched on to a kind of sinecure, a lifelong mass-grant with plenty of money, no duties and no inspiration.

Now I am a professor myself, with many years of teaching behind me, and so my reaction (irritated amusement) is both natural and suspect. To me it seems obvious, though, that some people, having once found their own studies tedious and gray, do not understand the satisfactions or agonies of the academic experience. They do not realize that it is but one form, but a real and vital form for all that, which mature experience can take. They think it inimical to the creative spirit, although many poets are teachers and their poetry does not seem diminished thereby. I have just, in fact, finished preparing an anthology of American and British poetry since the last war. It contains work by 105 poets of every group and tendency, among them Beat, Black Mountain, Sixties, and confessional poets in this country, and "Movement" and "Group" poets and their opponents in Britain. In reviewing the availble information about these people, I find that at least 41 of them are full-time professional teachers, mostly at universities, and that at least 23 more are occasional or former teachers.

Whether this situation is good or bad for poets and poetry has almost become one of those set debating topics. To my mind, the statistics are more significant sociologically than artistically. What they show is that schools are to some extent a source of livelihood for poets, most of whom are after all suited for teaching through their love of language, their interest in ideas, and their humane sympathies. In another sense, the topic, as an *issue*, is irrelevant because the situation, like the poetry itself, is an expression of our moment in time, and because the individual poets concerned are so different from one another. I am sure that the motives of Robert Lowell in teaching are quite different from those of Donald Davie, who is a scholar and professor in the most complete meanings of those words. Mr. Lowell communicates well as a teacher, I understand, and has had a marked influence on the development of some younger poets whom he has taught; and I would suppose that his teaching satisfies important needs of his prodigious psychic energies, which present themselves so explosively in his poems.

Mr. Davie, at the University of Essex in England, writes with a certain cool, "scholarly" intellectuality and rigorous self-control. It would be tricky, however, to relate these qualities directly to his academic career. Probably they were deeply imbedded in his nature long before he decided to become a professor. Another tricky instance is that of the English poet Charles Tomlinson, who teaches at the University of Bristol. His poems reveal a sophisticated study of French and American models. But the knowledge is a *poet's* knowledge, acquired through a quite unacademic struggle to free himself of the comfortable laxness that has rotted so much current British poetry, by academic and non-academic authors alike.

More obviously, the gnarled and diffident and half anti-intellectual writing of the American poet-professor Robert Creeley or the rhetorical, satyr-posing, bourgeois-shocking writing of the Canadian Irving Layton will demonstrate at once how far apart a poet's adult vocation (by which he earns his bread, I mean) and the springs of his art must needs be.

The universities are hardly hotbeds of poets. For all the talk of encouraging creative people, there is precious little actually done, especially as the problem is a bit elusive in an institutional setting. To reach the higher professorial ranks (in the United States at least), the doctorate is still almost indispensable, and only a tiny number of poets have undertaken the necessary discipline:

> Poems are made by fools like me,
> But not while studying for the Ph.D.

Nevertheless, a certain number of colleges do make allowance for the poet's special abilities. Some of them, such as Iowa and Oregon, have highly developed special programs for writers. Some, like Dartmouth here or Leeds in England, have "resident poets." Some, like New York University, employ professional writers to teach composition. Some, like Bennington, choose their faculties as much as possible from the actively creative community. And there are all sorts of "exceptional cases" tucked away everywhere.

The real danger of this situation, I think, is not that some people will find themselves growing artistically timid, or dulled in sensibility, because of their academic experience. The danger, rather, is that the true poet—whose need to write is too fierce and idiosyncratic to be tamed all that easily—will turn his attention too exclusively to his work of teaching. The tasks of teaching assert themselves powerfully because they are unavoidably regular in their scheduling and because they are so *interesting*. They make for an intense, arduous life full of compelling deadlines and challenges and of significant personal relationships. There are temperaments that can manage this life fairly readily and combine it with that of the artist without too much violence to themselves and there are those that cannot do so.

Of course, *academic* is a dirty word in poetic circles. It *ought* to be, if it is used to disparage work that is tamely formal or pedantic, or that is a slavish exemplar of some established orthodoxy. Just a few days ago, a Scottish "Concretist" poet both amazed me and made me wince on my country's behalf by using the word in just this sense. He preferred American to British academic poetry, he said, because it was better constructed. As if, at this level, the question at all mattered! My own tastes are such that I have always, perhaps unjustly, been more interested in the poetry that storms and dreams past known boundaries than in the poetry that seeks to perfect itself within them. Nevertheless, anyone who does not know how to love the rich values of the latter kind of writing, and who does not remain alert to the deceptive originality and discoveries it may well embody, will not be able to understand the truly new either.

Behind the more blatant dislike of such work by people whose idea of poetry is purely external—to whom any junkie or hipster looks more "poetic" than a man quietly writing—lies the subtler contemporary tendency to discredit the whole creative meaning of the humanistic tradition. The grove outside Athens where Plato taught has the associations of this tradition, and of the pleasures of sweetly philosophical musings and reverie as well as of learning. It was called Academe.

The New York Times Book Review (7 March 1965)

Poets of the Dangerous Way

FOR THE UNION DEAD by Robert Lowell
ARIEL by Sylvia Plath

THE important news is that Robert Lowell, the chief figure of the "confessional" movement in American poetry, has begun to leave its methods behind. The poems in his *Life Studies* (1959) presented Lowell himself so vulnerably and humiliatingly that only his extraordinary artistic gifts enabled him to transcend the hysteria behind them. But the transcendence made for a revolutionary achievement. It encouraged other such poets as Anne Sexton, John Berryman and the late Sylvia Plath to take the same dangerous road. Lowell, working sophisticatedly in a direct line from various earlier masters, including the young Eliot and Hart Crane, catapulted his own, literal self into the centre of his poems and thereby brought the familiar themes of a betrayed civilisation and alienated psyche into startling new focus.

Now, in *For the Union Dead*, we can see that for him at least there is a further way, closer to the "main stream." It seems impossible to maintain indefinitely the violent pace of *Life Studies*. To do so would be to cultivate a poetry that fed on, and encouraged, suicidal madness. Instead, beyond a certain point at least, Lowell has been working free of the intolerable burden of his self-laceration. The problem is to hold on meanwhile to what he has gained in poetic conception (the painfully alert sensibility alive to the pressure of its own anxieties and those of the age) and in its embodiment in a brilliantly improvised formal technique. We can see now how invaluable his translations from poets like Montale and Pasternak have been for him, in their own right and also in helping him isolate certain qualities of the earlier work—the wry irony and humour, for instance—and use them in new ways. Thus the boisterous poem to his first wife, "The Old Flame," is really for him a *gay* poem in spite of its picture of the tormented couple's "quivering and fierce" life in Maine, "simmering like wasps/in our tent of books." At the same time, he can project as beautifully as ever that peculiar identification of inward anguish with the public ills of the nuclear age that is the idiom of his genius:

Our end drifts nearer,
the moon lifts,
radiant with terror. . . .

A father's no shield
for his child.
We are like a lot of wild
spiders crying together,
but without tears. . . .

But I would note especially the poems in which something "quieter" is going on, among them "Water," "The Mouth of the Hudson," "The Lesson," "Law," "The Severed Head" and "The Flaw." In many of these everything is put into the concentrated evocation of a scene, within which is locked a tragically relevant personal and historical complex of meaning as well. Perhaps the single most original and surprising piece is the biazarre dream-poem "The Severed Head," with its overtones from Crane's "Passage" (his greatest short poem) and from the "familiar compound ghost" episode in "Little Gidding." The poetic courage of these new explorations in search of greater impersonality, and the variety and excitement of the poems as they hit us one by one, again suggest that Lowell is *the* American poet of this age.

Sylvia Plath, with her narrower range of technical resource and objective awareness than Lowell's, and with her absolute, almost demonically intense commitment by the end to the confessional mode, took what seems to me the one alternative advance position open to her. Only a few poems in her first book, *The Colossus* (1960), hint that she was destined to fulfil the implied suicidal programme of irreversible anguish beyond his limits. She was only thirty when, two years later, she threw herself into that last passionate burst of writing that culminated in *Ariel* and in her death, now forever inseparable. We shall never be able to sort out clearly the unresolved, unbearably exposed suggestibility and agitation of these poems from the purely aesthetic energy that shaped the best of them. Reading "Daddy" or "Fever 103°," you would say that if a poet is sensitive enough to the age and brave enough to face it directly it will kill him through the exacerbation of his awareness alone. Sometimes Sylvia Plath could not distinguish between herself and the facts of, say, Auschwitz or Hiroshima. She was victim, killer, and the place and process of horror all at once.

This is not the whole picture. Though Sylvia Plath may become a legend, we ought not to indulge in over-simplification. There are some lovely poems in the book ("Poppies in October," for instance) that are cries of joy despite a grim note or two. There is rhythmic experimentation looking to the future, in particular with an adaptation of Whitman's characteristic line; and beyond that, the sheer wild leap into absolute mastery of phrasing and the dynamics of poetic movement in the title-poem alone, despite its tragic dimension, cannot but be considered an important kind of affirmation. But there are poems too that are hard to penetrate in their morbid secretiveness, or that make a weirdly incantatory black magic against unspecified persons and situations, and these often seem to call for biographical rather than poetic explanation.

Under all the other motifs, however, is the confusion of terror at death with fascination by it. The visions of the speaker as already dead are so vivid that they become yearnings toward that condition. "Death & Co." is one of several nearly perfect embodiments of this deeply compulsive motif. It moves from a revolted imagery of death as a condor-like predator, a connoisseur of the beauty of dead babies, to a disgusted yet erotic picture of him as would-be lover, and at last to a vision of the speaker's own death such as I have mentioned:

I do not stir.
The frost makes a flower,
The dew makes a star,
The dead bell,
The dead bell.

Somebody's done for.

Thinking of this pitifully brief career, it is hard not to ask whether the cultivation of sensibility is after all worth the candle. The answer is yes, for reasons that I hope we all know—yet it seems important to raise the question anyway.

Spectator (19 March 1965)

❧

The Couch and Poetic Insight

THE FAR FIELD by Theodore Roethke
77 DREAM SONGS by John Berryman

I AM not sure how well Theodore Roethke's memory has been served by the publication of his very uneven last poems, which he had been readying for the press when he died in August, 1963. The poems are touching in at least two ways. First, they refer to his illness and seem aware of imminent death, though he was only fifty-five or younger when they were written. Second, behind their assumption of an achieved, transcendent quietude lies a deeper impression of inability to cope with the old, still unresolved hysteria that Roethke unloosed in his earlier work and of a consequent resort to the stock cosmic pieties of sagedom from Chuang-tzu on down. As V. S. Pritchett has written in another context, "It is often noticeable that tormented writers who seek a synthesis end by falling into self-complacency." This was indeed noticeable in Roethke long ago, in the poetic sequences of his early forties in which the characteristic structure was based on a progression of psychological states, more or less Freudian in their conception. "The Lost Son," for instance, took us from the stage of raw terror at the demands of actual life—the brutality of nature and of death, the challenge of adult sexuality—through a phase of self-repossession by accepting the father's daily world and so onward to a final, calmly affirmative, but really unearned resolution.

It is this last stage, unfortunately, at which Roethke was arrested in the poems of *The Far Field*, his posthumous volume. The vital tension had retreated some distance, leaving the poems free to attempt something like joyous acceptance of things as they are, immersion in nature in the old Romantic sense—that is, before Keats gave it the special modern twist of being a projection of man's own tragic paradoxicality. Sometimes Roethke almost achieved what he was after, notably in "Meditation at Oyster River" and "I Waited": a certain delicate precision, a light-spirited seriousness such as we are told the early Christians possessed, a sweetness of spirit deriving from a literal rendering of minutiae of nature and accepting their meaning wherever it may lead. But generally, even in the long, ambitious "Meditation at Oyster River," the work is marred by verbosity, clichés, and derivativeness. (Yeats, Whitman, Eliot, Dickinson, Crane—this sort of thing was always one of Roethke's besetting weaknesses.) But he was a real poet, and this volume had many lovely effects and interesting passages even though the poems as a whole failed of realization. He still had great tasks ahead.

Roethke came into his own as a poet in his group of short "greenhouse poems" published in 1948. (You will find them, with most of his other work before the present volume, in *Words for the Wind,* the collected edition of 1958.) After a weak start as a conventionally competent versifier, he made his essential artistic advance in these pieces. He had discovered, apparently simultaneously, that his great source of energy was his own uncontrolled, riotous psyche—he called it "the muck and welter, the dark, the *dreck*"—and that his youthful experience around his father's greenhouse in Michigan provided just the vivid, squirmingly uncomfortable, and concrete focus his poetry needed to channel and concentrate this emotional tumult. The equally exuberant and disgusted earthiness of these poems, their close relationship with plants and the slimy sublife of slugs and other such creatures, is unique. Although his later work sometimes carries forth their Rabelaisan gusto (see, for instance, "Give Way, Ye Gates" in the collected volume) and presents searching moments of psychological association, and though it can jolt us by its pure manic recklessness or its painfully gross and disturbing dejection, it seldom carries through with the same absolute conviction. One reason, no doubt, is the greater ambitiousness of the later work.

More important is the fact that for the most part Roethke had no subject apart from the excitements, illnesses, intensities of sensuous response, and inexplicable shiftings of his own sensibility. The greenhouse poems enabled him to objectify it for a time, but then he had nowhere to go but back inside himself. We have no other modern American poet of comparable reputation who has absorbed so little of the concerns of his times into his nerve-ends, in whom there is so little reference direct or remote to the character and experiences of the age—unless the damaged psyche out of which he spoke be taken as its very embodiment. But that was not quite enough. The confessional mode, reduced to this kind of self-recharging, becomes redundant and uses itself up after the first wild orgies of feeling. We are left, at best, with a thin exhausted bitterness or desire to be cheerful:

> The way grew steeper between stony walls,
> Then lost itself down through a rocky gorge.
> A donkey path led to a small plateau.
> Below, the bright sea was, the level waves,
> And all the winds came toward me. I was glad.

JOHN Berryman, in his *77 Dream Songs*, seriously enters the postwar current of confessional poetry. The general features of this kind of poetry—as represented especially in the writing of Robert Lowell but also in a number of his followers such as Anne Sexton, W. D. Snodgrass, and now Berryman—are that it not only makes use of private anguish and psychological disturbance but actually exploits them through putting them forward nakedly, and to some degree exhibitionistically, as the poet's predominant theme. In most of the new confessional poetry an exact correlation is suggested between the poet's private predicaments and those of the nation and the culture at large. Berryman is the first poet (except Allen Ginsberg, whom he resembles more than he would like to think, perhaps, but whose writing is essentially of a different cast) to pick up Mr. Lowell's cues on so sweeping a scale. The genius of the latter poet lies partly in his having that quality so conspicuously lacking in Roethke, of having absorbed "the concerns of his age into his nerve-ends." But he has shown a terrible courage, as well, in the way he speaks in his own person, and of course there is the pure force and virtuosity of his art. We must respect Berryman's effort to match this achievement in his own way.

The *77 Dream Songs* were perhaps foreshadowed in the tension of *The Dispossessed* (1948), and in the special quality of his repossession of (and identification with) the psyche of the seventeenth-century poet Anne Bradstreet in *Homage to Mistress Bradstreet* (1956). In this latter book, with its high pitch of intensity, Mr. Berryman presents a kind of dialogue between himself and the woman poet in which their voices sometimes merge, and in an important sense the effect is of two voices of a divided self. The technique involved is carried forward in the *Dream Songs,* but this time the character Henry and the other voices are literally of this nature. "Unappeasable Henry" and the "I" of the poem and other voices, often including strong infusions of vaudeville and plantation Negro dialect, are all facets of the central sensibility.

In this device, and in presenting his book as "one version, of a poem in progress," as well as in giving the reader various leads and allusions to be worked on through research on Berryman's private life and reading, he resembles Ezra Pound. But since the element of innovation here is truly minimal, and since the quality of Berryman's art does not really make him the Pound to Lowell's Eliot, we may decline that part of his gambit which invites us to consider the book a major work and may view it rather as a collection of lyric and dramatic poems all in basically the same form (three six-line stanzas of varying rhyme scheme and line lengths). It then becomes a modern equivalent of the traditional sonnet sequence, with a few nuggets of gold among the lesser pieces, with much wit and interest but offering no real justification intrinsically for further development. It is "in progress" in the sense that it would benefit considerably from rigorous reduction and revision, but that is the lot of all poets, especially of compulsively self-repetitive ones.

Of these seventy-seven poems, then, perhaps a score stand out from the rest, two of them (Poems 29 and 53) supremely. These two poems are so much epitomes of what is best in this book that one might almost say—but it would be wrong—that they render the rest superfluous. Poem 29 begins on a deeply moving and beautiful note, stating private misery and unlocatable guilt in the most immediate, humanly available manner; and it realizes itself perfectly:

There sat down, once, a thing on Henry's heart
só heavy, if he had a hundred years
& more, & weeping, sleepless, in all them time
Henry could not make good.
Starts again always in Henry's ears
the little cough somewhere, an odour, a chime.

And there is another thing he has in mind
like a grave Sienese face a thousand years
would fail to blur the still profiled approach of. Ghastly,
with open eyes, he attends, blind.
All the bells say: too late. This is not for tears;
thinking.

But never did Henry, as he thought he did,
end anyone and hacks her body up
and hide the pieces, where they may be found.
He knows: he went over everyone, & nobody's missing.
Often he reckons, in the dawn, them up.
Nobody is ever missing.

Faint echoes of other poets touch these lines—Hopkins and Eliot mostly, yet without the intrusiveness of some others among the *Dream Songs*. It is the essential predicament of the speaker that is presented here, and even the Lowell-like final line does not violate the poem's purity. A fine gift for distorting syntax for emphasis and yet holding onto the clarity of his sentences is one of Berryman's chief stylistic strengths. What is elsewhere a slightly offensive buffoonery in the use of Negro dialect, and a probably unwarranted assumption that the griefs of the Negro and the griefs of Berryman are aspects of one another, becomes in a few poems like this one a wry effect of childlike vulnerability—"in all them time," "end anyone and hacks her body up." Even the elsewhere often gimmicky "&" contributes to this effect by helping to compress the statement and make it look less formal. Poem 53, which takes off, as it were, where this one leaves off—"He lay in the middle of the world, and twitcht"—gives us what might be called the social and cultural correlative of this private condition. It is a poem about the compulsion to shut out what cannot be shut out, the "outside world":

Kiekegaard wanted a society, to refuse to read 'papers,
and that was not, friends, his worst idea.
Tiny Hardy, toward the end, refused to say *anything*,
a programme adopted early on by long Housman,
and Gottfried Benn
said:—We are using our own skins for wallpaper and we cannot win.

This poem, as so often here, modulates clearly toward the familiar theme of the *poète maudit*. But unlike, say, Poem I, it neither sentimentalizes the theme nor oversimplifies it. Nor, as so many of these pieces do, does it commandeer political themes facilely or fashionably. (See, for example, the easy satire on Eisenhower in Poem 23, or the presumed identification with the Jews of the Warsaw ghetto in Poem 41, or the comment on America's betrayal of Jefferson's meanings in the incantatory Poem 22.) There are many aspects of the book I have neglected—the elegiac group on Frost, the poems about sexual desire, the various autobiographical and self-analytical notations, and so on—which cast a good deal of light on this poet's admirable range and flexibility, and on his own motives and the attitudes of literary and intellectual circles with whom he is associated. A longer essay would be required to sort out the real thing from the attitudinizing and elite-gossipy chaff. But even this brief close-up may suggest that, whatever individually poignant and accomplished poems it may still bring to us, the confessional movement as a startling new factor in our art may be just about played out, or more accurately, may now be beginning to be absorbed and taken for granted as part of the extremely varied new poetic scene. With that development comes the danger that its practitioners may in the future be overindulging themselves if they think that every nuance of suffering brought out on the couch or in reverie is a mighty flood of poetic insight, or the key to a new aesthetic.

The Reporter (25 March 1965)

❧

Smailliw Solrac Mailliw (William Carlos Williams Backward)

THE COLLECTED LATER POEMS by William Carlos Williams

I WISH there were some kind of chronological mirror-reading one could devise to undo the effects of the way William Carlos Williams is being published in England. Of all the myriad ironies of his career—and the fact that arrangements for his first British publication were not announced until the day of his funeral in 1963 surely ranks high among them—the counter-chronological order of his posthumous presentation to this country may be the weirdest. Last year we had *Pictures from Brueghel* and *Paterson*. The former volume collects his books of shorter poems printed after 1950—that is, between his sixty-seventh birthday and his death at seventy-nine. The latter volume is a long sequence begun during the last War and continued at odd intervals over the whole final period. Now we have *The Collected Later Poems*, taken mostly from books originally printed between 1944 and 1950, and we are promised *The Collected Earlier Poems* for some time in the future.

Truth to tell, I am so happy to see Williams finally becoming known in England that I am unwilling to remain frozen in this indignant, jaw-dropped attitude. Behind the situation, I am sure, are quite understandable publishing considerations of the kind that send us all into glaring retreat sometimes. But what a strange fate it is. Though even in America his recognition was painfully tardy, Williams' work came to us there in a more normal way, of course. It filtered through in the poetry and avant-garde magazines, the little early volumes, and the two "collected editions" from them in the 1930s; and then it came in the swelling later stream that brought him at last into the culminating efforts of the two books published here last year. Until the mid-1950s he was a hardworking pediatrician and obstetrician whose patients were mostly from the working class sections of the industrial complex of northern New Jersey, where Williams lived and had his practice. A number of his most moving yet toughminded poems and stories are about them; they contributed a great deal to both the wild despair and the hilarity of his art. His work as a doctor slowed him down a bit, but when he did make his mark it was through a certain re-education of readers in what real people are like and how the American language sounds. His exuberance, visual precision, and fine melodic ear served a mature intelligence concerned with cultural and sexual realities. He was different from his friend Pound and, even more, from Eliot in his conscious, unyielding effort to create a new, nativist American poetry, not provincially indifferent to European values but nevertheless based on a ground-sense of American life.

How conscious and cumulative this effort was became clear to us over the years not only through the poetry but also through the criticism, the "experimental" prose (especially that brilliant, compressed improvisation, *The Great American Novel*), the short stories and plays and novels, the half-poetic, half-documentary essay on America's "mythical history" called *In the American Grain*, and the *Autobiography*. Despite the appeal of Europe (detailed in all its ambivalence in the novel *A Voyage to Pagany*), he resisted the temptation to go expatriate and led the revolution in American poetry on home ground. It was he who most bitterly deplored Eliot's betrayal (as Williams saw it) of that revolution, even while he admired Eliot's genius. Unlike Eliot and Pound, but like a great many of the rest of us, he was a second-generation American wholeheartedly engaged in the common struggle to assimilate the almost intractable realities of the United States. He could criticize those realities savagely and splendidly. Nevertheless, he made a certain commitment to whatever our life in the long run could discover its best meanings to be. His own role, he thought, was to try to "unravel" the "common language" of our sensibility. There are signs now that his influence may actually outlast Eliot's, whose background and concerns were in important ways so alien to most Americans.

Re-reading this collection has made me more aware than ever before of the way that a writer prepares his own readers' future appreciation of him. The early Williams' sensitive impressions of growing things, his birth-imagery, and his absorption in the violence and change that mark ordinary life—always with a certain suggestion, explicit or not, of their significance as keys to aesthetic process—conditioned his readers in a subtle fashion. Take for instance the poem "Catastrophic Birth," in this volume. Despite its concrete imagery, this poem presents a basically abstract, even formal argument about the "aesthetic process" I have just mentioned. Its explosive beginning ("Fury and counter fury! The volcano!") is one sign of the strong emotion that the experienced reader of Williams knows is always present in his rare abstract expositions. So is the way he punctuates the exposition with smaller outcries and ironic asides:

The
cone is subsiding, smoke rises as
a funnel into the blue unnatural sky—
The change impends! A change stutters
in the rocks. We believe nothing can change.

And in just one stanza of this poem, amid the concentrated theorising, we suddenly have a scene, or dialogue, from the poet's "other" existence as an obstetrician. Its relevance is joyously clear, especially if one has learned from Williams' past writing to expect the "unexpected" and enlightening intrusion of elemental life into his reveries:

Shut up! laughs the big she-Wop.
Wait till you have six like-a me.
Every year one. Come on! Push! Sure,
you said it! Maybe I have one next year.
Sweating like a volcano. It cleans you up,
makes you feel good inside. Come on! Push!

This is the "natural," "spontaneous" Williams, with a gift of empathy as acute as Lawrence's. In this volume we do not have as many of the brief, piercing, casual notations as in earlier books, but there are still a number of them—momentary, half-humorous sketches, such as the one of a half-Cherokee girl thumbing a ride while holding a bunch of wildflowers pressed "just below the belly"; or of the "disconsolate" male dog and the "frolicsome" bitch just after they have been "halving the compass." One of Williams' persistent themes is the heavenliness of the earthy. He realizes it touchingly but with great gaiety in the elegy "To Ford Madox Ford in Heaven":

Is it any better in Heaven, my friend Ford,
than you found it in Provence?

So the poem begins. The argument, excited and colloquial, transcends the commonplace familiarity of the plain thought:

Provence, the fat-assed Ford will never
again strain the chairs of your cafés
pull and pare for his dish your sacred garlic,
grunt and sweat and lick
his lips. Gross as the world he has left to
us he has become
a part of that of which you were the known
part, Provence, he loved so well.

Williams' exuberance entered his writing physically and shaped the poems through a kind of muscular pressure. The twelve-line poem "The Kermess" renders in two dizzy, rollicking sentences the heavy, drunken dancing to bagpipe, bugle, and fiddles of the peasants in Brueghel's painting. It is as close to a literal experience as a poem can well be. The quieter "Philomena Andronica" is a picture, at once charming and unsentimental, of the movements and languorously indefinable expectancy of a girl near puberty, playing with a younger child. "Choral: the Pink Church" is a witty and musically rich hymn in praise of the body's holiness.

The "musical" aspect of Williams has in the past been most elusive for British readers. His American speech-rhythms, the way he relies on an exquisitely improvisatory (but self-disciplined) cadence, and his audacious linking of unpretentious directness, sudden joking, outbursts, and pure lyricism and eloquence have apparently put people off. In the end, though, appreciation of him involves recognition that he was an original who took stylistic chances and yet spoke directly to us. The timid reader might try speaking the following moderate manifestation aloud a few times, just to get his ear in, as it were. It is the first stanza of "To All Gentleness":

> Like a cylindrical tank fresh silvered
> upended on the sidewalk to advertise
> some plumber's shop, a profusion
> of pink roses bending ragged in the rain—
> speaks to me of all gentleness and its
> enduring.

Or he might try the first stanza of "The Horse Show," one of the poems Williams wrote about his dying mother:

> Constantly near you, I never in my entire
> sixty-four years knew you so well as yesterday
> or half so well. We talked. You were never
> so lucid, so disengaged from all exigencies
> of place and time. We talked of ourselves,
> intimately, a thing never heard of between us.
> How long have we waited? almost a hundred years.

Williams' fusion of a deep, simple, normal humanity with an encompassing aestheticism became in his art a program for the redemption of what Yeats called "modern subjectivity" through a strategy for impersonality. Some of these poems express grief, frustration in love and in coming to terms with himself, or, sometimes, the mystery of fulfilment. Yet the essay opening this book says: "There's nothing sentimental about a machine, and: A Poem is a small (or large) machine made of words." Williams was like the other older masters of modern poetry in using such objective formulations to help him discipline the intense inwardness, chaotic and hyper-suggestible, that is the chief danger, because it can so easily plunge into ruined negation, to the art of this age. The masters used their "objectivity" to discipline that precarious perturbation—not to deny it but to contain and re-direct it.

Spectator (25 June 1965)

Yearning For a Change

IN his introduction to his Penguin anthology, *The New Poetry* (1962), the English critic A. Alvarez wrote: "Sometime in the twenties Thomas Hardy remarked to Robert Graves that 'vers libre could come to nothing in England. All we can do is to write on the old themes in the old styles, but try to do a little better than those who went before us.' Since about 1930 the machinery of modern English poetry seems to have been controlled by a series of negative feedbacks designed to produce precisely the effect Hardy wanted."

By "negative feedbacks" Alvarez meant the reactivation of the anti-experimental, anti-intellectual and anti-emotional "sets" or prejudices in English sensibility. He hoped to counteract this renewed conservatism by leading off his anthology with two fiercely emotional Americans, Robert Lowell and John Berryman, and by giving more space to Ted Hughes, a writer of highly charged if beautifully contained and directed violence, than to any of the other seventeen Britons represented.

He included, as well, the nervously energetic Peter Redgrove, the American-influenced Charles Tomlinson and Christopher Middleton, and the intellectually intense Donald Davie, among others who could to a greater or lesser degree be said to represent modulations toward the kind of vigor and relevance he advocates. Alvarez praised Philip Larkin's talent, but discounted his tone and his concerns. He included Thom Gunn without comment, as an acknowledgement (I would surmise) of a latent power that has only very recently begun to find its right formal expression.

Since the Alvarez anthology appeared, there have been other signs of yearning toward new orientations. The poetry of William Carlos Williams has belatedly begun to take hold on the English ear and imagination, partly in the wake of Allen Ginsberg and of a revival of interest in Pound. This development parallels a new attention to Russian and other European poetry and a vast proliferation of public readings, notably the highly publicized affair at Albert Hall some months ago. Not only did a wide array of Americans from Ginsberg to Harry Fainlight read there, but some quite unexpected Continental and English poets did so too (for instance, George MacBeth of the B. B. C., usually associated with the somewhat inhibited movement known as the Group), and there were such sidelights as the presence of Andrei Voznosensky in the audience.

The international Concretist movement has found wider recognition, thanks largely to the gentle but durable Scottish poet Ian Hamilton Finlay, who for a long time now has been putting out a whimsical little publication, with contributors from many countries, called *Poor.Old.Tired.Horse*.

Another sign of change was the extraordinary response in England to Sylvia Plath's posthumous volume, *Ariel*. This book by a young American, the wife of Ted Hughes, was written during the months before her suicide and remains inseparable from the suicide in its anguish, its insistent power and its explicit motifs. It brought home to many British readers the savage energies and full involvement of experience of which poetry is capable. For the first time, there is serious discussion in England as to whether or not such energies and such involvement are what a realized poetry *demands*.

It is hard to believe that out of so much ferment, so many readings, and so much openness to the outside world's doings, the English are not on the verge of a wonderful new period comparable to our own between the two World Wars.

There are scattered, if inclusive, signs of it everywhere—in a stray poem by Ted Hughes, for instance, that appeared in the magazine *Agenda* not long ago; or in the admittedly feeble experimentation with poetic dynamics in the Beat manner by Michael Horowitz and his group; or in the contributions to serious criticism by Ian Hamilton and his magazine *The Review* (now in some danger of being discontinued); or in Charles Tomlinson's neglected volume *A Peopled Landscape* (1963), which presents that rarity in current British verse—a concern for the rhythmic movement and balance, the over-all life of the sound, as well as for the thought and the moment-by-moment phrasing; or in the more recent work of Christopher Middleton, whose *Torse 3* (1963), though still dominated by a fairly traditional impulse, was already moving toward a new view of structure.

The title of Middleton's book was taken from a definition in the "Shorter Oxford English Dictionary," arranged as verse by the poet as an epigraph:

> *Torse* 3.
> [*f.med. L.* torsus,—um,
> *for L.* tortus *twisted.*]
> Geom. A *developable surface;*
> *a surface generated*
> *by a moving straight line*
> *which at every instant is turning,*
> *in some plane or other through it,*
> *about some point or other*
> *in its length.*

Yet these indications are all still exceptional, and an American reader of British poetry is on more alien ground than he may at first realize. He is likely to be repelled by what seems a morass of petty cleverness, effetely knowledgeable, spongy and talkative, and often derivative, that seems quite dead at the center. The poetic act, on many occasions socially rather than esthetically oriented, seems taken for granted, and a tolerance for facile mediocrity at times pervades poetic activity. One needs the experience of much re-reading, and if possible of actually hearing the poets and, indeed, of getting used to British speech in general to correct this overall impression.

That is, the nuances and pitch and style of thought and speed of movement in that speech are really different from ours and do make a great difference. Behind them lies another world of experience and background, a reaction against violence and overstatement in the wake of the last war, a political sharpness and class-feeling a great deal more European than ours, and some decisive differences in the character both of mass and elite education. That education encourages greater articulateness than ours, but not greater originality. A poet who deals with all this most sympathetically is Donald Davie, whose *Events and Wisdoms* reveals an attempt to forge a living poetics out of his own experience and voice, a method related to the tradition and yet in the middle of things—

> One sees the lately formless as most formal,
> The stanza most a unit when
> Open at both ends, all transition . . .

It is surprising, in a way, to see Davie, a poet of coldly intellectual distance in most of his earlier work (though with a keen enough gauge one could measure his remote volcanic seethings), begin to turn now toward the "confessional" mode of a few influential Americans. "Wide France" and "Across the Bay" are poems of family turbulence, and the sequence "After an Accident" (about the effects of a terrible automobile smash-up in which Davie was involved) is a serious effort to repossess a psychological state that was both traumatic and privately full of painful realizations.

The stubby thoughtfulness of most of Davie's other work is one kind of spiritual independence—suggesting an intellectual honesty that does not wish to preen itself on its virtues—but "After an Accident" makes a leap into emotional clarification beyond all that he has so far done. Some of the credit must be given, I think, to his acceptance of the possibilities of "confessional" writing.

The advance in another poet, Tony Connor, seems to have the same influence behind it. Connor's book *Lodgers* has naturalness and ease of formal movement far beyond his first book, *With Love Somehow* (1962). What he is being easy and natural about is his own embittered life, first as the child of a broken home, and then as a husband and father in an apparently difficult marriage. A more flexible stylist and exuberant spirit than Davie, he nevertheless does not get through as fully and meaningfully except in the elegiac half-dream poem "Beyond Hindley" and in the brilliantly executed "The Small Hours in the Kitchen," which brings him near the terrifying wellsprings of his own creative impulse.

Neither Davie nor Connor breaks drastically out of his previous voice; in fact, each one's discovery clarifies that voice more sharply, through an honest pursuit of private meaning. The weakness of John Wain's new book, *Wildtrack* (to be published in the U.S. this spring), is that it so seldom relies on his personal, idiosyncratic voice or knowledge. It is conceived as a sustained sequence that seeks out the "crucial mystery" of man by way of accurate identification of the subjective ego. (The language and bearing of this purpose are contained in a quotation from Joseph Campbell's "The Hero With a Thousand Faces," placed at the head of the poem.) Yet Wain writes in a truly lyrical and inward voice only at a very few points, particularly in the mystically visionary sections called "The Day-Self Contemplates the Defeat of Time" and "The Night-Self Sees All Women in One Woman."

These sections, together with a remarkable adaptation of Alexander Blok's "The Twelve," are interesting and powerful—as good as anything Wain has ever done. The Blok passage dwindles into tendentious political commentary, just as a good deal of the rest of the poem becomes an awkward machinery for the thematic contrasting of mass-man (creature of political, technological and economic manipulation—the "Day-Self") and subjective man (the "Night-Self"). This machinery is vaguely reminiscent of Hardy's poetic drama, *The Dynasts*; it involves Wain in some historical portraiture, especially some touching 18th-century close-ups. Intellectually worked through but not really resolved poetically, *Wildtrack* is nevertheless a doughty effort to break through the oppressive British thing of mere articulateness.

Roy Fuller's *Buff* and Paul West's *The Snow Leopard* barely overcome that condition, accomplished as both writers are. Fuller's sequence "To X" is the account of a furtive love-affair that the poet, at an advanced age, has found himself unexpectedly launched upon. In verse and diction after the manner of William Empson, it leaves no room for anything but a minimal sad clowning. Like much of Fuller's work, it is a wry shocker for the fashionably disillusioned.

The wit, the light play of imagination, the resourcefulness of language of this writer are a half-pleasure in poems like "Bagatelles" and "The Zouave," which yet leave the taste of the already often experienced, of attitudes struck rather than discovered. One hears voices—sometimes the poet's own, for a moment, but very likely Auden's as well (especially in the sonnet sequence "The Historian") or Yeats's or Stevens's; and most of all, the voices of a generation not lost but forever self-echoing. Even a truly fine piece like "Favouring the Creatures" adds up to very old reckonings and insights indeed.

West, too, though by no means as deft a craftsman, plays winningly with the *déja vu;* one almost doesn't notice his slight tendency to chase some elusive theme completely out of sight, to un-express the expressible, as it were, reversing a dictum of Eliot's. His feeling for the past and for the unnoticed or unstated is, like Fuller's, delicately colored by a sense of lost historical and political possibilities, and of individual lives gone awry.

In these motifs Fuller and West are joined by Bernard Spencer *(With Luck Lasting)* and C. A. Trypanis *(Pompeian Dog)*, both of whom write more concretely and with a more immediate evocativeness. Landscapes, memories of old loves, re-creation of notes from vanished civilizations—how winningly these poets and others like them conjure these things up, and how hard it will be for English poets to break the spell of the tradition they represent!

New York Times Book Review (6 February 1966)

Delmore Schwartz

I never knew Delmore Schwartz intimately. We met a number of times and had several long conversations, mostly about his poetry and about other poets. We shared certain friends, but there are many people who knew him better than I did. I took to his first book, *In Dreams Begin Responsibilities,* enormously when it appeared in 1938. It was not only its lyricism—those memorable lines and stanzas that make such a sad, isolated music—but the wryness, the contemporaneity of the intelligence, and that special big-city voice: of New York, to be exact. This was a poet who woke in the very early, still dark, winter morning of the insomniac, "In the naked bed, in Plato's cave," as he said, and was at the same time entirely of that unremitting other world of the streets outside, where "a fleet of trucks strained uphill, grinding," and where the heavy stillness of buildings and pavement bespoke the oppression of the city. There are poems in that book that are absolutely of New York City, of this age, and of a generation of displaced Americans whose sense of loss goes back to rural or immigrant parents or grandparents:

> Tired and unhappy, you think of houses
> Soft-carpeted and warm in the December evening,
> While snow's white pieces fall past the window,
> And the orange firelight leaps.
> A young girl sings
> That song of Gluck where Orpheus pleads with Death;
> Her elders watch, nodding their happiness
> To see time fresh again in her self-conscious eyes:
> The servants bring the coffee, the children retire,
> Elder and younger yawn and go to bed,
> The coals fade and glow, rose and ashen,
> It is time to shake yourself! and break this
> Banal dream, and turn your head
> Where the underground is charged, where the weight
> Of the lean buildings is seen,
> Where close in the subway rush, anonymous
> In the audience, well-dressed or mean,
> So many surround you, ringing your fate,
> Caught in an anger exact as a machine!

The handsome, bemused face (but in more recent years marked by the lines of anxiety and suspicion recorded in the Jane Lougee photograph), the almost mocking simplicity of manner, the melancholy idealism that could parody itself so easily and turn into pessimism, the wit that could be all gaiety or turn acidly sardonic concerning the games of the great—these remain fixed in our memories. Some of them are beautifully recorded in poems by John

Berryman and Robert Lowell. A difficult, unhappy life, aggravated by the special problems of the poet in America (its peculiar forms of loneliness and half-neglect after early recognition), this was also a representative life in its own way. The heart sickens to recall the names of poets prematurely dead within the past decade or so. "Let us," as Pasternak wrote in even more drastic circumstances of the deaths of so many of his friends, "bow our heads with compassion for their talents and their bright memory as well as for their sufferings."

There was an undefensive honesty in Delmore Schwartz's best poetry of vulnerability and self-knowledge. Almost joyous, almost whimsical, it made his sophisticated insight into philosophy and psychology suddenly innocent and new, as in the poem that begins:

A dog named Ego, the snowflakes as kisses
Fluttered, ran, came with me in December,
Snuffing the chill air, changing and halting,
There where I walked toward seven o'clock,
Sniffed at some interests hidden and open,
Whirled, descending, and stood still, attentive
Seeking their peace, the stranger, unknown,
With me, near me, kissed me, touched my wound,
My simple face, obsessed and pleasure bound. . . .

In the later poems, these earlier notes of burdened consciousness sometimes become the expression of an anguish so unbearable that only a very pure poetry could handle it. A few of these poems approach that point—it is the most precious tribute we can pay the poet, and the man, to recognize his purer voice and the cost behind it. Difficult as it is to make ourselves listen to it at this moment, when the living voice makes itself felt more than ever before because for the first time unrecallable, I wish to close by remembering one such poem, "All of the Fruits Had Fallen"—

All of the fruits had fallen,
The bears had fallen asleep,
And the pears were useless and soft
Like used hopes, under the starlight's
Small knowledge, scattered aloft
In a glittering senseless drift:
The jackals of remorse in a cage
Drugged beyond mirth and rage.

Then, then the dark hour flowered!
Under the silence, immense
And empty as far-off seas,
I wished for the innocence
Of my stars and my stones and my trees
All the brutality and inner sense
A dog and a bird possess,
The dog who barked at the moon

As an enemy's white fang,
The bird that thrashed up the bush
And soared to soar as it sang,
A being all present as touch,
Free of the future and past
—Until, in the dim window glass,
The fog or cloud of my face
Showed me my fear at last!

Poetry (December 1966)

British Poets of WWI

UP THE LINE TO DEATH: THE WAR POETS, 1914–1918
edited by Brian Gardner
RUPERT BROOKE: A BIOGRAPHY by Christopher Hassall
ENGLISH POETRY OF THE FIRST WORLD WAR by John H. Johnston
MEN WHO MARCH AWAY: POEMS OF THE FIRST WORLD WAR
edited by I. M. Parsons

TO recapture the poetry of a past moment, particularly a poetry that one had discounted, is a curious experience. The decision, or impulse, to regain it in its own terms generates a sympathy as of a contemporary. It is easy to summon up this feeling with the work of the young British poets of the Great War, most of them gifted innocents whose disillusionment, even, was that of an age that now seems a million years ago. At least, our writers seem a million years older at birth than the poet who could write at the outbreak of war:

> Now, God be thanked Who has matched us with His hour,
>   And caught our youth, and wakened us from sleeping,
> With hand made sure, clear eye, and sharpened power,
>   To turn, as swimmers into cleanness leaping,
> Glad from a world grown old and cold and weary,
>   Leave the sick hearts that honour could not move,
> And half-men, and their dirty songs and dreary,
>   And all the little emptiness of love!
>
> Oh! we, who have known shame, we have found release there,
>   Where there's no ill, no grief, but sleep has mending,

Naught broken save this body, lost but breath;
Nothing to shake the laughing heart's long peace there
But only agony, and that has ending;
And the worst friend and enemy is but Death.

I re-read Rupert Brooke's poems after I had put down Christopher Hassall's admiring biography of him, and that has made some difference. The sonnet just quoted does not become a better sonnet thereby. Its rhymes remain as obvious, its diction—much of it—as padded and cliché-ridden, its sentiments as derivative and almost as dreary as before. But to fill oneself with the biography (for all its sentimentality and its awestruck murmuring of famous names—the Asquiths, Keyneses, Stracheys, Stephenses, etc., with whom Brooke was intimate) and with Brooke's poetry and that of his wartime contemporaries again is necessarily to evoke the ambience of the poem's making.

Brooke had the music of a magnificent tradition behind him, but he was too much the amateur to carry that tradition to a perfection of personal craftsmanship, deeply colored by his private idiosyncrasies and therefore adapted somehow to his own age, as Swinburne, Bridges, and even De La Mare did. (Of course, it is in a sense idiotic to make this kind of judgment of a poet who died at twenty-seven. He *might* have become anything, but the stamp and the commitment of the poet seemed to lack a certain emphasis. Virginia Woolf's final estimate was that he was destined "to be a member of Parliament and edit the classics, a very powerful, ambitious man, but not a poet.") It is true that he shared the malaise, the restlessness, the urge toward the new and revolutionary in the modern spirit, and that his susceptibility to illness and his private torments and ultimate skepticism and despair might eventually have led him into that psychological experimentation and deeper candor that characterizes so many of the great moderns. He seems, however, to have suffered from a kind of arrested adolescence that made him depend too much on his charm and physical presence and on the approval of the elite groups of which he was a part from his university days onward. He was hardly the young man to break really new ground, as Eliot, for instance, was at the same time quietly doing.

The Hassall biography, despite my reservations, gives us a very full, almost satisfactory picture of Rupert Brooke and his world. It is often quite moving, especially in its depiction of his strangely unresolved relationship with Ka Cox, one of several not quite adult love-relationships in which he was involved. On the surface, this exhaustingly frustrated mutual tortureship, with its unaccountable brakes on fulfillment in sex and marriage, betrays the saddest kind of romantic infantilism. One can't help feeling that too much is left unsaid, or unrevealed to the biographer, but the account is one of the elements that makes Brooke's use of phrases like "half-men" and "the little emptiness of love" and his placing of "shame" and "release" in opposition to one another take on a poignancy that the overt meaning would not in itself give them. And on the wider plane, the accounts of his wanderings over half the globe and his sense of a pointlessness to existence, despite the socialist idealism that he forgot so quickly with the coming on of the war, explain the subjective relief—felt by so many young men of comparable background—uttered at the beginning of the sonnet. His great literary friend was Edward Marsh; his commission was obtained through his connection with Marsh and with Winston Churchill. The limits of his sensibility and artistry are hardly to be defined by these facts, and there is nothing discreditable about them; but it seems doubtful that he would ultimately have transcended the assumptions about life and poetry that he shared with these men.

Nevertheless, the Hassall biography, by taking him seriously as a man and as an artist, helps us re-focus attention on the best of Brooke—and by extension, of his Georgian contemporaries. Look, for instance, at the beginning of his poem "Retrospect"; the woman addressed is presumably Ka Cox:

In your arms was still delight,
Quiet as a street at night;
And thoughts of you, I do remember,
Were green leaves in a darkened chamber,
Were dark clouds in a moonless sky.
Love, in you, went passing by,
Penetrative, remote, and rare,
Like a bird in the wide air,
And, as the bird, it left no trace
In the heaven of your face.
In your stupidity I found
The sweet hush after a sweet sound. . . .

Some of this is uninteresting, but it is clear why Hassall felt that Brooke had more than a touch of Marvell's "lyric grace." The mildly wry simile "quiet as a street," the imagery of remoteness that counteracts the effects of passion, and the calm employment of the word "stupidity" in this context are modern modulations of the seventeenth-century master's irony, while the whole is borne through by a sub-Keatsian negation—

O mother quiet, breasts of peace,
Where love itself would faint and cease!
O infinite deep I never knew . . .

If we turn back to Brooke in a sympathetic mood, then, we begin to recover the impression of a valuable sensibility in process of development, discovering itself through "normal" lyric channels but deviating in minor ways—through certain unorthodoxies of diction and attitude, and unexpected turns of various sorts—that his own generation experienced in his work. We shall never, as Edward Thomas observed, be able to separate the man from his poetry. The poetry is in the personality, and in the poignancy or—as Wilfrid Owen said of his own poems—in the Pity. This is broadly true of the bulk of the war poets as well—the groups ably represented in the anthologies edited by Brian Gardner *(Up the Line to Death)* and I. M. Parsons *(Men Who March Away)* and crisply, if not always adequately, discussed by John H. Johnston *(English Poetry of the First World War)*. One would have to be one of those whom Owen allowed himself to hate—"But cursed are dullards whom no cannon stuns"—to remain aloof from this body of work, written by the flower of England's youthful intelligence and spirit, so many of them killed in action, often fairly early on. The relative lack of vitality in British poetry ever since can be largely traced to the slaughter of these young officers. The century grew old in the course of the few years of their war, which exploded them into the twentieth century so traumatically. Both Gardner and Parsons are constrained to organize their anthologies in basically the same way, under a series of headings suggesting the progress from innocent, patriotic enthusiasm to the experience of hell and the bitter aftermath. The very nature of the process made it impossible for the great poetry of the war, aesthetically speaking, to be written during it. *Hugh Selwyn Mauberley, The Waste Land,* and Yeats's great sequences "Nineteen Hundred and Nineteen" and "Meditations in Time of Civil War" (which, though they specifically refer to post-war developments in Ireland, appear to me to have the World War in their ultimate background nevertheless) assimilate the fragmenting force of that process into their very method and find the right structural form, the modern sequence, as well as the lyrical and dramatic methods appropriate to it.

But these poets marched out of the universities, as it were, with their heads full of Housman, Swinburne, Hardy, Browning, and the loveliest poems in the tradition, to meet meaningless, mechanized death of the most brutal sort. The shock of the *facts* was what they had to learn to set down, and quickly; and it is Sassoon, Owen, and Rosenberg who do it most remarkably, although Blunden's beautifully skilful art, never fully appreciated because of his Georgian associations, becomes extremely impressive in this context. The *point of view* of modern poetry was hardened and established by the war-experience as caught and set forth by these sensitive, suddenly shocked and embittered minds. It merged, naturally, with techniques and theoretical projections that had already been in the making, but the harshness, uncompromising anti-sentimentality, and satirical, anti-bourgeois edge of the best poetry since the war has much to do with that sudden, painful maturing. So does the modern insistence on a style cleansed of the traces of mere amateurism. One could very profitably, say, study the line of continuity between the war poets and Ted Hughes, the most vigorous poet, and most mordantly sharpened stylist, in England today.

Mr. Johnston's book is a clear, well-organized presentation of a number of these poets. He gives attention first to a group of "early poets": Brooke, Julian Grenfell, Robert Nichols, and Charles Sorley. All these save Nichols, who was invalided home after the Somme with shell-shock, were killed before the end of 1915; Sorley was only twenty, a brilliantly promising young Scotsman, when killed in the Battle of Loos. Johnston's main figures in subsequent chapters are Siegfried Sassoon, Edmund Blunden, Wilfrid Owen, Isaac Rosenberg, Herbert Read, and David Jones. Three aspects of his book require at least brief comment. First, the description of each poet's work is knowledgeable, scholarly, and in general discriminating. This is really the best, though the simplest, aspect, for what these poets now require of criticism is precisely a plain recounting of their identities and achievements from the vantage-point of the present age.

The second aspect is that Johnston rides, rather repetitively but not very persuasively, a notion that the war poets were for the most part too close to their subject, too "subjective" and "emotional" and caught up in the literal details of their experience. What was needed, Johnston asserts, was more objectivity and a larger perspective and organizing approach, on a tragic or epic scale, than the lyric mode permits. Parsons's introduction to *Men Who March Away* (which appeared in 1965, a year after the other books under review here) makes short shrift of these strictures. They rest, he says, "on a number of misconceptions, both about the nature of poetry and the work of the particular poets under discussion. The forces which impelled them to write in the lyric or elegiac mode rather than in the epic were, first, the physical conditions . . . and far more important, their realization that the epic, with its classical ancestry and time-hallowed associations with the heroic, was the very reverse of a suitable medium." Parsons disagrees, properly, with Johnston's assumption that "shorter poems, whether lyric or elegiac, are ipso facto incapable of expressing 'the vast tragic potentialities' of modern war." Finally, "as to the proposition that First World War poetry was almost exclusively concerned with the plight of the common soldier, who, an insignificant pawn . . . , was at once too close to actuality and too divorced from responsibility to provide a suitable vehicle for 'the tragic vision,' I can only say that I think this view totally misguided."

I would regard as equally misguided Mr. Johnston's exaltation of Herbert Read and David Jones as exemplars of approaches he thinks would have been more suitable for the other poets as well. Though I commend Mr. Johnston's appreciation of these poets, his abstractly oversimplified, a priori thesis has led him to a compensatory overstatement on their behalf, admirable as they are. But the important thing about his study is that it freshly and sharply reintroduces its subject, and in attentive detail. It recalls forcibly to attention a compelling body of poetry that for some reason, now, begins to take on renewed relevance.

Victorian Studies (March 1966)

Black Dada Nihilismus

THAT part of the white population of the United States that is willing to learn is now going to a segregated school. That is, Negro America is holding special classes for whites and especially for the despised group of "middle-class, intellectual, liberal" whites. In militant Negro eyes, that group seems to include everyone except the filthy, openly reactionary rich and the rarely mentioned (but really, and numerously, extant) semi-educated poor whites. The struggle for civil liberty, economic equality and social fraternity seems to the ordinary enlightened white citizen to call for the greatest possible unity and friendliness from all interested parties. Many Negro spokesmen, on the other hand, have been slapping the outstretched hand of late and have insisted on shock tactics of verbal violence, reverse-racist intransigence and revived slogans of Black Nationalism. The striking poem "Black Dada Nihilismus," by Leroi Jones, expresses the deepest disillusionment with the "white" culture that so ruthlessly "destroyed Byzantium, Tenochtitlan, Commanch" and calls for revenge:

> ... Come up, black dada
>
> nihilismus. Rape the white girls. Rape
> their fathers. Cut the mothers' throats.
> Black dada nihilismus, choke my friends
>
> in their bedrooms with their drinks spilling. . . .
>
> may a lost god dumballah, rest or save us
> against the murders we intend
> against his lost white children. . . .

The intransigence and bloodymindedness are easy enough to understand, just as the riots in the Watts District of Los Angeles are easy to understand. Beyond the historical oppression and local tensions, and beyond the fact that aggression finds its greatest release just when things promise to improve, there is still the enraged sense that nobody is actually looking or caring—that, as Owen wrote about the suffering of war, "God seems not to care." And it is true. It is painfully clear that the majority of Americans, though concerned about the insult and injury to the Negro, are not at all aware of his literal day-to-day life with its imposed barrenness and deprivations and the ghetto-like entrapment implicit even in his pleasures. It is hard, perhaps impossible, for the ordinary person, however great his goodwill, to have that kind of continuously sensitized awareness. I suppose that is why the Negro community suffered no great trauma from the fate of the six million Jews under Hitler, and why the few empathy-crazed people who have burned themselves alive out of an unbearable identification with the Vietnamese victims of napalm-bombing have hardly touched the feelings of their fellow Americans.

At any rate, under the present conditions of American Negro life, a new body of leaders and thinkers have arisen who make no concessions. Why should they? If they are Americans, why not have all the prerogatives of Americans without having to go through so much struggle and bloodshed? And if they are *not* Americans, but a special form of semi-enslaved or semi-colonial population, then it is clear they must fight with all the weapons they can command and without gratitude for partial concessions. And so we have the photograph, so irritating and touching and absurd, in the *New York Times* of April 15, showing Sargent Shriver, the director of the Office of Economic Opportunity, trying to get his thoughts across to three disgusted-looking Negro delegates to the "poor people's convention" in Washington. These delegates, among others, wouldn't listen. They shouted him down with cries of "You're lying!" I do not think he *was* lying. He has been working hard, and so has the government, but the problems are miles ahead of them and require national commitment on the scale of a war effort if they are to be handled promptly and properly.

Out of this new situation of accelerated activity by the government and accelerated impatience by the people most concerned, and out of the whole welter of recent events evoked by the names, say, of the Reverend Martin Luther King and of Malcolm X, comes a new body of Negro writers taking their bearings at once from two very different sources. One is the existential condition of the mass of American Negroes; the other is a sophisticated intellectual self-knowledge, the common property of all educated people in the modern world. The double identification is particularly tormenting at this stormy historical moment, and the tendency is to avoid the crushing task of constructing a private personality that will be self-sustaining without betraying either "cause." The temptation at the moment is to put on a mask of revolutionary violence and to use the knowledge of the general crisis of modern man as a weapon against white morale.

Leroi Jones is the newest Negro writer to charge his work with the materials of this dangerously unstable complex. Born in 1934, the son of a postman and a social worker in Newark, NJ, he studied at Rutgers and Howard Universities, served in the air force, and has held various literary fellowships—in short, now belongs to the intellectually privileged class in America. He first came to attention as a promising young poet associated with some of the "Black Mountain" poets (the Olson-Creeley-Duncan constellation) and has published two interesting volumes of poetry, *Preface to a Twenty Volume Suicide Note* and *The Dead Lecturer*. His use of rhythmic movements, improvised spirallings of thought, and mood-tones comparable to those of jazz and his sardonic wit were striking in the first book, and the second is preoccupied with the implications of the "double identification" and the "mask of revolutionary violence" I mentioned earlier on. The subtlety of mind and ear in these books, and their intellectual honesty, place Jones among the younger poets of genuine energy and formal control and with something important to say.

At the same time he has been prolific in other directions. He has published a study of American Negro music, *Blues People*, that is not only valuable as history and as critical interpretation, but is also a keen attempt to see the music in a cultural perspective. This study must have helped him to clarify his insight into the whole "national" question of the role of the Negro as an unwilling American who has been allowed neither to enter the pale completely nor to escape from it. It is alive with the love of the music and lyrics of the tradition and throws light on the deep feeling for idiomatic language and rhythms of his poetry. He has published, in addition, a book of two plays, *Dutchman* and *The Slave;* a novel, half realistic and half free-associative, called *The System of Dante's Hell;* and, just now, a book of "social essays" called *Home*.

Read one at a time, the books and essays provoke one to continual quarrelling with the author. The positions are wilful, self-pitying, insensitive to logical and humanistic considerations of the most obvious sort. But Jones is disarming, because he himself, or his characters, points out these objections often enough. Clay, the hero of *Dutchman*, is a confused and silly boy. Walker, the hero of *The Slave*, indulges in the wildest self-serving in everything he says. The "I" of the novel disgraces himself ethically, and so somehow even deserves the conditions of the white-man-given Hell. Still, the evolution of a coldly analytical, intelligent rationale for an uncompromising Negro Nationalist position is made clear and given a vital body in Jones's work. It adds up to a plea for understanding at the highest level, to appreciate the full anger in the air and to accept its presence and try to dissipate it through the workings of a truly responsive national sensitivity on the part of élite America.

Spectator (29 April 1966)

❧

Poet and Public Figure

IT is ten years since Allen Ginsberg's *Howl and Other Poems* exploded out of nowhere and, simultaneously, Beats appeared everywhere. The movement now seems to have been inevitable. It expressed a "secret" side of American life, and helped catapult a whole forbidden realm into the open. Plenty of antecedents can be found in our own and other literatures for the sexual (often, homosexual) frankness of Ginsberg's writings, for their freedom of vocabulary, and for their drug-oriented mystique of private release, as well as for their formal characteristics. They mirror something that has been going on for a long time—the discrediting by many people of traditional concepts of a nobly disciplined life.

The timing of their first appearance is another matter. A delayed reaction against the impersonal violence of the total war during which Ginsberg's generation came to maturity is involved in the hysteria of his rhetoric. In addition, the intellectual intimidations of the McCarthy period had much to do with this counterburst against genteel complacency. The *Howl* poems definitely foreshadowed the new political and moral radicalism of the decade that followed.

Ginsberg has always been the major figure of his constellation. He has an international following based as much on his dramatic personality as on his works, if the two can really be separated. He marches for peace, fights to legalize marijuana, has been expelled from Cuba for strictly nonpolitical reasons, and once appeared in a loin-cloth playing the flute at a busy Warsaw street-corner. That performance was one result of his sojourn in India where he conferred with holy men and seems to have exerted his own influence on impressionable young people.

Viewed unsympathetically, Ginsberg is an exhibitionist and egotist whose politics may be sincere but are beclouded by his attitudinizing self-indulgence. His poetry, in the same light, has merits but is too often dedicated to advertising himself and his coterie and to advocating a messy, irresponsible, self-destructive way of life. One can understand Senator Jacob Javits's irritation when Ginsberg testified concerning LSD at a hearing of the Senate's subcommittee on juvenile delinquency.

Ginsberg was lyrical about the drug's uses, and Javits, quite properly, asked: "Do you consider yourself qualified to give medical advice? Do you consider yourself qualified to give medical advice to my 16½-year-old-son?" With some justification, one may consider Ginsberg's donning of the seer's mantle presumptuous and his detailed announcements concerning his homosexual love-bouts disgusting. After all, the words "presumptuous" and "disgusting" still mean something, no matter how libertarian we may have become.

There is a sympathetic side as well. Even if there were not, the vitality of Ginsberg's public presence and the affection with which he is widely regarded are real and important. In significant ways, even in certain surface qualities of his poetry and in the kind of disagreement it stirs up among critics, he is a Whitman of our era. If Whitman were alive, he would doubtless bring his personal life into the open as Ginsberg has done. He would have as sharp things to say about the age of the concentration camp, the Bomb, and computer totalitarianism, and very possibly be as stung to despair by the Vietnam situation.

Whitman might even speak much as Ginsberg did to that Senate subcommittee. The burden of that testimony was that LSD is but one means among others to achieve universal love. That aim is the root of Ginsberg's appeal, together with the impression of absolute commitment to truthfulness and to the right of an individual to follow his psyche wherever it may lead at whatever private cost.

What was touching about Ginsberg's testimony (and won the hearts of young admirers of his with whom I have talked) was his attempt to magnetize the Senators into the orbit of his private "magic." He wanted to induce in them the same emotional openness and vulnerability that he feels. LSD, he said, had tamed the threatening Hell's Angels and prevented them from assaulting peace-marchers in California. LSD had enabled him to overcome hatred toward the President and to pray for him as a victim of his own problems and policies rather than to view him as a criminal.

Ginsberg took these positions unselfconsciously and undefensively. He assumed they were natural and inevitable and his authority among young sensitives is closely related to that sort of assumption of rightness. To them he seems very much like the angel in a too-little known poem by his beloved Blake:

I asked a thief to steal me a peach:
He turned up his eyes.
I ask'd a lithe lady to lie her down:
Holy & meek she cries.
As soon as I went an angel came:
He wink'd at the thief
And smil'd at the dame,
And without one work spoke
Had a peach from the tree,
And 'twixt earnest & joke
Enjoy'd the Lady.

In the wake of the traumatic history of this century, along with our absorption with power and efficiency, has come an ever more drastic sense of individual disorientation. The tendency was long ago foreshadowed in the effects of the Industrial Revolution on poetic sensibility, and we have now come perilously close to maximum anxiety about the point of existence and about the relevance of prevailing social expectations to the ego's need for reassuring identity.

Ginsberg's emphasis on the primary importance of intense self-awareness, on experience so keen and revealing that it opens one increasingly to one's self as a physical and highly sensitized being (and therefore opens one at the same time to other persons and to the whole revealed universe) strikes many people with a force at once religious and esthetic. It is a new and active Romanticism that he offers.

The esthetic life—the life of sensation, of creative self-exploration and of the transformation of existence through imposing on it the visions of the artist—becomes the clue to general liberation. The dynamic, affectionate, unashamed poet comes into his own as leader and prophet of a personalist revolution.

What about the poetry itself? I have already suggested that it is difficult to sort it out from the impact of Ginsberg's personality. Since his public readings have contributed much to that impact, the difficulty is twice compounded. However, it is still basically true that his reputation rests on four books, the "Howl" volume of 1956 and three later ones, and that in them only a fairly small number of poems are of genuinely artistic interest.

These poems include the title-poem of the first book (together with the short "Footnote to Howl," really a fourth section of the same poem) and, in the same tiny collection, the ironically charming "A Supermarket in California," the visionary "Sunflower Sutra" and "In the Baggage Room at Greyhound," and the jeering "America."

In the later collections—*Kaddish and Other Poems* (1961), *Empty Mirror: Early Poems* (1961) and *Reality Sandwiches* (1963)—only the long "Kaddish" stands out with any real power. A confessional sequence based on the madness of the poet's mother, it is in many ways comparable to Robert Lowell's *Life Studies*, which was published the year that *Kaddish* was completed. The *Kaddish* volume has "To Aunt Rose," a sentimentally moving piece, and "Ignu" an attractive bit of buffoonery. Otherwise, its chief interest apart from the title-poem lies in a number of improvisational poems written under the influence of laughing gas, mescaline, lysergic acid, and ayahuasca.

As contributions to a "psychodelic" anthology they, together with the very long "Aether" in *Reality Sandwiches*, would surely have an important place. As poetry, they intermingle predictable notations with some fine moments. The poems in *Empty Mirror* are interesting mainly as indications that the later Ginsberg was prefigured even in the cocoon, but most of even *Reality Sandwiches* was written at about the same time as the pieces in *Howl* or earlier. In short, Ginsberg's reputation rests most surely on two poems completed between 1956 and 1959: "Howl" and "Kaddish." There are many flashes elsewhere of his unique vigor, wit and capacity for feeling, but these are the most striking works so far.

The initial thrust of "Howl" was sensational. For the first time in the history of serious, yet relatively popular American poetry, full use was being made of the arsenal of obscene and scatalogical colloquialisms of this ingenious nation. The purely verbal shock, however, was supported by Ginsberg's bitter rhetoric, the burden of which was that a generation of young Americans had been betrayed and psychically crippled—sacrificed to the ruthlessness of Moloch, not only the god of war but also the very embodiment of the principle of impersonal power worshipped by America. At the same time, the effect was leavened by a wildly whimsical humor (as in the poet's pledge in the final line of "America"—"America I'm putting my queer shoulder to the wheel") and by a rhapsodic momentum.

But Ginsberg does not give us the unadulteratedly elemental speech of street, farm and factory after all. The surrounding thought makes a great difference, and usually the more basic language is engulfed in deliberately intellectual phrasing.

Moreover, Ginsberg's imagery of sexuality is so hysterically frenzied that it suggests not a wanton self-indulgence, but a compulsive search for love and acceptance through ceaselessly self-defeating, almost automatic, activity. One hardly ever discerns those "lineaments of gratified desire" that, according to William Blake, are what men and women do "most admire" in one another as the result of love.

The visionary side of Ginsberg's poetry—the search for exaltation that can sometimes express itself, for instance, in a mystical identification of joy in the sunrise with sexual rapture—does have its affinities with Blake, though it is qualitatively different in itself and in its psychological derivation.

Looking back to the beginning of "Howl," one sees that the motif of neurotically intensified activity enters the very first line: "I saw the best minds of my generation destroyed by madness, starving hysterical naked." The phrase "best minds" has been harped on by hostile critics. I take it that Ginsberg means by it the most vulnerable, or suggestible, spirits, seismographic responders in their very character formation to the atmosphere of the times. He thrusts their predicament upon us with a half-comic violence that implies a revolutionary attitude in which social and political criticism are inseparable from private psychological and moral breakdown. His heroes have forgotten normal manly pride and responsibility as they "cowered in unshaven rooms in underwear, burning their money in wastebaskets and listening to the Terror through the wall."

The clue to all this is really given in "Kaddish." It was implied in a few elusive references to his mother Naomi's madness in "Howl" and "Footnote to Howl" and also in his obsession with the theme of madness and confinement in these poems, as well as with the theme of anguished neglect. "Children screaming under the stairways! Boys sobbing in armies! Old men weeping in the parks!" Underlying the need for prophetic vision are the terror expressed in "Howl" and the disgust, guilt, and fear of following in his mother's footsteps revealed in "Kaddish."

The full title is "Kaddish for Naomi Ginsberg 1894–1956." The kaddish is the Hebrew lament for the dead, which is at the same time a hymn of praise to God. Modeling his poem on the traditional form, Ginsberg divides it into a six-part sequence: "Proem," "Narrative." "Hymmnn," "Lament," "Litany" and "Fugue." Of these the "Narrative" is the most important both in substance and in length; it makes up two-thirds of the whole sequence.

Here we have the story of Naomi's paranoia, degeneration, and death. It is told in humiliating detail, far more harrowing than that in Robert Lowell's

Life Studies. Not that Ginsberg is a poet of greater power; his technical resources and ability to channel his materials to greatest effect are inferior to Lowell's. But Naomi's case and its traumatic effect on young Allen were terrible, desperate. The family's poverty, combined with the hysterical atmosphere, deprived it of dignity; nor could the children be at all protected against the violence of the experience.

To handle all these well-nigh uncontrollable elements, Ginsberg resorted to a line, or prose-paragraph, that does not so much contain them as release them and keep them moving. He has described the method as "the long line breaking up within itself into short staccato breath units—notations of one spontaneous phrase after another linked within the line by dashes mostly: the long line now perhaps a variable stanzaic unit, measuring groups of related ideas, marking them—a method of notation." It is the line of Whitman, Lawrence, Fearing without their syntactic ear.

The pathos and hideous squalor and waste of Naomi's life, her terrible transformation whereby an ardent young revolutionary idealist came to suspect the whole world (including her mother and her sister, whom she would kick mercilessly) of plotting against her on behalf of capitalists and Trotskyites, are the real source of the emotion of "Howl" and the revulsion against himself in so many of Ginsberg's other writings.

In "Mescaline," the association between the "smell of Naomi" and the notion of himself as "familiar rotting Ginsberg" is stated so casually as to be one of our few examples of the facetious statement of despondency. It is somehow a betrayal of the wonderful effort in "Kaddish" to be perfectly true to the bestial reality of Naomi's life and still to counter-assert the need for human transcendence, for there are indeed beautiful moments of such realization in that poem.

Despite all that can be said in criticism, though—and it is a great deal—there is sure energy in much of Ginsberg's writing. It is partly élan, partly sheer ability to give rhythmic body to emotion—an essential poetic gift. In poems whose over-all structure absolutely goes to pieces, he often, nevertheless, holds us captive at certain moments.

In a sense he is best in small, unpretentious poems like the "Dream Record: June 8, 1955," in which he is disciplined by the desire to be true to the reality of a dead friend's humanity, or "My Sad Self," with its quiet lyric intensity. The *Empty Mirror* poems make perfectly clear how at one stage he immersed himself in the masters from Shakespeare to Yeats. Now that he is 40, they have all the more to teach him about the directions he must take for the perfecting of his art.

However, apart from the fact that "perfecting his art" may seem to him a secondary, overly formalistic consideration, there are various barriers to further progress. The writing has always been uneven in quality and usually confused in its motives. As a poet, Ginsberg has one good ear and one bad ear. If, given these facts, the poetry has nevertheless generated its own power and been interesting, it remains true that the drama of Naomi's life and of the poet's inescapable identification with her was the driving force behind "Howl" and "Kaddish."

It compelled him to improvise a unifying form, but by the same token the impulse toward structured work seems to have exhausted itself with the completion of the latter poem. However internalized, the objective details of the family history that had to be brought out into the open prevented rhetoric, on the one hand, and exhibitionism or a variety of half-gloating, subjective gossip, on the other, from taking over completely. Almost all the later work that I have seen points to a relaxing of tension and blurring of perspective, while the poet awaits some reinvigorating change to occur that will carry him to another high point. One poem though—"The Change: Kyoto-Tokyo Express," written in 1963—has an unusually tight concentrated structure. It is a passionate attempt by the poet to exorcise self-revulsion and thus to ready himself for that "change" which involves not only himself but the whole vile pattern of war and human suffering of our world. (This poem appears in a collection of Ginsberg's work, in English and Italian, published in 1965, in Milan, by Arnoldo Mondadore Editore under the title *Jukebox All'Idrogeno*. The translation into Italian is by Fernanda Pivano, who also provides an excellent introduction and notes.)

Ginsberg, in his roles both as poet and as public figure, attracts, repels, confuses—and does these things to himself, I am sure, as much as to the rest of us. He is one embodiment of our new fascination with the idea of a cast into the unknown to discover who we really are and what we really want, lest we become finally convinced that the present drift of all our enterprises has irretrievably become our fate.

New York Times Book Review (14 August 1966)

William Carlos Williams: More Than Meets the Eye

(Introduction to *The William Carlos Williams Reader*, edited by M. L. Rosenthal)

1.

THE death of William Carlos Williams on March 4, 1963, at the age of seventy-nine, ended his unusual career, at once so brilliant and so humble, in the most literal sense only. Two days later, the news broke that finally a British publisher was going to bring out his poems—a special irony because he had waged bitter war against the English influence on American poetry and because the English had been largely deaf to his voice in the past. In May he received posthumously both the Pulitzer Prize and the Gold Medal for Poetry of the National Institute of Arts and Letters. In the same year the expanded edition of *The Collected Later Poems* and the paperback edition of the complete *Paterson* sequence appeared. The present volume is a response to the widening and deepening interest in Williams. It is a selection from the whole range of his writings: poetry, drama, fiction, and other prose.

Prolific as he was in various genres, Dr. Williams was clearly a poet first of all, as the whole emphasis of his career and of his development as a craftsman proves. The rest of his work, therefore, is from a critical standpoint important primarily for its relationship to his poetry. Yet it is misleading to put the matter so, for much of that work is absorbing in its own right even if the reader has no great interest in poetry. Williams's short stories are often vital evocations of ordinary American reality—its toughness, squalor, pathos, intensities. Many have to do with his relation as a doctor to poor folk and their children in the industrialized section of New Jersey in which he lived and had his practice. (Medicine not only enabled him to support his family. It gave him emotional ballast and was itself the source of some of his most impressive writing.) His method in these stories approaches that of Anderson and Hemingway, but when he becomes white-hot in his excitement over the characters, as in "Jean Beicke" or "A Face of Stone," the work is essential Williams and nobody else.

So also in the Stecher trilogy, in which the author seeks to repossess the childhood of his wife: her babyhood, her parents' characters, her relation to her older sister, the total quality of this immigrant family on the rise in the years before the first World War. The novels of this trilogy, which appeared at distant intervals (1937, 1940, 1952), are uneven and sometimes sketchy and derivative. Again, though, the most striking chapters are informed by Williams's experience as pediatrician and obstetrician, a fact that may well account for the superiority of the earlier volumes, *White Mule* and *In the Money,* to the last one, *The Build-Up*. The interpretations of a baby's awareness (in pleasure, illness, fears), the accurate pictures of the mentality and anxieties of mothers, the understanding of what we might call the imperturbability of physiological fact—all with its Rabelaisian aspects as well as its anguish—are unique, and uniquely interesting, in our literature. The driving, insensitive ambition of the mother and the contrastingly introverted individualism of the highly intelligent father are set against one another with unforgettable authority. Sometimes, as in the story of Joe Stecher's triumph over crookedness and bribery in his fight to get a government printing contract, Williams gives sharp glimpses of a world of business and power outside the one of women and babies and the local ecology of family life. The scene in which Joe Stecher and Teddy Roosevelt face each other in a momentary tangency of their so different orbits, the public man speaking of "my policy" and the ironic creative man whose whole sense of value centers on concrete techniques, is based on an actual incident in the life of Williams's father-in-law.

Behind the Stecher trilogy we can see some overriding preoccupations relevant to all of Williams's work. His special interest in women—what they are really like, how they grow into their maturity, their sources of strength and weakness, their real relationship to the oversimplified visions of male sexuality—is certainly implied in this extensive imaginative exploration of his wife's early life and ambience. *The Autobiography,* short stories, and poems give further emphasis, explicitly, to this preoccupation. It is at once a matter of the normal erotic range of interest and curiosity and of something else, a romantic sense of mystery pursued through the unorthodox methods of the realist. (See, for instance, the short story "The Burden of Loveliness" and the poem "The Raper from Passenack.") It sometimes appears that the more gross or brutal the details, the more the mystery is heightened for Williams, and the more he is in love with the female principle in all its bewildering variations. Compassion is an important ingredient, but also there is a curious bafflement at once challenging and discouraging, and perhaps a sense of the entrapment of the demonic male in a kind of maze of domesticities characteristic of the whole modern relationship between men and women. More than a hint of his bafflement is given in the scene printed in the present collection from the play *A Dream of Love,* and his essay "Jacataqua" locates its source as specifically American. But this is only the negative side of Williams's romantic preoccupation with certain mysteries. *The Autobiography* gives us the other side, in a passage concerning the meaning to him of his medical career:

> And my "medicine" was the thing that gained me entrance to . . . [the] secret gardens of the self. It lay there, another world, in the self. I was permitted by my medical badge to follow the poor, defeated body into those gulfs and grottos. And the astonishing thing is that at such times and in such places—foul as they may be with the stinking ischio-rectal abscesses of our comings and goings—just there, the thing, in all its greatest beauty, may for a moment be freed to fly for a moment guiltily about the room. In illness, in the permission I as a physician have had to be present at deaths and births, at the tormented battles between daughter and diabolic mother, shattered by a gone brain—just there—for a split second—from one side or the other, it has fluttered before me for a moment . . .
>
> (*The Autobiography,* pp. 288–289)

Another preoccupation of Williams's thought and art reflected in the Stecher novels is the meaning of the American relationship to Europe. The well-known native ambivalence on this subject is not lacking in Williams, himself a second-generation American. The familiar contradictory pulls of attraction to the culture of Europe, determination to make a new start in terms as indigenous to the United States as possible, and a sense of the distorting and demeaning effect on personality of the American absorption in power, wealth, and abstract process are important in the novels. An insistent longing to restore or at least rediscover lost continuities without surrendering to them asserts itself in different ways in all the important characters. In an earlier autobiographical novel, *A Voyage to Pagany* (1928), and then in *The Autobiography* (1951), the poet pursues the meaning for himself of these warring feelings and attitudes. German medicine, the artistic and intellectual vitality of Paris, the self-acceptance of European women are placed, in *A Voyage to Pagany,* in direct confrontation with the hero's sense of his "hard, barren life" at home, "where I am 'alone' and unmolested (work as I do in the thick of it) though in constant danger lest some slip send me to perdition but which, being covetous not at all, I enjoy for the seclusion and primitive air of it."

Both this book and *The Autobiography* show how important European study and experience were to Williams as a boy and again as a grown man with a certain reputation in avant-garde circles, the literary associate of Ezra Pound, Robert McAlmon, and other Americans of some recognition in Paris and London. Equally, they show how impossible for him the life of the expatriate artist would have been. As he goes on to explain in the passage just quoted, America possessed for him, despite his isolation there and despite its "primitive" character, "an attraction in all the inanimate associations of my youth, shapes, foliage, trees to which I am used—and a love of place and the characteristics of place—good or bad, rich or poor." (Incidentally, the chapter in which these remarks are made was omitted from the printed version of the novel because the publisher considered the book too long, though Williams considered it "the best chapter." It was later published as a short story, "The Venus," and is therefore included separately under that title in the present collection.)

Williams was not precocious, though he was constantly and intimately in touch with precocious people. He was in his early thirties when he began to find himself as a poet, and in his later thirties when he did really find himself. His development was a slow one for an artist of such spontaneous and passionate energies. This fact, together with his feeling for place and the effects of having had a medical rather than a literary education, accounts for his resistance to the expatriate life of so many of his friends.

It also, quite obviously, helps account for his interest in making his work idiosyncratically American, but in a cosmopolitan rather than merely a provincial sense. He well understood the advantages of European culture and manners but taught himself to redirect those values in the American context. One might note with surprise the way in which his "early" prose poems in *Kora in Hell* and his prose-poetic chapters in *The Great American Novel* parallel French models and are nevertheless American in much of their substance and attitude—their humor, for instance, and their frank homeliness: "*A man watches his wife clean house. He is filled with knowledge by his wife's exertions. This is incomprehensible to her. Knowing she will never understand his excitement he consoles himself with the thought of art.*" (*Kora in Hell*, p. 67). But then one should remind oneself that he was thirty-seven when the former book was published and forty—just the age of the hero of *A Voyage to Pagany*—when the latter book appeared.

The "Prologue" to *Kora in Hell*[1] is too lengthy and diffuse, despite its importance for students of poetry, to be published in this volume. But it is significant for the light it throws on Williams's literary position at a critical point in his development. It is partly an account and evaluation of various fellow poets, partly a defense and proliferation of the "improvisations" in his book, and partly a presentation and consideration of criticisms by other poets of his work so far. Thus, he quotes from a letter of Pound's attacking his pretensions to being especially American in his poetry:

1. Reprinted in *Selected Essays*, pp. 3–29.

> . . . What the h–l do you a blooming foreigner know about the place. Your *père* only penetrated the edge, and you've never been west of Upper Darby, or the Maunchunk switchback.
>
> Would H. [Harriet Monroe] with the swirl of the prairie wind in her underwear, or the Virile Sandburg recognize you, an effete Easterner as a REAL American? INCONCEIVABLE!!!!!
>
> My dear boy you have never felt the woop of the PEEraries. . . .
>
> The thing that saves your work is opacity, and don't forget it. Opacity is NOT an American quality. Fizz, swish, gabble, and verbiage, these are *echt americanisch*. . . .

Williams replies indirectly, but what he says is especially interesting in that he implies that there is some truth to what Pound is saying but suggests that he is getting at a nativist poetry in a new way. He will use European methods but at the same time will turn his back on Europe and allow the methods to find their American expression:

> I like to think of the Greeks as setting out for the colonies in Sicily and the Italian peninsula. The Greek temperament lent itself to a certain symmetrical sculptural phase and to a fat poetical balance of line that produced important work but I like better the Greeks setting their backs to Athens. The ferment was always richer in Rome, the dispersive explosion was always nearer, the influence carried further and remained hot longer. . . .

Again, he considers a criticism by Hilda Doolittle of one of his poems. H. D. had written:

> I trust you will not hate me for wanting to delete from your poem all the flippancies. The reason I want to do this is that the beautiful lines are so very beautiful . . . and real beauty is a rare and sacred thing in this generation. . . . I don't know what you think but I consider this business of writing a very sacred thing! . . . I feel in the hey-ding-ding touch running through your poem a derivative tendency which, to me, is not *you*—not your very self. It is as if you were ashamed of your Spirit, ashamed of your inspiration!—as if you mocked at your own song! It's very well to mock at yourself—it is a spiritual sin to mock at your inspiration.

Williams defends his buffoonery because it helps him liberate imaginative energy and counteract the too confining expectations of formal perfectionism:

> . . . There is nothing sacred about literature, it is damned from one end to the other. There is nothing in literature but change and change is mockery. I'll write whatever I damn please, whenever I damn please and it'll be good if the authentic spirit of change is on it.
>
> But in any case H. D. misses the entire intent of what I am doing no matter how just her remarks concerning that particular poem happen to have been. The hey-ding-ding touch *was* derivative, but it filled a gap

> that I did not know how better to fill at the time. It might be said that that touch is the prototype of the improvisations.
>
> It is to the inventive imagination we look for deliverance from every other misfortune as from the desolation of a flat Hellenic perfection of style. . . . If the inventive imagination must look, as I think, to the field of art for its richest discoveries today it will best make its way by compass and follow no path.
>
> But before any material progress can be accomplished there must be someone to draw a discriminating line between true and false values.
>
> The true value is that particularity which gives an object a character by itself. The associational or sentimental value is the false. Its imposition is due to lack of imagination, to an easy lateral sliding. The attention has been held too rigid on the one plane instead of following a more flexible, jagged resort. It is to loosen the attention, my attention since I occupy part of the field, that I write these improvisations.

The defense against H. D.'s strictures turned without warning into a reply to objections by Wallace Stevens in still another letter. Stevens had complained about the "casual character" of Williams's poems. His letter, containing the famous observation that "a book of poems is a damned serious affair," argued for a consistency of method and viewpoint such as one does find, indeed, in Stevens's own poetry:

> . . . My idea is that in order to carry a thing to the extreme necessity to convey it one has to stick to it . . . Given a fixed point of view, realistic, imagistic, or what you will, everything adjusts itself to that point of view; the process of adjustment is a world in flux, as it should be for a poet. But to fidget with points of view leads always to new beginnings and incessant new beginnings lead to sterility. . . .

Williams felt that his reply to H. D. was a reply to Stevens as well. It is easy, he wrote, to fall under the spell of Stevens's mode of work, but the real problem is that of "lifting to the imagination those things which lie under the direct scrutiny of the senses, close to the nose. It is this difficulty that sets a value upon all works of art and makes them a necessity."

In all these instances, Williams makes allowance for the validity of his friends' *descriptions* of his work, but he also readjusts the perspective, as it were. What they consider weaknesses he views as veerings in a new direction. Taken together, the letters and his responses give us the context and kernel of his attitudes as a practicing poet.

I have grouped *The Great American Novel* with *Kora in Hell* because the term "improvisations" applies to it equally well. In both these experimental forays Williams reworks the prose poem in such a way as to allow for free narrative movement and association, for outbursts of exuberant buffoonery, for the introduction of critical assertions and of historical data and theory, and for autobiographical and confessional details. But *The Great American Novel* is far less "literary" and precious than *Kora in Hell,* though I do not mean, obviously, to disparage the germinal inventiveness of the latter book. In a short time, Williams had advanced toward the sure voice of a poetic master, taking the best qualities of *Kora in Hell* and widening their usefulness. He was now able to involve his immediate experiences as a doctor and his personal knowledge of the sexual and marital problems of a mature adult in his poems, and to bring sharply to bear, for instance, the role of the automobile in all its ludicrous, ironic, and deadly serious and deeply American importance. The gaiety and melancholy that result, and the total relevance, far surpass those of *Kora in Hell*. It is easy to see *Paterson* and the other work of the older Williams emphatically foreshadowed here.

Williams, then, had over a period of time given himself room and time to study his own possibilities and to formulate them. Not unlike Yeats, he "re-made" himself and opted for new beginnings, brutal and abrupt if necessary, using himself as the embodiment of an American self-awareness free of that kind of innocence which is actually ignorance. His prose matrix for the poems of *Spring and All*, dropped after the first publication of 1923,[2] was already the work of a mature thinker with a good idea of what he was doing. So was his recapitulation of what Horace Gregory called America's "mythical history": *In the American Grain* (1925). An explosive, freshly improvisatory intelligence, able to think imagistically and to see thoughts as new, sensuously felt insights, was being put to the service of a long-pondered program.

2.

I have already noted that Williams was of course a poet first of all, and it is in the poetry that his deep contemplation of his principles as a writer counts the most finally. We have no other poet so intriguing, and so misleading, to a reader who takes up his work for the first time. How vulnerable to imitation, how simple and spontaneous he seems!

> The sea that encloses her young body
> ula lu la lu
> is the sea of many arms—

But have a care! Even this fragment, the beginning stanza of "The Sea," has more than spontaneity and immediacy alone—though these are in themselves a great deal. It has the accurate pitch, the sure music, of "When that Aprille with his shoures soote" or "Shall I compare thee to a summer's day." Williams's disingenuousness of technique reveals itself in the counterpointing of front and back vowels, in the "light" rhymes and repetitions ("sea," "body," "many"), and in the intruded lullabying break that prepares us for similar refrain effects later in the poem. With this stanza as a start the poet goes into a varied contemplation of the multiple symbolism of woman and sea, maintain-

2. The poems were later printed in sequence without the prose, and still later given individual titles instead of being merely numbered, though they are still grouped in *The Collected Later Poems* as "Spring and All." I have included a selection from the original prose in this book, and kept the original whimsical numbering in the portions here reprinted, though the simple typographical foolery of shuffling the order of numbers, printing upside-down, and shifting from Arabic to Roman numerals cannot be fully represented in our shortened text.

ing a penumbra of mystery through varied shiftings of intensity and shadings of thought:

> In the sea the young flesh playing
> floats with the cries of far off men
> who rise in the sea...

Beneath the impromptu surface many associations are made to converge in a single vision of all-embracing sexuality; the sea has been psychologically—that is, humanly—re-embodied.

Quite as deceptive, many of Williams's shorter poems seem at first glance mere impressionistic notes or figures caught shimmering in a momentary visual frame. Among the best known of these pieces is "The Red Wheelbarrow":

> so much depends
> upon
>
> a red wheel
> barrow
>
> glazed with rain
> water
>
> beside the white
> chickens.

The sense of being alive, this poem and many others imply, depends on our viewing the familiar world with a fresh eye. The standpoint from which we view that world and its intensities determines the scope of life's meaning for us. The humblest objects of perception are also elements in a symbolic design with a transcendent aesthetic function. To see them thus is to liberate ourselves and them from the rut and squalor in which the mass of men lead their "lives of quiet desperation." It is to bring to bear upon any momentary observation or set of circumstances the whole of imagination and sensibility, and to gain courage from the application.

> ... the thing that stands eternally in the way of really good writing is always one: the virtual impossibility of lifting to the imagination those things which lie under the direct scrutiny of the senses, close to the nose. It is this difficulty that sets a value upon all works of art and makes them a necessity. The senses witnessing what is immediately before them in detail see a finality which they cling to in despair, not knowing which way to turn. Thus the so-called natural or scientific array becomes fixed, the walking devil of modern life. He who even nicks the solidity of this apparition does a piece of work superior to that of Hercules when he cleaned the Augean stables.
>
> ("Prologue," *Kora in Hell*)

To Williams it seemed a natural corollary of this emphasis to remain close to native American sources. Moreover, this program seemed the way to get out from under the derivativeness that saddled his peers and rivals:

> But our prize poems [he wrote in 1920] are especially to be damned not because of superficial bad workmanship, but because they are rehash, repetition—just as Eliot's more exquisite work is rehash, repetition in another way of Verlaine, Baudelaire, Maeterlinck—conscious or unconscious—just as there were Pound's early paraphrases from Yeats and his constant later cribbing from the Renaissance, Provence and the modern French: Men content with the connotations of their masters.
>
> . . . Eliot is a subtle conformist. . . .
>
> ("Prologue," *Kora in Hell*)

No wonder Pound (always a close friend) was irritated into replying:

> There is a blood poison in America; you can idealize the place (easier now that Europe is so damn shaky) all you like, but you haven't a drop of the cursed blood in you, and you don't need to fight the disease day and night; you never have had to. Eliot has it worse than I—poor devil.
>
> You have the advantage of arriving in the milieu with a fresh flood of Europe in your veins, Spanish, French, English, Danish. You had not the thin milk of New York and New England from the pap; and you can therefore keep the environment outside you, and decently objective.[3]

But one has only to read "To Elsie"—

> The pure products of America
> go crazy—

to realize that Williams had a sense as bitter as Pound's of the "poison" in the native blood. In fact, he *stayed* in America just as angrily and vigorously as Pound *left* America. Each of them is in a curious way an alternative possibility of the other. Simply to contemplate this fact is to see something of Williams's role and location in contemporary poetry.

The two poets met at the University of Pennsylvania, shortly after the turn of the century. Pound exerted a tremendous influence from the start, though in part this influence generated a movement in poetry directly opposed to his own conceptions. The first thing Williams's preface to the *Selected Essays* tells us, for instance, is how he came to know Pound. And if we glance, however idly, through the pages of that collection of essays and reviews, we can hardly help noting the many reminders of Pound and his passions. Thus, we find a defense of Antheil's music, a scattering of enthusiastic comments on *The Cantos*, a deep though cagey and sometimes determinedly hostile interest in "the tradition," and sympathetic interpretations of Joyce, Gertrude Stein, and Marianne Moore. Pound, Joyce, and Stein are held up to younger writers as models. *The Cantos* are criticized frankly in some respects, yet an

3. *The Letters of Ezra Pound: 1907–1941*, ed. by D.D. Paige (N.Y.: Harcourt, Brace, 1950), p. 158.

essential admiration and rapport is the dominant note: "We have, examining the work, successes—great ones—the first molds—clear cut, never turgid, not following the heated trivial—staying cold, 'classical' but swift with a movement of thought." ("Excerpts from a Critical Sketch")

In both writers, too, an attack on the main direction of American society goes together with a radical rejection of modern economic practices and a call for the violent breakthrough of human creativity. Williams's insertion of a Social-Credit propaganda leaflet in the poem *Paterson* and his portrait of Poe striving desperately to originate a truly American poetry amid the corruption and imitativeness of the national drift are two obvious examples among many of this identity or at least overlap of attitude. Certainly Williams and Pound are at one in a driving conviction, evangelical in nature, that man's best possibilities, brutally subverted and driven underground, must be brought to the surface through a freeing of pagan impulses—a "revelation" which is also a moral and cultural revolution: "to get at the actual values that concern man where they frequently lie buried in his mind." ("Revelation," *Selected Essays*, p. 271) Here is their kinship with Blake, Whitman, and the Romantic spirit. The Romantic aim of actualizing the ideal becomes that of reactivating natural men's motives through art. Thinking in his *Autobiography* of Pound's "mission," Williams says:

> The poem is a capsule where we wrap up our punishable secrets. And as they confine in themselves the only "life," the ability to sprout at a more favorable time, to come true in their secret structure to the very minutest details of our thoughts, so they get their specific virtue.
>
> (*The Autobiography*, p. 343)

But Williams was his own man, and one of his most striking characteristics is the fashion in which he worked his shared interests toward unique, idiosyncratic ends. For instance, he tells us that he began to be interested in Laforgue, an important figure for Pound and Eliot, only when he read an article by Kenneth Burke demonstrating how the French poet "has taken what he finds most suitable to his own wants, what at least he has, and made it *the* thing" by "building upon the basis of what is observed, what is proved, and what is of value to the man in the welter as he found it." By a similar shift of emphasis, Williams's essay on Poe finds that the nineteenth-century poet was struggling with precisely the problems of technique and of the meaning of an American art that Williams struggled with. This essay, therefore, becomes one of our clearest expositions of Williams's own poetic rationale. Similarly, he praises a Matisse painting not because of its relation either to tradition or to "modernism," but because it is so easily and rightly of its own place, as American art should be of *its* place:

> No man in my country has seen a woman naked and painted her as if he knew anything except that she was naked. No woman in my country is naked except at night.
>
> In the french sun, on the french grass in a room on Fifth Ave., a french girl lies and smiles at the sun without seeing us.
>
> ("A Matisse," *Selected Essays*, p. 31)

The work of Ford Madox Ford is valued for the same reason: "His British are British in a way the American, Henry James, never grasped. They fairly smell of it." In the poem "To Ford Madox Ford in Heaven," a further implication of this conception of the values inherent in place is brought into the open. The novelist is beatified as the apostle of the sensual and earthy:

A heavenly man you seem to me now, never
  having been for me a saintly one.
It lived about you, a certain grossness that
  was not like the world.
The world is cleanly, polished and well
  made but heavenly man
is filthy with his flesh and corrupt that
  loves to eat and drink and whore . . .

Williams's enthusiasm for local values, then, carries readily with it a sense of the paradoxical "heavenliness" of the physical and the ordinary. America, impatient to loose its own still unexplored meanings, is the more open to the new because of the past suppression of American sensibility in favor of European and English standards. Hence, it was natural, as Williams points out in his devastating defense of Joyce against Rebecca West's strictures, for Americans to respond more quickly to Joyce than the British could:

> Joyce is breaking with a culture older than England's when he goes into his greatest work. It is the spirit liberated to run through everything, that makes him insist on unexpurgated lines and will not brook the limitations which good taste would enforce. It is to break the limitations, not to conform to the taste that his spirit runs.
>
> ("A Point for American Criticism," *Selected Essays*, p. 88)

These are recurring motifs in Williams's criticism. What he says about Joyce is very much like what he says about Whitman, and seeing the quotations side by side may help dispel any notion that his nativism is at all parochial:

> Whitman. . . . For God's sake! He broke through the deadness of copied forms which keep shouting above everything that wants to get said today drowning out one man with the accumulated weight of a thousand voices in the past—re-establishing the tyrannies of the past . . . The structure of the old is active, it says no! to everything in propaganda and poetry that wants to say yes. Whitman broke through that.
>
> ("Against the Weather," *Selected Essays*, p. 218)

All these considerations carry with them the danger that we may forget we are talking about a poet, and one whose chief talent, at that, lies in the writing of "simple, sensuous, and passionate" rather than ratiocinative verse. "All I do," Pound quotes Williams as saying, "is to try to understand something in its natural colours and shapes"; and Pound observes: "There could be no better effort underlying any literary process, or used as preparative for literary process."[4] The claim Williams makes for himself may be too modest, but his

4. *The Literary Essays of Ezra Pound* (N.Y.: New Directions, 1954), p. 390.

amazingly vivid sense of the life around him is certainly the foundation of everything he writes. Randall Jarrell's characterization is arch but to the point.

> Williams' poetry is more remarkable for its empathy, sympathy, its muscular and emotional identification with its subject, than any other contemporary poetry except Rilke's. When you have read *Paterson* you know for the rest of your life what it is like to be a waterfall; and what other poet has turned so many of his readers into trees? Occasionally one realizes that this latest tree of Williams' is considerably more active than anyone else's grizzly bear; but usually the identification is so natural, the feel and rhythm of the poem so hypnotic, that the problem of belief never arises.[5]

This extraordinary empathic responsiveness, to trees and flowers especially, recalls D. H. Lawrence, with whom Williams has other affinities also. By the time he was nine or ten, the poet tells us in his *Autobiography*, he had learned

> the way moss climbed about a tree's roots, what growing dogwood and iron wood looked like; the way rotten leaves will mat down in a hole—and their smell when turned over—every patch among those trees had its character, moist or dry. . . .
>
> It is a pleasure for me now to think of these things, but especially of the flowers I got to know. . . . The slender neck of the anemone particularly haunts me for some reason and the various sorts of violets. . . . My curiosity in these things was unbounded—secret certainly. There is a long history in each of us that comes as not only a reawakening but a repossession when confronted by this world. . . .
>
> (*The Autobiography*, p. 19)

In the poems this repossession is visceral, complete. We see a young tree rising

> bodily
>
> into the air with
> one undulant
> thrust half its height. . . .
> ("Young Sycamore")

Other trees, seen on a winter night, present a grotesque Tam O'Shanter dance vision:

> Limb to limb, mouth to mouth
> with the bleached grass
> silver mist lies upon the back yards
> among the outhouses.
> The dwarf trees
> pirouette awkwardly to it—

5. "Introduction" to Williams's *Selected Poems* (N.Y.: New Directions, 1949), p. xii.

whirling round on one toe;
the big tree smiles and glances
upward!
("Winter Quiet")

Williams never wanted to wear his mind on his sleeve, but it is hard to attribute his reputation as a completely unintellectual poet, in fact an anti-intellectual one, to any cause but unsympathetic reading. "Almost everything in Dr. Williams's poetry," says R.P. Blackmur,

> almost everything, ... including the rendering, is unexpanded notation. He isolates and calls attention to what we are already presently in possession of. Observation of which any good novelist must be constantly capable, here makes a solo appearance: the advantage is the strength of isolation as an attention-caller to the terrible persistence of the obvious, the unrelenting significance of the banal. Dr. Williams perhaps tries to write as the average man—that man who even less than the normal man hardly exists but is immanent. The conviction which attaches to such fine poems as ... "Spring and All" perhaps has its source, its rationale, in our instinctive willingness to find ourselves immanently average; just as, perhaps, the conviction attaching to tragic poetry is connected with our fascinated dread of seeing ourselves as normal. Dr. Williams has no perception of the normal; no perspective, no finality—for these involve, for imaginative expression, both the intellect which he distrusts and the imposed form which he cannot understand. What he does provide is a constant freshness and purity of language which infects with its own qualities an otherwise gratuitous exhibition of the sense and sentiment of humanity run-down—averaged—without a trace of significance or a vestige of fate in the fresh familiar face.[6]

Mr. Blackmur is, of course, a critic from whose "expanded notations"—to alter his phrase—many of us have learned a good deal. Misled by Williams's anti-academic stance, however, he made the mistake of seeing the poem's surface as the whole work. In February 1922, when all the world was new, Kenneth Burke had written that in Williams's poetry "the process is simply this: There is the eye, and there is the thing upon which the eye alights; while the relationship existing between the two is a poem." But Burke's mind would take for granted the whole process between germination and completion, and would hardly choose—either then or seventeen years later, when Blackmur's comment was first published—to beat the poet over the head with his talent. Other critics, following such judgments too literally and overstressing Williams's early imagism and objectivism, have discounted his "perspective," "finality," and "formal power" (Blackmur's criteria) despite the many clear evidences, several of which we have noted, to the contrary in Williams's poetry and prose.[7] Doubtless this development was unavoidable, since any

6. R.P. Blackmur, *Language As Gesture* (N.Y.: Harcourt, Brace, 1952), pp. 349–350.
7. Two notable exceptions to this kind of critical discounting were René Taupin, *L'Influence du symbolisme français sur la poésie américaine* (Paris: H. Champion, 1929) and Yvor Winters, *Primitivism and Decadence* (N.Y.: Arrow Editions, 1937).

continued attempt to absorb the exact inner "feel" of things outside oneself would inevitably lead to an initial effect of glancing impressionism, however successful or unsuccessful the full effort might turn out to be.

Actually, Williams worked out of a sophisticated and developed tradition, in whose principles he slowly educated himself throughout his career. Implicit in it is the avowal of the assumptions of the religion of art by which the symbolists and their successors have lived. (René Taupin, indeed, sought to locate Williams as a direct heir, though not a slavish imitator, of Rimbaud and the French symbolists.) The fundamental premise is that the meanest of experiential data have their transcendent aesthetic potentiality, and hence that experience is the key to realization. Characteristically, the formal structure of a Williams poem involves a closing in on the realization involving several shifts of attention or focus along the way. It is not that nothing has significance, but that everything has it; not that eye and object alone make the poem, but that these, together with ear and intellect and formal movement, shape a poem through their convergence. Conception, empathy, compassion, and technique become functions of the same thing in many of the pieces; that is, they become inseparable functions of poetic process. Hence Williams's irritation with Wallace Stevens's praise of his use of the "anti-poetic." Poor Stevens had only wished to find an elegantly paradoxical way to appreciate the process.

Here again, it is useful to recall the resemblance between Williams's sensibility and that of D. H. Lawrence. Think of the close-ups which strengthen our knowledge of the individual flame behind the common mask of anonymity. Or think of Lawrence's anguished description of the carnage winter wreaks on the birds, or of his sense of the blazing life of flowers. In "To a Dog Injured in the Street," Williams recalls further instances of suffering innocence summoned up by sight of the screaming dog. Remembering these moments of cruelty and pain, he cries out his kinship with still another poet, René Char, whose theme has like his own been the imaginative or aesthetic resolution of the violence man's condition subjects him to.

René Char
you are a poet who believes
in the power of beauty
to right all wrongs.
I believe it also.

Though Williams parts company with Lawrence in his unfaltering confidence in art's redeeming and healing powers, the difference between them on this score can easily be exaggerated. For example, the motifs of symbolic death and rebirth are important in both poets, and in parallel forms. (See, for instance, Lawrence's "New Heaven and Earth," a poem which might almost serve as a credo, in all its aspects, for Williams quite as much as for Lawrence.) But the salvation implied in the localist program of Williams, and in his many poems informed primarily by compassion, is finally aesthetic rather than purely religious, mystical, or social. In an early poem, "The Wanderer," whose motifs are later absorbed into the *Paterson* sequence, the poet shows himself attempting to awaken the people to their own rich possibility. Finally, though, it is he himself who is awakened and purified, by taking into himself the whole degradation of modern industrial life bereft of all traditional graces. The waters of the "filthy Passaic" enter his heart and soul and transform him. But it is a transformation like that in Yeats's "Byzantium" or "The Circus Animals' Desertion"—from the "foul rag-and-bone shop of the heart" to the "masterful images" of the "pure mind." As he says to René Char, it is "beauty" that will "right all wrongs."

So there's more to Williams, putting the matter very gently, than meets the eye. Even the sharp, objective snapshots which Blackmur calls "obvious"—"what we are already in possession of"—have the "more" buried in them, and not really so very deeply. The *Paterson* sequence is the outgrowth of Williams's need to bring the inner meanings out into the open and to pursue them more explicitly:

> The first idea centering upon the poem, *Paterson,* came alive early: to find an image large enough to embody the whole knowable world about me. The longer I lived in my place, among the details of my life, I realized that these isolated observations and experiences needed pulling together to gain "profundity." I already had the river . . . I wanted, if I was to write in a larger way than of the birds and flowers, to write about the people close about me: to know in detail, minutely what I was talking about—to the whites of their eyes, to their very smells.
>
> That is the poet's business. Not to talk in vague categories but to write particularly, as a physician works, upon a patient, upon the thing before him, in the particular to discover the universal. . . .
>
> (*The Autobiography,* p. 391)

If we follow the main currents of *Paterson* through its several books we find that the effort to create "an image large enough to embody the whole knowable world" of the poet is also an effort to deal with the bleakness of that world. There is first of all its imperviousness to meaning, projected at the very start in the personification of the city as a sleeping stone-giant:

> Eternally asleep,
> his dreams walk about the city where he persists
> incognito. Butterflies settle on his stone ear.
> Immortal he neither moves nor rouses and is seldom
> seen, though he breathes and the subtleties of his machinations . . .
> animate a thousand automatons. Who because they
> neither know their sources nor the sills of their
> disappointments walk outside their bodies aimlessly for the most part,
> locked and forgot in their desires—unroused.

The whole problem is failure of communication. The people "walk incommunicado"—

> The language is missing them
> they die also
> incommunicado.

Against this failure is set the primary symbolism of primitive or peasant cultures. A picture in the *National Geographic* is described:

. . . the 9 women
of some African chief semi-naked
astraddle a log. . . .

In a "descending scale of freshness" from the proud, youngest queen, "conscious of her power"—with "uppointed breasts" that are "charged with pressures unrelieved"—to the oldest, with

. . . careworn eyes
serious, menacing—but unabashed; breasts
sagging from hard use

we see the organic relationship of natural and social orders; there is communication and wholeness here. But our modern theme is divorce: "the sign of knowledge in our time." Nature offers the same resources to us as it does to other cultures—the swirling, roaring river, the greenness of spring, or "half-grown girls hailing hallowed Easter." But our minds are rarely in harmony with nature's energies. Williams reaches into local history to find the backgrounds of a world lacking in the language of personal awakening, and finds emblems of destructive violence in the origins of the Jackson's Whites community north of Paterson, in the story of Sam Patch and his daring leaps, in the account of the death by falling of Mrs. Cummings. In the second section of Part I the poet closes in on a more personal theme: the failure of communication in love and friendship. And in the third section he faces his own hard artistic task within the limits he has set himself, recalling Pound's old taunt: "Your interest is in the bloody loam but what I am interested in is the finished product." Williams wants both, but seems unconvinced he can get them.

The quarrel with Pound continues into Part II, which explores and on the whole rejects the usefulness of libraries and traditional resources for Williams's present purposes. On Sunday in the park, we pass with him among the people, locating what he calls "the modern replicas" of the motifs already delineated in Paterson's past. What he sees still attracts and repels him in the same fashion as in "The Wanderer":

. . the ugly legs of the young girls,
pistons too powerful for delicacy! .
the men's arms, red, used to heat and cold,
to toss quartered beeves and

Yah! Yah! Yah! Yah!

—over-riding

the risks:

pouring down!

For the flower of a day!

Pound's Canto 45 had blamed the loss of standards and perspectives on *Usura*, the triumph of the principle of usury in the banking system:

with usura the line grows thick
with usura is no clear demarcation

Williams, without denying the charge, shifts the emphasis entirely in a passage that appears to be a reply to Pound:

> Without invention nothing is well spaced,
> unless the mind change, unless
> the stars are new measured, according
> to their relative positions, the
> line will not change. . . .

The call is for new constructs, new poetic measures, taking the risk of loss and immersion in the amorphous, pleasure-seeking, undirected mass of energies that is our American scene.

Everywhere, though, there is interference. The second section of Part II begins with the word "blocked." "An orchestral dullness overlays their world." The "massive church," the mulcters of cash, the political interests all interfere with creative invention: "I see they—the Senate, is trying to block Lilienthal and deliver 'the bomb' over to a few industrialists." The closest we seem to come to beauty is the kind of free-wheeling evangelism heard from a vigorous speaker in the park—an irresponsibly sharpshooting, half-deadly-accurate, half-charlatanish operator. The pessimistic prayer, growing out of the poet's bitter love for America, with which this section ends, and the almost unrelieved negations of the next section make Part II the most intense and concentrated writing of the book.

There is a "prose correlative" running through the poem—in the form of letters, news items, and other documentary passages, interesting in themselves but as it were providing a continual "outside" commentary as well as the raw material out of which the high poetic moments seem to arise. One voice in particular makes itself felt in the prose correlative, that of a woman writer whose utter loneliness and inability to come to terms with herself or to develop her poetic talents are seen as a function of the national indifference to the ideals of civilization. Her reproaches to the poet—the cry of failure reaching up to him, irrevocable and tragic, from the sea of desolation (that sea pictured so brilliantly and painfully in "The Yachts")—are part of the burden of the creative spirit in America. The block to communication between man and man, man and woman, man and his land is the result of centuries of violation of the human need for *concern*—the rape of the land pictured in *In the American Grain*, betrayal of the Indian, power monomania, brutalizing of the frontier woman, terror, and civil war. *Paterson* recalls this background at scattered moments, adds the figures of the Jackson's Whites, and presents the complaint of the woman writer as a sort of chorus, climactically effective at the end of Part II. As D. H. Lawrence's review of *In the American Grain* puts it, "The author sees the genius of the continent as a woman with exquisite, super-subtle tenderness and recoiling cruelty," who will "demand of men sensitive awareness, sensuous delicacy, infinitely tempered resistance."[8]

In *Paterson* as a whole, the poet is seen exploring the resources of the modern city, using its history, its population, its institutions as a "second body

8. D. H. Lawrence, *Phoenix* (N. Y.: Viking, 1936), p. 335.

for the human mind" (Santayana's phrase, quoted as epigraph to Part III). He is seeking to close the sexual circuit, to re-establish the contact between the male and female components of life. Unfortunately, like Lincoln as portrayed in *In the American Grain,* the poet is faced with the characteristic American confusion of the functions of the sexes. The library, symbolizing the accumulated civilization of the past, cannot help him face the "roar of the present," and there are no rules of law or love that will guide him. The poem as originally planned ends, in Part IV, with a group of tentative approaches to the meaning of love and of the future; Williams was bravely following Lawrence's challenge in the review just noted: "*Touch* America as she is; dare to touch her!" A series of brief "pastoral" dialogues involving the poet himself, a younger woman called "Phyllis," and an older woman (a Lesbian who calls herself "Corydon" and employs Phyllis as a masseuse) brings us to the heart of the sexual confusion, and to the entire cultural confusion around it.[9] Pound's ideas on economics and art, and his Odyssean theme in *Mauberley* and *The Cantos,* are brought to bear on the situation, but in such a way that Part IV ends modestly and familiarly—as it began—in the midst of things, finding something like an inner calm despite the turmoil and scramble of events and things.

Then, in the unexpectedly added fifth book, Williams refocused the issues. The transforming and saving power of the aesthetic imagination plays like a brilliant light over the old oppositions of sexuality and chastity, and of reality and the ideal. The Virgin and the Whore, the hunted-down Unicorn pictured (in a famous tapestry) in the midst of nature—images such as these do the refocusing. The poet's own perspectives have been put into sharper relation to the confused perspectives of the culture at large.

Is *Paterson* a success structurally? On the whole we should say yes, with these qualifications: *Paterson* is an *open* sequence, like *The Cantos*. As many critics have noted, the first two parts hold together as a single aesthetic compartment more beautifully and convincingly than does the whole poem finally. However, the scheme of the poem is based on a search, on a continuity, rather than on the containment of a watertight finality. It is the flow of a *river* Williams is after. "From the beginning," he wrote, "I decided there would be four books following the course of the river whose life seemed more and more to resemble my own life . . . : above the Falls, the catastrophe of the Falls itself, . . . below the Falls, and the entrance at the end into the great sea." It would have been easier to end with Part II ("catastrophe"), but twice Williams chose to reopen the poem, to stick with his own understanding of the nature of things, pragmatically and stubbornly in the midst of tragedy and confusion: "Say it, no ideas but in things." So long as the poet does not accept the "failure of speech" in modern civilization as final, so long (as Williams wrote in a comment on *Paterson*) does he "hold the key to . . . final rescue" among his still undiscovered resources. For himself, certainly, *this* poet won a decisive release through his completion of *Paterson*.

The fact lies outside the strict domain of criticism, perhaps, but it is instructive to read "Asphodel, That Greeny Flower" in the light of the search of

9. Some of the passages in these dialogues, "casual" or "slight" in their first impact, are among the most original in *Paterson* and have perhaps touched off new tendencies in verse.

Paterson. It is the work of a man who did in some fashion "come through." In it, simply, naturally, he was able to bring together the motifs of the meaning of old age and death, the nature of love, the function of poetry—all as aspects of his awareness of his relation to his wife. Even the three-unit, stanzaic broken line employed in "Asphodel" represents a coming-through. It is the line Williams always looked for—free-flowing and organic yet tightly disciplined, a beautifully patterned musical involvement of form and feeling within one another, the earned prize of Williams's poetic development:

So let us love
            confident as is the light
                        in its struggle with darkness
that there is as much to say
            and more
                        for the one side
and that not the darker . . .

3.

I came to know William Carlos Williams only a couple of years after the last war, when he had already begun to suffer those strokes that cruelly, and often, marked in his last years. It was characteristic of the man that, death being on his mind, he began to speak to me of it without preliminaries—"I think constantly of death." Of all the distinguished elderly writers I have met, he was certainly the one who stood least on ceremony. Perhaps in earlier years he had been less accessible, and vulnerable, to others. Some of his letters at the beginning of his career show that he could be short with people, and even difficult. But as he grew older he came to be bathed in the affection of many younger writers, and because he was unfailingly courteous and had the great gift of enthusiasm for the work of other poets, whether known or unknown, his influence grew. Some of the younger people who admired him never realized, I believe, the rigorous self-perfecting implied in his achievements. They never saw that what he called beauty and what his arch-"enemy" Eliot called beauty had many points in common despite their differences.

The two had other attitudes in common as well, including that unfortunate tendency to make racial generalizations often found in people educated before the first World War. Some of the comments on Jews and "niggers" one finds in Williams seem to belie his finest virtues, but they do not recur in his writing after the beginning of World War II. The issues of that war, in which his own sons served, and his revulsion against the ideas of Ezra Pound concerning it, probably brought him up to date with a jolt, although as early as "Impromptu: The Suckers," his 1927 poem on Sacco and Vanzetti, he had given evidence that he was very far indeed from anything that could be reduced to stereotype. Looking for the colorfully energetic and the interesting grotesque, writers of his generation stumbled over a psychic landscape the full danger of which had not been revealed to them in time.

I remember Williams best as a serious, wonderfully articulate, and good man talking about ordinary life and about poetry with an absolute immediacy of involvement. His thoughts, like his published criticism, were not always consistent and were certainly not uniformly original or impressive. But they were the product of long contemplation of a few principles brought to bear on the accidental issues of the moment. He admired the young and the unknown too much perhaps, and was always saying that he had learned something from any kind of passing manuscript. This made for a "soft" criticism, some people said, but he strengthened the hand of many a young man and woman by his generous, unsqueamish praise—such names as Allen Ginsberg's and Charles Olson's are only the ones that have come to some public attention, and he was equally able to praise more conventionally perfectionist poets like Lowell and Shapiro if he felt the kick of life and commitment in them. I know several young people, unpublished save in student magazines, who possess long appreciations by Williams of poems they sent him in the mail. A personal relationship, even with a stranger in this way, held sacred meaning for Williams,[10] as did any vivid experience. Not long before his death, he and Mrs. Williams came to see us on the dirty old Erie Railroad, a frail-looking couple whose anonymous presence nevertheless awoke delicate instincts of courtesy in everyone involved with the railroad all the way from Rutherford, New Jersey, to Suffern, New York. The later memory of Dr. Williams on a living-room sofa, explaining to a sixteen-year-old boy who wished to be a poet the meaning of the "variable foot"—starting his sentences, losing track of them, but keeping the inward thought fully in view all the while—is of the order of things too rich and too sad to describe. But it is of the essence of so much that made his art the moving force that it is.

I have not reproduced any of Dr. Williams's letters in this collection. Despite their interesting and illuminating passages, very few of them stand up from beginning to end as examples of his best writing. I do, however, want to quote from one letter that somehow is of a piece with the incident just described and perhaps, in its very quiet way, the best brief comment the poet could give us on the relationship between his writing and his personality. He wrote this letter to Marianne Moore on May 2, 1934, when his health and work were in full, vigorous career. She had spoken, in a review, of the "inner security" of his poems.

> The inner security . . . is something which occurred once when I was about twenty, a sudden resignation to existence, a despair—if you wish to call it that, but a despair which made everything a unit and at the same time a part of myself. I suppose it might be called a sort of nameless religious experience. I resigned, I gave up. I decided there was nothing else in life for me but to work. It is the explanation for the calumny that is heaped on my head by women and men alike once they know me long enough. I won't follow causes. I can't. The reason is that it seems so much more important to me that I *am*. Where shall one go? What shall one do? Things have no names for me and places have no significance. As a reward for this anonymity I feel as much a part of things as trees and stones. Heaven seems frankly impossible. I am damned as I succeed. I have no particular hope save to repair, to rescue, to complete. . . .[11]

The William Carlos Williams Reader (*New Directions*, 1966)

10. "He bore with me sixty years," wrote Pound in his message of condolence to Mrs. Williams. "I shall never find another friend like him."

11. *The Selected Letters of William Carlos Williams*, edited by John C. Thirlwall (N.Y.: McDowell, Obolensky, 1957), p. 147.

Dilys Laing

(Introduction to *The Collected Poems of Dilys Laing*)

ALTHOUGH Dilys Laing was not famous, many other poets admired her work. There were always people who recognized her quality. Three books of her poetry appeared in her lifetime; the fourth and best, *Poems from a Cage* (1961), appeared a year after her death at the age of fifty-three. With her husband, the poet Alexander Laing, and with their old friend and neighbor, the poet Ramon Guthrie, I shared the pleasure and the pain of editing that posthumous volume.

It was then that I first experienced one of the most shocking of artistic realities—that a poet's voice comes most piercingly to life in his work after his literal voice is unrecallable. Dilys had been a beloved friend. Her poems had always won me, and I had published a number of them when I was poetry editor of *The Nation* and had encouraged her to get the fourth book together after ten years of "silence." Yet now the purity, the compassion, the suffering, the vividness came through as never before. I understood in a new way how *human* the true poetic voice is, how gallantly it stands out against all that is precarious and brutal and dooming in life. The slightest effects, if they are the real thing, can stop the heart for a moment, as when Dilys sings so debonairly of her own coming death at the beginning of "To David":

When I go to the Capital
where I dream of going. . . .

In "Transience of Pain," a poem that came to her while she was "listening to Rudolf Serkin," we can see in cameo the precise structure of her spirit against a background of half dream-reverie. An image of the human predicament arises, summoned up by the music and endlessly relevant. The poem is at once clear in its realism and psychologically accurate in its projection of both the passionate need for solutions and the elusiveness of the exact source of that need. All this is complex enough, yet the poem makes everything simple. It is the *grief* in the voice that does it:

It happens and unhappens
in the recording cortex:
structures of love and
images of suffering
rise and resolve

Wounded fawn in the thicket
I must go to him I must go
Antlers caught in the branches
I cannot bear his terror
I must go to him and I go
but there are no antlers
there is no fawn

One more instance—the first and last stanzas of "Emanation," so apt to the particular point I am making now. Here Dilys, with her implicit poet's belief in the literal magic of language, projects the most poignantly modest modulation toward immortality that I know of:

The poet sweats to build himself a ghost
of words to haunt the world with, lest he be lost
out of the mind of men with his own dust. . . .

Stay, my ghost, and claim a slender space
amongst these others. Sleep, my dust, in peace,
if my words breathe an hour above the grass.

These elegiac recognitions and, in "Transience of Pain," the cruel confrontation of the conscientious and loving self with the elusiveness of its task when seeking to undo the tragic are made with the most economical, unpretentious immediacy. There is nothing extreme about Dilys's work. It *is* personal; it reveals a vulnerable sensibility. But though, at times, it approaches the confessional, and perhaps even the suicidal, it is never exhibitionistic. Nor, accomplished and versatile as it is, does it make a show of being drastically experimental. I have often paid close and respectful attention to violent or extremist writing, as Dilys did too. Wonderful, powerful things have been done in these modes, especially in our time. But one must always remember the persistence of the clear lyric tradition, its way of working through some of the finest spirits by drawing flame from their intensity and honesty of feeling and from their sheer intrinsic pressure to be directly articulate. We shall never be sure that when the "siftings on siftings in oblivion" are completed it will not be their writings alone that will remain. On this subject, a friend wrote me recently that "people are missing the point of this time. What is wanted is not experiment, and extensions of experience. . . . If technology and all that means anything, doesn't it really mean that the centuries of experiment are over and that now we have to face the fact of choice—choice of world, choice of what man is to be—a situation which doesn't call for 'experiment' at all, but rather something much more ethical . . . ?" In the prevailing current view, he says, "even the Death Camps come to seem a kind of 'good' because they seem more profound or 'interesting'—deeper—than had been suspected. And poetry becomes something of the same sort. . . . I want to ask, what is the value of this kind of depth, or isn't there another kind of depth . . . ?"

I am far from agreeing with some of the assumptions behind my friend's thoughts, but they are most provocative. If there is "another kind of depth" to be taken into account, I do think it is represented by Dilys Laing. Hers is not an alternative, in my way of thinking, to the dangerous exploration of man's repressed nature and to the formal aspects of that exploration. Rather, it goes side by side with it, a lyrical correlative. Dilys's chief talent was to write beautifully and simply, with ardor, candor, wit. But the reader will see in poem after poem—for instance, in "In Horror of History"—that the dark psychological and historical depths of man are her subject as well as Robert Lowell's or Charles Olson's:

In horror of history
the reading spirit shuts the book of wounds
wakes from the dungeon dream. . . .

In horror of history
the reasoning angel shuts the book of wars
begs an eighth day of God.

She can be bitter, though never with the bile of life-hatred. Humor and humanism combine with imagination to save her from that fate. Thus, she is a feminist, but of the most *womanly* kind. Old-fashioned militant feminists had their points, and Dilys shared their uncompromising refusal to accept second place in the human universe. Coming upon St. Paul's admonition in I Corinthians 14:35 ("And if they will learn anything let them ask their husbands at home: for it is a shame for women to speak in the church"), she descanted wryly on one of her favorite ideas—that God is *female*. In "Let Them Ask Their Husbands," she writes:

In human need
of the familiar
I see God
woman-shaped

for God created
woman in Her own image
and I have
my Pauline pride.

Political tendentiousness is likely to be humorless, most of all where self-irony is involved, and so I am not sure whether any of the noble heroines of women's rights would have found this poem as amusing, or its first two lines as charmingly self-corrective, as we can today. The poem "Villanelle," with its frank tribute to male sexuality, certainly marks an advance in the feminine right of self-expression that would have shocked those ladies if they could have believed what they were reading. There never was any stridency in Dilys's work, but there was very often a clean accuracy buoyed up by her love of high-spirited speech and of sound for its own sake:

Proud inclination of the flesh,
most upright tendency, salute
in honor of the secret wish.

Slant attitude. When anglers fish
they hold their rods in this acute
proud inclination of the flesh. . . .

The thought, *naturally,* is a woman's. The skill and exuberance, however, are neither masculine nor feminine but human. They are alive, of the very essence of the poetic. Merely gross language, the shortcut that semipoets occasionally take to sensual expression, would have been impossible to such a writer. It might have been adequate as the self-expression of a pornographically oriented mind, but not as that of a person speaking out of the whole complex of subtle perceptiveness and resourceful artistry as well as of responsive desire that "Villanelle" distills. The person speaking is the same who at the beginning of "Aubade" can say:

My bed rocks me gently
in the pale shallows
of 5 A.M.

And at the end:

The great light of morning
shines and shakes
in my eyes.

That is, the most important organs are the delighted ear and eye. All feeling must come to us by way of them. A classical devotion to her art went hand in hand with Dilys Laing's classical tough-mindedness. "When I say exactly what I think," she once observed to me, "people always think I'm joking." Essential truthfulness is always unexpected—that is half the character of classical wit.

On the other hand, hers is not the dry classicism of an Yvor Winters or a J.V. Cunningham. She is close to the Sapphic tradition, that aspect of the pure lyric stream as we follow it through figures as varied as Catullus, Villon, Emily Dickinson, and the Pound outside the *Cantos* and of moments within them. This is of course a great poetic tradition. However, far more meaningful than the question of whether we are to call her "great" is the fact that Dilys Laing was a genuine poet who thought as a poet and respected her art and loved and stood in awe of it. When I speak of her as in the Sapphic tradition I am thinking of a disciplined lyricism in which there is no fear of passion, no *necessary* anti-Romanticism, but on the contrary a deep charge of feeling. The classical aspect is mainly embodied in her power of suggestive concentration, her reluctance to let go in mere expansiveness and self-indulgence.

But if there is no fear of feeling in this poet, there is by the same token no fear of intellect either. Gentle, pitying, passionately alert as she was in every private personal sense, she also brings abstract intelligence into play in her writing, and certain very strongly humane political and social concerns. The intelligence is modern—desperate over war and injustice, appalled by poverty, inclined toward that necessary set of openness to revolutionary possibility (but without dogmatism of any kind) that is indispensable if man is to survive the age and still remain man. In this respect she shares the anguish of such poets as Lowell and Sylvia Plath, though never going all out for the sheer power that the absolute release of such anguish can lead to, for it leads to loss of psychological self-control as well and is in danger of becoming too dependent on that which nourishes the destructive principle. In Dilys Laing's poems, too, we see a questioning modern intelligence combined with a genuine religious instinct. She returns again and again to Biblical notes, theological questions, figures of angels, visions, quarrels with God and with her own conscience. Aztec life and religion fascinated her imagination, as some of the poems show and as her friends know from her plans to make deeper poetic studies of that civilization. So much of this many-sided person makes itself manifest in her writings that we can well say that here was a poet who brought the whole of life into her work—and that life includes marriage and motherhood as well as all the other motifs I have noted. The poems are rich with that personal reality which only an art impersonal in its discipline can realize. A familiar principle, admittedly, but surely the poems here collected reveal its validity in a fresh and special way.

The Collected Poems of Dilys Laing (The Press of Case Western Reserve University, 1967)

Poetic Theory of Some Contemporary Poets or Notes From the Front

POETIC theory, as set forth by poets themselves as an adjunct of their working apparatus, usually has a makeshift air. Their aperçus, their occasional comments and reviews, even their more abstract forays take on importance less from what they say literally than from their relation to the qualities of the poets' best work. What Pound has to tell us about Guido Cavalcanti has its real center in, say, his translations of *Donna mi prega* and in his own poetry somewhere between "The Return" and some of the more complex Cantos. What Eliot says about Shakespeare refers to Eliot's own attempt, throughout his career, to "express the inexpressible," as he puts it. That is to say, the real magnetic center of a poet's criticism lies in his poetry.

Looking broadly at the range of poetry today, and of the related theoretical formulations by its practitioners, one sees the usual raggedly improvisational picture. Take Robert Lowell, our great poet of the middle generation. He has written scattered comments that at times would scarcely interest us save for their incidental illumination of his practice. "Writing," he said in accepting the National Book Award for his *Life Studies* in 1960, "is neither transport nor technique. My own owes everything to a few of our poets who have tried to write directly about what mattered to them, and yet to keep faith with their calling's tricky, specialized, unpopular possibilities for good workmanship." In a private letter he had written: "I know what my book intends and what went into its making. Its final character is another matter. I have no way of telling whether there was enough energy and skill behind the projectile to carry it home. Something not to be said again was said. . . ."

Now these remarks, despite their apparent obviousness, do contain clues to Lowell's operational theory. It would take several hours' exposition to show just how *Life Studies* carries through the double program stated in the speech and implied in the letter. The exposition would have to show the particular sense in which, despite the intimate and insistent importance of Lowell's subject-matter to him, he was dominated by his standards of objective artistry. No one any longer denies the organic inseparability of form and content (though I think one could show that certain American schools of poetry do in fact reduce their emphasis to one or the other.) Hardly anyone would even deny the absurdity of conceiving, in the juxtaposition of these terms, any significant opposition between them. Yet there is actually a world of difference between Robert Creeley's formula, "Form is never more than an extension of content," and Lowell's search for self-transcendence by way of objective artistry as the *shaping* motivation of his work. In *Life Studies*, his hot pursuit of the realities of his own nature—his breakdown of his family's past and of his childhood relation to it, and his slow reconstruction of an adult self from the depths of that breakdown—is aesthetic in character despite its self-analytic, autobiographical relevance. The state of vulnerable but poised openness at which the pursuit aims has self-destruction as its worst possibility, and reintegration at a deep level as its promise.

To a poet in search of such an equilibrium, the psychological and artistic motives come together beyond a certain point. Yet Lowell remains sufficiently detached to subordinate the former to the latter in finding the curve of the poem. I was struck, in a conversation with Sylvia Plath in 1960, with her absolute certainty about what could be achieved through Lowell's methods, if only one could be dauntless enough and gifted enough. And after her posthumous *Ariel*, with its suicidal leap toward a perfection of death-realization, had appeared earlier this year in England, Lowell wrote in another letter: "Maybe it's an irrelevant accident that she actually carried out the death she predicted . . . but somehow her death is part of the imaginative risk. In the best poems, one is torn by saying, 'This is so true and lived that most other poetry seems like an exercise,' and then one can back off and admire the dazzling technique and invention. Perfect control, like the control of a skier who avoids every death-trap until reaching the final drop. There should have been a great drawing-short poem, but I guess, like Crane, the momentum was out of control." These remarks remind me of Pasternak's passage, in *I Remember*, on the suicides of the Russian poets. Pasternak, however, is making a different sort of point. He associates the suicides of the poets with their sense of a hopeless irrelevance of the life about them to the life that had realized itself in their work.

Lowell's position is closer to that of Hart Crane, except that he is so far the one American master to survive the suicidal "imaginative risk" both in his life and in his art. The reasons are too complex for analysis here, but his insistence on remembering the impersonal motivation of his art even while private memory threatened to sweep him away from it made the difference in *Life Studies*. He was, for instance, the one younger poet since Crane to advance the art of the sequence, that single real contribution to the art of the longer poem by the modern age. Indeed, the sequence, with its shorter units and looser structure, has replaced the older forms—or anyway given them a new disguise to fit contemporary sensibility. Then again, he has brought to a certain culmination the evolution of confessional poetry—poetry that uses the poet's literal self, at its most vulnerable, as its central voice and as the major symbol of the modern predicament. Lowell pushed its possibilities to the uttermost limit (for this moment, at least) in *Life Studies*. Even so, he went at the poem's problems as formal ones:

> When I was writing *Life Studies* [he said in an interview published in the *Paris Review*], a good number of the poems were started in very strict meter, and I found that, more than the rhymes, the regular beat was what I didn't want. I have a long poem in there about my father, called "Commander Lowell," which actually is largely in couplets. Well, with that form it's hard not to have echoes of Marvell. That regularity just seemed to ruin the honesty of sentiment, and became rhetorical; it said, "I'm a poem"—though it was a great help when I was revising having this original skeleton. I could keep the couplets where I wanted them and drop them where I didn't; there'd be a form to come back to.

To which we might add: *Life Studies* gives us the naked psyche of a suffering man in a hostile world. Lowell's way to manage this material, to *keep* it, is by his insistent emphasis on form. The natural heir to Eliot and Pound as well as to Crane, he extends their methods. What he says about "the couplets" and so on is like Pound's talk, half a century earlier, about "absolute rhythm" and Eliot's about an "objective correlative," but is openly tied in with his own idiosyncratic practice rather than presented as a general poetic principle.

Sylvia Plath's "explanations" of her poems in *Ariel* are curiously comparable. "These new poems of mine," she wrote in an unpublished typescript, "have one thing in common. They were all written at about four in the morning—that still, blue, almost eternal hour before cockcrow, before the baby's cry, before the glassy music of the milkman, settling his bottles." That is, at any rate, the symbolic scene of their creation, as distinct from the hellish symbolic scene of their psychic predicament. Some of her comments on particular poems in the same typescript (prepared for a radio broadcast that was never made) give a related impression of her sense of an ordered setting or consciousness of motivating elements within which the paradoxically doughty terror of the poems is framed. Of "Lady Lazarus": "The speaker is a woman who has the great and terrible gift of being reborn. The only trouble is, she has to die first. She is the phoenix, the libertarian spirit, what you will. She is also just a good, plain, very resourceful woman." Of "Death and Co.": "This poem . . . is about the double or schizophrenic nature of death—the marmoreal coldness of Blake's death mask, say, hand in hand with the fearful softness of worms, water and the other katabolists. I imagine these two aspects of death as two men, two business friends, who have come to call." In these descriptions, and others, we see the confessional being given external order by an artist's balancing of the elements involved, even though the active impulse in the poems is the suicidal urge and purpose in which they are caught up. In no instance—and the same is true of Lowell—does the poet confine the account of a poem to the interpretation of a purely subjective state.

The term "confessional poetry" came naturally to my mind when I reviewed *Life Studies* in 1959, and perhaps it came to the minds of others just as naturally. Whoever invented it, the term was both useful and too limited; very possibly the conception of a confessional school has by now done some damage. Any concretely usable suggestion about poetic practice is likely to catch on quickly if it is noticed at all. It may be large or small, important or unimportant. It may be almost purely formal, or almost purely attitudinal, though usually it involves the simultaneous acquisition of an idiom of thought and of technique. Among examples of varying significance that one could adduce are William Carlos Williams's flexible three-part rhythmic unit, the "variable foot" that worked so happily for him in his later work; Robert Bly's reminders that surrealist imagery can be used effectively in an otherwise straightforward poem; and Robert Creeley's reductionist use of subject-matter and style. Such "discoveries" need only be recoveries of neglected insights or principles, but they always have a certain "new" effect when they reappear. On the other hand, their further transmission is likely to seem immediately stale and mechanical, for the borrower often merely exploits them without regard to the subjective need that led to their discovery. Lowell's major discovery of the confessional mode as he practices it is no less susceptible to borrowing than these other discoveries. Indeed, it seems more subject to mechanical and trivial imitation than most.

Incidentally, the least realized imitations, because of a basic failure of sympathy with American use of language and with American mentality, include some by English writers like Elizabeth Jennings, Edwin Brock, and George MacBeth who do not seem to realize the kind of resources that must be brought to bear in such poems. American followers of Lowell like W. D. Snodgrass, Anne Sexton, Sylvia Plath, and—sometimes—the John Berryman of *77 Dream Songs* are able to tap the same sources as Lowell, if not as deeply. Even the best English and Irish poets who have in some degree tried to exploit private sensibility in any way comparable to Lowell's are not led to try to improvise new formal modes or even to adapt Lowell's methods to British speech and thought in any striking new way. Such remarkably gifted poets as Ted Hughes, Peter Redgrove, and Thomas Kinsella do not move far from the familiar discursive framework. They simply have learned very well indeed the modern standards of concreteness, compression, and unsentimental adherence to what one actually sees and to one's own voice within the confines of the traditional line. None of them (except Hughes in a single recently published poem) approaches the revolutionary formal conception underlying, for instance, "A Mad Negro Soldier Confined at Munich," in which an accumulation of pure speed and power is the aim of Lowell's hurtling language. A wild release of psychic energy is catapulted by this poem, sparked off by the speaker's uncontrolled sexual intensity and the confused savagery of the war and its issues. Many Americans have had the same aim, one of them Allen Ginsberg, who describes his poem *Kaddish* as "completely free composition, the long line breaking up within itself into short staccato breath units—notations of one spontaneous phrase after another linked within the line by dashes mostly. . . ."

Prosodic and technical theory remains weak and uncertain, however, even among the post-Williamsites who are so hot on the subject. "Who knows what a poem ought to sound like? Until it's thar?" I am quoting Leroi Jones quoting Charles Olson. Yet the one essay by a poet specifically intended to point the new way, as it were, that has achieved any wide currency is by Olson. It is his essay "Projective Verse," which first appeared in *Poetry New York* in 1950. This piece has affected writers as far apart in every way as Williams and Donald Davie. Williams saw it as an extension and clarification of his own vague but germinative idea of the "variable foot." Announcing that "an advance of estimable proportions is made by looking at the poem as a field rather than an assembly of more or less ankylosed lines," he linked the essay's importance to the fact that, as he put it, "the reconstruction of the poem [is] one of the major occupations of the intelligence in our day." He also saw it as justifying his well-known absorption in local American rhythmic and other values: "Nothing can grow unless it taps into the soil." He was quite right to show fatherly pride in Olson's ideas, a direct outgrowth of Pound's influence but also, and more especially, of his own. The cluster of poets usually associated with Olson—Robert Creeley, Robert Duncan, Denise Levertov, and Paul Blackburn, as well as a number of others—bear a closer relationship to Williams on the whole than they do to Pound.

Davie's interest in Olson is quite another matter. British awareness of the achievements of the great older American masters, including Pound after *Mauberley*, has been long a-coming. It is still far from empathy with the violence and intensity, the high valuation put on what I have called cumulative energy, of our most vital work. It tends to isolate the usable externals of approach and technique in American poetry from their original functions and to view them with a far cooler eye than do the practitioners. The connection of the Olson group with the Concretist movement in the United Kingdom, particularly by way of Ian Hamilton Finlay in Scotland, is a strange, extreme example, since not even Creeley in this country denies himself (as Finlay does) the satisfaction of fiery or at any rate rhapsodic "moments." Indeed, the rhapsodic aspect is an essential value in the practice of the Olson group. The British poet of greatest reputation who has deliberately associated himself with this group is Charles Tomlinson, who took his earliest cues from French Symbolism, though again "coolly," and from more deliberately calm and precisionist achievements of Marianne Moore and Wallace Stevens. He has managed to transplant the "field" approach of Olson in a limited but effective way to the British scene and sensibility, though with none of the reckless self-investment it has demanded of the most successful American practitioners.

To return to Davie for a moment. In his study *Ezra Pound: Poet as Sculptor*, he finds Olson's essay a helpful aid to understanding the precise nature of Pound's revolutionary experimentation with rhythmic structure. Davie describes this experimentation as aiming "to reconstitute a longer poetic unit than the line while still holding on to the rhythmical dismemberment of the line from within." He regards Olson's ideas as support for his own argument that Pound, together with the poets he has influenced, has worked for a poetry of presentative simultaneity rather than of energy and of time sequence. I think he is mistaken. It seems clear that the new poetry has been as much concerned with the one kind of structure as with the other—an illogical equality of concern only when looked at syllogistically rather than aesthetically. After all, the logic of artistic sensibility is precisely involved with the encompassing of paradoxically apposed motifs. Nevertheless, Davie is right to call sharp attention, however lopsided, to the effort toward presentative simultaneity. What he seems to overlook in talking about both Pound and Olson is the relation between Pound's conception of *periplum*—defined by Hugh Kenner as "the image of successive discoveries breaking upon the consciousness of the voyager"—and Olson's conception of the poetic "process":

> ONE PERCEPTION MUST IMMEDIATELY AND DIRECTLY LEAD TO A FURTHER PERCEPTION. It . . . is a matter of, at *all* points (even, I should say, of our management of daily reality as of the daily work) get on with it, keep moving, keep in, speed, the nerves, their speed, the perceptions, theirs, the acts, the split second acts, the whole business, keep it moving as fast as you can, citizen. And if you also set up as a poet, USE USE USE the process at all points, in any given poem always, always one perception must must must MOVE, INSTANTER, ON ANOTHER!
>
> So there we are, fast, there's the dogma. And its excuse, its useableness, in practice. . . .

Olson speaks, of course, as one who is in on the work, rather than as a scholar or pure theoretician. His points of reference are to poetic *action;* hence the resemblance of his language to that of a coach or team captain—almost a sort of literary Casey Stengel. But it is from such clues, thrown out by artists, that critical theory recurrently makes its new starts. Olson, in turn, may have picked up a notion or two from Dylan Thomas's description of his poetry as a "moving column of words" and from his image of "blaspheming down the stations of the breath," as well as from his sexually colored notion of the dialectical process by which a poem grows, finding its own antitheses to the original impulses and then its syntheses beyond that. Olson describes the process as "composition by field." Such composition, he says, involves feeling the poem as, "at all points, a high energy-construct" and at the same time,

> at all points, an energy discharge. . . . And it involves a whole series of new recognitions. From the moment he ventures into FIELD COMPOSITION—puts himself into the open—[the poet] can go by no track other than the poem under hand declares for itself.

The principle behind the process is that "FORM IS NEVER MORE THAN AN EXTENSION OF CONTENT. (Or so it got phrased by one, R. Creeley . . .)"

It is perfectly true, I think, that what Olson calls "projective verse" is very far neither from Pound's *periplum* nor, for that matter (however it horrify the projectivists), from Eliot's "objective correlative." The terms are shifted, however, from attention to the sequence of images and other concrete effects to any form of externalization of the speaking psyche by way of the medium of language. Davie was somewhat misled because Olson's essay points to some further incidentals of this process of setting the poem in action. Thus, Olson notes the ways in which a poet working by ear rather than by eye suggests the spacing of movement and of silences, his suspension of layers of lines, as it were, in relation to one another as well as of smaller sweeps of breath and their pauses. Now, British poetry has not for a long time concerned itself very much with such considerations. British poetry is self-conscious but not about the language and its rhythms—only about attitudes and nuances of sensibility. It is for this reason that Olson seems to have taken Davie by surprise with his *spatial* formulations—for instance, his observation that "it is the advantage of the typewriter that, due to its rigidity and its space precisions, it can, for a poet, indicate exactly the breath, the pauses, the suspensions even of syllables, the juxtapositions even of parts of phrases, which he intends. For the first time the poet has the stave and bar a musician has had. For the first time he can, without the convention of rime and meter, record the listening he has done to his own speech and by that one act indicate how he would want any reader, silently or otherwise, to voice his work. It is time we picked the fruits of the experiments of Cummings, Pound, Williams, each of whom has, after his way, already used the machine as a scoring to his composing, as a script to its vocalizations."

The argument is not revolutionary in itself, though its emphasis sets up the danger of a certain confusion between visual or spatial arrangements on the one hand and the movement of the poem in time on the other. If there is a significant formal weakness in the method of Charles Olson and Robert Duncan, it shows up precisely in this confusion. The avowed intention to "get on with it, keep moving," is blocked by a certain narcissism of form, the poet's over-absorption in his own voice not as the embodying element of the curve of the poem but as a reflection of his own self-awareness. Robert Creeley, apparently less ambitious, is able to exploit the formal narcissism without attempting any major constructions. In the preface to his *For Love: Poems 1950–1960*, he writes: "Wherever it is one stumbles (to get to wherever) at least one way will exist, so to speak, as and when a man takes this or that step—for which, god bless him." And: "Not more, say, to live than what there is, to live. I want the poem as close to this fact as I can bring it; or it, me." The "modest" tone (and, doubtless, feeling) cannot hide the preoccupation with a personal rhythm in the sense that the discovery of an external equivalent of the speaking self is felt to be the true object of poetry. The transcendence of that self—the great aim of modern romanticism—is not the issue. *That* issue is held in abeyance in this movement, in this crucial respect so very different from its models in Pound and Williams. Yet the rhapsodic side I have mentioned—the structuring so that the poem comes into its own when it most approaches pure melody—is still an important factor. Because certain bearings have been neglected despite the theory, however, the feeling that such a moment is the sacred center or ultimate justification of the poem has been weakened. The richly musical Duncan, with his very considerable natural gifts, resists the whole conception in the interests of a collagist art full of arbitrary interferences with the movement of his poems. We thus have a poetic theory implicitly more vulnerable even than Whitman's—but a trifle less unjustly so accused—to the charge of being anti-aesthetic.

Salmagundi (1967)

❧

Poet of a Cold Climate

THE LETTERS OF WALLACE STEVENS edited by Holly Stevens

WALLACE Stevens was a tall, overweight Keats with normal temperature and an important position in an insurance firm. For a long time his primary energies went into his professional career as a lawyer and businessman. He developed slowly as a poet and was in his late thirties when his talent began to be recognised by *Poetry* magazine and by a small group of his peers; and he was forty-four when his first book, *Harmonium*, appeared in 1923. The pieces in that book are marvels of gay, gaudy, witty, dauntlessly pessimistic but humane writing. Little noticed at first, it has become a classic (in its revised form) for thousands of readers. This is the book that has "Sunday Morning," "Thirteen Ways of Looking at a Blackbird," "Peter Quince at the Clavier," and a dozen other poems the very names of which summon envy and delight.

After *Harmonium* there was a long silence while Stevens went about the work of his firm. There are wry comments in this volume and odd sparks in the poems, about his self-chosen prison of dollars, but no overt self-pity. After all, he hadn't been *forced* to play it safe. The timidity was in his own nature, though reinforced by the influence of his father and, perhaps, by his marriage to a not very robust and hardly bohemian girl from his home town in Pennsylvania. The nearest he comes to outright complaint is in a letter he wrote, at sixty-three, to his daughter Holly Stevens when she decided to drop out of Vassar College and find herself a job. "Take my word for it," he wrote, "that making your living is a waste of time. None of the great things in life have anything to do with making your living. . . ."

If it were not clear that his own way of making a living—and his *echt*-bourgeois way of life—were important expressions of his personality, this admonition would seem pitiful indeed. He dreamed of riotous colour and passionate release, but was thrown into a panic when he learned that a mildly unconventional couple, on a walking tour and wearing walking shorts, were planning to drop in on him in the fortress of his insurance company in Hartford, Connecticut.

He had a romantic love of France and her language and literature—the poems swarm with Symbolist echoes and Anglo-French puns like "*Le Monocle de Mon Oncle*"—but was in fact as provincially landbound as most good Frenchmen. You'd have expected him to follow his exotic imagination, not so far as to become an American Malraux but at least to get to *one* of the places he dreamed about—China, Yucatan, the Near East. But he was far too passive. Instead of going abroad, he manipulated all sorts of people to send him things from those places: tea, carved objects, paintings, surprises. He purchased, appreciated, imagined, rather than experiencing directly. Granted, it made for some amusing letters, and it *was* a mode of experience, after all. Still, he isolated and protected himself from the very wildness and dangers that magnetised his inward attention.

One of the reasons for the ultimately depressed feeling in his poems lies deep in all this. There seems to have been a kind of early inward surrender, so that beauty became a consolation rather than something to be won, let alone anything like salvation. The poems say in many ways that the chaotic and death-oriented character of reality must finally prevail over the ordering imagination that culminates in art. Art can, however, intensify and make exquisite what is otherwise intrinsically meaningless.

A number of the letters suggest these half-Keatsian motifs finely, often in the course of clarifying particular poems. These letters are more helpful than all but a tiny fraction of the great mass of critical commentary on Stevens, most of it quite inert. They make fascinating reading, for they are casual distillations of his dearest contemplative themes. He wanted very much to be understood, though he sometimes deplored the need to explain. Like all true poets, he detested mere appreciation of his technique, his "sound and music," though his poetry is so rich formally.

The conservative practicality of the whole background out of which Stevens came, provincial Pennsylvania with a strong Pennsylvania-Dutch strain, must have had a good deal to do with the walling-in of his sensibility. His method was to accept circumstances while keeping the inward life intact. He was like the Maine man whose epitaph reads, "He et what was sot before him." The *Letters* include some letters written to him by his father, a man whose mind seems to have been lively and who was affectionate enough, apparently, but who kept continually cracking the whip of worldly self-discipline over his head. "I am convinced," one letter written to him while he was at Harvard goes, "from the Poetry (?) you write your Mother that the afflatus is not serious—and does not interfere with some real hard work."

When Stevens was invited to write for the Harvard *Advocate*, his father wrote: "It is all right to talk gush and nonsense—but to see it in cold type don't seem worth while." Some of Stevens's journal entries are also included in the volume, and one of them concedes, after what seems a very short-lived difference of opinion about devoting his time to writing rather than to earning a living, that his father "seems always to have reason on his side, confound him." The depressingly stupid views he sometimes expressed may go back to the same influence: "I am pro-Mussolini personally. . . . The Italians have as much right to take Ethiopia from the coons as the coons had to take it from the boa-constrictors." (On the other hand, he *could* express unusually sophisticated, enlightened views.)

There is a curious chilliness in these letters. Some of them seem to slap correspondents in the face with an icy glove, for no very valid reason. The young Stevens worried about his coldness in an early journal entry, but later seems to have accepted it as he accepted other limiting aspects of his life and personality—and, of course, he could be warm and charming, and had the faculty of being aloofly kind. You will not find any very intimate revelations about his private life and feelings in this highly selective edition of his letters. There are delicately chosen letters of courtship to Mrs. Stevens and cordial enough letters to such writers as William Carlos Williams (whom he regarded, apparently, with unusual camaraderie), Marianne Moore, and Allen Tate, as well as to a host of other people, but everything is under control.

Even the letters to and about Holly on the occasion of her leaving Vassar are finally rather restrained, despite their obvious disappointment. But then there are vast gaps—only two letters available, for instance, for 1879–1906. The physically restless young man who went for giant walks of forty miles or more on a single day is lost in the whimsically reflective, not quite committed voice that dominates these pages. Coldness is a theme of many of his poems, and pops up as well in a little poem that is inserted in one of the letters.

The Widow

The cold wife lay with her husband after his death,
His ashen reliquiae contained in gold
Under her pillow, on which he had never slept.

Spectator (24 March 1967)

Metamorphosis of a Book

THE COLOSSUS by Sylvia Plath

SYLVIA Plath's *The Colossus* was first published in 1960 by Heinemann, and then was issued two years later in the United States by Knopf in a new edition with ten of the original poems omitted. Miss Plath's promise was quickly recognised, despite a general impression of academic precisionism. Except for a few poems whose bitter, concentrated force made them unlike the rest, her work seemed "craft"-centered and a bit derivative. In 1963 came the shocking news of her suicide. Soon afterwards we began to read in the *Observer* and elsewhere those extraordinary last poems that went into the 1965 volume *Ariel* and all but swamped the memory of the earlier book.

Now *The Colossus* has been reissued in its original form, though Miss Plath's cuts for the American edition had actually improved the book. For me at least, it has become almost an entirely different organism. After one has experienced *Ariel,* the poet's death-obsession and its deep link with her fear of yielding to the impersonal processes of her body stand out in *The Colossus* with morbid emphasis. The way in which many of the poems are haunted by images of cold terror, and the empathy involved in her poems about dead animals, are more striking now, and the theme of suicide is seen to be more pervasive than was at first evident.

The psychological horror of "Daddy" is revealed to have a less drastic forerunner in the title poem of the earlier book. Familiarity with later poems like "Lady Lazarus" and with the autobiographical novel *The Bell Jar* has sensitized me to the orientation of much of *The Colossus*. *Ariel* was not a completely new direction for its author, but the realization and clarification of irresistible motives that were seeking their way to the surface from the start. I do not mean that *The Colossus* is artistically on the same level as *Ariel,* but that it has become far more interesting than it was at first. It has flashes of Sylvia Plath's final, and special, kind of awareness. We see it, for instance, in one macabre line of her "Two Views of a Cadaver Room," with its grisly echo of "Prufrock": "In their jars the snail-nosed babies moon and glow."

We see it, in fact, in the whole of this poem. The first of its two sections is about a girl's visit to a dissecting room, where she sees "white-smocked boys" working on four cadavers, "black as burnt turkey," and where her friend (one of these boys) hands her "the cut-out heart like a cracked heirloom"—a gross love token that seems to foreshadow the morbidity of the lover hinted at in "Lady Lazarus." The second section describes a Brueghel painting of a war scene, but with a romantic love-scene painted in the lower right-hand corner showing two lovers absorbed in one another and "deaf to the fiddle in the hands/Of the death's-head shadowing their song."

Her attempt here to relate by simple juxtaposition her painful private experience in the dissecting room to the general theme of war represented in Brueghel's "panorama of smoke and slaughter" and to Brueghel's other implied themes of love and of the transcendent character of art points to Sylvia Plath's major preoccupations just a short time later. So does her attempt in "Suicide off Egg Rock" to reconstruct exactly how the protagonist of the poem felt at the moment when he drowned himself and how it was with him afterwards when his body was an inert object.

Sylvia Plath was a true "literalist of the imagination." When we use the word "vision" about her poems, it must have a concrete, not a philosophically general, sense. Thus "The Disquieting Muses" gives us a literal account of her "muses." After her death, her husband, Ted Hughes, said in a memorial note that in her later poems "there is a strange muse, bald, white, and wild in her 'hood of bone,' floating over a landscape like that of the primitive painters, a burningly luminous vision of Paradise. A Paradise which is at the same time eerily frightening, an unalterably spotlit vision of death." The evolution of her muse is one sign of the growth and clarification, within a brief span of months, of Sylvia Plath's peculiar awareness of the burden of her sensibility in the whole context of the lifelong "association" with such visions.

The happier side of her poetic character is revealed in poems and passages of entrancement within nature, moments of the subordination of that sensibility to the pure rapture of existence. A marvellous moment of such entrancement comes at the beginning of "The Eye-mote":

> Blameless as daylight I stood looking
> At a field of horses, necks bent, manes blown,
> Tails streaming against the green
> Backdrop of sycamores. . . .

It is all turned into merely nostalgic, rueful memory, however, by a splinter that flies into the speaker's eye, as if with the deliberate intention of knocking the Wordsworth out of her—leaving only a doleful, Larkin-like sense of loss behind. Only one poem of this volume, "Flute Notes from a Reedy Pond," ends more joyfully than it began.

More characteristic are "Hardcastle Crags," a poem of absolute alienation from town and landscape both, without an ounce of self-pity or sentimentality, but as concrete and irrefutable as the rocks of which it speaks, and "The Stones." This last poem, with which the book closes, is one of those whose bearing is clearer and more harshly moving now that *Ariel* and *The Bell Jar* have illuminated the mind behind them for us. I feel rebuked not to have sensed all these meanings in the first place, for now they seem to call out from nearly every poem.

Spectator (21 April 1967)

West of the Park

NEAR THE OCEAN by Robert Lowell

THE best poem in Robert Lowell's new volume, *Near the Ocean*, is one of the shorter pieces, "The Opposite House." It describes a scene to be viewed, presumably, from the windows of the poet's elegant New York flat on a street just west of Central Park. Though quite different from them in a strictly formal sense, the feeling and even the sound of the poem recall several of Yeats's pieces in "Meditations in Time of Civil War." It, too, moves into a tragic, existential knowledge of the present moment's irreversible realities. Helpless to change the present (whatever the future may become), we can but get its meaning as far as our powers of penetration into our moment permit:

A stringy policeman is crooked
in the doorway, one hand on his revolver.
He counts his bullets like beads.
Two on horseback sidle
the crowd to the curb. A red light
whirls on the roof of an armed car,
plodding slower than a turtle.
Deterrent terror!
Viva la muerte!

So ends "The Opposite House." Its contemporaneity is peculiarly American; the dynamics of the summer riots to come are packed into it. Needless to say that an awareness not *merely* American is involved, and that the outcry at the end summons up at once the fascist terror of prewar Europe and all the world's present disorders as well. Here Lowell's technique is superb: the economy of the line introducing the theme of the religion of death ("He counts his bullets like beads") that is picked up again, in full volume, at the end; the unobtrusive yet subtly echoing series of feminine endings; the extraordinary concentration of relevant detail, packed in tight and reinforced by the harsh alliterations and the internal rhymes.

The same prophetic, helpless anger enters another of the outstanding poems in the volume: "Central Park." In this poem we cross the street, as it were, into the great park, seen literally and at the same time allegorically as emblematic of the human, and certainly the American, condition. There we find yearning, entrapped mankind, symbolized especially by the lovers in the park:

I watched the lovers occupy
every inch of earth and sky:
one figure of geometry,
multiplied to infinity,
straps down, and sunning openly . . .
each precious, public, pubic tangle
an equilateral triangle,
lost in the park, half covered by
the shade of some low stone or tree.
The stain of fear and poverty
spread through each trapped anatomy,
and darkened every mote of dust. . . .

Perhaps this passage is slightly condescending. Lowell follows the scene of crowded lust with impressions of the rank zoo-smell near by and of an abandoned day-old kitten whose owner has left it in the park, with heaps of food for it lying not far off and yet "out of reach." The whole line, "Welfare lying out of reach," suggests the failure of the "War against Poverty" to reach those whose need is greatest. Impressions of the wealthier class in Manhattan come next. They, too, are trapped and isolated by their advantages: "Old Pharaohs starving in your foxholes"—"tyrants with little food to spare." The poem concludes, climactically:

all your plunder and gold leaf
only served to draw the thief...

We beg delinquents for our life.
Behind each bush, perhaps a knife;
each landscaped crag, each flowering shrub,
hides a policeman with a club.

The rhyming tetrameter couplets, deliberately rough and colloquial yet beautifully deployed, recall Swift in, say, "Phyllis, or the Progress of Love." The form is very effective. Yet over a span of fifty-five lines (there is one triplet), despite the varieties of off-rhyme occasionally introduced and despite Lowell's usual masterly massing of concrete detail, the effect is finally too contrived and even derivative to have the force of this poet at his best. That is the trouble with someone's being as good as Lowell is. One cannot be satisfied with anything less than his original energy at its peak. I prefer the title-poem, the third of the three really interesting pieces in this collection. It is the most difficult poem in the book, involving an attempt to distance the speaker from his confessional materials while drawing heavily upon them. "Near the Ocean" adds a new turn to the experimenting in this direction that marked Lowell's volume before this one, *For the Union Dead*.

The rest of the book consists of four less successful original pieces and a half-dozen translations. The former group includes an elegiac tribute to the poet Theodore Roethke, a brief private outburst that recalls the mood of *Life Studies*, and two long verse-essays, again in rhyming couplets, on our present spiritual and political conditions. The translations, which take up twenty-six of the book's forty-three pages, are from the *Odes* of Horace, from Juvenal's tenth *Satire*, from the *Inferno*, and from Quevedo and Góngora. "The theme that connects my translations," Lowell says in his introductory note, "is Rome, the greatness and the horror of the Empire." Then, wryly, he adds: "How one jumps from Rome to the American of my own poems is a mystery to me."

Actually, the connection is self-evident between Lowell's grieving over the lost soul of modern imperial America and the hyper-sophisticated unease of imperial Rome, with its thematic extensions to the marvellous pathos of Dante's conversation with Ser Brunett in the fifteenth canto of the *Inferno* and to the Roman examples in the two Spanish poets' treatments of the mutability theme. Some of the translations are in the free mode of his earlier *Imitations*. In others, he adheres more closely to the text with which he is working. All, however, reflect his disciplined artistic versatility. The most immediate is probably the translation from Horace's *Odes* I, 4 ("*Solvitur acri hiems*"), so touched with nostalgia for the passing present moment; the most vigorous is the Juvenal; the most moving is the Dante—all as we would expect from the nature of the originals, whose life Lowell catches so well. Lowell has not quite made a *book* of these materials. They do hold together. They are all variations on the theme of the poet's despair as nevertheless, with wit, imagination and anger, he shores these several fragments against the general ruin.

And yet it seems to me that he is trying to leave this theme, and this method of dealing with it, a little behind him by now. The passion of the earlier books enters this one only occasionally. He is on his way somewhere else, perhaps by way of all his recent activity in the theatre.

Spectator (1 September 1967)

Journey Toward Rebirth

THE HEIGHTS OF MACCHU PICCHU by Pablo Neruda
Translation by Nathaniel Tarn

IN 1949 the Chilean poet Pablo Neruda, then forty-five, made a speech in which he turned against the work of his youth. That work included the very popular *Twenty Love Poems and a Song of Despair* (1924) and his surrealist-oriented poetry of private disillusionment in the two-volume *Residence Upon the Earth* (1933 and 1935).

The self-denunciation was political. Neruda had been assigned by the Chilean diplomatic service to Spain just before the Civil War broke out. He sympathized with the Loyalists; the iron of revolutionary militancy entered his poetry, and he became a Communist who wrote his quota of "heroic" rhetorical verse. By the time of the 1949 speech he was able to attack such figures as Eliot and even Sartre as "apostles of the great charnel-house that is being prepared" and as "active microbes of destruction" engaged in "annihilating men morally." His own early writings, he said, were of the same order, bearing "the marks of bitterness of a dead epoch."

> A whole decaying system has spread deadly vapors over the field of culture; and many of us have contributed in good faith to making more unbreathable the air which belongs not only to us but to all men, those living as well as those to come. . . .

Interestingly, the beautiful twelve-part sequence *The Heights of Macchu Picchu,* written in 1945, is not among the poems thus repudiated. Neruda allowed it to be printed in the selected translated editions of his work, including one in English that appeared in 1949 and 1950. As Robert Pring-Mill points out in his fine introduction to Nathaniel Tarn's new translation, the first five poems of the sequence are "almost a recapitulatory survey of the different moods and settings of his previous poetry." To sustain the figure developed in Neruda's speech, a certain Baudelairean despair still pollutes the atmosphere in this work despite the poet's attempt through his central image to get beyond the despair to a more wholesome ambiance—to move "from air to air," as he says in his opening line. Marxism and "decadent" estheticism collaborate oddly here. They create an incompletely convincing yet most suggestive structure.

The Heights of Macchu Picchu is, in fact, a typical modern poetic sequence: an account and contemplation of a symbolic journey through our malaise of spirit toward a vision of rebirth or renewal or at least possibility. Certain of its effects suggest comparable ones in Hart Crane and in T. S. Eliot—the subtle shifts of association and of tone, the feeling for the musical structure of a poem, the introspection that touches all contemporary sensibility. In his very thinking Neruda is part of the international movement, involving these two poets and many others, that has subjected the life of urban man to severe and intimate scrutiny. The city is the new, secular Inferno. It destroys the life-energy of man, reduces him to a "rodent wanderer through dense streets" *("el roedor de las calles espesas")*.

Probing for "the jasmine of our exhausted human spring," in an imagery at once indirect and erotic, the sequence tries to get beneath the exhausted surface of life to the quick of things within. The speaker searches out the elusive source of the vital creativity that alone can make even death meaningful because in its wake human achievement—"permanence of stone and language"—can persist. The remarkable first poem in the sequence introduces the quest with exquisite subtlety and urgency. The next four show the reduction of man from the greater and graver dimensions of which he is capable to the meanly personal and scavenging animalism imposed by a squalid age. In the sixth poem the Macchu Picchu of the title is introduced—the abandoned Inca city in the Peruvian Andes whose ruins were rediscovered only in our century and which Neruda visited in 1943.

The second half of the sequence is then devoted to contemplation of the geometrically designed city as a transcendent "life of stone after so many lives," symbol of our need to repossess the past of American man before he was demeaned by a system of industrial exploitation and mass-life. Macchu Picchu—at least, the Macchu Picchu of the revolutionary poet's imagination—becomes the embodiment of truly human vision which alone can counteract "the condor's shadow" that "cruises as ravenous as would a pirate ship." *("La sombra sanguinaria / del cóndor cruza como una nave negra.")* The time-mysticism of all this is not identical with Eliot's or even with the more secular Hart Crane's, but it approaches the perspectives developed by these poets and many other moderns including Ezra Pound. A more specifically humanitarian and Marxian emphasis is introduced in the final three poems, which recall that the labor which went into the building of the Inca city was that of living men, slaves, who share a certain forced anonymity with their latter-day brothers but who, by the poet's spokesmanship for the myriads of exploited through the centuries, are summoned into the fellowship of creative mankind nevertheless.

The Heights of Macchu Picchu is judged by Pring-Mill to be Neruda's finest poem, and this may well be the case. It is marred by some momentarily facile oratorical notes, and by a tendentiousness—admittedly muted—inseparable from the public role Neruda has felt he must play since his early thirties. However, the poem's richly varied dynamics and swelling symphonic structure, as well as its miraculous effects of rhythm and phrasing in individual sections, far outweigh its weaknesses for the most part. Nathaniel Tarn's translation, conscientious and suggestive, misses some of the rhythmic and echoing cues and too often sacrifices a chance to evoke the sound and syntax of the original. It does, though, catch the luxuriant ambiguity, the delicate exploration, and the power of many passages. Since the Spanish and English are given on facing pages, the reader may compete with the translator.

Saturday Review (2 September 1967)

Poems in Embryo

THE NOTEBOOKS OF DYLAN THOMAS edited by Ralph Maud

DYLAN Thomas, who had the air of a precocious baby, actually was one. He was not much of a student, and did so badly at school that a university education would have been out of the question. The reason, obviously, was that, like other bright drop-outs, he was just not interested. But the precocity was there, and all of it that did not go into such activities as daydreaming about sex and greedy reading went into his writing. Born in 1914, he came into quick poetic maturity (which became a sort of *arrested* maturity, his very youthful preoccupations forever frozen into unresolved attitudes because his art did not advance very far beyond the early achievement) in the 1930s. By his twenty-fifth birthday he had published three volumes of poems. His youthful prolificacy is further revealed by Ralph Maud's edition of four manuscript notebooks, containing some two hundred poems, which Thomas filled during 1930–1933, plus a number of other poems written during the same period and available from other sources than the notebooks.

Among these poems printed from manuscripts of Thomas's teens are forty or so familiar to readers of the *Collected Poems*, published in this country the year after Thomas's death at the age of thirty-nine. One finds in Mr. Maud's collection early versions of such poems as "The Hunchback in the Park," "In Memory of Ann Jones," "The Marriage of a Virgin," "The Hand That Signed the Paper," "The Force That through the Green Fuse Drives the Flower," and "Especially When the October Wind." In one sense, what we have here is an oddly limited, semi-variorum edition of these poems, in which only the changes Thomas made, by deletion and revision, in the *manuscript versions in the notebooks* are recorded, though the notes do tell us where those poems that eventually were printed appeared. It is thus a source-book for scholars and critics, and a useful one. Thomas said of the notebooks for the year 1933 that "they show the growth of poems over a period of just more than a year, one extremely creative, productive year, in all their stages and alternations *(sic)*, and—in many instances—show how a quite different poem emerges, years later, from the original."

The latter part of this enthusiastic claim is a bit ambiguous, but one must remember the circumstances. It was 1941, Thomas was hard up, and—precocious baby that he was—he was trying to sell his manuscripts for a good price. Or, as Mr. Maud puts it, he "balanced future possible use of the Notebooks against immediate financial gain, and decided to sell them." In the event, the manuscript books and some other manuscript materials went to the Lockwood Library at the University of Buffalo for a total of $140, from which no doubt the British bookseller involved in the transaction deducted his commission. Charles Abbott of the Lockwood Library fully understood the importance of the materials, but it was the library's "policy" not to pay for worksheets of living poets and so the money was supplied by Thomas B. Lockwood, the library's leading patron. It was, wrote Abbott, "a transaction . . . most unlikely to occur again." In fact, though, various university libraries are still trying to seduce writers into giving up their properties for little or nothing, and probably succeeding now and again despite the good prices sometimes paid for manuscripts.

Now, in the best of all possible worlds such a thing could not happen. A young writer should not give up his working manuscripts—in fact, should not be *allowed* to do so out of penury. The university, library, or other institution interested in him would do better to persuade him to hold on to his manuscripts while they are of any use to him, rather than closing in on him voraciously in the midst of the living process, and should subsidize him if they are all that interested. Or at least they might work out some long-term arrangement satisfactory to both, with the help of the ingenious legal talent at their command. But this is not (you will be shocked to learn) the best of all possible worlds, and the process of accumulation of scholarly materials becomes increasingly impersonal and subject to market considerations.

In this light, the publication of *The Notebooks of Dylan Thomas* bears some relationship to the unpleasant circumstances of the notebooks' acquisition. The book is a nice piece of scholarship, and I'm glad to have it. At the same time, its aims are not limited to the purely scholarly. "The aim of this edition," writes Mr. Maud at the start of his introduction, "is to provide a pleasant reading text of the four manuscript exercise books" in the Lockwood Library. There is a "sense in which they are finished poems"—namely, that Thomas wrote his very first versions on scrap paper but then, as the poems developed, copied them into the notebooks. "However," Mr. Maud himself points out, "Thomas later came to think of these Notebooks poems as first drafts."

So they were *not*, we all agree, *the* finished poems, and one can genuinely doubt whether the poet—whether any good poet, in fact—would really want intermediate versions of his poems published in a "pleasant reading" edition. Similarly one may doubt whether he would want *all* the poems he had set down in manuscript but chosen not to publish in his lifetime to be published in such an edition. (Of course, Mr. Maud does not publish *all* of Thomas's poetry that exists only in manuscript. There are other exercise books and manuscripts of the period that were not accessible to him, as he notes.) Not to put too hard a case, for Mr. Maud has done a professionally excellent job and an admirable one, the impersonal processes of modern scholarship have perhaps led to certain humanistically questionable procedures. One still feels constrained to respect the poet's own reticences and decisions concerning what is to be printed and what not. And critical evaluation, for a number of reasons, had best concern itself with what was the "finished" work in the literal sense, by the poet's own choice. After all, Thomas did write, in his prefatory Note to the *Collected Poems*, that "this book contains most of the poems I have written, and all, up to the present year, that I wish to preserve."

But like the Hollywood producer who announced that he had just made a fearless film on the subject of divorce, with a definite point of view—"straight down the middle"—I am willing to grant points, and even to argue them, on the other side of the question. For one thing, having objected to the idea of a "pleasant" edition, presumably for the general reader, of such materials, I think that—given such a conception—it was a mistake to omit from the printed texts of poems Thomas's interlinear insertions. In the 1932 version of "The Hunchback in the Park," for instance, Thomas has one line that Mr. Maud prints as follows: "[A][2] figure without fault." One has to turn to the back of the book, to the footnote indicated after the brackets, to discover that the line first read "A figure without fault" and that Thomas crossed out the "A" and inserted, just above the line, the words "Created a"—so that the reading obviously intended was "Created a figure without fault." This kind of practice is neither pleasant nor necessary, even if one grants the headaches involved in trying to print the poems in such a way as to give an accurate sense of the process reflected in the manuscripts.

The main thing, though, is the poetry itself. To stick with "The Hunchback in the Park," it was first actually published, much altered by then, in 1941. Since this and various other poems by Thomas did not appear in any of the three books he had published by 1939, some people have assumed that they must have been composed only after that date. Mr. Maud makes a point of this matter of dating, and it will doubtless become another weapon in the arsenal of those scholars who claim that criticism should maintain discreet silence until all textual facts are in. But the later version, written into the Notebook nine years later and dated July 1941, is far more sophisticated and effective than the earlier one. Both begin with the touching evocation of the lonely, half-mad hero of the poem—

> The hunchback in the park
> A solitary mister
> Propped between trees and water. . . .

And both develop the same double contrast between the hunchback and the lively boys who mock him (the simple-minded solitary taunted by everyday reality) and between the hunchback and the dream-woman he creates in his imagination to give him solace and inward security. The early version has one image, of a frozen vision, that is misleading and that interferes with the central effect. Also, once this version develops the fact of the double contrast it has nowhere to go, and falls off into some punning on "mister" and "mistier," and into an obviously sentimental ending. (The hunchback hears the dream-woman calling him, romantically, in the same words with which the truant boys have mocked him: "Mister . . . hey mister.") The poem was simply unrealized at this point. The later version does away with the intrusive image and the puns and facile sentimentality (much of it, anyway) but becomes far more evocative. The leap into the final version of a poem will always have a certain mystery about it. Hence, it would be a treacherous enterprise to try to explain that final version by earlier drafts, shed like snakeskins as the poem discovers itself.

So there is much to think about in this edition of Mr. Maud's, and we must be grateful to him for helping us reconsider all these issues. Most important, though, it is interesting to see, not only the variations great and small in the well-known poems, but all those "secret" poems, conceived but never brought to birth, which have now become vulnerable to study by a broader range of readers. Some of the writing is merely adolescent, some has the kick of Thomas's greatest power without quite making it, and some will seem to many readers to warrant a birth-certificate in spite of the decisiveness of the poet's prefatory Note in *Collected Poems*. Thomas's rich ear, his tendency to let complex and paradoxical imagery and thought have their way in giving shape to a poem, and his overriding motifs of death-consciousness and of a sexually and physiologically suffused view of the universe mark many of these early pieces. They are often striking even when the poetry is getting nowhere and being a bit tiresome. One's curiosity finds much to feed on and sort out in this quarryful of poems and pre-poems. Thomas himself returned to it several times to plunder and to refine it for his several books. And now the scholars are beginning to excavate it and him—alas, poor quarries!—completely.

Saturday Review (30 December 1967)

Poet of Ghetto Tragedy

IN THE MECCA: POEMS by Gwendolyn Brooks

THE real interest of Gwendolyn Brooks's new collection lies in her title-piece, a long, essentially grim narrative poem that dominates the few slight, mainly topical poems that follow it. This tale of the murder of a little black girl in the Chicago ghetto ought to have the unrelenting directness of Crabbe's "Peter Grimes" but is overwrought with effects—alliterations, internal rhymes, whimsical and arch observations—that distract from its horror almost as if to conceal the wound at its center.

Perhaps a certain backing off from her overpowering subject is the whole answer to the puzzle of Miss Brooks's baroque method here. An appropriately remorseless, driving style would not only be hard for any poet to sustain but would also call for an absolute toughmindedness. The setting is a sprawling tenement, once a garishly posh apartment "palace" but now, seventy years or more after it was built, a microcosm of the world of the Negro poor. Sallie Smith, who works as a servant, returns home to get supper for her large, fatherless family and discovers that tiny Pepita is missing. The hunt, which involves some indifferent policemen, begins. At last the poem moves ahead of the searchers and shows us the murdered child hidden under the cot of "Jamaican Edward." On the way we are given portraits of good, hardworking people and sinister ones, of old folk with crazed wits, of flamboyant girls and nobly or madly dreaming young men—while, in her desire to express her love and compassion and understanding, the poet indulges herself in the forced, occasionally grotesque effects I have noted. Except in isolated passages, we are held off from the pain at the center almost as if the author were an old-fashioned local colorist commenting from a distance. Meanwhile, the plot is left to make its own way by the sheer force of its intrinsic elements.

Incidentally, The Mecca is a real building, but we are nowhere told that the story of Pepita is based on an actual incident. We must in any case find the poem's meaning in its own structure, and it is interesting that its closing focus is on a *foreign* black man as the murderer. It is as though, despite the familiar squalor and violence and terror—the ambience of rats, roaches, and poisoned fantasies fermenting in thwarted American souls—it would be unbearable to point up a native son's literal guilt as well. The displacement at this crucial point is like the stylistic distortions. Nevertheless, the poem has the power of its materials and holds the imagination fixed on the horrid predicament of real Americans whose everyday world haunts the nation's conscience intolerably. Miss Brooks herself puts the matter succinctly at the beginning of another poem, "The Blackstone Rangers" (about the well-publicized Chicago gang of that name), in this collection:

Black, raw, ready.
Sores in the city
That do not want to heal.

The New York Times Book Review (2 March 1968)

❧

Living Action In Language

SELECTED WRITINGS OF CHARLES OLSON
edited, with an introduction, by Robert Creeley
HUMAN UNIVERSE by Charles Olson, edited by Donald Allen

"THE basic idea anyway for me is that one, that form is never any more than an extension of content—a non-literary sense, certainly. I believe in Truth! (Wahrheit) My sense is that beauty (Schönheit) better stay in the thing-itself: das Ding—Ja!—macht ring (the attack, I suppose, on the 'completed thought'—or, the Idea, yes? Thus the syntax question: what is the sentence?)"

That is the poet-essayist Charles Olson speaking, and rather reminding us of Henry James's crack that Walt Whitman "knew too many foreign languages." As for the *English* language, how it looks in this fairly characteristic quotation is nobody's business. I should not "explain" these remarks of Olson's. After all, he was the man doing the explaining, in a letter he wrote in 1959 to Elaine Feinstein about his "poetics."

You might think that the whole thing was just a way of showing off to a girl who had asked for this kind of treatment, but actually Olson often writes this way, in his poetry as well as in his prose. It is his method of showing the kind of living action that language is and should be, as opposed to the dead decorum of what we usually think of as beautiful style. As he says, he is for *Wahrheit*, let the *Schönheit* fall where it will—and all our old Platonic and Keatsian notions about the identity of the two along with it.

I do not agree with the implication that Olson's way is *the* way, the *only* way, to get on with the task of bringing the true speech-rhythms and deepest pulsations of a civilization to bear on its literature. And when reading a passage like the following one from his poem "The Kingfishers," I am not sure that he has finally resolved the "syntax question" in his favor as opposed to the votaries of the "completed thought":

I thought of the E on the stone, and of what Mao said
la lumiere"
                    but the kingfisher
de l'aurore"
                    but the kingfisher flew west
est devant nous!
                    he got the color of his breast
                    from the heat of the setting sun!

Henry James, I surmise, would have said about this passage what he sarcastically said about Whitman's *Drum-Taps* just over a century ago, that the poet "prides himself especially on the substance—the life of his poetry. It may be rough, it may be grim, it may be clumsy—such we take to be the author's argument—but it is sincere, it is sublime, it appeals to the soul of man, it is the voice of a people. He tells us . . . that the words of his book are nothing. To our perception they are everything, and very little at that."

The young James was being terribly bright, but was dead wrong in taking literally Whitman's line: "The words of my book nothing, the life of it everything." The surface pose and mannerisms threw him off, as Olson's can throw off people today who react too quickly against the apparently loose structuring and punctuation and grammar, and cavalier deployment of syntax and levels of speech, of much of his work. And Olson, like Whitman, irritates by proclaiming that his way is the true way of the future.

But the fact that he does not at all point the only way is no refutation of his accomplishment. It is, rather, a fact that the reader has to get past, as he must get past the obvious objections based on a purely traditionalist view of the limits of poetry. Olson is himself a sophisticated thinker. He obviously knows his poetic history and is capable of writing passages and whole poems that by most standards have elegance as well as power. He is, in fact, a solid theorist and practitioner in what by this time can well be called the tradition of the experimental.

The prose quotation at the head of this review is keyed in with Olson's thinking about Goethe and Kant. Its playfulness and insistent, self-interrupting colloquial emphasis are intended to present a concept of the process of poem-formation at a pitch of involvement that communicates itself actively rather than through conventional exposition. Such exposition, Olson seems to feel, would always be at a remove from the process and would, therefore, falsify it.

In the same way, the passage from "The Kingfishers" packs a good many diverse elements in tightly together that are clarified by the poem as a whole: ponderings of Mayan symbols (the undecipherable "E," the highly valued kingfisher) and their meaning for our moment; an attempt to relate that meaning to the more idealistic side of Communist activism; a lyrical image for the beauty taken on by the emblems of a culture as the culture itself approaches its death.

A good deal is going on in the passage. It is in a sense a self-contained lyrical universe—a "field" of poetic discovery that is rich within itself and richer within the context of the whole poem, as well as a delight to contemplate. One needs more space than I have here to demonstrate Olson's achievement, but even this one passage will reward anyone who allows himself a little time to get the hang of the method and tone.

Robert Creeley's edition of Olson's "Selected Writings" includes a goodly gathering of poems, including eleven from the "Maximus" group. On the whole, he has picked the most immediately communicative and musical pieces. The reader unfamiliar with Olson might well begin with "The K," "The Moebius Strip," "The Ring Of," "The Songs of Maximus" and "Maximus, to Himself." In all these poems the musical curve is pure and realized and one is at once aware in them of an original intelligence saturated with memories of the ideas and phrasings of the past, both remote and recent.

Leafing through them now, casually, I note echoes of Yeats, Eliot, Shakespeare, Williams, Pound, Cummings, and allusions out of Egyptian, Roman,

Renaissance, Grecian and early American sources. These echoes and allusions are integral yet lightly involved—balanced elements in poems at once emotionally expressive and intellectually oriented.

The other poems are often, perhaps, overly involved structures. They push forward, nevertheless, by a strong thrust of argument and of sheer will, and in most cases they come through to a difficult triumph. Olson's struggles with intractable and awkward elements are deliberate enterprises. He keeps his form true to his own abrasive and self-sabotaging tendencies and still discovers right melodies for his work, winning us to the speaking personality in spite of ourselves. His central drive keeps the writing ultimately simple and passionate, and sensuousness often resides in his variously shouting, muttering, explaining, confessing voice.

Both Creeley's edition and Donald Allen's collection of Olson's prose represent the poet's ideas on "projective" or "field" composition—as he calls it—rather fully. The letter to Elaine Feinstein and a number of other germinative pieces appear in both books. These pieces include the relatively well-known essay "Projective Verse" and several other essays hitherto hard to come by: "Quantity in Verse, and Shakespeare's Last Plays," "Equal, That Is, to the Real Itself" (on Melville), "Human Universe" and "Apollonius of Tyana."

In addition, the Creeley collection contains the very interesting "Mayan Letters," in which Olson develops a number of his basic ideas about the neglected values and possibilities implicit in earlier civilizations and forgotten in the wake of the destructiveness of the European-oriented modern state. These ideas are closely related to his esthetic, which sees such literary figures as Shakespeare, Melville and Pound as discoverers, through their relation to the living language, of ways of recovering those neglected human motifs.

The wider range of the prose in Allen's collection makes it a useful companion volume to Creeley's, despite the unfortunate overlapping. One sees revealed in it more of the specifically American preoccupation of Olson—his localist side and his sense of the historically pertinent documents—that point up his kinship with William Carlos Williams and with Ezra Pound in his role as what Gertrude Stein called a "village explainer." It is his continuity with these writers, together with the energetic, informed engagement of his thinking and, of course, the exploration of new forward positions in poetry, that has proved so magnetic to a number of other poets in recent years.

The New York Times Book Review (27 October 1968)

❧

Poemas Humanos

HUMAN POEMS by César Vallejo
Translation by Clayton Eshleman

THERE is a well-known sense in which all real poetry is irreducible experience in its own right, just as it is, and therefore not accessible either to paraphrase or to translation. César Vallejo's poetry is even more its own world than most, and we may be grateful to Clayton Eshleman for his brave attempt to give us Vallejo's major volume, *Human Poems [Poemas Humanos]* in English versions side by side with the originals.

Vallejo was a Peruvian who, after his twenty-first birthday, spent the rest of his short, hard life in Europe: Paris mostly, but Spain as well, with brief travels elsewhere. His life-span, 1892–1938, marks him as of that generation of Spanish-speaking poets who shared the experience of exile, whether political or psychological, between two hemispheres, as they shared the blows of the civil war and its results.

In his own person, Vallejo, both of whose grandmothers were full-blooded Indians, embodied a vast leap from provincial, backward origins to the advanced political and literary nerve centers of Europe. It was a leap he made in imagination and personality long before his literal migration. Moreover, it was not so much a break from his sources as a way of bringing them with him into the telescoped, accelerated time of this century.

The two poles of his world of time are well represented in the way he sometimes alludes to his mother and to Paris in poems written shortly after he had made the journey. "I'm going to Paris now to be a son," he writes in "Loin of the Scriptures"; and the prose-poem "Common Sense" begins: "There is, mother, a place in the world called Paris. A very big place and far off and once again big." But that "big place" is the new, unnourishing mother of an agony and a deprivation that are magnified transpositions of those left behind, and the completed leap is the discovery of the huge hunger in modern man. "The Starving Man's Rack" ends:

> A piece of bread—that too denied to me?
> Now I no longer have to be what I always have to be,
> but give me
> a stone to sit down on
> but give me
> por favor, a piece of bread to sit down on
> but give me
> in Spanish
> something, in the end, to drink, to eat, to live, to let me sleep,

then I'll go away . . .
I find a strange form, my shirt's
all ripped and filthy—
and now I have nothing, this is horror.

It seems important that Vallejo was himself a "starving man" who never prospered in ordinary ways. Much of his work is still unpublished. Though he became a Communist, he experienced no lasting political triumph in his lifetime and was anyway intractably untendentious and never a popular poet. The beating down of the Spanish Republic, though not yet complete at his death, contributed to the despair of his last days reflected in the poems.

Slightly more than half the manuscripts of *Poemas Humanos* were dated by the poet; they appear to have been written, or at any rate to have reached final form, over a three months' period at the end of 1937. As Eshleman observes, they form "an amazing curve, totally coherent, of a build in intensity through September and October into the half-dozen or so truly magnificent poems written in November" and the one poem, "Sermon on Death," written in December.

The question of what the dating signifies is a somewhat open one. Vallejo's widow put together earlier editions of the book from manuscripts that had been piling up since 1923. Eshleman gives the clear impression that, though friendly, she has not permitted anyone access to the manuscripts themselves. Hence, some sticky problems remain for future scholars to deal with.

Be that as it may, the 52 dated poems are indeed a unique constellation. These are poems of cruel suffering, physical and mental, which yet have a kind of joy of realization in their singular music, harshness, humor and pain. They are clear as brookwater; you can see through them to the specific awareness and feeling, the sharply exuberant self, green and alive, growing at the bottom, while at the same time they are elusive and changing.

Motifs flow together, and an imagery of bitter, impotent male love moves through transferences of direction into wider implications, perhaps political, perhaps philosophical, and constantly elegiac; often some witty reversal of image will suddenly and unsentimentally turn the tone into one of affirmation as if in spite of itself. Even when Vallejo seems to *want* to be sentimental (as in the untitled poem beginning "There comes over me days a feeling so abundant, political"), his phrasing crackles so brilliantly with its own life that it carries him into an original statement of the predicament of a would-be generous, truthful spirit.

The technical range of these poems, as well as of many of the undated ones, is striking in its variety and its functional virtuosity. They are sometimes tightly formal structures and sometimes quite improvisational ones, and they move easily between colloquial directness and the most exquisitely pure and imaginative language reaching toward complex and concentrated effects. A poem like "Yokes" is a triumph at once of structural simplicity and of emotional projection through sheer mastery of syntax. And although Vallejo, described by Pierre Lagarde as having "invented Surrealism before the Surrealists," could proliferate metaphors like meteors, he shows by his endings that he was not just "letting go"—fascinating as that can be—but was able to recognize and control the design of image-motifs despite the tremendous speed with which they *emerged* in his poems.

Vallejo is like Keats in his enhanced sense, related to his illness and concerned anguish, of life-on-the-edge-of-death. He adds certain dimensions of a later sensibility—of the literal, the violent, the seedy, the hard-pressed. He is the essential poet of the modern city, the infinitely charitable man himself in need of charity who can summon up Dante and Chaplin as alternative selves in the same line.

Though Eshleman's method of translation sometimes lets him down a bit, he has worked devotedly and on the whole done an invaluable job of helping us see Vallejo's passion, beauty, control, and real presence. In this poet's work rather than Neruda's, he insists, "the entire consciousness of modern South American man is suffered and partially redeemed. . . . The *Poemas Humanos* of Vallejo are still in South America not read, because the consciousness is *altered*." Many of the best minds there, Eshleman argues, are still dominated by a "Catholic-racist-colonial culture" whose roots Vallejo cuts away by his emphasis on universal suffering and its demands on poetic sensibility. In both his translations and his deeply felt introduction, Clayton Eshleman has made us a very rich gift.

The New York Times Book Review (23 March 1969)

❧

from *Poets & Critics & Poet-Critics*

FORMS OF DISCOVERY by Yvor Winters
DEFENDING ANCIENT SPRINGS by Kathleen Raine
THE COMPLETE POEMS OF MARIANNE MOORE
COLLECTED SHORTER POEMS 1927–1957 by W. H. Auden
THE CITIES by Paul Blackburn
PREPOSITIONS: THE COLLECTED CRITICAL ESSAYS by Louis Zukofsky

THE late Yvor Winters's *Forms of Discovery*, like most of his writing, affords a clear view of *criticus irritabilis*. In the first paragraph of his introduction, Winters lays the groundwork of his authority: "I have devoted my life to the study of poetry. . . . I have taught English and American poetry for well over thirty years. . . ." Later in the introduction he tells us that he was a breeder and exhibitor of Airedale dogs for many years and has developed an extraordinary knowledge of them, far beyond that of most of his readers, as a result. The clear implication is that he stands in the same relation to the rest of us in his understanding of poetry. Now, such an argument could cut no ice with some passionate young critic, full of ideas, of hunches, and, especially, of empathy with kindred sensibilities. As for those others of us who, like Winters, have devoted our lives to the study of poetry and, by and by, realize that thirty years or so have passed, we can see the force of his self-regard without being unduly impressed by the reason. But Winters knew about himself what he did not know about a single one of the rest of us: that he had disciplined himself, had immersed himself in poetry, had developed a rigorous, astringent, intellectually searching approach to it. He realized about himself, too, I think, but somehow translated it into a virtue, that he had to a large degree sacrificed immediacy of responsiveness—the quality that puts one in touch with the developing feeling and tone of a poem sympathetically—to a carping sort of quarreling with the poet's thought.

Winters, naturally, did not feel this last point in the way that I have put it, which is a partially unjust way perhaps. He felt he just knew his Airedales better than anyone else, and he was sufficiently talented and wilful so that natural modesty did not inhibit him. So we find his discussion of Shakespeare and Milton centering on their weaknesses and supposed weaknesses. (The opening quatrain of Shakespeare's Sonnet XXIX, for instance, "is facile melancholy at its worst.") As for Donne, "A Valediction Forbidding Mourning" is on the whole scorned, though it gets a few good marks; the first half of "The Canonization" is "badly written"; and "nothing intelligent can be said in defense of the first twelve lines of 'The Extasie.'" Blake's "The Tyger" is inferior to Fulke Greville's "Down in the depth" or Robert Bridges's "Low Barometer." Wordsworth? "A very bad poet who nevertheless wrote a few good lines." Coleridge? Except for "The Rime of the Ancient Mariner," which is finally, though, after all, suitable only for children, "Coleridge is merely one of the indistinguishably bad poets of an unfortunate period." Ditto Shelley, Keats, Tennyson, Yeats, others.

Well, do we really care about all this? It would be really smashing, it would put us all down beautifully, if a critic could actually demolish a Wordsworth or a Coleridge or a Yeats through rational argument that centered on the poet's inadequate moral intelligence and on important flaws in his craft. But the truth is that you cannot *argue* a poem either into or out of being a real presence, and Winters tried to do both things. I personally am more grateful to him for the way he forced certain poets onto our attention. Even the greatest poet has his "magic" that makes us at once respond to the magnetic achievement of his work and discount the inevitable weaknesses—not discount them entirely, it goes without saying, but keep them within the bounds of proportion set by the true force of the work when sympathetically read and understood. Winters was constrained to demonstrate the magic of work akin to his own: repressed in its external dynamics, and revealing its passion mainly through its precision, its force of argument, and its syntactic structurings. The bias was too eccentric; he cut so much out of the tradition that if he had really changed our taste all that much he would have made poetry itself seem rather tiresome.

Yet his insistence on the fineness of a poem like Edgar Bowers's "Dark Earth and Summer" or like J.V. Cunningham's "To the Reader," two pieces that are at once direct, literal, and simple on their brief surfaces and emotionally more richly suggestive at the level of what Winters calls "tenor," is a reminder that poetry is not made up of reputations and generalizations but of individual poems, and that evaluation is never to be taken for granted. When his antennae were in proper working order, Winters's eccentric sensibility could close in on what was especially *interesting* about a poem in a serious and engaging way. Then, as in his paragraphs on these two poems, he could show that generous but accurate sympathy which poems demand of a good reader. What he was particularly sensitive to is shown in a comment on Cunningham's "plain style." "The plain style", he says, "if mastered as it was by Jonson, is unmannered; it is free of the eccentricities of the time, the place, and the man; it is perennially useful." Cunningham's style is of this order, though his "matter" is different. "Cunningham's spiritual situation is much more difficult, and by that measure"—for the "Christian character" of Jonson "is no longer possible for an intelligent man"—"his achievement has been more difficult." Cunningham's style cannot date as "the styles of pseudomythic hypertension" of Yeats and Crane, and the style of "aimless associationism" of Pound and his followers, must. "*'What then?' sang Plato's ghost*"—and I would agree with that mocking apparition, though not without the misgivings and further thoughts and partial internalizing that a forceful, knowledgeable intelligence like Winters's always imposes even when its range of sympathy is too narrow.

MR. Winters's critical crankiness had behind it an aesthetic ideal related to his hatred of the chaotic principle and of the death-principle. The plain style, if only it was based on genuine thought, had a better chance of surviving fashions in intellectual idiom than did the elaborations of the "pseudo-mythic" and of unrestrained "associationism." Kathleen Raine's collection of essays, *Defending Ancient Springs*, derives its fury from romantic daemons whose existence Winters denied. Because of her bitterness at the influence of Richards and Empson, she rejects the vigorous aesthetic criteria that their work, like Winters's, assumes—this in the name of a "beauty" that she strangely claims is a concept of no interest to other contemporary critics. Her "beauty" is a matter of conception first of all:

> I am one of those who hold the unfashionable belief that talent cannot make a poet, and that the *what* of art is more important than the *how;* and also that "technique" does not exist in itself but only as a means to an end, an idea that is to be realized. Nor are all poetic ideas of equal value. Donne or Dryden cannot be as great as Milton or Dante because these poets do not attempt themes that bring into play so great a range of imaginative experience. . . .

Here is one of those ringing defiances that everyone agrees with, and disagrees with, and qualifies, and sighs over because there would be so much to explain in showing how ambiguous and half-truthful the ringing defiance really is. It is perfectly safe to rank Milton and Dante above Donne and Dryden, even on the spongy grounds of "range of imaginative experience." The real test, though, would lie in showing, not the epic range of Milton and Dante, but the imaginative range implicit in, packed into, and underlying

Donne and Dryden. That is, one real test of the critic lies in the way he examines the apparently self-evident. As it happens, the passage I have just quoted appears in an essay on Edwin Muir. It leads up to an observation that, although Muir wrote no epics, "an epic sense haunts his work." This is true enough, but it changes the subject. An epic or tragic sense, and often vision, "haunts" much serious lyric poetry—the qualitative differences involve crucial formal questions, which of course cannot be isolated from questions of meaning and feeling. It is instructive simply to remember the function of the lyric in Greek tragedy; the choral odes grew out of the specific context of tragic action. Although most lyric poems lack a visible dramatic context, we nevertheless assume an invisible one something like it. The pressures on the poet's voice come from the human condition around him and the tradition behind him. The way they penetrate the voice, the way the voice to some degree "controls" them, are qualities of meaning that enter the form.

Miss Raine very probably knows all this quite as well as your correspondent, but she exploits the knowledge rather than illuminating and particularizing it by really looking at Muir's poems. Muir wrote: "I think that if any of us examines his life, he will find that most good has come to him from a few loyalties, and a few discoveries, made many generations before he was born." Miss Raine translates this statement about "any of us," a straightforward statement about how one gets down into one's own essential and primal meanings, into a battle-cry against modernity and unorthodoxy: "Fast vanishing in Ireland and Scotland, all but gone in England and America, this vital sense of the life of a race that bears, as if a single life, a destiny to unfold and fulfil, is still to be found among those Jews who are loyal to their inheritance. . . ." Speaking from outside that last *particular* pale, and yet from a closer vantage-point than Miss Raine's own, I should say that this formulation contradicts the plain, active wisdom of Muir's thought.

Miss Raine's whole argument, in fact, revolves around the idea of "the learning of the poets," a traditional symbolic language in which they are expert that is the key to "the beautiful order of 'eternity'" as grasped by Blake, Shelley, Yeats, St. John Perse, Muir, and others. Her odd belligerency is painful and personal. It interferes to a serious extent with her ability to deal unforensically with poems. But again, as with Winters, it can make for certain strengths. Her ultimate position, obvious as it is, enables her to make passionately insistent statements on a relatively neglected figure like David Gascoyne or a relatively slighted one like Vernon Watkins that bring them forcibly to our attention in a new frame. Herein she resembles Winters, though she is far less precise an instrument. Moreover, her essay "David Gascoyne and the Prophetic Role" is unusual, for Miss Raine, in providing little known details about Gascoyne's development as a thinker and artist and about the history of modern British poetry. Marxian and Freudian influences, the entry of surrealism and irrationalism into the British poetic scene (and the roles of Charles Madge and Humphrey Jennings, as well as Gascoyne, in the process) are recalled in sensitive detail and perspective. Her attempt to pinpoint the decisive turn in British poetry is bold and suggestive:

> The context of Gascoyne's poetic development was swept away by the war. The communications between the poets of England and France

> were broken, never to be resumed; the moment of the Surrealist Exhibition in 1936 (in which both David Gascoyne and Humphrey Jennings were active) marks the climax of the last literary movement to unite the two countries. . . .

Whatever over-narrowing of focus is involved in these assertions, and whatever fault one may find with Miss Raine's evaluation of Gascoyne, the whole level of her thinking here is finely enough engaged with the poetry and with the world in which it existed to hold itself intact. We are not being challenged to yield or fight or make our polite excuses. We are helped to *see*. When Miss Raine writes in this way we can only be grateful, and forgive her her efforts elsewhere to disdain the opposition out of existence, and rebuke ourselves for any impatience with the merely local and petulant side of her argument. It is a good experience to be instructed by a voice that is so warmly engaged with its subject, that opens the subject out so thoughtfully, and that leaves itself vulnerable not out of self-indulgence but out of sheer sympathetic interest. . . .

TWO events of ritual as well as intrinsic significance, *The Complete Poems of Marianne Moore* and W. H. Auden's *Collected Shorter Poems 1927–1957*, are in the nature of retrospective exhibitions. Both poets have been incessant revisers and excluders of their earlier work, evading, in the time-honored and scholar-cursed way of poets, commitments to "definitive" texts. (The "definitive" text! That will-o'-the-wisp in pursuit of which scholars go dancing over cliffs maddened into Yeatsian Romantic frenzy by their dreams of perfection!) This is hardly the place for a full-length revaluation of the accomplishment of Miss Moore or of Mr. Auden. I shall assume a certain consensus: they exist, they are sufficiently present, and for the most part we are fairly sure of the ways in which we admire them or qualify that admiration. Both have made certain kinds of statements alive for us in a new way by incorporating special prose-rhythms into our feeling for the scope of lyric possibility—that is, by showing how certain kinds of intellectual exposition are poetically involved in the imagination (the moral imagination, at least, but more than that). But in the light of my true subject on this occasion—the openness of poetic reality to rediscovery, the impossibility of assuming that we yet know enough either about what the "canon" consists of or even about what the individual poem consists of—the constant self-remaking of these two bodies of poems is of some special interest.

No better proof could be offered than the history of these poets' work that the endings of most poems are really arbitrary sealings-off, and that poems are never, even when seemingly "perfect," quite the closed systems (even in the most restrictive critical terms) they are usually assumed to be. The original version of Miss Moore's "Poetry," to take the most obvious example, had one of those purse-mouthed, conversation-stopping lines that she still retains to close off a number of her pieces. But the poem underwent a number of changes, and in the latest she gives us only the first three lines of the version printed in the 1951 *Collected Poems*. The change makes it a fine aphoristic little paradox of a poem but loses the finely accomplished and pointed rhetorical development of the once new poetics that the original versions were after.

But soft! hold! Miss Moore includes the 1951 version in the notes (the only such instance of counter-balancing two versions in the book). She is taking the mickey out of us, or at any rate playing with the two alternative versions in order to liberate herself from the chains of critical solemnity.

Her "new" version of "Poetry," then, in its relation to the previous "fixed" form, exists almost as a witticism. To my mind it dramatizes the insistent fact that many poems are comprised of what we might call a kernel and a context, and that often, in fact, the kernel does reside in the first line or lines. The amusing, and nevertheless real and serious, implications of this fact—especially, what it suggests about the energizing center of a poem—have been thrust upon us by Miss Moore's decision, no matter what her specific intention. On the other hand, the *Complete Poems* gives us other sorts of revisions as well, perhaps most notably in the expansion of the opening poem, "The Steeple-Jack," by more than twenty lines—a change that restores the structure of the original version (considerably cut for *Collected Poems*) in the sense of proliferating complexities that strain against the final simplifying and patterning resolution of the poem. The *Complete Poems* adds the pieces that have been published in Miss Moore's volumes since 1951, and includes a selection from her translations of La Fontaine and four hitherto uncollected poems as well.

MR. Auden has done another reshuffling of his poems in the new collection, this time arranging them "in the main" chronologically, instead of alphabetically by first lines as he did twenty-four years ago in the *Collected Poetry*. That order, he says,

> may have been a silly thing to do, but I had a reason. At the age of thirty-seven I was still too young to have any sure sense of the direction in which I was moving, and I did not wish critics to waste their time, and mislead readers, making guesses about it which would almost certainly turn out to be wrong. To-day, nearing sixty, I believe that I know myself and my poetic intentions better and, if anybody wants to look at my writings from an historical perspective, I have no objection.

These prefatory remarks are surely not disingenuous, but they are self-deceptive. Though this is not the place to subject them to detailed analysis, it is striking that Mr. Auden describes himself as confusing his role as a poet, both in 1944 and now, with that of his critics. . . .

The desire not to have one's poems looked at absolutely objectively by others is not only understandable but justifiable. Though in practice it is impossible for a critic to be absolutely objective, nevertheless any writer is guilty enough and unsure enough to fear that such a monstrous instrument might at any moment be in the offing—and the danger of having some damage done to the internal dynamics of his work and development by being made to look at it too hard and coldly is perfectly real. Still, I am sorry that Mr. Auden has dropped "Petition" and "Spain, 1937" and "September 1, 1939" (though he has, quite properly, retained "The Decoys" and "1929") from his new book. He explains these omissions on moral grounds. Such poems are "dishonest", he says, for they express "feelings or beliefs . . . never felt or entertained" by him. But these poems cannot be unwritten, the feelings in them *were* at least "entertained" by the poet, and each, despite its inadequacies (shared, to a certain extent, by many of the other poems, including the popular "In Memory of W. B. Yeats"), contributed a certain music of its own kind that remains cherishable. The Spain poem, especially, while reflecting the intellectual shakiness of its moment, also caught the improvisational bravery and the pathos and made a music of political rhetoric that is sufficiently rare. I do not believe that a tired poem like "We Too Had Known Golden Hours," with its post-Yeatsian diction and mannerisms, is more "honest" than those ardent assertions of a younger man's idealistic interests. On the other hand, Mr. Auden is certainly right, though his use of this particular quotation implies a double-meaning for him that he apparently did not quite catch, when he writes: "On revisions as a matter of principle, I agree with Valéry: 'A poem is never finished; it is only abandoned'".

OR, as Paul Blackburn puts it in his poem "Canción de las Hormigas" (in his new book *The Cities*), which is about a tirelessly moving line of ants but possibly about poetry too:

> And I do not know what the job is
> or when it will be finished.

At least, to shift my point of attention here, the Blackburn emphasis is always on the quality of movement of something when one is in the middle of it. The dominant motif in *The Cities*, the speaker going through the motions of living, thinking, and sensing the passing moments in the wake of a broken marriage, sets the pitch and direction for a number of the poems. Mr. Blackburn's love of the American lingo and capacity to be absorbed in any moment of existential awareness as though he were married to it lead the poems out in various directions—humorous, sensuously recreative of the concrete outside world, speculative (especially about sex and love and their contemporary meaning or, rather, the way we are changing in our experience of them), and collagist. But the harsh central situation keeps reasserting itself in a number of poems that present its different emotional phases through a precisely weighted rhythmic ordering, as in the balanced phrases at the start of "The Quarrel":

> Dried green leaf on the door
> Blackened leaf below it
>
> Under that a metal leaf, blackened also
> Below that the leafy ace of clubs
>
> Outside the window the tree I thought a friend
> has undressed all its branches & is ugly to me
>
> Returning home defenseless. . . .

AS the poet says in his "Author's Note," this poetry "is a construct out of my own isolations, eyes, ears, nose, and breath, my recognitions of those constructs not my own that I can live in. . . . Let me use Lorca's term: *duende* is that faculty of making/into which you subsume yourself. . . ." Mr. Blackburn, like some others among our contemporaries, has but focused on the essential process engaging the poet as the poem gets under way, making the process itself a disciplining *subject* of the poem as well as its range of action. Part of the background of this kind of thinking in poetry comes from the work of Louis Zukofsky, whose new book has the pleasing title *Prepositions: The Collected Critical Essays*. This is a gentle witticism, sustained by the titles of the book's three sections ("For," "With," and "About"). Like Mr. Zukofsky's poetry, these short, gnarled, tendentious, self-assured, inward, rather pedantic, rather touching pieces give an impression of restraint whose bearing is toward some integrity of self that is itself a kind of restraint. They are pieces mostly yellowed with time. I am glad to have again the famous (to me) essay on Pound that comes down to us from that infamous year 1929. And from the next year we have the essay "American Poetry 1920–1930," with its ambience of Ez and Bill and Co. Important data of that moment, and, come to think of it, why not of this?—"Pound's first three *Cantos* preceded Joyce's *Ulysses* by some years." "Marianne Moore has allowed the 'neatness of finish' of her 'octopus of ice' to clarify ubiquitously the texture of at least a hundred images with a capacity for fact." "Eliot has always been more interesting in his effects with quantity than in his effects with accent." (Open to argument, but arguments about poetry are most interesting when they force us back into the specifics of poems for whatever answers will suggest themselves afterwards.) The author's modest prefatory note concedes that his insights of the past may have become dated. However, they are still in touch with the process that continues—notes of involvement with it, slight but genuine realities of our continuing poetic moment.

Poetry (May 1969)

Ramon Guthrie's Asbestos Phoenix

LET'S put aside words like "important" and "significant." Ramon Guthrie is a lovely poet, and it is a pity he is not better known. Here is a passage from "Pattern for a Brocade Shroud: After Watteau," his brilliant poem on death that is better known in France than here:

Naked
I want to lie   naked to the
naked earth,
                              on my left side
facing the point on the horizon's rim
the sun first notches at the vernal equinox.

Will I get that? Damn right I won't!
Whole sheaves of laws, rules, statues, ordinances
stand counter to such senile whims.

Well, what about a dolmen? I'd settle for
a dolmen. No, not a phony nor even
a dismantled, reassembled one. A small
one-owner dolmen second-hand would do.
What I have in mind is something in the line
of the one I stumbled on that summer afternoon
hidden among the yellow-blossomed broom
on the downs above a loop of the Vézère. . . .

This is characteristic Guthrie: the quick shifts and shadings of tone, the lightly worn learning, the human naturalness and clarity. The passage is followed by another, too long to quote here, that focuses entirely on that one summer moment in the downs. The moment, the whole literal feel of it, is there recaptured in active language of an exquisite evocativeness. Throughout Guthrie's work, such lyrically exalted moments become enchanted centers that transform the thought-juggling, humorously melancholy speaker into a pure visionary.

As a poet of a certain kind of sensibility, Guthrie carries on from the best directions of the twenties in his special mixture of liveliness with seriousness, and of artistic exploration with a deeply informed sense of structure. His three-part love sequence "Suite by the River," which opens the book, may for instance suggest a certain ambience of Hemingway and Pound (he has shared their wars and their Europe) yet is indisputably his own. Not only does it have his particular relaxed, sensuous grace—

this smooth knoll of your shoulder,
this cwm of flank, this moss-delineated quite
un-Platonic cave . . .

—it also reflects, in the reciprocity of its three parts, a half-century's experience by our poets in making sequences that work.

The first part, "Brittle as Threads of Glass," projects a long last afternoon together of parting lovers. The second, "Alba for Mélusine," is an incantation, darkly lost in contemplation of Mélusine's beauties, against her future lovers. Finally, "Stalled Meteor"—in the striking image of its title—places the two, "in the caduceus orbit of each other's arms," in a perspective at once intellectually playful and cosmic. Each poem in the sequence has a distinct formal character, while the mounting intensity and the echoings of sound and pattern make the development of the whole sequence a sustained, single movement.

Whimsy plays a role of some importance in Guthrie's work, as a bridge between his erudite, wild imagination and normal communication. It must have worked the same way in his life as a teacher; though "privately educated by myself," he became one of the unique college teachers of the century, giving famous courses on Proust and other writers at Dartmouth. Whimsy has in many poems enabled him to be serious without solemnity, by piling in disparate associations and bits of knowledge toward some climactic, piercing moment.

The Tristram Shandyish buffoonery is suddenly caught up short (as indeed Sterne himself sometimes does it), so that you realize how the familiar, amiable voice has been easing you into a close-up of a drastic realization. "Unveiling a Statue to a One-Time Poet" is Guthrie's poem about the terror underlying this process. In this fantasy, a poet has caught the phoenix and, for an instant, held it with his bare hands. It befouls, half-cripples, and blinds him before tearing free, but thereafter he claims to have "learned of it to sing/in modes too sublimate for mortal ears." The poem bitterly mock-celebrates this hero; the supercilious speaker is one of those who have found his claims intolerable and therefore have killed him and then set up a plaster effigy of him. "Unveiling a Statue" is one of the few modern poems that, in a truly original way, use the phoenix motif and the related motif of the alienated poet who nevertheless insists on the renewing function of his art as well.

This poem, more subtly and brutally ironic than at first it seems, represents a kind of culmination of modern romanticism. That fact suggests another: that Guthrie has mastered the difficult art of reaching through to the rhapsodic by means of the vernacular and the comic, in combination with traditional lyric methods. He has the music of older poetries and of many possible new melodic combinations of language running through his head.

It is a happy event to find a poem that *sings* marvelously all the way like his "L'Enfance de la Sirène"—sings without directly echoing any other poet, and talks wittily and realistically and in our current idiom at the same time. "It Happens" has the music of awe. It tells us how the Muse works by shock upon the artist, still without bullying us intellectually or even insisting on Guthrie's own absolute centrality. "Laura, Age Eight," about a child asleep, is something Marvell might have thrown off if he spoke modern and saw through our eyes:

> This abrupt repose is of no single kingdom
> Cats and catkins have it
> colts and ferns and wild
> columbine
>
> And in the mineral realm
> some of the more improbably
> spontaneous crystals
>
> Patterns akin to this sometimes turn up
> on beaches
> as intricately twined
> roots of driftwood.

Speaking modern and seeing through our eyes has its political aspects, a fact Guthrie knows fully though his main drive is not at all political. His satirical pieces, such as "Homage to John Foster Dulles" and "To a Face in the Métro," show a range from outright contempt to sympathetic, humorous chiding. His "Postlude: For Goya" is a poem of bitter affirmation in the face of horror and disillusionment. Like other pieces in "Asbestos Phoenix," it shows Guthrie unafraid to speak forcefully, though always undogmatically, to the point of his convictions. "Scherzo for a Dirge" ends:

> . . . When I close my eyes,
> my sight turns back to Guernica, Oradour, Lidice,
> Ben Tre and goes sick with shame and grief.
> My only prayer would be, "Listen, Lord God of Hosts,
> whatever it is that you are up to, please
> lay off it, for Jesus' sake. Amen."

This many-sided, richly endowed American poet is 73 years old. What has he been doing all these years, while others were making it in the public eye? Just teaching, living, and writing his poems, mostly in Hanover, New Hampshire; in Norwich, Vermont and, sometimes, in Paris, France.

The New York Times Book Review (3 August 1969)

Dynamics of Form and Motive in Some Representative Twentieth-Century Lyric Poems

I shall put my topic in the context of two questions I recently discussed with a meeting of poets in London.[1] The questions were: What is the present state of British and American poetry? and What do we mean by poetic experimentation today? I developed a number of the thoughts for the London conference with the present essay in mind, for if it is well for scholars to remember that poets are practical men whose mode of action is poetry, it is also well for poets to remember that what they do has a history behind it. Kenneth Fearing

1. Conference on "British and American Poetry Today," U.S. Embassy, April 26, 1968.

may have been *too* practical when he used to say, with his bitter garret-wit, that books of poetry should be printed on some edible substance; the fewer copies sold, the more the author would be able to eat. It was Fearing, too, who warned his fellow-poets of the American Depression that the invasion of our literary scene by their British opposite numbers would cost the Americans both readers and critical attention. This was a realistic observation of the absurd fact that in poetry as in polity the groups, or gangs, in the ascendancy are not necessarily the best qualified. The Wordsworth-Coleridge gang, the Rossetti gang, the Pound-Eliot gang were doubtless exceptions, though dissenters among their rivals and victims would not be all that hard to find.

But all this is just cuisine and gossip and politics. Poetry is what poets *write*, and the real practical issues are always a matter of specific poems. My intention at the conference of poets was to recall with them certain perspectives that are neither so limited and extraneous as those of gang warfare nor so inward and elusive as the literal details of the process through which a poet goes as he makes a poem. Rather, they were perspectives intimately involved with the character of the poem that emerges from that process. The point of view was simply that of the continuing struggle for poetic form. Working poets at a certain level of consciousness have the dangerous knowledge of the possibilities of form. They know, for instance, that there is a kind of secret reciprocity between the structural assumptions of traditional closed poetic forms and those of the more open and free arrangements in individual units and in whole sequences of the sort sometimes thought to be especially modern.

The reciprocity to which I refer is not just a matter of planting echoes, quotations, parodies, and allusions within a free structure so that there is a constant reference to a traditional heritage of sensibility. The classic modern instance, of course, is *The Waste Land,* in which this kind of planting is clearly exploited for purposes of irony and ambiguity, both reversible. (That is, the present and the past throw an ironic light on one another; and the ambiguous religious character of the modern mind throws a corrosive light as well over the meaning of the religious certainties of the past.) In a more organic, formal sense, though, Eliot had discovered the mutually supportive relationship of traditional and free motifs both of form and of tone, and had placed them into relationship through his feeling for dynamics and modulation. *The Oxford Companion to Music* defines *dynamics* as "that part of musical expression concerned with the varying degrees of intensity (loudness) of the sound produced" and *modulation* as "a method of key-change without pain," by which "the adoption of the new set of tonal conditions is softened, or at any rate, made intelligible." I do not wish to invent a new critical terminology, let alone a new critical religion, and so will not labor the simple musical analogy implied. I would only point to the usefulness of these concepts for helping us to see a poem as a series of tonal effects and varied intensities and balancings of motion and rest, all related to an essential overall curve of movement. It is interesting how often we find specifically musical images and motifs introduced into modern sequences, as if by them the poet was guiding not only his reader but himself into an openness to what might appear superficially as mere improvisation but is in reality a drawing on the widest range of poetic resources.

Good poets have something like an instinctive sense of such matters as these, which makes them remarkably articulate in their qualitative insights, often at a youthful age. And indeed, they are "poetical" in the sense that composers are "musical"; they are engaged in recognizing, in making, in realizing, rather than in constructing arguments, for they are in on the process as practical involvement. You cannot get evaluative judgment from non-poets with quite the authority of Laforgue writing on Corbière, or Pasternak on Mayakovsky, instances in which one poet realizes the irreversible presence of another despite his instant, and ruthless, recognition of essential weaknesses. Of course, poets are capable of ridiculous judgments of one another's work based on refusal of sympathy, or on the misreading of someone else's work as an extension of one's own. But where there is genuine openness and readiness to respond, there is also a generosity of spirit that is free to fasten on the necessary points of attention. Yvor Winters, for all his odd acuteness, was grievously lacking in this sort of right generosity. Astringent standards are useful, but when applied as Winters often applied them (so as to exclude Coleridge, say, from the reading-list) they are only a nuisance.

What I am getting at is that poets have always sensed the principle of dynamics as the key to structure, and have generally been reluctant to be dominated by a petty perfectionism. In the past, and often in our own time, this principle has been concealed to some extent by traditional considerations of formal patterning and of rhetorical ordering. Without pursuing the point much further, I would just suggest that the question of dynamics is related not only to the poet's control over his materials but also to the nature of the materials he is trying to deploy. Some of Shakespeare's sonnets in which the endings seem, from one perfectionist standpoint, to be thrown away; some of the passages in which a poet like Yeats seems to lapse into the commonplace or the trite; some of the supposedly weak links in poetic sequences like *The Bridge* and *Paterson* are less aesthetic failures than aspects of the intransigence of certain necessary materials. The structure is felt to be moving, while certain improvisations within it are just sufficient to keep it going in its own way. This is one use of the traditional formal effects often introduced into an essentially open poem, as when Williams in "The Yachts" begins in *terza rima* but drops the rhyme as soon as it is, so to speak, established. He does keep the three-line stanza, and the purpose of the Dantean reminiscence is revealed when the poem shifts from literal impressions to allegorical vision.

I shall forgo here the sort of extended analysis that I have elsewhere given to the moving structure of Robert Lowell's *Life Studies*—both the individual poems and the whole sequence—and to other works. But I do want to look quickly now at two poems that are very much of the present moment, poems of real interest though not generally well known, in the light of these first observations. Both these poems, the second of them more complex than the first, have in common, at the center, a speaking self seeking to put itself in perspective. Each poem is absorbed in a certain perplexity of identification; but the speaker in each, instead of remaining locked into his sweating if unlocated self, is liberated through an extension of the initial predicament into further contexts. The process turns these contexts around and around the focal point of feeling or bemusement, encompassing it aesthetically without losing touch with its literal reality.

The first is a poem of love: "Losing Track," by Denise Levertov.[2]

Long after you have swung back
away from me
I think you are still with me:

you come in close to the shore
on the tide
and nudge me awake the way

a boat adrift nudges the pier:
am I a pier
half-in half-out of the water?

and in the pleasure of that communion
I lose track,
the moon I watch goes down, the

tide swings you away before
I know I'm
alone again long since,

mud sucking at gray and black
timbers of me,
a light growth of green dreams drying.

The woman who speaks in this poem defines herself existentially, in relation to the man. Though real and present, she is ordinarily hardly conscious (in the special sense being developed here) until the man's love enters and awakens her, "nudges" her awake. Then, long after the act of love, the sense of achieved communion remains with her. She has "lost track," not only of time but of separate identity. Eventually, however, she must know herself "alone" again. But what she is has been made clearer in the extended image of the pier that closes the poem.

That is the literal situation of the poem, though the act of love is never explicitly mentioned. At first, the poem appears to be a very happy expression of the meaning of love to the speaker—she is transported by it, if not into a state of undying bliss at least into one that changes her sense of being memorably over a long period of time: the nearest state to undying bliss that secular rapture can attain to.

I said "at first," as though I meant to imply that the poem's surface is thoroughly deceptive, and that the poem is not really so very happy an expression. But I do not mean that exactly. It is only that something else is operating beneath the perfectly genuine surface. There are really three centers of attention, or focal images, that have been placed in relation in this poem, as if it were a mobile construct consisting of three elements. There are the

2. *O Taste and See* (New York: New Directions, 1964).

image of the pier, the phallic boat-image, and the transformed, awakened consciousness of the woman.

The central *aperçu* lies in the image of the boat coming in on the tide and nudging the pier. That is a sensuous, revealing image. When, however, the speaker focuses attention on the pier image itself, in its own right, the question of identity is brought into the open rather clumsily:

am I a pier
half-in half-out of the water?

The speaker's refocusing on the image of herself as a pier has a rather inert quality; the pier is no longer just that which has been touched by the boat in momentary communion—an image that worked happily as long as our attention shifted quickly to the speaking woman herself. When the boat recedes again, this inertness is combined with associations of a slightly brackish sort:

mud sucking at gray and black
timbers of me,
a light growth of green dreams drying.

The dynamics of the poem involve a movement from the initial abstract statement of the sense of time transcendence, which is the result of lovemaking, into the central *aperçu* of the boat-image, toward this final projection of the self as an inert, isolated being whose physical attributes are desolate and unpleasant if not repulsive. The sequence of intensities takes us from the abstract bemusement of the beginning to a moment of startled happiness *(mezzo forte)*, then back to the bemused state of reverie, and then into a relatively prolonged, moderately desolate mood at the end that at least matches in degree of emphasis the earlier mood of joy. This movement can be broken down further and more subtly. I do not want to make too much of it, or even too much of the poem, but only to suggest that the poem combines unresolved elements through modes of juxtaposition that have more to do with structural considerations than with considerations of meaning. The poem rests momentarily at the point I have suggested, but that is not finally necessary. The fairly regular stanza, and the irregular pattern of rhyming and other echoing effects, suggest a structure at once superficially stable and basically open and unresolved. In this quality, Miss Levertov's poem is representative of a good deal of interesting work of the present era.

Next I should like to turn to a longer poem, Robert Duncan's "Strains of Sight."[3] This seems to me one kind of ideally illustrative poem for this particular discussion. Divided into two parts, it is a "field" of association around three motifs: first, the condition of Adam and Eve after the Fall; second, the implications of artistic process; and third, the bearing of the two motifs just mentioned on the poet's search into his own being—that is, on the way his sensibility confronts fatality. I would ask the reader who does not know the

3. *Roots and Branches* (New York: Charles Scribner's Sons, 1964).

poem simply to "listen," at first—perhaps by reading it aloud—to the way in which Duncan's lyric voice touches on his themes so as to put them into a simple relationship that keeps working after the poem has ended.

1

He brought a light so she could see
Adam move nakedly in the lighted room.
It was a window in the tree.
It was a shelter where there was none.

She saw his naked back and thigh
and heard the notes of a melody
where Adam out of his nature came
into four walls, roof and floor.

He turnd on the light and turnd back,
moving with grace to catch her eye.
She saw his naked loneliness.

Now I shall never rest, she sighd,
until he strips his heart for me.
The body flashes such thoughts of death
so that time leaps up, and a man's hand

seen naked catches upon my breath
the risk we took in Paradise.
The serpent thought before the tomb
laid naked, naked, naked before the eyes,

reflects upon itself in a bare room.

2

In the questioning phrase the voice
—he raises his eyes from the page—
follows towards some last
curve of the air, suspended above

its sign, that point, that .
And asks, Who am I then?
Where am I going? There is no time
like now that is not like now.

Who? turns upon some body where
the hand striving to tune
curves of the first lute whose strings are nerves
sees in the touch the phrase will

rise . break
as the voice does? above some moving obscurity

ripples out in the disturbd pool,
shadows and showings where we would read
—raising his eyes from the body's lure—

what the question is,
where the heart reflects.

I know that I shall again be mixing my aesthetic metaphors when I say that "Strains of Sight," which is very possibly Mr. Duncan's best piece of work so far, can be viewed as a delicately articulated verbal mobile. I have been talking about "dynamics" in language derived partly from musical theory, but actually intended to suggest the values implicit in poetry as moving structure. Some of the other dictionary definitions of "dynamics" are almost as useful as the musical one. For instance, dynamics is that "branch of physics that treats of the action of force on bodies in motion or at rest"; and more generally, the term refers to "the various forces, physical or moral, operating in any field." In a good deal of our poetry, the problem is to sustain rival forces, of containment and of dispersion and redistribution, within a single moving structure. The poem as a whole moves forward, while disparate elements are placed in relation to one another in a momentarily spatial relationship as in a mobile. This process, implicit in the nature of poetry, has received a special emphasis in the attempts by modern poets to bring the inner workings of the poem, the "real" poem, to the surface of consciousness.

A literal vision, of a man exposing his nakedness to a woman, is related to—all but superimposed on—the Biblical scene. The whole progress of postlapsarian man is compressed into the image, at once passionate and domesticated, of sexual revelation as the key to the poignancy of mortality and of the "burden of consciousness," as Delmore Schwartz once called it. It is not necessary to spell out how much of the whole tradition from, say, Milton to Keats to Wallace Stevens and Hart Crane is referred to in the vision here presented, and in the particular phrasing and rhythms employed.[4] In the second half of the poem, the ambiguous "he" of the poem's first line who "brought a light" so that the vision could be seen is reintroduced. He has been reading the Biblical text, or his re-vision of it, and in relation to it tries to follow the very rhythmic essence of his own idiom of thought and feeling.

4. Mr. Duncan's dialogue with the tradition—or perhaps "*duet* with it" would be more accurate—is beautifully illustrated in another poem of his, "Shelley's *Arethusa* Set to New Measures." The title speaks for itself. The poem is a sort of translation, or recasting, based on the poetic methods of another age than the original, and to some extent resulting in a final balance or set of the kind I have been describing in "Losing Track" and "Strains of Sight." This whole subject of the assimilation of specific formal motifs into modern poems throws valuable light on the energy of tradition as something not only formative but also contributory to change, an aspect of poetry that every modern poem of importance cries out to illustrate. Robert Lowell's trilogy of poetic plays, *The Old Glory,* which recasts fictional works by Hawthorne and Melville in new forms and by way of an altered sensibility, comprises a similar dialogue with the past.

It is a parallel movement to the lines in the first part that describe the reaction of the "she" of the poem to sight of his "naked loneliness"—

> Now I shall never rest, she sighd,
> until he strips his heart for me.

In the exquisite balance of this poem, each part has nineteen lines and, as with Denise Levertov's "Losing Track," elements of structural patterning that modulate toward traditional form are grafted onto less predictable and stable elements. The whole movement here is far more complex than in "Losing Track"—witness even such technical details as the incomplete abandonment in the second part of the four-stress pattern sustained in the first part, and the more insistent variations from the quatrains that are the basic units of the poem. But the essential duality of the movement, self-completing and final in one sense, open and tentative in the other, is unmistakably of the same order.

By holding off literal identification of the central situation in a poem, many poets gain the sense of open possibility, of involvement with but freedom from the literal, implied long ago in Williams' little poem "The Red Wheelbarrow." This is the method of the two poems we have just looked at. In another, but subtly related, mode, an undefined state of sensibility seeks a momentary frame of identity through attaching itself to some situation, scene, or ambience. Thom Gunn, Charles Tomlinson, and Paul Blackburn are among a fair number of poets writing in this latter mode. Robert Creeley often tries to do both things by whittling poems down to a hard center of suggested relationship between the central situation of the poem and the universalizing extensions, without necessarily defining either. In these general tendencies American and British poetry show few differences of national character apart from those of idiom, locale, and certain qualities of wit.

Almost all our poets have been cultivating something close to the bone, the "natural" tone, unpresuming yet significant, of the self in its own milieu. And yet, actually, the aim has not at all been self-portraiture. Even in the very personal poetry of Robert Lowell and Sylvia Plath, the speaking voice creates a rush of impersonal energy through the intensity of its self-entrancement. Analysis of *Life Studies* and of the poems in *Ariel* will show their deep reliance on the pressure of formal design based on effects of psychological excitement or of literal motion. But there are tendencies as well toward a formal letting-go, either through an extremely relaxed reliance on colloquial speech-patterns or through what may be called the rhetoric of expanding reverie or proliferative association.

British poetry does not take this risk of letting-go. Even a poet with such brilliant talent for the colloquial note and for comic mimicry as Philip Larkin forgoes this relaxation of form—"forgoes" is probably too strong a word, since he probably feels no temptation toward it. By stubbornly adhering to formal traditionalism in this sense, and by making his poems move in the preordained direction of slightly pessimistic melancholy—*that* kind of "classicism"—he gains not only compression but the inward reverberation of a closed yet meaningful system. The strength of R. S. Thomas, of Norman MacCaig (even in his recent more loosely ordered verse), and at times of Elizabeth Jennings lies in a similar reservation of energies and limiting of form. In the same way, the best confessional poetry of the British Isles, such as Donald Davie's "After an Accident," Austin Clarke's "Mnemosyne Lay in Dust," and Thomas Kinsella's "Wormwood," has avoided the presumptuousness of American confessionalism at its worst. (I am of course not referring to Robert Lowell or Sylvia Plath.) It is true that God gave us hysteria as well as capacity to reason, but self-induced hysteria does not *automatically* equal poetic insight. The discipline imposed on themselves by Davie, Clarke, and Kinsella has enabled them to work relatively purely, taking little for granted. Perhaps they *could* seize the fortress of the wider identification by main force, through sheer stormy intensity as do Lowell and Plath; but that is not their aim. Their poetry does not take us far in a new direction. Yet its vitality is undeniable, and has created a surprising new current in British and Irish verse only very recently.

The last three poems I have mentioned are all sequences, and there is no question that the dynamics latent in this form, which is so adaptable, have been in process of exploration throughout the century, with a renewal of interest during the past decade or so. It lends itself readily to the impression that one is using it in a new way, for it allows for so many idiosyncratic facets in its several parts. Americans, so far, have worked the most with the experimental sequence, but this fact, in turn, leads to some questions.

What, in fact, does it mean for poetry to "advance"? to "experiment"? I do not think that in poetry, any more than in science, the repetition of a method that someone else has already employed successfully can be considered an experiment in any sense but that of a classroom exercise or of a practitioner's confirmation of techniques. If we use the good old touchstone method, and if we know where the touchstones are, it should not be hard to sort out the question of the originality of a given piece or mode of work. Of course, the question is complicated by qualitative considerations of the precision and sensitivity of diction, rhythmic movement, and voice, as well as of the bearing and force of the overall structure.

Take a classic—or perhaps I should say "*secret* classic"—of the modern age like Pound's Canto 39, written about thirty-five years ago. It is one culmination of a method Pound had been developing for some fifteen years or more. I cannot imagine that a poet who has at all allowed himself to be instructed by the *Cantos* in the kind of possibilities for poetic statement and design that they reveal could fail to pick up important cues from Canto 39. Looked at first in the simplest way, it is a constellation of rather brilliant lyric and imagistic passages, somehow linked by allusions to events in the *Odyssey,* to certain Latin and medieval lyrical motifs, to traditional sex-based cosmogonic mythology, and to aspects of private experience barely hinted at. As a structured constellation, it is in itself part of a relatively modern tradition that includes *The Waste Land* and other earlier poems in various languages and therefore is but one perfecting of an experimental tendency. Its frank sensuality comes through as purely as anything in the language. Pound has learned from his study of Latin and Provençal poetry and from such a figure as Villon to use the elementary language of sex unselfconsciously and rightly in context, so that it gets past—beyond—the compulsiveness and sensationalism of mere pornography. Suddenly he lifts the faintly pornographic veil of insidious suggestiveness that flutters like a figleaf over so much of the best nineteenth-century poetry, with its repressions and reticences and strange hints of darkness and evil. Here is how the opening section of the poem goes:

> Desolate is the roof where the cat sat,
> Desolate is the iron rail that he walked
> And the corner post whence he greeted the sunrise.
> In hill path: "thkk, thgk"
>   of the loom
> "Thgk, thkk" and the sharp sound of a song
>   under olives
> When I lay in the ingle of Circe
> I heard a song of that kind.
>   Fat panther lay by me
> Girls talked there of fucking, beasts talked there of eating,
> All heavy with sleep, fucked girls and fat leopards,
> Lions loggy with Circe's tisane,
> Girls leery with Circe's tisane.
>   κακὰ φάρμακ' ἔδωκεν
>   kaka pharmak edōken. . . .

So, then, here is a poem saturated with realizations of the sexual principle as experience, both literally physical and as the informing element of poetry, song and myth. The marvelous opening passage begins with the imagistic closeup of the scene where the cat lived his happy night. That three-line closeup is, so to speak, a full-length Creeley poem, especially if we accept its tone as expressing the speaker's own post-coital sadness as the real referent of the emotion of wry desolation. The speaker then becomes Odysseus, or one who thinks of himself as Odysseus in the particular context of the ambience and of his own feelings. He has been with a woman, he has been Odysseus with Circe—and then the very sense of happy satiety, a stupefied utter enchantment of replete sensuality is brought into the foreground and framed by the Homeric phrase that is repeated like a refrain.

I shall not follow the poem through any further, or do more than mention its relation to the whole method of the *Cantos*—the projection of lines and fields of association in relation to certain radiating centers of value and of affect. Essentially, most structural experimentation that interests us today—even the self-interferences intended to strangle rhetoric and to untrack poetic logic itself in poets like Duncan and Olson—is fully anticipated in the *Cantos*. What is it that is being experimented with? First of all, the absorption of the Romantics in the reciprocities of subjective and objective. Secondly, the possibilities implicit in the open sequences of Whitman. Thirdly, the adaptation of Symbolist technique to longer structures. Incidental to these, a proliferation of by-products: rhythmic improvisations; assimilation into the poetic tradition of more and more supposedly unpoetic words and levels of formless expression; visual arrangements that are aspects of internal structure, rather than superficial elegances; the use of casual or purely functional cultural objects (comic strips, mechanical cranes, etc.) not as symbols of the age but as objects of contemplation, as though they were Grecian urns or Wordsworthian hills. Exploring some of these lines of possibility has become for many poets what "research" means for a certain kind of scholar: accumulation of more and more data toward the finally redundant ends of mere process. I do not pretend that we are dealing with the predictable, however. We all know that the individual voice and wit and imagination can change what would ordinarily be stale and unprofitable into something that really tells.

Charles Olson in *The Maximus Poems* and Robert Duncan in his "Passages," as well as David Jones in his *The Anathémata,* have written, each out of his own center, along Poundian lines, and I do not believe it can be said of any of them that he has simply repeated the work of Pound. Yet even as I write this, I suspect that the method is not entirely functional for them, that it has created obligations even for Pound at the end of the long effort over the years that do not quite match his present needs, as it were. I do not want to overstress the point, for I am not altogether sure of it, but the paraphernalia of the method tend to weigh it down even though Pound's and Eliot's sequences had such original vivacity and relevance that one scorned to notice that aspect. But now the stripped-down sequences of Davie, Clarke, and Kinsella seem to point the way to a rebirth of the sequence as a more organic structure than the loose contrivances of, say, Whitman or Yeats (in "Song of Myself" or "Nineteen Hundred and Nineteen") but less bristling with intellectual weaponry than the Poundian sort.

In insisting that *Wodwo,* his book of poems, stories and a play, be read as "a single work," Ted Hughes clearly implies that it is a sequence. If so—I shall not analyze it here—he has done a valuable work of simplifying the issue still further. That is, the sequence must be a relatively open structure, a complex of magnetic relationships, in its essential character; if it has a clear narrative or rhetorical line, that fact will be significant but not decisive for its character. Hughes has death-terror as his basic motif; and war-terror, the terror of the essential bestiality of man in his own nature and as revealed in the rest of nature, as the reinforcing motif. The play, "The Wound," is a war-horror nightmare. In the whole of *Wodwo* there are occasional vibrations from the work of Theodore Roethke—certain rhythms, certain states of feeling—but Roethke as he did not allow himself to be: mercilessly unflinching *vis-à-vis* the cruelty of our condition. There is a subdued autobiographical element in the poems, but this is the most objectified of the sequences I have mentioned, though only a talent as fiercely rigorous as Hughes's could hold these poems apart from one another as he does and yet keep them within a single poetic universe. I should note, incidentally, that we quite take for granted now what we might call the miniature sequence, a form that Roethke handled well except for his concluding sections but that Hughes manages superbly—as Sylvia Plath did—in a poem like "Song of a Rat."

I have been suggesting some thoughts on the overall situation without in any way hoping for an exhaustive survey, though the situation actually, literally, importantly, is made up of every single poem of interest written during the past decade or two. A poet at once so sensitive and so boldly frank as Harry Fainlight, the Concretists in their own right and in their incidental but valuable influence on a poet like Christopher Middleton, Jon Silkin in his "flower poems" that to some degree recall the spirit of René Char—all these, and many others, apart from the ultimate questions of achievement, make for a rich matrix of poetic life in our moment. It seems to me that the question of poetic engagement or commitment, especially in the political sense, is bound up with this fact. The whole history of modern poetry, at least since Yeats, Pound, and Eliot but actually going back over a century and a half, is in a vital sense a critique of the whole range of modern life, with revolutionary implications. Those three arch-conservatives, or reactionaries, whom I have just named were, despite their literal politics, radical critics of the system, the quality of life, that have emerged into the modern era. The experiments of Auden, Muriel Rukeyser, and others who have at times felt the political situation as *experience* rather than as the subject of polemical verse-argument alone have helped create a body of three-dimensional political verse. One sort of reflection lies in a poem like James Dickey's "The Firebombing," a poem of guilt, terror, and moral ambiguity. Another lies in a poem like Galway Kinnell's "Vapor Trail Reflected in the Frog Pond."[5] It was Yeats who discovered, in the sequences "Nineteen Hundred and Nineteen" and "Meditations in Time of Civil War," how political motifs may be related to other motifs in a sequence in such a way that their force is clarified and relieved of tendentious effect because of the context established. Kinnell does something similar in this poem, which is really what I have called a miniature sequence. The first and third sections are concrete, sensuous apprehensions of the atmosphere of war. The middle section is a brief closeup of the cruelties of day-to-day American reality that most of us, nevertheless, do not experience directly, however much we may bear their existence in mind. Kinnell begins this section with a sardonic echo of a passage in Whitman—

> And I hear,
> coming over the hills, America singing,
> her varied carols I hear:
> crack of deputies' rifles practicing their aims on stray dogs at night,
> spur of cattle-prod,
> TV groaning at the smells of the human body,
> curses of the soldier as he poisons, burns, grinds, and stabs
> the rice of the world,
> with open mouth, crying strong hysterical curses.

Whether Kinnell's poem actually succeeds I am not sure. He sketches his motifs and countermotifs in very briefly and slightly. Perhaps the section just quoted rises in pitch too abruptly and finds itself forced to rely less on experiential conviction than on the strong meat of a strident insistence. In the curious way of poetic affect, such insistence does not take hold of us quite as irrefutably as the ironic echo of Whitman or the four lines that conclude the first section of the poem—

> In the frog pond
> the vapor of a SAC bomber creeps,
>
> I hear its drone, drifting, high up
> in immaculate ozone.

5. *Body Rags* (Boston: Houghton Mifflin, 1967).

I do not think there was ever a time when the range of possibilities, both of the form and of the raw materials, for poets was as rich as it is now. With the general acceptance that this is so has come a new body of readers who take less delight in the shock-quality of formal effects than in their authenticity, their relevance to what is being projected. The poetry of easy rhetoric and easy didacticism was never more suspect. The poetry that realizes qualities of experience and feeling precisely will be followed wherever it leads, however abstract its constructions may at times seem, or however oblique its associations. If it does have the pressure of such realization, the pressure of the times will be in it as well, whatever its literal subject-matter. I should like to end by quoting a brief poem, "First Light," by Thomas Kinsella,[6] which does seem to me to be the result of both these sorts of pressure. You will notice how, as the little poem progresses, we are given, first, the external physical world that surrounds the protagonists, and then—surprisingly—not the protagonists themselves but the sound of a child's wail in the midst of a dream. Kinsella, like Yeats and like Wallace Stevens, is one of those poets whose modernity finds itself within a traditionally ordered structure. The inner structure of the poem, however, is a matter of the dynamics, the succession of emotional intensities as they relate to the meeting of the two kinds of force—that of intransigent reality and that of naked human suffering and fear. Poems of this kind seem to me, in the essential quality of their concern and their subjective realism, one of the true triumphs of poetry in English of this moment.

A prone couple still sleeps.
Light ascends like a pale gas
Out of the sea: dawn-
Light, reaching across the hill
To the dark garden. The grass
Emerges, soaking with grey dew.

Inside, in silence, an empty
Kitchen takes form, tidied and swept,
Blank with marriage—where shrill
Lover and beloved have kept
Another vigil far
Into the night, and raved and wept.

Upstairs a whimper or sigh
Comes from an open bedroom door
And lengthens to an ugly wail
—A child enduring a dream
That grows, at the first touch of day,
Unendurable.

ELH (March 1970)

6. *Nightwalker and Other Poems* (New York: Alfred A. Knopf, 1968).

Poetry of the Main Chance

JUST a few years ago one could distinguish more easily between British and American verse than one can now. Taking a kindly view of each, one could say that a finely humane articulateness was the typical British ideal, while American poetry was out for the main chance. Mind you, distinctions like this never really carry you to some of the more interesting, *quieter* questions, such as how many poems in English one can find that have a quality comparable to that of Robert Lowell's "Water." This is a poem that could not, I am sure, have been written had Lowell not gone through the Confessional phase embodied in his *Life Studies*. But it is not itself a confessional poem—not exactly—but just a very beautiful, very searching one that blends into the lyric tradition:

> Remember? We sat on a slab of rock.
> From this distance in time,
> it seems the color
> of iris, rotting and turning purpler,
>
> but it was only
> the usual gray rock
> turning the usual green
> when drenched by the sea. . . .

Just think how different the whole tradition, and even the whole body of work of individual poets, begins to look if we take it one poem at a time—how much closer we are to the actuality of poetry if we stop cataloguing forests and try to remember particular trees. Whole drifts of poems then disappear, non-existent save as representatives of a tendency for historians to record.

Still, the tendencies exist, and thinking about them may protect us from using poetry merely as a subjective opiate. The distinction I have mentioned, between American and British poetry, does persist though now it is beginning to blur.

What is poetry of the main chance? It is not altogether in good taste, even by the highest standards. It is often in danger of being thought pretentious. It is out to change our sense of reality, sometimes by removing the barriers of reticence, sometimes by penetrating the subjective life so as to affect our sense of what counts for us as important awareness. It may, most simply, be a poetry of brute energy. You can have brute energy of feeling without significant artistic power, as with Allen Ginsberg. You cannot have it the other way around, though. The qualities of form we find in Robert Lowell or in Sylvia Plath could not exist without the release and re-channelling of a stormy emotional state, driving but not blind. Those slamming effects, shifts of tempo and dynamics, and mobilizations of imagery come from a psychic life whose expression must strain against the limits of linguistic and poetic tradition. This is not the same thing, obviously, as ignoring these limits.

Lowell and Plath, like Eliot before them, but unlike Ezra Pound or William Carlos Williams apparently, have taken many English readers almost against their wills, if I read the criticism correctly and remember accurately the remarks about "exhibitionism" and "baby talk" I used to hear not too long ago. At their most demanding they force us to endure something like revulsion before wringing consent from us—a consent that most English criticism, with its expectations of emotional control and the form of speech appropriate to it, would ordinarily be reluctant to grant. Their emotion—hysteria that is transcended in the process of resolving the poem—is, however, contained in sentences conventional enough to reassure the reader and allow him to pick up their meaning fairly readily. Hence, Lowell and Plath profited from their control of syntax by winning the respect of those critics who are the most sensitive analysts of "normal" phrasing and style. At the same time they cleared the way for critical acceptance of other poets more or less of their school, some of whom do not come through very often in their own right.

But the emotional drive of such poets might just as well have pushed them into directions that made for difficult because unfamiliar reading (the real reason for people's hostility to experimental writing). That the general chaos of modern sensibility is a condition of our art is hardly by now open to argument. Some artists compress their responses to this disturbed state into recognizable channels, especially when, as so often, the chief need is to hold on to a saving perspective of intelligence. If their underlying sense of disturbance is violent enough, their struggle to control it will be evident in many ways. When Yeats wrote that all his life he had "tried to get rid of modern subjectivity by insisting on construction and contemporary words and syntax," he was speaking to just this point. He solved the problem very consciously, and moved from being a beautifully engaging poet to being an overpowering one who made a great art out of the struggle within himself. But there is another direction poetry of the main chance can take in the course of this struggle. It is the direction of an at least partially anti-syntactic mode projected in the image of the poetic process itself, as if the sort of thing done by Lowell and Plath had been pushed an erg harder and a different—not necessarily superior—field of action were now discovered.

Here is the true realm of the experimental if the term means anything more than the imitation of what others have done to see if it works for oneself too. A. Alvarez cannot be praised too highly for insisting that a world "under pressure," with the reek of the concentration camps and the knowledge of things as bad still going on and to come hanging in the air, must find room for a few poetic notes beyond those of wryness, nostalgia, irony, and dry common sense. But that is perhaps an old story by now. It began to be an old story a half-century ago, *before* the concentration camps. Even if one expands the characteristic British option to include the whole range of what I have called "a finely humane articulateness" it is not really enough, for the same reasons. (The main chance involves a bitter grappling with the gross, the anti-human, the inarticulable.) Yet that too is a familiar enough argument, a little tiresome by this time, and in any case it is stupid to try to instruct individual poets in how they should feel and write. The question is not a matter of the limitations of particular poets who may be doing exquisite work of the kind they can do best, but of the position of the art as a whole.

For this reason the inordinate amount of critical attention given to a poet like Philip Larkin seems largely wasted. To admire his writing is easy; to make too much of it is almost sentimental. Donald Davie was not wrong to praise him for the "humanism" of his writing. His insights, with their make-do despair, are certainly suited, in the short view, to the day-by-day quality of much English life. But putting aside Mr. Larkin's actual achievement within this circumscribed context, one can see—if one thinks of the possibilities of *poetry*—that the dissatisfaction of critics like Mr. Alvarez and Colin Falck with what he represents is natural and inevitable, though its roots lie less in what Mr. Larkin does so well than in the sense that alternative modes are being neglected. Mr. Falck's reply to Professor Davie in *The Modern Poet* helps to define the issue:

> Larkin has probably captured the feel of life as it is for a great many people much of the time and this gives his poetry a certain kind of humanity. But he has done this only at the expense of a deeper and more important humanity, because he has done it ultimately at the expense of poetry. . . . The last and truest humanism in art is the truthful expression of emotion, and this . . . concerns only the honesty or corruption of our own consciousness. If this means barbarism then let us have barbarism.

Despite his moralistic vocabulary and the implication that the issue has developed only since the Nazis, Mr. Falck's argument is in the right direction. He is calling for the real thing, appropriate to the sense of this age. At least, I think this is what he is calling for. The language he employs recalls that of D.H. Lawrence and others who long ago saw that the abyss has already opened beneath us. But the real thing, when it comes, is often unexpected in the way it sounds and looks—unfamiliar not only in attitude but in what it assumes a poem can be. The conception here is that projected by Robert Duncan at the end of his poem "After a Passage in Baudelaire":

> *L'idée poétique*, the idea of a poetry,
> that rises from the movement, from the
> outswirling curves and imaginary figures
> round this ship, this fate, this sure thing,
>
> *est l'hypothèse d'un être vaste, immense,*
>
> *compliqué, mais eurythmique*.

Robert Duncan, the late Charles Olson and Robert Creeley are the American experimentalists best known in England. They have won a following here among certain readers, found mainly in the universities so far, who are interested as well in Pound and Williams as earlier models and in Concrete poetry. Without wishing either to exaggerate or even to describe in detail their individual accomplishments, I suggest that they offer useful clues toward the kind of poetry that is now possible for us in the English language. All are uneven writers. Mr. Duncan's special gift is for a rather romantic lyricism, Olson's for a hard, concrete, yet melodic poetry sometimes like Hart Crane's, and Mr. Creeley's for a classical restraint and grace of the sort that Yvor Winters valued so highly. Yet often they go against the grain of their own gifts and deliberately refuse to develop their poems in a simple, organic way. A poem by Mr. Duncan or Olson is quite likely to interrupt its own movement several times, constantly redirecting itself so that a "field" of disparate elements is established. Mr. Creeley's poems are likely to be reduced to suggestive possibility only, the central situation or motif or *aperçu* being hinted at only, like one of those fragments of Greek sculpture in the British Museum that might be anything but which has tempted the experts to label it as a bit off the heel of Laocoön, or perhaps (if only they were *deliberately* a little more facetious) a petrified piece of the sculptor's own heel or hand or shoulder. The real object of imitation—to borrow an ancient phrase—is the inward shifting of the mind as it spots its own hesitant rhythms and associations in the elusive context of deep reverie when objective self-observation is all but impossible. As Mr. Duncan puts it in "Strains of Sight," the process

> above some moving obscurity
> ripples out in the disturbd pool,
> shadows and showings where we would read. . . .
>
> what the question is.
> where the heart reflects.

Neither Mr. Creeley's reductionist methods nor the proliferating open structures of Mr. Duncan (especially in his "Passages") and Olson are really new. There is almost nothing in the technique of these poets that one cannot find in *Mauberley, The Cantos, The Waste Land, Four Quartets, The Bridge,* or *Paterson*. The real change lies in their focusing on the inwardness of the caught moment of consciousness as it flickers across the surface of deep awareness. This focusing, however, is crucial to the new thinking about form, the premise of which is that form is always intrinsically open, a continuing process despite the illusion of completion. (Probably this question is far more germane to the problem of "Kubla Khan" than any number of speculations about Coleridge's dream life and the person from Porlock.)

The great modern sequences I have named are all trickily entangled in the contradiction between traditional conceptions of aesthetic completeness ("closure") and the resistance of the materials to being sealed off. There is something arbitrary about the structure of any poem, no matter how beautifully articulated. Even more arbitrary is the structure of any sequence, which is a poem writ large by being made up of a number of separate relatively independent units that form a kind of constellation. Yet Pound and the others did discipline their tendency to send out more and more sprouts in a single work; they held in mind certain established models of poetic form—*The Odyssey, The Divine Comedy*—or of musical structure. From another viewpoint they conceived of these long, sometimes sprawling works as adaptations of essentially lyrical poetry to complex uses involving narrative, dramatic, and rhetorical functions.

Theoretically, this insistence of the masters on purposeful structure, allied to continuing faith in humanistic perspectives, no longer prevails in much of the more recent experimental work. But poets still yearn to contain the widening gyres, they still refuse to vote for absolute disintegration, and so the real situation is that they still struggle for form although the new emphasis on process has altered the conception of form itself.

English criticism has somewhat lagged in recognizing these untidy developments. Still, *Mauberley, The Waste Land* and *The Bridge* were written before the Nazis came to power, and *The Cantos* too began to be published before that event. We should add Yeats's sequences *Meditations in Time of Civil War* and *Nineteen Hundred and Nineteen* to the list here, despite some important differences in character from the work of Pound, Eliot, and Crane. I have already recalled that poetry of the "truthful expression of emotion [even] if this means barbarism" (Mr. Falck) and of "violence" (Mr. Alvarez) began to exist in the most contemporary sense for us before Hitler came to power. Because for various reasons the continuity with the immediate poetic past had been virtually broken in England, it was easier for a while after the war to forget the history of modern poetry and to reject, as merely the sensational outpourings of people with low boiling points and no feeling for the language, some of the most interesting work being done. Hence the initiative for further work along the two lines of the main chance that I have mentioned more or less remained with the Americans until quite recently. It has produced many tiresome things, of course. Doctrinaire aesthetics are even more boring than doctrinaire politics. At the same time it has helped make the individual voice of the poet a focus for form as well as for thought. The "barbarism" here consists in the departure from familiar expectations as to what a poem is and how it must work; it is not just a matter of scorching the page with the vehemence of one's flaming passions.

There are many signs that poetry of the main chance has been becoming less and less an American speciality. Thus the sequence has taken on a renewed life in the British Isles. At least three Irish poets—Austin Clarke, Thomas Kinsella, and John Montague—have experimented with the form in the manner of Mr. Lowell, as have Donald Davie and others in England. But there has been more daring work conceptually as well, especially represented perhaps in the violent confrontations of sensibility in Ted Hughes's *Wodwo* and Peter Redgrove's *Work in Progress*. (Mr. Redgrove's inner poetics, the kinetic forces underlying poems that were outwardly descriptive or narrative, have always taken him toward a monstrous psychic closeup of the universe as self; see his earlier "Required of You This Night," for instance.) Not quite in another world yet seriously engaged in what they are doing are poets like Ian Hamilton Finlay and critics like Stephen Bann or Michael Weaver who must be respected though the question of the carrying power of Concrete remains open.

Ultimately, the results of experimentation that count come from the struggle of poets to handle their problems of expression through means already familiar. If their improvisations work, they have added to the store of real resources; and what they do is absorbed into the central tradition and affects it in turn. Already we see the effect of the new sense of open structure in the work of talented poets who are not themselves innovators: such British figures for instance as Christopher Middleton and Charles Tomlinson. To mention these names and a dozen others, though, is only to begin a very long discussion of how the mode of fine articulateness is being assimilated to the sense of the main chance. As this occurs, criticism returns naturally, once more, to absorption in the individual poem and loses interest in the battles of the schools and tendencies.

Times Literary Supplement (29 January 1970)

Olson / His Poetry

HOW shall we think of Charles Olson's poetry? He made a very brave run, and did some brilliant things, and pushed into some difficult problems. *Was* he a "lance," a "metal hot from boiling water," compounded of "jewels and miracles," as he calls himself in the first of *The Maximus Poems?* For that matter, *was* Walt Whitman a "kosmos"? Yes, if you allow them their magic, let them earn it by listening to what their poems tell you. I should like to suggest some of the issues that Olson gets us into, for the whole question of his success has to do with the way they are built into the poems, the way the poems find a language and a system for them.

The leading issue—but it is involved with a complex of others—is that of the identity created in the speaking voice of the poems. Any poem, necessarily, has its voice, its guiding sensibility. But Olson makes this identity a major theme and a center of poetic method. In "Maximus to Gloucester: Letter 27" (published in the 1968 volume *Maximus Poems* IV, V, VI), he tries to locate the time-context and cultural context of the identity being developed, starting with his own childhood memories that include a grotesque incident in the life of his parents. The process, he says, is

the generation of those facts
which are my words, it is coming

from all that I no longer am, yet am,
the slow westward motion of

more than I am. . . .

And:

An American

is a complex of occasions

themselves a geometry

of spatial nature.

I have this sense,

that I am one

with my skin

Plus this—plus this:

that forever the geography

which leans in

on me I compell

backwards I compell Gloucester

to yield, to

change

Polis

is this

We can see the connection between Olson's sense here of the speaking self as embodied history and culture and something very similar in works as disparate otherwise as *Song of Myself*, the *Cantos*, *The Bridge*, *Four Quartets*, and *Paterson*. Olson comes closest to the last of these in the way he converts an affirmation into its personal idiom. His syntactic compression projects a resistance and a reciprocal outward pressure of the private self, which is also being molded by "the slow westward motion" of a more inclusive identity. The slightly involved elliptical thought-movement becomes his fingerprint.

Now this is all a rather difficult tack to sustain. Olson was using the still unclarified form of the poetic sequence, for which he was heavily dependent on the models I have named. These sequences combine narrative, lyric, and expository elements in possibly overloaded structures, and most of them use a good many documentary passages as well. Again, they all develop principles of overall movement and patterning, if not of dynamic progression, with various hesitations, interferences, or repetitions. But Olson wants more than the others to get the whole range of tones, intensities, and materials back into his own skin, as he suggests in the passage just quoted. American meanings, and the local data of Gloucester, Massachusetts, are going to be *compelled,* made to yield, to this purpose.[1] It is a confusing task for a poet to keep this sort of intention clear over the long haul, and impossible to make one's own idiom stand entirely clear of one's models. Olson, however, with his rugged and sophisticated intelligence, his humor, his curmudgeonly independence, and his language of inwardness and modesty, helped us all to see what was at stake poetically.

In a curious way, Laura Riding's experience illuminates his problem. Despite obvious differences, her aim was critically comparable to Olson's. She viewed her poems, she said, as "a long exploration of the possibility of using words in poetry with the true voice and the true mind of oneself." After 1938, she changed her view, not of poetry's aims but of its capacities. "I began to see poetry differently, even to see it as a harmful ingredient of our linguistic life. . . . As I reflected on my past poetic activity, I perceived that, in casting my voice and my mind in the poetic mold of speech, I had shut out the realization of the very thing I sought. The equivalence between poetry and truth that I had tried to establish was inconsistent with the relation they have to each other as—the one—*art* and —the other—*the reality*. I came close to achieving, in my poems, trueness of intonation and direct presence of mind in word. But what I achieved in this direction was ever sucked into the whorl of poetic artifice, with its overpowering necessities of patterned rhythm and harmonic sound-play, which work distortions upon the natural proprieties of tone and word."

Miss Riding characterized her own work—all this in a special statement for the BBC some years ago—as "poetry *in extremis,* poetry caught in and confronted with its factitious nature as a mode of linguistic expression." She had learned, she said, "that poets, to be poets, must function as if they were people . . . on the inside track of linguistic expression, people endowed with the highest language-powers." This assumption she found erroneous, for it "blocks the discovery that everyone is on this inside track" and the poet's very successes "leave ordinary speech, and its literary counterpart, prose, sunk in their essential monotony and uninspiringness." She concluded that "the only style that can yield a natural and happy use of words is the style of truth, a rule of trueness of voice and mind sustained in every morsel of one's speech," and that "for the practice of the style of truth to become a thing of the present, poetry must become a thing of the past."

The history of modern poetry, beginning at least as far back as Blake and the *Lyrical Ballads,* is the history of this struggle, or attempted mutual assimilation, or overlapping, of modes. American poetry has added to it the straining for a language at once indigenous and not provincial—dominating motifs of *Paterson* and of *In the American Grain,* to cite the most obvious instance, that of Williams. The American as what Olson calls "a complex of occasions," his private self "the slow westward motion of/more than I am," comes up against the "despair" of which Williams spoke, the sense of making "poetry

1. It is to emphasize this intention—to *will* its success, I think—that he doubles the *l* at the end of "compel" in this passage.

in extremis" that Laura Riding felt, the "barbaric glass" of impersonal reality that Stevens nevertheless looked through (though this last example may be changing the subject slightly). Of course, Laura Riding was wrong in thinking that she had come to a dead end in her own efforts. As Spender says, her poems show "intense personal seriousness, an anguish of being," and embody "the pain of being a woman of genius." I would add that the anguish and pain could not be resolved through poetry, but only realized; and that even if this one poet felt she had reached her limits, this was clearly no proof for others. Olson seems to have felt the issue less as a personal crisis than as a challenge to reorientation organically related to nineteenth-century findings in science and to the character of American local and national experience. There are certainly moments of anguish and pain in his poetry, but they do not involve despair for the art, unless the call for reorientation of method be thought the positive side of despair. The program, however, is no more despairing than Mallarmé's comment on what happened to French poetry after Hugo. "Poetry," he wrote, had "waited patiently and respectfully until this giant (whose ever more grasping, ever firmer blacksmith's hand was coming to be the definition of verse) had disappeared; then it broke up. The entire language was fitted out for prosody, and therein it rediscovered its vital sense of pause. Now it could fly off, freely scattering its numberless and irreducible elements. Or we might well compare it to the multiple sounds issuing from a purely verbal orchestration."[2]

The great issue of form with which Olson contends is implicit in that conception of an "entire language fitted out for prosody" and then suddenly broken up into "numberless and irreducible elements." His greatest immediate predecessors had been forced to let their sense of form make way for another sense—that of the process creating an *illusion* of form. Their insistence was nevertheless on the ultimate, if possibly desolate, expectation of humanized form that would dominate mere process. They felt, and both resisted and yielded to, the great, new pull toward the void: reality abandoned by the human imagination. And yet we always have an instinctive confidence in the congruence, or at least reciprocity, of the objective and subjective, external reality and our inner selves. It is what makes the recordings of whale-songs that I heard recently so absorbing. Not only do whales sing, but each has its own characteristic song, which can be heard for hundreds of miles at sufficient depth. The songs are strange, something like electronic music. We recognize that strange musicality, for the referent, present in the very sound, is a living being whose every note is counterpointed by the wash and roar of the sea: a perfect reciprocity by the very nature of things. The strangeness, the idiosyncratic curve of sound expressing the whole of a vibrant, massive being in its own—but still destructive—element, is its idiom. Old wooden sailing ships used to transmit the sound, and the sailors thought they heard sirens or mermaids. "I await a thing unknown," says the heroine in Mallarmé's *Hérodiade*. Process and expectation do not require the actual realization of humanized form to suggest its presence; their reciprocity suggests it. This is what is really meant by open form. It is the reason that all form in poetry,

2. "Crisis in Poetry," in *Selected Prose Poems, Essays, and Letters*, translated by Bradford Cook (Baltimore: Johns Hopkins Press, 1956), pp. 34ff.

poetry that *counts,* is ultimately open, dependent on arbitrary juxtapositions that create a tentative balance only.

Once we accept—and, more important, *absorb*—this principle, it is possible to move with greater ease within a centrifugal structure like *The Maximus Poems* and to take it on its own terms. I have had occasion elsewhere to argue that the basic method of these poems is not really new, that there is virtually nothing in it for which we cannot find certain predecessors. "The real change," I have suggested, "lies in their focusing on the inwardness of the caught moment of consciousness as it flickers across the surface of deep awareness. This focusing, however, is crucial to the new thinking about form." It is not that the struggle for form has been abandoned, but that the greater emphasis on process—as opposed to older efforts at integration in terms of revised definitions of the possibilities of traditional form—"has altered the conception of form itself."[3]

An anonymous recent reviewer of *The Maximus Poems* in the *Times Literary Supplement* (13 November 1970) thinks to denigrate the poems by saying that they are derivatively modeled on the great earlier sequences of the century, that their syntax is awkwardly idiosyncratic, and that they allude to obscure colonial American history and contain obscure documentary snatches. Furthermore, the reviewer charges that "in accordance with his literary programme, Olson leaps in midline from the poet's surroundings while writing to the memories his impressions provoke, or from minute autobiography to extracts from historical documents, or from economic theory to invective against America." Again, Olson's "language is deliberately flat, slangy, anti-poetic. But the surface of toughness dissolves in the few lyric passages, which could not be softer or more conventional." I quote from this review simply to show how little many people have learned after a half-century or more of the modern sequence. Only the comment on the "few" lyric passages (there are in fact many lyric passages) calls for anything like refutation. The rest of the critique explodes the same kind of little paper percussion-caps that have been used against most of the great earlier American poets of the Pound-generation. The only difference is that the names of those poets, once the intended victims of the same toy pistols, are now being used as caps themselves.

"The unhappy few," says this reviewer, "who listen for lines that engrave themselves on the tablets of memory, for rhythmic subtlety or the undeniably right choice of words, for grace of sound or felicity of perception, for a fresh, true insight into the human condition—in other words, for significant art—will feel generally thwarted." This writer reminds me of those British critics—and a fair number of American ones—who for years never could catch the quick music of Williams because of the way he tasted the beauty of everyday speech and related it to the more familiar poetic values. I suspect that the unknown reviewer would consider a passage like the following one non-lyrical and infelicitous. It is "Song 3" of "The Songs of Maximus."

3. See "Dynamics of Form and Motive in Some Representative Twentieth-Century Lyric Poems," pp. 286–298, above.

This morning of the small snow
I count the blessings, the leak in the faucet
which makes of the sink time, the drop
of the water on water as sweet
as the Seth Thomas
in the old kitchen
my father stood in his drawers to wind (always
he forgot the 30th day, as I don't want to remember
the rent
a house these days
so much somebody else's,
especially,
Congoleum's

Or the plumbing,
that it doesn't work, this I like, have even used paper clips
as well as string to hold the ball up And flush it
with my hand
But that the car doesn't, that no moving thing moves
without that song I'd void my ear of, the musickracket
of all ownership . . .
Holes
in my shoes, that's all right, my fly
gaping, me out
at the elbows, the blessing
that difficulties are once more

"In the midst of plenty, walk
as close to
bare
In the face of sweetness,
piss
In the time of goodness,
go side, go
smashing, beat them, go as
(as near as you can

tear

In the land of plenty, have
nothing to do with it
take the way of
the lowest,
including
your legs, go
contrary, go

sing

This song is one of many nearly invisible lyric passages in the sequence. There are things in it I would criticize, rhythmic effects I would not care to try for myself. But the conformation of diction, rhythm, sentence-movement—that is, its *music*—is absolutely inseparable from the speaking self of the poem: his tone, his sense of life, his posture that is as natural to him as that of Yeats when he writes: "Others, because you did not keep/ That deep-sworn vow, have been friends of mine." Yeats's understatement, his beautifully subdued internal rhyme ("you did not *keep* that *deep*-sworn vow"), his colloquial edge are not actually far removed from the effects of Olson's poem. Here too we have some exquisite echoings of sound, and a powerful emotion at first held in check by a certain minimizing effect—in the word "small," in the attention to minutiae ("the leak in the faucet," the domestic detail, the water-drops):

> This morning of the small snow
> I count the blessings, the leak in the faucet
> which makes of the sink time, the drop
> of water on water. . . .

Both poems, too, move later into violently emotional, even melodramatic statement, though Olson's goes through more phases—from a slightly wry ecstasy to comic play to sheer anger and then song. But to look solely at Olson's poem now: the details of his idyllic dream are of a sufficiently simple, sufficiently physical and laborious existence. He wilfully rejects the pressure of an abstract, organizing force in our economic life that drains men of significant personality, experience, and memory all at once, bribing them with conveniences. Behind the song lies an informed neo-primitivism, unreconciled to modern states and economies. The *argument* may in itself be oversimplified; the speaking personality is nevertheless alive, humorously cross-grained, and deliberately using the vernacular to sustain an image of itself without romantic clichés. Isn't this, in what is after all a minor passage, just such a "fresh, true insight into the human condition" as the *TLS* reviewer requires, with considerable "grace of sound" in its own terms—"Holes/ in my shoes, that's all right, my fly/ gaping, me out/ at the elbows, the blessing/ the difficulties are once more." Among other things, this is high-spirited modern pastoral.

One more point concerning this song. Its intimacy, its sheer vulnerability, is the best clue to Olson's talent—partly, no doubt, because when he gives the game away, almost mumbling to himself at times (showing us the view from the peacock's back, as it were), we still receive enough evidence in the long run of artistic and intellectual rigor. Passages like "Song 3," their musicality and formal modulations always playing on the ear, are spotted throughout his work. They provide perfectly clear points of reference to his strong but self-correcting dominating sensibility.

At any rate, within this context of ultimate rigor and highly developed sensibility, Olson's way of letting go, tuning in on himself without inhibition, serves to give a special kind of subjective body to his work. It seems to me that he has influenced some poets to think that this is the whole of the real thing, the only honest, candid, immediate thing in poetry; that the whole process consists in catching some fleeting memory, in mid-sentence, the grammar turned awry perhaps because it is really a note of association caught in midstream:

> after the passage-way of the toilets
> and the whores
>
> (as that movie-house,
> Boston, you buy your ticket
> but you don't enter, you find yourself
> in an alleyway. . . .

On the other hand, a serious poet like LeRoi Jones has learned to use Olson's sort of inwardness of speech brilliantly:

> I am inside someone
> who hates me. I look
> out from his eyes. Smell
> what fouled tunes come in
> to his breath. Love his
> wretched women.

("An Agony. As Now.")

Jones, like Olson, deploys such effects to feed the language of literal awareness and free association into firmly realized structures. In *The Maximus Poems*, passages like these go side by side with a myriad other kinds. Sometimes they are extremely concentrated and organized lyrical moments, such as that which begins "Tyrian Businesses":

> The waist of a lion,
> for a man to move properly
>
> And for a woman,
> who should move lazily,
> the weight of breasts
>
> This is the exercise for the morning

The narrative passages, historical, personal, and fantasied, have a lyrical dimension too. They not only give clarity of reference and description to a good part of the sequence, but often are a kind of primitive story-telling, touched with pure imagination:

> She sat down and sang a song, a great foam
> or froth rose to the surface and in it appeared the back and tail
> of a great serpent, an immense beast. The woman
> who had taken off her clothes, embraced
> the creature, which twined around her, winding inside
> her arms and legs, until her body was one mass
> of his. . . .

But this is not the occasion for an exhaustive account of the various types of poetic effect that Olson balances off against one another, or for extended analysis of even one passage. My aim, rather, has been to suggest the character and elements of the process in this loosely articulated structure. The character, the bearing, and the affect of Olson's verse, its human involvement with the issues of poetry *in extremis*, makes it a telling witness to that continuing pressure which has extended the limits of the poetic almost unrecognizably in our century. It is a curious gathering, the congregation of American poets of our moment, trying in their separate yet related ways to see their own inner selves, and the volatile historical situation, and the crisis of art, in the same single organic vision. They must define the very landscape of their lives, the very language they are to use, the very sense of personality. Here is Lowell, whose frenzied sense of his own suffering is meant to be the key to reality for all of us. Not far off is the late Sylvia Plath, who marked out a pure, all but obscene curve of death, naked and beautiful—that was a kind of suicide of poetry. And Jarrell, who kept reaching for a lost individual possibility, buried somewhere perhaps still in the neglected common life. But the list need not be further proliferated here and now. Charles Olson, who snapped his sentences open like twigs as he wrote, and whose mind moved outward in a series of intersecting ripples pushing against his syntax, sought to mobilize all that he could of language and local human reality and the most cherished memories of tradition against the new "pejorocracy." He was conceivably the unacknowledged leader of all these unacknowledged legislators. Poetic leadership, I suppose, consists not in directives and programs but in accurate perceptions—

> It is undone business
> I speak of, this morning,
> with the sea
> stretching out
> from my feet

And, finally:

> I set out now
> in a box upon the sea.

The Massachusetts Review (February 1971)

"The Unconsenting Spirit": Poetry and Politics

I was long ago struck by the closing lines of the *Aeneid*. There, at the single point of irreversible emphasis, the poem's attention leaps from the wrathful power of Aeneas to the refusal by Turnus, after all, to grant the hero anything but physical primacy. Aeneas, harbinger of the imperial Roman state, has mercilessly slain Turnus, who embodies the resistance of a primal, kinship-oriented, locally idiosyncratic mode of life. As the poem ends, we are told (in the Day Lewis translation) that "with a deep sigh" Turnus' "unconsenting spirit fled to the shades below."

This is the divine elusiveness of poetic process. By its very nature it can turn an epic designed to glorify the state into its opposite—a "protest poem," if you will. Aeneas and Turnus are, say, the two faces of Mayakovsky. The poetic process, through its fluid medium the language, subverts all established positions or formulations, whether revolutionary or counterrevolutionary.

Modern poetry isolates the process from superimposed argument or narrative. It moves in a volatile context. History dramatizes itself in broad, crude sweeps, but the realities of minute experience and of our emotional dynamics make up the crystal particles of the dreaming, creative sensibility that is our subjective life. Many critics, most recently Michael Hamburger in *The Truth of Poetry,* have noted the reactionary political bent of some of our greatest poets, such as Yeats, Pound, Eliot and Rilke, as well as the curious veering between political extremes of many poets from Baudelaire to Gottfried Benn. Yet these same poets, I believe, have given us by far the most revolutionary critique available of the whole range of bourgeois life and thought, of the philistinism of power, and of the totalitarian impersonality toward which the present age, in whatever ideological guise, is ever more tending. The horror of violence in Yeats's great political sequences, and of war—specifically, World War I—in Pound's *Mauberley* are inseparable from this critique, quite apart from the explicit political statements and actions of these poets.

Modern poetry is revolutionary—not your revolution or mine, however, but *its*. It subverts dogmas, liberating the intelligence to improvise a deeply "human universe" (Charles Olson's phrase) out of our true needs. It does not accept the cant phrases deployed for the subjection and murder of millions, but it does accept the danger and treachery that lurk within our thoughts as a tragic condition of existence. It is thoroughly international. One can as readily compare Cafavy, Vallejo, LeRoi Jones with one another as with their compatriots. They can be seen as at three different but related phases of the historic explosion and re-formation of modern sensibility, though each of course conveys as well the personal and national coloration of his innermost self.

Cafavy's "Waiting for the Barbarians," for instance, takes us to no political program but to a sense of dead loss precisely in that innermost self. The poem arrays the traditional symbols and language of political authority and of advanced civilization, especially in their Grecian manifestations, against the advancing terror of nothingness. We are free to discern the ironic coexistence of many possible contexts within this simple poem.

César Vallejo, the Peruvian poet whose *Poemas Humanos* was recently translated by Clayton Eshleman, far exceeded those English-speaking poets who tried to give body to Spain's agony in the Civil War. He did not write programmatically. He did not need to prove anything. He assimilated the Spanish agony to his own childhood hunger, as it were; his language was true to his entire consciousness. A revolutionary, he did not resort to slogans and ideological clichés. No one has had to write of him, as Ben Belitt did of Neruda, that "the tyranny of the partisan position is apparent throughout." Belitt did go on to say that Neruda is redeemed by what Rilke, in the *Ninth Elegy,* calls "the other relation," arising from his poetic subjectivity, which "constantly draws the poet away from the entrenched point and the limited commitment; from 'false astrologies'... and all the apparatus of historical and theoretical positivism, to the 'enigmas' which have always been the 'general song' of creation."

The "other relation" is what dominates Vallejo, who had a poet's sense even of the word "political" and who wrote (in Clayton Eshleman's translation):

> There comes over me days a feeling so abundant, political,
> for passion, for kissing tenderness on its two faces,
> and comes over me from far away a demonstrative
> passion, other passion to love, willingly or by force,
> whoever hates me, whoever tears up the child's paper,
> the woman who weeps for the man who was weeping....
> whoever gives me what I forgot in my breast
> in his Dante, in his Chaplin, in his shoulders.
>
> I want, in order to end,
> when I'm at violence's celebrated edge
> or my heart swollen size of my chest, I'd like...
> to care for the sick exasperating them,
> to buy from the salesman,
> to help the killer kill—terrible thing—
> and to have been in everything
> straight with myself.

In this untitled poem, from which I have quoted the beginning, a middle passage, and the ending, the concept of the "political" enters the speaking personality as an energizer of universal relatedness. The poet's sensibility becomes an encourager of everything that is, including things and forces he hates, with a certain confidence that the process will bring out the Dante and Chaplin in everyone—the risk of thought and feeling that I mentioned earlier. The volatile context of aroused awareness is limited only by the mind's capacity for conception and empathy. It would be easy to show exact correlations between what goes on here and what goes on in Yeats's political sequences, despite great technical differences.

Whatever one thinks of Vallejo's or of Yeats's explicit positions, neither of them was cowed by commitment. Both followed through into that objectified involvement that allows a poet to place a given moment in which a poem is centered into a context at once tragic and comic. Auden's "Spain 1937," with its refrain "But today the struggle," moves nobly into the voice of a revolutionary orator haunted by tragic vision and by a comic sense of infantile inadequacy; but it is finally limited, despite some beautiful, unforgettable notes, by its self-conscious politicality. How unspeakably greater was the failure of Roy Campbell's counterrevolutionary voice in *Flowering Rifle*. Campbell worked himself into a state of political frenzy but not of poetic awareness. It was not only his reactionary position (just a starting point, as Yeats's famous account of the composition of "Leda and the Swan" shows) but even more his boring inability to rise out of a peculiarly vile literalness, that defeated him. Jerzy Pieterkiewicz, in *The Other Side of Silence*, observes penetratingly that Campbell's real success in projecting what Spain meant to him poetically came in his apparently apolitical translation of St. John of the Cross. I would add a further point. The Popular Front in Spain seemed to Campbell a violation of an order of mysteries that he falsely identified with the political Right. Actually, no poet, however Left, could resist the poems of St. John as a cluster of perceptions true to subjective reality.

Closer to our own moment, a complex example of poetic involvement with political motives comes in LeRoi Jones's "An Agony. As Now." Jones, best known as a literary spokesman for Black Power, has in recent years advocated a rather fierce black racism. Yet the ambivalence of his plays, and, even more, of his poems, gives us an inward psychological view closer to the reality of his world than such terms as "Black Power" and "racism" could possibly suggest. The poem "An Agony. As Now." holds several psychological states in related suspension. Among these are a state of inarticulate suffering and frustration, a state of outward aggressiveness, and a state of confused desire to reject persons and relationships to which the speaker is greatly attached. Clearly, the ambivalence of Jones's split existence is at the poem's center. For instance, he has been close to a group of other poets from whom, because they are white and because he has wished to devote himself to the black struggle, he may have felt he must turn away. The poem says nothing of the sort, though, and nothing about other similar circumstances that come to mind. Detached from its literal referents, yet crammed with concrete images, it takes on the character of mystical vision: "I am inside someone/who hates me. I look /out from his eyes. . . ."

In these words the speaker, at the start of this poem, presents himself as double in nature. His outer self, toughened and adaptable, loathes and represses and gives pain to his inward self. Jones's poem is an attempt to fuse the elements of a fragmented emotional life into a single epiphany. It is only in art and particularly in poetry, that in our time we find a recurrent effort of this sort. The poet may have lost a certain bardic authority, but it is he alone whose word we accept when he reports to us on spiritual experience. Politicians and divines would be suspect; they are alienated from the language of immediacy, nor can they use language as psychically plastic material. The poet alone retains our assent through never being allowed to forget the volatile, treacherous nature of that material.

Implicit in a good deal of current thought is a protest against poetry itself.

Both Pieterkiewicz and Hamburger, in the books I have mentioned, trace this development to the self-defeating romantic and symbolist tendency to view poetry as the royal road to metaphysical or political revelation, and to the intrusion of political determinism into art as a result of activist motives. A resulting reaction has been to condemn poetry because of its failure as prophecy in the omniscient sense. In their valuable introduction to *Modern German Poetry 1910–1960,* Hamburger and Christopher Middleton stress the deterioration of German expressionism after 1914, when it tended more toward the programmatically political, whereas early expressionism, like symbolism and imagism, had rediscovered poetry as its own kind of action. One finds, however, in more recent German poetry, a nonprogrammatic negativism centered on a diminished, dispiriting social and psychological landscape. The dreary staunchness of a poem like Ingeborg Bachmann's "Every Day" suggests the best this body of poets can do in the way of morale. It recalls Herbert Read's "To a Conscript of 1940" in its fear of false idealism. The same fear damps down the work of such poets as Enzensberger, Grass, Piontek and Fried—an echo of the world Oskar Loerke sensed coming in 1933, when he wrote of "the anguish of being confronted with terrible consequences, without having done or even known the least thing." Much of this poetry, like that of such Frenchmen as Pierre Seghers, Georges Hénein, and Henri Michaux (in poems with such titles as "Dead in the Midst of Life, the Days That Are No More," "The Obscurest Sigh," and "Peace amid the Shattering"), suggests an exhaustion of psychic energy in the culture.

The French, it is true, give more of a suggestion of movement to remobilize that energy despite obstacles. On both sides, though, the simplifications and quietism are really sloughings-off of traditional ideological burdens. We seem to be returning everywhere to the essential position Pasternak stated in *Safe Conduct:* "The clearest, most memorable and important fact about art is its conception, and the world's best creations, those which tell of the most diverse things, in reality describe their own birth."

Finally, the cry of André Frenaud in his poem contrarily entitled "Night"—that "I am not afraid of joy I am there for it"—does not consent to the dwindling of possibility with which so many poets are today engaged. Sometimes I feel, because I hope, that a new world poetry, unaffected, of the common life and linked to common speech, yet with the high freedom of the great older moderns, is coming to birth—in protest against history, ideology and joylessness. I do not mean that some direct and passionate poetic thrust against the exploitation and torment to which rulers, systems, and the often unwittingly brutal beneficiaries of oppression subject their victims is ever out of order. Nor is that rarer sort of true poem, a vision of the genuinely joyous kindness and love and human purpose of which we are capable. But the soul of a man or a woman is a complex thing no matter how plain, ignorant and unheeding a given person may seem to be. The furthest reaches of feeling and the imagination, the darkest and most brilliant subtleties of thought, are the heritage of all the people, for whom the poets (like other artists and thinkers) serve as transmitters of whole fields of consciousness and possibility.

The Nation (1 February 1971)

❧

The "Crisis" in Criticism

VLADIMIR: Moron!
ESTRAGON: That's the idea, let's abuse each other.

They turn, move apart, turn again, and face each other.

VLADIMIR: Moron!
ESTRAGON: Vermin!
VLADIMIR: Abortion!
ESTRAGON: Morpion!
VLADIMIR: Sewer-rat!
ESTRAGON: Curate!
VLADIMIR: Cretin!
ESTRAGON: *(with finality)* Crritic!
VLADIMIR: Oh!

He wilts, vanquished, and turns away.

—Samuel Beckett, *Waiting for Godot*

THUS Beckett shows us where the critic stands: lowest in the scale of Creation. But I shall now quote from P. E. N.'s statement, to recall the points at issue:

> Never has criticism in literature and the other arts been more visible and many will say more inadequate. Some will even say purposeless. Whether this situation is due to lack of philosophic depth or faulty critical tools or whether critics, like grammarians, chart only the past and are therefore of no use to the present or whether the fault lies in the works of art themselves, the fact remains that criticism appears to be in a state of crisis. It is either a hothouse product of the academy, scarcely touching the life of art, or it has become a merchandising vehicle in the marketplace.

Now, as so often in literary matters, this attack on criticism goes counter to my own apparent experience: my own writing, what I read, what I study and teach.

There *is* a crisis in criticism, but it is part of the crisis of sensibility that has been developing continuously for about two centuries. It has created a multiplicity of reciprocally related critical approaches. Anyone who wants to think truly while ignoring the cultural crisis and the complexity of modes and levels of understanding is going to miss the point.

From the point of view of the writer—and that category includes the critic—the real crisis is in publishing. There is no single center of critical communication—nor even a group of publications that on the whole bring the issues out. The leading reviews (defining the term for the moment as those with the widest circulation) do not really seem to believe in literature. At best their attitude is that of selective neglect. The situation in poetic criticism, with which I have the closest relationship, is truly scandalous. One ought to be able to expect reasonably inclusive reviewing of new books of poetry of some promise or achievement. Books of criticism receive, if anything, even shorter shrift. And I am sure that novelists and short-story writers have their complaints as well, especially the latter.

An English writer can expect notice in several publications at least, however shallow the treatment may be. Not so in this country. And then it follows that serious literary discussion of basic critical questions has no place in the more popular weekly reviews because people, by and large, have not been given the basic news: who is writing what, and what its character is. This, despite the fact that the daily reviewers on the *Times*, and a few others, contend as ably as the situation allows with the great mass of books that appear.

The situation is reflected in the awards of national prizes. Except for William Troy's *very* posthumous book, no award has been given by the National Book Committee judges to a work of pure criticism. In the last round of these awards, an eminent political figure—admirable for his struggle against the war in Vietnam but hardly an outstanding poet or critic—was appointed one of the poetry judges. The Pulitzer prizes are meaningless from an artistic standpoint, for comparable reasons.

There is a whole world of literature and criticism in this country of which the reading public, who get their information from newspapers and weekly magazines for the most part, is kept largely unaware. It makes its way into the serious small circulation magazines sometimes, into the little magazines that appear and disappear, and into books that very often go unreviewed, or for which reviews are commissioned in the most haphazard way.

But to turn from the publicity situation to criticism itself: Criticism is thinking about literature—about any art, but we are concentrating on literature here.

As poetry is what poets write, and not what we say they should write, so too criticism is what the people who think about literature write.

To be lost in a book, however compelling, is not criticism. But when I begin to find language for what I have been experiencing, I both embody and examine the experience at one and the same time. To that degree I am a critic, and taking the risks of criticism, which is a deep engagement with everything in a culture that resolves itself as art.

The language of criticism is never adequate to the experience of literature. The impossibility of its being so—the poverty of criticism—does not mean the effort is not worth the candle.

Criticism is improvisation, because that is the way thought is made. If there are rules, someone improvised them, and then others elaborated on, corrected, transposed, rearranged them in new contexts, so that by now we hardly know the difference between tragedy and comedy, or between unity and disorder. The catchword of our moment is "process." We are, we think, interested in process rather than in static formal measurements. Still, the germinative critics, thinkers, and artists of the past were always more interested in the mystery of becoming than in formulas; so, after all, we are not so very revolutionary.

We should not fear the uncertainties of critical thinking. If it is improvisatory, remember that it occurs in the midst of action. That is, it occurs amid chaos and in the parentheses, themselves illusory, between confusions. It is at the mercy of everything that vulgarizes clear thought. Its vulnerability begins at the point at which one decides what to think about and what to isolate within that object. The "main critical trends" always begin with the struggle of a coterie to make its way into the foreground. (The vulgar term is "making it," but that is another matter!)

The critical decision to think about work by a writer not "established" is so rare that virtually no such writer ever receives a prize. The committees that award the prizes do not, *cannot,* read his work. The carapace of their past interest has hardened, though they are likely to have the best will in the world. Surely Matthew Arnold, writing "The Function of Criticism in the Present Time," did have the best will in the world, and yet he was unresponsive to what French literature of his own century had accomplished. I would have said "amazingly unresponsive," but the phenomenon is inevitable. Arnold submitted that the influence of the French Revolution had been, not toward a poetry of genius but toward "enthusiasm for pure reason" and toward a condition in which France became "the country in Europe in which *the people* is most alive." We should not blame him for this necessary blindness. Twenty-three years later, his remarks on Villon show why he could not appreciate the genius of a Baudelaire:

> A voice from the slums of Paris, fifty or sixty years after Chaucer, the voice of poor Villon out of his life of riot and crime has at its happy moments (as, for instance, in the last stanza of *La Belle Heaulmière*) more of this important poetic virtue of seriousness than all the productions of Chaucer. But its apparition in Villon, and in men like Villon, is fitful; the greatness of the great poets, the power of their criticism of life, is that their virtue is sustained.

This is, to use Arnold's own sort of rhetoric, great and noble thinking, but calculated to blot out the "virtue" of, say, *Les Fleurs du Mal*. It is the unconscious dismissive criticism which only the most fortunate critics avoid. However open-spirited, they may slip into the sleepy, stuffy complacency of the critics mimicked in Pound's *Mauberley*. "The case presents," they say, "no adjunct to the Muses' diadem."

In a theoretical sense, I have never before felt so acutely the dilemma of criticism. Criticism is in a most important light *the* theory of literature, based on a profound body of knowledge—the traditional knowledge of the history and genres of literatures, of the various modes or approaches to it that scholars and critics have employed, and of many individual works in themselves. I agree completely with people like Kenneth Burke and I. A. Richards and William Empson who have worked out strategies for using our complex, modern sense of process and of reality to watch what goes on in a literary work and what is, richly, involved in its literal and its sunken meanings—what Northrop Frye means by the anagogic mode or approach. And I agree, too, with Frye who, in his *Anatomy of Criticsm,* rather beautifully proposes ways of organizing the whole of literature and its various genres into a scheme of archetypes and functions and definitions that will help us see what criticism as a whole is up to in treating of the nature of literature. Frye's classifications, like those of the Chicago Aristotelians who first battered into my head the need for formal analysis and for seeing how systems connect with each other (Richard McKeon), are full of value for the person who has done enough reading and thinking on his own to enter into a discussion about basic premises with other critical philosophers. I don't care that Frye uses *mythos* for what we ordinarily call plot, or structure; or that in discussing dramatic and fictional structures he does not pay as much attention as I would like to the pressure of the given initial situation and of the laws of the given world on the protagonist—as he himself says, the important thing is *not* that one be right about everything.

My own personal problem with all of this has been that so much of my own work has been driven by the idea of restoring, or reasserting, the primary place of literary experience—imaginative empathy, participation in the process that is the work—in criticism. There is an elementary form of this experience, the child's simple, entranced pleasure of involvement that makes him sad when the book is coming to an end. That feeling needs to be cherished, but at an informed, disciplined, mature adult level, that enables us to see and formulate implications and relationships and principles without denying the work its own magic. How to combine participation with objective study?—that is the dilemma, which can be solved only through the critic's assumption that it can be done. One does it by confident engagement with individual works, using the knowledge and theoretical equipment one has at that particular moment but bearing in mind their tentativeness so as to avoid dogmatism or presumptuousness. The confidence comes from the certainty that the works themselves will give us our bearings and suggest their own structural process and correct us if we check our hypotheses against them again and again.

The American Pen (1971)

Poet of Brooklyn, Ulster & Paris

A CHOSEN LIGHT by John Montague

THE Irish poet John Montague is one of the most interesting now writing in English. He tells a story, paints a picture, evokes an atmosphere, suggests the complexities and torments of adult love and marriage—all in the most direct, concrete, involving way. The poems come out of a deeply human speaking personality for whom language and reality are more than just a source of a plastic design of nuances. Montague does have a highly developed sense of the craft; he is a real poet, who works at his desk and drinks of the tradition. But he brings all his engagement with his art directly to bear on the world of our common life, as Frost and Williams so often did, and thus makes immediate contact with his readers. He thinks and talks like a grownup man, and that fact alone makes him better literary company than most of his poetic contemporaries.

The poems of *A Chosen Light* fall naturally into four large groups. The first ones we encounter, and with some exceptions the most striking, have to do with love. More particularly, they deal with love in a marriage that, it is suggested, has suffered a grievous, unnamed wound and yet survives with a unique meaning and purity. The group includes at least five truly memorable pieces, chief among them "All Legendary Obstacles," a poem about the troubled reunion of lovers after long separation. It is closely rivaled by "That Room," about the traumatic discovery by husband and wife of some disastrous reality, and by "The Trout," literally about the sensation of trapping a trout with one's bare hands but with overtones of sexual and psychological intensity that keep reverberating in the mind. I would add, as well, the dedicatory poem, whose protagonists find their house symbolically disappearing—first the roof, then the walls, and finally the floor under them; and "A Private Reason," a further development of the theme of "All Legendary Obstacles." Montague has a classic lyric gift. Lines like "Kissing, still unable to speak," "Side by side on the narrow bed," "Rarely in a lifetime comes such news," and "To this day I can/ Taste his terror on my hands" are not rare in his work.

A second grouping has to do with rural Ulster. This is not quite "his native Ulster" (as the book jacket has it); Montague was born in Brooklyn, where his father, as one of the most touching poems, "The Cage," tells us, worked in a subway change booth. Ulster was nevertheless the family base. The poet lived there many years and does indeed write of it with a native ground sense both loving and harsh. Local realities of landscape, personality and indigenous experience are sharply sketched in with a bitter yet tender truthfulness reminiscent of the older Irish master poet Austin Clarke. Unlike Clarke, though, Montague has lived much of his adult life away from Ireland, mostly in Paris. His poems have a distancing and a nostalgia peculiar to this situation and not uncharacteristic of much modern Irish writing that grows out of the self-exiling of many Irish writers. (In a group of poems not yet published in this country, Montague has written powerfully of Irish political history and the current struggles in Ulster from the same intimately concerned yet "objective" standpoint.)

Montague's Parisian experience constitutes the center of the book's third section. Although this section brings his political awareness, Irish interests and marital situation into play again, its true concern lies in his situation as an artist of this moment. The brief title sequence moves into this focus of sensibility with a special accuracy and beauty. First we see the night view from the door of his atelier, where he can "smell the earth of the garden" and range all the impressions of that tiny, unluxurious Eden against the lights and dark outlines of working-class Paris in the vicinity. Then, in imagination, he follows one rigorous "voyager," a "strict master" with his "fastidious mask," as he moves sustaining his disciplined inner aesthetic among the children and lovers in the Luxembourg Gardens and "weathers to how man is." Finally, we have a poem anchored in the marvelous image of the radiometers in rue Jacob, symbolic "not of help, but of neutral energy" that is forever "casting its pale light/ Over unhappiness." The effect of this image is to conjure up the peculiarly impersonal empathy that life demands of the poet. The final group of poems ranges among primal and broadly symbolic motifs that place this guiding sensibility in the widest possible context. With this book John Montague reinforces his position among the humanly genuine poets now writing.

The Nation (17 May 1971)

❧

Under the Freeway, in the Hotel of Lost Light

THE BOOK OF NIGHTMARES by Galway Kinnell

GALWAY Kinnell's title for his new book of poems suggests its preoccupation: the world of terror raging beneath the sill of daylight consciousness. It is the world of Eliot's "Rhapsody on a Windy Night," where destructive reality invades the naked psyche. *The Book of Nightmares* is a sequence of ten poems, each in seven sections, that takes us on an extended inward journey toward the state of the speaker's soul at a specified moment—

> in March, of the year Seventy,
> on my sixteen-thousandth night of war and madness,
> in the Hotel of Lost Light, under the freeway
> which roams out into the dark
> of the moon, in the absolute spell
> of departure, and by the light
> from the joined hemispheres of the spider's eyes.

This key passage shows how much of a piece the book is with the whole post-Romantic tradition. The first pair of lines links social and private horror with the contemporary instant. The next two extend the horror to a meaningless cosmos; man is in the dark whether he seeks refuge or risks the unknown. The final lines charge the desolate scene with a malign spell. The ten poems of the sequence accept the implications of such a universe while holding on to lines of human meaning.

Each of the elementary motifs around which the work is built is conceived in this double light, as a reaching toward glimmers of transcendence beyond the acutely depressed vision of existence. They include the births of a son and daughter, the speaker's love for his wife, his abortive affair with another woman, his life-communion with other animals (brilliantly and morbidly explored in a poem about the killing of a hen), his identification with a drunk found dead in a hotel room, the gross violence (culminating in Vietnam) done by Christian man to himself and to others, and the spider-fly principle in human life. These basic motifs are interwoven in subtle ways, and all contribute to a dominant sense of mystical self-orientation in circumstances beyond control; the yearning implicit in the living flesh is the only shadow of hope in this interim dominion of death.

The surrender, the despair, that gives these poems their very pitch and melody is all the more striking because the natural symbols of affirmation—the wife's happy pregnancy, the birth of their children, and the couple's sexual harmony—come through with such tenderness and, sometimes, humor. Some readers might well consider Kinnell's description of the birth process as grimly realistic, but the net effect of the reconstructed experience is rather glorious and buoyant:

> and she skids out on her face into light,
> this peck
> of stunned flesh
> clotted with celestial cheesiness, glowing
> with the astral violet
> of the underlife. . . .

Indeed, the closer one looks at the sequence, the more clearly one sees that the real triumph, which is considerable, lies in just such moments of concrete realization, when the language exults at and transforms literal reality. The music of Kinnell's projections of reality is quite extraordinary. What is more dubious is his further projection of some unclarified personal complex of sufferings onto the same materials. Naturally, the unresolved sexual guilts and the broodings over war and death that saturate the poems are irrefutable sources of depression. But they are, if in varying proportions, our common lot, and there is nothing in the way Kinnell handles these themes that makes them particularly his.

To reinforce the psychological state he is trying to evoke, of a condition of visionary awareness heightened by private disorientation, Kinnell deploys a good deal of zodiacal, occult and religious symbolism. This aspect gives the volume much of its feeling of being heavily structured, with the sequence—and each poem within it—seeming to progress from a kind of despair to a kind of affirmation with many ups and downs and swirlings on the way. A "system" like that of Yeats's *A Vision* may be implied. The atmosphere is rich, sometimes thick, with allusions to the mysteries of augury and of the Crucifixion, and to such emblems and traditions as "the Archer," "the Bear," "the Crone" and "the sothic year."

Although some exciting effects of cosmic imperviousness to human affairs, heartbreaking and beautiful, are achieved, the structure is overloaded. Like that of Ted Hughes's *Crow,* it proliferates its symbolism to cast a net over a superhuman range of reference. In both works, repeated readings do open up much of the wider meaning the poets seek to mobilize, but the problem remains. And at the end of *The Book of Nightmares,* we are after all back to the original lonely sensibility of the speaker. He is still on his isolated "path among the stones," yet passionately a part of the common life of all "who live out our plain lives," locating the sources of possibility however minimal:

On the body,
on the blued flesh, when it is
laid out, see if you can find
the one flea which is laughing.

Thus the sequence ends. Intellectually, the program isn't much, is it? Kinnell has echoed all the great, sad questions of the past concerning our destiny, and he has summoned up the famous masks of the poet, especially the crucified, freely confessing sinner-saint and the sufferer beyond all telling. Something like an astrologically oriented prophetic role attracts him too, and so we have a renewal of the poet as seer. But the real power of his book comes from its pressure of feeling, its remarkable empathy and keenness of observation, and its qualities of phrasing—far more than from its structural thoroughness or philosophical implications. It needs stripping down. But no matter. Whatever its weaknesses, *The Book of Nightmares* grapples mightily with its depressive view of reality and with essential issues of love, and it leaves us with something splendid: a true voice, a true song, memorably human.

The New York Times Book Review (21 November 1971)

The Waste Land *as an Open Structure*

THE recovery of the lost version of *The Waste Land*—"the original drafts including the annotations of Ezra Pound" reproduced in the Valerie Eliot edition of 1971—compels a new recognition of the open character of the poem's structure. I do not mean that the earlier version shows us what Eliot was "really" doing in the later one; only the text a poet finally decides on takes the responsibility for itself. But because of certain different emphases while the poem was still in the making, the sense of improvisation at the high pitch of genius that struck the first readers of the printed text is reinforced. One almost does well to forget Pound and think of someone as unlikely as Lawrence, with his idea of Whitman as the poet of the "open road," and of a poetry "of the present"; Lawrence wrote in 1918 of "the poetry of that which is at hand: the immediate present. In the immediate present there is no perfection, no consummation, nothing finished. The strands are all flying, quivering, intermingling into the web, the waters are shaking the moon. . . . This is the unrestful, ungraspable poetry of the sheer present, poetry whose very permanency lies in its wind-like transit. Whitman's is the best poetry of this kind." This was in Lawrence's introduction to the American edition of his *New Poems*. But five years earlier still he had written, in a letter: "I have always tried to get an emotion out in its own course, without altering it. It needs the finest instinct imaginable, much finer than the skill of craftsmen."

One could assemble a huge battery of statements by Lawrence and others, even by Pound and Eliot, to show how much a renewed fascination with the organic and "wind-harp" conceptions of Romantic poetics affected the young advance-guard poets and theorists of the time. Even those who made something of a show of their intellectual rigor—their learning and "classicism" and formal self-discipline—were infected with this desire to write directly out of the "immediate present," to use the language and the experience and the whole context of life that was "at hand." To isolate, release, recognize, and ride the real emotional direction of the poem—such an aim involves the sense of improvisation at the pitch of genius that I have mentioned. The true poem, in this perspective, consists of a series of affects that together create the life of the poem; their order is a tentative satisfying of the need to explore the emotional range they embody that is felt by the poem's ultimate sensibility or speaking voice. It is interesting that Eliot, in the face of his poem's obvious preoccupations with large moral, religious, and social issues and with philosophical and cultural meanings of a very inclusive kind, should have remarked that "to me it was only the relief of a personal and wholly insignificant grouse against life; it is just a piece of rhythmic grumbling."[1] It was not that those broad and deep preoccupations, which enable us to see a certain clear rhetorical order in the progression of the poem, are not actually present. But they are present as dimensions of a speaking consciousness, rather than as the main point or purpose of the poem. Eliot himself, in his doctoral dissertation, had concerned himself with F. H. Bradley's concept of "Immediate Experience" as the ambiguous, undifferentiated condition of the living self in the midst of its world but hardly sorted out from the reality that engulfs and saturates it.

The context of Bradleyan thought brought to bear on the sensibility that broods over the shifting moments of *The Waste Land* has been discussed by a number of scholars. Eliot spells the key-formulation out for us by quoting directly, in his notes, from Bradley's *Appearance and Reality:*

1. Quoted in the Valerie Eliot edition, p. xxiii.

> My external sensations are no less private to myself than are my thoughts and my feelings. In either case my experience falls within my own circle, a circle closed on the outside; and, with all its elements alike, every sphere is opaque to the others which surround it. . . . In brief, regarded as an existence which appears in a soul, the whole world for each is peculiar and private to that soul.

The passage is applied directly, of course, to lines 412–417 of *The Waste Land*, in which the isolation of the speaking self by pride and by failure of sympathy is presented as a hapless condition after all.

> I have heard the key
> Turn in the door once and turn once only
> We think of the key, each in his prison
> Thinking of the key, each confirms a prison
> Only at nightfall, aethereal rumours
> Revive for a moment a broken Coriolanus

Eliot refers us as well to *Inferno*, xxxiii, 46, the point at which Ugolino, imprisoned with his sons in the Tower of Hunger, awakes to find they are being sealed into their prison. The relevance of one motif of tragic isolation to another is obvious, though the full hideousness of the Ugolino tale can hardly be assumed to be evoked in Eliot's lines through the mediation of a footnote (especially since the allusion to Coriolanus in the passage itself takes us in a quite different direction). The Bradleyan approach, indeed, implies for the poet a continuously depressive condition that was not at all the concern of the philosopher: that state in which the psyche is so invaded and possessed by "outside" reality that it cannot define itself and its purposes in any actively formed perspective.

Poetically speaking, this is the state of readiness shared by the poet and his work—readiness to receive the unavoidable impact of reality and readiness to move out of this open and vulnerable position into the exploration of possible new sets of attitude and awareness. The characteristic lyric poem of the past two centuries begins with recognition of a real situation that has perhaps elusively melancholy overtones, or with a direct statement of a feeling of sadness or of precarious balance. It moves into a sense of the complexity of the relationships and feelings it is contemplating, often marked by a sense of confusion and of the breaking down of normal distinctions. It ends with something like reconciliation, but on closer observation the reconciliation consists in the speaker's recognition of a drastically and tragically unchangeable reality. Paradoxically, this recognition has the ring of a joyous affirmation. Eliot's "Shantih shantih shantih," which picks up from the gloriously elated language of ascetic abnegation in lines 419–423 ("The boat responded/Gaily" etc.), is but one of a very long series that would include such endings as Wallace Stevens's "Downward to darkness on extended wings" and Yeats's

> Hermits upon Mount Meru or Everest,
> Caverned in night under the drifted snow,
> Or where that snow and winter's dreadful blast

Beat down upon their naked bodies, know
That day brings round the night, that before dawn
His glory and his monuments are gone.

The movement, in other words, is from a state of depressive awareness to one of depressive transcendence. It is not usually a straight-line movement, particularly in a sequence; except in relatively short pieces, it tends to be a series of balancings, in which the depressive state inseparable from a sufficiently open sensitivity is countered by momentary holdings against the chaos threatening the speaker both from without and from within. A lyric poem is in this way of seeing it a sensibility in motion. The motion is toward a tentative reconciliation by way of a number of poised balancings interspersed among movements of loss and dissolution. These balancings hold off absolute loss of morale, if only through the purity with which a negative recognition is evoked and sustained. Let us again cite lines 412–417, both because we have already noted the Bradleyan reference attached to it and because it is a strategically placed passage. It presents sharp and striking images for the speaker's sense of spiritual isolation and self-defeated pride; at the same time, it has positive tonalities mostly contradicted by the literal context. I say "mostly" because the image of a key that locks one into oneself does not exclude the possibility of the key's being turned the other way, and because there are associations of transcendence and tragic heroism implicit in the thought of "aetherial rumours" that "revive" even for only "a moment" even a "broken Coriolanus." This is a balancing, though on the whole negative in its implications. Another "positive" tonality is created by the word "confirms," though what is being confirmed is "a prison." The music of the passage sustains its balancing of motifs and tones. The confessional voice at the start, followed by the meditative voice that shifts from "I" to "we" and then by the exalted melancholy of the closing two lines, introduces a play on the word "key" that induces contemplation of its varied suggestiveness partly through sheer repetition and partly because it is alliterative with "confirms" and "Coriolanus" and has an insistent vowel echoed in "we" and in "aetherial." By the time the passage concludes we are thinking of "keys" to the poem's psychological frustrations and to its largest possible meanings as against the dead pressure of a continuum of undifferentiated reality.[2]

In its formal movement the passage epitomizes *The Waste Land* as a whole. Its final balance is not really final at all; it is a precarious stay only against breakdown, a set of notes that might easily enough be extended with other groupings of images—as in fact the next six lines do brilliantly, and as the next eleven lines, which end the poem, do once again. Those final eleven lines, too, "handle" the problem that was projected at the very beginning of the poem by jumbling together the basic tonalities of morale that punctuate the whole poem. These are, in order of appearance, the breakdown in madness and meaninglessness that comes with loss of sustaining vision, the passion to

2. See Richard Wollheim's excellent "Eliot and F. H. Bradley: An Account," in Graham Martin, ed., *Eliot in Perspective: A Symposium* (N.Y.: Humanities Press, 1970). Wollheim takes up this passage, but without regard to its poetic character.

search out purification by discipline and mortification, the inseparable linking of tragedy and transporting desire in mythical and literary tradition, the emptiness felt by the speaker himself (coming forward, at last, as the poet who has "shored" the "fragments" of which the poem is made "against my ruins"), and the counter-motifs of spiritual redemption and calm at the end, themselves concealed as nonsense words until the English-speaking reader is properly indoctrinated.

The poem no more necessarily ends here than if it were one of Pound's *Cantos*. The real movement of *The Waste Land* is of brief, irregularly alternating cycles of depressive letdown and of resistance to it. As Lawrence said he tried to do, Eliot "gets an emotion out in its own course, without altering it"; he lets himself be carried by it but improvises ways of coping with it, for the "emotion" is actually a complex of feelings and attitudes informing what Eliot downgraded, half-humorously, as the "personal and wholly insignificant grouse against life" that he used the poem to "relieve."

Not to go into too tedious detail, we may trace the alternations of affect that define the progress of "The Burial of the Dead," and then add a few notes about later sections. The exquisite and poignant music of the first four lines, with their vital and painful challenge to meet the self-renewing demands of life, has a curious echo without resonance in the ensuing three lines. These are deliberately dulled and casually diffident in tone though they sustain the participial rhyming and general rhythmic character of the opening. Marie's expanded, more relaxed lines provide another kind of echo of the opening. Memory and desire are evoked once more, but are rendered trivial by the life-patterns within which they are held; the loose rhythm of the opening of this section, and the anticlimactic ending, make Marie's speech that of one of the dull roots of lines 4–7. If one still feels a certain bravery and touching love of excitement in what she says, the deeper voice of lines 19–30, turning on such roots and branches as could possibly grow "out of this stony rubbish," introduces the sound of prophetic horror at human reality seen in its terrifyingly amoral emptiness. The new voice's compulsive repetitions balance this terror at our loss against the promise of a revelation that may be yet more terrible. Then the music of rhetorical prophetic insistence drops away. It was another reverberation, we should note, of the atmosphere of challenge suggested in the opening lines, and even of their romantic intensity. But now something more similarly evocative of the world of erotic desire and its full implication of painful self-awareness re-enters the poem in the lines from *Tristan und Isolde* and in the "hyacinth girl" passage. Madame Sosostris, another dull root, presents a welcome comic and satiric variation while introducing themes from the deeper world of prophetic mystery though she does not understand them. At last, in its turn, the "Unreal City" passage (one of the three or four most powerful and concentrated climactic points in the whole sequence) transposes the comic and satirical effects to something grimly fantastic and grotesque and appalled.

My point is that we have been carried through a process of emotional clarification that is musically ordered, a music of feeling rather than a music of ideas, its dynamics determined by shifts in the intensity and lyric deployment of the successive passages. Attraction to life's most magnetic sources in body and spirit vies with fear of its consequences in the opening lines, and all the ensuing variations and modulations and transpositions open out and narrow down this central, active motive caught into the poem by the opening words, "April is the cruellest month. . . ." The two opposed sets of dramatic speech, one hysterically inward and the other savagely comic and externalized, of "A Game of Chess" provide yet another context for the same polar oppositions. Richness, then sheer need and distraction of spirit, then sardonic notes that pick up from those concealed in the serious Shakespearian parody at the start, then jazzy rhythms like those in Madame Sosostris's speech, then the chill paralysis of the sheer failure of feeling, and then the protracted, complex mixture of low comedy, desperate grossness, and doomsday warning—these are, on the whole, the dominant succeeding affects here. Still "mixing memory and desire" and the fear of pain and of barrenness with both, the poem's genius lies in its prolificacy of variations and of new tones that yet are controlled by the one original emotional complex with which it began. The possibilities for more and more variation, with a cumulative effect so long as redundancy is avoided and the extent of the poem does not stifle the emotion, are not inexhaustible although the limits of the power of any given sequence are easier to discern than to characterize.

In any case, the extraordinary stylistic variations, and in particular the varied lyric forms that interact with one another within this poetic constellation and yet remain superbly independent, are what make this poem the unique achievement it is. The possibilities of the initial emotion are realized in a large number of directions within the same magnetic field. The Bradleyan perspective serves the poet as a reminder of the gulf between what we can actually know and the self-transcendence to which we aspire. It makes any state of awareness keyed to sharply defined insight (as opposed to passive immersion in experience) in some sense an affirmation. States of ecstasy and horror can in this sense be balanced on one side of the scale against sheer entropy. It can, I think, be argued—though to demonstrate in detail would take many pages—that *The Waste Land* despite some aberrations proceeds through purer and purer intensities to extend and weigh the polarities with which it begins, but that it need not necessarily have stopped where it did. The surface rhetoric is in this sense an interference with the real process of the poem.

Recovery of the earlier drafts shows us what some of the alternative possibilities were. One needs to be open, not only to the deleted passages as given to us in the Valerie Eliot edition, but also to the possibilities they represent. Whatever, for instance, one may think of the original first section of "He Do the Police in Different Voices," it is important to remember that its very presence would have changed the character of the whole poem and that Eliot would probably have revised and developed it differently in a final draft had he decided to keep it—as he did, say, with the Tiresias passage whose first line originally read: "The typist home at teatime, who begins. . . ." To start "The Burial of the Dead" ("He Do the Police in Different Voices: Part I") with the long account of a night out in Boston was a more daring idea than has been recognized. It got the sequence off in low gear rather than at the highly concentrated lyric pitch of the present opening. Thus the poem would have lacked the advantage of an initial powerful center of reference around which the rest of the sections would appear to be developed. On the other hand, the idea of establishing a context of colloquialism and of commonplace urban life from the start had its own advantages:

> First we had a couple of feelers down at Tom's place,
> There was old Tom, boiled to the eyes, blind. . . .

The idiom becomes more specifically American a bit further on, and at the same time introduces the sexual theme without the romantic and emotional force it takes on a little later in the poem:

> —("I turned up an hour later down at Myrtle's place.
> What d'y'mean, she says, at two o'clock in the morning,
> I'm not in business here for guys like you;
> We've only had a raid last week. I've been warned twice. . . .

All this was difficult to manage, technically. Eliot had to get Boston Irish speech right, and also the normal hesitations and crude phrasing of most uncultivated conversation. Perhaps he meant to mingle the diction of college students with that of Myrtle and the local Irish-American speech. The cadences are abrupt though syncopated, and the allusions to current songs and Boston places are almost parochial. It is easy to dismiss what he does here, and yet the modulation toward a genuine poetry based on the speech of the streets is suggestive of a possibility for which the poetic situation was on the whole not yet ready. An atmosphere of casual and commercialized licentiousness is quickly established, as trivial and yet as cheating to the protagonist's real desires as the life of Marie. A certain ambience of confusion is established too. The love of music, theatre, erotic experience, and joy for its own sake, and the importance of magnanimity, are set forward as values despite the vulgarity of their manifestations. At the end of the passage the protagonist separates himself from the others—"I got out to see the sunrise, and walked home." It is the beginning of the journey among the levels of feeling and of moral condition that *The Waste Land* reports. And suddenly, in the next passage, we are reading: "April is the cruellest month. . . ." The shift is a wrenching one, between extremes that mark out the opposite poles of consciousness in the poem. This was surely a potentially fruitful direction of the poem, one that might have informed it with a dimension of ordinary reality had the orientation been somewhat different.

In this context, the original beginning of "Death by Water," with its knowledgeable depiction of the life of sailors and the circumstances of serving on old sailing ships, also linked common experience with the larger motifs of the sequence. It is extremely interesting to see Eliot employing materials not unlike Masefield's while sustaining a highly formal precision of language in his own right and at the same time writing with a candor and a deliberate interrupting of his own formal tone that foreshadows the method of a poet like Charles Olson:

> The sailor, attentive to the chart and to the sheets,
> A concentrated will against the tempest and the tide,

Retains, even ashore, in public bars and streets
Something inhuman, clean, and dignified.

Even the drunken ruffian who descends
Illicit backstreet stairs, to reappear,
For the derision of his sober friends,
Staggering, or limping with a comic gonorrhea,

From his trade with wind and sea and snow, as they
Are, he is, with "much seen and much endured,"
Foolish, impersonal, innocent or gay,
Liking to be shaved, combed, scented, manicured. . . .

Elimination of this passage, and of the account of a ship's strange and sinister journey that follows, left only the brief Phlebas the Phoenician passage as Part IV. As with the deletion of the original opening lines of the poem, what was retained made for greater emphasis and clearer outlines. Yet if both passages had been retained, at the beginnings of "The Burial of the Dead" and of "Death by Water," they would have constituted a continuing journey or quest pattern that would have prepared the reader for the Grail motif of "What the Thunder Said." The loose, halting rhythms of the deleted passage at the start were to be replaced by the firmer ones of the passage on the sailors' journey. Tragic proportion would thereby have been lent to the common life as we saw the sailors inexorably having to face their fate under a supernatural compulsion. The speaker's yearning toward that common life is now suggested only incidentally in a few lines of the poem. With retention of these two passages, it would have entered the poem's music more penetratingly whatever the effect on the total balance of the poem would have been.

Finally, had Eliot retained the Fresca passage at the head of "The Fire Sermon" and kept certain omitted lines about the "young man carbuncular" in the passage about the typist's seduction, a strong personal note of disgust and contempt would have altered the whole atmosphere of *The Waste Land*. His Swiftian revulsion at Fresca, the chic, vulgar female poetaster at her toilet and in society, violates the generous and emotionally open sensibility that seems to preside, otherwise, over most of the poem. A pettiness and meanness pervades the satire here, and the wit dissipates itself against a hardly formidable victim. That "Fresca slips softly to the needful stool" is hardly a powerful satirical point, and the following lines about her seem pathologically inflamed:

This ended, to her steaming bath she moves,
Her tresses fanned by little flutt'ring Loves;
Odours, confected by the artful French,
Disguise the good old hearty female stench.

These lines, and much of the rest that goes with them, give a bitchy flavor to Eliot's style that carries over to the scenes in "A Game of Chess" and to other scenes elsewhere in the poem. If retained, they would have destroyed the fine distancing generally maintained between the ultimate voice of the poem and the characters seen in closeup. Similarly, the contempt shown toward the young man and the typist in the original draft for their cultural pretensions obscures the essential bearing of the scene that depends in part on their viciousness being seen as ignorant and even innocent. And yet Eliot, had he kept these passages, would have committed himself to a much more confessional and vulnerable role in the structure of the poem. He would have had to set his own finicky and precious attitudes, and his abysmal feelings about female physicality, into the scale with other predominant motifs. These were possibilities of commitment toward which he went a fairly long way. In the era of Robert Lowell and Allen Ginsberg, he might well have gone the whole distance. Neither his nor Pound's taste was ready to be confident about doing so in 1922, and doubtless the best available reading public for poetry would not have been ready either. When he wrote, in the typist's seduction scene, that the young man

> Bestows one final patronising kiss,
> And gropes his way, finding the stairs unlit;
> And at the corner where the stable is,
> Delays only to urinate, and spit,

Pound crossed out the last two lines and wrote in the margin: "probably over the mark."

So *The Waste Land* is an open structure in two senses. The first sense is the one developed at the start of this essay, and has to do with the dynamics of the poem's movement as an extended lyric structure in sequence form. The structural principle resides not in ideas but in affects within a float of memories and associations in an ambiguous realm of consciousness, their direction determined by a driving emotional preoccupation. Intensities and modes of language define the structure; no story ends or argument completes itself here, but a momentary sense of balance provides a tentative sense of closure now and then.

The second kind of openness lies in the undeveloped potentialities suggested by excised portions of the earlier draft. We have not looked at all those passages, but have noted enough to show that certain colloquial modes of verse, and certain unattractive dimensions of personal feeling, were suppressed in the interests of an advanced poetics that was nevertheless not yet ready for them in the early 1920s. The feelings of the desired audience were a factor as well, as Pound's comment that I have just quoted would seem to indicate. A definite critical success was sought for *The Waste Land,* and that fact, and the two poets' stage of development at just that point, and Eliot's nervous condition all militated toward the inhibition of certain lines of exploration. Every poem is after all open in the sense that it could be developed further, it could be improved, if only the poet's energies and state of readiness were a trifle beyond their actual state. But *The Waste Land,* because of its place in the history of modern poetry and the peculiar history of its text, and because of its pioneering inward voyage by way of externalized images and other points of reference, is a particularly fascinating instance and problem.

Mosaic (Fall 1972)

Poetic Power—Free the Swan!

IN THE OUTER DARK by Stanley Plumly
UPLANDS: NEW POEMS by A.R. Ammons
GROWING INTO LOVE by X.J. Kennedy

THE title of Stanley Plumly's first volume of poems is a fine image for the dramatic scene implicit in much lyric poetry: *in the outer dark*. That is where the sensibility finds itself as it confronts objective reality; it is the confusing yet involving place described at the start of the title-poem:

> In the outer dark we come to where
> we are, all-fathering waters, the wind
> that led us here, the stillness in the air,
> the star, the slow beginnings in the mind . . .

A state of depression, caused by the invasion of the self by more than it can grasp, is implied, but as a phase of a process of realization and not as a final set of mind. The book's epigraph, from Hermann Broch, provides a kindred image and perspective:

> . . . *it was the immeasurable gulf that stretches between the obverse and the reverse sides of darkness, a tension without equilibrium.*

All this suggests a heavily gloomy metaphysical writer. Plumly does have a little of that, in an oddly youthful and exuberant way. Like some lovely sparkling-eyed girl with bitter views on life, his "darkness" is touched with grace—a quality embodied in his handling of light and shadow in some of his better poems. Such a poem, perhaps his best, is "Now That My Father Lies Down Beside Me," a visionary repossession of a dream-experience in which he was reunited with his dead father. Exquisite in its concreteness and simplicity, the poem is completely convincing:

> We lie in that other darkness, ourselves.
> There is less than the width of my left hand
> between us. I can barely breathe,
> but the light breathes easily,
> wind on water across our two still bodies.

Thus it begins, later picking up variations on the light-shadow-water ambience that gives the poem its strange accuracy, its sense of being at one, though not directly communicating, with the dead in an alien element that suggests "life" beyond death and "awareness" beyond consciousness:

(There is no star in the sky of this room,
only the light fashioning fish along the walls.
They swim and swallow one another.)

and

A window, white shadow, trembles over us.
Light breaks into a moving circle.
He would not speak and I would not touch him.

One thinks of Dante's famous figure of the shadow of the *Argo* cast on the sea-floor below; and Pound's brilliant "Fish and the Shadow" suddenly came to my mind, evoked no doubt by Plumly's line "at the sleeping center—no fish, no shadow."

I don't mean to claim that *In the Outer Dark* is consistently splendid, though this poem and a love poem—equally precise in its imagery of light in motion but more concentrated and "hard"—called "Circulating Epiphany" would alone make any book of poems vitally interesting. When I first opened the book, the initial poem seemed to me alive and intense but unfocused. The second and third, called "Angst" and "The Celestial Ennui of Apartments," made the facile assumption of automatic despair that one might expect from their titles. The fourth seemed centered on a forced image, all the more tiresome for its insistently elegiac feeling and the sincerity with which that feeling was being so brutally jammed into an inappropriate conceit. The fifth poem has strong echoes of Lowell's *Life Studies*. Etc.—Plenty of faults to be found, but the genuine notes of poetry are to be found everywhere too, and, sooner or later along the way, a poem will strike even the most begrudging bawd of euphony as something he'd rather not quarrel with at all, just absorb. The first of these, for me, was the downright plain poem "Digging Potatoes, 1950." A little bit like Frost, a little bit like Lowell, it nevertheless has its own sturdy authenticity. The speaker's memory of working alongside his father is given depth by the merging of separate experiences and times, so that the poem is at once elegiac without straying from sensuous recall to rhetoric and zestful without buffoonery. Turning the page, I next found "A Late Summer Storm Come to Southern Ohio," a poem totally in motion first set off by an accumulation of observed detail and then realized through the speaker's internalization of the storm atmosphere. I've oversimplified; there's more to the poem than that. But the point I really want to make is that I suddenly realized the fact that this poem, without calling itself "Angst," actually has the shape and impact toward which the intention of the other poem had been moving. Here, in other words, is a *poet*. The resonances implicit in the effort may not always, perhaps not even usually, find their decisive form, but the dynamics are sensed even in that relative failure.

One grows into the sense of the real poet by such stages, and it is a sign of Plumly's genuineness that he lets some uneven and uncertain poems into the early part of his book and gives us the richest work toward the end. It is all part of the same vision, for him, though it has to be arranged poem by poem. Finally, one comes to cherish the whole vision through those individual poems that show the speaker's voice and level of imagination precisely in phase with it.

One of Plumly's poems, "From Fossil, Wyoming," happens to share A. R. Ammons' major preoccupation in *Uplands:* the organic unity, a kind of life-principle, underlying the complexities of formation and movement in suborganic nature. The mystery in this unity is for Ammons a key to the place of individual life and consciousness within the vast swirling chaos of natural process and, by the same token, a key to the principles of poetics. Plumly's poem begins:

> Like the fish
> whose bones are little horizontal
> ladders embellishing the silence
> of Lake Gosiute, itself bone-dry,
> a maria wind deep in death,
> we learn to swim in stone.
> The light breaks down on our heads
> until the day is white and brittle
> in our hands, but we still break water with the dead. . . .

And Ammons, in the characteristic "Cascadilla Falls," tells how he

> picked up a
> handsized stone
> kidney-shaped, testicular, and
>
> thought all its motions into it,
> the 800 mph earth spin,
> the 190-million-mile yearly
> displacement around the sun,

until he had "thought all the interweaving/motions/into myself" and stood looking into the sky in rapt cosmic confusion about his own life-direction. Where Plumly finds a half-blessed, half-awestruck (and probably terrified) vision of where he is, Ammons almost makes a comedy of it. He is serious, all right, but he loves to play with ambiguous and temporary hypostatizations of form and meaning emerging from the endless motions of nature; meaninglessness and meaning, dissolution and structure, seem imponderably inseparable concepts, and man's soul less a dark center accumulating transcendent energy than a ludicrous shimmer of morale dependent entirely on illusion. "Shadows," he says in the closing line of "Transaction," "are bodiless shapes, yet they have a song." Or, as he puts it more lightheartedly at the end of the very sardonic and ingenious "Spiel":

> nip and tuck
> scoops
> scopes
> scrimps &
> scroungings

Many of Ammons' poems are metaphysically framed sketches from nature. Some are realistic, some a kind of animated cubism, and some abstractly patterned. The "metaphysical" aspect is rather like that in Wallace Stevens:

the same issue of reality and illusion. It almost seems obvious that Ammons' opening poem, "Snow Log," is a conscious allusion to Stevens' "The Snow Man," as a starting point from which *Uplands* goes on to explore possible directions of form and phrasing on a wider range than Stevens engaged himself with. Ammons does have certain advantages over Stevens: his knowledge of geological phenomena (an *experienced* knowledge) and his ability to use language informally and to create open rhythms. Everything he writes has the authority of his intelligence, of his humor, and of his plastic control of materials. What he lacks, as compared to Stevens, is a certain passionate confrontation of the implicit issues such as makes Stevens' music a richer, deeper force. There *is* a great deal of feeling in Ammons; but in the interest of ironic self-control he seems afraid of letting the feeling have its way, in the sense that Stevens lets his bitterness flood through "The Emperor of Ice-Cream." Stevens was certainly self-ironic, and hardly an emotional screamer, yet he *hated* the illusoriness of human ideals and understanding that the fact of death forced him to face. What Ammons presents is a certain delight or dismay at the imponderable, while at the same time he refuses to strike for effects of power we yearn for in a poet with such a mind and such an ear.

He shows the promise of power in one poem especially: "Transaction," whose paradoxical closing line I have already quoted. This poem is an elusive, allegorical report on a tragic and crucial turn in the speaker's life. Its beginning recalls, despite differences of rhythm and style, any number of Emily Dickinson's cryptic accounts:

> I attended the burial of all my rosy feelings:
> I performed the rites, simple and decisive:
> the long box took the spilling of the gray ground in
> with little evidence of note: I traded slow
>
> work for the usual grief: the services were private:
> there was little cause for show, though no cause not
> to show: it went indifferently, with an appropriate
> gravity and lack of noise. . . .

The effect in this twenty-four line poem is of the slow unfolding of the acceptance of disaster. (Each major pause, marked by a colon, emphasizes this process.) Part of the acceptance is to leave nature, with the human element buried, as the decisive, ultimate scene: "the sun, the breeze, the woods," and "the little mound of troublesome tufts of/grass." Reconciliation consists in noting that one can find a music even in "shadows"—that is, in the loss of hope, or even of life. This seems very different, but is only the opposite extreme of the same spectrum, from Ammons' outcry of joy at the swirling, heady excitement of nature remembered in "Runoff":

> that was a place! what a place!
> the soggy small marsh, nutgrass and swordweed!

"Transaction" is the most interesting, though not the most brilliant, poem in *Uplands*, for it comes closest to taking the risk of tragic vision. The most ingenious and lively, though it runs out of steam, is "Summer Session, 1968," which has some of the glorious, open proliferation of keen sensuous awareness we find in, say Browning's "The Englishman in Italy." It lacks Browning's sustained and exalted exuberance, however. At the end one has to ask, both of the conception and of the expansive form: *Where is this taking us?* Ammons, putting himself down as poet, teacher, and man and sometimes resorting to a slackly colloquial wit as he does so, is behaving too fashionably and not doing justice to himself. Given his talents, it is fair to hold up such figures for comparison as Browning, Dickinson, and Stevens. None of them eluded the whole challenge of poetry; none feared the rhetoric of ecstasy or terror when the right moment for it arrived.

At first glance, the poems of X. J. Kennedy seem free of the Romantic challenge that I have been, perhaps unjustly, urging upon Mr. Ammons. The stakes and risks of that challenge are high; superb artistic courage is needed to get beyond sensitive reporting and simple introspection into the realm in which outward observation is transformed and re-directed by its internalization. Kennedy, in any first reading, seems clearly of the order of classical ironists: worldly, satirical, wry, astringent. His sonnet "Nothing In Heaven Functions As It Ought" wittily transposes certain conventional notions of Heaven and Hell and manages, at the same time, to bury its hatchet in the totally anaesthetic skull of computerized technology. A coolly "modern" candor pervades the poems of love and marriage. The crushingly knowledgeable "The Korean Emergency" hits hard, not through polemic but through its closeup of men on a destroyer in the Mediterranean and their behavior when they "hit the beach with fifty bucks to burn"—a comment, not so much on the men (though the realities of their world are, not very admirably, there) as on the whole situation and attitude inevitable in such circumstances. Kennedy's little witticisms in "Apocrypha" and elsewhere, too, place *Growing into Love*, like his earlier book, in the light verse tradition of what A. J. M. Smith has called "the worldly muse."

Some of Kennedy's work, though, is so passionate in its sense of life and art that, despite his surface amusement at romantic mystification and its magical symbols, he exposes himself as vulnerable and sympathetic to their magnetism after all. An interesting instance is his poem called "Poets." It is built around two epigraphs. The first comes from a letter written by D. H. Lawrence in 1923 while he was staying in Kennedy's native town, Dover, N. J. "These people," wrote Lawrence, "are . . . quenched. I mean the natives." The quotation is both simple and ambiguous. (I take it on faith, without checking, that the quotation is authentic and not a whimsical improvisation by Kennedy.) The second epigraph is Mallarmé's famous opening line—*"Le vierge, le vivace, et le bel aujourd'hui"*—in his sonnet about a swan trapped by ice that has formed around him in a frozen lake.

"Poets" consists of five iambic pentameter quatrains. Its rhyme-scheme (*abba, cddc,* etc.) somewhat parallels the Petrarchan scheme of Mallarmé. Its structure is intrinsically looser, however; and the tone is superficially far lighter because each stanza makes a joke or two and because the tone appears to mock the mentality of poets and their use of swans as glamorous poetic symbols. It is easy, then, to overlook certain implications of the form and the theme. The long lines and the sustained stanza patterns make their own serious insistence. So do the themes of poet and swan although their surface treatment is disdainfully negative. When poets are young schoolboys, we are told, they are unmanly, self-conscious, squeamish, and "moody, a little dull." And swans, when caught in ice (it happened every winter in Dover) are stupid, vicious, and disgusting:

> A fireman with a blowtorch had to come
>
> Thaw the dopes loose. Sun-silvered, plumes aflap,
> Weren't they grand, though?—not that you'd notice it,
> Crawling along a ladder, getting bit,
> Numb to the bone, enduring all their crap.

Yet the presence of beauty, even if he says the swans are "so beautiful, so dumb," is stressed by the poet. He sees it as inseparable from the unworldliness, as it were, of these birds that let the ice form around them because they cannot focus on it "through their dreams." They are exactly like the poets when the poets were inept children—and Kennedy says the swans are "birds of their quill," kindred beings. He has, in the first half of the poem, gradually made these poet-children grave, intense beings who interest him as they might have interested Lawrence: "Quenchers of their own wicks, their eyes turned down/And smoldering."

What emerges is a view of swan and poet in Romantic perspective after all. A great deal rides on such words and phrases as "smoldering," "beautiful," "dreams," and "sun-silvered," on the sheer weight of the form despite the apparent tone, and on the evocation of Lawrence's feelings against the repression ("quenching") of psychic energies and of Mallarmé's marvelous poignancy and pride.

It is a pleasure to see Kennedy being a poet of power in this way, and using common speech and experience and humor toward such ends. All three of the poets, Plumly, Ammons, and Kennedy, seem to have the strength to draw the Odyssean bow. It is no belittling of their fine talents to recognize this strength and hope they will give it more practice in the future through an even fuller use of the gifts they already display.

Shenandoah (Fall 1972)

Randall Jarrell

1

ALTHOUGH Randall Jarrell wrote a very witty novel and a good deal of lively criticism as well, his most enduring interest as a writer lies in his poems. Between the appearance of an early group in the New Directions anthology *Five Young American Poets* in 1940 and his death at fifty-one in 1965, he prepared seven books of verse. Their usually melancholy titles suggest the desolation with which he constantly contended and which seems to have won out in the breakdown he finally suffered.

To review very briefly the curve of this psychological struggle as it manifests itself in the succeeding volumes: The first book, *Blood for a Stranger* (1942), reveals amid its many echoes of Auden and others certain underlying motifs of loss and confused focus. The next volumes, *Little Friend, Little Friend* (1945) and *Losses* (1948), take their main strength from a number of elegiac war poems. In these poems Jarrell was often able, because of their concreteness and directness, to objectify the motifs that had knotted up so much of his previous work. Also, he learned a good deal about immediacy from such poets of World War I as Siegfried Sassoon and Wilfred Owen. A period of broadening perspectives followed, marked by the appearance in 1951 of *The Seven-League Crutches*, in 1954 of the novel *Pictures from an Institution*, and in 1955 of *Selected Poems*. This last-named volume, containing only two new pieces, was the result of careful reconsideration and, often, revision of past work.

It was not until 1960, actually, that Jarrell published his first book of new poems since *The Seven-League Crutches*. But in the decade and a half after the war he had had a varied experience. He had been literary editor of the *Nation*, poetry consultant at the Library of Congress, visiting lecturer in American colleges and abroad, and, with occasional interruptions, a professor in the Woman's College of the University of North Carolina. He had established himself as one of a small, elite group of poets, protégés originally of Allen Tate and John Crowe Ransom. But Jarrell's outward successes did not anesthetize him against his painful need to gain inward clarification, which finally led him to write the autobiographical poems of *The Woman at the Washington Zoo* (1960) and *The Lost World* (1965).

In a sense, Jarrell tried to make a European of himself, to change over from a bright young American Southerner to a sort of German-Austrian-Jewish refugee of the spirit. His interest in Rilke, in the German *Märchen*, and in the neglected European heritage of Americans seems in part an effort to repossess for himself a nourishment denied him in his childhood. Yet this effort, by a process analogous with that described in Keats's "Nightingale" ode, eventually "tolled him back to his sole self."

The word *fey*, meaning both *intensely excited or gay* and *doomed*, is perhaps too grim for Jarrell's poetic personality. Yet it is useful when we think of that side of him which is at once high-spiritedly brilliant and superciliously over-insistent, engaging yet irritating, and which assorts so ill with his capacity for gentleness and for an almost sentimental love of the quieter and more pedestrian virtues—and with the absorption of his imagination by bleakness and horror. The impact on others of this complex of qualities comes through strikingly in the collection of affectionate essays and reminiscences, *Randall Jarrell, 1914–1965*, that appeared in 1967 as a memorial volume. An unusually valuable piece in this excellent collection is "A Group of Two," written by his widow. It is a lovingly drawn portrait of a baffling man: his varied enthusiasms, his childlike ebullience and depressions, his sparkling if somewhat shrill spirit. Mrs. Jarrell is straightforward but protective. She never spells out the nature of his psychic disturbance or the exact circumstances of his death while walking on a highway. She does nevertheless suggest that he carried about with him throughout his life the burden of childhood insecurity, both psychological and financial. His parents were divorced, and for a while he lived happily with his paternal grandparents and great-grandmother, working-class people, in Hollywood, California, before his reluctant return to his mother in Nashville, Tennessee. The gifted, volatile child never "grew up" entirely. The intensity, the traumatic moments, and the accumulated guilt and resentment behind these experiences were never resolved.

He recurs to the Hollywood period a number of times in his poetry, most notably in the title sequence of *The Lost World*. The confusion and displacement of that period are crucial, though many of their implications are suppressed. "Mama" and "Pop" in Jarrell's poems are the *grandparents*, while his mother is "Anna." The sense of universal sadness, betrayed vulnerability, and emptiness at the center of the self in Jarrell's work is rooted in these childhood events and relationships, and doubtless helps account for his strong attraction to European literature of tragic consciousness.

In his poems there is at times a false current of sentimental condescension toward his subjects, especially when they are female. But more often another current carries us toward a realization of the ineradicable innocence and pity of the common life in all its alienating reality. This current did not really show itself, as a directive element in Jarrell's art, until the war poems of his second volume. In the first, *Blood for a Stranger*, some of his major themes were visible but neither voice nor tone was yet quite his own. One hears a sort of Auden-static everywhere, with other voices cutting in every so often. In the most accomplished poem of the book, "The Skaters," the voice seems a duet of Hart Crane and Edwin Muir:

I stood among my sheep
As silent as my staff;
Up the sea's massy floor
I saw the skaters pass.

Long like the wind, as light
I flowed upon their track
Until at evening's edge
I marked their breathless flocks.

I sped among them then
Like light along its lands—
Love wreathed their lips, and speed
Stiffened their tissue limbs. . . .

Half vision, half nightmare, the poem closes in on a note of lost personal focus. The speaker discerns in the stars the image of "one obsessing face," with which he comes into a precarious sympathy or relationship while caught up in the swirling skaters' movement that controls the curve of the poem. But finally, abandoned and abandoning, he is whirled into "the abyss":

But the iron's dazzling ring, the roar
Of the starred ice black below
Whirl our dazed and headlong strides
Through the whirling night into

The abyss where my dead limbs forget
The cold mouth's dumb assent;
The skaters like swallows flicker
Around us in the long descent.

These motifs of coldness and distance, and of a fantasy realm that is only a heightening of desolate reality, persist throughout Jarrell's career. It is hard not to see "The Skaters" as a suicidal projection of the symbolic search for the irretrievably lost mother:

The million faces flecked
Upon my flickering gaze
Bent to me in the stars
Of one obsessing face . . .

A hopeless distance, a bewildering cosmos. Another poem in the volume, "The Bad Music," is addressed to "Anna" and uses the same pattern of symbolic imagery as "The Skaters" without reaching the glitteringly impersonal final set of that poem. Here the speaker sits by a window watching students as they return home from caroling. They carry candles that "wink out and on and out, like mixed-up stars," and

I sit here like a mixed-up star:
Where can I shine? What use is it to shine?
I say; and see, all the miles north inside my head,
You looking down across the city, puzzling. . . .
High over the millions who breathe and wait and sparkle . . .

"The Bad Music" makes almost embarrassingly explicit the buried reference, which is not the literal meaning, of "The Skaters." In its first stanza, the speaker blurts out his accusation of abandonment to Anna:

The breast opening for me, the breaths gasped
From the mouth pressed helplessly against my wrist

Were lies you too believed; but what you wanted
And possessed was, really, nothing but yourself:
A joy private as a grave, the song of death. . . .

Poetically, what is interesting in the relation of the two poems is the similarity of their *process*. Each starts in a state of passive melancholy and moves into active despair. Under surface differences of tone and theme, they share a configuration of feeling and imagery. The "mixed-up star" symbolism in both poems projects the speaker's relation to the elusive object of his love. Faces appear as part of a subjective constellation in which confusion reigns, and it is all but impossible to sort out lover from beloved (son from mother) or either one from the shifting mass of other people, or, indeed, from the whole objective universe. The pattern of movement is characteristic of Jarrell: a static initial state of sadness; then a phase of confusion that lets deeper depression flood into the poem; and then a final bitter thrust. We see it working in the famous five-line war poem "The Death of the Ball Turret Gunner":

From my mother's sleep I fell into the State,
And I hunched in its belly till my wet fur froze.
Six miles from earth, loosed from its dream of life,
I woke to black flak and the nightmare fighters.
When I died they washed me out of the turret with a hose.

This poem is "impersonal." The speaker is not the poet himself but a dramatic character, a soldier who has been killed in the war. Yet the ironic womb imagery recalls the earlier mother theme, as of course the word *mother* itself does. We begin with the abstract yet unhappy assertion in the first line, an assertion that the young man received into the military world from the dreaming family world of childhood has hardly had time to emerge from fetal unconsciousness before he is in a new womb, that of war. Attention shifts in the next line to the chill, metallic character of that new womb. Suddenly then, the next two lines transport us to the gunner's moment of "waking" into nightmarish vision, at the moment his plane is hit by flak in the sky. The image is fetal; a note by Jarrell in *Selected Poems* stresses the fact that, "hunched upside-down in his little sphere," the gunner "looked like the foetus in the womb." The scene itself here is close to the confused cosmos of the two poems already discussed. Life is seen as only a "dream," whereas death is the reality into which the protagonist is born. In the harshly distorted womb images of this poem, we have once again the motif of love betrayed.

What Jarrell forces on our imaginations through his grotesque symbolism is the obscenity of war, its total subversion of human values. In highly compressed form, he has summoned up his subconscious preoccupations and the dynamics of poetic association they generate to make a poem that gets outside his own skin. The conversion process was not simple, though the result is emphatically clear in its narrative movement and in its succession of tones and intensities. Instead of the anapests that launch the first two lines, a suddenly lurching hovering-accent gets the third line off to a wobbling start that helps shake the poem open to let in wider ranges of felt meaning. (Effects of confusion and ambiguity, in rhythmic shifts as in the literal suggestion of language, often have this function in poems.) The brutal nastiness of the closing line refocuses the poem sharply, yet the final effect is not abrupt. The line is in hexameter, longer by a foot than any of the preceding lines. It has the impact of a final "proof" of war's nature as a mockery of all that is life-giving.

It is easy to see how such a poem was prefigured in *Blood for a Stranger*. If we think of that book as comprising a definite unit of sensibility, we shall perceive it as, in large part, a complaint against loss of the world of childhood. (Jarrell specialized in psychology as an undergraduate at Vanderbilt University and was, in his omnivorous way, a reader of Freud; he is very likely to have "psychoanalyzed" himself to some degree at least.) The unresolved discontents of childhood are certainly present, but the real complaint is against separation, against initiation into adulthood, against the loss of an insufficiently discovered and savored life of innocence. "What we leave," mourns the opening poem ("On the Railway Platform"), "we leave forever." Another poem, "90 North," makes explicit the contrast between the secure childhood where

> At home, in my flannel gown, like a bear to its floe,
> I clambered to bed,

and the present, "meaningless" moment where

> all lines, all winds
> End in the whirlpool I at last discover.

True enough, a bear climbing onto its floe is not the most secure of beasts; but the nightmares of childhood, in Jarrell's poem, do end in "rest" and a "warm world" of dependable certainties where "I reached my North and it had meaning." Of the poems in *Blood for a Stranger* specifically about childhood and separation, the most poignant is "A Story," a monologue by a boy sent away to school. It has none of the portentous phrasing that mars "90 North" and other poems of this volume. Its thoughts are always appropriate to the speaker. "I liked home better, I don't like these boys" is more to the point than the generalizations in "90 North" and "wisdom" and "pain."

Not to linger overlong with this first book, it has other, though related, points of interest besides this central one of the child soul's vulnerability. In "Children Selecting Books in a Library," for instance, Jarrell meditates charmingly, if slightly pedantically, on the value of reading fairy tales. Another piece, "The Cow Wandering in the Bare Field," has been praised by Allen Tate, who remembers seeing it when Jarrell, then a freshman at Vanderbilt, was seventeen. Its beginning at least is slightly reminiscent of Hart Crane's "Black Tambourine," the details at once starkly literal and accusatory:

> The cow wandering in the bare field,
> Her chain dangling, aimless,—
> The Negro sitting in the ashes,
> Staring, humming to the cat. . . .

Jarrell rarely again tried this kind of distanced yet incisive presentation. Indeed, he loses track of it later on in this very poem; he was after a faint modulation toward a theme of social protest, perhaps, and he did think of himself as a "radical" in his youth. But that side of him is seen in poems strongly indebted to Auden and Spender, with such titles as "The Machine-Gun," "The Refugees," "A Poem for Someone Killed in Spain," and "For an Emigrant." Part I of the last-named poem, with its final stanza greatly altered, was salvaged for the *Selected Poems* and retitled there as "To the New World." It was interesting as showing special sympathy for the victims of the Nazis and for its insight into the life of exiles:

> Free—to be homeless, to be friendless, to be nameless,
> To stammer the hard words in the foreign night. . . .

"For an Emigrant" shows, also, Jarrell's early realization that, ultimately, the refugee condition is universal; the balm of America is only a salve:

> You escaped from nothing; the westering soul
> Finds Europe waiting for it over every sea. . . .

"For an Emigrant," despite its political clichés and its sermonizing, meant something for Jarrell's future development. Much of it has to do with the effect of anti-Semitism and fascism on a *child's* life in Europe, and it attempts to assimilate the political lessons of the thirties in such a way as to bring the poet's childhood-obsession into a wider, more adult context of awareness. The poem anticipates, as well, Jarrell's later tendency to assume a European consciousness and graft it onto his American personality—a tendency for which Pound and Eliot had doubtless provided models. Jarrell, however, differed from them by playing the role of an exile in his own land, if far more modestly than they and with a lesser genius though a real, and kindred, sense of cultural mission.

2

Jarrell served in the Army Air Force between 1942 and 1946. "In the first months of the War," Robert Lowell writes in an "appreciation" appended to the 1966 paperback edition of *The Lost World*, "Jarrell became a pilot. He was rather old for a beginner, and soon 'washed out,' and spent the remaining war years as an aviation instructor. Even earlier, he had an expert's knowledge. . . . Nine-tenths of his war poems are air force poems, and are about planes and their personnel, the flyers, crews, and mechanics who attended them. No other imaginative writer had his precise knowledge of aviation, or knew so well how to draw inspiration from this knowledge." His mind was similar to Hardy's and to Owen's in its fusion of informed objectivity with a compassion as close to sentimentality as intelligence and taste would allow. Of course, the world of which he wrote was very far from Hardy's, and he lacked Owen's combat experience. But in his war poetry he was like Hardy in bringing to bear on it his whole, extraordinarily literate intelligence—an intelligence of the kind that feels imaginative literature as the distillation of considered experience, the usable treasure of a contemplative mind. And he was like Owen in the way the pressure of his empathy with the pilots he knew made him envision their war experience in a vivid, accurate manner unmatched by most of his writing having to do with civilian life. The poetry of their condition lay for him, as for Owen, "in the Pity." For both poets this is a sort of passionately apprehended disproportion between the young soldiers' ultimate innocence and the terror they both suffer and inflict. It is realized not in sentiment but in action.

Jarrell's war poems are found mainly in his *Little Friend, Little Friend* and *Losses* volumes, which came directly out of the war years, and there are a few more in *The Seven-League Crutches*. His vision of the soldier as betrayed child is clearly epitomized in "The Death of the Ball Turret Gunner," a poem strategically placed at the end of *Little Friend, Little Friend*. As with most American and British poets of the second world war, the ultimate implied attitude is an ambiguous, or at any rate a tentative, one. The shock, horror, and questioning that mark the poetry of the first world war were the discovery of a generation, a discovery crystallized on the run, in the midst of death—the discovery that war *was* the trenches, the barbed wire, the humanly pointless slaughter while, in Owen's words, "God seems not to care." Jarrell and his contemporaries had been teethed on that earlier work; for them it was the definition of war experience. All later war poetry is in an important sense informed by the World War I "tradition." However, there are at least two significant differences for Jarrell's generation. First, they felt a far greater initial detachment from official rhetoric and from the assumptions of the social system. And second, though there was a good deal of old-fashioned combat in the later war, the over-all organization and the far greater importance of the air forces and long-range technology and communication made the involvement of most soldier-poets far less immediate than before.

These differences may be overstressed, but I am trying to suggest that the poetry of Jarrell's generation feels the impact of war with a double awareness. It is still in touch with the original shock of World War I, but is further away from the almost tribal sense of participation in a ritual gone wrong. Herbert Read's poem "To a Conscript of 1940" is a bridge between the two positions in time. The ghost of a soldier of 1914-18 speaks to the poet, a survivor who now faces the new war situation:

> We think we gave in vain. The world was not renewed.
> There was hope in the homestead and anger in the streets
> But the old world was restored and we returned
> To the dreary field and workshop, and the immemorial feud
>
> Of rich and poor. Our victory was our defeat.
> Power was retained where power had been misused
> And youth was left to sweep away
> The ashes that the fire had strewn beneath our feet.
>
> But one thing we learned: there is no glory in the deed
> Until the soldier wears a badge of tarnish'd braid;
> There are heroes who have heard the rally and have seen
> The glitter of a garland round their head.

Theirs is the hollow victory. They are deceived.
But you, my brother and my ghost, if you can go
Knowing that there is no reward, no certain use
In all your sacrifice, then honour is reprieved.

To fight without hope is to fight with grace,
The self reconstructed, the false heart repaired. . . .

Basically, this is the position—acceptance of the war (presumably because of the policies and aggression of the Nazi government) but without any chivalric or apocalyptic illusions. The history of the between-wars governments was too well known; certain Marxian and pacifist conceptions, admittedly contradictory, had irrevocably entered Western sensibility; and the fact that military victory would not solve the great social problems of the age was widely understood. Jarrell's way of encompassing all this was, on the whole, to adopt an existential approach. Here were men—*child*-men, really—in circumstances beyond their control or even their comprehension. It was not existential*ist*—neither a revolutionary perspective, nor a challenge to men to be as fully and heroically human as possible in the circumstances of limited choice open to them, is implied. Jarrell's emphasis is on the saving innocence of those whom these circumstances have after all made, as he says in "Eighth Air Force" *(Losses)*, "murderers." That is a bitter word, yet Jarrell uses it a bit lightly and ironically. Because the young American airmen also run the risk of death, as he himself does not, he compares them with Christ. The comparison has some validity. Whitman, in "A Sight in Camp in the Daybreak Gray and Dim," had used it for the soldier as *victim;* and even when the soldier is constrained to kill he is in some sense still a victim. Pressed too hard, though, the argument is obviously forced and sentimental. Could one have put the case otherwise about young German soldiers in the same situation? Hardly. And if not, must not one say also that the most hardened killer is ultimately an innocent victim, a Christ crucified on the cross of his particular fate? But Jarrell did not follow the logic through:

The other murderers troop in yawning;
Three of them play Pitch, one sleeps, and one
Lies counting missions, lies there sweating
Till even his heart beats: One; One; One.
O murderers! . . . Still, this is how it's done:

This is a war. . . . But since these play, before they die,
Like puppies with their puppy; since, a man,
I did as these have done, but did not die—
I will content the people as I can
And give up these to them: Behold the man!

I have suffered, in a dream, because of him,
Many things; for this last saviour, man,
I have lied as I lie now. But what is lying?
Men wash their hands, in blood, as best they can:
I find no fault in this just man.

In these lines Jarrell makes explicit the prevailing social assumption about war: that men cannot be held responsible for what history compels them to do, especially when they are on the "just" side of the struggle. But he tries, too, to make a subtly paradoxical argument to get past the objections to this assumption, and his style turns to putty in the process because the thought is too contrived. The reality of the situation requires the most relentless intellectual toughness and unwillingness to be an apologist for war mentality. Otherwise, the paradoxical fact that one can, in a sense, be good and innocent while behaving murderously becomes merely another sophistical argument for further mass murder. Jarrell himself recognizes this problem by his play on the word *lie*, but self-irony does not always purge a speaker of the error he confesses by it. Indeed, Jarrell's note on this poem, given in his introduction to *Selected Poems*, has no self-irony at all: "'Eighth Air Force' is a poem about the air force which bombed the Continent from England. The man who lies counting missions has one to go before being sent home. The phrases from the Gospels compare such criminals and scapegoats as these with that earlier criminal and scapegoat about whom the Gospels were written."

The limitation in Jarrell's war poetry is not, however, political or intellectual. It is a matter of energy. He focuses on the literal data of war—their irreversible actuality, and the pity of the human predicament implicit in that actuality. The poems stop short of anger, of programs, of anything that would constitute a challenge to soldiers or to their commanders or to the statesmen who make policy. Letting the facts of war experience speak for themselves, Jarrell sank all his real poetic imagination into primary acts of empathy; ordinarily he resisted any obvious political rhetoric. In "Eighth Air Force" we have a rare instance of his swinging out of his usual orbit to deal with the moral issues of mass bombing. His failure to handle the problem poetically lay in inadequate resources of emotional complexity and intellectual power.

But within the narrower limits of its engagement, Jarrell's war poetry is often superb. In poems like "A Front," "A Pilot from the Carrier," "Pilots, Man Your Planes," and "The Dead Wingman"—the last of these a dream poem, but one that presents the essence of a familiar situation: a pilot searching for a sign of a shot-down wingman—the poet's entire effort is to project the sense of men and machines in action, from the viewpoint of a participant. In all the poems just named, Jarrell has a double aim. First, he wishes to get the technical and atmospheric details in coherent order (a bombing plane whose radio has gone bad, so that the pilot cannot be diverted from a closed landing field to another still open and therefore crashes; a plane that has been hit and is burning, from which the pilot parachutes; a carrier under attack from a Japanese torpedo plane; the situation of the airman hunting for a lost comrade). And second, he desires to make the perspective that of a living, suffering man. "A Pilot from the Carrier" and "A Front" are in the same volume, *Little Friend, Little Friend,* as "The Death of the Ball Turret Gunner." They carry a kindred birth-death motif, though less explicitly. The pilot in the plane from the carrier, "strapped at the center of his blazing wheel," tears himself loose from that tomb of death and is reborn via parachute

Into the sunlight of the upper sky—
And falls, a quiet bundle in the sky,

The miles to warmth, to air, to waking:
To the great flowering of his life. . . .

The pilot in "A Front" cannot be wrenched free in time, and perishes. In *Losses,* the men on the carrier in "Pilots, Man Your Planes" are sleeping "hunched in the punk of Death" until awakened into their own literal deaths unless they escape in time. The pilot in "The Dead Wingman" searches in his dream over that same amniotic sea into which so many figures of "Pilots, Man Your Planes" have disappeared, but he never finds the dreadful evidence of the birth into death that he seems to need for deep inward confirmation of his own reality:

The plane circles stubbornly: the eyes distending
With hatred and misery and longing, stare
Over the blackening Ocean for a corpse. . . .

I have not really meant to labor this womb referent, which appears and disappears, usually very fleetingly, in Jarrell's shifting float of associations. His creation of an ambience of confused details, a dream of total self-loss, before a final note of profound sadness is equally important in all the poems I have just mentioned. What gives them more authority than the poems of *Blood for a Stranger* is not only the precision within the confusion, but also the definiteness of the military setting within which the lost, childlike psyche of Jarrell's soldiers (with the poet's voice standing in for them, as it were) speaks its pain. Several times in the two "war" books the persons spoken for are women or children. The title of *Little Friend, Little Friend,* which evokes just the childlike psyche to which I have referred, is taken from a phrase used in the book's opening poem, "2nd Air Force." Here, as Jarrell's note tells us, a "woman visiting her son remembers what she has read on the front page of her newspaper the week before, a conversation between a bomber, in flames over Germany, and one of the fighters protecting it: 'Then I heard the bomber call me in: "Little Friend, Little Friend, I got two engines on fire. Can you see me, Little Friend?" I said, "I'm crossing right over you. Let's go home."'"

The woman of this poem might just as well have been the mother of the ball turret gunner in the closing poem. Her son—this is the whole burden of the poem—has indeed fallen from her womb into that of the state. The barren and dangerous world of the air base appears amid "buses and weariness and loss," with its "sand roads, tar-paper barracks," and "bubbling asphalt of the runways." A specific womb image dramatizes what has happened to her transplanted son: "The head withdraws into its hatch (a boy's)." This alien world—"The years meant *this?*"—is her and our bleak introduction to what the war means for the soldiers as Jarrell understands them. Between "2nd Air Force" and "The Death of the Ball Turret Gunner," then, the volume makes its journey through a wasteland of deadly machinery and pathetic soldiers who "pass like beasts, unquestioning," through their new life where "the bombers answer everything."

Both *Little Friend, Little Friend* and *Losses* contain many closeups and vignettes of soldiers: men being classified, a soldier whose leg has been amputated, prisoners, a soldier being visited in the hospital by his wife and baby, men being discharged from service, a field hospital. Politically and historically, the war may have been unavoidable, but for Jarrell this is more an existential than a moral reality. Despite his recognition of the monstrousness of the Nazis in "A Camp in the Prussian Forest" *(Losses)*—

> Here men were drunk like water, burnt like wood.
> The fat of good
> And evil, the breast's star of hope
> Were rendered into soap—

it is the pointlessness and cruelty of the war that emerges as the poet's repeated insight. Each soldier, as the mother sees in "2nd Air Force," is "heavy with someone else's death" and a "cold carrier" of "someone else's victory." The poem "Losses," in the earlier book but clearly the source of the later one's title, utters a complaint on behalf of all the young *and* of their victims. Although its speaker does not explore the moral dilemma involved, he does raise an ultimate question:

> In bombers named for girls, we burned
> The cities we had learned about in school—
> Till our lives wore out; our bodies lay among
> The people we had killed and never seen.
> When we lasted long enough they gave us medals;
> When we died they said, "Our casualties were low."
> They said, "Here are the maps"; we burned the cities.
>
> It was not dying—no, not ever dying;
> But the night I died I dreamed that I was dead,
> And the cities said to me: "Why are you dying?
> We are satisfied, if you are; but why did I die?"

It is interesting that World War II produced no great poem at once absolutely ruthless in its fidelity to the realities of human experience in the war and encompassing in its understanding of all their complex contradictions: particularly, the crushing choice seemingly thrust on the most advanced spirits between pure pacifism and accepting the need to destroy the Nazi power. The rhetorical questions at the end of "Losses"—slightly confused because of the ambiguous use of the word "I" in the closing line—suggest the epic psychological exploration needed, but not furnished, to give body to their meaning. At a pragmatic and popular level the questions were certainly answerable by reference to recent history. The answers were both moral and practical, involving the fate of nations and of ethnic groups as well as of political and economic systems. The contradiction lay, as Malraux perceived in an only slightly different context, the Spanish Civil War, in the fact that the methods of war compel imitation of the enemy and indeed outstripping him in his own methods. It is indeed possible to present the voice of an innocent and ignorant soldier asking "Why?" Yet even the boys Jarrell wrote about had more of a sense, however inarticulately they might express themselves, of "why" than he quite gives them credit for. As for the poet himself, a number of the pieces show the usual intellectual's grasp of the economic and historical aspects of modern war. Of the American poets who emerged immediately after the war, only Robert Lowell was keyed to the demands of the materials, but on the other hand he had neither the literal experience nor the inclination to work on *the* war poem. Perhaps Pound and Eliot, by their keen location of the inner contradictions of Western culture, had rendered a large effort of this sort redundant for later poets.

That Jarrell wanted to suggest large historical and mythological considerations is clear from "The Wide Prospect," which comes just before "The Death of the Ball Turret Gunner" at the end of *Little Friend, Little Friend,* and from the two poems that close *Losses:* "In the Ward: The Sacred Wood" and "Orestes at Tauris." The influence of Marx via Auden is obvious in the opening stanza of "The Wide Prospect":

> Who could have figured, when the harnesses improved
> And men pumped kobolds from the coal's young seams
> There to the west, on Asia's unrewarding cape—
> The interest on that first raw capital?
> The hegemony only the corpses have escaped?

The poem ends, after a determinedly sustained exposition along these lines, with an imagery of ritual sacrifice that links Marxian, Freudian, and myth-and-ritual oriented motifs:

> the man-eaters die
> Under the cross of their long-eaten Kin.
>
> All die for all. And the planes rise from the years . . .
> When men see men once more the food of Man
> And their bare lives His last commodity.

The poems at the end of *Losses* are superior in being free of the long, expository sections, with a forced liveliness of imagery but without driving energy, of "The Wide Prospect." "Orestes at Tauris," the closing poem, was according to Jarrell an early composition written before any of the poems from *Blood for a Stranger* included in the *Selected Poems*. Very different in character from anything else in the war books, it shows Orestes arriving in Tauris after being pursued relentlessly by the Furies, under compulsion "in expiation for his crime, to bring back to Greece that image of Artemis to which the Tauri sacrificed the strangers cast up on their shores" (Jarrell's note in *Losses*). This long, partially surrealist narrative poem imagines the sacrificial beheading of Orestes by his sister Iphigenia, now a priestess, instead of their triumphant escape. Jarrell's recasting of the myth, in a well-sustained unrhymed pattern of four- and five-stress lines, focuses on the succession of impressions, states of feeling, and sensations that Orestes experiences, striving for an effect of terror amidst psychological confusion and barbaric splendors. The condition of Orestes and Iphigenia at the end then becomes a perfect mythic embodiment of Jarrell's vision of war as the sacrifice of driven innocents for the sake of a savage, mindless determinism inherent in our natures:

The people, silent, watching with grave faces
Their priestess, who stands there
Holding out her hands, staring at her hands
With her brother's blood drenching her hands.

"In the Ward: The Sacred Wood," which precedes "Orestes at Tauris," is perhaps Jarrell's most determined effort to give mythic dimensions to his theme of the sacrificed innocent in war. His own description of the poem, in his introduction to *Selected Poems*, goes: "The wounded man has cut trees from paper, and made for himself a sacred wood; with these, the bed-clothes, the nurse, the doctor, he works his own way through the Garden of Eden, the dove and its olive-leaf, the years in the wilderness, the burning bush, the wars of God and the rebel angels, the birth and death and resurrection of Christ." This account, and the style of the poem, somewhat recall the symbolic distortions of thought and syntax of Lowell's early poems—

Is the nurse damned who looked on my nakedness?
The sheets stretch like the wilderness
Up which my fingers wander, the sick tribes,
To a match's flare, a rain or bush of fire. . . .

But Jarrell's movement does not rip free into Lowell's frenzied piling up of associations and allusions. In this poem, however, he surpasses Lowell in one important respect though he does not achieve that state of passionate intensity of speech which makes the whole language an electric field of highly charged, crackling movements of realization. At each point along the way, as the wounded soldier ponders the symbolic analogies with Christ implicit in his condition, he nevertheless at the same time maintains a basic simplicity and a distance from the mental game he is playing. Unlike "Eighth Air Force," this poem does not press an identity between the dying soldier and Christ. The dominant tone is one of a real man, without hope, letting go though aware of a dream of divinity incarnate—a tone corresponding to the wry twist of negative heroism in Read's "To a Conscript of 1940." Negation is accepted quietly; this is one of Jarrell's most touching and thoughtful poems:

And beneath the coverlet
My limbs are swaddled in their sleep, and shade
Flows from the cave beyond the olives, falls
Into the garden where no messenger
Comes to gesture, "Go"—to whisper, "He is gone."

The trees rise to me from the world
That made me, I call to the grove
That stretches inch on inch without one God:
"I have unmade you, now; but I must die."

Earlier, in discussing "The Death of the Ball Turret Gunner," I ventured a description of the characteristic structural dynamics of Jarrell's poems as involving a static initial state of sadness, then a phase of confusion that lets deeper depression flood into the poem, and then a final bitter thrust. Most lyric-contemplative poetry since the early Romantics has, in fact, a comparable structure. That is, an initial state of unease or depressed feeling is followed by the introduction of complicating matter for contemplation: any of a number of contexts of awareness that enlarge and, very likely, confuse the original perspective. The final "resolution" of the poem is a reorientation of the speaker's initial attitude in the light of the intervening complication. It may take the form of acceptance or reconciliation though at the same time what is being "affirmed" is defeat of a sort—what we might call "depressive transcendence." Needless to add that shifts of style, rhythm, intensity, and level of diction are as important as the literal statements.

Without forcing the point, we can say that Jarrell's whole poetic career follows a similar pattern of movement. After the early poems of childhood desolation, the speaking psyche confronts three bodies of material external to itself: war experience, the world of myth and folk legend (to which are added, often, the associations of music, painting, and literature), and individual human suffering. In the final phase of his career, the poet objectifies himself, in relation to his childhood life, as one of the sufferers over whom his attention has hovered with such empathy. That is, he has brought back his earliest preoccupations into the center of his work, but in a focus altered by the discipline through which he has passed and the knowledge he has accumulated. He has learned to isolate the pity of the irrecoverable and, therefore, of the irredeemable in existence and is free to present sharp, concrete memories and to play with them in a number of ways.

In *Losses*, we see the three bodies of "external" material (war, myth and legend, and suffering individual people) already present. War is of course the overwhelming major subject. But there are other myth-involved poems besides the two we have already examined, among them "The Märchen" and "The Child of Courts"; Jarrell's fascination with the German *Märchen* (folk-tales, in this case those of the brothers Grimm) is at this point related to the historical fatalism induced by his response to the war. The dreams and terrors of primitive life foreshadowed those of the modern age with its discovery of the limitations of man's hopes and prospects:

Listening, listening; it is never still.
This is the forest: long ago the lives
Edged armed into its tides (the axes were its stone
Lashed with the skins of dwellers to its boughs);
We felled our islands there, at last, with iron.
The sunlight fell to them, according to our wish,
And we believed, till nightfall, in that wish;
And we believed, till nightfall, in our lives.

These are the opening, and on the whole the best, lines of "The Märchen," a somewhat preciously proliferative poem which nevertheless shows Jarrell's characteristic wit, ingenuity, and sympathy with the common lot. He had learned, in his war poems, how to write with economy, but there is no economy in this poem of over a hundred lines of moderately roughened blank verse. Jarrell luxuriates in the way the *Märchen* bring folk motifs and folk wisdom, simple and often comic materials related to the life of peasants, together with the symbolic and archetypal motifs of religious or mythical tradition: Christ and the old gods, Hell, "the Scapegoat," "Paradise," and "the Cross, the Ark, the Tree." The perspective he introduces has to do with primitive man's desire, never fulfilled but never forgotten or relinquished either, even in our time, to make reality conform to his wish. Herein, for Jarrell, lies the inescapable pathos of the human condition, of which the vulnerable innocence of children is the most obvious embodiment. The *Märchen* show that it is not so much our inability to make wishes come true as the paltriness of the wishes themselves that is defeating. In Romantic tradition generally, it is the disparity between desire and reality, between subjective and objective "truths," with which the poet is obsessed—ultimately, the pity that we cannot stamp our own images on nature. In Jarrell there is a curious turn of emphasis: the inadequacy of imagination, driven as it is already by conditions imposed on it by nature, is the heart of the problem—

> Poor Hänsel, once too powerless
> To shelter your own children from the cold
> Or quiet their bellies with the thinnest gruel,
> It was not power that you lacked, but wishes.
> Had you not learned—have we not learned, from tales
> Neither of beasts nor kingdoms nor their Lord,
> But of our own hearts, the realm of death—
> Neither to rule nor die? to change! to change!

"The Child of Courts" (reprinted in *Selected Poems* as "The Prince") presents the ambivalent night-terror of a child who fears that the ghost of a buried man has come up out of the grave toward him but who then is disappointed: "I start to weep because—because there are no ghosts." The poem at first ambiguously suggests a prison atmosphere. But the child calls out "Mother?"—in an equally ambiguous context, however—and thus there is a suggestion not so much of a prison as of a castle or palace in which there is intrigue and insecurity. One thinks of young Prince Edward after Henry's death, a thought mildly encouraged by the two titles. The situation of this brief and simple poem suggests, at one and the same time, the well-known situations of Edward and other English princes, the grisly circumstances of certain folk legends, and the excited imagination of any sensitive child at certain times.

> After the door shuts, and the footsteps die,
> I call out, "Mother?" No one answers.
> I chafe my numb feet with my quaking hands
> And hunch beneath the covers, in my curled
> Red ball of darkness; but the floor creaks, someone stirs
> In the other darkness—and the hairs all rise
> Along my neck, I whisper: "It is he!"

Many years after *Losses*, in his 1965 volume *The Lost World*, Jarrell published "A Hunt in the Black Forest," which begins exactly as "The Child of Courts" does, except for a shift to the third person that heralds a new, or at least a redirected, point of view toward the same situation:

After the door shuts and the footsteps die,
He calls out: "Mother?"

The speaker now, however, is not the child but an omniscient narrator. The circumstances, like the title, suggest the world of the *Märchen*, projected in a Freudian nightmare fantasy. A king, out hunting, comes to a hut in the forest where a deaf-mute feeds him a stew that poisons him while a red dwarf watches through the window. At the end of this poem, whose every stage is brilliantly and dramatically clear and sinister, there is a blending of supernatural and psychologically pointed details that brings us all the way over from the climax of the king's death to the further, greater climax of the child sensibility underlying the entire story.

Then a bubbled, gobbling sound begins,
The sound of the pot laughing on the fire.
—The pot, overturned among the ashes,
Is cold as death.

Something is scratching, panting. A little voice
Says, "Let *me!* Let *me!*" The mute
Puts his arms around the dwarf and raises him.

The pane is clouded with their soft slow breaths
The mute's arms tire; but they gaze on and on,
Like children watching something wrong.
Their blurred faces, caught up in one wish,
Are blurred into one face: a child's set face.

The mute, the dwarf, and the child thus share horrified, guilty fascination; they are three facets of innocence, despite their involvement in a primal tragic scene. It would not be difficult to "interpret" the story as one in which the child (into whose face the other faces blend at the very end of the poem) is both the victim—the stew that the king his father ate—and the killer who destroys his father through the very act of being devoured by him. If we put "The Child of Courts" and "A Hunt in the Black Forest" side by side and consider each a gloss on the other, it becomes clear that the addition of the third-person narrator enabled Jarrell to fill out the symbolic context of the original poem's conception. But he added to it the distanced understanding of an adult voice presenting the unresolved anguish of one kind of disturbed childhood. "A Hunt in the Black Forest" brings both its psychological and its archetypal motives directly to bear on the tale it has been telling by a final refocusing of elements present in the story from the start. It represents, as do the more literally autobiographical poems of the final volume, an achieved objectification of the speaking self and an achieved clarity as well. Thought is presented experientially, with sharply sketched action and description that leave room for shadows, depths, and implied complexities.

One poem in *Losses*, "Lady Bates," especially foreshadows Jarrell's turn, after the war period, to poems centered on suffering individual persons, often women. The Lady Bates of the title is, says Jarrell in his notes to *Selected*

Poems, "a little Negro girl whose Christian name is *Lady*." The child has died, and the poem is addressed to her as an epitome of everything helpless and betrayed in human existence. Viewed unsympathetically, the poem is an example of sophisticated sentimentality, a humanitarian Southerner's attempt to speak to his knowledge of the hurt done to Negroes in a language appropriate to both. "Lady Bates," significantly, comes first in *Losses*, the only poem quite of its kind in this book, preceding all the war pieces. A certain oversimplification of the meaning of ordinary people's lives, comparable to that we have seen in the war poems, comes through in "Lady Bates" despite its genuinely touching aspects. The worst of Jarrell is concentrated into parts of this poem that mercilessly expose both his condescension and the presumptuousness of his spokesmanship for the girl:

> Poor black trash,
> The wind has blown you away forever
> By mistake; and they sent the wind to the chain-gang
> And it worked in the governor's kitchen, a trusty for life;
> And it was all written in the Book of Life;
> Day and Night met in the twilight by your tomb
> And shot craps for you; and Day said, pointing to your soul,
> "This *bad* young colored lady,"
> And Night said, "Poor little nigger girl."

"Lady Bates," with its weaknesses, continues Jarrell's development toward the objectification of the speaking self that I have suggested is the chief triumph of *The Lost World*. Like the many soldiers who are his subjects in the war volumes, the little black girl in this poem serves two functions in this development. First and most obviously, she is one of the many figures in his poems whose reality he seeks to repossess as persons outside himself. Secondly, though, she and the other figures are the beneficiaries (victims) of an empathy that enables him to project onto them certain basic features of the child psyche familiar in his earlier poems—its confusion, innocence, and betrayal by life. It would be accurate to say that each of these figures is at once himself or herself *and* Randall Jarrell; not, of course, Jarrell the wit, translator of Rilke, and edgily competitive poet, but the essential Jarrell whose sensibility defines itself in his poems in the way we have been tracing.

3

This essential sensibility enters many of the speaking voices in Jarrell's next volume, *The Seven-League Crutches*. In fact, reading through this volume, one is pierced by the realization of how completely possessed by it his writing is and what a chilling desolateness he coped with. It is not only the specific *child* minds he presents that make the realization so forcible, though indeed this volume gives us several such characterizations to add to "Lady Bates." The one closest to "Lady Bates" in tone is "The Truth," in which, Jarrell explains in *Selected Poems*, "the little boy who speaks . . . has had his father, his sister, and his dog killed in one of the early fire-raids on London, and has been taken to the country, to a sort of mental institution for children." This poem has none of the cultural overlay of "Lady Bates," the treacherous sense of "understanding" the black child's world that cuts across Jarrell's finer sense of her as one abandoned by life in her own idiosyncratic way. "The Truth" is stripped down to the essential anguish and bewilderment:

> When I was four my father went to Scotland.
> They *said* he went to Scotland.
>
> When I woke up I think I thought that I was dreaming—
> I was so little then that I thought dreams
> Are in the room with you, like the cinema.
> That's why you don't dream when it's still light—
> They pull the shades down when it is, so you can sleep.
> I thought that then, but that's not right.
> Really it's in your head.
>
> And it was light then—light at *night*. . . .

And yet, as with the play of thought in "Lady Bates," one can well ask of this poem whether the anguish and bewilderment are really the little boy's or Jarrell's. All that charming talk about a child's notion of what dreams are is really in Jarrell's grown-up voice, reminiscing about his own memories. Naturally, these thoughts about dreams being like the cinema might occur to any child, and my only point is that Jarrell is using this kind of situation, so close to his own constant preoccupation, as a suitable instrument on which to play. He is a virtuoso of pity, and the form his virtuosity takes is to work his own voice into his materials so as to bring out their intrinsic pathos and his active insight simultaneously.

In "The Black Swan," a poem about another child, this fusion of sensibilities works superbly. The preface to *Selected Poems* tells us that this poem was "said, long ago, by a girl whose sister is buried under the white stones of the green churchyard." "The Black Swan" and a number of other poems in *The Seven-League Crutches* mark a considerable advance in the artistic isolation and redirection of Jarrell's deepest motifs. The loneliness, the sense of a chaotic universe, and the lost focus of identity (expressed as a shared or confused identity) of his best later work are all present at the very start of "The Black Swan":

> When the swans turned my sister into a swan
>   I would go to the lake, at night, from milking:
> The sun would look out through the reeds like a swan,
>   A swan's red beak; and the beak would open
> And inside there was darkness, the stars and the moon. . . .

This beginning, a decisive act of empathic imagination, opens up a world of associations to the end of recovering the stab of primal pathos. The swan images proliferate, and the mad or nightmare-ridden speaker becomes a swan herself as, out of the calm of heartless nature and death, her sister responds to her call. This poem alone would make it clear that Jarrell's poetic control had grown enormously by 1951. He could now deal purely and forcefully with psychological and mythic or archetypal materials and could write his own thoughts directly without over-intellectualizing and without superciliousness. "The Orient Express" opens *The Seven-League Crutches* on a note of unpretentious intimacy that combines his ever-present child-mindedness with his adult intelligence:

> One looks from the train
> Almost as one looked as a child. In the sunlight
> What I see still seems to me plain,
> I am safe; but at evening
> As the lands darken, a questioning
> Precariousness comes over everything. . . .

All of Jarrell is there, as simply apparent as possible. But the form itself has a new sort of interest when compared to much of Jarrell's earlier work. The ease and grace of movement, the sustained clarity of speech, and the engaging, concrete thoughtfulness keep the reader listening and moving along with the speaker. The lines of this passage, as in the poem as a whole, tend toward a three-stress unit but often—here in the two opening lines—depart from it. Rhyming effects (an exact rhyme in lines one and three, the echoing of *-ing* in lines four, five, and six, the repetitions of "look" and "one," and the sequence of the monosyllabic verbs "look" and "looked" and "see" and "seems" and "comes") are introduced lightly yet saturate the sound structure as in the even richer "The Black Swan." One finds a similar felicity and immediacy in the two poems that close the book, "The Venetian Blind" and "Seele im Raum"—poems which both recall, the former in its literal theme and the latter in its title, a poem of Rilke's. "The Venetian Blind" does indeed present its protagonist as a "Seele im Raum" or "soul in space."

> He is lost in himself forever.
>
> And the Angel he makes from the sunlight
> Says in mocking tenderness:
> "Poor stateless one, wert thou the world?" . . .
>
> The bars of the sunlight fall to his face.
>
> And yet something calls, as it has called:
> "But where am *I*? But where am *I*?"

Rilke's "Seele im Raum," written in 1917, has as its literal subject the condition of a soul torn from its body and suddenly become pure potentiality in a realm of pure being. The soul feels stripped of comforts, exposed, and tremulously fearful in its ignorance of its own destiny. Jarrell's "Seele im Raum" has in part the same theme, but the central situation of his poem is that of a woman who once had the grotesque illusion that an eland was present wherever she was. The woman's pathetic obsession would be hilariously absurd were it not, as her monologue shows, symptomatic of her sense of being a lost self despite the fact that she was a wife and mother. Her period of madness is now over; but in an important way she misses the eland, which was so tangibly and oppressively present to her and yet was the only thing that was hers alone: her soul's embodiment of its own misery—

> Today, in a German dictionary, I saw *elend*
> And the heart in my breast turned over, it was—
>
> It was a word one translates *wretched*. . . .
>
> —It was worse than impossible, it was a joke.
>
> And yet when it was, I *was*—
> Even to think that I once thought
> That I could see it is to feel the sweat
> Like needles at my hair-roots, I am blind
>
> —It was not even a joke, not even a joke.
>
> Yet how can I believe it? Or believe that I
> Owned it, a husband, children? Is my voice the voice
> Of that skin of being—of what owns, is owned
> In honor or dishonor, that is borne and bears—
> Or of that raw thing, the being inside it
> That has neither a wife, a husband, nor a child
> But goes at last as naked from this world
> As it was born into it—
>
> And the eland comes and grazes on its grave. . . .

The passage I have just quoted takes us from the punning proof that the eland had been for the speaker a projection of her soul's *elend* condition, its misery, to the bitter sense she has now of all that she has lost and then, finally, to that sense of being stripped of a human past and utterly out in space of which Rilke writes. Jarrell's absorption in Rilke was one of his great passions; it must have been of tremendous importance to him in the progress of his art that I have described. He immersed himself in the greater poet, whose themes were so close to his own. The sensibilities of children and of women dominate the attention of both poets. Both are in search of points of directive contact with chaotic reality—both are "souls in space." Both, incidentally, had noncombatant military service involving a certain disillusionment, and there were temperamental affinities as well (as in their mixture of endearing traits with ruthless critical attitudes).

Rilke's essential influence on Jarrell seems to have been to encourage him to widen his poetic thought and to reach for a more concentrated and evocative imagery, a more personal and vital poetic speech and rhythmic movement, and a style both natural to him and in touch with European cultural tradition. It is interesting that *The Seven-League Crutches* begins with a section called

"Europe"—poems with European settings to which Jarrell attaches his American awareness. The displacement of context enables him to convert old sets of thought into deepened historical and philosophical musings. Looking out from the Orient Express, he can see that the whole world (not just his own empirical life) is unassimilable to the soul in space and yet has its own aesthetic magnetism we cannot avoid:

> It is like any other work of art.
> It is and never can be changed.
> Behind everything there is always
> The unknown unwanted life.

One could conceivably make the same observation looking from an American train, but just that kind of consideration is involved in the implied comparison. It is just the sensed history behind the fields, people, houses, and villages that makes the feeling of an essential changelessness of existence such a powerful one. In "A Game at Salzburg," the same principle is at work. Jarrell's explanation in *Selected Poems* shows how much he relishes the knowledgeableness behind the poem, the kind of Europeanized wit its subject enables him to cultivate: "I put into 'A Game at Salzburg' a little game that Germans and Austrians play with very young children. The child says to the grown-up, *Here I am,* and the grown-up answers, *There you are;* the children use the same little rising tune, and the grown-ups the same resolving, conclusive one. It seemed to me that if there could be a conversation between the world and God, this would be it." And so, in the poem, the whole style is delightfully relaxed until the very end. The poet (during the year in which he was a participant in the Salzburg Seminar in American Civilization) is seen passing lazy, happy days amid the innumerable tokens not only of an old civilization but also of the recent war. One notices with some surprise and interest that his juxtapositions of a modern American intelligence like his own with all these surrounding signs and symbols, under circumstances at once so congenial and so poignantly and volatilely suggestive, have led him into a tone and rhythm that must have influenced Robert Lowell's style in *Life Studies:*

> A little ragged girl, our ball-boy;
> A partner—ex-Afrika-Korps—
> In khaki shorts, P.W. illegible.
> (He said: "To have been a prisoner of war
> In Colorado iss a *privilege*.")
> The evergreens, concessions, carrousels,
> And D.P. camp at Franz Joseph Park;
> A gray-green river, evergreen-dark hills.
> Last, a long way off in the sky,
> Snow-mountains.

These are the social and political and historical realities, all within the unchanged ancient landscape. When, later on, the poet finds himself playing the little game of *Hier bin i'—Da bist du*, with a three-year-old, there is an inevitably ironic echo from that opening scene. Reality is intractably itself, and the fact is softly underlined in the persistence of a language and a ritual even in a tiny girl "licking sherbet from a wooden spoon" as she engages the poet in the game. Later still, he moves "past Maria Theresa's sleigh" and the statues, mostly broken, in the garden where "the nymphs look down with the faces of Negroes." The two worlds suddenly related in this image are one world after all, as is the prewar world that became the one at war and then the postwar one. At the end, Jarrell's old, persistent insight is thrust into the foreground, but the voice adopted is a European one recalling the "dreamy" American to the imponderable:

In anguish, in expectant acceptance
The world whispers: *Hier bin i'*.

We cannot pursue all the examples of Jarrell's "Europeanization" in *The Seven-League Crutches*. One further instance is the translation of Corbière's "Le Poète Contumace." Corbière's tough-mindedness and scathing but funny self-characterizations show up the sentimental limits of Jarrell's own work. Nevertheless, Jarrell admired Corbière and aspired to his kind of mentality.

Jarrell's one novel, *Pictures from an Institution*, bears extended analysis because so much that was important to him is packed into it, and also because it is an extremely clever work of satire as well as a humanely intelligent book. It is set in a progressive women's college not altogether unlike Sarah Lawrence College, and its pictures of the academic and personal life of all concerned remain extremely amusing. I shall discuss it only very briefly, in relation to Jarrell's poetic development. It represents, I think, a completion of his attempt to assimilate his own frame of thought to that of cultivated and sensitive Europeans. The novel is written in the first person, from the viewpoint of a poet who has been teaching at Benton College for a number of years. The real hero, though, is an Austrian-Jewish composer named Gottfried Rosenbaum through whose eyes the provincialism, complacency, and emptiness of much of American education is made, somewhat lovingly, clear, while certain genuine American strengths and potentialities are seen as goods after all. Dr. Rosenbaum's mind is razor-keen, though he does not ordinarily use it to slash people. That role is taken by a visiting novelist, Gertrude Johnson, whose analytical savagery has no kindness in it and who is often malignantly inventive in her sizing up of people, all grist for her novels. She is going to do a novel about the college, and it will be merciless—presumably far more so than *Pictures from an Institution* itself. Yet this necessary comparison gives one to think. Gertrude, as it were, discharges the hostile and supercilious side of Jarrell's critical intelligence, while Gottfried represents a more genial ideal. John Crowe Ransom, in his contribution to *Randall Jarrell, 1914–1965*, notes the indications that Gertrude undergoes something like a "conversion" to a more humane attitude in the course of the novel, and I would suggest that the improvement of Gertrude is something in the nature of a purgation for Jarrell himself. The "I" of the novel, the poet who is ready to leave the limited campus scene at the end of the year, has been close to both Gertrude and Gottfried. Gottfried, with his elderly Russian wife who shares his cultivation and his sense of tragic history, will remain after the writers have left. With them will stay the talented and loyal Constance Morgan, who in her life embodies the best of American openness and possibility as Gottfried and Irene embody the living tradition of European art with which we must remain in vital touch. Constance, an orphan, is thus one of four figures who represent ideals or characteristics of Jarrell himself. The book reaches a certain serenity and insight into the best qualities of each of the characters, despite the fun at the expense of most of them along the way.

What an injustice I have done to this novel, with its marvelously amusing passages that Jarrell wrote in an ecstasy of acerbic release. It is his most balanced work, done not long after his marriage to Mary von Schrader in 1952, and it helped him gain a precarious personal balance. It was also a self-deceptive balance, a standoff between barely repressed total revulsion and sentimental voting for the triumph, in any one person, of decency over stupidity and mean-spirited worldliness. A variety of sexual repression is involved as well. In the novel, as in Jarrell's poetry, sexuality in itself seems hardly present as a factor in his own thought and emotions or in those of his characters. His attitude toward women is a little like his attitude toward unhappy children and a little like Sophocles' toward "the Mothers": awe, mystification, and, sometimes, a cozy sympathy with a bitter edge nevertheless. The sense of a life ridden by despair that comes through in his last two books of poems is linked with that bitter sympathy. The balanced feeling of control of the mid-1950s dissolves into something harsher, more convincing finally, and at its best more brilliant.

4

The three poems that open the 1960 volume, *The Woman at the Washington Zoo*, are rather precise examples of Jarrell's feeling for women. He thinks about them a great deal, and passionately, but in the ways I have suggested. The title poem is one of a number written from the point of view of a woman, usually aging, who feels that, as she says, "The world goes by my cage and never sees me." (Jarrell discusses the composition of this poem brilliantly in one of his essays in *A Sad Day at the Supermarket*, 1962.) The poem begins with a tone of quiet desperation and in a sometimes banal cadence of a sort occasionally cultivated by Eliot, but rises to a hysterical pitch at the end—an accusation against fate and an appeal to be transformed. The woman's outcry is directed toward a vulture, both real and symbolic. She wants to be devoured and transformed, and her language suggests that the bird of prey to which her protest and prayer are addressed embodies the male principle:

> Vulture,
> When you come for the white rat that the foxes left,
> Take off the red helmet of your head, the black
> Wings that have shadowed me, and step to me as man:
> The wild brother at whose feet the white wolves fawn,
> To whose hand of power the great lioness
> Stalks, purring. . . .
> You know what I was,
> You see what I am: change me, change me!

It is the first time in his poems that Jarrell speaks so fiercely through a woman's voice. In the next poem, "Cinderella," he does so again, but here, for once, female toughness—and even hardness—of spirit comes through. Both Cinderella and her fairy godmother are presented as coolly anti-male. Cinderella, on her very wedding day, under the "pulsing marble" of her wedding lace, "wished it all a widow's coal-black weeds." Later she became "a sullen wife and a reluctant mother." The godmother is sophisticated into an archetypal "God's Mother" who comes into her own whenever her son is away. At these times she invites Cinderella into the "gold-gauzed door" of her Heaven that exists only in the flames of the male-created Hell, and they gossip comfortably apart from male ideas, ideals, and laws. This poem is far more effective than the long, rather involved, and precious one that follows: "The End of the Rainbow." In this latter poem, about a woman "old enough to be invisible," Jarrell's proliferating details carry a certain pathos but, even more, suggest the poet's extraordinary identification with his protagonist.

After these opening poems of human sensibility gratingly out of phase come the four most striking pieces of the book—poems that, together with those in the title sequence of *The Lost World,* complete Jarrell's work by closing in on intimate realities of his own actual life and memory. Again we have an interesting parallel to Lowell, for both poets were moving into their confessional period at the same time. Lowell's *Life Studies* had appeared the year before, an enormous gathering of concentrated neurotic energy centered on his childhood and the personalities of his parents as somehow symptomatic of America's and the world's malaise. Although Jarrell's confessional poems are less ambitious formally and symbolically than Lowell's, they are in many ways closer to the anomie and the disturbances that mark the common life in our day.

Jarrell is in his own way as much an exotic as Lowell. The strains of his boyhood are as atypical as those of the privileged Bostonian, and the adult lives of both men have been atypical too. But often in these poems he summons up the world of plain-living, laboring souls and of the hardships and pleasures of ordinary life. The confusing images of his beloved grandmother wringing a chicken's neck, and of the already dead bird still running about in circles, recur, for instance, in a number of the poems. Each is an image of the brutal nature of existence and cannot be separated out from the meaning of love. Millions of ordinary folk know the experience described in "A Street off Sunset" (in *The Lost World*):

> Mama comes out and takes in the clothes
> From the clothesline. She looks with righteous love
> At all of us, her spare face half a girl's.
> She enters a chicken coop, and the hens shove
> And flap and squawk, in fear; the whole flock whirls
> Into the farthest corner. She chooses one,
> Comes out, and wrings its neck. The body hurls
> Itself out—lunging, reeling, it begins to run
> Away from Something, to fly away from Something
> In great flopping circles. Mama stands like a nun
> In the center of each awful, anguished ring.

The thudding and scrambling go on, go on—then they fade,
I open my eyes, it's over . . . Could such a thing
Happen to anything? It could to a rabbit, I'm afraid;
It could to . . .

The details here are as plain, and as hideous, as, say, those in John Clare's "Badger." Where Jarrell differs from a true *naïf*, though, is in his superimposed notes of observation, themselves simple in tone but implying meditative and informed intelligence: "righteous love" (a note of psychological insight, for the woman's look is a gesture both of self-encouragement and of apology and self-justification); "away from Something" (a note to underline the presence of universal terror); "like a nun" (again, the note of reaffirmed innocence, which is yet "the center of each awful, anguished ring"); and at last the deliberate pointing up of the child's reactions. The easily colloquial iambic pentameter lines run on quite naturally; one hardly notices the alternating rhymes that help rock the movement into hysteria—that is, into the child's momentarily traumatized hypnosis by the impossible thing that is happening. Jarrell uses this pattern throughout the "Lost World" sequence. It makes for a slightly relaxed, anecdotal tone that drags boringly at times but provides a frame at others for effects such as this one. This weakness, in itself, is a reflection of Jarrell's desire to keep his form open to common speech and common psychology—something he much admired in Robert Frost's work.

Returning to *The Woman in the Washington Zoo* and the four poems there that I have noted, we can see that "In Those Days" and "The Elementary Scene" are both exceedingly simple in form. "In Those Days" consists of four quatrains with the simplest of rhyme schemes, *abcb*, and is in a basic iambic tetrameter with much variation for naturalness and dramatic immediacy. It reads, except for the deliberate avoidance of smoothness of meter, like an afterbeat from Heine, particularly in the last stanza:

How poor and miserable we were,
How seldom together!
And yet after so long one thinks:
In those days everything was better.

Almost doggerel—but this ending shrugs off a painful nostalgia for a past love, the whole adolescent atmosphere of which has been evoked, with all its bittersweet frustration and sense of wintry isolation of the two young people, in the preceding stanzas. The poem strikes a new personal key for Jarrell, and serves as an overture to the further exploration of the speaker's lost past. Then come "The Elementary Scene" and "Windows," still quite simple in their diction and the scenes they envision: the first a rural elementary school at Hallowe'en, the second the home of dead elders who once loved and cherished the speaker. Jarrell's ability to suggest, with utmost economy, a milieu at once provincial and inarticulate and yet full of unmet challenge—the reality of an irretrievable folk past that might have led to a far different life for the speaker, less to be regretted, perhaps—is his greatest strength.

> The thin grass by the girls' door,
> Trodden on, straggling, yellow and rotten,
> And the gaunt field with its one tied cow...

—the lines recall his very early "The Cow Wandering in the Bare Field" and the curious persistence of images demanding clarification again and again during a poet's lifetime. The self-reproach at the end of "The Elementary Scene"—"I, I, the future that mends everything"—is the final evidence that this is one of his purest poems, a poem of unearned but heavily felt depression, in which the speaker takes upon himself the guilt of time's passing. So also in "Windows," it is the unbearable irrevocability of the past that the speaker lives with and endures (in this respect a true heir to Frost and E. A. Robinson). The beloved dead, imagined alive in their time, are compared in their vivid presence to "dead actors, on a rainy afternoon," who "move in a darkened living-room" on a television screen.

> *These* actors, surely, have known nothing of today,
> That time of troubles and of me. . . .
> They move along in peace. . . . If only I were they!
> Could act out, in longing, the impossibility
> That haunts me like happiness!

Sentimentality is held at a distance in this poem by the sheer force of illusion: the construction of a moment of the recaptured past so keenly present to the speaker's desire that it goes beyond imagination—

> It blurs, and there is drawn across my face
> As my eyes close, a hand's slow fire-warmed flesh.
>
> It moves so slowly that it does not move.

The poem "Aging," which follows, does not have the fine sensuous conviction of "Windows" and does lapse into sentimentality. When, in the "Lost World" sequence and in "Remembering the Lost World," literal memory again picks up these motifs, the intensity and concentration are sacrificed for the anecdotal colloquialism we have seen. These are poems banking on total rather than on selected recall and striving to hold their recovered, or reimagined, reality intact against the poisonous fact of elapsed time. Theirs is an opposite method, allowing room for something like a novelistic play of mind over bizarre contradictions of a child's life in Hollywood, a life at once disciplined by good gray work and indulged by an almost sensually remembered aunt and her friends, one of thom owned the MGM lion. It is a bath of charming, touching, and heartbreaking memory in the new open mode that Jarrell had discovered. The new mode seems to have freed him from a vision too sharp to be endured, and to have taken him over the line of belief in the present reality of the past. "Thinking of the Lost World" ends:

> LOST—NOTHING. STRAYED FROM NOWHERE. NO REWARD.
> I hold in my own hands, in happiness,
> Nothing: the nothing for which there's no reward.

"I felt at first," writes John Crowe Ransom in the essay I quoted from earlier, "that this was a tragic ending. But I have studied it till I give up that notion. The NOTHING is the fiction, the transformation; to which both boy and man are given. That World is not Lost because it never existed; but it is as precious now as ever. I have come to think that Randall was announcing the beginning of his 'second childhood.' There is nothing wrong about that, to the best of my knowledge." Perhaps, but what Mr. Ransom is describing is the letdown, or failure of nerve, in the face of the issues (which Jarrell nevertheless did to a certain important extent face) that often takes the form of a paradoxically melancholy complacency in writers just below the energy level of genius. Jarrell himself approaches the issue wryly in the quoted lines, and also in the self-ironically named poem "Hope," which takes us into the poet's grown-up life with all its gaiety, fears, and gallant playing of roles. It is almost as though he had given the tragic its due in "The Elementary Scene," "Windows," and the very dark-spirited Rilke translations of *The Woman at the Washington Zoo* and then turned his back on the discipline of greatness.

But this would be too harsh a judgment. At fifty-one, Jarrell was still expanding his range of technique and of personal sympathies. He might well have reversed his direction once more and made another fresh start as he had done in the war poems and again in *The Seven-League Crutches* and the last books. With all the intelligence and openness to varied literary influences reflected in his criticism and his translations during the two postwar decades, he was surely capable of a great deal of further development despite a deep formal conservatism. Our poetry—and it is Jarrell's *poetry* almost exclusively that we have been concerned with—is today struggling in a new way with the question of the role of an active, many-sided intellectuality in essential poetic structure. Jarrell might conceivably have contributed something of interest to this exploration. Meanwhile, he remains a force among us as a poet of defeat and loneliness who nevertheless does not allow himself to become less spirited. He is like that ex-P. W. in his poem "A Game at Salzburg" who says, "To have been a prisoner of war in Colorado iss a *privilege*."

Randall Jarrell (Minneapolis: University of Minnesota Press, 1972)

PART III

1973–1988

❧

Israeli Poetry: Pagis and Carmi

(Introduction to *Selected Poems of T. Carmi and Dan Pagis)*

AN outsider coming to Israeli poetry for the first time will inevitably be tempted to see the obvious. He is going to see, more clearly and crudely than an Israeli reader could do, the pressure of Jewish history and culture—the centuries in the Diaspora, the drama of the return, the horror of the Holocaust, the Biblican resonance—on whatever he reads. It is a little like the foreigner's overriding consciousness, in reading Baudelaire, that this is an expression of *France:* something a Frenchman would naturally discount in weighing Baudelaire's or any other French poet's quality. But the discounting would be superficial only, a matter of balancing the whole experience. Ultimately, the historical, cultural, national relevance reveals itself sensitively only to intimates of a country's life and language. It reveals itself in a leap from the poem's fingertips to the nerve-ends of such readers. It is not to be coded through a list of motifs and topics, such as may exist in a piece of writing that is itself dead and therefore uncommunicative.

We come to the poems of Dan Pagis and T. Carmi, in the present collection, through the translations of Stephen Mitchell. Mr. Mitchell's problem has been enormous; no English version can show us the combinations of harshness and sweetness, and of tradition—deep allusiveness and abrupt colloquial immediacy, of the Hebrew originals. One small instance may suggest the character of the challenge to the translator. In line 6 of Carmi's "To the Pomegranate Tree," a whole complex of association is involved with one simple visual effect because of the *sound* within which the effect is imbedded. The translator cannot begin to imply the connotations of the repeated Hebrew word *adóm* when it is rendered, properly, into the English *red*.

TO THE POMEGRANATE TREE

Go away. Go.
Go to other eyes.
I wrote about you yesterday.

I said green
to your branches bowing in the wind,
and red—red—red—
to your fruit shining like dew.
I called light to your dank
obstinate root.

Now you don't exist.
Now you're blocking the day
and the moon that has not yet risen.

Come, beloved
(I wrote about you two days ago,
and your young memory
stings my hands like nettle),
come look at the strange pomegranate tree:
its blood is in my veins, on my head, on my hands,
and it still is planted in its place!

"In line 6," writes Harold Schimmel, "the threefold repetition *adóm adóm adóm* ('red red red') echoes the praise of the seraphim in the heavenly spheres: *kadósh, kadósh, kadósh* ('Holy, holy, holy is the Lord of Hosts') of the Hebrew prayerbook."[1] While the translator can often weave compensatory effects into the poem, we must nevertheless reconcile ourselves to the loss of such essential values as Mr. Schimmel describes. The Mitchell translation of "To the Pomegranate Tree" does sustain Carmi's atmosphere of inspired though resistant celebration. It was impossible, though, to catch alive that splendid note that re-enacts, in a single line, Carmi's conversion of ritual adoration into a secular, aesthetic exaltation.

Still, translation is not the hopeless affair it seems in our saner moments. Look again at Mitchell's version. He has given us, after all, a window onto Carmi's poem, not only its incantatory imperiousness and wonder but its helpless quarrel with an overmastering symbol. The speaker had at first thought the pomegranate tree merely a source of vivid impressions. Now he sees it possessing his whole being. A striking turn of thought shows him summoning his new love to bear witness to this change. She too has begun to enter his existence in the same way as the tree. The erotic is thus, casually but powerfully, brought into the process the poem describes. Carmi's preoccupation is with the way passionately regarded external reality invades his own very nature. Like an Israeli Lawrence, he has his pomegranate personify a world of fierce knowledge, blood-drenched, sexual and intractable.

Read one way, the poem is clearly touched with the tragic awareness of modern Israel—its possession by a landscape and a history which it wished merely to use for its own creative purpose—but only if we do not labour the point. With most of Carmi's work, indeed, we do better to wait for him to spell out this side of things, in his own usually subtle way. Poems like "Memorial Day, 1969" and "A View of Jerusalem" speak explicitly and elegiacally of Israel's griefs and terrors, but such poems make up only a small fraction of his writing. Dan Pagis, on the other hand, is centrally engaged with those griefs and terrors and with a prophetic vision related to them. His full strength is realized in his somewhat Yeatsian poem of coming universal catastrophe, "The Beginning":

1. In Stanley Burnshaw, T. Carmi, and Ezra Spicehandler, eds., *The Modern Hebrew Poem Itself* (N.Y.: Holt, Rinehart & Winston, 1965), p. 169.

In the ice-filled chaos before the end of creation,
distant fleets of steel are waiting.
Boundaries, in secret, mark themselves.
High above the smoke and the odour of fat and skins hovers
a yellow magnetic stain.
Oblique rays at the pole, alert, quick-eyed,
search for the signal. The code is cracked.
Now that all is prepared for darkness,
a wind, with savage fur, from the horizon, blows
in the hollow bones of mountains,
and at the zero-hour
the Great Bear, blazing, strides forth
in heat. The heavens stand now,
and the earth, and all their hosts.
A time of war.

Despite the grandeur of this vision, its terror is of almost pathological proportions. Chaos resolves itself in a violence all the more frightful because it makes murderous technology a function of the life-principle reduced to mere savagery. "The odour of fat and skins" that recalls the German concentration camps becomes but a detail in the universal readiness for the coming "end of creation."

Pagis lives with the memory of annihilation as something he has both experienced and, of course, been spared. In early adolescence he was a prisoner in a concentration camp in the Ukraine; he escaped in 1944. The past will not hold still in his poems, which cannot help assuming it must return. His work is coloured, too, by guilt at having survived. This guilt is expressed, not through self-castigation, but through a rueful sense of unearned reprieve, neither undesired nor completely welcomed either:

Ready for parting, as if my back were turned,
I see my dead come toward me, transparent and breathing.
I do not accept:
one walk around the square, one rain,
and I am another, with imperfect rims, like clouds.
Grey in the passing town, passing and glad,
among transitory streetlamps,
wearing my strangeness like a coat, I am free to stand . . .
("Ready for Parting")

Pagis is a poet of survival. He is comparable to Zbigniew Herbert and other Eastern European poets who write out of memories of the concentration camps and the Resistance. But he does not resort to their anti-rhetoric, their almost deadpan restraint. Pagis and other Israeli poets have certainly been affected by the reaction against overt emotionalism in the wake of violence to the human spirit that no verbal violence could match. It is as clear to them as to anyone else that the unspeakable cannot be spoken even though the unbearable has to be borne, and they too have often mastered an astringent and ironic style. They have not, however, had the paralyzing political experience, leading to spiritual isolation, of moving from one kind of brutal repression directly into another. An ultimately humanistic and even romantic affirmation is implicit in Israeli thought and life. As Pagis's "The Beginning" has shown us, this affirmation is anything but a sentimentally optimistic one. It is tragic in character, an affirmation of human meanings however disastrous the human predicament.

"The Beginning" is a total expression of Pagis's tragic and prophetic vision. But he does not devote himself exclusively to the apocalyptic, and I would not wish to discount his simple humanity. We can see it in a quietly compassionate and plainspoken poem such as "Moments of Old Age" and in the mocking tenderness of "Europe, Late"—a repossession of that moment when too many people still ignored what was upon them and clung to the illusion that "everything will be all right." Pagis unites his prophetic and his colloquial voices in the remarkable poem called "Written in Pencil in the Scaled Railway-Car." The title itself would seem to make anything that follows in the poem anticlimactic. It isn't:

here in this carload
i am eve
with abel my son
if you see my other son
cain son of man
tell him i

Despite one's first impression, the poem's actual power soon shows itself. Partly this is a matter of the sepulchral force of the Hebrew, the sonorous authority of the primal Biblical names. Partly it is the projected realization of the unspeakable. Sacred text and secular understanding both prove inarticulate before the literal situation commemorated in the title. Eve's thought cannot be completed; identity cannot go beyond the naming of names. The tension between title and poem is between two determinants of Jewish and, by extension, all human consciousness. The poem calls up the implications of an ancient myth whose full meaning, and inadequacy to account for our condition, could not be grasped until our own day.

To write something as crucially relevant and at the same time as brilliantly compressed as this poem may be a matter of inspired luck. The result is almost non-verbal, a breathing archetype. Pagis has projected names and phrases as pigments of bitter consciousness. Or, to change the metaphor, they are acts of invocation that conjure up archaic guilt echoing undiminished into our own moment. He gives us no other poem as directly physical in its utterance as this one in which immediacy and traditional resonance ring out as a single clang of feeling. But three of his short poems ("The Roll Call," "Testimony," and "Instructions for Crossing the Border"—separate poems with a shared frame of reference) and one longer poem ("Footprints") have a different and more characteristic sort of success. Literal data of the Holocaust appear in these poems too, but their stress is on the begrudging acceptance of survival by one whose real destiny, as it were, was to have been killed as one of the six million. A sense of unreality, almost yet not quite fantasy, is inseparable from being oneself. The thinking in these poems is necessarily metaphorical and paradoxical, and so the poet's idiosyncratic personality and imagination are brought fully into play.

The three shorter poems present the survivor as an "imaginary man," one who does not appear at the "roll call" in heaven and who is therefore a "mistake." He should be deleted from the records, his eyes "turned off", his shadow "erased." At best, he was made by a "different creator" from the others and remains curiously unsubstantial:

> And he in his mercy left nothing of me that would die.
> And I fled to him, rose weightless, blue,
> forgiving—I would even say: apologizing—
> smoke to omnipotent smoke
> without image or likeness.
>
> ("Testimony")

Rueful at having avoided annihilation, the "imaginary man" is at once "not allowed to remember" and "not allowed to forget." The long poem "Footprints" grounds all the paradox and half-fantasy in its literal and personal source, the memory of the time of the "unloading of the cattle-cars" when the speaker was somehow spared:

> It's true, I was a mistake, I was forgotten
> in the sealed car, my body tied up
> in the sack of life . . .

"Footprints" is a difficult poem. It moves within an ambience of opposed states of existence: escape from death into other-worldly life, and then return once more to the dangerous, death-ridden life of this world. As in the three shorter pieces, Pagis employs an imagery of ambiguous existence in the form of a cloud that moves mysteriously from one state and level of being to another. For instance, the smoke from the bodies cremated in the gas-ovens is an image that blends into the cloud-phase of the speaker's existence. This imagery is intermingled with a birth-imagery sometimes reminiscent of Dylan Thomas's—there are some real affinities between these two poets—with impressions of an imagined realm where seraphim move, and with harshly cruel axe-strokes of realism based on Nazi atrocities. The feeling that this mixture produces is a combined helpless anger, self-directed sarcasm, and visionary buoyancy. The poem moves through recollection of despair and utter moral confusion and *anomie* to a widened view of desolation in the very heavens and then back to something like acceptance of the world's realities without fatuousness or illusion—

> against my will guessing that it's very near,
> inside, imprisoned by hopes, there flickers
> this ball of the earth,
> scarred, covered with footprints.

Too rich for easy summary, the poem proliferates points of reference that sometimes appear as unrelated as the couplets of a *ghazal*. But they do form a complexly unified whole, whose volatile, dynamic, humour-splashed shiftings make this the most rewarding poem by Pagis in the present collection.

Carmi's work hardly ever touches, directly, the nerve of burning historical memory and chagrin that Pagis's does. Indirectly, though, a number of his poems reveal the two poets' reciprocal concerns. Carmi's "Examination of Conscience Before Going to Sleep" is dedicated, rather pointedly, to Pagis, as though through it Carmi was making a point in a continued friendly debate about the function of poetry. The "examination of conscience" referred to has no connection, on the surface, with great historical events. It is about a small bird killed by a motor car on the street, passed over by speeding truck drivers and at last kicked into the gutter by a pedestrian. Carmi gives us a sharply drawn vignette of the scene—the people, the sounds, the work going on all around, "all . . . in broad daylight." The poem ends:

> I suppose the bird
> is still there, clinging
> to the gutter's edge.
> I note it among the things
> I should forget.

The reverberations of this unpretentious poem are greater than Carmi pretends. It assumes responsibility for what the speaker could hardly have helped, and finds a challenge to conscience in any living being that has been destroyed while oneself has survived. A comparable reverberation arises from Carmi's tiny sequence of two poems called "Landscape." The landscapes are views from a moving train. The first is a charming contemplation of the poetic problem of selecting focal points from among the innumerable apparently trivial details dancing before the eye. The poet makes a necessarily arbitrary decision to use one such detail only, the "white bird over a green river" with which the poem begins. Yet even this one detail at once splits up into smaller elements, and so the choice must be narrowed even further.

> In fact, I think I'll note
> just one bird.
> Maybe just its wings.

The pathetic bird of "Examination of Conscience Before Going to Sleep" need not come to mind here, but there *is* a relationship. Carmi's method of structuring his poem engages him with the fundamental aesthetic principle that everything involves everything else, that—as William Carlos Williams's "The Red Wheelbarrow" has it—"so much depends" on the implied relationship of sensations and perceptions. He moves from "a white bird over a green river" to other birds seen in other places, and then to the bushes along the tracks, and then to the whole chaotic mass of things, all the roofs and clouds and blades of grass:

> hard to count from a train,
> so I won't mention them.

But of course he *has* mentioned them. And so, when he returns to the one bird, or at any rate "just its wings," the whole of life, including the human life that created—and dwells under—the roofs he sees from the train, has been concentered in the one arbitrarily chosen detail of focus.

If it stood alone, the first "Landscape" would suggest the richness of life rather than its sufferings or our existential guilt at all the pain and death we can do nothing to prevent. The second "Landscape" alters the case completely. The view glimpsed from the train this time is of a man working with a saw at the top of a tree. Suddenly the passenger sees the man, face contorted with terror and body twisting helplessly, slip and fall. The tone and perspective at the end both parody and deepen the ending of the first "Landscape." Though Carmi's literal subject remains far different, these closing lines bring us sharply into the world where Pagis's poetry moves:

All this I saw
from the window of a train,
after a green meadow
and before a team of horses.
I note only the fact
of his falling.
I didn't hear
the scream.

Whether or not so intended, this poem "justifies" Carmi's natural preference for writing a purely lyrical poetry. It suggests what "Examination of Conscience Before Going to Sleep" states explicitly: the hideous realities that the mind, whatever its state of empathy or level of consciousness, is always to some degree burdened with. In other poems, often, the only sign of such a burden is a melancholy shading of tone as the speaker pursues an elusive notion or feeling—the "tears from the depth of some divine despair" that are so distinguishing a mark of the lyrical tradition, East or West. One such poem is "Somebody Like You," about the difficulty of discovering the true mind of a sleeping child. Another is "No News," about a moment of unexpectedly felt emptiness in the midst of deep and lonely meditation. Carmi's love-poems, too, depend for their intensity of feeling on a sense of loss and guilt as well as on their exploration of the subjective meaning of passion. These poems, especially "The Sacrifice," "The Claim," and "Those Who Go on Voyages," are not self-lacerating in the manner of Lowell or Plath. They plunge, rather, into the actual sense of an infinitely valued personal unfolding within an experience. But each experience has had its cost which must be explored as well, in the same way that the train-ride of "Landscapes" exacted its emotional expenditure.

Carmi's finely responsive and resilient sensibility stamps his poems with a pervasive anticipation of discovery. They are magnetically engaging. A poem like "Through the Windows" is an absolutely delightful composition of lights and darks and touches of sound. "Girl in the Closet" is touching and sympathetic and yet "heartless"—"simple and faithless"—in the age-old sense of the poet as objective observer of his own emotional relationships. Carmi has an elegant, intimate disinterestedness that is the obverse side of his capacity for empathy. He is one of those who, in the midst of tragic life and themselves committed to humane loyalties, still insist on savouring whatever life genuinely has to offer.

I have, perhaps, not given enough attention to some parallel qualities of Pagis's. Certainly his poetry does not exist at a lower level of "purity"—that is, of poetic rigour—than Carmi's, but his expressed concerns are more drastic. He succeeds in making a singing poetry out of the materials of disaster and in getting beyond the clichés of politics and of a Spenglerian portentousness to which he might be prone. When he turns away from historical and prophetic concerns, the tone is usually still drastic. Often, as in "Snake" and "Already" and many other poems, he has the same doom-driven dismay that we find in Dylan Thomas. He, too, is obsessed with the knowledge that death rides hard on the heels of birth, and that we are hurried irresistibly through the process by the force that through the green fuse drives the flower. Carmi's dead bird in the gutter and his man falling from the tree are equally victims of this pressing force of natural change, but Pagis is far more taken up with the indignity of our condition, the fact that we are quick-marched through life's changes before we can even think to get anything in order. Even when Pagis's poems are abstractly metaphysical in character, as in "Final Examination" or in the beautiful "Twelve Faces of the Emerald," in which he comes closer than anywhere else to a purely image-centred technique, they remain chained to reality by an armed and uncompromising sensibility. But sometimes, just sometimes, as in "Come" or in "Seashell," he shows himself a mystic of the same sensed awareness as I have attributed to Carmi. An urgent desire—a lust—to isolate spiritual resources that will make us as strong as possible in the face of history's savage blows while we remain responsively open to reality and the creative possibilities within it may be endemic to the modern mind. If so, these two Israeli poets are compellingly accurate spokesmen for that mind, as well as for their own country's special and precarious poise and for their own very individual natures.

The Nation (2 April 1973)[2]

2. Advance publication of the foregoing introduction to *Selected Poems of T. Carmi and Dan Pagis*, translated by Stephen Mitchell (London: Penguin Books, 1976).

Problems of Robert Creeley

A DAY BOOK by Robert Creeley
LISTEN: A PLAY by Robert Creeley
CONTEXTS OF POETRY: INTERVIEWS 1961–1971 by Robert Creeley

DESPITE a tendency to regard as quintessential poetry any twist of phrase that happens into his mind, Robert Creeley has written some real poems—the lovely "Koré," for instance, and the self-fraught, intellectually engaging "I Keep to Myself Such Measures." His new volume, *A Day Book*, adds a few more poems of interest among its many varied offerings. Like his 1969 volume, *Pieces*, it presents a mixture of rather diffuse and arbitrary notes with a number of short, lively poems and with several longer, serious ones that give the book its most decisive coloration.

A Day Book, though, is more than merely a new collection. It is, actually, a sequence. It could have become, I think, a rather marvelous sequence had the poet removed the dead matter, edited himself rigorously, and waited himself out. One thing he needed to wait for was an appropriate poetic line to carry the full surge of thought and feeling at peak moments along the way. But that problem aside, the reader who wants to ride with *A Day Book* from beginning to end has to step around a welter of hasty, awkward, ill-written passages and of dropped names—Alan and Allen and Louis and Charles and Stan and whomever else the book concerns.

The basic organizational plan, the jacket explains, is of "a record of experience." The implicit aim is to embody poetic process, the way we get from our daily empirical consciousness into a self-transcendent art. Almost half the book's approximately 165 pages is made up of prose entries in a journal; the rest consists of poetic entries, often parallel or at least reciprocal to the prose. Since the book is unpaginated (an annoyance, given its size, whenever one wants to go back and find anything in it), and since no time divisions within its span of more than thirty months are specified, we have the impression of an almost undifferentiated drift of consciousness. Yet the sequence retains a fundamental, sometimes absorbing *promise*. Who can tell what will show up next in the float, partly confessional and partly atmospheric, of events, conversations, gossip, crumbs of literary or philosophical thought, introspective moments, *aperçus*, outbursts of erotic fantasy and memory, and moments of defeat by or triumph over depression that the drift carries along with it? If we take into consideration the poet's varied interests in jazz, drugs, varieties of sexual behavior, being on the move, and the confusions of love and family life, we have an ambience not unlike the television documentary *An American Family*, with modulations—would God that side were more consciously striven for!—toward Proustian recollection. When that Proustian effort does occur, as in the long poem "People," we see how moving the whole work might have been.

The link between the chaotic ambience of day-to-day life and the nature of poetic process is one clear motif of the book. There is a strong implication (or perhaps only a strong hope) that the real poem lies in the ambience, the casual drift of consciousness. At the same time, the overall organization—the prose entries followed by a partial recapitulation and heightening of the same material in poetry—would also suggest that Mr. Creeley wants to demonstrate an interaction between his raw materials and the results of aesthetic conversion, as Lowell does in *Life Studies*. Now there is nothing shocking or new in this kind of thing, but the problem is perhaps the most difficult and central one in both art and criticism, as Pound once pointed out very harshly to Williams: "Your interest is in the bloody loam but what I am interested in is the finished product." Everything depends, finally, on the quality of conception and execution. "Among School Children" and *The Man with the Blue Guitar* are certainly about the process and, at the same time, embodiments of it. So too, at least in good part, is *Paterson*. And so, in quite another way, are Lowell's excursions round and about his *Notebooks*. What counts is the pitch of language and realization, and the discovery of a dynamics that defines the poem's right curve of movement and helps strip bare the issues at its heart.

A Day Book does not get that far, yet it has its thread of progression and its emotional soundings. Its protagonist must deal with a depressed sense of loss, waste, and inadequacy, dramatized in the initial ambiguous indications of a personal crisis involving his wife's infidelity or at least his fear of it. There are counter-effects—assertions of energy (often in memories or fantasies of sexual experience, especially fellatio, as a sweet relief that is more an almost infantile addiction than a delighted relationship) and confidence and a kind of joy. The depressive element remains, too heavy to be overcome though each of the two sections ends with a sufficiently "positive" emphasis: both the prose section and the verse section indicate a desire to continue in the real world despite the suicidal note at certain moments.

Looked at with complete sympathy, the sequence is an opening out in each section from the initially disturbed situation into the speaker's whole wide float of subjective associations, and then into an acceptance of despair without absolute surrender. In both sections the depression is traced to childhood sorrows and family tragedy. In the prose section the speaker asks: "Was my father, like they say, a deadbeat? . . . Now son makes deathly silence, in return, as though he were the tradition somehow of that deadening silence. . . . At least I won't live to see the end of it." And in the poetry love is seen as an anodyne (which indeed it often is) rather than a source of adult strength:

> Love
> Tracking through this
> interminable sadness—
>
> like somebody said,
> change the record.

I hope that I have suggested how interesting the play of thought can be in

A Day Book. With more power and depth, and with less clutter, it would be something to range alongside the truly accomplished American sequences rather than being a catchall with some finely interesting things in it. There are too many passages, too, done either in telegraphese or in a comma-spiked, anti-idiomatic style that befuddles one's memory of the English tongue. Some examples:

(1)

When Leslie comes he speaks, in his lecture, of the fact, to him, that prose has rejected the self image or the sorrows of Werther kind of fiction.

(2)

He wanted to fuck his wife all the time now. Yet having done so, would have his head fill with "things to do," almost lists of them, as if the relief of coming, like they say—and though understandable, it's an odd phrase finally to mean emission of semen, but must mean something like, *it's me, I'm here?*, whereas "emission" would have the slightly military sense of, that which has been sent forth . . .

(3)

There was a joke of girl at water fountain in factory who bending over to drink finds herself then caught by nipples of each breast by fingers which pinch, twisting them. The sharp, quick flood of wanting. She gasps. But couldn't it be equally, someone else's voice interrupts, it just hurts like hell? That the joke probably, either way. And for years in sense of, if one does it, that way, the consequence is as stated.

(4)

I'm almost
done, the hour
echoes, what

are those words
I heard, was
it *flower, stream,*

Nashe's, as Allen's
saying it, "Brightness
falls from the air"?

It hardly seems necessary to spell out why the first three of these quotations are bad prose. Their cozy gawkiness (including Mr. Creeley's most obsessive mannerism: "like they say") evades an essential problem of style; to write intimately and informally and well is not just to muck about with language. Similarly, the fourth passage exploits our modern openness to the colloquial tone in poetry. Few effects are as satisfying as the assimilation of natural speech into a powerful and melodic poem—one could demonstrate from all the masters, past and present. But again, this does not mean there are not enormous qualitative differences possible, or that a loose and stumbling casualness automatically makes for good writing. I have just quoted the opening stanzas of Mr. Creeley's poem "Echo." The first two of these stanzas are relaxed and facile, but suggestive in their dreamy, halting, listening movement; and the poem will return to that tone in the unquoted portion after the third stanza. But that third stanza! I *think* Mr. Creeley is alluding to the way Allen Ginsberg recites Nashe's line, mutilated here, of course, by the way it is broken. But that is not as important as the sheer failure of the language and rhythm.

This problem of breakdown of diction and syntax is pervasive, though it is interesting that in the best Creeley poems—such as the short, witty, musical "Walking the Dog" or the long, beautifully serious "People"—the incidence of distracting mannerisms and limb-tangled syntax is sharply reduced. But not entirely. In "People," we find a passage like this one:

If you twist one
even insignificant part
of your body

to another, imagined
situation of where it
might be . . .

The intensity of the poem's concentration, however, enables us to discount such lapses, and even to attribute them to a desire to hold so much in the mind simultaneously: a remembered world of childhood fantasy, and the transmutations of that set of memories in patterns of adult awareness and longing. The abstractions do get out of hand, as does the language at times, yet these problems do not defeat the poem. "People," with one or two of the other longer efforts, is the main reason we can feel that *A Day Book* is concerned to make a sustained voyage of inward emotional discovery.

Before leaving *A Day Book,* I shall turn to just one more of the better poems in it to suggest a possibly important consideration. The poem is called "The Edge." Within the larger sequence, it is part of a brief series of poems and fragments on the theme of love: a movement of meditative tones that is calmly appealing. "The Edge" itself is a brief variation on a poem by William Carlos Williams, curiously unacknowledged considering how often Mr. Creeley speaks of the significance to him of Williams' work. I shall quote "The Edge" first, and then Williams' poem, "Love Song."

Place it,
make the space

of it. Yellow,
that was a time.

He saw the stain of love
was upon the world,

a selvage, a faint
afteredge of color fading

at the edge of the world,
the edge beyond that edge.

And:

I lie here thinking of you:—

the stain of love
is upon the world!
Yellow, yellow, yellow
it eats into the leaves,
smears with saffron
the horned branches that lean
heavily
against a smooth purple sky!
There is no light
only a honey-thick stain
that drips from leaf to leaf
and limb to limb
spoiling the colors
of the whole world—
you far off there under
the wine-red selvage of the west!

Williams' poem is rich and full-bodied. It isn't just that, as Mr. Creeley has it, "He saw the stain of love/ was upon the world." Williams' "yellow, yellow, yellow" is an active image, the projection of the lover's desire over the visible universe. In "Love Song," that universe is tangibly out there. Its organic, natural patterns are absorbed ("eaten," "stained," "spoiled") into the driving emotion of the speaker until its limits are reached in that wonderful image, "the wine-red selvage of the west," which receives and contains the poem's male force and suggests female response and sexual fulfillment. The Creeley poem echoes all this but makes it almost static and reduces the emotion to an abstraction. Without Williams' phrasing—"yellow," "stain of love," "upon the world," "selvage"—it would have neither vigor nor concrete reference. It is a pulling back from Williams and toward Louis Zukofsky, another of Mr. Creeley's chosen ancestors but one more congenial to a less robust imagination than Williams', with a thinner melodic line and less possibility for technical variation.

When I came upon "The Edge," I first thought to look into Williams' 1948 play *A Dream of Love* to find "Love Song," which the play's poet-doctor hero reads to his wife in the brilliant opening scene. The scene underlines the fact that the poem is directed by a real, grown-up man in the real, everyday world to a real woman. Both characters are intelligent, sensitive, but durable people baffled by the complexity of their relationship and even of their identities. The dialogue certainly reveals a whole philosopher's-bookcase-full of problems, but without belying the earthy realities in which the characters are rooted. The original poem had been written more than a quarter-century earlier, and Williams repossessed it for the play.

The accident of going back to *A Dream of Love* first instead of to *The Collected Earlier Poems* led me to another, related realization. The scene between the hero and his wife that I have mentioned parallels the dialogue in Mr. Creeley's play *Listen,* which I had been reading just before *A Day Book*. The difference between the plays is like that between the two poems. *A Dream of Love,* whatever its weaknesses by the time it comes to its end, is physically very much alive. It strives to imply the co-presence of many different selves in the literal, often absurd situations of its characters. *Listen,* with its two characters named "He" and "She" and its quotations from R. D. Laing and from Wittgenstein (e.g., "The I, the I is what is deeply mysterious" and "The I is not an object") is a gently, pleasingly abstract treatment of the same theme. It is somewhat academic and derivative, with traces of Eliot here and Williams there and Pirandello somewhere else, and with charmingly pedantic interruptions of the "action" while He gives instructions to the director which also instruct the reader in what he is to appreciate. There is also an appendix of "production notes" by Mrs. Bobbie Creeley to instruct us in how the lines should be read. Her "monoprints" in this edition, incidentally, are imaginative examples of photomontage, and in a sense they illustrate the drift of the He-She conversation in the play. Because of their necessarily visual combination of literal human figures (the same man and woman in the same shot, but seen in different degrees of clarity and in different contexts) with a vague landscape and abstract forms around them, they lend a sensuous conviction and lyrical vibration mostly absent from the text.

Mr. Creeley's vague but assertive poetics may be examined at length in *Contexts of Poetry,* a collection of ten interviews with him by various people between 1961 and 1971. The interview as a way of getting at people's ideas and artistic practice is a not altogether satisfactory form, but it does bring out what the victim is likely to say when compelled to be relatively spontaneous in the face of his own self-consciousness. I found these interviews particularly useful for biographical information; the one with Lewis MacAdams, especially, throws light on the psychological background of the poet's interest in inarticulateness as a mode of expression, but the conversations with David Ossman and with John Sinclair and Robin Eichele are helpful in this way, too. The most *articulate* interview, on the other hand, is the well-prepared one with the very intelligent and purposeful Linda Wagner. Interesting points concerning rhyme and structure arise here, and Mr. Creeley points to Williams' observation that "a poet thinks with his poem" as a valuable touchstone of method. In this interview, too, he quarrels with Eliot's thoughts on the "objective correlative." He cites his own poem, "The Immoral Proposition," to show that an apparently abstract statement about feeling can convey its emotion through the weight and distribution of the words when it is spoken in the right way. He rather oversimplifies Eliot's thought; Eliot would doubtless agree with his general theoretical statement, though he might well disagree about the quality of "The Immoral Proposition." The important thing, though, is the way Miss Wagner gets Mr. Creeley to state his positions more clearly than he has in his essays.

On the whole, these interviews do bring out the range of the poet's concerns. There is plenty here to agree and to disagree with—the great point is that, as he says, "What is interesting . . . is that which one *does* say, over and over, without being really aware of it. For better or for worse, these insistences must be the measure of one's acts." I agree, and should like to speak to one of those measuring insistences—the notion that Whitman and Williams were neglected until quite recently. "The figure the New Critics and the universities to this day have conspired to ignore," we are told, "is Walt Whitman." So much scholarly work and criticism has been done on Whitman (Newton Arvin, F.O. Matthiessen, Gay W. Allen, and many others) and he has been well anthologized in so many scholarly anthologies, such as Harry Hayden Clark's *Major American Poets* (1936) and Matthiessen's superb *Oxford Book of American Verse* (1950), and taught in so many courses, that one does not know what to make of this assertion. As for Williams, Mr. Creeley is equally wrong in saying that "in 1945, I don't think [he] was even regarded as a minor poet." Just for starters, I suggest he look into Fred B. Millett's *Contemporary American Authors* (1943).

To get back to *A Day Book*, it's there, I think, that the lessons of Whitman and Williams have been, not neglected, but incompletely studied.

Parnassus (Fall/Winter 1973)

❧

Continuities in Modern American Poetry

LET us avoid the pedantic view of literary history that has recently led to a certain amount of nonsense about what is called "modernism" and "post-modernism." The modern poetic movement is to my mind still in full swing, and recent poetry at its best has been following through on possibilities opened up during the second, third, and fourth decades of this century. A specifically Left poetry, for instance, flourished for a while during the 1930s in our country and then re-emerged far more explosively in the late 1950s. It has had a new life, unhampered by Communist dogma, ever since. In matters of form, the most striking tendency is that the development of image-centered poetry in English has led to the evolution of the modern sequence, a relatively long poem whose structure and life depend on a series of radiating centers or affects.

As it had in French poetry, this reorientation of the long poem came to rely strongly on improvised associative dynamics, but it has always carried within it important references to traditional forms and symbolic motifs. It helped in the process of freeing the poet to work directly out of his subjective awareness even when the realities uncovered were humiliating, nasty or dangerous. There were plenty of 19th-century forerunners in English. *Song of Myself* comes to mind first of all, perhaps, but one could assemble a long list of titles such as Tennyson's *Maud* and Browning's "Childe Roland to the Dark Tower Came." It would be a great pleasure to contemplate such works and their relation to the great 20th-century sequences, but simple reference to the obvious connection must suffice here. One might point, though, to some similarities of psychological and sexual unease, with surprising corollaries of a political and social character.

Let me touch on a few salient aspects of the poetic situation as coherently as my brief space allows. One never really *knows* a living art. Hundreds of between-wars poets wrote poems of some interest that no one is any longer aware of. But even among the score or so poets of the period whose names are still fairly well known, their actual work remains largely unexplored. Nothing has brought out this fact so strikingly as the publication of Valerie Eliot's edition of *The Waste Land*, with the early manuscript drafts and other relevant materials. As soon as a view of the manuscripts became possible, various scholars began applauding this acceptance, and that rejection, by Eliot of Pound's advice; and this change, or that retention, decided upon by Eliot all on his own. Curious! People of the sort who in the early 1920s would have paid no attention to *The Waste Land*, any more than they now pay attention, say, to Ramon Guthrie's *Maximum Security Ward*, or to Galway Kinnell's *The Book of Nightmares*, suddenly were able to tell at a glance just what belonged in it and what did not. On the whole, according to them, everything Eliot finally did was right and all omissions, except in the case of one line, were very properly omitted. Indeed, *The Waste Land* as we have it is the best of all possible *The Waste Lands*.

But what the manuscripts show is something much more intrinsic to what happens in a poem. They show elements the poet tried to work with and was not always able to handle, partly because they were intractable at the particular point he had reached in his development and partly because of insufficient reinforcement from contemporary sensibility. Despite its double embalmment by Eliot's self-created later public image and by saturation in certain half-official modes of interpretation, *The Waste Land* had since World War II decayed in some spots and ossified in others. The manuscripts reminded us of its primary character as a poetic sequence, its mobilization of diverse elements of tone, awareness, intellectual preoccupation, and social attitudes under the pressure of a psyche struggling to transcend its disturbances by a unifying vision. It was open, improvisatory, tentative, yet firm in that larger, self-organizing purpose. It was a young man's poem, impure and unsimple. His head was full of melodies—speech rhythms, lyrical lines and phrases, operatic and poetic snatches, sardonic raspings, gusts of feeling, echoes of voices, bits of internal dialogue. Redeemed from exegetes, archetypists, anthropologists and Christian illuminators, the poem's original life clarified itself. It begins in something like pure music and ends in self-mocking confusion. Like Pound's *Hugh Selwyn Mauberley* and *Homage to Sextus Propertius* and first groups of *Cantos* it is a discovery whose poetic achievement remains to be explored. The real symbiosis of the two poets is revealed in their parallel enterprises during their 30s and 40s.

Obviously, there is a direct continuity between such works and the sequences by Hart Crane and William Carlos Williams that came along a little later—and then the sequences of our own decades by Olson, Duncan, Guthrie, Kinnell, Muriel Rukeyser and others. The influence intermingles with the energies generated by Yeats's longer works, a continuing force in American as in British poetry, and by those of Stevens. The authority of these germinative works derives both from the achievement of their most intense and beautiful passages and from the courage of letting the associative process lead where it will. As Stevens puts it in *The Man with the Blue Guitar,* at once savagely and charmingly:

> Ah, but to play man number one,
> To drive the dagger in his heart,
>
> To lay his brain upon the board
> And pick the acrid colors out,
>
> To nail his thought across the door,
> Its wings spread wide to rain and snow,
>
> To strike his living hi and ho,
> To tick it, tock it, turn it true,
>
> To bang it from a savage blue,
> Jangling the metal of the strings . . .

Among much else in modern poetry that remains to be explored, the savage side of Stevens, and his centrality, call for more attention. His playful comment on Blackmur's criticism was in fact a pointed indication of his own poetic interests. "Blackmur," he wrote, "fails, not for lack of ideas, but for not knowing what his ideas are. Nothing shows this more clearly than ten or twelve pages of his work from which one usually comes away—longing for sex and politics." Poetic courage consists in getting into the real thing, the real awareness within which the poem is born, regardless of whether anyone, even the poet himself, considers the subjective states involved admirable ones. A predilection for the aristocratic, fear or disgust at the thought of sex, self-hatred, racial prejudice, the sense of paranoid or unstable qualities in oneself (I am thinking of motifs present in some of our most distinguished poets)—*are* subjective realities. The ambiguities of social and psychological experience, converted into volatile, many-dimensioned possibilities of language and image, are mobilized by the dynamics of a poem into aesthetic perspectives.

A number of black poets at this moment, with Imamu Amiri Baraka (LeRoi Jones) in the foreground, are playing with dynamite morally somewhat as Pound and Eliot have done in their anti-Semitic passages. They project warped, but real sensibilities in which violent, caricaturing racial images are combined with a language of uncompromising and sometimes vile abuse.

With a poet as gifted and as aware of the implications of what he is doing as Baraka is, and as able to write with exquisite psychological accuracy and subtlety, we are confronted by the use of political consciousness as a volatile element of poetic dynamics. One cannot help being reminded of the two sides of Pound, to some degree embodied in his brilliant portrait of Blake "before hell-mouth" in Canto 16 on the one hand, and his more blatant passages in the "Hell Cantos" on the other hand. At the same time, this *dangerous* use of poetry is premised on the assumption that poetry counts. Auden to the contrary, it is not true that "poetry makes nothing happen." What happens, I admit, takes place mainly at the level of qualitative subjective awareness: the "agony of flame that cannot singe a sleeve" nevertheless transforms modes of perception. The great generation of early moderns certainly felt this way, and Williams devoted *Paterson* to what he called his need to find a "common language to unravel" and thus help unify a people.

The belief, or hope, is that getting the real life of the psyche out into the open is the difficult but right path of the poet; that art is the testing ground of attitudes without bloodshed. Baraka's poem "Black Art" includes the following passage, which I suppose speaks for itself:

> Look at the Liberal
> Spokesman for the jews clutch his throat
> & puke himself into eternity . . . rrrrrrr
> There's a negroleader pinned to
> a bar stool in Sardi's eyeballs melting
> in hot flame. Another negroleader
> on the steps of the white house one
> kneeling between the sheriff's thighs
> negotiating coolly for his people.

This is not Baraka's best writing or thinking, to put the matter as mildly as one can. It is infantile and repulsive. But that is not the end of the matter. Baraka is a pupil of Pound in his recklessness of attitude testing, and I can only admire Adrienne Rich's reaction to such passages as well as to the rest of his work in her poem, "The Blue Ghazals." One section of the poem is addressed directly to him. She sees his racism as an expression of suffering and as a means of distancing himself from even the most sympathetic white mentality. The following passage shows, in a number of ways, the continuing strength of poetic attitudes of the 1920s and 1930s:

> Late at night I went walking through your difficult wood,
> half-sleepy, half-alert in that thicket of bitter roots.
>
> Who doesn't speak to me, who speaks to me more and more,
> but from a face turned off, turned away, a light shut out.
>
> Most of the old lecturers are inaudible or dead.
> Prince of the night there are explosions in the hall.
>
> The blackboard scribbled over with dead languages
> is falling and killing our children.

Terribly far away I saw your mouth in the wild light:
it seemed to me you were shouting instructions to us all.

Miss Rich's lines refer specifically to Baraka's novel, *The System of Dante's Hell,* and a collection of his poems, *The Dead Lecturer*. Baraka has in his own way picked up from Pound's and Eliot's heavy redeployment of motifs and tones from Dante. It is odd to see Miss Rich recognizing the modern Inferno in which he moves and at the same time proposing that "most of the old lecturers are inaudible or dead" and that "the blackboard scribbled over with dead languages/is falling and killing our children." The recognition of the interdependence of tradition and invention was one important key to the liberation of form in twentieth-century poetry; it is the same kind of key to significant social change. Nevertheless, Miss Rich sees the real interior landscape of the speaker in Baraka's poetry and reaches out with an overstatement that is part of her empathy. The deliberately averted face of Baraka, the voice that speaks to her and yet does not speak, the wild sense of shouted instructions that cannot be heard are images both personal and political, ambiguous images of a nightmare world that resemble effects in poets as different from one another as Eliot and Muriel Rukeyser. Like the poets of the 1930s, who were so strongly influenced by Eliot and Lawrence, she sees the interchangeability of the personal and the political. As she says later in "The Blue Ghazals":

The moment when a feeling enters the body
is political. This touch is political.

That insight has to do with the free-floating universal relevance of sensation and emotion. This is a constant in aesthetic process, one whose full significance is brought to bear in modern poetic method. We see manifestations of it in each of the longer sequences I have mentioned. One reason the *ghazal* has interested our poets recently is that it allows for a float of tonal association in which such connections can emerge in an almost amniotic context without the organizing demands of the developed forms in our own tradition. The formal laxness is not a total blessing for it encourages Delphic utterances in a vacuum and sometimes is hard to distinguish from talking in one's sleep.

Be that as it may, the name of Adrienne Rich brings me back to Stevens' remark about sex and politics, which of course come together sharply in the poetry of women's liberation. One thing we have been witnessing is the reawakening of continuities with the social and revolutionary poetry of the 1930s. The poetry of the late 1950s and early 1960s, for instance, when the Beats came into their own, was foreshadowed by Kenneth Fearing. There is no poem more desolate than his "Green Light," a masterpiece of depressive candor more devastating and less pretentious in its vision of urban emptiness than any other poem I know. Now that the era of wildly rhetorical and humorous poetry associated with the new radicalism is past, Muriel Rukeyser stands out as both a precursor and an exemplar of the half-political, half-personalist tendencies of the present moment. The passage by Adrienne Rich I have quoted has a good deal of Rukeyser in it, including the refusal to challenge Baraka on ideological grounds.

Well, there is much left to say, to bear out my conviction that the poetic tendencies set in motion earlier in this century are still in full career. Let me end by quoting a short poem by Williams and making a very few remarks about it. It is called "Love Song":

> I lie here thinking of you:—
>
> the stain of love
> is upon the world!
> Yellow, yellow, yellow
> it eats into the leaves,
> smears with saffron
> the horned branches that lean
> heavily
> against a smooth purple sky!
> There is no light
> only a honey-thick stain
> that drips from leaf to leaf
> and limb to limb
> spoiling the colors
> of the whole world—
>
> you far off there under
> the wine-red selvage of the west!

I pull this one poem out of the treasure-hoard of unexamined modern work because its original energy puts to shame a great deal of the poetry that is supposed to be rendering modernism obsolete. "Yellow, yellow, yellow" is an active image, the projection over the whole visible universe of a man's urge toward a woman he is thinking of. That universe is tangibly out there: the leafy, "horned," actively thrusting branches, the colors of the sky and of "the whole world," and the sunset's "red selvage of the west," waiting to receive the spreading yellow. Everything in the external universe is absorbed—"eaten," "stained," "spoiled"—into the driving emotion of the speaker until its limits are reached in the wonderful image of the "wine-red selvage." This image not only receives but contains the poem's male force and suggests female response and sexual fulfillment.

The "stain of love" of which the lover sings is like the personified "blind loving wrestling touch" in *Song of Myself* and like the "body" that "stubbornly pushes out of the" speaker in Mayakovsky's "I." To think of its source is to see Williams' daring. His linking of "yellow" with "stains," "smears," "honey," "thick," "drips" and "spoiling" is rooted in associations of the sexual with the excremental and with such richly sweet bodily sensations as the taste of honey. The idea of passion that obliterates clear vision is linked, too, with a kind of primitive or infantile guilt over being nasty and sticky. The poem reflects a subconscious feeling that the world is made up of clearly defined objects bathed in light until the sexual principle takes over, staining and smearing and eating into the beauty of natural things—*spoiling* them. Yet the whole set of the poem is not sad or disgusted but exuberant. It *is* a "love song" and it asserts desire in an abundant sexual image that converts all the elements I have been describing into a joyous reaching for fulfillment. This effect is so convincing because the successive tones and impressions correspond to actual human feelings. The varying associations of "yellow" as each image emerges are directly related to the ways people experience and think about love. The order of images corresponds, in a sense, with the maturing process. Somewhere along the way, in their early psychological development, people are likely to feel at least some revulsion at the proximity of the body's sexual and excremental functions. But ordinarily, through normal maturing, we learn to subordinate such revulsion and, in fact, to reverse it so that it contributes to the exaltation of love. This whole development of feeling in love-experience is recapitulated in "Love Song."

Why have I gone into such detail just here? Because the poem is so alive and interesting. Do you suppose we have got to the bottom of this kind of modernism yet? The whole body of poetry of our age is bursting with it.

The Nation (2 February 1974)

Voyage into Neruda

RESIDENCE ON EARTH by Pablo Neruda
Translation by Donald D. Walsh

WHERE the poem takes you is the question. Leaving aside important objections that have been raised about Donald Walsh's original texts as well as about his translation of *Residencia en la tierra*, I simply want to think a little about what kind of voyages the best poems in this book are. I shall discuss only a few as they come through to me, using Mr. Walsh's English as a point of reference wtihout being bound by it. The best translation, after all, is but a crib to rock us toward the original, which we must catch at as we can.

What genius Neruda showed in his twenties and thirties! How well he saw what he was doing is shown in the remarkable little poem "Ars Poetica" in which the theory is all laid out. Here, with passion, humor, self-irony, and an unabashed conviction of his own power to deal with tragic knowledge, he defines for us, with the fingerprint of his own particular sensibility, essential poetic process—the internalizing of haphazard external reality and the redirection of it in human perspective. Working through images at once commonplace and almost mystically riddling ("invisible water that I drink somnolently," "nights of infinite substance fallen in my bedroom") or intimately direct, he reveals an absolute confidence in the power of his intensity to carry him through. This confidence struggles constantly with the "ceaseless movement" of the world and its "swarm of objects" to invade him and confuse his sense of his own identity.

But the most beautiful exploration into poetic process comes in Neruda's opening poem, "Dead Gallop." In it we are drawn inexorably into a painful movement of awareness. Intransigent reality grows human, not in a sentimental way but through the natural, ordering means of response and imaginative repossession. Neruda suggests what is going on in language true to his feeling and absolutely rigorous in itself.

> Like ashes, like seas peopling themselves,
> in the submerged slowness, in the shapelessness,
> or as one hears from the crest of the roads
> the crossed bells crossing,
> having that sound now sundered from the metal,
> confused, ponderous, turning to dust
> in the very milling of the too distant forms,
> either remembered or not seen,
> and the perfume of the plums that rolling on the ground
> rot in time, infinitely green.

Thus the first stanza, in Mr. Walsh's translation. We can see his abilities and limitations in the way the stanza moves. Something of the original tone comes across through the boldness of Neruda's images, but at the same time one can sympathize with the problem of translating a line like "*o recordados o no vistas*" in the eighth line above. It is not easy to catch the clear yet elusive music in English without losing Neruda's grave seriousness at the same time. Mr. Walsh catches only the elusiveness with his "either remembered or not seen." I make this point less to criticize his translation than to indicate what Neruda accomplishes. Such a poem demands every ounce of the poet's ability to discover and yield to the implicit energies of language in following the true track of his insights.

Notice that there are no complete sentences in this stanza. It is made up, rather, of fragments of image, an accumulation of similes without referent. Indeed, the referent is defined only by all these disparate notes of comparison. From the translation one can observe that the poem's dominant feeling is not quite melancholy but something partly akin to it. It is at once oppressed and insistent, the result of an emotionally demanding concentration on the way disparate impressions impinge on a consciousness seeking to fuse them into a whole vision. Paradox is the first step in such a poetic formulation. It unites opposites: "ashes" and "peopling," "shapelessness" and "form" ("*informe*" and "*formas*"), plums that "rot" and yet remain "infinitely green." In general, images of death and destruction are reconciled with images of life and generation. What one does not, however, get from the translation is the extraordinary individual clarity of the separate impressions. Neruda brings this out by his very pure handling of sound, which stresses the particular quality of each sensuous effect:

> *teniendo ese sonido ya aparte del metal,*
> *confuso, pesando, haciéndose polvo*
> *en el mismo molino de las formas demasiado lejos . . .*

Compare these lines with their English rendering in lines 5–7. The *o*'s alone provide a musical stress and punctuation that are lost in the translation. The hard explosives of *"aparte"* stress the active separation in the speaker's mind of sensuous effects from their sources. Here Mr. Walsh certainly misses an opportunity to get closer to Neruda just by writing "holding that sound now apart from the metal"—a phrasing that would find echoes in the next line as it does in the original.

The burdened concentration involved in absorbing and holding in balance a wider and wider range of images is increased as the poem progresses. Except for two questions, Neruda holds off forming complete sentences until his closing stanza. There we find a surge of affirmation at last, after the poem has all but sunk into a surrender to death-consciousness—that is, consciousness of the world's "oceanic" disorder—and then been aroused to anticipation through a double image of possibility:

> upsurge of doves
> that exists between night and time, like a moist ravine.

Almost humorously, the poet had, just before presenting this erotically suggestive image of the "moist ravine," introduced himself as "me who enter singing as if with a sword among the defenseless." It had seemed a desperately self-savaging picture, since he was entering the realm of "vast disorder" with nothing but his sensitivity and his art. But now we see the phallic functioning (however muted the statement) of his song, placed in relation—as so often in these poems—to the "moist" *("húmeda")* receptivity of reality. The poem ends with a quiet, almost plain image of the growth of life and form out of this confrontation of the poet's active openness and a tragically destructive universe:

> the great calabash trees once listen,
> stretching out their pity-laden plants,
> it is made of that, of what with much wooing,
> of the fullness, dark with heavy drops.

"Dead Gallop" is quite special, but it epitomizes Neruda's poetic genius. Other poems make fuller use of the erotic impulse that shapes "Dead Gallop" so effectively if unemphatically, but all are enmeshed in the same process: the creation of form out of accumulated effects whose initial ambiguity of direction prepares the way for every sort of use by the sensibility gathering them in. Take the beginning of "Alliance (Sonata):"

> Of dusty glances fallen to the ground
> or of soundless leaves burying themselves.
> Of metals without light, with the emptiness,
> with the absence of the suddenly dead day.
> At the tip of the hands the dazzlement of butterflies,
> the upflight of butterflies whose light has no end.

Ignoring (for one thing) that word "upflight," we see once more a procession of fragmented images in paradoxical relation. This time the procession leads directly to the language of love, though the images introduced make for an address to time and reality as well:

> The spying days cross in secret
> but they fall within your voice of light.
> Oh mistress of love, in your rest
> I established my dream, my silent attitude.

This image of a "mistress of love" grew out of the contrast between notes of negation ("dusty glances fallen to the ground," "soundless leaves burying themselves," "metals without light," "suddenly dead day") and the images of touch, brightness, and soaring at the end of the first stanza. The "mistress" is thus a formation and realization of earth and time. At the end she becomes a memory of possible joy within the very domain of nature's murderous and "smashing" fury:

> the waves are crashing, smashing themselves to death:
> their movement is moist, drifting, ultimate.

One could argue that these early poems of gathering vision, these voyages into the dreaming self guided by splinters of illumination leading to their own felt meaning, are Neruda's finest. Certainly all but one or two of his political poems drop far below their level. "Dead Gallop," by its very nature, casts derision upon such outright propaganda as "Song to the Red Army on Its Arrival at the Gates of Prussia." It makes the sequence "Spain in our Hearts" seem shallow, though Mr. Walsh calls it "the noblest poem" produced by the Spanish Civil War. Vallejo, I believe, wrote more nobly out of the same experience because he could not compromise with his own voice. Even *The Heights of Macchu Picchu* is somewhat compromised by comparison with the rigorous consistency of "Dead Gallop." The magnificent side of that sequence comes from the aspect most akin to the best poems in *Residencia*, the evocation of a lost past that becomes a promise through conversions of a kind that Neruda understood quite early on.

Not to end with matters of rhetoric, let me speak of other vital poems in this book. The clever, somewhat odd "Ritual of My Legs" traces the poet's literal body lines down to the points at which his feet press the world outside themselves. We protect ourselves from that "foreign and hostile" world and its "dense and cold constancy." The speaker's loneliness is at the poem's center here—characteristically. But in one poem at least, "We Together," something almost altogether different happens. This exultant love-chant begins with exuberant praise of a woman: "How pure you are by sunlight or by fallen night." Very quickly she is created by images taken from the real world that do not usually reflect Neruda's usual sense of apartness: her "bosom of bread," her "crown of black trees," her "lone-animal nose, nose of a wild sheep/that smells of shadow and of precipitous tyrannical flight." For a while in the poem, until the very last lines, the speaker becomes the "invader," his maleness cockily intent on possessing and penetrating this woman who embodies the physical universe. For once he does not receive but bestows the initial "shock" of union with reality. The imagery is sensual and thrusting until, after an affect of thrilled and trembling possession, the vision collapses into a sense of peril and illusion "like swords' edges or inheritance of smoke."

Hoping to give some idea of its exciting movement, I have over-simplified this poem in my description. I would place it, except for its sheer power and approach to joy, with such sensual and bitter poems as "Single Gentleman," "The Widower's Tango," and "Josie Bliss." These poems, each unique, are rooted in normal life but wildly volatile at the same time. They are fantasies of the real. They take us through points of magnetically charged contact between the self and its inner and outer worlds and are voyages into the mystery of identity.

Review 74 (Spring, 1974)

❧

Paul Blackburn, Poet

THE poet Paul Blackburn died of cancer almost three years ago, at the age of 44. He had published seven volumes of his poems, mostly very slender volumes printed by little presses with names like Divers and Totem and Trobar and Perishable, as well as five books of translations from the Spanish and the Occitan. Associated with the Black Mountain group, he was a gentle, affectionate person with devoted friends all over the country. As the moving force behind the readings at the Dr. Generosity Café and what he called "St. Mark's-in-the-Bouwerie," he must have encouraged innumerable younger writers. He was accomplished but unpretentious, one of those poets whose work shows more than most how ridiculous the barrier is that separates the general reader from poetry.

Blackburn was so naturally, so humanly a poet that to read him is to tune in at once, intimately, on our own inner selves. He called the world of our common life as it penetrated his reverie "the half-cultivated country of meditation." The poems are always immediate. They isolate a situation or atmosphere or mood and let the poet's aroused and varied feelings play over it. Blackburn was never embarrassed at sharing the emotional values of ordinary folk. In "7th Game: 1960 Series," for instance, he is one man in a cityful of men all under the enchantment of a championship baseball game in far-off Pittsburgh:

> Nice day,
> sweet October afternoon

Men walk the sun-shot avenues
                                        Second, Third, eyes
                                        intent elsewhere
ears communing with transistors in shirt pockets. . . .

In these few lines we can see how Blackburn uses the full richness of the spoken language. The apparently casual, prosaic phrasing becomes exquisitely lyrical through his handling of pauses and linebreaks—his colloquial syncopation. Certain echoing adjectives ("sweet," "sun-shot," "intent"), together with graver tones fleetingly introduced in "Men walk" and "communing," add shadings of intensity and evocativeness. Much of the special genius of one strain of American poetry resides in such almost invisible effects. They give their own order to chaotic perception if we really attend to them, really listen.

Blackburn was probably our finest poet of city life since Kenneth Fearing. He knew the lingo and tempo of New York. His subway poems are at once sardonic and delighted as they rock us through their grimy, lurching, sometimes Rabelaisian underground voyages. They are apt vehicles for Blackburn's emotional rangings, from his manic fantasies of poetic declamation and sexual conquest on a crowded train ("Clickety-Clack") to his melancholy close-ups of urban squalor in early spring ("Meditation on the BMT"). His voice is often a sounding board for the whole sense of a New York moment. "The wet streets of my city speak to me," says one poem. The filth of the sidewalks, the patterns of light, the street voices, conversations in McSorley's, all the soiled and passionate life of the city enter Blackburn's voice:

Windows are
steps of light
running down into darkness
From the lowest yellow step
one falls into backyard blackness. . . .

Some of the poems find their structure in the rhythms of dialogue, at times just amusing or mildly abrasive, at times rigorously beautiful with a severe, sculptured formality that makes of sheer perception itself a compressed emotional state. Despite what I have said, Blackburn was far more than a poet of one American milieu. He can sense the absolute stillness of a moment in the Spanish countryside, the perplexity of anyone's inarticulateness before the stunning dilemmas of existence, the triumph of joy at the incongruity of things under the most dismaying literal conditions. His elegiac gifts and poetic repossessions of love-longing—but I am selecting these motifs almost desperately, almost at random, to indicate in this limited space Blackburn's lyric scope and many-sided sensibility.

If indeed there were space here I would discuss his style a great deal more: for example, his engaging mannerism of strewing wittily itemized little catalogues, like a facetious Whitman, throughout his poems. I would give pages to his poems of marriage going out of whack and of sexual encounter. Certainly I would discuss the superb translations of Peire Vidal and other Provençal poets: they should have been in print these 15 years and more. He learned a great deal from those poets about the whole scale of volatile poetic possibilities, which transcends narrow ideas about "conventional" and "free" verse. And I would recur again and again to the way a man walks through the poems of Paul Blackburn—the man of "The Sea and the Shadow," not his best poem perhaps but the one that most frankly expresses the despair, humiliation, bright awareness, and affirmative, loving energy balanced and combined in so much of his writing.

For the interested reader three books are most available. They are *The Cities*, published by Grove Press in 1966, and two posthumous volumes: *Early Selected y Mas* (Black Sparrow Press, 1972) and *Peire Vidal: Translations* (Mulch Press, 1972. What a difference there is between the quiet authenticity of these books and the chic slickness of what Cummings called the "talentgang" running most of the show.

The New York Times Book Review (11 August 1974)

"Like the Shark, It Contains a Shoe"

WHAT is American poetry today? Louis Simpson tries to tell us in six uneasy lines:

AMERICAN POETRY

Whatever it is, it must have
A stomach that can digest
Rubber, coal, uranium, moons, poems.

Like the shark, it contains a shoe.
It must swim for miles through the desert
Uttering cries that are almost human.

That is a view as grim as it is witty. Simpson, looking at a terrifying new world, sees a subhuman future for the race. Our changed sense of life's prospects is one drastic condition of our poetry. Many of our poets write as though we had already been defeated, an obsolete species trying to swim in the desert.

This is not, thank God, the whole truth of where our poetry stands today. Just as characteristic is this quietly human piece by Jill Hoffman:

RENDEZVOUS

Summoned from a dream of your summoning
by your cry, I steal out of bed and leave
my doting husband deaf to the world.
We meet, couple, and cling, in the dim light—
your soft mouth tugs and fills and empties me.

We stay that way a long time it seems, till
on your brimming face, where milky drops glide,
I see my body's pleasure flood and yawn.
We turn each other loose to sleep. Smiling
your smile of innocence, I return
to the bed of your begetting, and a man's warm side.

The pleasure of poetry comes first of all from its aroused language, an active discovery through words of our actual states of awareness. Jill Hoffman's poem begins with a situation familiar to parents: having a dream penetrated by a baby's cry and then being awakened by that same cry. Almost at once, though, the poem takes us elsewhere, into the submerged world of the elements floating in every reasonably happy young nursing mother's mind—the secret bond with her baby (as if she has stolen away from a fatuously "doting" husband to meet a lover) created by the sensual pleasure of suckling; the mingled states of dreaming and waking; the whole cavelike atmosphere of primitive sexuality enfolding the tiny family at night.

Remember all the talk about drugs and "expanded consciousness"? But the real expanded consciousness comes when imagination fastens itself on reality. What is discovered can be like the primal paradise of "Rendezvous." It can also be a realm of hell, as in Michael S. Harper's poem about the death of his two-day-old son:

REUBEN, REUBEN

I reached from pain
to music great enough
to bring me back,
swollenhead, madness,
lovefruit; a pickle of hate
so sour my mouth twicked
up and would not sing;
there's nothing in the beat
to hold it in
melody and turn human skin;
a brown berry gone
to rot just two days on the branch;
we've lost a son,
the music, jazz, comes in.

"Rendezvous" and "Reuben, Reuben" show that, regardless of the world's great changes, poetry still comes intimately out of our everyday lives and speech and psyches. (Simpson's poem shows the same thing, but more through its tone and images than through the immediate scene it presents.) Whatever the latest fad or movement, the basis of poetry remains powerfully emotional. The more a poet succeeds in closing in on the emotional center of a subjective state, the more he speaks for many other people as well.

Poetry gives a tongue to the unrealized meanings of many lives. It also reflects, sometimes almost imperceptibly, the assumptions of a generation. Jill Hoffman's confident sense of her own womanliness testifies to subtly altered feelings women now have about themselves. Michael Harper's assumption that we will understand his turning to jazz for strength after his child's death, inadequate as he says the attempt must finally be, demonstrates a comparable new self-assurance in black culture. The social role of jazz in helping people cope with harsh and desolate realities has something to do, as have certain turns of colloquial black speech, with the raggedly nervous, concentrated passion of "Reuben, Reuben."

These are but two poems, growing out of two states of feeling, in two styles, among the myriads of poems now pouring forth in every conceivable idiom and formal guise. *Multiplicity* may be the outstanding fact about our poetry now. A higher proportion of people than ever before in our country have gone on to some degree of advanced education. The general level of sophisticated anxiety about the world's problems, as well as of psychological self-knowledge, has risen. An army of ambitious young poets, often encouraged by college "workshops" and by governmental arts programs, are proliferating and starting new publications.

All this is not just a matter of numbers alone. Another kind of multiplicity comes from the popularity of dissent and of nonconforming positions, the discounting of traditional learning and morality and esthetics. A restless sense of decay and violence and imminent explosion is once more in the ascendancy.

To get some sense of these developments over the past three decades, interested readers might well immerse themselves in the "30th Anniversary Poetry Retrospective Issue," recently out, of the *Quarterly Review of Literature*, a magazine of consistently high standards that has been sensitively open to new talent. We move in it from poems written in the nineteen-forties by such masters as Wallace Stevens, E. E. Cummings, and William Carlos Williams to those by the latest talented youngsters.

But for a quick close-up of the immediate present, I would propose plunging into the latest *American Poetry Review*. This is the most sparkling, hospitable and excitable of the new poetry journals, the one most likely to take over the role once played by *Poetry: A Magazine of Verse*. It's tabloid format is ideally suited to the current atmosphere of young poets swarming onto the scene and jostling their slightly insecure elders. It has plenty of space for both verse and prose in its long pages as each issue rocks through oceans of newsprint. The atmosphere is as of a combined literary pub, monster reading rally, assassins' den, and Hyde Park or Bughouse Square of poetry. The reader who is not too solemn can pick up any number of cues in these pages. He will not miss the pervasive American interest in translation (represented in the *Q.R.L.* retrospective issue as well) that has helped our poetry become such an open affair; the cultivation of prose poems (for example, some coolly sardonic ones in the May/June issue by Michael Benedikt; and of long-lined poems making extreme use of prose rhythms (in the same issue, several by C. K. Williams); and the focusing on commonplace subjects and autobiographical soundings by many young poets.

The editors of numerous other magazines such as *Mulch, Antaeus, Shenandoah, Open Places, Salamagundi* and *New York Quarterly* would have a perfect right were there but world enough and time, to protest my not discussing them here. The new poetry explosion is indeed remarkable, especially when one considers how few readers poetry has. One editor (the first issue of her magazine has not yet even appeared!) wrote me recently that "poetry submissions have been coming in like a small avalanche—welcome, of course—but it's painful to realize how much good poetry is being written, and that so very little of it can possibly be published." Those of us who know young poets and are familiar with the whole situation never cease being amazed and dismayed.

The position is even shakier with books. Even when a good book of poems by a young writer appears at last, after all the ignorant rejections and agonizing delays, it will be poorly distributed and is almost certain to go unreviewed in any publication that is widely read. Possible readers will be unaware of its existence unless they happen to take a critical magazine like *Parnassus,* which devotes itself to the lively reviewing of new books of verse. But few people among even the supposed literati are all that interested to find out what is happening in the one art most intimately rooted in the common sensibility of their time.

I will not dwell at length here on this paradoxical situation. Its complexities demand more than a cursory summing up. Yet some obvious realities do underlie the fact that so very few books of poems sell even 1,000 copies. One uncomfortable reason is the mass indifference to poetry, reinforced by the neglect of literature in the lower schools. (What do they *do* during those 12 long years?) And linked to that indifference, like a Siamese twin in the same cultural placenta, is what a friend of mine calls the "cash-over-culture policy" that, on the whole, dominates publishing despite the presence of so many fine editorial minds. Essentially, the publishers' irresponsibility toward poetry, as toward other kinds of original and demanding writing, is a means of not facing the problem forthrightly. It is traceable to the fact that the supposed market, rather than professional concern to print the best books available, dictates their day-in, day-out preoccupations. Luckily for the poets, tiny spaces for them are always being grudgingly cleared here and there, and almost every publisher has had a streak or two of intensive poetry publishing—inspired usually by a single inside conspirator who thus jeopardizes his future reputation for practical good sense. And certain presses, including university presses like those at Connecticut Wesleyan, Pittsburgh and Louisiana State, have devoted themselves to poetry programs. Generally, though, the creed is simply that "poetry doesn't sell." And though poetry would sell a great deal better if enough attention were given to making it happen (as Lawrence Ferlinghetti's City Lights Books proved long ago when it made best sellers of poets like Allen Ginsberg and Ferlinghetti himself), by and large the main chance does not lie that way.

But putting aside the practical obstacles and the centrifugal diversity of the modern scene, can one size up the poetry itself in any coherent way? It will help, I think, if one has some notion of its background, of what has happened to poetry since, say, the days of Walt Whitman. A sense of such recent tendencies as "confessionalism" and "projectivism" and the resurgence of political engagement is equally helpful. And because poetry is first of all an art, one needs some insight into "open form" and the "modern sequence," concepts similar to those that have revolutionized music and the other arts and, indeed, philosophy and science.

In various ways, Walt Whitman is connected with all these developments. Most of our more interesting poets today are in some measure the sons and daughters of Walt, fulfilling his boast: "I am large, I contain multitudes." I have mentioned the modern sequence. It is a long poetic work made up of more-or-less independent poems and fragments; these can vary greatly in form and style, yet they reinforce each other in the larger structure and movement of the whole work. Whitman's *Song of Myself* is the prototype of the modern sequence, an ancestor of such efforts as Ezra Pound's *Mauberley* and the *Cantos*, T. S. Eliot's *The Waste Land* and *Four Quartets*, Hart Crane's *The Bridge*, William Carlos Williams's *Paterson*, Charles Olson's *The Maximus Poems*, Ramon Guthrie's *Maximum Security Ward*, Robert Duncan's "Passages," Robert Lowell's *Life Studies*, and Galway Kinnell's *The Book of Nightmares*.

These are key works of the past half-century, exposing their authors' nervous systems by the network of private feelings and associations running through each of them and at the same time throwing a glaring light on the age. They present devastating social criticism but also reveal untapped resources latent in our traditions. In all of them, as in *Song of Myself*, the poet has to relate his lyric gifts and deep subjectivity to his larger intellectual vision, which always has a definite political dimension. The problem creates awkward situations of focus and transition, like trying to lift a submarine over a bridge. But it mirrors the predicament of the modern divided sensibility.

The sequence, by allowing a poet to put together a number of poems and fragments with separate emotional centers and kinds of rhythmic patterning, meets this problem of reconciling conflicting motivations. As he moves through the fifty-two poems of *Song of Myself*, Whitman mixes many tones and styles. Some of the poems are broadly general in their proclamation of attitudes; some are mystically exalted; some are stabs of feeling, short and sharp; some resemble impressionist paintings in their play of light and color and shadow; and the most intense poems reveal an extraordinary sensitivity to "blind loving wrestling touch, sheath'd hooded sharp-tooth'd touch" that charges the whole sequence with a sexual glow of imagination and richly heightens its impact in surprising ways.

But even a single poem often contains such a mixture of many levels of intensity. To think of a poem as moving among radiating centers of energy, through a series of emotional tones that create its shifting dynamics, is to alter the conventional approach importantly. The elements of chance and improvisation are always essential in the real processes of art and thought. They become more visible when we stop looking at poems as straight lines of narrative or argument or description. This altered, "open" view of poetry has reoriented poetic practice. Again Whitman helped show the way. Thus, he begins poem 21 of *Song of Myself* with a prophetic pronouncement: "I am the poet of the Body and I am the poet of the Soul." He ends it in the swooning language of desire: "Prodigal, you have given me love—therefore I to you give love!/O unspeakable passionate love." Near the middle of the poem (lines 10–14) he gives us a passage that foreshadows modern method in the way it moves without transition between points that at first seem unrelated:

> Have you outstript the rest? are you the President?
> It is a trifle, they will more than arrive there every one, and still pass on.
>
> I am he that walks with the tender and growing night,
> I call to the earth and sea half-held by the night.
>
> Press close bare-bosom'd night—press close magnetic nourishing night!

The first two lines have a serious political bearing (though not the fortuitously comic one they inevitably suggest in the year of our Lord 1974). Whitman is insisting on the importance of self-regard for ordinary persons—they are every bit as important as presidents and aristocrats. Yet after he makes this centrally democratic point, he leaps into a totally different mode of statement, lyrically and mystically evocative. And after that comes an outcry of desire, and within it an erotically tinged image—"bare-bosom'd night"—whose tone is even further removed from that of the political pair of lines. It is easy enough to step back and see the connection. The poet is putting his democratic spokesmanship into action; he is assuming the reverberating significance of private feelings, his own and everyone else's. But we can only infer this, for he does leap between effects without warning or explanation.

All our "modern" ideas about art actually have a long history and many antecedents behind them. Whitman is the American wellhead of modern poetry, though it has sources in European Romanticism and French Symbolism and other sources going much further back. Whatever his weaknesses, he broke away from the confinement of closed, self-limiting structures based on conventional metrics and sensed the promise of poetic dynamics based on almost subconscious response to the demands of language under the pressure of his psychic preoccupations. Like us, he lived under the stress of both extreme political and extreme psychological crisis. Not only was he desperately susceptible to sense stimuli, especially touch, but he was a homosexual in nineteenth-century America. His language and art veer back and forth between large controlling perspectives and irresistible sensation and emotion. The twentieth-century sequences I have mentioned veer back and forth in the same way. Whitman's pulsing, rhythmic improvisations, his sheer energy of projection, his abrupt changes of focus and his unabashed pursuit of his own emotions remain touchstones for a later age despite all differences.

Later poets carry his methods forward and, of course, change them greatly in the process. The modern confessional poet for instance, puts his literal self on the page far more than did Whitman (vulnerable as he sometimes made himself). With photographic accuracy, he presents his own self-blackmailing dossier as inherently representative of the civilization as a whole—a tormenting example of Whitman's "divine average." Robert Lowell's *Life Studies* and *Notebook*, Allen Ginsberg's *Kaddish*, and John Berryman's 77 *Dream Songs*—to name just a few such books—bombard us with close-ups of the poets' most shameful or distressing moments. Lowell's family miseries, manic sexual behavior and divorces; Ginsberg's homosexual loves and hallucinogenic adventures and hideous memories of his poor paranoid mother; Berryman's alcoholism and suicidal depression; Anne Sexton's and Sylvia Plath's breakdowns—of such was the Kingdom of the Higher Literary Gossip for quite some time, especially in the nineteen-sixties. The poets wandered in and out of their poems—and many still do—as though their beds and their books were interchangeable.

The open exploitation of experience once considered too intimate or scandalous to mention has proven highly contagious for younger poets in an age when psychiatric treatment and "letting it all hang out" have become normal in many circles. Make no mistake, I am talking about people who can *write*. They do not merely exploit the desolate mirror image of themselves that they display to us, but seek through the objectification of art to exorcise it and end the waste of their keen perceptiveness and of the very life force by which they are driven. In the best confessional poetry there is a kind of Dionysian ecstasy of powerful realization despite the speaker's condition. Nothing could be more beautiful or painful than the ending of Sylvia Plath's "Ariel":

And now I
Foam to wheat, a glitter of seas.
The child's cry

Melts in the wall.
And I
Am the arrow,

The dew that flies
Suicidal, at one with the drive
Into the red

Eye, the cauldron of morning.

As one might expect, the great danger in writing like this lies in its becoming mere self-indulgence. The best of the confessional poets were disciplined by their knowledge of poetry of the past, including that of the truly great masters of poetry in English who formed the older poetic generation between the two world wars. Younger poets, growing up in the shadow of the confessionals, often devote their talents to revealing how sensitive they are, and how much they have therefore suffered and been saddened into depression—Whitmanian men or women with the sulks, as it were. At their best, however, they seek to be less melodramatic about themselves than the confessional poets were and yet to hover over their literal memories and their present relationships, testing the emotional quality of their lives with a fine, questioning ardor. One of the most promising of the younger American poets, Stanley

Plumly, begins a poem about a dream of being with his dead father with a gentle directness:

> We lie in that other darkness, ourselves,
> There is less than the width of my left hand
> between us. I can barely breathe,
> but the light breathes easily,
> wind on water across our two still bodies.

Dream memories are often found in Plumly's work as in that of many of his contemporaries. Dreams are after all real experiences, and their symbolic resonance and emotional strangeness readily suggest a lost past that remains desirable despite its sadness. Getting a purchase on deep meanings in one's life is the issue, very likely as a way to overcome the increasing dispiritedness of so much modern life. It is interesting that Plumly's latest book, *Giraffe,* has a poem on Randall Jarrell's suicide. A number of Jarrell's most moving poems were written late in his career. In them he tried to repossess his lost childhood and somehow to make up for having, as it were, abandoned himself as he once had been. There may be some connection between a preoccupation with an irredeemable past and the suicidal drive so terribly at work in the confessional generation. Memory is equally important in such other recent books as William Heyen's *Noise in the Trees* and Karen Swenson's *An Attic of Ideals,* though Miss Swenson and other young women poets keep their work harder and more bitter than that of most of the young men. Miss Swenson devotes much attention to the sour side of woman's lot and of love, yet she too is haunted by the past in ways resembling Plumly's and Heyen's.

I have mentioned the projectivist movement, in which memory works in a different way. Its chief figures (Olson, Duncan, Robert Creeley, Denise Levertov, Paul Blackburn, and a few others—like Gary Snyder—not strictly in the movement) have interested themselves in what I would call the rhythms of inner awareness, which involve all the hesitations and clumsinesses and sudden drops into unresolved conflict of the mind's continuous dialogue with itself. Robert Duncan describes the process in his poem "At the Loom (Passage 2)":

> my mind a shuttle among
> set strings of the music
> lets a weft of dream grow in the day time,
> an increment of associations,
> luminous soft threads,
> the thrown glamour, crossing and recrossing,
> the twisted sinews underlying the work.
>
> Back of the images, the few cords that bind
> meaning in the word-flow,
> the rivering web
> rises among wits and senses
> gathering the wool into its full cloth.

To catch the rhythms of the "rivering web," the mind's "increment of associations," and within them the vulnerable subjective preoccupations that are profoundly confessional in content, is to catch both general consciousness and memory in action. It is an extremely difficult task if one wants also to create coherent poems, and the task is often complicated by the tendency of these poets to throw abstract theorizing about their art into the poetic hopper alongside more poignant and suggestive elements. The phrasing can become deliberately graceless and opaque in order to accommodate the projection of actual mental process. For instance these lines of Charles Olson's:

> metric then is mapping. and so,
> to speak in modern cant, congruent means of
> making a statement . . .

But Olson did not write this way because he had no ear. He was able to write exquisitely and with power when his material demanded it:

> The waist of a lion
> for a man to move properly
>
> And for a woman,
> who should move lazily,
> the weight of breasts
>
> This is the exercise for this morning

The projectivist school has been the only one to lend itself wholeheartedly and uncompromisingly to the continuation of the experiments of such earlier poets as Pound and Williams and others who had discovered the vast prospects of open form. (The passage I have quoted from Duncan, for instance, is, like the poem as a whole, the development of a set of images to be found in the superb opening lines of Pound's "Canto 39.") Although it is difficult for younger poets to learn how to work in the extremely sophisticated way of an Olson or a Duncan, they have been influenced by the great store projectivism sets by tuning in on one's own associative processes and using one's own nature and interests at all points along the way. These concerns parallel and sometimes use the new interest in primitive, cultural and mythic structures, just as the concerns of T. S. Eliot's generation found reinforcement in the studies in comparative myth and ritual of the Cambridge anthropologists.

I want now to return briefly to one pervasive aspect of all the poetry I have been discussing in this essay: the insistent interlocking in it of the personal and the political. Poets want to please us with their works, but not at the expense of our discounting the depth of their involvement with actual life. Even when they, and other artists, speak mockingly of politics and moral attitudes, it is really clichés and the masks of hypocrisy they mean. Such lines as the following in Adrienne Rich's "The Blue Ghazals" express an insight characteristic of our time:

> The moment when a feeling enters the body
> is political. This touch is political.

Sometimes I dream we are floating on water
hand-in-hand; and sinking without terror.

Adrienne Rich is one of a number of poets who have come into the renewed conviction, reminiscent of the nineteen-thirties but less heavily Marxian, of the politics implicit in sensibility itself. "The Blue Ghazals" is a sequence that relates such themes as love and marriage and esthetic process to political considerations—the oppressions of urban life, for example, and the effects of revolutionary hatred. One poem in the sequence is addressed to Imamu Amiri Baraka (LeRoi Jones), the black poet whose work has also moved from a primarily artistic to a basically political orientation. The comparison is not totally accurate, for Baraka has gone much further along the purely activist road, even since he wrote "Black Dada Nihilismus" a number of years ago, with its ringing call for

A cult of death

need of the simple striking arm under
the streetlamp . . .

Baraka has written some grossly violent poems of hatred against whites generally, Jews, and liberal blacks whose attitudes are less intransigent than his own. Adrienne Rich's poem to him sees his posture of hatred as a significant reality without accepting it on Baraka's terms. He is a figure in a hellish world we all know about, or should know about: his refusal to communicate with white poets who were once friends is more a gesture from his own hell than anything else. Baraka has in fact written a book based on Dante's *Inferno*, and his *Black Magic Poetry* is a series of poems by an alert, intelligent man coaching himself into the role of black prophet and knowingly distorting his own genius. The state of furious alienation he can create within himself is sometimes countered by a different sort of recognition:

I walk the streets confused and half sick
with despair at what I must do, yet the doing
as it's finally possible, drags me on . . .

These few quotations only barely suggest how deeply political consciousness has invaded our sense of ourselves and our daily world. The sense of a life under too much pressure, of cherished values forsaken because of dangerous, unassimilable change, and—more happily—of the need to stop the destructive spiral of hatred feeding on fear and affirm our sympathies and possibilities has been the burden of all true souls for a long time now.

The New York Times Magazine (24 November 1974)

The British Poetries

BRITISH poetry today is, sometimes amusingly, threatening to get out of hand. The spasms that have convulsed Western art in the wake of modern history are affecting British poetry too. A post-Black Mountain school now exists, represented most recently in the books put out by Stuart Montgomery's Fulcrum Press and in the avant-garde magazine *Poetry Review*, edited by Eric Mottram. A list of germinative names sent me in 1972 by Mottram suggests the American-oriented, post-modernist nature of his interests: "Cage, Cunningham, Olson, Duncan, Zukofsky, Ginsberg, Jones (Baraka), a number of black poets, Ashbery, Elliott Carter, M.C. Richards, Fuller, the Gestalt therapists, Brakhage, McClure, Pynchon, Burroughs, Mailer, Goodman, Halprin, Chomsky, and so on." Of course, the new movements are not merely derivative. For instance, though Montgomery and Mottram have encouraged the young poet Tom Pickard, it is in part because he brings Northumbrian working-class attitudes and speech into his poetry so freshly and originally. And a poet like Jeff Nuttall thrives in the new atmosphere because of his wild imagination and satirical joy and hectic realism. At the same time, among England's most accomplished poets, certain individual voices such as Peter Redgrove's and Ted Hughes's can be heard to have a vigor beyond that of the prevailing tone of quietly controlled feeling still dominating English verse.

Most of that verse remains basically conventional in form as well as sensitively humane and highly articulate. The most influential models remain Auden, Empson and Larkin, and behind them, Yeats—not Yeats the mystical symbolist and passionate explorer of elemental reality but Yeats the advocate of straightforward syntax and of the use of intelligence as an active poetic energy. Too often, poetry that violates the premises implied in this list of names—one could add a few more, naturally—is likely to fall on what sometimes seem literally deaf ears. Hughes's *Crow* has been savaged by *The Times Literary Supplement* (that is, by one of its anonymous reviewers), and Charles Olson has been given his lumps, and Robert Lowell has been raked over, however respectfully. On the other hand, a poet like Ian Hamilton Finlay, the Scottish Concretist, has been received with surprising courtesy and attention. This has happened, I fear, not so much out of appreciation of his poetic accomplishment as because of the tidiness of his witty little structures.

A good deal of power, as power goes in the tiny world of the poets all over the globe, is wielded by a small band of rigorists under the leadership of the young poet Ian Hamilton. Founder and editor of the serious poetry journal *The Review*, and for a time poetry editor of the *T.L.S.* as well, he has now launched a magazine of broad literary scope: *The New Review*. From an American standpoint, the Hamilton group are a little baffling in their combined sensitivity and conservatism. They are watchful against exaggerated emotionalism and against what they would consider the irrationalism of poetry that goes all out for drastic confrontation with the uncontrollable and terrifying aspects of life. The poetry they favor is short, intense, confessional—but restrained. It is in effect an imagist poetry of personal suffering. The imagist aspect, the focusing on a concrete object or scene or situation before the poem turns for a swift moment into a view of the speaker's inward feeling, provides the essential discipline and restraint. Hamilton's own poems, collected in his book *The Visit*, are perfect examples. They reveal personal agony but do not examine it; their intelligence is used, rather, to protect the speaker from letting go.

The Modern Poet, Hamilton's anthology of poems, essays and interviews from *The Review*, reveals how imagism and the new confessionalism have been brought together in a manner peculiarly appropriate to one strain in British sensibility. The poems by Hamilton, John Fuller, A. Alvarez, Hugo Williams and others share this kind of expression in varying degrees and illustrate the need felt for the *protective* use of intelligence. The essays, too, bring out this chief preoccupation of current British verse. Colin Falck's "Dreams and Responsibilities," for instance, speaks of "the kind of reflection-within-experience which provides the basic strength of poetry" and warns against the way Americans like Lowell and Berryman "mirror the chaos of experience without controlling it." Of Ted Hughes, Falck writes that "the real limitation of Hughes's animal poems is precisely that they conjure emotions without bringing us nearer to understanding them." (Alvarez, in his anthology *The New Poetry*, struck out against this attitude over a decade ago, but it persists even among those who seem to have listened to him.) In another essay, Falck distrusts even Empson because his intelligence has been "authoritarian" and non-imagistic and hence has made for a refusal of poetry."

All this may sound like a variety of neophilistinism, but I do not think it is. The keenness of the critics of *The Review* is unquestionable even when one disagrees with them. They are interested in questioning a wide range of poetic positions too often merely taken for granted, and they have held out pretty well against various vulgarizing tendencies endemic to the British situation. But they do tend to be precisians, and the problem with art is that it *will* squirm away from its guardians. While they stand firm at the gates of purity, whole new encampments are being formed in the country round about.

John Matthias's anthology *23 Modern British Poets* provides one overview of these encampments. I have mentioned the Yeats-Auden-Empson-Larkin axis, but Matthias means something beyond that: "There *is* a contemporary British poetry which is modern." He wisely opens his anthology with three older poets, all in their seventies, who still are not fully honored in their own country (except in that doughty magazine, *Agenda*, edited by William Cookson). These poets are David Jones, Hugh MacDiarmid and Basil Bunting. Matthias, himself an American, speaks of his "growing irritation" at their neglect in the United States; but I think it can be argued that much of the new interest in them was initiated by Americans. In any case, each has shared the larger glory of their poetic generation, working out of sources both native and international, experimenting in the long poetic sequence and bringing a rich historical sense to bear on moments of lyrical realization. With some exceptions, though, younger British poets have not scoured through and assimilated their work as younger Americans have done with, say, Pound and

Williams. The resistance to the "difficult," British or foreign, has been enormous. That is one reason that British modernism has, on the whole, been so shaky.

The younger poets in Matthias's anthology range in age from just over thirty to fifty. The best known are Hughes, Finlay, Charles Tomlinson, George MacBeth and an Irish ringer, John Montague. All these are strikingly interesting figures. Hughes began early to show his eerie genius as a poet fascinated by the impersonal terror in nature—a projection, undoubtedly, of his sense of the uncontrollable depths of man's own destructive psyche. In *Crow* (not represented in Matthias's book) he draws on primitive sources to handle a vision inimical to modern humanism. Finlay is the victim of his identification with Concrete poetry, a movement easily vulgarized into a nice parlor game. He is beautifully represented by Matthias, and I should like to refer readers to Stephen Bann's brilliant pamphlet on him (*Ian Hamilton Finlay,* published by Wild Hawthorn Press in Scotland). Bann shows how Finlay embodies a new classicism, intimately though paradoxically "linked to a sense of estrangement from the Classical." His art has "its most clear affinities with the art of those epochs when estrangement from the past was the dominant tone," and "Finlay's case is precisely that of the traditional culture forced into the small-scale venture and the hazardous channel of communication . . . periodically interrupted by the ravages of the long ships." This remarkably accurate formulation *proclaims* as Finlay's achievement what Ezra Pound, in *Mauberley, feared* would be the outcome of his effort to create a heroic classical art for this century.

"The ravages of the long ships" are the incursions of barbarism. Poets who do not revel in the prospect of cultural breakdown are nevertheless often obsessed by the possibility. Tomlinson, despite the cool precision of his esthetic preoccupations, is concerned with the dissolution (and in love with the persistence) of traditional patterns the world over. A less seriously concentrated poet and one who broods less over the loved English past, MacBeth swoops into and out of the prevailing vision of terror. He is a sort of bright, humorous clown-moth teasing himself all around the flame. His virtuosity is engaging but, as he uses it, costs him a certain conviction. Montague, however, talks like a grown man in his poems. He deals directly and sincerely with a grown man's concerns, including the tragedy of Northern Ireland. Modern English and Irish poetry, given necessary differences of national emphasis, are reciprocally related, and Matthias is to be praised for including Montague, who has the gift of combining clarity and subtlety, simplicity and formal inventiveness. It is too bad he did not find space for a few other Irish figures as well. He should certainly have included Austin Clarke with the elder masters, and probably Patrick Kavanagh. The subtly intense Thomas Kinsella belongs to this collection and would give it needed depth.

Among the other poets included by Matthias, the acerbic Christopher Middleton is notable for his harshly self-undercutting style and the constant reorienting of his poems from any tendency toward sentimentality or complacency. The hard cutting edge of his poetry—his handling of phrase and line and shifts of tone and association, not just his basic thought—is an unusual quality in English verse. Christopher Logue's translations from Homer are exciting in their active force and formal freedom. They remind me, in their empathy and powerful release, of some of Paul Blackburn's best translations from the Provençal—both poets discover a dramatic energy in their translations not quite present in their own original less formally structured work. Gael Turnbull, a pleasantly personal, rambling old hand at a relaxed, anecdotally open form, is represented, as well as the bitterly unrelaxed Roy Fisher. Totally unknown in this country, Fisher's experiments in the blending of prose-poetry and patterned free verse are remarkably sustained and alive. His poetry reflects a continued trauma and depression because of the destruction wrought on English families and neighborhoods in World War II. The mood carries over to the general sense of a deteriorating civilization. His gifts of sharp, economical observation and lyrical precision resemble Middleton's somewhat, but he is more committed to direct communication with his reader. Finally, I should mention just a few of Matthias's younger poets and compare them for a moment with some included in another anthology, Jeremy Robson's *The Young British Poets*.

The three poets in Matthias, all in their mid-thirties, who are due to receive more recognition are Lee Harwood, Tom Raworth and Gavin Bantock. The first two of these men combine a certain hard, ironic distancing of themselves from their feelings (a familiar modern British tone) with fashionable current American modes that they handle expertly: painterly improvisations of a series of surface effects, the "deep image," and a whimsical ordering of apparent non sequiturs punctuated by serious psychological and historical notes. Bantock, a prophetically inclined writer, is miles apart from Harwood and Raworth in his refusal to trivialize his concerns. He was first brought to attention by the magazine *New Measure*, whose editor, Peter Jay, now publishes him for Anvil Press. He is the sort of poet who demands—and with justice, for he has a feeling for the dynamics and the whole music of a poem—complete acquiescence by the reader so that the poem can work its full spell upon him.

Robson's young poets ("none born before 1935") are all far closer than Matthias's to the conventional norm of English verse, and we find some of the same people in *The Young British Poets* as in *The Modern Poet:* Ian Hamilton, John Fuller and Hugo Williams. In addition, there are Robson himself, Stewart Conn, Douglas Dunn, Tony Harrison, Angela Langfield, Jon Stallworthy, the Irish poets Seamus Heaney and Derek Mahon, and the Indian poet Dom Moraes. Reading through their work again, I am struck by a thought half-disturbing, half-pleasing. Not one of these poets breaks the mold in any sense, and yet all are most interesting in what they reveal about their thoughts and feelings and observations. Conn, Dunn, and Stallworthy in his more recent work have a nervous power of awareness that carries them a bit further than most of the others; and Heaney and Mahon—both, like Montague, Ulstermen—have a welcome edge of rough localism. It would be possible to consider that modern British verse has hit a kind of golden mean, allowing for genuine communication of sensibility without imposing any overly demanding formal devices, special vocabulary, or pitch of passion on the reasonably literate reader. It's remarkable that so many of these younger poets are slipping so readily into the ranks of their immediate elders—poets like Dannie Abse, Donald Davie, Michael Hamburger, David Wright, Anne Beresford, Fleur Adcock and many others one could name who are, indeed, real and lively and suggestive poets of our age, with styles of their own that nevertheless owe something to a generally shared personality. Indeed, even those who have taken up the challenge to conventional verse can hardly be said to be experimenting in the hope of discovering ways to "make it new." They too have found an almost comfortable way of exchanging reports on their admittedly finely gauged subjective lives. The Robson group do not seem to be struggling with resistant materials as young American poets who are in a way comparable—Stanley Plumly or Raphael Rudnik, for instance—do. Nor do the Matthias group deliberately undertake Sisyphean tasks in the model of Olson; they seem to be out to handle rough labors smoothly rather than to challenge the apparently intractable.

But I don't altogether go along with what I have been saying. If you want to read a British poet who leaps with manic glory into sets of perceptions unreducible through art, Peter Redgrove is a pretty close approximation. His 1972 book, *Dr. Faust's Sea-Spiral Spirit*, is according to its jacket (almost certainly written by him) "about changing fear into a growing vision," and I take the feeling to be not very different in conception from Hughes's in *Crow*. Redgrove's private self, however, comes much more directly into his difficult and troubling and exhilarating poems than Hughes allows to happen in any of his work. He always has invited the whole absurdity and awkwardness of being human in the midst of physical nature, and of the torment of desires and dreams and intimations of perhaps supernatural transcendence beyond our ability to deal with, into the wild and yet bravely controlled movement of his poems. All the world's sharp angles and unmanageable realities, the sexual and psychic and cosmic intractabilities, are Redgrove's materials. He and Hughes, in their very separate ways, have given a contemporary turn to the meaning of that once popular Nietzschean catch-phrase: "tragic joy." In that context, they (like Thomas Kinsella) have reached as far as any American poet of our day. It may, indeed, be that the continuous sway of a relatively contained poetry of English sensibility, a poetry that really communicates at a high level, has become the context of the greater daring and power of a Hughes or a Redgrove of late. The connections, the readiness, the openness to new directions have been growing ever more evident in recent years.

The New York Times Book Review (19 January 1975)

Irish Memories, Irish Poetry

SELECTED POEMS by Austin Clarke
A SLOW DANCE by John Montague
THE NEW ESTATE by Ciarán Carson

YOU can feel the whole direction of Irish poetry since Yeats in Austin Clarke's *Selected Poems* and in John Montague's *A Slow Dance*. Clarke, who died two years ago at 77, was despite his distinction hardly known outside his country. Montague, now entering his late forties, is together with Thomas Kinsella the poetic spokesman for his newly graying generation. In a small, old provincial country that mantle of "spokesmanship" settles on a poet's shoulders like an iron yoke.

Ireland's assorted burdens are all too familiar—poverty, religious puritanism, sexual repression, ready violence, a crippled history. "Great hatred, little room," Yeats said. Rooted in ancient mists and forever nourished by rural speech and a tradition of eloquence, Irish poetry keeps learning how to assimilate harsh experience without being broken on it. There would be something grievously wrong if it did not sometimes grate on our nerves and ears as it jolts toward 2000 A.D. With its great past and its current pressures, it must take some necessary risks.

Clarke is a world unto himself, something like a black hole in space, very concentrated and absorbent. He drew into his innermost depths some richly suggestive, highly lyrical modes of medieval poetic thought and technique together with a plain Irish citizen's bitterest practical concerns. His most accomplished longer work is the narrative sequence "Mnemosyne Lay in Dust." Years in the making, this is a hardly disguised autobiographical account of hysterical personal breakdown accompanied by loss of memory. Life's pressures and terrors have built up in the protagonist, "Maurice Devane," until he has to be committed for treatment to the mental asylum founded by Jonathan Swift. The misery and the depth of revulsion in this poem, one of the important sequences of the century, are compounded of Maurice's anguish and sense of irreparable loss, but these are not purely personal in origin. The poem's sexual horror is inseparable from the social atmosphere of frustration and also from its reaction against compensatory images of a long forgotten priapic Eden. The squalor of modern commercial Ireland mingles with other oppressive realities—terrorism, the shadow of the State, the murderous political hostilities—like a confluence of foul odors, and all blend in turn with the more intimate motifs of private guilt and insecurity. The poem is saturated with brilliantly concrete moments: sudden memories, panicky outbursts, flashes of gentleness or joy, paranoid visions, closeups of grossness, glimpses of modern Dublin.

This was a work of Clarke's old age. But even as a young poet of barely thirty, Clarke had revealed an exquisite ear and a gift for balancing opposed states of feeling. The best known example is his "The Young Woman of Beare," which coolly echoes and redirects the famous tenth-century Irish lament "The Old Woman of Beare." The original speaker was a miraculously oft-rejuvenated beauty finally grown old after the seventh time around. Clarke shows her in her voluptuous prime, in lawless mockery of the parochial moralism of a later Ireland. While she exults she moralizes ironically; she warns good girls not to follow her example even while a happily pornographic imagination is glorifying her. Ah, the sweet fantasies Eros brings to young men of conscience!

Clarke's progress between these works was a matter of putting his virtuosity and love of melody to work in the service of his indignant intelligence and the freedom of his own sensibility. He wanted, too, to speak out about homely matters not ordinarily thought suitable for poetry: the practical problems of unmarried lovers or even of married couples lacking contraceptives; the cruelty of religious hatred in small children; the vulgarity of Church and government and their neglect of the people, even the export of horses for butchering—no issue was too prosaic for Clarke's withering tongue.

What he embodies is the great turn from a primarily aristocratic or genteel Irish poetry to a poetry that speaks directly out of the world of working folk and peasants and the less prosperous middle class, without however forgetting the poetic past. Clarke's "Martha Blake at Fifty-One" is a devastating piece of compassionate satire. The Martha of the title is exploited and ignored by the Church, to whose service she has given herself with humble devotion. The reader coming to Clarke for the first time will perhaps be put off by local references and quirky, old-fashioned concerns. Yet certain poems and passages will stick in the mind like burrs, and others will be remembered as pure song. These lines breathe modern Ireland, including her cherished (and repeatedly betrayed) memories from the heroic age.

One may say all this about John Montague's work as well, although it is more cosmopolitan in its influences and outlook than Clarke's. What they have in common is clear yet elusive, a crossgrained esthetic and the ability to move easily between traditional lyric and rougher, flatter statement. Montague has for some time been working with large sequences that relate his personal life and psyche to his family's background in rural Ulster and to the whole of Ireland's catastrophic history. *A Slow Dance* is of this order—a self-contained afterbeat of his very ambitious *The Rough Field*, which has been called an "Ulster epic." This new book is both a deep immersion in the poet's search to identify himself with his land and people and an effort to liberate himself at the same time. It begins with a group of poems that present the identification as a ritual sexual dance primitive in spirit but rather sophisticated in its tragic consciousness. At least two of these are among the most beautiful and telling in the book.

Other groups follow: one centering on the atmosphere of various Irish localities north and south; another on the long memory of war and atrocity in Ireland; another on "coldness," associated with Ulster; a fifth on Montague's family, and particularly his father, and the painful circumstances of removal to America (Montague was born in Brooklyn); and finally an elegiac group centered literally on the death of the composer Sean Ó Riada but focusing too on the poet's displacement and isolation, partly willed because of his need for detachment from his country's narrowness and madness. I can only suggest the range of feeling and of poetic method in this compelling work. Prolonged discipline by national crisis has sensitized the best Irish poets in a special way, making their explorations seem less arbitrary, often, than those of our comparable poets.

A third Irish volume, *The New Estate,* is by the 25-year-old poet Ciarán Carson. It contains translations of some lovely, rather "imagistic" Welsh and early Irish poems and, among a number of rather slight pieces, a few that promise work to come of greater strength. "Visiting the Dead" and "Our Country Cousins" engage with crude realities. "The Half-Moon Lake" risks (and achieves) sentimentality but wins through to the understanding of a child's death similar to Frost's "Out, Out—" or some of Ransom's poetry. "O'Carolan's Complaint" (spoken by a blind harpist who lived over two centuries ago) is a moving piece reminiscent of Clarke's combined realism and musicality.

The New York Times Book Review (19 September 1976)

"Poor Innocent"

(Introduction to A. J. M. Smith, *The Classic Shade: Selected Poems*)

IT has often struck me that A. J. M. Smith has something like perfect pitch in poetry. He has the ability to read a poem for the first time and, almost at once, catch its tones and associations. One might say that this was a critical rather than a creative gift, and, indeed, it is what makes his anthologies such triumphs of taste and makes conversations with him about poetry such interesting and delightful adventures. But the gift carries over into his poetry, most obviously in such a poem as "To Henry Vaughan," in which his mimetic empathy fills the lines with the light of a kindred sensibility aroused by his sheer love of Vaughan's phrasing.

More subtly, though, the empathy has to do with the nature of poetic process. It lies in Smith's feeling for the process—its traditions and its possibilities, the rich opportunities it provides for the convergence of creative energy with critical responsiveness. I am not speaking of an abstraction but of the way he writes his poems, the kind of play of form and private emotion that gives them their movement. Let me suggest an early instance, the half-light, half-serious poem called "Poor Innocent":

It is a gentle natural (is it I?) who
Visits timidly the big world of
The heart, and stares a little while at love
As at a plaited and ringleted paleblue
Seascape, whence escapes a new, untrue,
Refracted light, a shade or two above
The infra fringe beyond which does he move
He moves unsurely in an air askew.

This pretty simpleton, myself or not,
Squints at the filigree of wind and wave,
Scanning the frothing for the Lord knows what—
The foam-born rising, maybe, nude and swell,
Or—*Back to your kennel, varlet! Fool, you rave!*
Unbind that seaweed, throw away that shell!

One has to stop, and go back and notice, to see that this sweetly intense, self-ironic poem is a Petrarchan sonnet. Its lively surface-effects conceal the formal insistences of rhyme and turn and conclusion. The voice is witty and sophisticated, and yet the speaker *is* a "gentle natural"—an educated one, to be sure, skeptical about his own romantic vision and feelings and in all too great a hurry to tell himself to *come off it*. But he's still a "gentle natural" all the same. You can tell by the sheer fun he has looking at himself in the mirror of his supposedly deluded wonderment. Even the zest of his closing lines belies their claim to disillusionment. Aphrodite is truly being born again for him out there. He was right to go slangy with excitement just thinking how she would arrive: "The foam-born rising, maybe, nude and swell."

The sonnet-tradition, the Shakespearean phrase I have twice quoted, the effects in the octave slightly reminiscent of E. E. Cummings, the play on the Greek name of the goddess, the Romantic self-teasing at the end—these are all but details of the element in which the poet lives and breathes and in which his originality finds itself. Smith, an important force in modern Canadian poetry though still but little known in the United States, is an active esthetic intelligence whose life's work (like that of most other genuine poets of matured intelligence) refutes the very notion of an "anxiety of influence" that reduces the power of poetry to renew its energies because of the burden of its great past. Communion—dialogue—with the past, and repossession of it in his own new, idiosyncratic way is the artist's enormous pleasure as he engages with everything that the present is. The epigraph from an essay by George Santayana printed in all four of Smith's books of poetry, and again at the close of his selected essays, describes this pleasure with wry elegance. Smith obviously took a great fancy to his way of putting things. It renders pomposity nil. "Every animal," writes Santayana, "has his festive and ceremonious moments, when he poses, or plumes himself, or thinks; sometimes he even sings and flies aloft in a sort of ecstasy." Here is the perfect creed for the gentle, sophisticated natural, whose joy in the creations of his predecessors and of his contemporaries could hardly diminish his own song.

Smith's poem "Ballade un peu banale" should be cited first of all, I think, if one wishes to understand why the Santayana quotation attracts him so strongly. The "Ballade" is an exquisitely bawdy embodiment of Santayana's idea. This is especially true, perhaps, of stanza 1 and stanzas 4–7:

The bellow of good Master Bull
  Astoundeth gentil Cow
That standeth in the meadow cool
  Where cuckoo singeth now . . .

Bull boometh from the briary bush,
  Advanceth, tail aloft—
The meadow grass is long and lush,
  The oozy turf is soft.

He stampeth with his foremost foot,
  His nostrils breathing bale;
Uncouth, unhallowed is his suit;
  The vestal turneth tail.

He feinteth with his ivory horn,
  Bites rump, bites flank, bites nape—
Sweet Saviour of a Virgin born,
  How shall this maid escape!

He chaseth her to pasture wall;
  She maketh stand, poor bird!
He wields his tail like an iron flail.
  Alas! he presseth hard!

We're listening to something like pure poetic engagement, the poet's happy engagement with this parody of sexual melodrama and with all the lovely paraphernalia of medieval lyric, of pastoral romance, and of earthy piety he can deploy in it. And then there is the simple sweetness of absurd erotic fantasy in which he indulges himself. This poem is in a cherished tradition, at once popular and learned, running twin risks of preciosity and vulgarity but certainly worth the effort. It goes back, obviously, to Rabelais and Chaucer and earlier. My favorite contemporary example beside this one, and exceedingly close to it in spirit, is the opening section of Basil Bunting's *Briggflatts*. There too we find a Master Bull in a state of pastoral arousal, although the hilarity is muted for the sake of a different kind of lyricism. Bunting's sequence as a whole has deeply serious, even depressed tones to contend with and develop. A whole world of personal and historical memory, the whole idiom of regional culture—the very grain of a people's self-regard—is being eroded. Moreover, the speaker feels something akin to all this in his own nature: a self-betrayal and a disloyalty to the simple folk and their ways that nourished his childhood and youth. If we viewed Smith's complete oeuvre as a unit, we would find in it analogous balancings of joy in the life-force and more depressive visions. But I do not want to touch on that side of things quite yet, except indirectly by pointing to another apparently frivolous poem or two. Take the memorably silly beginning of the one called "Political Intelligence."

Nobody said Apples for nearly a minute—
I thought I should die.
Finally, though, the second sardine
from the end, on the left,
converted a try.
(It brought down the house.
The noise was terrific.
I dropped my glass eye.)

This is unforgettable nonsense, especially the first two lines. One should, I know, hesitate to suggest that, nevertheless, it contains notes of the sinister and the disturbing and the seriously political, and that those notes lurk in the words "die" and "left" and in the phrases "brought down the house" and "glass eye." The next two stanzas, however, have strongly satiric and sombre tones that reinforce the suggestion:

Meanwhile the P.M.
managed to make himself heard.
He looked sad
but with characteristic aplomb said
Keep calm there is no cause for alarm.

Two soldiers' crutches
crossed up a little bit of fluff
from a lint bandage
in the firing chamber of a 12-inch gun.
People agreed not to notice.
The band played a little bit louder.
It was all very British.

But of those poems which can conceivably be called light or humorous, the one I most love is "Brigadier," translated from a French-Canadian song. The song is a dialogue between an egotistical general and his sardonically deferential sergeant, Pandore: variants on the Don Quixote-Sancho Panza pairing. Smith's English version beautifully juxtaposes the general's expansive, complacent romanticism (you *might* call it) and the sergeant's ironic detachment. The language of the one grows ever more fustian; the other's remains a reticent constant. In the two final stanzas, the teller of the tale takes over the general's style and echoes it mockingly, but Pandore's refrain has the last word:

As 'Right you are,' replied Pandore,
'Right you are, my Brigadier.'

All our dreams, and all the mere literalness of whatever we experience, are implicit in the contrast. The poem is a music of opposing tones, joyous and melancholy and at the same time remarkably, ecstatically impersonal.

The two characters, General and Sergeant, were a happy discovery for a poet at once full of luxurious dreams and all too ready to deflate them. In the Romantic-Classical debate, Smith tends to vote Classical on principle while his poems actually throw the balance of feeling and imagination a little the other way. Both his collected volumes, for instance, begin with the poem "Like an Old Proud King in a Parable." It starts out with Yeatsian flourishes although, as is usual in Smith's work, the discernible literary influences do not finally dominate the poem:

A bitter king in anger to be gone
From fawning courtier and doting queen
Flung hollow sceptre and gilt crown away,
And breaking bound of all his counties green
He made a meadow in the northern stone
And breathed a palace of inviolable air
To cage a heart that carolled like a swan,
And slept alone, immaculate and gay,
With only his pride for a paramour.

Thus the first stanza. It is followed by a single line set off by itself, in which the poet rejects the facile dream-notion that he is this king—some alienated Fergus ruling over the land of the imagination: "O who is that bitter king? It is not I." The poem should end just here. But what happens is that the speaker picks up the Yeatsian dream after all and indulges in the identification. The poet prays to be able to learn a proud, isolated art in spite of having (as in "Poor Innocent") placed himself abruptly in his own reality:

And I will sing to the barren rock
Your difficult, lonely music, heart,
Like an old proud king in a parable.

But the second poem in both collected volumes, "Shadows There Are," is more deeply accurate. Modern classicism must be, not some bullying demand for superficially formal tightness or for demeaned and shrunken vision, but a hard pursuit of the implications of contemporary mentality and sensibility. The pursuit leads primarily to formal concentration, a pressing of the issues of realization beyond showing one has "interesting" sensitivities. That is, it involves a certain impersonality and distancing, just to get past the self-betrayal of the ego mirroring itself hungrily but falsely in passionate stereotypes. We can see the really serious classical poet at work in "Shadows There Are"—*and* the really serious romantic poet too, of course—

Shadows there are, but shadows such as these
Are shadows only in the mortal mind
Blown by the spirit, or the spirit's wind.

Yet shadows I have seen, of me deemed deeper,
That backed on nothing in the horrid air,

And try as try, I cannot limn the form
That some of them assume where I shall pass.
They grow transparent, and as sharp, as glass.

The two three-line stanzas enclosing the light-rhyming couplet (and each containing another couplet, one with exact, the other with consonantal, rhyme) formally present us, as it were, with three distorted mirrors in their relationship of sound. They play with the idea of shadow and form in a way that suggests the mind's bafflement when confronting its own limitations. It is not far from a poem like this one to the death-obsessed pieces that have accumulated in Smith's successive volumes. Where I said "mind's bafflement," indeed, I should have said "self's bafflement," and perhaps have used the word "death" instead of "limitations." The ambiguity here is true to the lyric tradition. Smith reaches back to Elizabethan forerunners who flung a mood to the mercy of the language—to ravishing evocations, rhythms, echoes—and thereby discovered how a mood was a world of involvement and how the phrasing needed to evoke that world was, despite its quite possibly melancholy meaning, a sort of ecstasy in itself.

I suppose it's because he found in it an analogue to his own fascination with this paradox—our delight in finding the right language even for inescapable horror; the illusion of triumph over fatality this discovery brings us—that Smith translated Mallarmé's swan-poem beginning *"Le vierge, le vivace et le bel aujourd'hui."* His is the best rendering we have in English. It catches precisely the vision of romantic energy trapped within its own need for form (the *pressure* to be "classical") that Smith, as much as any modern writer in our language, shares with Mallarmé. The elusive glory of our dreams and desires, richly and tragically presented in the figure of the swan, is held ice-bound in language as "transparent, and as sharp, [to quote the poem we have just been looking at—"Shadows There Are"] as glass."

The author of this translation and of a poem like "Shadows There Are" is unlikely to engage in proliferative rhetoric or witless exhibitionism to prove he has normal human feelings and a common touch. Naturally, he has both. His ordinary humanity is evident in his obvious preoccupation with love and death and joy, and in his sense of the language. I realize that this proposition may not be self-evident to people who do not really believe that poetry is an art, or who disapprove of writing that does not, as they say, "let it all hang out," or who prefer their authors' commitments to be packaged in familiar slogans. Yet it should be clear that, loving wit and the evocative exploration of feeling as he does—and revealing them at every turn—Smith is inevitably an engaged poet in his own clear fashion. He does not know the answers any more than the rest of us do, but he knows the questions better than all but those other poets who, being his peers, can see what he is doing. One poem best illustrates my point: "A Soldier's Ghost," which begins:

How shall I speak
To the regiment of young
Whose throats break
Saluting the god?

I prefer this poem to the ones by Smith that, if never blatant, yet spell out their fear of war and of the hypocrisy of governments more explicitly—or even to his other poem of comparable helpless compassion, "The Dead." "A Soldier's Ghost" asks for a message but has none to give save that the speaker knows no word to keep future generations from suffering the same betrayal (and he does not even call it betrayal) that he has experienced. The poem begins with his cry of inarticulateness; it ends with a delphic utterance of love expressed through an emblem of loss and perhaps of ultimate meaninglessness: "the hieroglyph of ash." The opening stanza might almost have come from the Greek Anthology; while the closing stanza, unpretentious yet transcendent, focuses the speaker's unmanageable emotion—not hysteria but just as real—in the words "hieroglyph" and "love." The poem's force derives from its rhythmic restraint of that emotion and from the beautifully modulated phrasing: the controlled intensity of the first stanza, the hard, technical literalness of the sound, the deftly colloquial characterization of the third, the questioning of the fourth stanza, which echoes that in the first two, and then the closing mystical half-assertion. The issue of youthful sacrifice in war has involved the whole emotional range of the speaking sensibility, rather than merely being the subject of rhetoric.

But now I should like to return for a moment to the frivolous Smith who so gaily and charmingly lets his imagination wander over meadowlands of erotic fancy, with such a mixture of classical and between-wars worldliness—or rather, would-be worldly playfulness. Take the poem "An Iliad for His Summer Sweetheart," with its epigraph from Pound's *Homage to Sextus Propertius:* "And if she play with me with her shirt off, / We shall construct many Iliads." It's hard to think of another contemporary who takes such innocent pleasure in innocent pleasure as Smith does, not to prove he has the usual male endowment or to suggest he's Don Juan redivivus but just out of glee that such things can be.

I love to see my Amaryllis toss her shirt
  Away and kick her panties off, and loll,
  Languid and lazy, by the lily pool,
While old Silenus leers and laughing Cupids squirt.

My fancies swarm like bees about her golden head
  And golden thighs, where love's best ore is found.
  When she sinks softly to the sun-warmed ground
We need no silken walls, no blinds, no feather bed.

To read this poem in the same volume as "A Soldier's Ghost" *(Poems New and Collected)* is to glimpse the connections of humane intelligence and human love that bind the various aspects of the poet's sensibility. For Smith is, in his own way, a libertarian, with a mind free to move beyond constraints of inhibition and gentility absolutely without notice. In some moods, it is true, he would like to see himself as a rigorously conservative intelligence—and why not? Ultimately, there's no contradiction there, just as there is none between his pleasantries about Amaryllis' panties and his frequent preoccupation with death. If, incidentally, he had written Pound's little poem "April," which presents a twin vision of death and delight, he would probably have changed the epigraph from "scattered limbs of the nymphs" *(nympharum disjecta membra)* to "scattered panties of the nymphs." Be that as it may, "April" speaks well for the kind of association that occurs in Smith's mind too:

Three spirits came to me
And drew me apart
To where the olive boughs
Lay stripped upon the ground:
Pale carnage beneath bright mist.

It's the carnage, the presence of ever-raging death, that absorbs his deepest poetic attention. It informs his strongest poems. You can see, in "What the Emanation of Casey Jones Said to the Medium," how it fuses all his characteristic tones and modes. Here is the ending:

the make-up of the mind

Embellishes and protects,
Draws beards between fabulous tits,
Endorses the stranger's cheques,
Judges and always acquits.

Turn inward to the brain:
The signal stars are green,
Unheard the ghost train
Time, and Death can not be seen.

The comic title recalls, as the poem itself does more richly, the combination in the original folksong "Casey Jones" of rollicking colloquial speech and lively music with elegy. Smith picks up both the exuberance of the railroaders' lament and the grimmer note implicit in the mechanical power and speed of the engine and in the fatalistic symbolism of railroad tracks. The language of even the few lines I have quoted unites many levels of expression and consciousness—the speech of Amaryllis' lover, a metaphysical thinker's musings, a working stiff's lingo, and the imagination of a poet who thinks in metaphor at once original and popular: "The signal stars are green," "the ghost train."

Smith's combined life-exuberance, humanity, and death-obsession also produce some of his *noblest* effects of high lyrical evocation—for instance:

A sigh of the inconsequential dead,
A murmur in a drain,
Lapping a severed head,
Unlaurelled, unlamented, vain.

This is the ending of "What Is That Music High in the Air," whose title is a line in Eliot's *The Waste Land*. The tone, however, is Smith's own, something evolved by a process of contemplation and correction from the poem's ringing opening lines, whose mood was exalted but finally unacceptable:

A voice from the heroic dead,
Unfaltering and clear . . .

The nobility of his finest work has many aspects. I believe it can partly be accounted for by his high degree of empathic sensitization to the rhetoric of the most truly accomplished lyrical poetry generally. But his unabashedly human hatred of death is somehow another, and of necessity a more passionate, source. One rarely finds the position held with such thrilling clarity in poetry. The language is the pure, sustained, and subtle speech of a poet who sees his own nature as a relationship between his art and his fate. He commands the inevitable to happen in a manner that makes it seem subordinate to his own shaping will.

Bend back thy bow, O Archer, till the string
Is level with thine ear, thy body taut,
Its nature art, thyself thy statue wrought
Of marble blood, thy weapon the poised wing
Of coiled and aquiline Fate. Then, loosening, fling
The hissing arrow like a burning thought
Into the empty sky that smokes as the hot
Shaft plunges to the bullseye's quenching ring.

So for a moment, motionless, serene,
Fixed between time and time, I aim and wait;
Nothing remains for breath now but to waive
His prior claim and let the barb fly clean
Into the heart of what I know and hate—
That central black, the ringed and targeted grave.

That's giving our poor innocent, speaking for all the rest of us poor innocents, the very last word—or very nearly. The closest thing to it that I can think of readily is Cummings' "who's most afraid of death? thou," a poem much admired by Smith himself. But the prize for nobility and formal rigor must, clearly, go to Smith's "The Archer."

Modern Poetry Studies (Spring 1977)[1]

1. Advance publication of foregoing introduction to A. J. M. Smith, *The Classic Shade: Selected Poems* (Toronto: McClelland and Stewart, 1978).

Hebrew, Arabic and Death

AMEN by Yehuda Amichai

YEHUDA Amichai is Israel's best-known living poet. His work is so volatile—heart-burdened, ironic, sometimes terribly funny, sometimes very gentle and tender—that I was about to call it archetypally Jewish. It isn't; it's archetypally poetic. In "Amen," his third book to appear in English, Amichai reaches pure states of intimate, aroused awareness unusually often. As in, say, Plath or Esenin or Vallejo, the best poems present themselves with simple immediacy even when their sense is elusive or complex:

> Oh, touch me, touch me, you good woman!
> This is not a scar you feel under my shirt.
> It's a letter of recommendation, folded, from my father:
> "He is still a good boy and full of love."

But Amichai is certainly deeply Jewish—an "'ebrew Jew," as Falstaff would have put it. That side of him is rooted in specifics of place and of memory. His "Letter of Recommendation," from which I have just quoted, begins as a sort of Jewish joke about the permanent imminence of disaster:

> On summer nights I sleep naked
> in Jerusalem on my bed,
> which stands on the brink
> of a deep valley
> without rolling into it.

Another poem, the first one in the sequence "Seven Laments for the Fallen in the War," closes in on one figure, the father of a dead soldier whom the poet recognizes amid the swirling city crowds—

> He has become very thin, has lost
> his son's weight.
> Therefore he is floating lightly
> through the alleys . . .

The pathos here is an all too faithful echo of daily life in Israel; Amichai's poetry breathes a people's worst experiences. Yet it is always intensely private, driven by a wildly associative imagination that attaches itself to quickly changing emotional states. It is political because human reality is political, but Amichai's politics are wryness and candor. "A flag loses contact with reality and flies off," he writes in his Memorial Day "lament," whose disgusted refrain is the great theologico-political Pollyannism that "Behind all this some great happiness is hiding." The proper languages for Memorial Day in Israel, the same poem tells us, are "Hebrew, Arabic and Death."

Many of the best poems in "Amen" have to do with the joys and disasters of love. The themes of sexual power gone awry and of lost relationships and broken marriage darken the book with a bitterness matching its pain at all the death and suffering in Israel's wars, so much so that the two sets of feeling merge inseparably. The very curious poem "Harlem, a Dead Story"—which I dare not discuss because it would take us into convolutions of sensuality, thoughts of the Holocaust and personal desolation that would burst the limits of a brief review—is only one instance. Hardness, and even nastiness, mingle with poignancy in a number of Catullan mixtures—"A Dog After Love," for example:

> After you left me
> I let a dog smell at
> My chest and my belly. It will fill its nose
> And set out to find you.
> I hope it will tear the
> Testicles of your lover and bite off his penis
> Or at least
> Will bring me your stockings between his teeth.

I have by no means touched on the whole range of tones and preoccupations, and particularly the subtler modulations and musics, in "Amen." One sees everywhere in the book an absorbed spirit that contemplates the world not to explain things but to get into focus the subjective and emotional ambiance of whatever is remembered or experienced. The position is expressed, a bit more cheerily than usual, in "Sometimes I'm Very Happy and Desperate":

> Sometimes I'm very happy and desperate,
> Then I'm stuck deeply
> in the fleece
> of the world-sheep
> like a tick
> I'm happy so.

This is a harshly lovely, exhilarating, depressing book. It proves once more that when the real thing comes along the chic critical passwords—"post-modernism," "anti-poetic." etc.—are useless. Amichai has for the most part done a fine job of translating his work into English that is idiomatically alive and suggestive. I wish, though, that Ted Hughes, who helped him, had given him more help or encouraged someone else to do so. Sometimes the phrasing goes badly awkward or unnecessarily ambiguous or the rhythm or sound becomes impossible. But the successes are admirably frequent.

The New York Times Book Review (3 July 1977)

❧

Modern British and American Poetic Sequences

WE are faced with a remarkable and curious phenomenon. My subject is the modern poetic sequence in Britain and the United States over the past few decades. But I cannot take the obvious for granted. I cannot assume general knowledge of the nature or importance of this genre, which is nothing less than the outstanding formal development in our poetry for over a century. Examples abound—I despair of being able to touch on enough of them in so short a space. A litany of outstanding poets since Whitman will show that most have been makers of sequences. This form of the long poem—intimate fragmented, self-analytical, open, emotionally volatile—meets the needs of modern sensibility, even when the poet aspires to tragic scope. Yet because of the stultifying critical and scholarly situation, it remains one of those fine things that need much laboring but are largely ignored by our supposed theorists.

The modern sequence is a grouping of mainly lyric poems and passages, rarely uniform in pattern, tending to interact as an organic whole. It usually includes narrative and dramatic elements, and ratiocinative ones as well; but its ordering is finally lyrical, a succession of *affects*—that is, of units of phrasing that generate specific intensities of feeling and awareness. Because of these separate radiating centers, the sequence meets Poe's significantly modern objection to the idea of a long poem: namely, that it is impossible because of the limited duration of any one surge of emotional energy.

The sequence is openly improvisational and tentative in structure—a condition, in fact, of all art, but often papered over by the conventions of set forms. From this standpoint, every successful long work of the past is, after all, a sequence beneath its surface continuity and uniformity. Tennyson's superb *Maud: A Monodrama* is a clear example. Its hero's psychic state gives the poet his excuse to juxtapose varied states of naked feeling, with minimal need to justify the emotional dynamics that are the work's real movement. We have earlier prototypes, such as Blake's *Song of Innocence and Experience*, in which, moreover, the varied arrangements foreshadow the open structuring of many later sequences. Closer to us, some of Emily Dickinson's fascicles may well be experimental models of sequences, for in them she groups poems within a float of reciprocal emotional states and gives them direction through her mercilessly precise insights and her search for realistic transcendence. A related consideration is that any volume of poems, if it somehow involves a single impulse of realization, may be a sequence.

The characteristic speaking voice of a sequence operates under pressure. Sometimes the speaker is *in extremis;* more often, he or she is oppressed by what Delmore Schwartz called "the burden of consciousness"—locked in Laocoön-like struggle with a moribund yet murderous civilization. Seeking to objectify itself, the speaking sensibility calls up sunken dimensions of its consciousness from the depths, moving through confusions and ambiguities toward a precarious balance. The process is cultural as much as psychological. It involves the feeling of obsolescence, the need to recover one's identifying past. The heroic or epic aspect of the sequence lies in the protagonist's effort to pit personal, historical, and artistic memory and vision against anomie or alienation. In short, the modern sequence has evolved out of a serious need for an encompassing poetry, one really involved with what our lives mean and at the same time self-contained—a poetry that projects and reorients our consciousness in action. That need reflects the ultimate pressure on modern sensibility to understand itself and the importance of regaining what Charles Olson called the "human universe." The pressure is felt inescapably by poets even when they hardly realize why they write as they do.

There is, as a result, a pervasive politics of altered consciousness in the modern sequence. We find it strikingly in American works as diverse as those by William Carlos Williams, Charles Olson, Robert Lowell, Robert Duncan, Muriel Rukeyser, Galway Kinnell, and Imamu Amiri Baraka. (I am thinking of post-World War II sequences, but we find it as well in the earlier examples.) It is the politics of shared awareness and urgency; and the world of the sequence is one of adult intelligence and candor, of a truthfulness about oneself and one's views that need not be forced, because it is simply a condition of existence. All the issues of empirical politics—war and peace, sexual and racial repression, ecology, atomic energy—seem to enter these sequences naturally, as part of their awareness, just as they do in one's intimate personal relationships. So we find Muriel Rukeyser, in "Waterlily Fire," seeing profound, necessary correlations between her own private disastrous experiences and two public ones: a fire at the Museum of Modern Art endangering some famous Monet paintings and the rise of war mentality in the United States. Galway Kinnell's *The Book of Nightmares* relates personal crises to the Vietnam war and to every kind of social carelessness about the fate of suffering people. Adrienne Rich's "The Phenomenology of Anger" so conflates the political and the personal that each is a function of the other.

I do not want to labor this one point, however. Its extraordinary significance in the detailed working-out of sequences would require many pages of examination. I will just add that political awareness, experientially rather than just ideologically conceived, is consciousness of one's present moment as a focal point of history—that is, of the living context of one's sensibility. American awareness of this sort has relatively more to do with general social realities as they impinge on the individual, while British and Irish political awareness is more often charged with regional concerns and memories. This is not, obviously, an absolute distinction, and anyone can think of exceptions. But it has something to do with transatlantic differences in the sequence.

American sequences often strain to include more elements than they can handle. They run the risk of losing themselves in introspective voyages that can become self-indulgent mumbling when they lose sight of objective points of reference or of any sense of style. Perhaps this is the reason some of our poets have been allowing themselves to arrange their sequences simply in order of composition, marking off the sections by the dates on which they were written—a sort of wind-harp way of admitting all the materials trying to crowd their way in. But what I am saying may easily be an overstatement, to be corrected by attention to the actual affective structure of individual works. In any case, the British and Irish sequences are on the whole less sprawling than ours, more reminiscent of Yeats though pretty much stripped of his high rhetoric. An apt instance, and a model of the kind of sequence whose germinative center is a crisis in the life of the narrator, is Austin Clarke's "Mnemosyne Lay in Dust," written in the third person but based on Clarke's own experience of hysterical amnesia. Protagonist and speaker share the intimate subjectivity of this poem: its quick shifts of focus among hospital scenes, suddenly relived childhood memories, hallucinatory and dream passages that release free association in their sexual aspect especially, notes of pure evocation or pure horror, and depressed close-ups of modern Dublin. Despite all the changing perspectives, and partly because of his technical virtuosity, Clarke keeps a tight rein on the varied forms he deploys and on the whole movement of his sequence.

Compare Clarke's work, only a step away from *Maud: A Monodrama*, with two brilliant American works whose protagonists are in even more critical situations: Ezra Pound's *Pisan Cantos* and Ramon Guthrie's *Maximum Security Ward*. Both are composed on complex scales. Each has a wider range of voices than Clarke's, a more demanding dynamics of varied tones and intensities, and many more facets—whole sets of allusions and cultural layerings. At one point in Canto 74, for instance, in the brief passage beginning "A Ventadour," Pound swiftly alludes to a number of French places, persons, and associations. He has remembered them in a surge of nostalgia: "we will see those old roads again, question, / possibly / but nothing appears much less likely." Brought low and humiliated, under arrest for treason, he has as his only riches his memory and his imagination, both of which provide vast drifts of thought—whole worlds present in his mind—free of the prison camp's confines. In Guthrie's sequence the poet, dying of cancer, is confined in a hospital, where memories comparable to Pound's assail him. Also, as with Pound, Guthrie's allusions often suggest alternative personae and existences to his own, possibilities lived out, say, by a Robert Desnos or a Rimbaud, or already explored by Proust. Obviously, the orchestration of such elements involves greater risks of overloading and losing direction in a wilderness of mirrors than most poetry of the British Isles has dared attempt.

No invidious comparison is intended. We are dealing with the most advanced poets on both sides of the ocean, well aware of each other's art and of their relation to one another. There are, for instance, "American" aspects to Basil Bunting's *Briggflatts: An Autobiography*, but it has a certain British self-containment nevertheless. This exquisitely modulated work begins pastorally with a lovely fantasy of "sweet tenor bull" dancing. Quickly, however, it introduces Hardyesque notes of fatality and then memories of young love and working-class life that the protagonist feels he has abandoned and betrayed. A mood of cultural despair invades the sequence, especially in Part 3, a Poundian hell-canto. The mood is subdued but not resolved in the mature perspective of the rest of the sequence.

Most sequences link reaction against capitalistic culture with insistence on primal values: an atavistic feeling for place and for the older, fully involved folk-cultures. Bunting sets Northumbrian historical memory and speech against the oppression of "southron," London-based customs. *Briggflatts* is one expression among many of the shallowly buried nationalisms always flaring back to separatist life in long-conquered European regions. We can easily see its kinship with the localism in American works like William Carlos Williams' *Paterson* and Charles Olson's *The Maximus Poems*. All these sequences, as I have suggested, pursue the continuing, ingrained realities of common experience, the people's and the protagonist's underlying history and identity.

David Jones's *Anathemata* tries to run all the cultural layers of British history together in one rich gathering symbolically concentrated, in part at least, in Jones's own family history and in his particular linguistic interests. A relative lack of intensity, however, together with a sometimes coyly riddling style and a complacent religious tendentiousness, makes this work blander than it should be. By contrast, the nervous inwardness of Thomas Kinsella's sequences, especially his deep diving into the world of his childhood and into family memory in *Notes from the Land of the Dead*, makes for a disturbing mental voyage into a private, unpretentious, yet tragic and sometimes monstrous Irish world. Kinsella's uneasy self-probing is interestingly reciprocal to John Montague's *The Rough Field*, an extended recovery of Catholic Ulster by one whose boyhood memories are tempered by his knowledge of the outside world. The blood and violence of Ulster history have their intimate counterpart in the narrator's own family; and the imposition on the people of an alien language and culture, imaged in the figure of "a severed head with a grafted tongue," has its reflex in the narrator's stammer and his other problems. *The Rough Field*, a montage of documentary materials, old songs, and a wide range of emotional and dramatic moments, comes closer to the American sequence than do most other British and Irish works. Its major rival in this respect is doubtless Ted Hughes's *Crow*, a rather overloaded but highly original projection, by way of mythopoeic fantasy, of the void awaiting us should the whole humanistic tradition be brought down. *Crow* moves in blocks of poems through many phases—gross violence, grotesque hilarity, surprising tenderness mixed with fear.

But I cannot describe all these sequences here. I can only mention them and try to insist on their primary importance. It is unfortunate that our criticism should have become so abstracted that a whole major genre could evolve, mature, and metamorphose without even being noticed. The sequence seems to have heaved itself into being and to have been cultivated half-consciously by poets who have felt their way along—fortunately perhaps?—without benefit of any school but one another's work.

Contemporary Literature (Summer 1977)

❧

Zukofsky: "All My Hushed Sources"

A good deal of nonsense has been written about Zukofsky—that is, since people began writing about him at all. You won't find him mentioned in early books on modern American poetry like Kreymborg's *Our Singing Strength* (1929) and the Gregories' *A History of American Poetry 1900–1940* (1946), or in Millett's *Contemporary American Authors* (1943). The most intelligent comments remain those by William Carlos Williams, appended to the 1959 edition of "A" *1–12*. They are intelligent because Williams sweetly respects Zukofsky's talents and interests without exaggerating his accomplishment. "There was always a part of this poet which would not blend. . . . I for one was baffled by him. I often did not know what he was driving at."

Williams speaks with deferential interest of Zukofsky's involvement with musical structure, of parallels between his work and the *Cantos*, of his careful, "meticulous" art, of his intellectuality, and of the Jewish dimension of his writing. But the sense of bafflement is pervasive: "The concentration and breaks in the language didn't add anything to my ease in the interpretation of the meaning." Also, "an obscure music, at least to me obscure, related to the music of . . . Bach, has dominated the poet's mind, beliefs, and emotions." Yet Williams can also say: "It is amazing how clean and effective Zukofsky has kept his composition . . . [he is] a poet devoted to working out by the intelligence the intricacies of his craft; he is imbedded in a matrix of his art and the multiple addictions which govern him, make him, of this time."

These apparently self-contradictory observations pretty much sum up the situation. As a fellow poet with certain affinities, Williams could appreciate the tonal delicacy and attenuated music of many passages in Zukofsky. He saw him, too, as sharing his own relationship with imagism; that is, the movement had had a necessary impact, inseparable from the Pound connection, without making either of them a complete imagist. Williams, the more robustly vivid and emotionally direct of the two poets, nevertheless sympathized with Zukofsky's kindred effort to deploy a precise, subtly associational poetic speech, weighted melodically. Subtlety can sometimes produce warping, however, and Williams was too honest and too normally human to pretend to love the extended monologues, full of tangential and muted rhetoric and going on forever in pretty much the same tone, that Zukofsky often indulged in. That is, Williams found Zukofsky's mentality and methods more interesting than his poetry, but distrusted his own instinctive reaction.

In the world of grown-up poets and critics one can feel this way and say so and be showing genuine regard at the same time. Williams' essay sustains Zukofsky's reputation as the unqualified praise of some of the Black Mountain poets, who have borrowed his mannerisms, does not. The play with grammatical ambiguity, the introduction of highly private references, the identification as essential poetic process of one's own halting movement into clarification of emotion and perception, and the extreme academicism of a poetry larded with literary puns and allusions—all these provide poetic opportunities and obvious pitfalls of preciosity at the same time. The most damaging instance of the latter that Zukofsky provides comes in his Catullus "translations." Robert Creeley's introduction to the 1967 edition of *"A" 1–12* suggests—if I understand the opaque prose correctly—that Zukofsky has caught a special music in these translations. Creeley has at this point been quoting, without commentary, a passage to illustrate the musical character—that is, the intimate music of poetic composition in action—of Zukofsky's method. He introduces the Catullus reference as a further instance.

> Thus to *hear*, as he would hear Catullus, in the translation he has made with his wife—"fact that delights as living hint and its cues" being "facit delicias libidinesque"—"which is much more simple in the Latin. It has to do with pleasures and desires. . . ."

Creeley has a little trick, throughout his introduction, of suggesting a commitment to admiration of Zukofsky while in practice quoting him almost all the time and avoiding clear statements of his own—as in the odd sentences just cited. But I think it is necessary to point out that the Catullus "translation" is merely spiritless bilingual punning. Anyone can do it who sets himself the task of doggedly transliterating from one language into another, wringing words out of the sounds of the original that make a certain strained sense. The passion, the wit, the art of the original are replaced by a display of low-level ingenuity, just as when some verbose wag breaks up serious conversation by turning everything other people say into material for puns and jokes. The inner music of Zukofsky's method was not always worth hearing. Take for another sad example, two candidates for the worst lines of verse ever written: the opening lines of his serious poem "Peri Poietikes":

> What about measure, I learnt:
> *Look in your own ear and read.*

But. The other side of Zukofsky was the true poet. I shall risk the wrath of those who think that to have an ear is a positive hindrance to poets and their readers (unless the ear be a purely visual object), and shall cite a lovely early poem:

> Not much more than being,
> Thoughts of isolate, beautiful
> Being at evening, to expect
> at a river-front:
>
> A shaft dims
> With a turning wheel;
>
> Men work on a jetty
> By a broken wagon;

Leopard, glowing-spotted,
    The summer river—
Under: The Dragon:

Like Williams, and not—a shared mode of sensibility, but with a modulation toward philosophical reverie that arrives like a glow of insight, finds the quiet particulars out of which it emerged, and then notices more encompassing instances as well, remaining open and entranced throughout. "Not much more than being" finds an echo over thirty years later in the more active "The Ways," whose movement is similarly widening and whose absorption is similarly keen but which introduces an altered idiom in its second half (not unlike the closing stanza of the earlier piece in its shift of emphasis but much more freely handled):

The wakes that boats make
and after they are out of sight
the ways they have made in water:
loops, straight paths,
to do with mirror-like,
tides, the clouds the deep day blue
of the unclouded parts of the sky,
currents, gray sevens or darker shadows
against lighter in and out weaving
of mercurial vanishing eights,
or imaginably sights
instantaneously a duration and sun,
and the leaping silver
as of rain-pelted nipples
of the water itself.

After reading, a song

a light snow
a had been fallen

the brown most showed
knoll trunk knot treelings' U's

The Sound marsh water

ice clump
sparkling root etc

and so far out.

The contradiction between beautiful Z and tiresome Z is simply a given of the man's artistic life, of interest mainly because of the continuum between the extremes we have been observing. A fair amount of the work falls somewhere between Z^b and Z^t; that is, it has elements of both. One might suggest a curious doubleness related to a confusion of traditions, a possible result of Zukofsky's immigrant family background and of Jewish traditions of the display of cleverness and subtlety for their own sakes. An infatuation with thought-process (apart from its aims and content), with the tone of linguistic ingenuity (apart from whether the play of speech is sparkling or not, penetrating or not, pointed or simply continuous), and with the pleasures of just feeling intelligent because one is articulating something keeps Zukofsky going as a kind of secular talmudist even when the poet is fast asleep. (Samuel Greenberg, although much less developed than Zukofsky, seems to have had the same verbal proliferativeness.) The influence of Pound's allusiveness and constant show of learning must have fed this side of Zukofsky's intellectual personality. But Pound's psychopathology—his projection of the role of hero-leader and visionary summoning a civilization to its salvation—was not Zukofsky's. It could not convert the younger man's complex of thought into poetry of power. Many of the poems, including the innumerable personal messages and valentines in verse, are coy exhibitions, counting heavily on the recipient's affection for their acceptance.

Yet the poetry is full of strong political interest and specifically Jewish memories and preoccupations. Here we are not speaking of cultural nuances but of the most familiar kind of alienation—and struggle for recognition—and superimposed on that the equally familiar and natural reaction to the outrages of the Nazis. Zukofsky was in his early 20's when Pound accepted his "Poem beginning 'The'" for *Exile*. Heavily saturated with *Mauberley, The Waste Land,* and *Ulysses* (and associated works and authors, including Vachel Lindsay and Virginia Woolf), the poem showed revolutionary sympathies and the poet's conflict between being a "Jewish boy" and his need to depart from home ties and give himself up to mastery of the dominant literary culture. The young man's self-consciousness and hostility are striking, especially in the section called "*FIFTH MOVEMENT: Autobiography*":

> Assimilation is not hard,
> And once the Faith's askew
> I might as well look Shagetz just as much as Jew.
> I'll read their Donne as mine,
> And leopard in their spots
> I'll do what says their Coleridge,
> Twist red hot pokers into knots.
> The villainy they teach me I will execute
> And it shall go hard with them,
> For I'll better their instruction,
> Having learned, so to speak, in their colleges.
>   It is engendered in the eyes
>   With gazing fed, and fancy dies
>   In the cradle where it lies . . .

The notes from *Hamlet* and *The Merchant of Venice* suggest self-irony toward the speaker's own feelings. Elsewhere in this most indicative poem we find an apparently hostile reference to Mussolini and a sentimental address to the speaker's mother, alluding to her childhood in Russia and recalling (and distorting) a Yiddish folksong:

Speaking about epics, mother,
How long is it since you gathered mushrooms,
Gathered mushrooms while you mayed.
It is your mate, my father, boating.
A stove burns like a full moon in a desert night.
Un in hoyze is kalt. You think of a new grave,
In the fields, flowers.
Night on the bladed grass, bayonets dewed.
It is your mate, my father, boating.
Speaking about epics, mother,—
Down here among the gastanks, ruts, cemetery-tenements—
It is your Russia that is free.

We find echoes and developments of these deeply felt motifs in a number of Zukofsky's later works, among them "A Song for the Year's End," "Song of Degrees: 3," "The Old Poet Moves to a New Apartment 14 Times: 10," passages in the "A" sequence, and "Anew: 14." The motifs—strong emotional currents, rather—surface very effectively at times and yet are never fully explored or resolved. They are not *assimilated*, either psychologically or artistically, and seem at odds both with the weaker rhetorical stretches in Zukofsky and with the gentler intensities of his most successful writing. Somehow the touching manifesto of the clever and boisterous boy who speaks in "Poem beginning 'The'" has been carried through at the level of a word-game rather than of the most highly realized art. The poem "Anew: 42," written in his early 50's, reveals to a rare degree Zukofsky's potential power but also his innate secretiveness of manner and ultimate inability to mobilize his efforts into an original poem of tragic force. It is a poem that starts out with an intriguing combination of Dantean and colloquial idioms, grave and compelling despite some lapses, and passionately cumulative in its charge. Later, it somehow slips into the idiom of Marianne Moore, gaining a certain wry humor and personal appeal but losing its true affect in the process. At its height the poem promises:

like the devil in the book of *Job*

Having come back from going to and fro in the earth
I will give the world all my hushed sources
In this poem, (maybe the world wanted them)

I will be so frank everyone
Will be sure I am hiding—a maniac—
And no one will speak to me.

And the poet mocks his own cleverness, his tendency to be one of Job's comforters rather than a Job (let alone "the devil"!), to clear the way for something finer and greater:

(I am, after all, of the people whose wisdom
May die with them)

In the wake of the Holocaust, the double thrust of these lines is irresistible.

But moving as the inner pressure is in "Anew," and pure-spirited and clear as its conclusion is, the poem remains but a promise to develop what it has begun. The "hushed sources" remain so. A fierce energy of pathos, engaging our affection but never resolved, is the most advanced point of arousal in Zukofsky's most serious vein. Yet notes of genius remain notes of genius, even if unresolved. Zukofsky's poems are full of love and need, reverberating perceptions and keen awareness of their own process, and idiosyncratic formations that compel us although they often lose us at last.

Louis Zukofsky: Man and Poet, ed. Carroll F. Terrell
(Orono, Maine: The National Poetry Foundation, 1979)

❧

Intimate and Alien

SELECTED POEMS 1950–75 by Thom Gunn

TWO decades ago Thom Gunn and Ted Hughes were generally considered outstanding among the English poets just entering their thirties. They were beginning to write the harder, passionately concentrated, artistically alive verse that Britain sorely needed. Their names were so closely associated that in 1962 Faber and Faber brought out a joint volume of their selected work.

But in truth they were unalike. Mr. Gunn never grew vampire teeth the way Ted Hughes did in his boldly grotesque, increasingly sensational poems. He was not after sensational violence, even in his poems about California killers and motorcycle gangs, storm troopers, wolf-boys and murderously jealous lovers. Those poems were few and far between; besides, he has always kept his philosophical distance—though keeping his distance while sidling toward disaster may be the underlying psychic pressure in his writing. We can feel it in the very youthful "Wind in the Street," with its refrain: "I may return, meanwhile I'll look elsewhere," and in the desolately impressive "My Sad Captains." A stanza from his best-known poem, "On the Move," will show how even in his twenties Mr. Gunn recognized the fascination of the brutal yet managed to hold it off:

On motorcycles, up the road, they come:
Small, black, as flies hanging in heat, the Boys,
Until the distance throws them forth, their hum
Bulges to thunder held by calf and thigh.
In goggles, donned impersonality,
In gleaming jackets trophied with the dust,

They strap in doubt—by hiding it, robust—
And almost hear a meaning in their noise.

The poem lapses into abstractions that muffle the pounding heartbeat of these excited lines. Yet the stanza is serious journeywork, beyond the apprentice level of what follows it. The rhyming couplets and delayed rhymes—especially the one connecting the second and final lines—help create its ironic and pitying clarity. It echoes Pope and Eliot, no question, but uses effects learned from those masters to convey a genuine, complex impact. Never merely imitative, Mr. Gunn has developed his craft so that by now even his freest compositions have a disciplined music.

In his quietly intense way, he seems a more involuted modern sensibility than Ted Hughes or Philip Larkin. He has neither the cruel fantasy of the one nor the flat anti-romantic wit of the other, though a kind of wryly alienated, sometimes almost furtive tone suggests a certain double kinship. He is unusual among English poets in allowing himself to reveal vulnerability. Without self-pity, and often hesitantly inward, he implies a half-reluctant, all but passive fascination with the unknown and the forbidden. We can follow its progress through the years, from the wavering "Wind in the Street" through the astringent "A Map of the City" (in which private and social "malady" is linked with "endless potentiality" and "my love of chance") to the disillusioned yet persistent "The Idea of Trust." These poems, especially the third, reflect a peculiarly contemporary habit of mind: the hope that one throw of the dice can redeem *something*, make room for significant experience, no matter how depressive the general terms of life.

And yet Mr. Gunn is not lugubrious. His best work is exploratory in a courageously candid way. In it the heavy youthful pondering has been drained off in some unpublished draft; a precise evocation of inner awareness remains. In "Touch" a lover enters the dream-world and sensuous darkness of his sleeping beloved. In "Bringing to Light," lost moments, among them the repressed sources of sexual guilt, are startlingly retrieved in reverie. In "Moly" and the group of poems that follow, the bestial and the human in ourselves are seen struggling to engulf one another; the agony is projected in allegorical symbols borrowed from the *Odyssey* but suggestive of drug-induced hallucinatory states.

In many of Mr. Gunn's poems, introspection rises to a sort of surrealistic, terrified pitch reminiscent of the work of Sylvia Plath and Ramon Guthrie. Reading "For Signs," I could not help thinking of Mr. Guthrie's exquisite, eerie "Homage to Paul Delvaux (1897–)":

Death in temporary form
of Paul Delvaux's discreetly pubic girls
bedmates of gone goddesses walking in gardens of
undeflowered music and undeciphered roses
while waiting for their mutual dream to bring about
eclipses of the moon

And here is Thom Gunn:

> I dream: the real is shattered and combined,
> Until the moon comes back into that sign
> It stood in at my birth hour; and I pass
> Back to the field where, statued in the shine,
> Someone is gazing upward from the grass
> As if toward vaults that honeycomb the mind.

At the same time, Mr. Gunn can be very humanly direct, as in the plain-spoken monologue called "Sparrow." He can also combine richness, subtlety and forthright compassion, as in the remarkably orchestrated "In Santa Maria del Popolo." Here esthetic and sacred vision, slowly unfolding in a dark painting seen in difficult, changing conditions of light, comes painfully into view.

> I see how shadow in the painting brims
> With a real shadow, drowning all shapes out
> But a dim horse's haunch and various limbs,
> Until the very subject is in doubt.
>
> But evening gives the act, beneath the horse
> And one indifferent groom, I see him sprawl,
> Foreshortened from the head, with hidden face,
> Where he has fallen, Saul becoming Paul.

In the same church poor women, "each head closeted/In tiny fists," pray for the miracle that artist and saint (Caravaggio and Paul) have not yet brought to them after all. The vision won through to at such cost remains elusive even at the moment of triumph—and not for the visionary alone, but for mankind in general, longing for revelation. As Mr. Gunn writes in another, very recent poem, "The Outdoor Concert":

> At the edge
> of the understanding:
>   it's the secret.
>
> You recognize not
> the content of it but
> the fact that it is
> there to be recognized.

It is fortunate that American readers now have a single volume of Thom Gunn's selected poems. With their undemonstrative virtuosity, their slightly corrupt openness, their atmosphere of unfathomable secrets and their intimacy, so like that of a reticent friend who has something crucial to confess, these poems strike a chord at once insinuatingly familiar and infinitely alien.

The New York Times Book Review (20 January 1980)

Landscape with Figures

POEMS 1956–1973 by Thomas Kinsella
PEPPERCANISTER POEMS 1972–1978 by Thomas Kinsella

OURS is more than ever a poetry of the recapture of lost worlds—a nation's or a region's deep history, the buried memories of families, the primal impressions of early childhood. A poet like the Irishman Thomas Kinsella, who engages these worlds ably and bravely, can reach past surface charm and nostalgia to discovery. He is coping with the intractable, with what he calls in "Ritual of Departure"

> Landscape with ancestral figures . . . names
> Settling and intermixing on the earth,
> The seed in slow retreat, through time and blood,
> Into bestial silence.
> Faces sharpen and grow blank,
> With eyes for nothing . . .

Mr. Kinsella is a true elegist with a bitter, grieving, melodious tongue. Now that he has assembled his poetry in two volumes, Americans will have ready access for the first time to the whole range of his work since 1956 (including his superb translation of the Cuchulain saga, *The Táin*). It is a great deal to try to absorb at once. The rich elegiac strain and the painful note of reminiscence involve extremes of tonality: subtle wit, easy humor, flat candor, bursts of visionary transport, burning anger, speculative openness—all deployed in a mature exploratory poetry.

Mr. Kinsella's most powerful poems tend to open quietly, perhaps humorously, in the midst of reverie or of a familiar situation, and then to unfold through "natural" modulations. The very recent "His Father's Hands" (in *Peppercanister Poems*, which contains Mr. Kinsella's "occasional poems" of 1972–73, together with his major poetry since then) begins with a close-up of the poet and his father drinking and arguing, their gestures comically intimate: "I drank firmly/ and set the glass down between us firmly," while "His finger prodded and prodded,/ marring his point."

A quick association recalls the childhood memory of the poet's grandfather, a cobbler, pressing tobacco into his pipe and cutting new leather; the details culminate in a nostalgic, vivid repossession. Suddenly we are with the grandfather, now very old, playing the fiddle with "his bow hand scarcely moving" and "whispering with the tune." The poem breaks into song, combining the words of an old ballad with the poet's interpolations:

with breaking heart
whene'er I hear
in privacy, across a blocked void,

the wind that shakes the barley . . .

A sweet yet piercing rapport across the generations has been evoked, and next we hear the grandfather's voice telling the boy something about family history: "Your family, Thomas, met with and helped/ many of the Croppies in hiding from the Yeos. . . ." It is, as it were, the personal history of Ireland's common people—the battles, the escapes, the hangings, the migrations, the available occupations and trades. At the end of the poem an impersonal, terrified vision of a menacing landscape and an evil history gives a hard, dark gleam to the language, which casts an ironic and tragic mood over the final references to the grandfather's "blocked gentleness" and the child's memories.

"His Father's Hands" is only part of a complex sequence entitled "One," a nightmarish plunge into the "ghost companionship" of past worlds; but it does touch on most of Mr. Kinsella's preoccupations and may incidentally serve as an introduction to his work. Readers approaching this poet for the first time are advised to begin with "Ancestor," "A Hand of Solo" and "Tear," which fuse intense revulsion and love in a precise rendering of childhood; and "Traveller," "First Light," and the sixth and seventh poems of "A Technical Supplement" (in *Peppercanister Poems*) for the emotional shocks they register. The demanding marriage-sequence, "Wormwood," embodies an agonized emotional struggle that is won by sheer moral and human endurance—intelligence in action.

No one could be more Irish than Thomas Kinsella. Witness the rough-hewn, deliberately populist dream-visionary poem "Butcher's Dozen," on the shooting down of thirteen demonstrators in Derry by British troops; or the relatively early "A Country Walk," a pitiless account of the depredations wreaked on modern Dublin, and the implied betrayal of republican ideals; or the portrayal of his father's experiences as a political organizer in the first labor struggles against Guinness. Yet there is nothing parochial about his work. At fifty-one, he is among the true poets, not only of Ireland but among all who write in English in our day.

The New York Times Book Review (24 February 1980)

❧

Streams of Tonality in Bunting's Briggflatts

BRIGGFLATTS came to us in Ezra's long wake, a gathering of Basil Bunting's finest possibilities after what seemed a long poetic slumber. The affinities and derivations are clear. *Briggflatts* even has its hell-canto: Part III, with the requisite scatological smell. In general, the sequence presents the usual Poundian mixture of tonalities that has influenced so many other works as well—the affirmations amidst bitter alienation, the rhetorical fulminations against the evils of modern urban culture, the moments of sharpest observation or dancing fantasy or passionate memory, the flash of ironic or exalted insight connecting the real or mythical past with the present instant, and the devout aestheticism that yet does not blur an essential harsh clarity and even fatalism about life as it is.

Bunting has neither the master's scope and copiousness nor his powerful originality. Yet within the Poundian shell he has made a small, pure creation of his own: a living stream of verse that makes its way from beginning to end, disappearing from sight at times when the urge to bluster and convince takes over or the voices of other poets (not only Pound but a chorus of others from Tennyson to Austin Clarke and Auden) create a kind of static. Or one should say, rather, that certain streams of tonality combine to form an essentially elegiac poem compounded of lyrically celebratory elements and tormenting personal memories of young love and the hard but wholesome life of artisans—memories betrayed by the poet's abandonment of the provincial world of his youth. This is the world of Northumbria and its Anglo-Saxon past, evoked by direct historical reference and by the recurrent use of a starkly alliterative, compressed line. The evocation of a more primitive native culture, with its axe-swinging warriors, earthy basic language, and immersion in raw contact with resistant nature, is a parallel stream of tonality intermingling with the others. It contributes an insistent melancholy to the sequence and reinforces the idealized memory of the stonemason at the center of the poet's nostalgia for his youthful past. The stonemason's materials and cutting skills were exercised against the same resistant nature with which ancient folk contended. To have left his tutelage, and the love of his daughter, is identified with turning one's back on the life and language and history of the region.

Part I of *Briggflatts* is the heart of the sequence and its most fully successful section. Its dozen thirteen-line stanzas, each ending in a rhyming couplet, combine Anglo-Saxon with modern versification in flexible units allowing for complex development and for many shifts of feeling and intensity. The exquisite opening stanza is at once sheer song, charming comedy, and ominous vision; it is saturated with a sense of local place and with the mixture of elated spirits and near-lugubriousness characteristic of the whole work:

Brag, sweet tenor bull,
descant on Rawthey's madrigal,
each pebble its part
for the fells' late spring.
Dance tiptoe, bull,
black against may.
Ridiculous and lovely
chase hurdling shadows
morning into noon.
May on the bull's hide
and through the dale
furrows fill with may,
paving the slowworm's way.

The familiar linking of vital sexuality with the death-principle is implicit here, but held at a distance by the sheer delightful buffoonery of the first half of the stanza. We have been charmed into the dominant tonal realm of the sequence, where currents of buoyancy and power and decay and fatality constantly flow together in varying proportions. Then, in the second stanza, the mingling of opposites (spring and fertility, intractable reality and death) continues in a grimmer key; notice how much more emphatic the final couplet is here:

A mason times his mallet
to a lark's twitter,
listening while the marble rests,
lays his rule
at a letter's edge,
fingertips checking,
till the stone spells a name
naming none,
a man abolished.
Painful lark, labouring to rise!
The solemn mallet says:
In the grave's slot
he lies. We rot.

The middle stanzas (5–9) of this opening poem center on the very young (pubescent?) lovers. The fifth stanza, especially, evokes the homespun passion and magic of that remembered time, placing it within its context of a world of hardworking folk whose speech and history are vividly related to their everyday life. We see the "children" in their astringent Eden, lying together in the horse-drawn lorry the mason uses to fetch marble for his trade:

Stocking to stocking, jersey to jersey,
head to a hard arm,
they kiss under the rain,
bruised by their marble bed.
In Garsdale, dawn;

at Hawes, tea from the can.
Rain stops, sacks
steam in the sun, they sit up.
Copper-wire moustache,
sea-reflecting eyes
and Baltic plainsong speech
declare: By such rocks
men killed Bloodaxe.

Apart from the key lyricism of the poem's opening lines, Bunting's great achievement in this first movement of *Briggflatts* is his recovery of a lost world of reality: its decisive sensuous detail, the body of its physical presence. Thus, two stanzas further on, the journeyers are home again.

Rain rinses the road,
the bull streams and laments.
Sour rye porridge from the hob
with cream and black tea,
meat, crust and crumb.
Her parents in bed
the children dry their clothes.
He has untied the tape
of her striped flannel drawers
before the range. Naked
on the pricked rag mat
his fingers comb
thatch of his manhood's home.

The nostalgia here may be too pungent, the baby-sexuality recalled may seem at once sentimental and a little brackish, but the atmosphere summoned up in this stanza and in the quotation preceding it has the authority of deeply significant memory. The authority is reinforced by the more impersonal memory imbedded in the older regional language throughout this section: "Their becks ring on limestone," "fellside bleat," "fog on fells"—and with it the heavy stresses and echoes of an ancient poetry. Neither the historical nor the impersonal past can be restored: "No hope of going back." Even the recovery in words alone is painfully difficult, like the mason's work: "It is easier to die than to remember." And yet the opening poem *has* remembered, in the face of a debilitating depression that rides almost every stanza and that controls the whole sequence except in certain limited respects.

The four remaining sections of *Briggflatts* cope with the work's prevailing depressive perspective in various ways. One way is the exaltation of disciplined workmanship with intractable materials: "No worn tool / whittles stone." The axe swung by fighting forebears, and their language that was a sharp, rock-splitting weapon in its own right, were tools for a different kind of stone-masonry. So the work presents a staunch ideal, although the imagery of cultural defeat is pervasive. In Part II, the inevitable defeat of the axe-wielders is presented in terms suggesting a cultural betrayal comparable to the Poundian view of the modern world:

Loaded with mail of linked lies,
what weapon can the king lift to fight
when chance-met enemies employ sly
sword and shoulder-piercing pike,
pressed into the mire,
trampled and hewn till a knife
—in whose hand?—severs tight
neck cords? Axe rusts . . .

In the same section, music and mythology are mobilized as sources of morale for the poem. The struggle of the defeated king in the lines just quoted finds a curious parallel in men's efforts to encompass natural process in the organic structures of music and the myth of Pasiphaë. The musical theme is developed in four subtly unfolding sexains that take us from a simple, pleasant equation—

Starfish, poinsettia on a half-tide crag,
a galliard by Byrd—

to the more complex, deliberately unattractive proposition that a

rat, grey, rummaging
behind the compost heap has daring
to thread, lithe and alert, Schoenberg's maze.

The mythical motif is introduced in the concluding, and climactic, stanza of the section. This stanza reinforces the impression created in Part I of the sequence that the most intense notes of affirmation in *Briggflatts* will have an almost pornographic glow of erotic transport. Now Part II ends with the lines on Pasiphaë—who, we are told,

heard the god-bull's feet
scattering sand,
breathed byre stink, yet stood
with expectant hand
to guide his seed to its soil;
nor did flesh flinch
distended by the brute
nor loaded spirit sink
till it had gloried in unlike creation.

Part II has a rather wandering movement. It begins with the language of utter desolation, in a familiar, even trite, poetic mode. The alienated poet walks through London's streets, disheartened by the same things that have disheartened Blake, Wordsworth, and Eliot before him. (One difference, however, is the sexual obsessiveness that colors his sense of, and participation in, metropolitan squalor.) Then the poem turns away from the city with its available "sluts" and consequent opportunities for the poet to grow "sick, self-maimed, self-hating." Suddenly a language of self-questioning is introduced that lifts the poem's sensibility out of the romantically autobiographical morass.

And suddenly, again, we are in the midst of a fantasy-voyage in cold northern seas, its context that of the Anglo-Saxon "Wanderer." The shift of poetic focus culminates in a fatalistic intoning endemic to such verse. And after this passage, once more abruptly and arbitrarily, we are borne toward the appealingly sensual south—escape to Italy and lush experience, with the language reminiscent of Browning's "The Englishman in Italy." This mood, too, alters. It is too easy and free for Anglo-Saxon conscience to bear, a desertion of the worlds of chisel and mallet and rime-cold sea and the ever-presence of deprivation and uneaseful death: "wind, sun, sea upbraid / justly an unconvinced deserter."

So Italy is left behind. With its "white marble stained like a urinal" and its innumerable teeming dead, it is no genuine salvation. The poem must return to the true ground of its being. It must face directly into the challenge, despite near-hopelessness and a sense of helpless corruption, of certain native realities: the region of one's birth and early life and inherited history, the cultivation of a somehow indigenous art despite cosmopolitan seductions, and the repossession, sweatily and experientially, of certain mythical events—a repossession like Ovid's but at greater risk because crucial personal commitment is at stake. The events (Pasiphaë and the bull) are conceived as projections of agonizing, probably destructive elementary choices entailing an oddly hardpressed ecstasy.

From here on the sequence strikes various balances in the long struggle with a profoundly depressive state. Part III is the "hell-canto" of *Briggflatts*, seeing modern man as reduced to dung-selling in the marketplace. Only the cleansing rhythms of nature can purge away the vision of sheer foulness that presides over this section. Parts IV and V, after the drop of III into the abyss of total revulsion, settle into something like release through acceptance of life's meanness and living within one's emotional means. Part IV finds sources of energy in the candor and death-preoccupation of Cymric poetry. The poet accepts poverty, a new and very earthy love, the plainest satisfactions, along with his irrevocable separation from the stonemason's world. Separation nevertheless breaks the heart permanently:

> Stars disperse. We too,
> further from neighbours
> now the year ages.

These lines, at the end of IV, make a transition to the very lyrical Part V, which in many ways approaches Part I in its formal character. There is no rhetoric to mar the melody of this movement, which begins with winter-images rather than the images of spring in the opening stanza of I. The sequence has returned home, finding sufficient calm and an entrancement with the winter landscape that together make for a special music of sheer perception, even when what is perceived is chill and barren:

> Light lifts from the water.
> Frost has put rowan down,
> a russet blotch of bracken

tousled about the trunk.
Bleached sky. Cirrus
reflects sun that has left
nothing to badger eyes.

Because it is in part a reprise of earlier sections, and because it also moves into a wider, cosmic frame of reference, Section V is slightly overextended. Otherwise, however, its precise conversion of feeling into a distanced, impersonal language of impressionistic nature-description is as effective as it is surprising at this critical point in the sequence. Bunting chose to end, not with a bang *or* a whimper, but with a straightforward yet elegantly controlled movement whose reverberations are at once joyous and cool until a few notes of loss and regret chime in at the very last. Of course, the "Coda" that follows plunges the work into the sea of primordial despondency again. So be it. Bunting's real reputation will surely hang on *Briggflatts*. It is his one masterpiece of affective balancing, despite the problems I have suggested.

Basil Bunting: Man and Poet, ed. Carroll F. Terrell
(Orono, Maine: The National Poetry Foundation, 1981)

❧

from *Poems by the Packet*

THE MANUSCRIPT BOOKS OF EMILY DICKINSON
edited by R. W. Franklin

EVERYONE knows the basic facts. The author of some 1,800 poems, Emily Dickinson reluctantly published only seven of them during her lifetime (1830–86). Although she sent hundreds of poems to friends, she was resolute in her belief that "Publication—is the Auction / Of the mind of Man," reducing the human spirit to "Disgrace of Price." But after her death her sister Lavinia found the great mass of manuscripts and persuaded Mabel Loomis Todd and Thomas Wentworth Higginson to begin editing and publishing them. Their first selected volume, *Poems by Emily Dickinson* (1890), was an instant success. Since then five additional collections, all containing startling numbers of new poems, have appeared. The culmination of the series was T. H. Johnson's three-volume variorum edition, *The Poems of Emily Dickinson* (1955), containing 1,775 poems, with manuscript variants, and a wealth of essential bibliographical information.

R. W. Franklin's facsimile edition of *The Manuscript Books of Emily Dickinson* has brought us one step closer to a full understanding of her *oeuvre*. Ever since the 1955 *Poems* appeared, its sheer copiousness has made it difficult for criticism to deal with readily—to discriminate among the poems, to discern any sort of development, and (especially) to reconcile the most forceful and passionate of the poems with the lesser work, arch or whimsical or naively thoughtful or pious. But the Johnson edition, without being organized accordingly, drew attention to the fact that, beginning in 1858, Emily Dickinson began to arrange all her poems in fascicles—folded sheets of paper which she stitched together and on which she wrote fair copies of separate groups of the poems, not necessarily in order of composition. Each fascicle contains between eleven and twenty-five poems and constitutes a separate poetic sequence; the ordering and interrelatedness of the poems have an organic structure similar to that of the *Song of Myself* or *The Waste Land* or one of Pound's groupings of cantos. By the end of 1864 the poet had put together forty of these fascicles, containing almost half of all her known manuscripts. Thereafter, she continued making fair copies on sheets containing one or more poems but no longer stitched the sheets together. By 1862, in fact, she had begun putting some of her poems on separate sheets only, which Franklin has grouped by "sets" that seem to go together on the basis of their dates of composition and of other evidence, such as the kind of paper the poet used.

The Franklin edition reproduces the manuscripts of the separate fascicles and sets, so that we can see how Dickinson wrote out her poems and indicated variant phrasings she was considering. A crucial decision by Dickinson's first editors—made almost unconsciously in their zeal to find poems they thought especially worthy of publication—was to untie the fascicles and select poems without regard to the poet's arrangement. Mrs. Todd kept a record of where the pieces came from, but over the years confusion arose, partly because the manuscripts were divided between two households and partly because the editing was done by so many unprofessional hands. For these reasons, and because Dickinson's groupings were not taken seriously, the Franklin edition is the first to present the poems as she arranged them, in her very clear hand, with all her idiosyncrasies of punctuation, capitalization and spelling, and with her tidy notations of possible alternative words and phrases revealed. We thus see Dickinson's major work just as she did before it began to be sold in the "Auction / Of the Mind of Man." (The text does not include the many poems written on stray scraps of paper of all sorts, especially in the later years.)

It is to be hoped that a reader's edition of the fascicles alone will now also be published. Reading these sequences and near-sequences will allow the poems to be grasped as integral parts of larger though manageable structures. Franklin's labours in rearranging the poems within each fascicle and in arranging the fascicles in chronological order (as well as correcting earlier probable mistakes in the placing of a number of poems in the wrong fascicles) have been indispensable. *The Manuscript Books* comes to us now as tangible proof of the importance of the fascicles for an understanding of Emily Dickinson's art. The "sets," deliberately left unstitched by the poet, contain important poems but are not structured sequences; we do not know what internal order, if any, she may have intended among the sheets that supposedly may be grouped together. But the fascicles have a great deal to teach us.

It is easy now, for instance, to discern the development from the relatively slighter pieces of Fascicle 1 (1858), with its mixture of whimsy and elegiac tones, through the confrontations in the interlocking Fascicles 15 and 16 (about 1862) that make up a powerful double sequence, to the mature balance of Fascicle 40 (1864), its Yeatsian notes and parallels with Mallarmé's *Un Coup de dés* and with any number of twentieth-century poems. We should note something else: the way that Dickinson absorbed the pressure of the Civil War into her unique idiom of chillingly impersonal (that is, un-Confessional) familiarity with pain, grief, and death. "Death", she had written in Fascicle 1, is "but our rapt attention / To Immortality." In the fascicle's most arresting poem, "The feet of people walking home" (21 in Johnson's edition), this became an appalled detachment, almost cheerful if we ignore the skull beneath the skin. All this is echoed in the final fascicle in poem 970:

Color—Caste—Denomination—
These—are Time's Affair—
Death's diviner Clarifying
Does not know they are—

As in sleep—All Hue forgotten—
Tenets—put behind—
Death's large—Democratic fingers
Rub away the Brand—

and again, more subtly and daringly in poem 971:

Robbed by Death—but that was easy—
To the failing Eye
I could hold the latest Glowing—
Robbed by Liberty

For her Jugular Defences—
This, too, I endured—
Hint of Glory—it afforded—
For the Brave Beloved—

Fraud of Distance—Fraud of Danger,
Fraud of Death—to Bear—
It is Bounty—to Suspense's
Vague Calamity—

Staking our entire Possession
On a Hair's result—
Then—Seesawing—coolly—on it—
Trying if it split—

In reproducing the fascicles in their proper order, Franklin has found it necessary to re-number them. Originally Mrs. Todd assigned arbitrary numbers to them for reasons of practical convenience, and this numbering was followed by Johnson and his associate, Theodora Ward, in their monumental enterprise of sorting out the texts and trying to place the poems in their proper contexts and chronological order. Franklin, of course, provides careful comparative lists showing precisely how he has altered the Todd-Johnson-Ward numbering. Their Fascicles 26 and 32, for instance, are now numbered 15 and 16; and nine poems that they placed at the end of 26 now come at the end of 14.

I mention this technicality because it is the clue to the significance of Franklin's dating of the fascicles and of his publication of them in the most accurate order determinable. Some years ago S. M. Gall pointed out to me the probable importance of the fascicles as artistic constructs, rather than as mere devices of a desperate orderliness. Other students of Dickinson, notably Ruth Miller in *The Poetry of Emily Dickinson*, have given thought to the fascicles and their ordering: Miller finds that each fascicle repeats a symbolic narrative in which a woman learns Christian acceptance and patience, and that Dickinson's work is deeply influenced by Francis Quarles's *Emblems, Divine and Moral*. But apart from the fact that one is hard put to trace the suggested symbolic development in the actual poems, they can hardly be reduced to a formula. Dickinson wrote, over a relatively short period of time, a large number of poems of high intensity. She arranged them into physically linked, open and exploratory structures that enabled her to give tentative order to the chaos of emotions with which the writing was seized, and in so doing became along with Whitman but unbeknown to either, his fellow-inventor of the modern lyrical sequence.

This becomes evident when the fascicles are examined as poetic rather than thematic structures. Using the numbering and classification worked out by Johnson and Ward, Gall and I found that Fascicles 26 and 32 seemed the most powerful and, in fact, *reciprocal* in the sense in which Yeats's "Meditations in Time of Civil War" and "Nineteen Hundred and Nineteen" constitute a double sequence. In Franklin's redaction, it turns out that the two groups are close to one another in time, and the revised order (with the shifting of nine poems from Fascicle 15 to the fascicle just before them) gives them greater impact and reciprocity. They progress from the shock of destructive experience evoked in "The first Day's Night had come" (410), "The Color of the Grave is Green" (411), and "'Twas like a Maelstrom, with a Notch" (414)—three poems of pain, loss, and moral agony at the start of what is now Fascicle 15—to the remote, qualified affirmations of the final group of poems in what is now Fascicle 16, especially "When we stand on the tops of Things" (242) and "He showed me Hights I never saw" (446). The inner dynamics of the fascicles reveal the course of Dickinson's poetic maturing as nothing else can, while—not really paradoxically—throwing into relief major poems whose discovery will come as a surprise to even the most knowledgeable reader.

Times Literary Supplement (26 March 1982)

Unbroken Continuum

THE PENGUIN BOOK OF HEBREW VERSE
edited and translated by T. Carmi

> She said: 'Rejoice, for God has brought you to your fiftieth year in the world!' But she had no inkling that, for my part, there is no difference at all between my own days which have gone by and the distant days of Noah in the rumoured past. I have nothing in the world but the hour in which I am: it pauses for a moment, and then, like a cloud, moves on.

THIS is T. Carmi's prose translation of an eleventh century poem by Samuel Hanagid, whom he calls "the first major poet of the golden age" of Hebrew poetry in Spain and indeed one of "the greatest Hebrew poets of all time". Few people will have known of Hanagid's work, the bulk of which was not published even in Hebrew until 1934. Carmi's anthology is full of such revelations. In assembling a collection that would represent the 3000 years from the poetry of the Old Testament to that of his own contemporaries in modern Israel, the editor—himself a leading Israeli poet, who modestly (but regrettably) omits his own work from these pages—has performed a great service. The prose renderings, each printed facing its Hebrew original, are a fine achievement in themselves. The years of compilation and research have, however, resulted in something even more remarkable: the first presentation of the body of a continuous tradition in a single, coherent, absorbing volume.

The word "miracle" is justly used by Carmi in his introduction when he speaks of the crucial discovery, in the late 1890s of the Cairo Genizah ("hiding place"):

> This momentous event—momentous for almost every branch of Hebrew scholarship—has been aptly described as a cluster of miracles. It was a miracle that the community in Fostat (Old Cairo), which . . . bought its synagogue in the ninth century, perpetuated the . . . Palestinian rite. It was a miracle that they . . . held the written word in such esteem that any piece of writing in Hebrew . . . had to be stored in a special lumber-room. It was a miracle that hundreds of thousands of fragments were deposited . . . from the eleventh to the nineteenth century [and] were preserved from decay and were not discovered prematurely.

In 1896 "two ladies from Cambridge" bought some of the manuscripts as mementos of Cairo and, on their return, showed them to Solomon Schechter, Reader in Rabbinics at the University. Schechter "realized, to his amazement, that he was looking at a fragment of the Hebrew original of Ecclesiasticus" and "immediately travelled to Cairo and, with the permission of the keepers, crated some 100,000 fragments and shipped them to England." Thereafter began the publication of these fragments, and their piecing together with other manuscripts that had "somehow stolen out of Cairo before Schechter's arrival" and into many collections in cities all over the Western world. Almost half the material is poetry, much of it as yet unedited. "There can be little doubt that the Genizah and other manuscript collections hold many more revelations in their undeciphered leaves." The achievement of great poets such as Hanagid and Solomon Ibn Gabirol (1021/22–c1055), forty of whose poems were first published some five years ago, has, therefore, fully emerged only in recent times; others, hitherto unknown—Yannai (sixth century?), for example, and many anonymous authors of striking poems—have been resurrected from that "rumoured past" of which Hanagid wrote.

Behind the continuing miracle of retrieval, of course, is the miracle of the unbroken continuum of Hebrew poetry through centuries of exile and dispersal, expulsion and repression, massacre and partial assimilation. As Carmi notes, "its main centres were in Palestine and Spain, Babylonia and Italy and Germany and Eastern Europe. But it also had important branches in North Africa, the Balkans, Yemen and Holland." The periods of development in these main centres overlap and become intertwined with the stages of poetic style in each of the dominant cultures: Arabic, Iberian ("Andalusian"), Provençal, Italian, and so on. How intertwined may be seen in the description of Hanagid,

> born in Cordoba and . . . among those who fled the capital when the Berber hordes destroyed it in 1013. A renowned Talmudist and statesman, he was the first Spanish Jew to be granted the title "Nagid" ("Prince"). He was appointed vizier shortly after the accession to the throne (1038) of Badis, the Berber ruler of Granada. In this capacity [he] commanded the armies of Granada in a series of victorious campaigns . . . Hanagid's vast knowledge of Hebrew and Arabic culture is apparent in his . . . rich repertoire of forms and motifs.

As the poem I have quoted shows, Hanagid's deep sense of history and of the paradox of identity has, like so much of the poetry in this book, a sharply modern poignancy, combined with a tradition rooted in Biblical and liturgical origins.

Many questions of literary scholarship, and possibly much controversy, will inevitably be raised by this anthology. But the venture is thoroughly justified by the ancient Hebrew saying, "It is upon us to begin the work. It is not upon us to complete the work." And indeed, this sort of work can never really be completed. It should be read as a sequence by many hands, one that proceeds from the passionate primitivism of the Bible—with its savage warsongs, and its notes of compassion and holiness as well as eroticism—through later phases of widening sophistication and tragic awareness. The remarkable poem "You sold a brother", for example, by the eighth-century poet Phinehas Hakohen, recasts the tale of Joseph confronting his brothers in Egypt as a dramatic dialogue in ballad form (not unlike "Edward" in this respect) between Joseph and Judah. The psychological turn at the end exploits the initial charge of emotion in Joseph's accusations and in Judah's terrified pleading, and gives enormous power to the dénouement.

> . . . And he said, "I am your brother Joseph!"
> They shuddered at his words. They shook, dumbfounded, and could not answer him. Then he wept aloud, and they too wept. *And afterwards his brothers talked with him*.

Hakoken was also one of the authors of the imposing series of poems on the death of Moses written between the eighth and the eleventh centuries. These poems brood on death and destiny by way of a number of confrontations between God, who has decreed Moses' death, and the unwilling hero, seen as a Promethean figure—and by way of other forms of stark dialogue. In them we can see something like Greek tragedy in formation, the fusion of self-regarding piety and defiant questioning that we find in both *Oedipus* and *Job* and in so many later poems in the Hebrew tradition. (A simple example is the anonymous "You shall not withhold your answer"—a list of commandments to God instructing Him in the ways of mercy and understanding, and admonishing Him to abjure the premises of Original Sin: "You shall not prolong Your anger with Your sorrowing people to all generations.")

The most affecting quarrels with God—sometimes almost violent, sometimes as gently acquiescent as Abraham and Isaac, whose tale becomes a bitterly ironic symbol for later generations—come in poems centred on the mass-slaughter and mass-suicides of Jews during the Crusades. Whatever romance those expeditions may hold for some, they were sheer butchery for the Jewish people. "I shall speak out my grief," an anonymous poem about the massacre of Jews by Crusaders in Mainz on May 27, 1096, reproaches God for a moment, reminding him of the legend of Isaac, before turning to self-questioning:

> Almighty Lord, dwelling on high, in days of old the angels cried out to You to put a halt to one sacrifice. And now, so many are bound and slaughtered—why do they not clamour over my infants?

Brutality and horror break into many of these poems. "Let this sight come before You," David bar Meshullam of Speyer tells God: "young women, who put their trust in You, slaughtered naked in broad daylight; the fairest of women—their wombs slashed open and the afterbirth forced out from between their legs." One cannot help reading these dark poems as essential clues to the continuity of Hebrew poetry, carriers of terrible memories that it would be sinful to forget, and as challenges to poets to honour the possibilities of their art and not sink into triviality or mere anecdote.

It is not possible to convey here the enormous range of poetry in this anthology: the gradual evolution of liturgical verse and its several styles and verse-forms; the growth of secular verse from these liturgical origins, and the divergences of national and regional schools; and, most of all, the special qualities of particular poems of every kind. Carmi's introduction, his notes on individual poets and poems and on medieval Hebrew genres, and Benjamin Hrushovski's lucid "Note on the Systems of Hebrew Versification" are extremely apt and informative, and the book's overriding concern with poetry of quality rather than poetry that is merely representative of periods and schools is of decisive importance.

This is a book that opens up a world of poetic art and history. If anyone wishes to quarrel with its choices or emphases—well and good. I have rarely read anything so much worth arguing about.

Times Literary Supplement (11 June 1982)

❧

Dannie Abse: Gentle Existentialist

THE plain humanity of Dannie Abse's poetry is one of its attractive qualities. He speaks entirely as a domesticated city man—married, a father, with a profession (medicine), rather Left politically, but too decent and compassionate to contemplate violence really. And his background has kept him—London householder though he has been for these many years—from a complacent or a tatty insularity. He was born in Wales, but doubly saved from the provincialism that circumstance might have led to by his Jewish parentage and by his willy-nilly membership in the semi-bohemian companionship of the British theatre and, of course, of his fellow poets. And he is a good soul—not an ounce of the literary or academic backbiter in the man—with a wife (Joan Abse) whose own intelligence and literary skills are a pleasure (for him as for the rest of us) to behold.

In short, he is a normal modern man of sensibility living the good life despite the usual problems, including an all too normal income, most of us must face. His genius isn't a mad one; he's not a Lowell—and wouldn't capitalize on his private maladies if he were. There isn't a trace of the misogynist, or the region-proud Little Englander or archaeology-hip élitist or macho vampire or Willy-Wetleg-Weeping-Over-Its-Woeful-Childhood about him. And yet he is one of the true poets of the age and his work connects directly with what one whole tendency of British poetry embodies: a genuine, humane, yet tough-enough-minded, self-questioning civilization. The civilization is quietly, sanely European, with a touch perhaps of the kind of openness one might associate with the American mind when it is behaving itself. All this is part and parcel of Abse's poetry.

If anyone supposes I've been describing a rather unpoetic personality, let him or her think again. It's just that Dannie Abse is one of us (as Keats would have been). The daily streets of our twentieth-century lives are his streets too. On them he moves sensitively but unpresumptuously amid the traffic and the hopes, the heart-sickening memory of the Holocaust and the old idiocies of the new governments, thinking and feeling his kindhearted, sometimes anguished, often bemused and wondering way through routines that can amaze him. Meanwhile, his poetry connects with the life we know and with a tradition of modern poetry that speaks naturally in a mode developed by many poets since Wordsworth, including Hardy, Edward Thomas, and Auden. Abse's "Not Adlestrop," for instance, is a sort of curious conversation with Thomas's poem "Adlestrop," which goes (you remember):

Yes, I remember Adlestrop—
The name, because one afternoon
Of heat the express-train drew up there
Unwontedly. It was late June.

The steam hissed. Someone cleared his throat.
No one left and no one came
On the bare platform. What I saw
Was Adlestrop—only the name

And willows, willow-herb, and grass,
And meadowsweet, and haycocks dry,
No whit less still and lonely fair
Than the high cloudlets in the sky.

And for that minute a blackbird sang
Close by, and round him, mistier,
Farther and farther, all the birds
Of Oxfordshire and Gloucestershire.

"Adlestrop" develops slowly and quietly; not until the third stanza do we meet inversions and the sudden emergence of pastoral lyricism. Then, in the final stanza, the poem bursts into two kinds of Hardyesque music, somehow recalling the quixotic bird of "The Darkling Thrush" and, in the closing line, the ending of "Channel Fire."

Compare "Not Adlestrop," written by Abse a half-century later (about 1965) and sounding a little as though D.H. Lawrence had helped:

Not Adlestrop, no—besides, the name
hardly matters. Nor did I languish in June heat.
Simply, I stood, too early, on the empty platform,
and the wrong train came in slowly, surprised, stopped.
Directly facing me, from a window,
a very, *very* pretty girl leaned out.

When I, all instinct,
stared at her, she, all instinct, inclined her head away
as if she'd divined the much married life in me,
or as if she might spot, up platform,
some unlikely familiar.

For my part, under the clock, I continued
my scrutiny with unmitigated pleasure.
And she knew it, she certainly knew it, and would not
glance at me in the silence of not Adlestrop.

Only when the train heaved noisily, only
when it jolted, when it slid away, only *then*,
daring and secure, she smiled back at my smile,
and I, daring and secure, waved back at her waving.
And so it was, all the way down the hurrying platform
as the train gathered atrocious speed
towards Oxfordshire or Gloucestershire.

Thomas's quatrains, with their simple meter and rhyme-scheme (each significantly varied only once—the meter in the breath-caught, exquisite eleventh line; the rhyme in the closing line—but to beautiful effect) swell into pure music. Offhand realism, unromantic understatement, become transmuted (were it not for the time of day) into a medieval *aubade,* chorus of birds and all. Abse's free-verse lines begin as a kind of joke, as if he were having a conversation with a good friend—with Thomas, in fact—and telling about an experience that reminded him of the friend's poem. This sort of conversation does often occur in a pleasing way between poets who have some regard for one another's work. It happens among contemporaries who actually do know and speak with one another; and it happens—as here—over the years in imagination only, when a poet has absorbed a forerunner's writings into his or her own soul and then holds imagined converse with them. This is influence in the best sense—lovingly received and dealt with, like mother's milk and father's confirming presence. (Or, to step back from unintended Freudian suggestions, it is like the mannerisms and attitudes friends pick up from one another and absorb into their own characters. The way that Thomas and Robert Frost affected each other's verse makes a perfect instance.)

At any rate, Abse echoes Thomas's initial tone in a series of negatives that distinguish what he's about from that moment of something like anomie at the start of "Adlestrop." And there's a touch of that same anomie in Abse's first lines too; but at once, quickly, a lyrical vision fills the void. A Beatrice or a Blessed Damozel or a Madeleine (Abse, the modest urban understater, just calls her "a very, *very* pretty girl") leans out of a train-window—*et voilà,* we're just as much back in Provence as at the end of Thomas's poem! Of course, the psychological twist is sharper here: the sense of lost choices (not so much because of the girl's inaccessibility at just this moment as because of the poet's "much married" state and the whole existential surround of that state) but also the relief at the unreality of the challenge in the two protagonists, now "daring and secure," as they wave goodbye to one another. Humor, complacency, philosophizing—all come to soften the blow of defeat on the fields of glamour and free choice. The phrase "atrocious speed" at the end of the penultimate line is full of displaced dismay. Although the very place-names with which the poem concludes recall the end of Stephen Spender's "The Express" as well as of "Adlestrop," the tone is different—the wry surrender of a vision and a thrilling music.

Despite a certain burdened heaviness and evanescent melancholy in this evoked parting of two non-lovers who never met, "Not Adlestrop" is cheerful enough in much the same volatile way that "Adlestrop" is: wry, realistic, full of winning dreams, yet elegiac. To exhibit *some* sort of human morale within the elegiac mode is, precisely, one of the great pressures on modern poetry; a combined vivacity, intensity, and forthrightness is the natural response to that pressure, and in his deployment of these resources Abse again resembles Thomas and other poets of the Great War. His "Pathology of Colours" is a sharp reminder of the way Wilfred Owen and Siegfried Sassoon (in the remarkable poem "Repression of War Experience") dealt with the unbearable. Here Abse writes out of medical experience of horror just as they did out of the trenches, without squeamishness and with a blessed, unrhetorical seriousness:

> I know the colour rose, and it is lovely,
> but not when it ripens in a tumour;
> and healing greens, leaves and grass, so springlike,
> in limbs that fester are not springlike.
>
> I have seen red-blue tinged with hirsute mauve
> in the plum-skin face of a suicide.
> I have seen white, china white almost, stare
> from behind the smashed windscreen of a car.
>
> And the criminal, multi-coloured flash
> of an H-bomb is no more beautiful
> than an autopsy when the belly's opened—
> to show cathedral windows never opened.
>
> So in the simple blessing of a rainbow,
> in the bevelled edge of a sunlit mirror,
> I have seen, visible, Death's artifact
> like a soldier's ribbon on a tunic tacked.

This poem recalls the wrenched, awkward power of Owen's "Greater Love"—its impossible insistence on the greater, more exquisite and passionate feeling evoked by the battlefield dead than by the beauty of a loved woman. And the closing stanza goes further (as Sassoon's "Repression of War Experience" does) in suggesting how lovely or innocuous sights may evoke hideous associations—a reversal of our unwilling recognition of the distortions of beauty lurking in diseased and dead bodies. (The inescapable war-associations in our modern memories make themselves felt in the closing stanzas.) Perhaps Abse's most striking poem of those that cope directly with depressive knowledge in the elegiac mode, however, is the riddling "Hunt the Thimble." Here, in the guise of the children's game named in the title, a dialogue takes place in which one supposed speaker questions another about "it"—some ultimate source of fear and misery—and is constantly put off as the questions grow more and more suggestive of dreariness. ("Is it like heavy rain falling," or like "the brooding darkness" inside a provincial Spanish cathedral, or "like those old men in hospital dying" who "shout out, 'Mama,'" or like "the darkness inside a dead man's mouth"?)

"Hunt the Thimble" may well be Abse's purest poem, with an original turn in its subtly protective tone but nevertheless cumulatively dread-filled dynamics—a method reminiscent of Kenneth Fearing's but without the tough-guy New York rasp of that marvelous, neglected poet. In fact, it is remarkable how often Abse's work makes one think of the best work of other modern poets, not because of any mere derivativeness but because he speaks out of a world and a psyche and a complex of historical memory and anticipation that we recognize and share. His family poems, again, have that combination of idiosyncratic sensibility and a familiar realm of awareness that marks all his writing. They strike the confessional note again and again, but without hysteria or exhibitionism. The quiet poem "A Night Out" could hardly be more understated, and yet it gets at the heart of everything that gives such an ironic tinge to ordinary life these days—that is, the unavoidable pursuit of our daily needs and pleasures despite the dreadful knowledge of extreme suffering imposed on us at every turn. The poem is a simple anecdote. The poet and his wife have gone to see "the new Polish film" recommended by friends, an almost-documentary film about Auschwitz: "the human obscenity in close-up." The atmosphere of the "ever melancholy queue/of cinemas," and then of the theatre itself, and then of the Camp scenes (including an inner irony of the Camp orchestra performing "the solemn gaiety of Bach"), and of the confusions of real and unreal—"those striped victims merely actors"—in the passive receptivity of the audience is unfolded quietly but indelibly:

> We watched, as we munched milk chocolate,
> trustful children, no older than our own,
> strolling into the chambers without fuss,
> while smoke, black and curly, oozed from chimneys.

And then? The couple leave the theatre, have coffee "in a bored espresso bar nearby," drive home, and

> We asked the au pair girl from Germany
> if anyone had phoned at all, or called,
> and, of course, if the children had woken.
> Reassured, together we climbed the stairs,
> undressed together, and naked together,
> in the dark, in the marital bed, made love.

It's the plain helplessness about what to do with one's awareness, not only of the stench of continuing history but of all the ironies noted in so many details of the poem, that leaves such a coppery taste in one's mouth. The sense of being merely actors ourselves in some sort of irreversibly progressing film makes the sexual act at the end an embodiment of the elegiac, a possible contribution to the Auschwitz of the future, and a betrayal of grief. None of these thoughts are advanced by the poem itself; there is no lugubrious pontificating such as we might find in Auden or Larkin. The little anecdote about what is, after all, a common enough sort of experience presents itself and stops. Not that it lacks indicative language concerning its range of awareness; no, the whole of that range is part of the anecdote, and it includes all the depths of self-reproach at "living as usual" that constitute the abyss above which we hover in our time. But it also provides, with sufficient organic density, an atmosphere of normal human experience such as neither Auden nor Larkin, despite their considerable talents, provides.

In the same way, while Auden, say, is "European" by virtue of his reading and political interests, Abse is "European" without half trying, because he is so intimately Jewish without religious parochialism or defensiveness. Thus, the first stanzas of "Uncle Isidore":

> When I observe a toothless ex-violinist,
> with more hair than face, sprawled like Karl Marx
> on a park seat or slumped, dead or asleep,
> in the central heat of a public library
> I think of Uncle Isidore—smelly
> schnorrer and lemon-tea bolshevik—my foreign
> distant relative, not always distant.
>
> Before Auschwitz, Treblinka, he seemed near,
> those days of local pogroms, five-year programmes,
> until I heard him say, 'Master, Master
> of the Universe, blessed be your name,
> don't you know there's been no rain for years
> and your people are thirsty? Have you no shame,
> compassion? Don't you care at all?'

And in the touching portrait of his dying father's courage and indifference to suffering called "In Llandough Hospital," Abse gives us a simile out of the heart of modern Europe such as neither Larkin nor Auden would have conceived: "He's thin as Auschwitz in that bed." This is a natural image for a modern Jewish sensibility, at once internationalist, politically conscious, and, as it were, continuously in mourning whatever the context (even when it is boisterously comic, as in a few of the lines I have been quoting). It seems to me that this historically elegiac dimension enters even the least politically colored poems, such as "In the Theatre," that Abse has written. "In the Theatre" (subtitled "*A True Incident*") describes an operation in which the surgeon destroys a patient's brain as he probes (the date is 1938, before more precise methods had been developed) for a brain tumor.

> Lambert Rogers desperate, fingering still;
> his dresser thinking, 'Christ! Two more on the list,
> a cisternal puncture and a neural cyst.'
>
> Then, suddenly, the cracked record in the brain,
> a ventriloquist voice that cried, 'You sod,
> leave my soul alone, leave my soul alone,'—
> the patient's dummy lips moving to that refrain,
> the patient's eyes too wide. And, shocked,
> Lambert Rogers drawing out the probe
> with nurses, students, sister, petrified.

Abse doesn't even look for reassurance in his poems; and yet the morale remains—an energizing if thoroughly unpretentious sense of human coping, if only through sensitively accurate perception of things as they are and prevailing good will that is warm and humorous whenever given half a chance.

Of all the current English poets, he is the one who tries least to impress us—whether with athletic energies, or withering (and self-withering) wit, or scholarship in the service of nostalgia or local pride. More than the others, though, he speaks for our day and for the way we are moving through it. Without having any such thought in mind, doubtless, he is our gentlest existentialist.

The Poetry of Dannie Abse: Critical Essays and Reminiscences,
ed. Joseph Cohen (London: Robson Books, 1983)

❧

Laura Riding's Poetry: A Nice Problem

OUR usual expectations for lyric poetry that succeeds include a tonal dynamics leading to something realized, or an equilibrium among states of feeling. And yet just the opposite, a resistance to culmination or structural completion that is also a resistance to commitment or self-identification, can make for a genuine lyric poem as well. Laura Riding's poems, the work of her latter twenties and earliest thirties, are often of this order, foreshadowing certain current American developments.

Her writing is full of promises but preserved, as it were, in ambiguities, ironies, and near-solipsistic musings. Endlessly elusive, she gives of herself richly only on the rarest occasions. We are led to expect much—and don't usually get it yet are reluctant to leave: poor, ardent suitors who will never, really, feel welcomed into a clear, bright, shared world of climactic mutuality. Still, one doesn't want to lay aside a poem that begins with lines like "The rugged black of anger/Has an uncertain smile-border"—lines that remind of Emily Dickinson but have their own fingerprint. And so one submits to intolerably redundant soliloquies, always in hope. It is like being kept waiting for someone who has gone to another room to look through innumerable books for some vaguely remembered phrase that we know is unnecessary anyway, given her vivid originality. What prevents our leaving is what we're given on those rarest occasions I've mentioned, when a poem like "Faith Upon the Waters" presents itself:

A ghost rose when the waves rose,
When the waves sank stood columnwise
And broken: archaic is
The spirituality of sea,
Water haunted by an imagination
Like fire previously.

More ghost when no ghost,
When the waves explain
Eye to the eye

And dolphins tease,
And the ventriloquist gulls,
Their angular three-element cries.

Fancy ages.
A death-bed restlessness inflames the mind
And a warm mist attacks the face
With mortal premonition.

The delicate precisions here strike home in a manner that indeed recalls Dickinson, and moreover matches comparable poems by Stevens and Crane while maintaining its own integrity of tonal progression. The momentary illusion of the first line ("A ghost rose when the waves rose") touches off a vision that holds firm and then an *aperçu* (imagistically developed) that is charged, as the poem has it, with "mortal premonition."

So the upshot is that, much as one's tempted to turn one's back impatiently on Riding's off-putting sensibility, one can't do so and finally doesn't want to. In "Faith Upon the Waters," the line "A death-bed restlessness inflames the mind" insinuates her spell. One may want a more developed poetry than she usually offers, but what is there to do with that flickering restlessness of hers except to keep watching for it to flame up? The poems keep hinting that's about to happen. When it does, they expose a spirit restlessly intense as Plath's, abstract (though never as cool) as Moore's, inwardly torn yet insistent as Rich's. Often they suggest the potential drama of the psychoanalyst's couch; and their context, or predicament, is similar: the need for self-identification and the fear of it at the same time, together with an ambience of luxurious confusion. Riding offers something not altogether different from the ambiguous velleities of Pinter's later plays, at once so boring and so intriguing. Much of the riddling in her work does indeed, like her early decision to stop writing poems, point to unresolved psychoanalytical material. And the riddling, the invitation to guess at an unstated referent, is almost constant throughout her work in its implied source of disturbance. Take, for instance, the brief poem called "Mortal":

There is a man of me that sows.
There is a woman of me that reaps.
One for good,
And one for fair,
And they cannot find me anywhere.

Father and Mother, shadowy ancestry,
Can you make no more than this of me?

Riddle, nursery rhyme, chant, affect of touching bewilderment—and yet this is only the *beginning* of a poem, rather than one that is brought to completion. It's therefore more a bit of lyrically oriented discourse than a poem: vague, evasive, psychological discourse.

So too, the suggestively titled "Postponement of Self," though far more concrete, is ultimately psychoanalytical discourse rather than art. Its beginning and ending make the point self-evident:

> I took another day,
> I moved to another city,
> I opened a new door to me.
> Then again a last night came.
> My bed said: "To sleep and back again?"
> I said: "This time go forward."

and:

> At twenty I say She.
> Her face is like a flower.
> In a city we have no flower-names, forgive me.
> But flower-names not necessary
> To diary of identity.

In between these opening and closing passages we find a kind of autobiography, in the usual wearying post-Freudian identity-search shorthand: a telegraphic account of ambiguous, trying early relationships with Papa and Mama. Such poems curiously foreshadow the confessional preoccupations of a later generation of poets: Rukeyser, Sexton, Lowell, and others, male and female, whose work parallels Riding's narcissistic self-examinations. "Narcissistic," in this context, is not a personal but a literary term, implying self-absorbed non-poems, often both sexless and tiresomely portentous and unclear, by such poets at their least successful. After four opening lines strongly reminiscent of Emily Dickinson, "Postponement of Self" loses its way poetically.

But when Riding's poems are most successful, the sensibility is distinctly feminine and free of the thematically egocentric stress on identity that renders so many of her other pieces heavily quizzical and essentially discursive. Among her best poems, certainly, I would list "So Slight," "Dear Possible," "Lucrece and Nara," "Because I Sit Here So," and "Be Grave, Woman." The whole of "So Slight" is worth quoting here because it is colored by the preoccupations I have mentioned but is a lyrical distillation, not an introspective harangue:

> It was as near invisible
> As night in early dusk.
> So slight it was,
> It was as unbelievable
> As day in early dawn.
>
> The summer impulse of a leaf
> To flutter separately
> Gets death and autumn.
> Such faint rebellion
> Was lately love in me.

So slight, it had no hope or sorrow,
It could but choose
A passing flurry for its nuptial,
Drift off and fall
Like thistledown without a bruise.

Fear of commitment to identity is doubtless what gives "So Slight" its special depressive intensity. "The summer impulse . . . /To flutter separately" is equated with the impulse to love, described as "faint rebellion." Both modulations toward self-definition are "so slight" they have "no hope or sorrow." But the poem's incisive imagery and delicately evocative phrasing, again reminiscent of Dickinson without being merely derivative, give life to its movement independently of any imposed theme.

Similarly, "Dear Possible" maintains its pure direction despite its hovering identity-puzzlement and kindred concern (on which Riding's poetry rings many changes) about male dominance. Thus:

Dear scholar of love,
If by your own formula
I open heaven to you
When you knock punctually at the door,
Then you are there, but I where I was.

The unconscionably teasing arrogance of these lines is a delight all too infrequent in Riding. Elsewhere, the poem is even exuberant over the elusiveness of identity and roles in love. In this aspect it resembles the tonally very different "Lucrece and Nara," in which Riding's tendency toward solipsism is suborned by the emotion being traced—the sheer sense of love as ineradicable intimacy within whatever existential circumstance may occur. Here as elsewhere one becomes aware of a Blakean resonance in Riding at her most lyrical, something like the melancholy ecstasy of, say, "The Book of Thel." (Yeats caught a similar resonance in his "Ephemera," toughening and redirecting it in his later work.) The odd thing about "Lucrece and Nara" is that its complex of feeling is entirely self-reflexive. It embodies enduring love as two narcissistically mirroring reciprocal selves that are constantly transformed within the cycles of cosmic change:

Ghostly they clung and questioned
A thousand years, not yet eternal,
True to their fading,
Through their long watch defying
Time to make them whole, to part them.

A gentle clasp and fragrance played and hung
A thousand years and more
Around earth closely.
"Earth will be long enough,
Love has no elsewhere."

And when earth ended, was devoured
One shivering midsummer
At the dissolving border,
A sound of light was felt.
"Nara, is it you, the dark?"
"Lucrece, is it you, the quiet?"

Thus the reciprocal selves (or half-selves) retain their companionable shared isolation after earth itself finally dissolves and the one becomes "the dark," the other "the quiet." The poem gains its greatest confidence at the moment when identity, in any ordinary sense, disappears. An even subtler turn on this feeling of ineffable existential intimacy appears in the poem "Because I Sit Here So," with its threat of angry, unleashed power. This poem reveals, first, the volcanic vulnerability we sense, and sometimes hear asserted but hardly ever see released, in Riding's poems; and, second, her resistance to it:

Stir me not,
Demons of the storm.
Were I as you would have me,
Astart with anger,
Gnawing the self-fold chain
Until the spell of unity break,
Madness would but thunder
Where sorrow had once burned,
A sun to smile in
And sit waiting under.

The tone here is allied to the dark sensual rigor of "Be Grave, Woman," a poem that begins in harsh longing—

Be grave, woman, for love
Still hungering as gardens
For rain though flowerless—

and ends in the nobly proud acceptance of the single closing line:

Thou alone, stark mind.

Both the collected and the selected editions of Riding's poems attempt large divisional groupings that seem in search of an organic ordering principle, as if struggling to break free from the persistent existential isolation in which poems like "Be Grave, Woman" are trapped. Nothing strikingly coherent, poetically, comes of these efforts, but they do act out, in large, the volatility and reluctant closing-in on—and simultaneous repudiation of—identity we have observed. These paradoxical or self-neutralizing characteristics are closely allied to Riding's tendency to present affirmations and negations interchangeably (a sort of guerrilla warfare against being understood) and to riddle her way out of self-definition. The process presents itself sometimes fliply, sometimes desperately; sometimes as agony, sometimes as the mind's deliberate yet hesitant foray into universal empathy. Within such a context, the groupings move this way and that rather haphazardly, between modulations toward confession and modulations toward meditation. The whole tendency of modern poetry, with its intense subjectivity and radiant affective centers, has been toward becoming a poetry of psychological pressures and toward encompassing these pressures in the poem's structuring dynamics. Clearly, though decisive radiant centers of the most compelling kind are few and far between in her work, Riding's explorations fall well within this tendency.

In her case, I believe, we can see Laura Riding's riddling ambiguities as an affective context, at once projecting frustration and providing a psychological refuge. Had she cultivated a poetry of power more relentlessly, she might have carried her art into an irreversible commitment too drastic for her to bear, in the manner of Sylvia Plath and a number of other poets of genius whose merging of personal and aesthetic sensibility (like Aschenbach's in Thomas Mann's *Death in Venice*) has involved dangerous psychological risks. She certainly possessed the talent for such a cultivation although, perhaps, she lacked the sustained energy for it. Her problem was not that, as she claimed, poetry just cannot be reciprocal with felt reality. Rather, it was the fact that this possibly destructive reciprocity *can* be achieved. That fact, I suspect, is what led her to renounce her poetic career so abruptly at the age of thirty-seven. In a related sense, she may have been affected, in her expatriate phase, with the failure of nerve of British poetry after World War I, at the very time that other American poets of the between-wars period were finding their power. Riding went further than Marianne Moore toward a letting-go like Eliot's or Pound's, but in this ultimate commitment she could not go far enough.

The Southern Review (21 January 1985)

Psychological Pressure in Four Quartets

HELEN Gardner's brilliantly informative *The Composition of* Four Quartets (1978), with its account of successive drafts and of Eliot's developing conception and problems, is a model of its kind. If it has led me into further thoughts about what is going on artistically in these poems, in relation to the psychological pressures manifest in them, I do not intend these thoughts—despite some disagreement with Professor Gardner about formulations that were only secondary to her main purpose—as in any sense an attack on her finely intelligent scholarship. On the contrary, they are simply a foray in a somewhat different direction—and hardly as thoroughgoing as her studies.

My interest here is strictly poetic, and I have tried to relate what Gardner says to this interest. One aspect of her book, for example, is its revelation of John Hayward's special role as Eliot's sensitive, respectful confidant. He served as a not uncritical but far less challenging sparring partner than the *miglior fabbro* of *The Waste Land:* forthright Ezra would probably have slashed the text to ribbons and drawn enough blood to make what was left thoroughly, however painfully, alive all the way through.

Gardner, indeed, clearly shows the comfortably reassuring circle closest to Eliot while the sequence was in the making. It included Hayward, and the sophisticated Geoffrey Faber (how wonderful to have one's publisher so supportively in on the work!), and the Faber editor Frank Morley, who departed for America before the sequence was complete. There were also Bloomsbury-group readings at times, but these do not seem to have led to any severe criticism. The whole set of feeling was that the Master (as Hayward sometimes referred to him with lighthearted deference) was, at last, creating a new work of a scope and significance consonant with his genius. The essential piety of anticipation may be seen in a thought of Hayward's addressed to Morley in July 1941:

> My own view is that in these times the less delay the better in bringing into the world the kind of work that consolidates one's faith in the continuity of thought and sensibility when heaven is falling and earth's foundations fail.

Eliot, then, had to be his own most ruthless critic, as do most poets. But he had also to contend with a certain complacency because of his enormous reputation and a certain unease at the same time for the same reason. Peerless when at the top of his form, he nevertheless relied too systematically on giving the successive poems parallel structure and on a basically pointless symbolic scheme involving the four elements and the four seasons—pointless because without tonal resonance. In addition, he indulged repeatedly in a low-keyed rhythmic ruminating familiar in his plays. Even Hayward finally protested, in a letter on the first draft of "Little Gidding," that the first fifteen lines of Part III

> strike me as being imperfectly resolved into poetry, in fact rather laboured and prosy. I think I appreciate the difficulty of this kind of expository writing. It may be that it is too easy to cast such philosophical and ethical statements into the kind of long, fluid lines you use so ingeniously.

Hayward's unwonted acerbity was right on the mark. Ezra, though, would not have tempered his wrath with praise for the "long fluid lines you use so ingeniously"; those lines were precisely the "too easy" recourse that created the problem. Anyway, Eliot did not take the criticism seriously. It carried no authority of Poundian rigor, and he naturally preferred his own judgment. He did make small, deft improvements and add a single concrete image. But the phrasing remains a barrier to poetic assent from the start:

There are three conditions which often look alike
Yet differ completely, flourish in the same hedgerow:
Attachment to self and to things and to persons, detachment
From self and from things and from persons; and, growing
  between them, indifference
Which resembles the others as death resembles life,
Being between two lives—unflowering, between
The live and the dead nettle. This is the use of memory [etc.]

Hayward did not press the point again; actually, Eliot would have had to recast all four poems to deal with it. So there it is, this pontificating that resembles poetry "as death resembles life," with its "hedgerow" that quickens anticipation for a moment only because it echoes the beautiful start of "Little Gidding," and its not very clear nettle imagery as its only illusory hints that maybe the body is breathing after all. One *bad* line, just further on, stands touchingly in isolation, an arrested note of nostalgia: "The faces and places, with the self which, as it could, loved them." See, by contrast, Pound's moodily ebullient calling up of memory in Canto 74: e.g.,

we will see those old roads again, question
                                        possibly
but nothing appears much less likely,
                                        Mme Pujol,
and there was a smell of mint under the tent flaps

Poetic assent, whether the author be Eliot or an unknown, is won only when the work is at a different *pitch* from that of discourse (although tones and rhythms of discourse can certainly be deployed poetically). The starting point of a poem's movement lies in some psychological pressure that sparks verbal arousal, mobilizing the tonal resources of language—all those aspects that Paul Verlaine, in "Art Poétique," calls its "music":

De la musique encore et toujours!
Que ton vers soit la chose envolée
Qu'on sent qui fuit d'une âme en allée
Vers d'autres cieux à d'autres amours.

Que ton vers soit la bonne aventure
Éparse au vent crispé du matin
Qui va fleurant la menthe et le thym . . .
Et tout le reste est littérature.

[Music again and always!
Let your verse be a winged living thing
Fleeing, we feel, from a soul in flight
Towards other skies, to other loves.

Let your verse be sheer good luck
Scattered in the crisp gusts of morning wind

That arrive breathing mint and thyme . . .
And all the rest—just literature.]

"Music again and always!" We need to recognize how one of our greatest poets succumbed to a complacent flattening of his style that has contributed to a current general trend toward a minimal poetry, musically speaking. Poetry, let us remember, is the art that uses language to delight the heart or break it, but also to open the sensibility to itself. There is a uniquely continuous pressure of expression, a commitment, in vital poetry. This is a commitment to find the further language lurking in a nestful of perception, memory and association. And it is the music of poetry that frees its associations, turning apparent riddles into models of clarity. Eliot's successes in *Four Quartets* are of this order, furnishing a curious proof that he should never have tried to introduce straightforward discourse to reinforce his art. Take the beginning of part II of "Burnt Norton":

Garlic and sapphires in the mud
Clot the bedded axle-tree.
The trilling wire in the blood
Sings below inveterate scars
Appeasing long forgotten wars.
The dance along the artery
The circulation of the lymph
Are figured in the drift of stars
Ascend to summer in the tree
We move above the moving tree
In light upon the figured leaf
And hear upon the sodden floor
Below, the boarhound and the boar
Pursue their pattern as before
But reconciled among the stars.

Here we have the real thing. We can share the poem's space of associative freedom to net its own perceptions in their spectral mental haunt and fetch them out into the open. The passage follows through a strangely sensuous insight, in a manner foreign to "normal" speech yet clearing its way by the force of its dynamics. As it moves, conventional syntax dissolves into a syntax blurred by reverie. A self-induced mystical entrancement, bolstered by hypnotic sound-echoings, dominates the process. The passage begins with two complete sentences; but thereafter the grammatical units, like the images, collapse into one another, with no period until the very end and only one bit of internal punctuation (absolutely necessary to prevent syntactic disaster, but masterful in doing so with minimal fuss). The form is an intricate pattern of repetitions, irregularly occurring but frequent rhymes, and parallel phrasings, all contained within the densely concrete four-stress lines. It provides a rich lingering within the powerful but unstable visions of imagined ascent.

We may read many ideas into the passage, such as the assumption of an infinitely varied yet consistent rhythmic design throughout the universe, mirrored in the very form of the poem. We may detect a distanced personal complaint—a trapped sense of being mired in our muddy, clotted earth—and a related predicament of being compounded of filth and exaltation. The passage seems to speak of "scars" from repressed internal struggles as well as from humanity's "forgotten wars," both military and spiritual. And we can tell something of Eliot's reading from the echoes of Shakespeare, Chapman, Milton, Dryden, Mallarmé and others. Such observations, though not central, reflect notes of true if specialized interest that are floating realities of the poem and add to its atmosphere of inspired intelligence. Yet they would count for nothing were it not for the essential fusion of nervous intensity and visionary transport in the lines, which act out a progression from bafflement, loss and tragic memory to a cosmic grandeur and transcendence.

The fusion of tonalities here is precisely embodied in the vibrato image, at once fey and buoyant, of "the trilling wire in the blood" that "sings" a kind of faith in the ultimate meaning of all we undergo. This key affective pitch is reinforced by the insistent metrical beat, the almost unbroken momentum of the passage (virtually no emphatic stops along the way), and the heavy use of monosyllabic rhymes, often identical. ("Tree," for instance, is placed in end-rhyming position three times, and "stars" twice). So the passage presses toward exultant affirmation while also embodying something more fatalistic and bitterly resistant to such pressure. It flies high and is balked—and is simultaneously intimate and impersonal, like us!

Thus the "*bonne aventure*," the good luck of the poem: to find its balance among conflicting elements, in language that somehow escapes from the "soul in flight." The passage from "Burnt Norton" is but one verse-unit in one section of the whole poem; but it might well stand by itself, unlike the opening verse-unit in part III of "Little Gidding." Doubtless the passage has a certain abstruse quality if we try to translate its concentrated, resonant images into abstract ideas as we read along. But that way of reading is death to understanding, for the same reason that the "Little Gidding" passage is moribund writing. The whole freedom of the lines from "Burnt Norton" resides in the direct impact of the successive images and tones: the mingling of thrilled elation and passive dreariness, and of movement "above the moving tree" (and toward the stars) and immersion in the "sodden" cruelty of life below. These gather into a music of necessary contradiction that cannot be reduced to intellectual pronouncements. The poem's life (as in the brief Pound quotation) consists of simplicities we apprehend with alerted senses: "the trilling wire in the blood," "the dance along the artery," the "drift of stars."

The obvious problem of *Four Quartets*, then, lies in its mixture of such work with passages that hold forth rhetorically or "philosophically" with only the lowest charge of musical energy. Verlaine's image of the scent of mint and thyme in the fresh morning winds may not be entirely apt for the whole of *Four Quartets*, if we read over-literally. But the insight the image actually conveys is that poetry breathes its felt awareness, rather than spelling out positions pedagogically. The most famous line in the poem advises: "*Prends l'éloquence et tords-lui son cou!*" ("Take eloquence and wring its neck!") Living poetry foregrounds pressure of feeling, not logic.

What are the real psychological pressures invading the *Four Quartets* and shaping its responsive structure? According to Gardner (writing somewhat delphically),

> the strongly autobiographical element in all his poetry appears undisguised in *Four Quartets;* but the painful and deeply troubling experiences which lie behind the earlier poetry, and to which he could not give direct expression, were now in the past. The questions that *Four Quartets* provokes are not painful. It is a confessional poem, but not in the same sense as *Ash Wednesday* is a confessional poem.

This is her most specific statement on the subject, together with the suggestive if unpursued observation that "the circumstances of the war acted in rather the same way as overwork and personal distress operated on the composition of *The Waste Land* and its successors, 'The Hollow Men' and *Ash Wednesday*." This observation is echoed in a more general way by her comment that "the relevance of the whole discourse" in part III of "The Dry Salvages" (which orients itself around Krishna's address to Arjuna in the *Bhagavad Gita* concerning his duty as a warrior serving divine purposes), written "in 1941 with a fratricidal war raging in Europe," should "not need stressing." And one other rather general statement on the psychological pressures at work in the sequence should be mentioned. "The major sources of *Four Quartets*," she writes, "are experiences: . . . both actual experiences and experiences revived in memory. These last come back with a new power as their meaning is apprehended." The distinction between "actual" and "revived" experiences is not altogether clear; but at any rate, to illustrate her point about the latter kind, she quotes from part II of "The Dry Salvages":

> We had the experience but missed the meaning,
> And approach to the meaning restores the experience
> In a different form, beyond any meaning
> We can assign to happiness. . . .

Now, I do not agree about what this passage is saying. If I am right, of course, the fault in reading is by no means altogether Gardner's. Except for the telling first line, the passage is—like much of this part of "The Dry Salvages"—hopelessly gluey writing. Nevertheless, the sense of the passage, made more emphatic in its full context, has to do with the way in which, when we contemplate the meaning of experience, the nature of the experience itself seems to alter—particularly, perhaps, because private memory merges with cultural and historical memory. For one thing, we see that a passing moment of experience, when objectified by exploration, is after all imperishable. The closing dozen lines or so of the section, lines far better than the rest, press this insight with a kind of bitter triumph. They show how the realization is enhanced by closeness to "the agony of others," which

> remains an experience
> Unqualified, unworn by subsequent attrition.
> People change, and smile: but the agony abides.
> Time the destroyer is time the preserver,
> Like the river with its cargo of dead negroes, cows and chicken coops,
> The bitter apple and the bite in the apple,
> And the ragged rock in the restless waters.

This drift of association brings us back to the contradiction between Gardner's emphasis on the importance in the sequence of Eliot's "actual experiences and experiences revived in memory" and her initial assertion that "the painful and deeply troubling experiences which lie behind the earlier poetry, and to which he could not give direct expression, were now in the past." Or rather, it is not so much a self-contradiction as a tangential pair of formulations that do not quite connect with the poem's own language. Can we truly believe that the passage just quoted, with its reference to "the agony of others" that remains in the mind "unworn by subsequent attrition," has nothing to do with those "painful and deeply troubling experiences" of Eliot's earlier life (unspecified by Gardner but fairly well known by now)? The whole point here is the imperishability of the past. If so, how can one possibly dismiss certain memories whose "agony," Eliot's poem tells us, still "abides" as "now in the past"? And can one then go on to say, in the very next sentence, that "the questions that *Four Quartets* provokes are not painful"?

I raise these points because they matter acutely when we try to see the major driving pressures at work in the poems. For the same reason, I think there is a misplaced distinction in the contrast proposed between Eliot's alleged inability to "give direct expression" to the unhappy experiences underlying his earlier writing—presumably his psychological and marital problems—and his later alleged ability to do so because he was now free of those problems. For one thing, *Four Quartets* does not spell out the circumstances of guilt and humiliation, which must surely be part of the agony that "abides," any more explicitly than does *The Waste Land*. Rather, it masks them in similar ways. More centrally to the issue, however, "direct expression" in poetry (as Eliot long ago explained in his *Hamlet* essay) is a function of evocation, not of abstract statement, photographic description or literal confession.

In this artistic respect, the two works are not really different. Both evoke states of piercing feeling whose affective character they partly share despite important differences. One such difference is the overlay of guru-wisdom, quietistic religious intonation and sheer rhetoric in the later work. Another is its indulgence in personal grousing—to pick up Eliot's phrase for what he was doing in *The Waste Land*. He grouses about getting old, and about the undependable materials (i.e., words) of the poet's art, and about losses or betrayals all must endure. Some of this is a bit odd. For instance, he was writing *Four Quartets* between his early forties and early fifties—a pre-gerontic interval for most of us. And in general, the emotions that *Four Quartets* most openly displays to us (dismay at the impermanence of one's art, or a sudden awed exaltation in an epiphanic-seeming moment, or frustration at realizing one doesn't have time—even if one had the power—to right past error) are not really "confessional" in their context. They do not arise from self-exposure in some shameful way (like Wordsworth's boat-stealing scene and its depressive aftermath, or the situations in Robert Lowell's *Life Studies*). I am not quite sure why Gardner used this word, unless she simply means that Eliot describes his own feelings at certain points in *Four Quartets*. But putting this matter aside, we can say that *Four Quartets* shares some of the pressures, by way of the kind of memory that stings as though one were having the original experience again and again, of *The Waste Land* and other early poems; and at the same time, that it adds new pressures and perspective—in short, that the balance or proportion of formative pressures shifts between the one work and the other, but that there is also a stubbornly persistent continuity.

Gardner's account of the growth of *Four Quartets* reminds us of a point made several times by Eliot himself: namely, that he wrote "Burnt Norton" as an independent poem, with no notion of its being part of a sequence, and that it was only while he was writing "East Coker," a good five years or so later, "that the whole sequence began to emerge, with the symbolism of the four seasons and the four elements." "Burnt Norton" had its special pressure of movement: a deep sense of nostalgia and loss and of the ineradicability of whatever happens in action or in thought, and a beautiful yet melancholy dreaming into the opposite state. Its third and fourth sections resonate with tonalities akin to those in *The Waste Land* though lacking its dramatic closeups. Its vision of a childhood Eden would undo the horrors of experience (embodied in the very emptiness of Burnt Norton itself) and of all our disappointments—much as the intellectual conceit of using the persistence of memory and of the effects of the past as a token of a timeless, transcendent realm of being would do. In itself, the poem is an afterbeat of *The Waste Land* and "Ash Wednesday" in a different key from either.

"East Coker" has nothing like the purity of structure and lyrical fineness—the straining out of essences of feeling, the surface calm that delays but does not even pretend to conceal the intensity of reenactment of balked experience—of "Burnt Norton." Its most vivid moment is found in the opening eight lines of its second verse-unit (except for the portentous opening sentence, "In my beginning is my end"). These sharply project a momentary self-view, existential, isolated without context except a contrived one to be conjured up from the past by a slightly forced imaginative process in ensuing lines:

> In my beginning is my end. Now the light falls
> Across the open field, leaving the deep lane
> Shuttered with branches, dark in the afternoon,
> Where you lean against a bank while a van passes,
> And the deep lane insists on the direction
> Into the village, in the electric heat
> Hypnotised. In a warm haze the sultry light
> Is absorbed, not refracted, by grey stone.

Nothing else in the poem is at a comparable pitch, although of course there are lovely notes further on such as "Dawn points, and another day/Prepares for heat and silence" (another passage of isolated, keenly depressive sensibility) and—to similar effect at the very end (except, again, for the chiastically intrusive refrain): "The wave cry, the wind cry, the vast waters/Of the petrel and the porpoise. In my end is my beginning."

These existential stases, without context, position a finely tuned spirit at a dead loss. In them, nature and society seem ominously compelling and at the same time pointless. It seems to me that the eight-line passage I have just quoted, so impressionistically precise and charged with an imbalance of weak, hazy light and powerful darkness, is the key to Eliot's conception of a *sequence* while coping with bafflement in "East Coker."

Artistically he was reduced to a kind of anomie: "all passion spent." Five years had passed since "Burnt Norton," which placed the intensities of the earlier work in a subdued context of unforgotten but "unredeemable" time, and imagined itself into an Edenic new start. That did not make any the less "ridiculous" the "waste sad time/Stretching before and after," however. The discursive near-banalities of "East Coker" seem a way of priming the creative pump at all costs. The poem latches on to some of the phrasing of "Burnt Norton" (the "deception of the thrush," the failure of the vision) when it asks, somewhat inelegantly:

> Had they deceived us
> Or deceived themselves, the quiet-voiced elders,
> Bequeathing merely a receipt for deceit?

Other such echoes inhabit "East Coker," notably the opening verse-unit of section II ("What is the late November doing"), whose meter and high style recall—but too flamboyantly now—those of the parallel passage ("Garlic and sapphires in the mud") of "Burnt Norton." But then, in the long-lined discursive part of Section II that follows, the poem comes flat up against its motivating sense of futility:

> That was a way of putting it—not very satisfactory:
> A periphrastic study in a worn-out poetical fashion,
> Leaving one still with the intolerable wrestle
> With words and meanings. The poetry does not matter.

And again, at the start of section V:

> So here I am, in the middle way, having had twenty years—
> Twenty years largely wasted, the years of *l'entre deux guerres*
> Trying to learn to use words, and every attempt
> Is a wholly new start, and a different kind of failure
> Because one has only learnt to get the better of words
> For the thing one no longer has to say, or the way in which
> One is no longer disposed to say it. And so each venture
> Is a new beginning, a raid on the inarticulate
> With shabby equipment always deteriorating
> In the general mess of imprecision of feeling,
> Undisciplined squads of emotion. . . .

"Oh, Woe, woe, woe, etcetera. . . ."—as Pound says in "Mr. Housman's Message" (in case one can't help feeling a little unsympathetic). World War II had been under way for almost two years, and perhaps the military phrasing sprinkled through the passage suggests a twitch of stimulus to respond, as Gardner tells us the Krishna-Arjuna section of "The Dry Salvages" must have been. Given the realities of the war and of Nazi behavior, though, neither passage can be taken seriously in this sense. The one combines personal self-pity with a poet-workman's complaint about his medium. The other talks of a "field of battle" almost incidentally, and hardly in terms relevant to blitzkrieg and genocide. (What it actually reads like is a free-verse chorus

uttered by Longfellow and Emerson, competing to see who can be more profound and inspiring.)

It is only in the superb London-blitz passage in "Little Gidding," II, that something like an appropriate level of scorched intensity chimes with the brutal impact of the war:

In the uncertain hour before the morning
  Near the ending of interminable night
  At the recurrent end of the unending
After the dark dove with the flickering tongue
  Had passed below the horizon of his homing
  While the dead leaves still rattled on like tin
Over the asphalt where no other sound was
  Between three districts whence the smoke arose.

Yet the passage quickly moves away from the literal scene so powerfully conveyed here, though retaining the tone of tragic severity. The scene itself is left behind to float as a separate existential affect, like the scene we noted in the second verse-unit of "East Coker" ("Now the light falls . . ."). And what the "Little Gidding" passage turns to almost at once, both in spirit and in literal subject matter, is a concentratedly hell-like psychological atmosphere, a turbulent mixture of unresolved guilt and remorse very close to "Gerontion," *The Waste Land*, and *Ash Wednesday*. That atmosphere is embodied in the nature and speech of the "familiar compound ghost" of all tragic poets from Dante to Yeats: the purgatorial mirror image of the author himself, still wracked by the torments expressed in those earlier poems. *Four Quartets* is such a strange tour de force—oddly Little-Englandish, deeply moving, deeply boring, often beautiful and falsely inspirational (like the closing stanzas of "The Wreck of the *Deutschland*") at the end—that one might well forget how decisively the sulphuric Dantean resonances of this most savage passage connect with those in Eliot's previous work.

The Southern Review (October 1985)

A Thought or Two About J.V. Foix

A poet of this century; a "modern" who (like the others of his somewhat lonely kind) reaches toward an idealized lost past and lost world of myth about which, nevertheless, he has no illusions; a lyricist of the intractable; an ultra-realist whose intensity needs fantasy and buffoonery to make room for itself; hard, provincial, a bit reactionary, beautifully humane; absolutely alienated; absolutely at home.

The usual contradictions that a marvelous poet resolves by taking them all to his bosom: i.e., into his float of language, rhythms, and silences. It's all there in the very first stanza of one of his early sonnets:

> Sol, i de dol, i amb vetusta gonella,
> Em veig sovint per fosques solituds,
> En prats ignots i munts de llicorella
> I gorgs pregons que m'aturen, astuts.

> (Alone, in mourning, wearing an archaic black gown,
> I stray often into dark solitudes,
> Uncharted plains where high slate-mounds surround
> Me, and everywhere I'm blocked by ocean-deep whirlpools.)[1]

The lines are at once ravishing and loaded with stop-sounds, the imagery boisterously copious yet projecting frustration at every turn. The second line is Romantic, positively "Byronic" in its haughty, unbroken gloom. Still, there is a shade of self-parody in the stage directions, as it were, of the first line and the proliferation of images of balked confusion piled up so quickly in the two closing lines (the stanza is hardly comic, but it would need just one more push to match the hilarious exaggeration accompanying the truly terror-filled wasteland-passage in "The Hunting of the Snark"). The internal rhymes and half-rhymes and highly functional alliteration (to which all true poets are addicted and whose particular conformation is the individual poet's clearest fingerprint) indelibly trace the dominant currents of feeling.

And on the other hand (actually, two hands aren't enough for all the oppositions and minor calibrations between extremes in Foix!), the twentieth century and its machinery are happily cherished by this poet at times. The stanza just quoted presents a figure better suited, in his "vetusta gonella," for a past age than for this one. But another early sonnet gives us quite a different picture:

1. The translations in brackets are my own slightly free adaptations.

De matí em plau, amb ferries tenalles
I claus de tub, cercar la peça llosca
A l'embragat, o al coixinet que embosca
L'eix, i engegar per l'asfalt sense falles.

I enfilar colls, seguir per valls ombroses,
Vèncer, rabent, els guals. O món novell!

(It pleases me, mornings, to pick up my pliers and other tools
And get to work and tighten some snug-fitting pin
So the gear will mesh just right, or adjust a bushing that cushions
An axle, and then purr out with smooth power over the asphalt.

And snake up and down mountain-passes, towards valleys in shadow,
And ford streams in a furious rush: Ah, a new world!)

These lines are sandwiched between an opening stanza drenched in antiquarian nostalgia and an ending that combines detached, eclectic aestheticism with an air of breathlessly innocent excitement about *everything* (both very "modern"—no?) The ending:

Em plau, també, l'ombra suau d'un tell,

L'antic museu, les madones borroses,
I el pintar extrem d'avui! Càndid rampell:
M'exalta el nou i m'enamora el vell.

(Also, these things are pleasing: a linden's gentle shade,

A museum of antiquities, madonnas turning dark and fading,
And the far-out stuff of our painters nowadays! I'm a child:
Everything new thrills and exalts me, and I'm mad for everything old.)

Closer still to the psyche of our own century is the pressure in Foix to uncover some secret, saving revelation the very thought of which sends joy flashing through his verse—while, at the same time, an ultimate disbelief makes every such foray a possible source of desolation after all. In the sonnet from which I first quoted ("Sol, i de dol, . . ."), a powerful, willful act of imagination imposes on the baffling world a landscape closer to the heart's desire: "el paisatge/De fa mil anys" (the landscape/Of a thousand years ago). What a liberation—to recover the transcendent pre-modern Eden-like state of existence where alienation was inconceivable! The warm thought follows that this triumph is God's loving trap for the speaker ("el parany/Per heure'm tot"): a sweet paradox Gerard Manley Hopkins would have loved. But wait—at the poem's last moment comes the counter-thought that it is perhaps no triumph but the Devil's trick ("del diable engany") to checkmate both the speaker and God. The knot of unclarity at the heart of the most intense *sense* of transcendence and delight is a frustration Foix seems to exult in.

That is, a natural exuberance of discovery charges his spirit even when what's discovered is tragic. Thus, the sonnet "Jo tem la nit, però la nit m'emporta..." (I'm afraid at night, yet meanwhile night carries me away) begins in terror and one can't say it ends any other way. But the striking energy and dynamics with which it rings its changes somehow give an illusion of triumph. The opening lines are followed by images of incompetent offstage music ("la cobla se sent, confosa"), then of utter loneliness and a ruinous landscape, and then suddenly of a moment of transforming vision: "Però jo hi veig una selva frondosa,/I en erm desert imagín una porta" (But I peer deep and spy a lush woods in their midst,/And imagine a doorway in the wasteland).

What follows "should" be a paradisal evocation of some sort—and what we get, for the moment, is a child's version of delight. Suddenly "la fosca nit m'aparenta pissarra" (the pitch-black night seems to me a huge blackboard), on which one can draw anything one wishes: funny faces, pictures of the dream world we all desire, whatever the innocent imagination can create. But this, it turns out, is only a momentary respite. After it comes the stark realization of the ultimate impersonality of the cosmos. Foix ends this remarkable sonnet, whose dynamic scope is that of a far longer poem of epic density, in a welter of rival tonalities—a tremor of fear, a thrill of cold, pure understanding of the distance of "wisdom" from human needs, a strange half-note demeaning that thrill of awareness, and a brutal summing-up of our condition:

Me'n meravell, i tem—oh nit que afines
Astres i seny!—La mar omples de vestes,
I una veu diu: "Plou sang a les codines."

(I gape, I'm afraid—oh night that isolates naked and pure
Stars and wisdom! You fill the whole sea with cast-off clothes,
And I hear a voice saying: "Blood's raining into the cisterns.")

Here please let me digress on the point made in the footnote to my first bit of translation: that I am offering slightly free adaptations rather than strictly literal renderings. Not that I depart deliberately from Foix's lines; but I do want, rather emphatically, to suggest his evocative resonances as best I can in English. Thus "cisterns" is not quite the same as *catchments*, which might render "codines" more precisely. But in context the closing image has nothing to do with rural sanitary engineering and everything to do with gross fatality. *Catchments* is too blandly technical, for considerations of sound and immediacy of evocation must take precedence. For this reason, too, I have rendered "afines" as "isolates naked and pure" and "vestes" as "cast-off clothes". Ordinarily a poet strives to make a piece of translation as loyal to the original as possible: that is, as loyal as natural, idiomatic phrasing and one's talent will permit. Adaptation is inevitable (I should add here that in translating several of Foix's poems, partly to enter their world of feeling and artistic discipline, I have freely exploited the work of David H. Rosenthal as my crib. His translations are of course conditioned by the rigors of sensitively conscientious scholarship. As an accomplished poet making a whole body of Catalan writing available in translation for the first time, his responsibility has been far greater than that of someone just trying, like me, to tune in on Foix with what empathy he can muster).

To return to the dynamics in Foix's poetry, his place as a master of this crucial element in poetic structuring seems self-evident. We have seen its workings in "Jo tem la nit . . ." with its narrative surface that for a short time only conceals its basically lyrical method—i.e., its surprisingly abrupt associative juxtapositions. We find this even more strikingly in the brief, beautiful "Es feia fosc i miràvem l'estesa de pells a cal baster" (It Was Growing Dark and We Stared at the Hides Scattered about the Saddler's House), dated April 1928. Here too the poem presents itself as a sequence of events but unfolds into a collage or, more actively, a montage of images (Eisenstein's old film *Romance Sentimentale* comes to mind as I write this):

> Ja els fumerols acotxen els jardins;
> Les rels, per terra i murs, s'ajoquen al misteri.
> Tots dos, efígies de cuir abandonades
> A la fosca arenella de la nit,
> Cedim, fraterns, a l'hora fraudulosa.
> Abrivades, les egües, afolcades,
> Nades a l'ombra i a l'ombra nodrides,
> Assolen els poblats.
> Damunt la pell d'elefant del cel
> Els astres obren llurs camins airosos.

> (Already vapors enfold the gardens;
> Roots draw back into mystery, in earth and in walls—
> All the mock skins of things, now forgotten,
> Lost in the deep sandpits of the night,
> Friendly, we cede them to the deceitful hour.
> Aroused and nervous, herds of mares
> Born in shadow and nourished by shadow
> Reach the tiny hamlets.
> High above the elephant pelt of the sky
> The stars open out their airy pathways.)

This poem exists in a kind of nervous ecstasy of balances, between "Ja els fumerols acotxen els jardins" (the changing scene down below on earth) and "Els astres obren llurs camins airosos" (the vast expansion of perspective far up above the clouds). A succession of hardly related metaphors, each comprising three lines at most, make their momentary appearances between these parallel yet opposite opening and closing images. Although they seem independent of one another, the pressure of association among the several metaphors is nevertheless compelling; they accompany the sense, at once enchanted and foreboding, of the ever-encroaching night. And also, they are elements of a proliferating imagery of skins (or coverings, or contexts, or concealments, or even things merely connected with leather). Everything is an illusion or pelt of something else—so much so that perhaps the "saddler's house" of the title is simply the wide world with its endless nexus of secrets within secrets: the only "revelation" we're ever likely to get, though less harshly thrust at us here than in "Jo tem la nit, . . ." One by one, we are told, we "cede" the familiar appearances of things, themselves deceptive "efígies de cuir abandonades" (mock skins of things, now forgotten—or more literally: leather effigies, abandoned), in exchange for other mock appearances. The deceitful hour ("l'hora fraudulosa") of changing forms finds us friendly and receptive ("fraterns") to its trickery. And no wonder, given the lovely images of the darkening world as herds of mares galloping toward all the tiny hamlets, and of the clear open pathways of starlight above the "elephant pelt of the sky," that end the poem.

The charm of these images may make us forget, for a moment, that they are figments of a "deceitful hour" of a type to which the human mind is all too amenable. It is, indeed, a kind of conspiracy between ever-changing outward forms in nature and our subjective imaginations. The negative notes planted along the way in the poem are manifold despite the exquisite play of sound, rhythm, and visual impressions. The assonance, consonance, and internal rhymes alone (to say nothing of the gardens disappearing in shrouds of mist, the shadow-mares, or the gracious stars) could seduce an angel into losing sight of the implied malaise and insecurity.

Among Foix's most famous poems, I am told, is the one that was brought to my attention first:

VAIG ARRIBAR EN AQUELL POBLE, TOTHOM ME SALUDAVA I JO NO CONEIXIA NINGÚ; QUAN ANAVA A LLEGIR ELS MEUS VERSOS, EL DIMONI, AMAGAT DARRERE UN ARBRE, EM VA CRIDAR, SARCÀSTIC, I EM VA OMPLIR LES MANS DE RETALLS DE DIARIS

(I GOT TO THAT TOWN, THEY ALL GREETED ME, AND I DIDN'T RECOGNIZE A SOUL; WHEN I STARTED TO READ MY POEMS, THE DEVIL, LURKING IN BACK OF A TREE, CALLED OUT TO ME, JEERING, AND PILED CLIPPINGS INTO MY HANDS)

Titles like this one are an attractive mannerism of Foix's. They are little prose-poems in themselves, with an air of serious whimsy (read "surrealism" instead, if you wish); and they prepare us for the special bearing of the poem to come. In fact, they get the poem itself under way, like Japanese paper flowers that expand in water. In this instance we soon get to see that the whimsy is actually a bold psychological realism, that the lack of communication with the people in the town is grimly a sign of the times and of the crisis of poetry, and that the insolent presence of the Devil, at first sarcastically calling out and then confidently expectant, is a genuine pressure of evil and torment. The poem is dated September 1942, when Franco was at the height of his power. Repression and cruelty, together with the other accoutrements of Spanish fascism, were in the saddle, and public conversation in Catalan—let alone publication—was forbidden.

None of this is stated in the poem explicitly, and so it would be possible to argue that the "pool of blood . . . shining" ("Clareja un toll de sang") in the third stanza, the suggestions of the Church's association with state power in the first and sixth stanzas—"flors al campanar" (flowers on the steeple) and "El bisbe em condecora" (The bishop decorates me—doubtless by pinning a cross)—have no necessary political significance. Similarly, one could not necessarily *prove* that the "I" of the poem re-embodies—with his "naked foot" associated with a "pool of blood," his (carpenter's?) apron, and his confrontations with the Devil—Jesus in various phases of his life and his Crucifixion, although there are many such implications in the poem. The fusion of persecuted Jesus, the *poète maudit,* and the ordinary person abandoned to a heartlessly indifferent political order supported by the Church and given to propaganda without content is suggested everywhere—and everywhere ambiguously. Under the sway of this order, the composite protagonist is unsure of his own identity and mission and cannot make contact. The opening stanzas may illustrate:

Com se diu aquest poble
Amb flors al campanar
I un riu amb arbres foscos?
On he deixat les claus . . .

Tothom me diu: —Bon dia!
Jo vaig mig despullat;
N'hi ha que s'agenollen,
L'altre em dóna la mà.

—Com me dic?, els pregunto.
Em miro el peu descalç;
A l'ombra d'una bóta
Clareja un toll de sang.

(What's the name of this place
With flowers all over the steeple
And dark trees by the river?
Now where did I put my keys . . .

Everyone greets me: "Good morning!"
I'm walking around in tatters;
Some of them genuflect,
Another gives me his hand.

"What's my name?" I beg them.
I stare at my naked foot;
In the shadow of a barrel
A pool of blood is shining.)

The poem sinks further and further into desolation, interspersed with bits of wry pathos—touches of innocence again distantly suggesting the Christ figure—and of straightforward satire. Near the end the speaker asserts that he's headed for Font Vella: a place-name for many spots in Catalonia, cognate with Fontvieille in Provence. The "meaning" may be literal and therefore not especially pointed; or it may be taken symbolically if we translate it into "Old Wellspring" or "Old Fount"—in which case the suggestion is that he intends to return to his source: Godhead for Jesus, and an older, better world for the poet. But he still has the Devil to confront and resist at the very end. The poem has no "solution," whether political, moral, or existential. Extremely active in detail, it reaches the same bitter edge of unclear perspective—whose *character* is nevertheless clearly perceived—as the more privately oriented poems referred to earlier on:

Me'n vaig a la Font Vella:
N'han arrencat els bancs;
Ara veig el diable
Que m'espera al tombant.

(I'm headed for Font Vella:
They've cleared away the benches;
And now I spy the Devil
Waiting for me on the corner.)

Well, somehow it doesn't seem to matter that joy triumphant doesn't reign in Foix, and that a dark bafflement is never quite overcome. The life of poems lies in the way they cope artistically with the pressures informing them. In "Vaig arribar en aquell poble..." everything in the town the speaker has reached seems set for celebration, and he himself is under the impression he was invited to give a poetry-reading and that the crowds are waiting for him (he is a little like Kafka's hero in *The Castle*). But the whole festive occasion dissolves, the audience just drifts away, and the spots of horror and confusion reveal themselves. The unrhymed quatrains are both alert and terse, and there are no abstractions to interrupt the succession of events, expressions of feeling and sensation, and shifting grammatical formations that accompany the very concrete and colloquial account the poem gives us.

In these few examples of Foix's work I have discussed, we can see something of his authority as a poet of our century, and of the contradictions and the struggle to overcome alienation that color and dominate modern sensibility. A long historical memory and a deep love for the past contend with a helpless skepticism toward all certainties. Every hour is in this sense a "deceitful hour," to which we must yield however much we would have it otherwise. But all this would be irrelevant were it not for the rich and witty dance of sound, and the subtle yet vivacious phrasing, that possess and direct our attention. The combined intimacy, dignity, and half-clowning of this poet give him all sorts of affinities with Yeats, despite every difference of personality and literal technique.

Catalan Review (June 1986)

❧

Innocence Betrayed

PEOPLE LIVE HERE: Selected Poems 1949–83 by Louis Simpson

Carentan O Carentan
Before we met with you
We never yet had lost a man
Or known what death could do.

EVER since it appeared in his first volume, *The Arrivistes* (1949), Louis Simpson's ballad "Carentan O Carentan" has been one of a very few American touchstone-poems of World War II. Its ritualized near-doggerel rehearses the pastoral hell of fledgling soldiers cut down by enemy fire one lovely June day in the Normandy countryside. In its stunned lament for innocents betrayed into death, it is one key to Simpson's work generally. The same fresh horror persists, for instance, in a quite recent poem, "On the Ledge," that recalls yet another ambush like the Carentan one. This time the German unit was destroyed just in time by artillery rockets, but inwardly the poet has remained frozen on the edge of annihilation:

There is a page in Dostoevsky
about a man being given the choice
to die or stand on a ledge
through all eternity

and

like the man on the ledge
I still haven't moved . . .
watching an ant
climb a blade of grass and climb back down.

Simpson shares with the psychologically war-wounded everywhere a particular sort of alienation, based on the lesson that the powers that be, on whatever side, care nothing for the traumatized "man on the ledge." In this respect he is closer to British poets of Wilfred Owen's and David Jones's generation than to his American contemporaries. Perhaps the fact that he was born and grew up in Jamaica, the son of a "native" (his word) father of partly Scottish background, has something to do with this affinity. On the other hand, his mother was a Russian-Jewish immigrant and a naturalized American, and he has a natural family feeling for her childhood world and the life destroyed by the Holocaust. Also, he has lived in the United States since University days and identifies with his adopted country's exhausting spiritual struggle against self-corruption. Two wry passages will illustrate these Jewish and American preoccupations. The first is from "A Story about Chicken Soup":

> In my grandmother's house there was always chicken soup
> And talk about the old country—mud and boards,
> Poverty,
> The snow falling down the necks of lovers.
>
> Now and then, out of her savings
> She sent them a dowry. Imagine
> The rice-powdered faces!
> And the smell of the bride, like chicken soup.
>
> But the Germans killed them.
> I know it's bad taste to say it,
> But it's true. The Germans killed them all.

The second passage, from "Walt Whitman at Bear Mountain," is part of an imagined exchange with Whitman's statue:

> "Where are you, Walt?
> The Open Road goes to the used-car lot.
>
> "Where is the nation you promised?
> Those houses built of wood sustain
> Colossal snows,
> And the light above the street is sick to death."

As in the war poems, extreme alienation is implied in both these instances. Other poems show that the way to Simpson's bleak vision had been paved by what Hart Crane once called "the curse of sundered parentage." One of Simpson's most telling pieces, "Working Late," refers obliquely—but with that dazzling emotional clarity an "obscure" poem can sometimes have—to his parents' separation and his mother's occasional trips to Jamaica to see him. The atmosphere of the house is charged with loneliness. The father, a lawyer of coldly logical temperament, had once constructed a plaster head to show a murderer's angle of fire, and

> For years, all through my childhood,
> if I opened a closet . . . bang!
> There would be a dead man's head
> with a black hole in its forehead.

The half-joke hardly conceals the unresolved memory of fright. Meanwhile, the disappearing mother, in the image of the inconstant moon, is presented richly and longingly. His phrasing for her shows Simpson's ability to shift rapidly between jarring or prosaic tones and lyrically evocative flights:

All the arguing in the world
will not stay the moon.
She has come all the way from Russia
to gaze for a while in a mango tree
and light the wall of a veranda,
before resuming her interrupted journey
beyond the harbor and the lighthouse
at Port Royal, turning away
from land to open sea.

Somehow, these compelling sources of depression allow room for warmth and humor as well, especially in the poems devoted to the mother's childhood world in Russia. Here Simpson takes on the homely role of a Yiddish storyteller, a sort of English-speaking Sholem Aleichem freely deploying Chekhovian and Symbolist flourishes with an attractively modest virtuosity. These poems combine fantasy, pathos, nostalgia, and gaiety and leaven the whole collection. They stand in sharp contrast to bitter poems like "American Classic" and "Quiet Desperation," which see the United States drifting into sheer bourgeois emptiness; and to poems of revulsion like "The Inner Part," "Lines Written in San Francisco," and "Indian Country," which speak of modern Americans as "colonists of Death" and dwellers near "the Lethe of asphalt and dust." The blackest mood of all, perhaps, is found in the short, slightly mysterious "Back in the States," a poem that *seems* to be about a war-prisoner just back from the miseries of Vietnam and "already becoming like the rest of us."

Many of the poems, like the book as a whole, are complex mixtures of style and tonality. In particular, this is true of poems having to do with memories of women—most notably "Sway," about a wartime friendship with a waitress to whom the young poet read Rilke and whose intense though pointless life continues to haunt his imagination. Some of his purest writing focuses on remembered scenes or moments of relationship felt to hold important yet elusive, ultimately lost meaning. Such writing includes "Maria Roberts," "The Hour of Feeling," and "A River Running By"—each centered on a woman's remembered words or perplexing companionship.

People Live Here provides the fullest view thus far of Simpson's technical and emotional range. In an admirable sense, he is a representative American poet of this century: an intimate of that realm of "lost connections" of which Robert Lowell wrote and in which Kenneth Fearing lived, but nevertheless finely quickened by whatever life and language have brought his way.

Times Literary Supplement (4 July 1986)

❧

Notes on the "Memory"-Sequence in Yeats's The Wild Swans at Coole

SUBTLY controlling the exact center of Yeats's *The Wild Swans at Coole* is a sequence of eight intensely personal poems: "Memory," "Her Phoenix," "The People," "His Phoenix," "A Thought from Propertius," "Broken Dreams," "A Deep-sworn Vow," and "Presences." All these poems first appeared in 1916 or 1917 and were incorporated into the 1917 Cuala Press edition of *The Wild Swans at Coole*. The expanded 1919 Macmillan volume includes them in the same order, with "Her Phoenix" retitled "Her Praise."

The psychological moment of the sequence is the period preceding Yeats's marriage in October 1917: something not mentioned in the poems. Nor do they say "Maud Gonne"—even if the name springs inevitably to mind for obvious reasons, especially when one reads "The People." No matter. The poems, like those of Catullus and Propertius or Wordsworth's Lucy poems, hold up in their own right. One can hardly doubt their confessional immediacy, but it serves as affective energy within the sequence rather than as autobiographical documentation.

The most obvious unifying element in the "Memory"-sequence is that it consists of love poems. One must, however, immediately note that they are not the usual expressions of present rapture or anticipation or painful uncertainty or desire. Rather, their character is best indicated by the titles "Memory," "Broken Dreams," and "His Phoenix"—the last because the actual past intimacy, whatever its literal character, has vanished yet is constantly reborn as a commanding presence in the poet's emotional life. That is, the sequence is fixed on the persistent domination of his sensibility and imagination by the nature of the lost beloved. Her power is seen first in the simple and unforgettable physical image, in "Memory," of the hollow left in the mountain grass by the mountain hare. This image—although we meet it only once, and it is replaced further on by the slightly riddling "phoenix"-metaphor—remains the key image of reference of the entire sequence. It is mirrored in the more explicitly personal language of the penultimate poem, "A Deep-sworn Vow," and of the closing "Presences," which adds dimensions of supernatural awe and terror. Meanwhile, however, the reach of the beloved's force has, in successive poems, directed the poet toward unexpected moral and political apperceptions. And at the same time, the sequence plays with varied thoughts about her—a lover's thoughts, sometimes worshipful, sometimes playful, sometimes critical—as if indeed the relationship were an actual empirical reality. The pathos implicit in this dreaming gives the sequence an elegiac cast, while the larger effect is of a self-created world of passionate meanings rooted in a past that refuses to disappear.

For the length of these eight poems, we are totally within that world. It is interesting that they are preceded by "The Hawk," a poem of self-reproach in which the poet reminds himself how easily the "hawk of [his] mind" loses its self-possession. This sharp stab of humility clears the way for poems of submission to a nobler, tutelary spirit. Similarly, the sequence is followed by "The Balloon of the Mind," which pulls the volume back into its previous orbit after immersion in the haunted realm of unrequited love and its permutations. This sequence is an anticipatory reply to the question Yeats was later to raise in "The Tower": "Does the imagination dwell the most/Upon a woman won or woman lost?"

"Memory," a masterpiece of imagist resonance, sets the emotional pitch with its compressed power. It begins in cavalier fashion, its tone that of a man totally free of romantic enslavement—

> One had a lovely face,
> And two or three had charm,
> But charm and face were in vain...

—and then swerves wrenchingly into an image of irrevocable possession, at once delicate and vital, of one being by another:

> Because the mountain grass
> Cannot but keep the form
> Where the mountain hare has lain.

Because it is called "Memory," and because the mountain hare is no longer lying in the mountain grass, the poem expresses loss as well as undying passionate subjection to a stronger personality and its sexual force. The language of shallow, hardly caring gallantry is dropped for that of ungenteel, animal reality, a displacement made even more emphatic by the reversal of sexual roles implicit in the imagery. The sustained enjambment presses the displacement urgently.

This tiny poem of sheer yet complex power is quickly followed by "Her Praise," whose opening line—"She is foremost of those that I would hear praised"—becomes a refrain when repeated in line ten. (In retrospect it seems tinged with plaintive obsessiveness.) The word "praise" recurs three more times, the last time at the very end. The human situation is both homely and touching: a lover's desire to speak his beloved's name and introduce it in all conversation. Whereas "Memory" has the form of pure song and the impact of an arrow shot unerringly from a crossbow, "Her Praise" is more openly confessional, a confiding, unfolding, musing incantation. Its language is restless, impatient:

> I have gone about the house, gone up and down,
> As a man does who has published a new book,
> Or a young girl dressed out in her new gown....

This tone is not *passionate*—not exactly. What it conveys, in context, is a confusion of excited awareness, rather than a sense of being helpless under the spell of another's personal magnetism. The ending moves the celebratory tone into a mood of almost commemorative adoration and prepares us for the brilliant turn in the next poem, "The People." The "mountain hare" of the first poem has left her imperishable imprint, but not only on a man who finds all other loves tame by comparison. "Her Praise" concludes:

> I will talk no more of books or the long war
> But walk by the dry thorn until I have found
> Some beggar sheltering from the wind, and there
> Manage the talk until her name comes round.
> If there be rags enough he will know her name
> And be well pleased remembering it, for in the old days,
> Though she had young men's praise and old men's blame,
> Among the poor both old and young gave her praise.

Again sustained enjambment presses home a striking emotional recognition: in this instance, of the engulfing compassion of a woman. The insight carries the poem's celebratory momentum into something like an attribution of divine grace. An irresistible surge of illumination, transcending private concerns, has reoriented the whole current of association and emphasis. The lover's feelings at the beginning (the restless excitement already noted, and the need to praise the beloved everywhere—"I have turned the talk by hook or crook/ Until her praise should be the uppermost theme")—are still present, but a whole new world of social bearing now encompasses them without obliterating their private glow. The long, loosely four or five-stress lines (almost verging on free verse) and the intricately reflexive rhyme scheme give room for the more complex development of this poem. Yet ultimately it depends on the same kind of torque in its second half that marks the much shorter "Memory"; and by its end it too focuses on "remembering."

The third poem, "The People," is just over twice the length of the eighteen-line "Her Praise." Written in blank verse, it has an even higher frequency of enjambment and presents a deceptively expansive and leisurely surface in its opening verse-unit. In its rhetorical progression, "The People" is a dialogue reminiscent of "Adam's Curse," written some fourteen years earlier. It too centers on a vehement protest by the poet against the public's ingratitude, a rejoinder by a beautiful woman, and a startlingly intimate shift of feeling at the end. But it is much less of a set piece. It lacks the romantic mood-setting start, the carefully patterned rhyming couplets, and the lovely, fragile ninetyish desolation of the passage describing the waning moon "washed by time's waters" in "Adam's Curse." Instead, "The People" starts at once with its partly mean-spirited complaint:

> 'What have I earned for all that work,' I said,
> 'For all that I have done at my own charge?
> The daily spite of this unmannerly town. . . .'

The mountain hare ("my phoenix" in this poem) has bitter knowledge too, but refuses to let it influence her or even be made public. Her reply is sharply to the point, yet pitched on higher moral ground than the poet's combined grousing and eloquent daydreaming about the life he might have led in agreeable company and "among the images of the past—/The unperturbed and courtly images." She reminds him that she has suffered fiercer ingratitude than he without losing sight of her duty to the oppressed and ignorant. Her revolutionary faith is unshakable:

> 'The drunkards, pilferers of public funds,
> All the dishonest crowd I had driven away,
> When my luck changed and they dared meet my face,
> Crawled from obscurity, and set upon me
> Those I had served and some that I had fed;
> Yet never have I, now nor any time,
> Complained of the people.'

Her staunchness puts the poet on the defensive—to no avail, for it has compelled him to face his own self-indulgence and unconscious pettiness, reflected in the poem's opening question with its cash-metaphors: "What have I earned"; "at my own charge." The closing verse-paragraph begins with his rationalizing outward response but ends with a double stress on his inner abashment before her preternatural moral authority: a "natural force" like that of the mountain hare in "Memory." Its place in the buried sequence has enabled "The People" to build on the two previous poems. The initial poem of unresolved passionate domination by a wild life-force in another being gives a fierce, almost brute anchorage to the giddy obeisance paid the loved person and her divinely bountiful spirit in "Her Praise"—which, in turn, reveals the particular lustre of her political faithfulness and resistance to disillusionment in "The People." Suddenly we have the extraordinary experience of seeing the poet forced off his high horse of artistocratic pretentiousness with a pang of simple shame, just as he rises to sheer eloquence:

> All I could reply
> Was: 'You, that have not lived in thought but deed,
> Can have the purity of a natural force,
> But I, whose virtues are the definitions
> Of the analytic mind, can neither close
> The eye of the mind nor keep my tongue from speech.'
> And yet, because my heart leaped at her words,
> I was abashed, and now they come to mind
> After nine years, I sink my head abashed.

This is not the place to go into questions of poetic theory, but I believe we have here a magnificent instance of artistic self-transcendence. That is, the associative process has led the poet to a point beyond his ordinary expressed attitudes, a point of humble recognition of psychological self-deception and irrefutable human realities. The sequence has at this point reached a climax of introspective discovery. It has moved quickly from its opening metaphor of passionate obsession, centered on a private emotional state, through a phase of attention to the dominant other being (the beloved) and her beautiful humanity—and then back to the private self, now vulnerable and "abashed" at the core of its intellectual pride.

The ending of "The People" reminds us, too, of the double time-stream of the poems. The climactic moment described took place in the past, and the sequence derives much power from its refusal to relinquish the immediacy of what that past has embodied. Therefore the affective coloration of the sequence depends on its vibrant sense of repossession of the past, with its lost possibilities, in the *present* volatile circumstance. Memory here is by no means a tranquil recollection of emotion; it is the return of experience with all its original life, though necessarily in an added, elegiac dimension:

> And yet, because my heart leaped at her words,
> I was abashed, and now they come to mind
> After nine years, I sink my head abashed.

But the sequence must return to the primary object of its attention, must break loose from this transfixed attention to the goddess's irrevocable rebuke to her worshipper and go on to new forms of celebration and awareness. The next poem, "His Phoenix" breaks loose with a vengeance. It is a piece of deliberate buffoonery, almost doggerel, with a rollicking ballad rhythm and a cleverly overlapping rhyme scheme capped by the refrain, "I knew a phoenix in my youth, so let them have their day." Yet within this happy, drinking-song frame it rings many emotional changes: something the refrain itself, with its mixed nostalgia and jollity, would suggest. The range of reference, too, is sophisticated from the start despite the colloquial air so that the effect somewhat resembles that of Byron's *Don Juan:*

> There is a queen in China, or maybe it's in Spain,
> And birthdays and holidays such praises can be heard
> Of her unblemished lineaments, a whiteness with no stain,
> That she might be that sprightly girl trodden by a bird;
> And there's a score of duchesses, surpassing womankind,
> Or who have found a painter to make them so for pay
> And smooth out stain and blemish with the elegance of his mind:
> I knew a phoenix in my youth, so let them have their day.

"His Phoenix" is in its way a ballad of fair women of every sort: grand ladies, dancers, actresses, and beauties "who live in privacy." Until the final stanza, the phoenix of the refrain is but one among the many. There, however, the poem turns from its free and easy gaiety and exalts her unique glory in her youth. An added sharp turn comes in the closing lines, which swing the mood back into the strangely elegiac exaltation established in the previous poems:

> There'll be that crowd, that barbarous crowd, through all the centuries,
> And who can say but some young belle may walk and talk men wild
> Who is my beauty's equal, though that my heart denies,
> But not the exact likeness, the simplicity of a child,
> And that proud look as though she had gazed into the burning sun,
> And all the shapely body no tittle gone astray.
> I mourn for that most lonely thing; and yet God's will be done:
> I knew a phoenix in my youth, so let them have their day.

That final note is of bitter loss, of a vision as well as a reality. The next poem, "A Thought from Propertius," holds cleanly up to view what it was that the would-be lover once lost: both the real woman and the vision ("that most lonely thing") of ideal womanhood surrounding her like an aureole. This is the one poem in which she alone holds the stage:

She might, so noble from head
To great shapely knees
The long flowing line,
Have walked to the altar
Through the holy images
At Pallas Athena's side,
Or been fit spoil for a centaur
Drunk with the unmixed wine.

In this single, lapidary poetic sentence, with its careful rhythmic balances and almost secret off-rhyming *(abcdb'a'd'c)*, the tangible sexuality of "Memory" and the supernatural aura evoked in "Her Praise" and "The People" come together as they might in some marvelous piece of Grecian sculpture. The poem's shining isolation as an image of pure pagan divinity whose true life would have flourished in a world of mythical earthiness is enhanced by its placement between the largely boisterous "His Phoenix" and the touching, ordinarily human "Broken Dreams." In the latter poem, the lover addresses his lost beloved directly for the first time, as older man to older woman:

There is grey in your hair.
Young men no longer suddenly catch their breath
When you are passing. . . .

He even makes free to favor her with a denial of her perfection:

You are more beautiful than anyone,
And yet your body had a flaw:
Your small hands were not beautiful. . . .

In lines like these, she is for the first time brought into the ranks of normally mortal women, and made more believable thereby as an actual person. In this poem too, memory itself is for one poetic instant reduced to average proportions:

Your beauty can but leave among us
Vague memories, nothing but memories.

Although all this plain realism humanizes and makes familiar the figure of the beloved, its function in "Broken Dreams" is to arouse a counter-assertion—one that, in turn, only brings into the foreground of the sequence the anguish that has been lurking offstage all the while. The deeper music of this exquisitely articulated poem is that of irrevocable frustration. Hence its insistence on renewing the past from the altered standpoint of the dream-driven present:

Vague memories, nothing but memories,
But in the grave all, all, shall be renewed.
The certainty that I shall see that lady
Leaning or standing or walking
In the first loveliness of womanhood,
And with the fervour of my youthful eyes,
Has set me muttering like a fool.

The poignancy of this penultimate verse-unit, and of certain lines in the closing unit that imagine her changed to a swan and thus even further out of reach, is a corrective to any impression of reconciliation to loss. The poet sizes himself up accurately: not as a triumphant lover in his indomitable imagination, or as one who has gone beyond the follies of romantic desire, but as "the poet stubborn with his passion." At the end the mood sinks into self-dismissiveness:

The last stroke of midnight dies.
All day in the one chair
From dream to dream and rhyme to rhyme I have ranged
In rambling talk with an image of air:
Vague memories, nothing but memories.

Yet the sequence ends with two poems that renew the power of that inescapable "image of air." The first, "A Deep-sworn Vow," begins in bitterness: "Others because you did not keep/That deep-sworn vow have been friends of mine." The lines are a quickening of the negative or critical feelings advanced more gently in "Broken Dreams." They are an accusation and an apology, and they continue the humanizing direction of the preceding poem. Nevertheless, the image of the beloved once more takes over as powerfully as ever when the conscious mind lets down its guard. When the thought of his own death overcomes the speaker, or when he is "excited with wine" or with highly emotional dreams, then—the poem confesses—"suddenly I meet your face." The closing poem, "Presences," intensifies this new emphasis on states of fierce psychic arousal and leaves the sequence in a climactic context of unmediated vision clamoring for expression. The woman-figure who has been in control so far has split up into her three major aspects—sexual, innocently childlike, and regal—in the dream-life. She has become many women, all studying *him* to find the ultimate meaning of his theme: "that monstrous thing/Returned and yet unrequited love." The sequence ends on a note of awestruck bafflement and perturbation, but still entranced by the sexually charged mystery with which it has been coping.

The buried "Memory"-sequence has its unique character, and I shall not at this point elaborate on its place in *The Wild Swans at Coole* considered as a whole. It has obvious affinities with poems like "On Woman" and "The Double Vision of Michael Robartes"; and "Solomon to Sheba" might well be called a happier alternative vision. It provides another elegiac dimension besides those for Mabel Beardsley, Major Robert Gregory, and Alfred Pollexfen. And there are other shared concerns elsewhere: weariness with oneself, changes of perspective in old age, the desire to recapture the feelings of "burning youth." Most of all, these poems at the heart of the book reveal the deeply subjective current of introspection underlying—and implicit in—"The Phases of the Moon" and related pieces.

One more point of some interest (among many that might be adduced in connection with this sequence). *At the Hawk's Well* was published in the Cuala Press edition of *The Wild Swans at Coole*. This is a play without resolution, juxtaposing its elements (the chief of which are the irresistible attraction of Cuchulain to Aoife and the Old Man's frustration) very much as the contradictory elements in the "Memory" group are juxtaposed, though less complexly or subjectively. Yeats's process of increasingly seeing aspects of his own struggles and relationships in the Cuchulain he recreated seems to begin with *At the Hawk's Well,* in fact. That identification reaches its height in *The Only Jealousy of Emer* (the closest in emotional positioning to the "Memory"-sequence) and finds its furthest, darkest discoveries—beyond those of the "Memory" poems—in *The Death of Cuchulain*. But that is another turn on our subject, to be explored in a further discussion.

Yeats: An Annual of Critical and Textual Studies (1987)

❧

The "Actaeon-Principle": Political Aesthetic of Joyce and the Poets

"POLITICAL aesthetic": I mean this phrase to suggest a view of art as expression, rather than as discourse or sloganizing. Poets are certainly persons with opinions: creatures of their historical moments. Yeats held some reactionary views, as did Eliot; and Pound, as man and as citizen, disgraced himself. Hugh MacDiarmid was simultaneously a Communist and a Scots Nationalist. When an American customs official asked him if he had anything to declare, he answered, "Aye, I'm verra Left!" Edwin Muir was a Socialist. All very true. And yet, if one continues talking in this vein (nothing wrong with it; a cul-de-sac can be cozy), one isn't talking about art but about ideology and again ideology—in language that has little to do with how poems work.

Perfectly legitimate. Nevertheless, a work of art transforms all that generates or enters it. It absorbs, without obliterating, its elements into a plastic structure not reducible to the artist's stated motives and meanings. Its medium, which in literature is of course language with all its permutations of sound and association, will have its own history and resonances beyond the individual artist's full knowledge. The greater the work, the farther it carries beyond its master's conscious horizons. Great adventure, great risk.

A classic instance is *The Divine Comedy,* hardly to be accounted for by Dante's narrow politics or his wide theology.

I wish to propose here that the realignment of perspective called modernism has political implications, but of a special sort. Modernism is foreshadowed in past literature whenever the lyric spirit, expressing subjective awareness and the ambiguous, provisional character of our actual apperception, comes into its own. The pressure of ideological and political determinism has long been the curse of human thought, always allied to the winning or consolidation of power. But the lyrical is the wild card in human communion as in literature, in its insistence on tentative perception and intimate psychological accuracy. Tone, rhythm, concreteness of image, and coloration and intensity of phrasing are essential in making brilliantly precise the shadings of complex awareness by which we guide our lives.

Joyce, the most democratic sensibility among the modern masters, who nevertheless influenced the politically reactionary Pound and Eliot more than did any other of their contemporaries, points very clearly toward the triumph of lyrical perspective over ideology. *A Portrait of the Artist as a Young Man* is an exemplar of this triumph, presented through lyrical centers of prose-poetry disguised as broken narrative. (And not only of *prose*-poetry. A rough count shows some thirty-one pages containing poems, snatches or single lines of poems and songs, and prayers and bits of prose arranged as poetry. Except for some lines by Yeats and from a few folk songs or popular traditional songs, these are all identified by author or source—unobtrusively yet with quiet emphasis.) It is a mistake to see the book as largely an ironic mocking of Stephen's naive pretentiousness. Its sloughing off of enslavement to institutionalized religious, national, and familial commitment, and to conventional expectations of love and marriage, certainly has its comic delights; but the intensity of the main drive can hardly be questioned. Nor can the intention to replace that enslavement by a seriously dedicated aesthetic reorientation. The exchanges with the peasant lad Davin, Dedalus' fellow student who embodies a deep, pure nationalist spirit, are but one instance. Davin's tale of a chance encounter with a peasant woman, as innocent in her way as he, is deeply stirring and reveals the roots Stephen has to tear out of himself on his way to freedom. Davin has been shocked by Stephen's confidences, which no doubt were tinged with a Baudelairean affectation. Stephen is therefore constrained to spell out his feelings:

> —The soul is born, he said vaguely, first in those moments I told you of. It has a slow and dark birth, more mysterious than the birth of the body. When the soul of a man is born in this country there are nets flung at it to hold it back from flight. You talk to me of nationality, language, religion. I shall try to fly by those nets.

The progression of *Ulysses* is a far richer triumph of this order. From the start, the work foregrounds the young protagonist's superior sensibility. All but invisibly, this quality is allied with acid political comment, pointed yet evading set positions and subtly contrasted with a series of anti-Semitic jokes and utterances—most notably by Haines, from whom Stephen remains aloof, and by Mr. Deasy, who talks of "jew merchants . . . at their work of destruction" and is answered:

> —A merchant, Stephen said, is one who buys cheap and sells dear, jew or gentile, is he not?
>
> —They sinned against the light, Mr. Deasy said gravely. And you can see the darkness in their eyes. And that is why they are wanderers on the earth to this day.

This is the passage, full of whirling thought, in which Stephen says, "History . . . is a nightmare from which I am trying to awake." The text continues:

> On the steps of the Paris Stock Exchange the goldskinned men quoting prices on their gemmed fingers. Gabbles of geese. They swarmed loud, uncouth about the temple, their heads thick-plotting under maladroit silk hats. Not theirs: these clothes, this speech, these gestures. Their full slow eyes belied the words, the gestures eager and unoffending, but knew the rancours massed about them and knew their zeal was vain. Vain patience to heap and hoard. Time surely would scatter all. A hoard heaped by the roadside: plundered and passing on. Their eyes knew the years of wandering and, patient, knew the dishonours of their flesh.

In this paragraph on the imagined Stock Exchange scene, Stephen's fantasy takes over. A changing vision of "jews" emerges in reverie, moving from the Deasy stereotype to more and more empathy with the "goldskinned men." In the next section, which ends Part I of the book, we are taken along the beach with Stephen during his isolated, highly lyrical reverie. We have been readied for the appearance of Leopold Bloom, Stephen's Jewish co-protagonist, at the start of Part II. Bloom is less cultivated but equally sensitive and introspective, and is perforce a carrier of international historical memories. The political and the aesthetic have been fused—and the Odyssean voyage of dangerous departures is fully under way, having been foreshadowed in the words "wanderers on the earth" and "Their eyes knew the years of wandering."

A surprising instance of a similar fusion occurs in Yeats's "The People," in *The Wild Swans at Coole*. This poem undercuts any simple ideological reading based on Yeats's more backward pronouncements. Indeed, it undercuts its own initial postures of contempt for the mob and of yearning for aristocratic elegance. The poem begins in egoistic protest:

> "What have I earned for all that work," I said,
> "For all that I have done at my own charge?
> The daily spite of this unmannerly town,
> Where who has served the most is most defamed,
> The reputation of his lifetime lost
> Between the night and morning. I might have lived,
> And you know well how great the longing has been,
> Where every day my footfall should have lit
> In the green shadow of Ferrara wall;
> Or climbed among the images of the past—
> The unperturbed and courtly images . . ."

To all this, the unnamed woman called "my phoenix" replies that she has suffered far more from the people's ingratitude. "Yet never," she says, "have I, now nor any time, / Complained of the people." (This despite the greater bitterness of her description of mistreatment.) Although the poet has a ready, rational reply to her affirmation, he confesses, in the poem's final lines, the force and nobility of her words:

> And yet, because my heart leaped at her words,
> I was abashed, and now they come to mind
> After nine years, I sink my head abashed.

The passionate immediacy of this poem, humble and powerful at the same time, struck me long ago. In his reply to the woman, the poet has observed that, because she has "not lived in thought but deed," she "can have the purity of a natural force"—as opposed to the "analytic" probings of his mind. Her certainty comes from the fact that she herself is a living metaphor, indistinguishable from the democratic, revolutionary steadfastness of her words. Her faith in the people is uncalculating, in sharp distinction to the attitude in the poet's opening outburst, in which Yeats slyly deprecates himself by using the language of the marketplace: "'What have I earned for all that work,' I said, / 'For all that I have done at my own charge?'" No wonder he is "abashed" by her unqualified magnanimity.

"The People," in fact, is one of the most original love poems one is likely to read. To repeat a word just used, it is a *revolutionary* love poem of possession not only by another being but also by what that being embodies. With exquisite strategy, Yeats placed it third in a tiny sequence of eight poems quietly embedded in *The Wild Swans at Coole*. The sequence begins with the perfect six-line poem of persistent, ineradicable love called "Memory" (formally paralleled, with variations, in the equally memorable penultimate poem, "A Deep-sworn Vow"). It ends with "Presences," a half-nightmare poem of "that monstrous thing / Returned and yet unrequited love." That "The People" should emerge in such a setting, converting its love-preoccupation into a political one and reversing rhetorical expectations in the process, is one remarkable sign of art's volatile reciprocities. It is a poem of 1915 and a token of how, in the dangerous, challenging world in which the great modern masters dreamt and worked, they awoke to a special new sense of associative freedom closely allied to an epic burden.

I am speaking of a world of potentialities, experiments, explorations: the world in which artists pursue the psychic and aesthetic formations arising from the pressures of their own lives and times. The "epic burden" I have mentioned is an *expressive*, not a primarily didactic or tendentious, relation between a writer's ideology and his or her art. The freedom of art has to do with openness to subjective realities, however self-contradictory on the surface. There is hardly a writer of note who has not been subjected to criticism or praise based on a rigid assumption of iron attitudes actually belied in his or her practice. Poets' publicly stated positions are by no means reliable indications of where their poems' sources lie and whither the poems themselves may lead. The "case" of Ezra Pound is doubtless our most striking instance among the many from which one might have chosen, and I should like to turn now to the basic considerations his work compels us to be aware of.

There's not much use at this late date in laboring the well-known facts about Ezra Pound's politics. He made very bad mistakes. He harbored poisonous attitudes and, indeed, attitudinized himself into a corner—a case, a little like Mayakovsky's in Russia, of what he himself recognized as *ὑπὲρ μόρον* (beyond the foreseeable). He escaped a treason trial only by virtue of his supposed insanity. So be it. Eugenio Montale, a quieter poet who had coped bravely with the Mussolini government in his own fashion, basically forgave Pound as a self-deceived baby of genius. "That a poet remain a child," he wrote, "is a necessary condition for his poetry; but perhaps Pound stayed too much on this side of the proper dividing line." No doubt Montale wrote truly, although such babies can be grossly unpleasant (as of course Montale was implying).

But let's focus, without forgetting the enormities Pound ignored or rationalized, on the genius-side of the equation. He was a great poet, not only in his virtuosity but also in the way his work was a reflex of the passion behind his convictions and of his sense of artistic and personal predicament. Beyond the apprentice (or the simply hopeless) level, a poet does have to write out of the way he or she really is. This isn't a matter of just mirroring one's private self; that's not the point at all. Rather, it's a matter of working as best one can out of one's whole awareness, from the barely conscious images and moods of reverie to the clearest, most explicit logical thought. At his best, Pound is unsurpassed in the way his poems give objective form to the inchoate flux of subjective life: a result that is the special triumph of the lyrical as the decisive element in poetry.

Let me cite a relatively early poem of Pound's as illustration, and also as a means of leading into the issue of how the poet's ideology and convictions connect with his art. This is the poem "The Coming of War: Actaeon," first published in March 1915.

The Coming of War: Actaeon

An image of Lethe,
        and the fields
Full of faint light
        but golden,
Gray cliffs,
        and beneath them
A sea
Harsher than granite,
        unstill, never ceasing;
High forms
        with the movement of gods,
Perilous aspect;
        And one said:
"This is Actaeon."
        Actaeon of golden greaves!
Over fair meadows,
Over the cool face of that field,

Unstill, ever moving
Hosts of an ancient people,
The silent cortège.

The poem's title is an unusual gesture—for this poet at any rate—toward explicitly spelling out the psychological pressure underlying its associative complex. Without the title, only a preternaturally suggestible reader could readily see the connection between the poem and the recent outbreak of the Great War, let alone that between the War and Actaeon. But the title nudges us firmly toward these crucial associations and, as it happens, toward the essential nature of poetic process revealed in Pound's development and in the greatest poetry generally. Specifically, the process is one of conversion of private awareness by an artistic medium: the language of lyric poetry, with its melodic dimensions, its partnership with memory, and its love affair with sensations and feeling. This conversion makes the most intimately private, idiosyncratic states available through the plastic, aesthetic medium of language. The more serious and gifted the poet, the greater the risks both of self-exposure and of being carried to disastrous limits. *Immediacy of association has no defenses*.

What has all this to do with "The Coming of War: Actaeon"?

To return to the poem's title, the implied analogy is between two instances of tragic blundering, the one mythical, the other historical: the blundering of Actaeon into Artemis' grove of sacred female mysteries, so that he saw the goddess bathing and was punished by being turned into a stag and killed by his own hunting dogs; and the blundering of the nations, once again as countless times before, into war.

The analogy implicit in the title becomes the frame for the poem, which may be compared to a dream-based scenario. It begins in the realm of the dead, with Lethe, the river of forgetfulness that flows through Hades (here merged with the Elysian fields):

An image of Lethe,
        and the fields
Full of faint light
        but golden.

Eerie, sad, and lovely at once, these lines give a distanced and impersonal yet intense coloration, as of irrevocable loss, to the poem's opening. The coloration grows grimmer and threatening in the next four lines; their starker beauty has a nightmare edge of deadly risk:

Gray cliffs,
    and beneath them
A sea
Harsher than granite,
        unstill, never ceasing.

The gathering tonality has something to do with the drastic implications of the death-ridden title. At the same time, the two initial passages I have quoted—while not explicitly linked with one another as pictorially continuous (but metonymically attached)—provide an extended vision of the realm of death not given in Greek myth or in its attendant classical literature. That is, the sea dashing forever against the cliffs appears as the violent, intractable route to death although death's supernatural realm exists high above it. The succession of juxtaposed sentence fragments is completed by an ambiguous description of godlike figures and a phrase—"Perilous aspect"—that applies equally to their demeanor and to the extended scene itself:

> High forms
> with the movement of gods,
> Perilous aspect.

We may for a moment seem to be pressing things a bit to find, in this unfocused yet commanding imagery, a suggestion of the linked power and terror symbolized in the Actaeon myth and enacted in the very nature of war. Yet suddenly the poem takes a decisive turn to just this suggestion:

> And one said:
> "This is Actaeon."
> Actaeon of golden greaves!

This is one of those torques that mark Pound's finest work so unmistakably. A voice from within the realm of godlike shades that overlooks the murderous sea has recognized a new arrival: presumably Actaeon after his punishment for having profaned the sacred retreat of Artemis. Then the poem itself cries out the Homeric epithet, "Actaeon of golden greaves!"—an epithet more suitable to a warrior than to a hunter. After this outcry the extended image of the hordes of all the past dead forming a funeral procession for the newest arrival takes over the rest of the poem. In this closing passage, the quiet, impersonal intensity of the opening lines is recaptured and then powerfully deepened by that simultaneously grave and turbulent vision. If we recall the title once more, we shall see Actaeon's arrival as embodying the new deaths of the present war, and the "silent cortège"—the "hosts of an ancient people"—as including all their predecessors in all the wars of history:

> Over fair meadows,
> Over the cool face of that field,
> Unstill, ever moving
> Hosts of an ancient people,
> The silent cortège.

The poem's first line, "An image of Lethe," introduces a particular scene. It also, of course, introduces the whole poem, thus suggesting that part of mankind's blundering into war results from *forgetting* what the past has taught, for the word "Lethe" implies both death and the obliteration of memory. Thus, from the start, the poem begins to evoke a vast, subtle complex of concerns and attitudes related to war, historical memory, fatality, and human limitations. The greatest of our limitations, the Actaeon-myth reveals, is that we cannot foresee the consequences of what existential circumstance will drive us into being and doing.

All this is not discursively but lyrically presented. As Pound had written a couple of years earlier, "A poem is supposed to present the truth of passion, not the casuistic decision of a committee of philosophers." The associative movement of "The Coming of War: Actaeon" is a construct of "the truth of passion." Early on, Pound appears to have sensed the fated way of his own life as well as of history in the story of Actaeon, and to have begun to see the poet's art in the same light. The body of his major work reveals an implicit poetics related to the Actaeon-principle. The dominant concept implied is of a shaping pressure whose rigorous gravity and increasingly specter-ridden dread carry a poem into a state of passionate alertness beyond the reach of logic or of ideology in the usual sense. We see the horror of war and its inescapability, yet the poem professes neither pacifism nor determinism. We feel the continuing force of the inherited past, and the continuing vivid meaning of myth, yet the poem offers no conservative creed. The passionate alertness I have mentioned is an existential one. Its commitment is irreversible—I mean, its commitment to what it perceives, shared with us to the degree that we are drawn into its orbit. Nor can we resist being so drawn, I submit, so long as the "truth of passion" in its successive affective units conveys itself.

"The Coming of War: Actaeon" represents Pound in his purest aspect: thoroughly engaged as a poet with everything that human beings care about, and at the same time anything but tendentious. It is true that the gifts deployed in this poem did not prevent his holding fast elsewhere to his provincial American prejudices, which he assumed to be as valid as more self-evident realities like the history of ever-recurring wars and the pathetic vulnerability of societies to greed. In the between-wars European context, these prejudices lost their sheen of populist innocence and took on monstrous proportions. Racial clichés and certain glib economic and political dogmas merged with bloody atrocity—not of course committed personally by Ezra Pound. But we shall return a bit further on to this matter as it affects his poetry. It is the darkest side of what we may call his Actaeon-principle.[1]

I have suggested that Pound's whole *oeuvre* reveals not only a daring and dazzling technique but an implicit poetics closely related to the Actaeon-principle. Poetry isn't something to "get published," but a dangerous voyage—a process that is crucially subject to the swerve of the unforeseen, despite the importance to poets of supreme mastery of their art.

Pound comes closest to putting the case explicitly—if elusively—in a passage of Canto 4 (1919). Eight lines in all, it begins with an imagined scene in which the mad Provençal poet Peire Vidal, who like Actaeon is said to have been attacked by his own dogs (when he disguised himself in a wolfskin), is

> Stumbling, stumbling along in the wood,
> Muttering, muttering Ovid:
> "Pergusa . . . pool . . . pool . . . Gargaphia,
> "Pool . . . pool of Salmacis."

1. In Canto 80, however, there is a subtler identification with Actaeon, elusively implied in the suggestion that Pound, like him, has been victimized by Artemis. An allusion to Yeats's early poem "The Moods" in this context suggests the impersonality of the process that may advance or destroy us. I am indebted to Walter Baumann for pointing out this allusion to me.

As if he were Pound himself, Vidal is dreaming of scenes and transformations in Ovid's *Metamorphoses*, at once miraculous and shot through with a sort of doomed sexuality: the ravishment of Persephone near the lake Pergusa; Actaeon's tragic arrival at Gargaphia, sacred to Artemis; and the misfortunes of Hermaphroditus because of the water nymph Salmacis. Then, in the same verse-unit but no longer in Vidal's supposed voice, the single line "The empty armour shakes as the cygnet moves" evokes the escape of Neptune's son Cygnus in the form of a swan when Achilles was about to slay him. The line, exquisite in itself and ominously resonant, serves as a transition to three lines suggesting the uncontrollable context of artistic vision, seen in the metaphor of liquid light introduced by the troubadour Arnaut Daniel (and translated by Pound alongside it at the beginning of the new verse-unit):

> Thus the light rains, thus pours, *e lo soleills plovil*
> The liquid and rushing crystal
> beneath the knees of the gods.

Beauty is thus subtly related to unseen powers, and creation to tragic risk or error. Pound's larger identification in the *Cantos* as a whole is with Odysseus, who constantly ran the risk of the unknown. Actaeon and Vidal are minor alternatives to the Odyssean model, shading it toward a personal and tragic coloration: an emphasis on humiliation or remorse rather than sheer archaic heroism. The *Cantos* present scattered notes of self-reproach, as if written by an introspective Odysseus who pointedly recalls that not even he could exercise enough "care and craft" to forestall all folly. Sometimes they express a piercing regret for a failure of compassion (perhaps the result of rigorous artistic shunning of sentimentality):

> Les larmes que j'ai creées m'inondent
> Tard, très tard je t'ai connue, la Tristesse,
> I have been hard as youth sixty years.

Such a confession shows recognition that one has grown imperceptibly into a disastrous, perhaps irrevocable state, even if out of originally good or innocent motives. Among other things, it prepares us for the extraordinarily humanized passages later in the *Pisan Cantos*, particularly winning in Canto 83. These are passages acknowledging tragic transformation. In this sense they resemble Keats's *Hyperion* fragments: our first instances of the lyricization of epic form, and of the triumph of the lyrical as the essential poetic element—as opposed to the deceptions of rhetoric and the surface suspense of narrative.

But aren't there also instances of rhetoric in the *Cantos?* And if so, should they not be dismissed on the grounds just advanced? Oddly enough, Pound does not really give us extended passages of argument and exposition as such. He doesn't drone and intone endlessly like Robinson, Stevens, Frost, and Eliot in their later phases. Often he is too demanding for a poor beleaguered reader's spirit to go along willingly with his polyglot diction and polymath allusions. But on these occasions, nevertheless, there is usually artistic gain. A longish quotation from John Adams or another admired sage—or from some document—may serve to provide a shift in tonality as well as to introduce a thought for its own sake. In context, the quotation (often together with the poet's own surrounding or interspersed phrasing) is meant to have an evocative coloration comparable to that of an image.

For example, the following passage from Canto 88, consisting of a bit of commentary on British banking history and part of a quotation from the terms of the United States Bank Charter (somewhat freely edited by the poet), has a lyrical function. Within the canto as a whole, it contributes to a swiftly moving, often narrative construct that is charged with the white-hot fury of crucial political and personal conflict. The passage exploits the rhythms of emphatic rhetoric to help convey indignation at what is felt as ruthless human betrayal rooted in centuries-long practice. The deployment of such devices as parallel contructions and repeated phrases rising to climax, or the sudden, unexpected hovering over a single word for dramatic stress ("DEBT," "GERM"), or the broken lineation that choreographs the rhetorical movement—all this skillful technique—helps embody passionate thought in action. The passage reads:

Such
a bank tends to subjugate government;
It tends to collusions,
to borrow 50 and pay back one hundred,
it tends to create public DEBT.
1694: Loan One Million 200,000.
Interest 80,000, Expenses 4.
GERM, nucleus, and is now 900 Million
It tends to beget and prolong useless wars;
aggravate inequalities, make and break fortunes.
"To carry on trade of banking
upon the revenues,
and in the name of the
United States;
to pay revenues to the
Government
in its own (the bank's own) notes of promise. To
Hold United States moneys
in deposit, without making compensation;
To discredit other banks . . ."

These lines will not strike a casual reader as "poetic" in any conventional sense, but a minimal openness to their incantatory use of supposedly unpoetic language will bring out their hypnotic musical force. This will be especially true once one realizes the extraordinary virtuosity of the *Cantos* as a whole, for it then becomes clear that a passage like the one just quoted is written in but one tonal mode among many. Even those passages which are argumentative in character usually vary greatly. See for instance the famous chants against sentimentality in Canto 30 and against usuriousness in Canto 45. The former starts off as if it were going to be a pastoral love song:

Compleynt, compleynt I hearde upon a day,
Artemis singing, Artemis, Artemis
Against Pity lifted her wail.

Canto 45, though, begins as if it were a stern pronouncement from the pulpit—"With *Usura*"—and then launches into a gradually more and more fierce series of denunciatory items climaxed by images of gross disaster:

Usura slayeth the child in the womb
It stayeth the young man's courting
It hath brought palsey to bed, lyeth
between the young bride and her bridegroom
CONTRA NATURAM
They have brought whores for Eleusis
Corpses are set to banquet
at behest of usura.

Or again, to cite another well-known passage, there is the piece of hearty satire in Canto 80 that parodies Browning for a moment in the first line ("Oh to be in England now that Winston's out") and goes on to gloat over the financial crisis of postwar Britain:

Chesterton's England of has-been and why-not,
or is it all rust, ruin, death duties and mortgages
and the great carriage-yard empty
and more pictures gone to pay taxes

It is one of those stupidly unfortunate, thorny truths that Pound cast his lot with Mussolini's Fascists and gave voice to anti-Semitic and other political nonsense. His intellectual vanity, together with the populist provincialism I have mentioned, may well have been the Actaeon factor leading him to personal disaster. That is, it set him going on the hubristic road of asserting his personal authority that led to his arrest for treason and his subsequent humiliations and that infected his poetry, at times, with the authentic odor referred to in Shakespeare's line "Lilies that fester smell far worse than weeds." One comes upon the brief passages revealing his viler affinities with a sort of jolt or electric shock. Not only do they seem unbelievable in such a highly developed sensibility—the kind that could achieve the wonderfully humanistic Canto 47 and innumerable other passages of similar accomplishment. They also (and this is the deeper shock and closest to the very nature of true art) fit perfectly into their poetic setting in a canto as superb as the one opening *Pisan Cantos*. They represent what I would consider the greater risk of passionate alertness in and out of art, a risk Pound himself understood but could not altogether cope with.

This is the gist of what I have called the Actaeon-factor or Actaeon-principle: the inevitable blundering into violation of the forbidden that attends the free, exploring imagination. Put the matter simply. If you never fall in love, you'll never make the sometimes disastrous mistakes of commitment. If nothing arouses your hatred, you'll never suffer remorse at misdirecting your anger.

And (to get into the Poundian arena of the artist as engaged citizen) if you do not feel fury when you see whole nations at the mercy of armed gangs, billions squandered on armaments while so many go hungry, and official deceptions and fraudulence proliferating until you recognize how little information of vital importance most of us can ever hope for—if your gorge riseth not: why, then your imagination sleepeth, or it feareth to dwell on unmanageable realities.

If, however, you are susceptible to imaginative arousal, and must stare at naked cruelty and suffering as Actaeon stared at the goddess, your predicament will be perilous indeed. You will hardly find it easy to choose the best path of understanding—let alone of action if you feel bound to act. The tragic, insoluble problem of choosing among partisan ideologies will press hard upon you. For a poet it is like facing into the actuality of death or the intractability of past injustice. And quite possibly the bravest, and those whose feelings are the keenest, are destined to be among those who will lose their way without warning. There is enough truth in Pound's two most striking efforts at self-comforting, it may be, to enable each of us to cope with the inevitable in the short run at least:

> Here error is all in the not done,
> all in the diffidence that faltered . . .

and:

> nothing matters but the quality
> of the affection—
> in the end—that has carved the trace in the mind
> dove sta memoria

And if all this seems a trifle solemn, let me recommend, finally, the whimsically charmed, lightly self-mocking description of the baby wasp's descent to Hades (mimicking at once both the *Odyssey* and the *Cantos*) in Canto 83. Here Pound puts everything in wryly humble perspective, and kindly omits any attention to dire outcomes, focusing only on the life enterprise itself. If he started out as an *enfant terrible* and remained one for too long a time, he mirrors, in these lines, the best of himself as man and artist, immediately after revealing himself at his most vulnerable:

> When the mind swings by a grass-blade
> an ant's forefoot shall save you
> the clover leaf smells and tastes as its flower
>
> The infant has descended,
> from mud on the tent roof to Tellus,
> like to like colour he goes amid grass-blades
> greeting them that dwell under XTHONOS ΧΘΟΝΟΣ
> ΟΙ ΧΘΟΝΙΟΙ; to carry our news
> εις χθονιους to them that dwell under the earth,
> begotten of air, that shall sing in the bower
> of Kore, Περσεφόνεια
> and have speech with Tiresias, Thebae

Note

Yeats's poem "The Moods," referred to in the footnote, appeared in *The Wind Among the Reeds* (1899) and obviously, like "He Wishes for the Cloths of Heaven" in the same volume, impressed the young Pound as a model of melodic and tonal structure:

Time drops in decay,
Like a candle burnt out,
And the mountains and woods
Have their day, have their day;
What one in the rout
Of the fire-born moods
Has fallen away?

Almost fifty years later, in Canto 80, we find these lines (the "she" is Artemis):

At Ephesus she had compassion on silversmiths
    revealing the paraclete
standing in the cusp
    of the moon et in Monte Gioiosa
    as the larks rise at Allegre
                                        Cythera egoista
But for Actaeon
of the eternal moods has fallen away

Despite the allusiveness, rapid shifts, and discontinuous syntax, as well as the implied identification with Actaeon, the connection with Yeats's sense of what a poem is holds clear.

The Southern Review (July 1987)

"Nerved by What Chills / the Blood": Passion and Power in Marianne Moore

LAST year was Marianne Moore's centenary, and somehow she swam into the mind with a new intensity—the quality she most valued when she edited *The Dial:* "A thing must have 'intensity.' That seemed to be the criterion."

Those of us who grew up in the shadow of her great poetic generation sensed that quality in her work but were, for a while, held at arm's length by her protective surround of coolly incisive elegance. Yet the more one reads her, the clearer it becomes that she was far more the lyric poet than her reputation has allowed. Sententiousness leavened by wit has its graces, for which she has had ample praise, but a driven intensity carried her much further. Her poem "The Mind Is an Enchanting Thing" is an exquisite example:

THE MIND IS AN ENCHANTING THING

is an enchanted thing
    like the glaze on a
katydid-wing
        subdivided by sun
        till the nettings are legion.
Like Gieseking playing Scarlatti;

like the apteryx-awl
    as a beak, or the
kiwi's rain-shawl
        of haired feathers, the mind
        feeling its way as though blind,
walks along with its eyes on the ground.

It has memory's ear
    that can hear without
having to hear.
        Like the gyroscope's fall,
        truly unequivocal
because trued by regnant certainty,

it is a power of
    strong enchantment. It
is like the dove-
        neck eminated by
        sun; it is memory's eye;
it's conscientious inconsistency.

It tears off the veil; tears
    the temptation, the
mist the heart wears,
        from its eyes—if the heart
        has a face; it takes apart
defection. It's fire in the dove-neck's

iridescence; in the
    inconsistencies
of Scarlatti.
        Unconfusion submits
        its confusion to proof; it's
not a Herod's oath that cannot change.

The poem is a little unusual for Moore in beginning at such a melodic pitch: first, her engaging self-correction between title and first line ("THE MIND IS AN ENCHANTING THING//is an enchanted thing"); and then the pair of enraptured similes:

> like the glaze on a
> katydid-wing
> subdivided by sun
> till the nettings are legion.
> Like Gieseking playing Scarlatti;

The self-correction shifts the poem quickly from a level of spontaneous wonderment to one of dazzled excitement expressed with a precision put to the service of sheer song. The bright, elated images that follow project a state of transport within the space of the carefully choreographed dance of lines in this first stanza. Although the next stanzas are weightier in their assertions and their intellectual demand, they retain the memory of all this celebratory gaiety, which also introduces—without crushingly discursive emphasis—an unfamiliar conception of the mind. "Mind" here is neither an abstraction nor a mechanical process but something magically, and beautifully, alive: glittering, physical, infinitely magnetic. Although the succeeding stanzas do not sustain, in phrasing or in feeling, the high-spirited, sweetly soaring tone of the opening, their *form* recalls it all the way through, for in each case the form exactly matches the metrical, spatial, and rhyming arrangement of the first stanza.

Sustaining this formal memory of initial ecstasy prevents the poem from bogging down when it changes emotional key in the second stanza. There the image is introduced of the apteryx, or kiwi: a New Zealand bird with a long, sharp, awl-like beak and hairlike feathers; its wings are undeveloped, and so it seeks its food along the ground. Since this bird is unknown to most non-South Pacific readers, the stanza takes on a slower pace, partly riddling, partly interrupted by caesuras, to help us envision the kiwi and its slow, ground-searching movement: an image of the mind in action, at once deliberate, piercing in its search for nourishment, and instinctually compelled:

> the mind
> feeling its way as though blind,
> walks along with its eyes on the ground.

The phrases "the apteryx-awl/as a beak" and "the/kiwi's rain-shawl" do have a playfulness reminiscent of the first stanza's gaiety. They form a modulation into the new key of grave contemplation, which deepens as the second stanza progresses and continues through the third. Indeed, by the end of the third stanza the poem threatens to become lost in amazement at the mind's "regnant certainty" and at the solemn mystery underlying it. But the fourth stanza remembers the motif of "enchantment" and introduces a vitally seductive new image for the mind:

It
is like the dove-
neck animated by
sun;

This image counteracts the gathering sententiousness of the stanza's close. It echoes the sunlight imagery of the first stanza ("the glaze on a/katydid-wing/ subdivided by sun") and prepares us for some new departure. And then, suddenly, in the penultimate stanza, the poem takes off again with wrenching, shocking force. The mind's dazzlingly enchanting purposefulness within its complex involvements is now seen in a new light. It is necessarily ruthless in its penetration:

It tears off the veil; tears
the temptation, the
mist the heart wears,
from its eyes—if the heart
has a face; it takes apart
dejection.

Power, passion, and suffering are compressed in this language. The passage embodies confession of profoundly shaken and disabused ardor, and beyond that of resultant depression that only the most unsentimental probing can account for. (The poem does not even claim that the mind can *dispel* depression; it can only "take it apart.") The "fire in the dove-neck's//iridescence" and the "inconsistencies/of Scarlatti" are images charged with delight; but when reintroduced toward the poem's end, they connect with something less ravishing. They have their impersonal separateness from human desires and needs, just as the mind's irrevocable pursuit of reality—however much it may have to change direction in the process—remains impersonal even if the pressure behind it is grief. These lines are a brief aria totally beyond the level of the cool style with which Marianne Moore usually masked any susceptibility to emotional storm. Like Yeats's "Meru," they face into the desolation that the "ravening" mind must strip bare—and the only transcendence offered is the transport of dark recognition itself.

Comparable effects appear in the long poem "Marriage." In her preface to *A Marianne Moore Reader*, the author denied the poem has any personal bearing and called it merely "a little anthology of statements that took my fancy—phrasings that I liked." But amid all its ironies and its air of detachment, suddenly we find this passage:

Below the incandescent stars[1]
below the incandescent fruit,
the strange experience of beauty;
its existence is too much;
it tears one to pieces

1. This line curiously anticipates a striking passage in T.S. Eliot's "Burnt Norton."

and each fresh wave of consciousness
is poison.

"Marriage" is suavely cutting on the subjects of connubial love, sexual desire, and male presumptuousness. The passage just quoted swerves away from anything like emotional distancing, however; it begins with voluptuous Keatsian intensity and ends in outright bitterness. The whole poem's mocking absorption in the legend of Adam and Eve ("I wonder what Adam and Eve/ think of it by this time," the poet says early on) is willy-nilly an engagement with primal passions in any case. It leads to rhapsodic contemplation of Adam even while he is being depreciated:

that invaluable accident
exonerating Adam.
And he has beauty also;
it's distressing—the O thou
to whom from whom,
without whom nothing—Adam;
"something feline,
something colubrine"—how true!
a crouching mythological monster
in that Persian miniature of emerald mines,
raw silk—ivory white, snow white,
oyster white, and six others—
that paddock full of leopards and giraffes—
long lemon-yellow bodies
sown with trapezoids of blue.
Alive with words,
vibrating like a cymbal
touched before it has been struck . . .

This marvelous passage has richness of a kind rarely associated with Moore's style. The other passages I have quoted are more direct outbursts of feeling and show her kinship with other lyric poets of high volatility. Inner turmoil (like that in Emily Dickinson's " 'Twas like a Maelstrom, with a notch") and love-entrancement (like that in her "Come slowly, Eden!") surface irrepressibly in those earlier quotations. But in these lines on Adam we see the co-presence both of restraint and of letting go. The lines struggle valiantly, wittily, and more or less successfully to keep things under control. They do so, in part, by deliberately merging Adam and the Serpent for the moment, and by describing Eden as a sort of Gaudí-designed or "Persian miniature" artifact, such as one might wish to find in a special wing of the Museum of Modern Art. Aesthetically, the passage is pure joy. In its very individual mixture of Romantic and modern pigments, it is also reminiscent of the varied colors, bouncing details, and sensuous phrases jumping out of their skin with excitement in Browning's verse. This is a sort of intensity that in one direction approaches buffoonery and in another reaches toward those most acute tones of power, violence, danger, and passionate arousal that keep surfacing later in "Marriage." Those tones ring out in wild splashes of verbal color, as in the following instances:

(1) "the speedy stream
which violently bears all before it,
at one time silent as the air
and now as powerful as the wind."

(2) "Treading chasms
on the uncertain footing of a spear,"

(3) Plagued by the nightingale
in the new leaves,

(4) "It clothes me with a shirt of fire."

(5) Unnerved by the nightingale

I have plucked these instances at random from the text. Some are quotations set as verse by Moore; others are completely her own. What matters in the dynamics of the poem is their resonance within it.

But to return to the passage describing Adam in Eden, it is a perfect triumph of passion within restraint. The chief value of "restraint" in poetry emerges only when we see that, at the right moments, the poet can also release feeling in full measure, making himself or herself vulnerable by giving the game away. Adam-Lucifer "has beauty"—"distressing" beauty. He is indispensable and dwells (monster though he be) in a dream-realm, one that combines the bestial and the blazingly attractive and the vibrantly articulate. All the notes of passionate intensity in the passage—as in the whole poem—serve to violate the resolute pose of sophisticated amusement set up to resist engulfment in chaotic feeling. Goethe wrote of the *"Jammer und Glück"* forever contending under Eros' stormy, pitiless rule. He begged his muses to leave him in peace. Moore, in "Marriage," confronts that rule with all her resources. The poem is one of her triumphs. In it she discovers how to deploy her genius for mannered restraint to enhance expression of great psychic tensions.

I should like to make one more general observation on the link between the sources of pleasure and the sources of terror in her work. The major source of pleasure for the poet herself seems to be an ongoing internal conversation, in which she is her own best audience and responder. It is full of joy at apt and melodic language, at the mind's endlessly copious associations, and at the ever-enticing profusion of things to observe: all the surfaces of quirky reality. And yet a darker undertone often accompanies what at first seems undilutedly joy-giving. See for example the finally ironic "The Steeple-Jack," which so disingenuously reassures us that

It could not be dangerous to be living
    in a town like this, of simple people,
who have a steeple-jack placing danger signs by the church
while he is gilding the solid-
    pointed star, which on a steeple
stands for hope.

The pressure here is of tragic awareness amid the world's intriguing sources of exuberance. The poet's sense that the whole life-perspective on this town (or on the universe) can be seen in illusory, gratifying patterns is self-sardonic. The same kind of drastic undercutting of aestheticized complacency occurs in the more direct "A Grave." Nor could we find a more intensely savage and disheartened poem than the truly startling "Bird-Witted." This poem begins with delighted observation of a mother mockingbird and her young. It ends in fascinated horror:

A piebald cat observing them,
   is slowly creeping toward the trim
trio on the tree stem.
   Unused to him
the three make room—uneasy
new problem.
         A dangling foot that missed
         its grasp, is raised
and finds the twig on which it
planned to perch. The

parent darting down, nerved by what chills
   the blood, and by hope rewarded—
of toil—since nothing fills
   squeaking unfed
mouths, wages deadly combat,
and half kills
         with bayonet beak and
         cruel wings, the
intellectual cautious-
ly creeping cat.

One finds in Moore, then, powerful pressures of fear, uneasiness, and a sensuousness that is itself felt as extreme vulnerability. The careful verse-patterning, like the temptation to see existence in pleasing, almost static patterns, serves to steady the passionate expression that *will* surge forth, defying containment. But "Bird-Witted" defines all this in the single phrase: "nerved by what chills/the blood."

American Poetry Review (July/August 1988)

Hurrah for Longinus! Lyric Structure and Inductive Analysis

IT is truly curious that, despite centuries of study and scholarship, and libraries overflowing with books on the subject, most literature remains unexplored in its own artistic right. There has been too little progress in such exploration since Longinus wrote his brief, arresting analysis of Sappho's most famous poem. Here is my free version of the poem, which she composed in the seventh century B.C.:

> Peer of gods he seems to me, the man
> who sits facing you and, close to you,
> listens to your sweet words
>
> and honeyed laughter.
> How that sound stirs the heart in my breast!
> When I just glimpse you my voice goes,
>
> my tongue's helpless,
> exquisite fire runs through my body,
> my eyes fail, my ears throb thunder,
>
> sweat drenches me, I'm seized
> with tremors. I grow pale as autumn grass,
> as if death were upon me.

And here, probably some nine centuries later, is Longinus' comment (in the W. Rhys Roberts translation):

> We shall find one source of the sublime in the systematic selection of the most important elements, and the power of forming, by their mutual combination, what may be called one body. The former process attracts the hearer by the choice of the ideas, the latter by the aggregation of those chosen. For instance, Sappho everywhere chooses the emotions that attend delirious passion from its accompaniments in actual life. Wherein does she demonstrate her supreme excellence? In the skill with which she selects and binds together the most striking and vehement circumstances of passion. . . . Are you not amazed how at one instant she summons, as though they were all alien from herself and dispersed, soul, body, ears, tongue, eyes, color? Uniting contradictions, she is, at one and the same time, hot and cold, in her senses and out of her mind, for she is either terrified or at the point of death. The effect desired is that

> not one passion only should be seen in her, but a concourse of the passions. All such things occur in the case of lovers, but it is, as I have said, the selection of the most striking of them and their combination into a single whole that has produced the singular excellence of the passage.

This is a remarkable early instance of inductive analysis of a poem: an attempt to objectify a subjective creative process by which the elements forming the poem fuse into a single organic body. (Longinus actually speaks of the poem's "body.") It's hardly a thorough treatment of the kind that would, say, propose a tentative characterization of lyric poems, and their principles of structure, and the kind of evaluation they invite. Nevertheless, it introduces vital considerations in all these respects. Look through most current anthologies of contemporary literary criticism and you'll be hard put to find even one passage in which the critic quotes from a poem or a piece of fiction at any length and then attempts to account for its affective dynamics. I mean *its* dynamics—not those of a hypothetical reader's hypothetical responses, or of the author's supposed psychic ups and downs, but of the succession of tones or subjective states, and of their degrees of intensity, *in* the units of rhythmic phrasing that make up a work's patterned structure.

This procedure parallels the inductive method as seen by scientists. I think that, rightly understood, their perspective can be extremely helpful in bringing criticism to its senses again. There's no doubt that specific scientific fields, ranging from astronomy to psychology, constantly reveal findings and complexities that illuminate culture and art generally and influence their future directions, often through oversimplification. The names of Galileo, Newton, Darwin, Einstein, and Freud—among others—come instantly to mind. But I am thinking here, rather, of scientific method itself, as described in John A. Moore's *Science as a Way of Knowing III—Genetics*, published in 1985 by the American Society of Zoologists. What Moore says in the passage I am about to quote is the plain bread-and-butter of scientific thought, no doubt familiar even to humanists who have had anything like a decent basic education. But if we take it *seriously,* it can be heady medicine.

> Induction [writes Moore] means no more than that one begins a study with observation and experimentation relating to some natural phenomena, and uses the data obtained in attempting to reach some understanding of fundamental causes or associations of seemingly unrelated events. Selected data are used to frame provisional hypotheses and from these hypotheses deductions are made and tested. Deduction remains a powerful adjunct of analysis, but the deduction of modern scientists is not the same as the deductive reasoning that Bacon found so repugnant. In science today, deductions from a hypothesis are (hopefully) necessary conclusions from that hypothesis. Their value is to suggest what observations or experiments can be done in order to confirm or deny the hypothesis, nothing more. The deductions of the early philosophers and theologians were often regarded as eternal conclusions drawn from eternal truths, but in reality they were based on shared faith or bold imagination, not on evidence.

Now I take it that the "natural phenomena" with which literary criticism and literary theory are concerned are literary works—in particular, literary works of the variety called "imaginative": i.e., poems, stories long and short, plays, and various mixtures within and around these categories. If you think about what you're reading, no matter how simply, you're being a critic at some level; you're observing bodies of language streaming through time and gathering shape as they move toward a state of equilibrium within a contained process. The more developed your reading abilities, the more you'll be able to ride with the flow of the text: its float of sensibility through shifting phases of awareness and degrees of intensity, the interaction of its parts, and the various pressures and counter-pressures at work in it. And while this active empathy is going on, you will also be enabled to note the process, make comparisons among works, and let yourself be instructed by the works themselves about their nature and problems and possibilities. That is, whatever provisional hypotheses you venture, they can be tested against actual texts and lead to relevant theoretical propositions.

Admittedly, our instruments of observation are internal and subjective ones and therefore affected by many contingencies. But in the first place, I'm not at all sure that scientists, despite their microscopes and telescopes and other ingenious and sophisticated devices, are any more free of those contingencies than we are. And in the second (really the first) place, we have the same duty as they to *try* to avoid (as Moore has it) "rigidity of thought, emotion, acceptance of *a priori* statements, personal opinions not based on scientific data, and supernatural explanations." That's the human condition—we just have to do our best. And of course, we'd need to change Moore's terminology—but not his meaning—just a bit. Our "scientific data" are the elements and shaping processes that reveal themselves within a literary work, such as evocative effects, rhythmic patterns, levels of diction, imagery, use and alteration of literary conventions, and implicit social and psychological bearing, either literal or symbolic. (I've hardly exhausted the list of such "data.") And when Moore speaks of the need to exclude *emotion*, he is not speaking of emotion-charged language within the object of study, but rather of certain private emotions of the observer: the sort that might prevent someone from studying evolutionary data objectively, for instance. In the same sense, we might warn someone studying the glands and nerve structures involved in human emotions not to allow his or her own emotional attitudes to impede a study of manic states or of sexual arousal or of maternal feelings. So also, in literary study; at least, I hope it's obvious that, in considering works that have aroused passionate controversy—such as Joyce's *Ulysses* or Lawrence's *Lady Chatterley's Lover* or Pound's *Pisan Cantos*—dispassionate characterization of what's there is one thing, and one's private attitude toward the turbid depths of life into which these works plunge is another.

In addition there is a special turn to all this: namely, that it's impossible to appreciate the qualitative character of a work without giving it the benefit of the doubt to start with. Otherwise you cut off responsiveness to what's going on—much like a scientist who is quite convinced a certain line of experimentation must be wrong and therefore doesn't really carry it through.

That is exactly what seems to have happened to the efforts that flourished earlier in this century to objectify aesthetic process in literature. People like

I. A. Richards, the so-called New Critics (I say "so-called" because they were actually too diverse to be thought of as a single movement), the neo-Aristotelians, and a miscellaneous crew of poets and other artists made stimulating efforts in this direction. Behind those efforts lay genuine upheavals in the arts as well as in science and psychological understanding, and cataclysmic historical events, and experimental uprootings of past assumptions in the last century. More recently a fog of abstractions has obscured the clear lines of thought and discussion that were being developed. As I've already noted, I think it's time to return to a criticism and related theory rooted in actual literature rather than in anything and everything else. One result, incidentally, of the present situation is the vast indifference of the supposed "reading public" to so many of our most interesting current poets—not only younger poets like Deborah Digges and Li-Young Lee; but older ones with years of work behind them, such as Jeanne Hollander, Robert Dana, and Walter McDonald. A richly American poet like Ramon Guthrie, who wrote *Maximum Security Ward*, one of our twentieth-century masterpieces—tragic, satirical, generously humorous, and purely lyrical by turns—could spend a long lifetime virtually unread.

I mention these figures not because this is the occasion to discuss any of them in detail, but to introduce the third point I wish to make. The new starting point in criticism might well be attention to the lyrical structure of works, with the lyric poem as a clear model. A personal reason is that for some years I have given myself to making such poems and writing about them. I am interested in their qualitative life and formation: that is, in a poet's poetics. But insight into the dynamics of lyric poetry suggests an approach to the process within *any* literary work seen as a work of art. And that approach is hardly a matter of personal predilection.

From this starting point, it's useful to think of all literary works as *poems:* that is, as projections, by means of relatively compressed and patterned units of phrasing, of specific qualities and intensity of emotionally and sensuously charged awareness. We may call those units lyric or tonal centers, or *affects*. This last term, useful for its psychological overtones, is valuable because it suggests both a subjective state and its degree of intensity: the two axes of reference for the qualitative character of a passage or of a whole work.

Partly because I mean to discuss some of his fiction further along, let me illustrate first with a poem of Poe's, "The City in the Sea"—a work, I should say, both known and unknown:

> Lo! Death has reared himself a throne
> In a strange city lying alone
> Far down within the dim West,
> Where the good and the bad and the worst and the best
> Have gone to their eternal rest.
>
> There shrines and palaces and towers
> (Time-eaten towers that tremble not!)
> Resemble nothing that is ours.
> Around, by lifting winds forgot,
> Resignedly beneath the sky
> The melancholy waters lie.

No rays from the holy heaven come down
On the long night-time of that town;
But light from out the lurid sea
Streams up the turrets silently—
Gleams up the pinnacles far and free—
Up domes—up spires—up kingly halls—

Up fanes—up Babylon-like walls—
Up shadowy long-forgotten bowers
Of sculptured ivy and stone flowers—
Up many and many a marvellous shrine
Whose wreathéd friezes intertwine
The viol, the violet, and the vine.

Resignedly beneath the sky
The melancholy waters lie.
So blend the turrets and shadows there
That all seems pendulous in air,
While from a proud tower in the town
Death looks gigantically down.

There open fanes and gaping graves
Yawn level with the luminous waves;
But not the riches there that lie
In each idol's diamond eye—
Not the gaily jewelled dead
Tempt the waters from their bed;
For no ripples curl, alas!
Along that wilderness of glass—
No swellings tell that winds may be
Upon some far-off happier sea—
No heavings hint that winds have been
On seas less hideously serene.

But lo, a stir is in the air!
The wave—there is a movement there!
As if the towers had thrust aside,
In slightly sinking, the dull tide—
As if their tops had feebly given
A void within the filmy Heaven.
The waves have now a redder glow—
The hours are breathing faint and low—
And when, amid no earthly moans,
Down, down, that town shall settle hence,
Hell, rising from a thousand thrones,
Shall do it reverence.

The lyrical structure of this poem centers on coping with death-terror. Its affective dynamics, or progression, moves through several imagistic and tonal phases within a curious narrative envelope. It is, I think, Poe's best poem although, as usual with him, it's quite uneven. Lines 4–5, for instance, are totally banal: "Where the good and the bad and the worst and the best / Have gone to their eternal rest." And there is something idiotic in the repeated lines: "Resignedly beneath the sky / The melancholy waters lie"—a perfect instance of what Ruskin called "the pathetic fallacy," and all the more so because the language contradicts the ideas both of absolutely motionless waters and of a realm empty of all *human* meaning. Moreover, there is enough redundancy here and there to stuff a pillow with.

Nevertheless, the poem has a most daring movement. It fully exploits effects of grotesque eeriness, and it visualizes the supernatural shockingly. That is, it nakedly sets side by side notations of morbidly fascinating mortality and decay, personifications of Death and the powers of Hell, uncanny impressions of Necropolis and its watery stillness, and a changing, mysterious, insistently concentrated imagery of light.

The general eeriness establishes itself first, so much so that the opening personification—"Lo! Death has reared himself a throne"—seems almost muted, almost flatly allegorical, for the moment. (It returns later, however, and explosively.) Very soon, too, after the somewhat stumbling evocation in the first stanza of a charnel atmosphere, the poem's dominant vision comes strongly into the foreground. It emerges in the changing imagery of supernatural light that I have mentioned: light streaming upwards among replicas, frozen in stone, of once living natural things and human creations. The slightly maudlin impact of the opening stanza is replaced by the purer energy of the succeeding four lines—a powerful lyrical center:

> No rays from the holy heaven come down
> On the long night-time of that town;
> But light from out the lurid sea
> Streams up the turrets silently.

These lines provide a dynamic shift of key from the opening affect of Gothic strangeness intermixed with elegiac and sentimental tonalities. They introduce the poem's controlling play of light and dark, preparing us as well for the Keats-like imagery of life held changeless through art but at the cost of death, and of the relation of beauty to this dire form of transcendence. Indeed, the beauty of the imagined scene and its aesthetic associations ("the viol, the violet, and the vine") cast a spell of nostalgic glamour and nearly obliterate the darker, grislier drive of the poem's deeper psychological pressure—this despite that ominous word "lurid." Poe's stories, incidentally, often use the same device. That is, they spot their effects of horror with moments of seductive beauty that imply the magnetic allure of that drive into horror. An instance is the closing scene of *The Narrative of Arthur Gordon Pym;* another is the long section in "The Fall of the House of Usher" that dwells on Roderick Usher's sensibility—his paintings expressing what Poe calls his "highly distempered ideality" that "threw a sulphurous lustre over all," projecting "an intensity of intolerable awe." These affects precisely parallel those in "The City in the Sea." That is to say, Poe employs the same kind of qualitative dynamics in the stories as in his explicitly poetic writing. In fact, Usher's poem, "The Haunted Palace," is the climactic peak of the section of the story I've just mentioned, moving inexorably from nostalgia through elegy to horror.

But let's return to our first model, "The City in the Sea." After the moment of nostalgic enchantment with the beauty of art seen as the death-saturated celebration of life held in stasis, there comes, suddenly, a truly shocking corrective, albeit still in the glamorous mode of terrible grandeur. It comes in the lines

> While from a proud tower in the town
> Death looks gigantically down.

And in the wake of this couplet comes the poem's self-reminder of the horrid realm of individual death and decay in which it dwells, the realm of "open fanes and gaping graves" and of the "hideously serene" (Poe's phrase) reality they embody.

Moreover, beyond this particular *frisson* there is an even greater one—a grand *torque* or tonal wrench—in the closing stanza. Here dread fantasy takes over, in the aftermath of the earlier imagery of streams of unearthly light. There *is* motion after all! Necropolis is sinking (like Venice)! The "lurid," "luminous," unearthly light has a "redder glow" now, for we are closer to Hell. And at the very end we are told that all the principalities of Hell will, when Necropolis has at last reached bottom, rise to "do it reverence." A strange, inexplicable reversal, joyless and detached from human values, as though the poem has sloughed off its indulgence in the pathetic fallacy and even in the idea, dispiriting but at least comprehensible, of entropy. Hell will pay homage to Death—a doubling of "the fantastic." At any rate, the poem's lyrical structure has brought us to a realm of stunned, unfathomable terror beyond will or remedy—and also, by the same token, a realm of solemn-masked pre-Surrealist buffoonery of the grotesque.

If I may recur for a moment to John A. Moore's words about scientific induction, no *a priori* assumptions about lyric poetry or Poe's mentality would prepare us for the way this poem works; and speculation about its "meaning," either in conventional terms or semiotic ones, must fall far short of tracking its affective dynamics. These are part and parcel of its own phrasing and successive, interlinked surges of subjective resonance—objectified, however, in the phrasing itself, including its prosodic aspects. What goes on in a poem is not an abstract meaning but a body of gathering awareness and feeling.

I have suggested the usefulness, in clearing the critical decks, of thinking of all literary works as *poems;* for, as it happens, the lyric poem provides our clearest model of lyrical structure. This flexible yet ordering dynamic principle is decisive in literary art. Thus, if we turn to Poe's *The Narrative of Arthur Gordon Pym,* we can readily see affective parallels to "The City in the Sea." These parallels demonstrate the irrelevance of approaching such a work via abstract definitions, however ingenious, of "the fantastic"—definitions such as Tzvetan Todorov once proposed but has himself, apparently, grown weary of. This consideration will, I hope, justify my turning now to some classic works of American fictional fantasy to suggest how the search for "meaning" in all its current proliferations obscures the nature of aesthetic process and what it reveals.

Chief among the parallels between the two works by Poe, then, is the atmosphere of an intractable dread, inherent in fatality. In the *Narrative* this dread is almost ridiculously embodied in the way so very much of the action occurs in the midst of gale-force winds hurtling ships forward and men about. In this work, death and treachery are endemic in the malign nature of things. People may be cunning, and some may even be for the most part more or less decent; nevertheless you can never tell when they will kill or even *eat* you! Now, we all know, although we generally repress the knowledge, that indeed such is the worst side of human possibility, corresponding to historical experience and to horrors lurking within existence itself. When imagination fastens itself, doubtless masochistically but not altogether unrealistically, on this direst aspect of life, we have a fusion of nightmare fantasy and what we may call creative fantasy: that is, the kind that builds beyond our ability to penetrate its meaning even in the wildest, most farfetched terms. Such is the bearing of the closing passage in "The City in the Sea"—

> And when, amid no earthly moans,
> Down, down, that town shall settle hence,
> Hell, rising from a thousand thrones,
> Shall do it reverence—

and such is the bearing of the ending of *The Narrative of Arthur Gordon Pym:*

> *March 5*. The wind had entirely ceased, but it was evident that we were still hurrying on to the southward, under the influence of a powerful current. And now, indeed, it would seem reasonable that we should experience some alarm at the turn events were taking—but we felt none. The countenance of Peters indicated nothing of this nature, although it wore at times an expression I could not fathom. The Polar winter appeared to be coming on—but coming without its terrors. I felt a *numbness* of body and mind—a dreaminess of sensation—but this was all.
>
> *March 6*. The gray vapour had now arisen many more degrees above the horizon, and was gradually losing its grayness of tint. The heat of the water was extreme, even unpleasant to the touch, and its milky hue was more evident than ever. To-day a violent agitation of the water occurred very close to the canoe. It was attended, as usual, with a wild flaring up of the vapour at its summit, and a momentary division at its base. A fine white powder, resembling ashes—but certainly not such—fell over the canoe and over a large surface of the water, as the flickering died away among the vapour and the commotion subsided in the sea. Nu-Nu threw himself on his face in the bottom of the boat, and no persuasions could induce him to arise.
>
> *March 7*. This day we questioned Nu-Nu concerning the motives of his countrymen in destroying our companions; but he appeared to be too utterly overcome by terror to afford us any rational reply. He still obstinately lay in the bottom of the boat; and, upon our reiterating the questions as to the motive made use only of idiotic gesticulations, such as raising with his forefinger the upper lip, and displaying the teeth which lay beneath it. These were black. We had never before seen the teeth of an inhabitant of Tsalal.

March 8. To-day there floated by us one of the white animals whose appearance upon the beach at Tsalal had occasioned so wild a commotion among the savages. I would have picked it up, but there came over me a sudden listlessness, and I forebore. The heat of the water still increased, and the hand could no longer be endured within it. Peters spoke little, and I knew not what to think of his apathy. Nu-Nu breathed, and no more.

March 9. The whole ashy material fell now continually around us, and in vast quantities. The range of vapour to the southward had arisen prodigiously in the horizon, and began to assume more distinctness of form. I can liken it to nothing but a limitless cataract, rolling silently into the sea from some immense and far-distant rampart in the heaven. The gigantic curtain ranged along the whole extent of the southern horizon. It emitted no sound.

March 21. A sullen darkness now hovered above us—but from out the milky depths of the ocean a luminous glare arose, and stole up along the bulwarks of the boat. We were nearly overwhelmed by the white ashy shower which settled upon us and upon the canoe, but melted into the water as it fell. The summit of the cataract was utterly lost in the dimness and the distance. Yet we were evidently approaching it with a hideous velocity. At intervals there were visible in it wide, yawning, but momentary rents, and from out these rents, within which was a chaos of flitting and indistinct images, there came rushing and mighty, but soundless winds, tearing up the enkindled ocean in their course.

March 22. The darkness had materially increased, relieved only by the glare of the water thrown back from the white curtain before us. Many gigantic and pallidly white birds flew continuously now from beyond the veil, and their scream was the eternal *Tekeli-li!* as they retreated from our vision. Hereupon Nu-Nu stirred in the bottom of the boat; but upon touching him, we found his spirit departed. And now we rushed into the embraces of the cataract, where a chasm threw itself open to receive us. But there arose in our pathway a shrouded human figure, very far larger in its proportions than any dweller among men. And the hue of the skin of the figure was of the perfect whiteness of the snow.

Thus *The Narrative* ends—apart from a "Note" that follows, which neatly balances off the "Preface" in its air of journalistic and scholarly professionalism that attempts to give ballast to the tale's surges of flight. But in this final surge the full horror of the sheer dread implicit in the work as a whole hurtles into the grotesque unknowable. Black and white, modern and primitive humanity, all are involved in the concrete symbolism piled, terror-image upon terror-image, into the ending. The work can advance no further; imagination falters here, as at the close of "The City in the Sea," for it has nowhere to go. Even after the anticlimactic "Note," the sense of fathomless guilt and doom reasserts itself in the unattributed prophetic quotation at the very end: "*I have graven it within the hills, and my vengeance upon the dust within the rock.*" Like certain quotations in *The Waste Land*, this detached phrasing gives one last affective turn of baleful supernatural purpose. It is akin to the half-penetrable words and symbols encountered earlier on in the tale. (Suzanne Langer's phrase "a symbol without a referent" might well characterize the whole work: an exact equivalent, one might argue, to the scientific view of the natural universe.)

Without quoting from it any further, I would describe the lyrical structure of *The Narrative of Arthur Gordon Pym* as follows. At first the sense of danger it projects is "natural" enough, if just tinged with a sort of fever for trouble. Headstrong, willful young men seek uncontrollable situations of adventure, like taking a boat out to sea despite their inexperience as sailors. Then, fairly soon, they're beyond their depth in most senses, and the gale winds take charge of the work's movement toward Terror-Absolute-in-Motion, without surcease or hope or revealed meaning. *The Narrative* has a structure of loosely connected adventures—a sort of picaresque of the terrifying, related through more or less escalating intensities of dread: the cumulative major affect constantly reinforced by the sense of being catapulted through diverse experiences into irreversible disaster. This is essentially lyrical rather than narrative progression. Incidents do not build into one another by virtue of an organically developed plot; the progression has a stop-and-start character, each episode seeking its separate emotional maelstrom into which to plunge. The two most terror-drenched passages before the intractable final one are the encounter with the Dutch ship of the dead and the escape from the Tsalalians. The former is an exercise in the gruesome, reminiscent of "The Rime of the Ancient Mariner" but far more deliberately morbid in its detailed macabre impressions and its fascination with items of putrescence. But beyond this, a sense of supernatural vileness surpassing understanding pervades its confused mixture of illusion, hallucination, and something like a necromantic spell. It foreshadows the ending in its association of whiteness with horror and with the destructive, ever-present sea.

The other passage, of escape from the Tsalalians, comes later. It is not preoccupied with dead bodies and what becomes of them: i.e., with the obsessive fantasies of hypersensitive children when continued and embellished in adulthood. Instead, it concentrates on the *personal* dread, easily converted into a compulsion to risk everything and have done once and for all, that is the counterpart of those fantasies if they have not been dissolved or repressed in the usual fashion. Everything here is focused on this complex of feeling, expressed as a panicky fear of high places that becomes a self-induced suicidal urge. In the same passage, also, the images of a phantom scream and a phantom figure waiting for the victim in a phantom world both echo the death-ship section and anticipate the closing section.

Looking back over *The Narrative*, we see the two major pressures at work in it. On the one hand, it presents, by fits and starts, an atmosphere of ever-increasing external pressure, of being rushed forward into utterly unmanageable confrontations with disaster and death. On the other hand, as it does so, intense inward pressures of helpless fear and, at the same time, of the death wish accelerate proportionately. The result is total loss of control, understanding, and, finally, identity. Such is the affective poetics, the lyrical structure, of *The Narrative*.

I have dwelt on it at this length because its lyrical centers are so clearly identifiable and so readily mark out its intrinsic structure, as opposed to its ramshackle narration. The more compressed and complex structures of works like "Ligeia" and "The Fall of the House of Usher" surpass it in their subjective and sexual resonances. "Ligeia" is a hideous fantasy linking female sexuality, gross death-obsession, and overwhelmingly malign supernatural power—all just conceivably to be explained away by the narrator's opium haze, but no less gruesome in their impact. The single most powerful affect, radiating total shocked terror and dismay, is the dying Ligeia's poem "The Conqueror Worm"—and I need hardly labor the obvious import of Poe's using a poem to give affective guidance to the whole work, just as he does in "The Fall of the House of Usher."

In "The Conqueror Worm," weeping angels watch the tragic play *Man*. Human beings, created in the image of a phantom called God, are impelled by demonic figures to chase after that ungraspable phantom until the monstrous Worm of the title seizes them with its "vermin fangs / In human gore imbued" and devours them. Oddly yet significantly, the *named "hero"* of this cosmic tragedy is the Worm itself: the death principle, the unyielding supernal will that persists beyond individual mortality.

This heretical paradox can hardly be resolved logically. Like the triumph of Death over Hell in "The City in the Sea"—which it echoes—it portends nothing we can hold on to. It provides a chilling link *poetically*, however, with the initial presentation in the story of "the lady Ligeia." She is at once voluptuously beautiful, infinitely learned, artistically gifted, and the very essence of "the strange" (Poe's own phrase, and perhaps our best affective equivalent—in the figure of Ligeia—of "the fantastic"). In the very first paragraph, we learn that the narrator first met her "in some large, old, decaying city near the Rhine," and that her family origins are lost in antiquity. She has, in short, the quality of a goddess with certain Gothic and Romantic twists. That is, she is a doomed passionate goddess subject to death in her mortal, bodily aspect but not in her immortal will, as we learn later. It is interesting that the description of Ligeia takes up the first five pages or so. It constitutes a massive affective unit, introducing seductive tonalities of superhuman, death-linked power that are abruptly succeeded by the convulsive description of Ligeia's passionate struggle (*everything* about her is passionate) against death and then by her horror-drenched poem.

Two small paragraphs, which I am tempted to call "stanzas" or "verse-units," then form a sort of elegiac prose-poem, uttered mostly by Ligeia herself in her death throes. Each ends with an incantatory refrain echoing part of the epigraph (a quotation from Joseph Glanvill): "Man doth not yield him to the angels, nor unto death utterly, save only through the weakness of his feeble will." The first time this refrain appears, only the phrase "unto death utterly" is italicized. The second time, the whole quotation is in italics: a simple poetic device for increasing intensity.

Once Ligeia's hold is apparently released through her death, the narrator sinks into an opium retreat in a former abbey, a place of "gloomy and dreary grandeur" within a remote, "almost savage" landscape. There, inexplicably, he marries a cold if beautiful Englishwoman with whom he lives in mutual loathing. Indeed, he "loathes her with a hatred belonging more to demon than to man." The final affective phase of the story is under way, marked by this irrational but jolting turn. Another turn, and the dead Ligeia manages to poison the lady Rowena and, dybbuk-like, to enter her body and transform it into her own. She has possessed the narrator's spirit all along, and now she has willed an at least momentary triumph over her death. The work ends with the narrator's "shriek" of recognition as the formerly blue-eyed Rowena's corpse opens its eyes, which have now become "the full, and the black, and the wild" eyes of Ligeia.

The metamorphosis is presented in an aura of madness and fear more than of rapture at his beloved's resurrection. The tale, the *poem*, has moved from a state of vastly fulfilling yet sinisterly overwhelming entrancement to violent struggle against death the conqueror Worm, and thence to this final state of terrified arousal charged with "mad" confusion bordering on buffoonery. "Ligeia," like *The Narrative of Arthur Gordon Pym*, has no *narrative* resolution but rather a stasis, the balancing off of states of feeling and awareness such as lyrical structure always seeks. In "Ligeia" the states balanced against one another are various contexts and intensities of a spine-chilling sense of the supernally strange, of the cruel nightmare-ridden pressure of death-dread, and of morbid sensitization generally.

Poe's story "The Fall of the House of Usher" is comparable in its structure. It is even more thickly studded than "Ligeia" with lyrical centers. The most extended of them is the long detailing of Roderick Usher's sensibility, which resembles a gloomy wind harp that emits tones like those resonating from the narrator of "Ligeia." The description of the house itself and its setting is equally important. It is exactly reciprocal with Roderick's internal state, a combination of hereditary self-centeredness born of luxury, noblesse, and essential sterility mixed with hypersensitivity to familial doom as the law of Roderick's and his sister Madeline's lives.

Buffoonery, or sheer absurdity, threatens the tale's seriousness even more than in "Ligeia." The business of the fissure in the house is really quite ridiculous, symbolic though it be of the family that inhabits (or rather, haunts) the house. The senseless premature entombment of Madeline in the vault, and then her dreadful, bloody reappearance as if she were Ligeia the Second, are elements in the grisly horseplay that begins with the half-satirical epic catalogue of Roderick's forbidden, death-focused books. So is the "favorite tale" the narrator reads aloud to cheer Roderick out of his post-premature-burial depression. Finally, the props supporting the whole structure—its engulfing "melancholy" and the macabre ominousness of the well-placed black tarn—all collapse when, because of the for-some-reason-never-repaired fissure, the house slips mercifully into the bottomless tarn.

Thus we have, on the one hand, a shuddery, brilliant play on over-refined vulnerability; and on the other, a self-parody that never drops its solemn mask. The lyrical structure resides in the interaction between these two central streams of shifting tonalities. Obviously, dark human forces, the descendants of Anangke and the Furies, make the movement toward total collapse irreversible in the work. Just as obviously, though, the grave seriousness of Greek tragedy is somehow being mocked. Characteristically, Poe deploys an overtly melodramatic assumption of fatality, unsupported by the deeply shared sacred traditions underlying the work of the classical tragic playwrights. Yet the psychological terror remains.

Hawthorne's work—to turn to another set of examples—is basically less sensational, with none of Poe's vampirish exuberance and wild dread over corpses, the walking dead, and phantasmal torment. He is often content to build a structure about just one weird or eccentric circumstance that evokes the sense of the fantastic, either supernatural or merely beyond rational accountability. For instance, a minister suddenly begins to wear a black veil: the central image around which "The Minister's Black Veil" is developed. The tale then proceeds fairly rapidly, through successive tableaux showing his parishioners' reactions and the stages of his subsequent experience. When he presides over a young lady's funeral, for example, the veil seems to make the corpse shudder—an affect closer to Poe, after all, than I have just suggested. At a wedding ceremony, the veil naturally spoils the occasion; and the minister himself, glimpsing its reflection in a mirror apparently for the first time, feels "the horror with which it overwhelmed all others. His frame shuddered, his lips grew white, he spilt untasted wine upon the carpet, and rushed forth into the darkness." His fiancée rejects him because he refuses to remove it. And although in all other respects a model clergyman, especially when called to comfort dying sinners, he becomes a figure of dread to all about him and at last dies still wearing the veil. "Why do you tremble at me alone?" he cries to those about him. "When the friend shows his inmost heart to his friend; the lover to his best beloved; when man does not vainly shrink from the eye of his creator, loathsomely measuring up the secret of his sin; then deem me a monster . . . ! I look around me, and lo! on every visage a Black Veil!"

Each of these successive moments in Hawthorne's "parable" (as he called it) serves a double affective function, centered on the omnipresent veil. It sustains the cumulative sense of secret guilt implicit in each human soul. At the same time, it helps weave a design of changing tonalities associated with pleasant or solemn or merry or casual events—all darkened, however, by the veil, which increasingly isolates the minister, "good Mr. Hooper," from ordinary human contact. The structure, again, is essentially lyrical. Hawthorne might have added more incidents, or omitted one or two; no matter, for the progression here does not depend on a curve of *action* but on the escalating emphasis on the veil's dark, compelling power. The work's success depends on its overcoming its initial absurdity—on a quality and pressure of style that impose a sense of supernaturally inspired vision, rather than mere personal eccentricity or sheer stubbornness. Hawthorne's closing sentence adds one final hammer stroke toward this end: "The grass of many years has sprung up and withered on that [the minister's] grave, the burial stone is moss-grown, and good Mr. Hooper's face is dust; but awful is still the thought that it mouldered beneath the Black Veil!"

A more interesting structure, with more dramatic and energetic life, marks Hawthorne's "The Wedding Knell," praised by Poe as "full of the boldest imagination—an imagination controlled by taste." Yet there is a clear similarity, in the bizarre substitution of a death knell for wedding bells and, even more, in the groom's donning a shroud for the happy occasion. This singular gesture of symbolic madness is an act of sexual revenge upon the bride, who many years earlier had been "compelled" to spurn him. Afterwards she had been through two unhappy marriages, while her true love had endured a life of shy, eccentric seclusion. Now at last, on her initiative, the aging pair will marry: and the groom's long resentment is expressed through his arranging for the death knell and also for a funeral procession in whose midst he appears wearing the shroud and saying, "Come, my bride! the hearse is ready. The sexton stands waiting for us at the door of the tomb. Let us be married, and then to our coffins!"

The impact here is far beyond anything in "The Minister's Black Veil," given the psychological surround. The rest of the story moves swiftly. The shocked bride, "heart-stricken," groans "Cruel! cruel!" and receives a bitter, vehement reproach in reply—one so revealing and pathetic that she loses all worldly poise and responds with her former pure love for him. Thus the story ends, charged with irrevocable loss and sadness for the wasted years, and yet with "solemn triumph." The structure is essentially elegiac, moving through tones of wonder, gossip, and irony to stark contrasts of youthful loveliness with aging and death and then into the tragically welcome exchange, and finally into a kind of transcendence without buoyancy. The most grotesquely fantastic elements are absorbed into the larger emotional dynamics almost invisibly.

Of Hawthorne's stories built around just one weird or irrational circumstance, "Wakefield" is perhaps the most effective and original. It is also a prime instance, I think, of what we might call the *buried fantastic,* for there is no hint in it of miracle or wild imagination—only of the unfathomable and arbitrary twists of human behavior. A man suddenly, almost whimsically, decides to step out of the "system" (Hawthorne's word) of his life. As the story has it, "The man, under pretense of going a journey, took lodgings in the next street to his own house, and there, unheard of by his wife and his friends, and without the shadow of a reason for such self-banishment, dwelt upwards of twenty years. During that period, he beheld his home every day, and frequently the forlorn Mrs. Wakefield. And after so great a gap in his matrimonial felicity—when his death was reckoned certain, his estate settled, his name dismissed from memory, and his wife, long, long ago, resigned to her autumnal widowhood—he entered the door one evening, quietly, as from a day's absence, and became a loving spouse until death."

This in its way is "The Wedding Knell" in reverse, but without the macabre overlay. It is Kafka, tempered by extreme Anglo-Saxon restraint. It is the fantastic as a mode of something like "normal" experience. At the end Hawthorne comments: "Amid the seeming confusion of our mysterious world, individuals are so nicely adjusted to a system, and systems to one another and to a whole, that, by stepping aside for a moment, a man exposes himself to a fearful risk of losing his place forever. Like Wakefield, he may become, as it were, the Outcast of the Universe."

Between these two passages, "Wakefield" consists of a series of imagined closeups: the moment of matter-of-fact parting, casual, domestic, deceptive; then his incognito settling into a place barely a street away from his home (emphasis here is on his vain imagining anyone will care enough to notice what he's doing); then a moment when he thoughtlessly almost reenters home, catching a chance glimpse of his wife through a window before retreating; then other moments when he's seen her, and a time when he realizes she must be very ill; and a moment when they actually bump into one another, years later, and she does not recognize him—and at last, after twenty years, his return on a cold wet night. These are compressed "spots of time," as in Wordsworth's *The Prelude;* and indeed many of the observations Hawthorne weaves around them resemble the poet's—for instance: "He . . . is perplexed with a sense of change about the familiar edifice" when he sees it just the day after he leaves, a change "such as affects us all, when, after a separation of months or years, we again see some hill, or lake, or work of art, with which we were friends of old. . . . In Wakefield, the magic of a single night has wrought a similar transformation, because, in that brief period, a great moral change has been affected. But this is a secret from himself." And even more Wordsworthian: "An influence beyond our control lays its hand on every deed which we do, and weaves its consequences into an iron tissue of necessity. Wakefield is spell-bound."

As much as in anything he wrote, Hawthorne shows his prose-poetic mastery in "Wakefield." The intimate, insinuating character of these closeups provides instances. So do the narrator's little outcries and epithets ("Poor Wakefield!"; "the wide and solitary waste of the new unaccustomed bed" in the changed lodgings; "the crafty nincompoop") and bits of direct address to the protagonist ("Go quietly to thy bed, foolish man"; "Wakefield! whither are you going?"; "Fool!"; "Stay, Wakefield! Would you go to the sole home that is left you? Then step into your grave").

All this stylistic interplay helps make the work a triumph of the fantastic. It gives body to the puzzle of Wakefield and suggests the presence of a force beyond our understanding or control within the realm of the utterly commonplace. The initial impression of Wakefield is that he is the least adventurous or unpredictable sort of man imaginable, a creature of habit or inertia who nudges himself, as it were, out of one "system" into another and then back again. But the source, the impulse, behind that torpid double nudging? Therein lies the fearful buffoonery of human destiny, its arbitrary, uncontrollable compulsions. Besides, the deeper affect unfolded poetically is a sense of the pathetic waste of youth and passion, just as in "The Wedding Knell." Sexual deprivation, whether self-imposed or cruelly if perhaps unwittingly imposed by another, is the darker motif recurred to again and again by the phrasing. The motif makes itself felt partly through the condescending comments (sometimes couched as imagined direct address to him) on Wakefield, but also through the allusions to barren years in a solitary bed and through the carefully placed moments of near-meeting. The last one is on a crowded footwalk where husband and wife, unnoticing, are about to pass one another and

> a slight obstruction occurs, and brings these two figures directly in contact. Their hands touch; the pressure of the crowd forces her bosom against his shoulder; they stand, face to face, staring into each other's eyes. After ten years' separation, Wakefield meets his wife!
>
> The throng eddies away, and carries them asunder. The sober widow, resuming her former pace, proceeds to church, but pauses in the portal, and throws a perplexed glance along the street. She passes in, however, opening her prayer-book as she goes. And the man! with so wild a face that busy and selfish London stands to gaze after him, he hurries to his lodgings, bolts the door, and throws himself upon the bed. The latent feelings of years break out; his feeble mind acquires a brief energy from their strength; all the miserable strangeness of his life is revealed to him

at a glance: and he cries out, passionately, "Wakefield! Wakefield! You are mad!"

"His feeble mind" indeed! For it's another ten years before he returns home! This passage is the most poignant in the story, a climax of intensity, not in any sense a resolution in action. After it, as in Wordsworth's practice in *The Prelude*, a passage of awed, pondering wonder follows. The prose poem has penetrated its furthest and then become enrapt in its realization of a pathetic human mystery.

A similar play on missed marital joys colors not only the stories by Hawthorne so far noted but many others that flaunt their fantastic dimension far more sensationally—most notably "The Birthmark" and "Rappaccini's Daughter." In each of these, harmonious love is forgone or thwarted through scientific—i.e., magical—tampering. The issue is drawn in both almost as melodramatically as Poe might have done it. It appears partly as a result of the power of scientists to destroy nature's system through their modern forms of necromancy. Also, however, it manifests itself in physical markings that disfigure the central characters ever so slightly: sacred or diabolical stigmata, in the guise of natural imperfections. In "The Birthmark" there is the tiny blemish, shaped like a miniature hand, on Georgiana's cheek. In "Rappaccini's Daughter," it is the "purple print like that of four small fingers" on the back of Giovanni Guiscondi's right hand, together with "the likeness of a slender thumb upon his wrist"—the result of Giovanni's having gradually been rendered poisonous by Rappaccini to enable him to marry Beatrice—who meanwhile has been detoxifying herself to the same end (an O. Henry touch in advance of its time). In both stories, a Faustian outwitting of nature brings death to a miraculously beautiful and loving woman—and the tiny hands are like the mark of Cain, although they embody ambiguous supernatural presence, not guilt. Why this symbol should take the form of a *hand* is doubtless food for psychoanalytic thought. But again, the emphasis is on the gathering pressure of self-defeating willfulness and on the poignancy of losing infinitely desirable women: the romantic counterparts to the drably bourgeois context of the tale of Wakefield.

At this late point in my essay, I shall enter only a very few remarks concerning the lyrical structure of a twentieth-century model of fictional fantasy: William Faulkner's *As I Lay Dying*. There are two burningly serious centers of intense awareness in this novel. The first is that of the dying Addie, who hovers over the elemental scene at the start, a passionately dominating spirit whose will guides her sons. She is not *like* a presiding deity; she *is* one. The second is that of the clairvoyant, complex Darl, his heart broken to start with by the illegitimate Jewel's displacement of him in his mother's affection, his nerves disordered by war experience, and his sensibility eerily heightened by his very nature. All these conditions unite to make him seem mad (shades of Poe again) to ordinary eyes. His thoughts are the most lyrical of any character's; and this quality—plus his extraordinary intensity, volatility, and visionary range—merges, in the overarching drive of the book, with the fanatically concentrated authority of Addie's Ligeia-like purposefulness.

Extremely important in the work's lyrical structure, too, is the way Faulkner gives chapters to many more or less inarticulate characters. These chapters often speak for them in the idiom of their reverie rather than of their literal voices. This is especially true of his handling of Darl's chapters (almost a third of the book), but in any case these chapters are decisively piercing, even when a certain cruelty enters. His magical insight and ultra-sensitivity—he is a sort of Roderick Usher in his fashion—are as self-defeating as Aylmer's or Rappaccini's, and far more tragically so. Jewel, whose name is reminiscent of Hawthorne's equally "strange" little Pearl in *The Scarlet Letter* (which *As I Lay Dying* often echoes or parodies), is triumphant in his rigidly intent physicality; and the comic, thick-skinned Anse, eternal victor in the struggle of ignorance and sloth to prevail in this world, is even more triumphant. But Darl's tragic vision, divinely inspired in the novel's context, makes him the sacrificial victim of this brutally comic mock-epic. The vision of life's intractable terror, so defeating to the exploratory soul and imagination, is subserved by the fantastic and the grotesque in the brilliant structure of this work. When the visionary force centered in Addie and Darl is removed from the mobile community inhabiting the book, only squalor and grossness remain ascendant in its wake.

To conclude: I have been offering a few simple illustrations of inductive analysis of texts and the kind of theory—rooted in what the texts have to teach us, not in what we command them to prove—to which it leads: i.e., *literary* theory, to be tested against examination of the discernible affective structure that resides in a text in its own right. Whatever our further interests—philosophical, political, linguistic, or whatever—the relevance of their application to literary works depends on knowing what we're talking about.

The Southern Review (January 1989)

PART IV

Personal Coda 1976–1987

❧

We Begin These Sequences Lightly

1

RATHER painfully, I have been making my way into a new sequence of poems. Something has got hold of me, something at once inside and outside myself. I recognize the impulse of energy behind these poems and yet it eludes me. The poems are casting themselves like fishermen's lines to hook the impulse and bring it back to me in a net of words.

WE BEGIN THESE THINGS LIGHTLY

We begin these affairs lightly
with an obscure smile, or an unseeing glance.

The soul, flung like rags on a greasy floor,
wavers into oneness again, tiny flames flickering.

These things, these affairs that begin so lightly—you would think the speaker was a Restoration rake. But it is only I, or some little demon speaking through me. How unexpectedly we move into deep experience. How our dispersed inner selves, fragmented by the different roles we play and by our centrifugal daily existence, flame up and startle our slumbering minds. We enter this awakening lightly, in a sort of languor, because we had no notion it was upon us. Is this perhaps a love poem, then? Oh, yes. But it has not a trace of the erotic unless read by the light, and to the rhythm, of those flickering little flames. It tells me of an order of experience in which I am caught up. The word "love" defines the order but so do a hundred other words as well that float invisibly within it.

My sequence is still in the making, and so I can say nothing certain about it. But here is another poem that has entered it out of a kindred impulse.

RIDDLE OF THE SWAN

Once, beating through the air, you amazed us.
We smiled under your shadow.

Broken-winged and raucous now, you're borne
whithersoever the torrent lists.

She and I, flung high on that arc where you made your song, never before saw
our joined shadows beating and riding the torrent below.

There is a dangerous joy in being seized by some noble and passionate symbol that is at once natural and traditional: the swan in flight, or at his song, or as a form for Zeus when he ravished Leda, or in his ice-locked state as Mallarmé imagines him. But also, in "Riddle of the Swan," something else, the innocent word "flung," appears, as it did in "We Begin These Things Lightly." In the one poem I see everything after being flung onto the heights. In the other I am surprised into awakening after having been flung away by self-neglect.

What brought the flying swan's shadow into my mind must have been the irreversibility of love-awareness, once fully aroused. The greater the arousal, the harder our wings must beat and the more intimately do our mingled shadows join with the remembered shadows of the great swan flights of the past. If reality touches us awake at all, it does so in many ways. Awakening to love is awakening to anonymity, to loneliness, to the absence of all that has been lost, to the terror of uncontrolled vision.

The two poems have arrived kindly, to help me confront disaster from their two opposed starting points: the one from its memory of a condition hardly noticed at the time, the other from its ecstasy so alert that it sees everything. The images of "rags on a greasy floor" and of the "broken-winged and raucous" swan call up all squalor, the dump-heap we want life not to be; and they hold on to an anger turned aside by the sheer vastness of desolation—children starving, self-righteous murder, whatever. At this point, although no order has yet asserted itself, a poem without a name makes room for itself in my sequence.

> Suddenly at the edge, black ocean below,
> and over the edge, flight without wings,
> soughing of waves, stillness of star-pierced air,
> tight-clenched and silent motion.
>
> Soughing of leaves
> now in my memory
> holds, like your smile flickering towards me,
> buoyant tracers ablaze, as when you
> woke lovely and drowsy and lay down beside me
> and we played like dolphins, awash in the night.

I envy that anonymous, witty, sweet-voiced Elizabethan who wrote of swans and death and lost joys and silence fraught with tragedy in a spirit as flippantly uncommitted as his spelling. He flexed his muscle and showed us all suffering, then relaxed and grew playful and turned it all into satirical metaphor.

> The silver Swanne, who living had no Note,
> When deth approacht unlockt her silent throat,
> Leaning her breast against the reedie shore,
> Thus sung her first and last, and sung no more:
> Farewell all joyes, O death come close mine eyes,
> More Geese than Swannes now live, more fooles than wise.

When the tragic was but one chord in a world brimming over with melodies, it summoned to cheerful resurrections after melodramatic crucifixions. Even Shakespeare could let a mighty beginning like "Th'expense of spirit in a waste of shame" go glimmering in a waste of tedious antitheses. That old world of cornucopias is our world still—who else is there for the past or any part of it to belong to? All that has changed is the proportion of freedom and order. Overriding order prevailed in the thoughts of men from earliest times. It was taken for granted. Because order was assumed—necessary hierarchies, rituals, formal modes in the arts—the mind was freer to play at aristocratic freedom. No question that life had spiritual forms beyond death, no question there were presences all around though mere intelligence could not locate them. We do not seek out the thing we assume. But the modern age, which takes chaos and pointlessness for granted, seeks to make everything count and to create an ordered vision. Yet when the moment of glory comes we hesitate to proclaim it, fearing once again to discover what we already "know," that dissolution is more powerful than synthesis. The impulse to conceal vision in order to save it from knowledge and its corrosions is like the impulse to make our own deaths rather than simply being carried away into them.

BEQUEST

Burn our sweet story,
let the wind carry its smoke away.
Hasten, hasten—
leave no shred to betray
our names, where we went, why we lingered,
whom we loved, when we wept, on what day.

Perhaps that will be the final poem of my sequence, on the desperate day I declare it completed for the time being.

2

The key to making a sequence is the key of immediacy. It is struck in the quick of language. It animates ideas and makes them organs of the poem's body. (A sequence is a larger body made of smaller units, self-sufficient for the most part.) Ideas and archetypes, symbols and motifs, attitudes and qualities of morale do not define a poem. The key of immediacy, of language rooted in the idiom of the poet's nature, makes itself felt as the energizing agent of these otherwise inert, resistant mental furnishings. No one's theism, or image of the nature of woman, or idea of what a dying nightingale may or may not mean to a lovelorn maiden, or optimism or pessimism ever made a poem, let alone made it one whit better or worse. But anyone's feeling for the language as a plastic medium, with the resources of rhythm, sound, and association available within it, will do for a beginning. The ideas, symbols, "influences" flood into a poem in a way that counts only as aspects of charged poetic movement. That movement transforms them as it does the poet's own nature and memory. They are present, a part of the realization taking place in the real world of shared sensation and emotion we all inhabit. But they are not present, intact, in the poem any more than there is a real oily rag on a real greasy floor in "We Begin These Things Lightly," or a real swan with feathers in "Riddle of the Swan."

I have never seen a broken-winged swan. I did, once, see a wild, broken-winged goose calling raucously on the water. Her reflection sailed serenely under her, past reflected trees and over stones that were visible in the clear stream. That sight—bird, water, reflections, serene drifting movement combined with the distraught cries—is all in my poem, which has nothing to do with it nevertheless.

Late in my life I had a vision stronger than any I had experienced before, in a life filled with passionate debate with myself and with imagined states of experience. The poem teaches me, better than I had hitherto realized, the simultaneity of ecstasy and dread.

The reciprocity of these opposites has many sources: in family experience, in the deaths of people we love, in the history of the world's peoples. Certainly the destiny of the Jewish people teaches it to me. It teaches me to be open to the alien and unknown and to become part of it, and also to be detached—the implicit irony of the objective mind holding steady amid minds totally given to their traditional illusions. The Jews' displacements, their separateness even in Israel from what perforce they consider their native lands, the simultaneous working in them of more than one culture—all these lead to the self-undermining of both romanticism and realism. Yet the Jews are hardly the only nation betrayed into consciousness by their history. The need to go beyond mere survival has led us all into the barren sunlight of man's general condition today.

A poet, as a man or a woman, is like other men and women. What goes on in his or her other mind is a constant shifting—at one time a convergence of attention into the certainty of a single perception or feeling; at another time the balancing of many states of awareness and emotion in one vibrating system; at still another a frustration when all the currents and countercurrents are too much at odds for even a momentary reconciliation. Because it enables one to project these psychic shifts so readily, the poetic sequence is our form of both epic and bardic poetry. It embodies cultural tasks and it assumes prophecy. Its protean landmark is the private sensibility, against which we test everything. The touchstone of reality, now more than ever before, is intensity of experience. Moments of such intensity, high points of self-confirmation by the poem's ultimate voice, are almost essential to its genuineness and conviction.

I say "almost" essential because I can conceive of a sequence in which no one section would quite be the kind of nakedly experiential or personal poem I have in mind. In some way that tells, every part of a sequence needs its emotive dimension. It must present an *affect* that colors even an abstract thought or highly expository style and makes it a realization of a mind in the midst of life rather than the mere development of a point of argument or clarification. That kind of somewhat distanced poem still does the necessary work though its subtlety or remoteness or intellectuality may lessen its force—for there are many ways to create intensity whatever the surface character of a poem. Nevertheless, so forceful can a stripped-down, immediate, and personal lyric statement be that the absence of such a passage throws a certain pall over a sequence, while its presence seems to light up the poem as a whole and to make the less vivid movements reflect some of its vitality.

Of course, a sequence can be planned in detail, yet I doubt that a good one can be written according to any plan except the kind that simply envisions the sorts of affects and materials and themes that would necessarily be involved given certain preoccupations. The individual poems within it must ordinarily grow as any other poems do, though the pressure of closing in on the movement and patterning of a sequence will very likely speed up the process (just as preparing a book of poems does, and for the same reason—every volume of new poems all written within a limited time-span will tend to be a sequence, something a poet like Yeats was extremely conscious of in arranging his individual volumes). But a clear order will emerge, at least in the final stages, if the group of poems is anything like a true sequence generated in the heat of a strong overriding drive of feeling.

It *is* true, I think, that "we begin these affairs lightly" if we wish to be carried by more than we could possibly, at first, have understood was there. I had written sequences before "His Present Discontents," which appeared in *The View from the Peacock's Tail: Poems* (1972); and, without really formulating ideas in relation to my own practice, I had written a number of studies of sequences by various modern poets. But "His Present Discontents" began coming to me during a period, toward the end at least, already marked by the state of feeling I am still exploring in the poems from the unfinished sequence I have already quoted. At the same time, in the aftermath of the "revolutionary" 1960s, I was thinking a great deal about the connections between private intensities of all sorts and the claims of the political left, from Lenin to the Students for a Democratic Society and the Weathermen. Personal crisis and social crisis always seem to reflect one another. I took the whole range of tenderness for the willful young "into account," without quite knowing what I was doing, in the opening poem; as it happened, the experience of that poem changed my entire sense of myself and my work—*but* . . .

If I were looking at that sequence as a sympathetic reader, I would not be talking of such matters at all. I would be concerned with its structure and its varying tones that inform the structure and carry the work wherever it's going. It is made up, for instance, of poems in verse and of prose-poems, almost but not quite in regular alternation. The prose-poems vary from a relatively relaxed style to very concentrated, unmistakably poetic writing—"poetic" because of emphatic rhythmic elements and because there are so many points of evocatively sensitized phrasing. A wide range of personal notes establishes the speaker's character, anchoring the sequence in moments of extraordinary arousal that create a context of intimately inward preoccupations within the "larger" political and philosophical ones. The strongest poem, probably, comes at the beginning—such, at least, was my intention, so that the rest of the sequence would, as it were, arrange itself around it and take off from its various implied dimensions. There is a play throughout the sequence of the loving, introspective voice over the grossest and harshest, most dispiriting realities as well as over a joyous miracle or two that bemuse the delighted mind. The sequence makes its way toward the buffoonery that closes it, a juggling act typographically acted out on the page to suggest all that has been placed in the swinging balance of the sequence as a whole. The success of the poem, it seems to me, is entirely a matter of the conviction of each part, of the succession of the affects, and the placement of the sections in relation to the opening poem's closeup of one young person whose disastrous condition embodies many kinds of ambiguous and precarious predicaments. A powerful thrust forward, a number of hesitant forays thereafter, and then movements of great intensity (sometimes leavened by humor and irony) just before the circus balancing act at the end—such, at least, is the structural *aim* as finally conceived. The structure at first, when the sequence is in the making, seems impossibly arbitrary, "playing tennis without a net" in the most negative sense. But as the implicit dynamics come more and more into the foreground an order does emerge; we are improvising a game of considerable rigor in its own terms.

3

What did I forget to say just now? That "His Present Discontents" is "about" human murderousness, desire, the enterprise of beauty. I could certainly go on in this vein! But nothing matters of all I might say unless the play of feeling, the shifting tones, and the whole growing complex of elements speak for themselves.

But let me tell you something more about the new sequence (though I still know nothing about it). You have seen a few short bits of it. I think I shall call it "She," and begin it with a long first poem I have already, nearly, completed. I think my poem may have been touched off by an inadvertent but surely a real, if buried, sexual image in Wordsworth's *The Prelude*, in a passage in which one would never expect to find such a thing:

> lustily
> I dipped my oars into the silent lake,
> And, as I rose upon the stroke, my boat
> Went heaving through the water like a swan . . .

Swans again, too! And (in Wordsworth) what a moment in which, suddenly, ecstasy and dread become one, just a few lines further on!

Let me quote the first two stanzas of the title poem of "She."

> She writes of sunburnt thighs,
> a terrace of stone lions,
> and Naxos just barely visible from her window.
>
> This poor vessel, I,
> one-oared, rudderless, droops
> or, randy, unspent, shivers
> in the moist night
> towards gardens blowing where she sleeps or wakes. Dawn
> is breaking there. And at its eastern gate
> erratic trumpets blast their notes of war.
> I'll beat into the wind as best I can.

I too, as you can see, am inseparable from my vessel that is carrying me, to be sure, towards joy and disaster. But despite what I've already said, I don't mean to be all that passive in the process. Homer was clever indeed to think of the device that enabled the wily Odysseus to hear the sirens. There he showed us something I haven't really talked about, intellectual energy put to work as a shaping force. I think Homer's method probably better than Wordsworth's in one respect at least, that of the way thought is presented. Thought, even pure, abstract thought, has every bit as much a right to enter a poem as an image does. But it must not make the poetic line sag or the dynamics sputter. Interesting problem, but I won't bore you with the details—I mean, with the details of my suffering. Thinking in a poem has to come in the form of electricity or flame. My "She" is a woman who makes me think into her childhood and her humanity, something very difficult for "this poor vessel, I" at the start of the poem. He can solve the problem only by a kind of forgetting, in which thought flames up in its own right, by the same associative process that sets everything else in a poem burning.

American Poets in 1976, ed. William Heyen (Indianapolis: Bobbs-Merrill, 1976)

❧

On Being A Jewish Poet

IF you want to know what Jewish poetry is, or even whether or not such a thing exists, it's best to look at it from a poet's viewpoint, or at least that of an ordinary reader of poetry. People who want to know what British poetry is don't first define what it is to be British, or what the characteristic British themes are or should be. They find out some poets' names and begin reading them, and by and large don't care a bit about the poets' degree of Britishness—only how interesting they are and what sort of poetry they write. Of course, one does begin to notice certain tentatively national traits though there are always exceptions. A certain tidy articulateness and emotional self-braking, often forthcoming as a heartbroken little whimper, mark a good deal of current British verse, for instance. But plenty of Americans, and even Israelis, write that way too, and there are British poets who are wildly emotional and others who "experiment" as if they were San Franciscans.

"Jewish" characteristics wander in and out of poetry. My friend Dannie Abse, the Welsh-Jewish Londoner who is one of the most humanely direct poets writing, has a poem called "Uncle Isidore" that begins:

> When I observe a toothless ex-violinist,
> with more hair than face, sprawled like Karl Marx

on a park seat or slumped, dead or asleep,
in the central heat of a public library,
I think of Uncle Isidore—smelly
schnorrer and lemon-tea bolshevik—my foreign
distant relative, not always distant.

Before Auschwitz, Treblinka, he seemed near,
those days of local pogroms, five year programmes,
until I heard him say, "Master, Master
of the Universe, blessed be your name,
don't you know there's been no rain for years
and your people are thirsty? Have you no shame,
compassion? Don't you care at all?"

This poem, published in the *New Statesman* of March 21, 1975, is both English and Jewish in its ethnic self-consciousness and its slightly embarrassed attributions of stereotyped comic, radical and shabby qualities to Uncle Isidore. English Jews are literally closer than we to the memories of European ghetto life. Their knowledge that European, and even English, anti-Semitism persists makes them shakier and less self-confident than American Jews in certain ways. At the same time, "bolshevik" leanings are not as taboo in England as here. But when Uncle Isidore bursts into his speech, there's nothing English about him any more. He is arguing with God in a famous Jewish tradition that has been echoed by many modern poets, including (briefly) Allen Ginsberg in *Kaddish* and your humble servant here and there.

Special Jewish concerns and themes and ways of thinking do then exist, yet you will often find them deep in the camp of the Gentiles too. Take Longfellow's "The Jewish Cemetery at Newport," or several of the speeches in Shakespeare's *The Merchant of Venice*. Some of the Shylock passages are remarkable Jewish poems, because in them Shakespeare, dreaming into a stereotype, discovered—probably to his own amazement—a man. Say what you will about him (he gloats, he's a kosher swine), that man is recklessly courageous. When condescending Antonio asks for a loan, Shylock speaks his bitter mind forthrightly. Later on, in terrible peril, he exposes his judge's unconscious hypocrisy in expressing horror at his insistence on the pound of flesh. Shakespeare brilliantly discovered the ironic, democratic turn of analytic thought that would occur to an intelligent person in Shylock's despised circumstances. His argument, addressed to supposedly Christian (actually, British) gentlemen, is sardonically Swiftian in its nasty "Jewish" way:

You have among you many a purchased slave,
Which, like your asses and your dogs and mules,
You use in abject and in slavish parts,
Because you bought them—shall I say to you,
"Let them be free, marry them to your heirs?
Why sweat they under burthens? let their beds
Be made as soft as yours, and let their palates
Be seasoned with such viands?" You will answer,
"The slaves are ours." So do I answer you:

> The pound of flesh, which I demand of him
> Is dearly bought, 'tis mine, and I will have it.

Leaving Shakespeare out of it, though, let me propose a simple definition: A Jewish poem is a poem written by a Jew. I think this definition can help keep us from focusing on set motifs and attitudes, however significant, as the sole givens of Jewish poetry. The Holocaust is an over-powering subject, so much so that only Dan Pagis and a few others have occasionally been able, poetically, to make us see or feel more than the facts themselves, at once and blindingly, show. The prophetic or bardic or devotional tradition, set forth as the only proper Jewish "way" by Harold Bloom some years ago (*Commentary*, March 1972), long ago ceased being specifically Jewish, if it ever was. Whitman, historically speaking a latecomer, picked it up and used it to good "American" purpose. My first memories of Whitman, in fact, come not from reading him but from hearing him recited in Yiddish translation by Jewish poets whose tone and gesture were strongly influenced by Russian Futurist mannerisms and Mayakovskyan declamation. To me, in effect, he was a Jewish poet named Voltvétman, who was part of a Russian-Jewish movement of the twentieth century.

No doubt many Jews have a special memory and awareness engaged with the prophetic tradition that suffuses their whole sense of life and language. And the Holocaust is "ours" in a way that no Gentile—at least not one healthily affirmative about existence—would want to steal from us (though healthy affirmativeness is not necessarily the key either to wisdom or to poetic power). And there are all the kindred memories and associations of Jews the world over almost—the synagogue and its worlds of thought and reverie, the *shtetl*, idiosyncratic turns of exaltation and vulgarity, vision and deprivation. But a Jew may write about the sunlight on a Sussex hillside, or about love in a way that does not echo the *Song of Songs*. If his "non-Jewish" poems are good enough, then lo! they have willy-nilly added to the sum total of Jewish poetry. ("The heavy memories of Horeb, Sinai and the forty years"—Ezra Pound's line in a poem bemoaning the loss of significant tradition in the modern age—have nothing, on the surface at least, to do with the case.)

I don't want to deny the appeal of an explicitly Jewish voice on its own terms. Charles Reznikoff's work, well represented in his *By the Well of Living & Seeing*, is always rhythmically true to this voice though often too relaxed to be called lyric poetry:

> When I came for my laundry, I found a shirt missing.
> The laundryman—a Jew—considered the situation:
> "There are four ways of losing a shirt," he said thoughtfully;
> "in the first place, it may never have been delivered by the steam laundry;
> in the second place, it may be lying around here, unpacked;
> in the third place, it may have been delivered and packed in someone else's
> bundle;
> and in the fourth place it may really be lost.
> Come in again at the end of the week and I'll know what has happened."
> And his wife, recognizing a fellow Jew,
> smiled and spoke up in Yiddish, "We won't have to go to the rabbi about it,
> will we?"

This piece has a good deal of nostalgic charm—at least for those who recognize the combined incantatory and pedagogical tone of the laundryman's speech, nicely counterbalanced by his wife's folk-witticism. It is by no means representative of Reznikoff's most serious work, much of which (including a long series of Holocaust closeups) is couched in a plain, documentary style of great integrity and almost archaic strength—more moral than poetic, if that is possible.

Reznikoff, despite an early phase of some duration when he was very much a part of the Imagist and modernist tendencies of his youth (he was born in 1894), writes a poetry saturated with Jewish experience of an essentially traditional and unassimilated kind. The poems in Harvey Shapiro's newest book, *Lauds*, are at times equally Jewish in a literal sense but struggle against the limitations of such total immersion. "For the Yiddish Singers in the Lakewood Hotels of My Childhood" is an example:

I don't want to be sheltered here.
I don't want to keep crawling back
To this page, saying to myself,
This is what I have.

I never wanted to make
Sentimental music in the Brill Building.
It's not the voice of Frank Sinatra
I hear.

To be a Jew in Manhattan
Doesn't have to be this.
These lights flung like farfel.
These golden girls.

Shapiro's loving self-distancing from unavoidable Jewish consciousness is an earnest of his desire to write primarily out of his own independent sensibility. Another poem in the same book, "Riding Westward," begins wryly, placing the Jewish ritual experience of which he has been a part in our gasoline world:

It's holiday night
And crazy Jews are on the road,
Finished with fasting and high on prayer.
On either side of the Long Island Expressway
The lights go spinning
Like the twin ends of my tallis.
I hope I can make it to Utopia Parkway
Where my father lies at the end of his road.

I am far enough away from my own first book of poems, *Blue Boy on Skates* (1964), so that I can look back over it now a little objectively. I have never been a deliberately Jewish writer. Leafing through that book again, however, I am a little surprised that apparently no one else has ever thought of me that way either. More of the poems are on explicitly Jewish themes than I had remembered. Here I must catch myself up short—there are really only three. One of them links the threat of coming nuclear war with the hard memories of Eastern Europe Jews. It is in part addressed to my mother:

> I was thinking how the hunters will come to the shelters;
> They'll have war-heroes' hands, smelling of raw meat.
> They'll brain the babies and take the canned salmon.
> Then I remembered the smell of strawberries in Jónava.
>
> That's what you told me once—that when you were a girl,
> In Jónava, the smell of strawberries filled the countryside.
> When you were a girl! O happy Jews wandering
> Sober among strawberries, everywhere in Jónava.

Another has to do with my father's funeral, and another with a childhood fight with Polish boys who ganged up on me. Shylock would probably have approved one pair of lines along the way:

> When the Christian martyrs were burned, we agreed,
> Anonymous Jews were used for kindling.

But although virtually all the poems in this book are *not* explicitly Jewish in their literal themes and subjects, my first impulse on rereading the book was to say they were. That was because the voice in the poems is my own; the literal content may be simply human in its meaning, yet the innermost subjective reach is toward specific persons and experiences in ways shared by many Jews. Thus, in one poem, "The Gate," I present—in terms so nearly allegorical that the reader might not take them any more literally than he would the biblical tale of Jacob's wrestling with the angel—an actual experience. Late one night, in London, my son had not yet returned home and I went out searching for him in the streets of Hampstead and on the heath. My anxiety, the coldness and strangeness of my solitary walk under the stars, and the fact that I was living in a foreign country all conspired to produce a curiously painful state of transport. I felt the co-presence of different times—the days of my dead father, whose ghost-world I felt I had entered, the whole curve of my own life, and the world of my son and his generation. For the first time I realized the loneliness of the older immigrant generation of Jews, out of phase with the orbit of their own childhood, as their children were drawn into the centrifugal and secular whirl of American education and thought. Yet the poem says none of this explicitly.

> Have I passed through the gate without knowing?
> It is not so dreadful after all.
> Shadows and terrors, gather around me;
> I will teach you a trembling peace.
>
> I did not know where I was going
> Though voices sang to me of the irrevocable.

The cold stars were shining in the sad night,
And I went out searching for my son.

When I found him it was too late;
I had passed through the gate, without knowing.
Strange that not until tonight
Have I seen the stars in all their silence.

I welcome the dead. I hope they do not care—
Love broke their backs, but so long ago.
I have joined the mists where the old ones rustle.
Father! I am no longer immortal!

Father! I have believed I killed you.
My soul winged blindly and left yours alone.
I did not know of the gate, my dear.
I did not know. I did not know.

I quote this poem not to attract admiring attention to it, but to illustrate the elusiveness of whatever it is in a poem that could be called essentially Jewish (or, by the same tokens, Irish or whatever). The literal sense of "The Gate" inheres in a succession of tones projected by a speaker who has passed some terrifying boundary and come to terms with it. He went out to find his son but found, as well, the immense universe and in it the unforgotten world of the dead. Especially, he found his father, who, he now sees, also "passed through the gate" once, perhaps in search of the speaker. I should not force my private associations into the poem. They are merely part of the background of its feeling, though conceivably the sense of being in an alien universe and of coping with a devastating break between generations is presented in images and phrasing with some Jewish resonances.

I have used my poem for illustration because I can speak with authority about its psychological genesis. The tragic sense of irrevocably disappearing communion between the generations is a deep American motif because of all the constantly dissolving continuities of our complex and ever-changing culture. Each special group within the culture will share this sense in its own way; in addition each poet will use it and change its bearing to accommodate his own inner reality. Think of the reversals from the assumptions about the generations in both Shapiro's poems and my poem "The Gate" in the following passage from David Rosenthal's "Saudade do Towbin":

In the dark cemetery chapel,
the mumbled Hebrew liturgy begins.
Father and mother stand, mute and listless,
their sweetest agonies hidden within
the dulled blank lines of a forgotten middle-age.
Below them their only son, whom they had abandoned,
glows in the casket, his arms clotted with old needle-marks.
It is the ring-wraith! The phosphorescent fire
of the dead soul in autumn. The candied leaves and flowers

of this cemetery lane glow with a wild, unrelenting light.
Deep in the womb, another forgotten son sleeps.

Another young poet, Frederick Feirstein, has written at least two poems that summon up Jewish identity to give the speaker a clearer focus for his private feelings and observations. That is, he wills a Jewish identity for himself to give his sense of life a dramatic perspective, without which his energetic sense-responses and emotions would seem merely restless and chaotic. One of the poems, "The Boarder," appeared originally in *Present Tense* (Spring 1974). It presents a picture of lost continuities through the eyes of a Jewish poet, Yud Schwartz, whose New York-Jewish literary world disappeared long ago:

He read a poem:
About wind, papers wrapped tight on his calves
As he walked Sholem Aleichem's streets, the old shops
Gone, slush soaking his shoes—gone poor,
Spanish in the tenement rooms
Where he spent the Sabbath afternoons
With his young wife, his poet-friends . . .

Schwartz is made perfectly alive in this poem, a man with an enormous zest for everything natural and alive. But his past has disappeared from under him, his wife has been killed by an automobile, everything has "gone poor," and he himself is dead at the end of the poem—a figure out of a Robinson or a Masters or a Frost poem were not everything we were told about him totally Jewish. The first books of both these poets, David Rosenthal's *Eyes on the Street* and Frederick Feirstein's *Survivors*, are the work of young American Jews at once thoroughly assimilated into American culture (though, like most poets, highly critical too) and unselfconsciously alert to the Jewish presence in their minds at the same time.

I have so far been leaning mostly toward poems that, at least by implication, can be labeled Jewish in content, though I have been trying to suggest as well the ambiguity and openness of my subject. Freer examples of Jewish poetry—that is, poetry written by Jews, regardless of theme—can easily be found, however. Take the beginning of Muriel Rukeyser's lovely, painful "Among Grass," from her *The Speed of Darkness:*

Lying among grass, am I dead am I sleeping
Amazed among silences you touch me never
Here deep under, the small white moon
cries like a dime and do I hear?

Whenever I think of these lines, the vast space of the poem's loneliness comes back to me: "amazed among silences," "you touch me never/Here deep under." The effort is to reach out and mark the failure of love to carry, and the cosmic distances involved. It does not matter that the desolate courage of these opening lines is not sustained all the way through to the poem's very end. The true note has been struck and does find echoes in succeeding lines.

Muriel Rukeyser has a gift for opening her poems with a music of loss, abandonment, loneliness. One poem, indeed, starts out from her main strength, as it were, by proclaiming: "The motive of all of it was loneliness." This sense of broken connections is an insight Jewish poets often pursue, but in much the same way modern poets do generally. A striking poem in Delmore Schwartz' *Summer Knowledge,* ostensibly on a specific Christian theme—the feelings of Christ's disciples after his resurrection—begins and ends with this lonely insight into the bleakness of the universe. Here is the opening stanza:

> The starlight's intuitions pierced the twelve,
> The brittle night sky sparkled like a tune
> Tinkled and tapped out on the xylophone.
> Empty and vain, a glittering dune, the moon
> Arose too big, and, in the mood which ruled,
> Seemed like a useless beauty in a pit;
> And then one said, after he carefully spat:
> "No matter what we do, he looks at it!"

The poem ("Starlight Like Intuition Pierced the Twelve") ends: "This life will never be what once it was"—a thought spoken, like the one that closes the first stanza, not with joy but with bitterness. The sense of displacement is modern, American and Jewish, an existential realization.

But it is all too easy to give a lugubrious cast to what one says on this whole subject. Pressed too far, the tragic view of what is Jewish can become an inflated arrogation of all the sacred virtues, as in Muriel Rukeyser's well-known poem, "To Be a Jew in the Twentieth Century," which appears in her *Breaking Open*. I have read that this poem has been selected for printing in the Reform Jewish prayer book, but it is far from her beautiful best.

> To be a Jew in the Twentieth Century
> Is to be offered a gift. If you refuse,
> Wishing to be invisible, you choose
> Death of the spirit, the stone insanity.
> Accepting, take full life, full agonies:
> Your evening deep in labyrinthine blood
> Of those who resist, fall and resist; and God
> Reduced to a hostage among hostages.
>
> The gift is torment. Not alone the still
> Torture, isolation; or torture of the flesh.
> That will come also. But the accepting wish,
> The whole and fertile spirit as guarantee
> For every human freedom, suffering to be free,
> Daring to live for the impossible.

Though some of its phrasing reflects her passionate vision, the sonnet distorts Muriel Rukeyser's genius in much the same way as Walt Whitman's "O Captain! My Captain!" distorts his. One can read it as an inspirational call to the sacrificial destiny that Schwartz's poem treats so sourly, but the essential method of surrounding "Jew" and "Twentieth Century" with rhetorical abstractions is unconvincing. Besides, the thought is dubious—rather ruthless, a little like Portia and her friends when they really lower the boom. The speaker threatens the poor Jews severely if they refuse the gracious "gift" of torment, and just as severely if they accept it. At the end, she counsels cheery courage as one nails oneself to a cross for the principle of the thing.

Less ambitious, David Ignatow's "Get the Gasworks" is satisfyingly hard and concrete. The rasping American bluntness of its opening is his way of being a man who happens to be a Jew in the twentieth century (lower case this time):

> Get the gasworks in a poem
> and you've got the smoke and smokestacks,
> the mottled red and yellow tenements,
> and grimy kids who curse with the pungency
> of the odor of gas. You've got America, boy.

Anyone who reads Ignatow's *Selected Poems* can see that he carries his load of spiritual heaviness. But he doesn't try to smear it over the entire universe in the name of Jewish contemporaneity. I suppose he does show a particularly Jewish sort of whimsy sometimes. His "Love Poem for the Forty-Second Street Library" is Chagall-like, I'm a little sorry to say, though I do like it:

> With my eyes turned to the sky
> and my toes nearly touching pavement,
> floating along I'll approach Times Square

And then there's "The Bagel"—least tragic of Jewish themes—in which he imagines himself chasing a runaway bagel and then doubling over and rolling after it in great somersaults "like a bagel" and "strangely happy with myself."

But I never meant to catalogue all the Jewish poets. I've omitted a great many interesting names—Howard Nemerov, Karl Shapiro, Denise Levertov, Adrienne Rich, George Oppen, Samuel Greenberg (whose youthful energy was crippled by inadequate education and feeling for the English language and yet shone through touchingly), Ruth Whitman and many others. I have wished mainly to suggest that we make no *a priori* assumptions about the nature of that sweet beast, Jewish poetry, but that we simply read it for what it has to show us. Traditions intermingle in Jewish as in other sensibilities, and the truest Jewish poetry will be written out of the inward preoccupations of people who happen to be Jews.

Let me end with an illustration of the process whereby such poetry finds its way toward its own historical meaning: Theodore Weiss's "The Polish Question," published here for the first time.[1] I shall comment only on its first

1. *Present Tense*, 3 (Winter 1976), 32–3. See also Theodore Weiss, *Fireweeds: Poems* (New York: Macmillan, 1976), 123–30.

two sections, for I do not want to "explain" it to death. But those sections, like the poem as a whole, show how the poet discovers the presence of a heritage of terror within his carefully detached, witty estheticism.

Like a great many fine poems, Jewish or not, "The Polish Question" is a fairly sophisticated work and calls for readers who won't expect to "get" it without listening attentively. The speaker is a poet who, in fantasy, imagines himself a perfect master, able to control every element like some great painter whose work is always superbly conceived and executed. What would happen, he wonders, if indeed his powers were such? What he discovers, suddenly, is the role of terror guiding his work. That terror is the unresolved historic memory of Jewish life in Poland, center of the most virulent anti-Semitism in the Tsar's domains. That is what "the Polish question" means in this poem. It has to do with an associative cluster around that Jewish memory always present in the speaker no matter what he does or thinks.

Without the speaker's realizing it, all his thoughts and images are leading to this "Polish question." He issues a series of instructions to the reader, presented as half-comic notes on how to see what the master-poet is doing but actually dead serious. The first two reveal life's wintriness and emptiness—he commands the reader to drink "icy water" to realize the wintriness sensuously, inside himself; and he shows him a parenthesis with nothing in it, a "space" that pictures ominous emptiness. From here he leaps to the exact opposite of these effects. The reader is asked to think of "his beloved" in "her most memorable stance." But that image is threatened by "storms already storing up"—and suddenly, abruptly, at the end of the first section we are faced with the subject of "Poland/of your grandparents, of terrible/times thereafter, waiting everywhere."

Literary echoes are important in the rich substance of this section. Students of poetry will recognize tones from Browning, Keats, Stevens and others, and a related connection, familiar in Romantic poetry, between the emotions of despair and of sexual ecstasy as they inform an artist's effort to make something beautiful. Though he works out of a well-steeped tradition, Weiss has found his own voice and style within it, and they have led him directly to the source of his sense of something threatening—the pain of family and tribal memories.

This discovery is pursued in succeeding sections. In the second, for instance, the speaker sees the beloved's vulnerability to everything dangerous—another common Romantic motif, as in Yeats' poem "The Pity of Love." But the Jewish turn lies in the way "Poland" becomes the equivalent of all danger, especially the violence and brutality of humanity, and even Nazi brutality. Poland "lurks" in the mind, forever menacing. The domestic scene in the second section suggests contentment yet is throbbing with "Poland." Without high rhetoric or sensationalism, Weiss shows us the storm troopers in a cracked teacup: a Jewish version of Blake's "Eternity in a grain of sand."

The idea of a Jewish poetry is in part arbitrary. It is useful if one does not press too hard, more useful for inviting empathy with subtle, elusive processes than for establishing categories. "The Polish Question" reminds us of the curious paths of our shifting awareness as well as of the way a Jewish poet's art creates its own tentative context as it opens out.

Present Tense (Winter 1976)

❧

Adolescents Singing, Each to Each —When We and Eliot Were Young

I am trying to reach back to what it was in T. S. Eliot's poetry that so attracted me and my little gang of adolescent literati pals in the early 1930s. Although I don't like to think of myself as a hoary memory bank, facts must be faced. I speak of a time before "Burnt Norton" appeared, when Joyce's *Ulysses* had just been published in the United States—to the shocked fascination of Miss Hughes, my charming, encouraging English teacher in Cleveland, where in 1933–34 my stepfather had a job. The year before, we had lived in Boston, where my previous little gang and I had taken to Eliot over the dead bodies of our teachers. Free verse was still a topic of hot debate, especially on the part of people who hadn't a clue one way or another. As for me, at ages 15 and 16, I certainly thought well of the word "free."

It takes a bit of recalling—or rather, perhaps, believing—some things in Eliot that caught our unfledged attention. Not his "obscurity" or "erudition" or religion or thoughts on tradition and the individual talent. I look back (surprised that I still share it) to our glee over "The *Boston Evening Transcript*," a pre-20s Menckenish squib enlivened by an opening that is still visually hilarious: "The readers of the *Boston Evening Transcript* / Sway in the wind like a field of ripe corn."

The *Transcript*, with its marvelously leisurely front page, full of white space, and its understated title, was so sedate! After those two lines a subtler Eliot insinuated himself into our innocent souls with his play on the word "evening" and his deliberate air of intellectual superiority (not in this instance too far out of our ken) that stirred up hidden instincts for random snobbishness:

> When evening quickens faintly in the street,
> Wakening the appetites of life in some
> And to others bringing the *Boston Evening Transcript*,
> I mount the steps and ring the bell, turning
> Wearily, as one would turn to nod goodbye to Rochefoucauld,
> If the street were time and he at the end of the street,
> And I say, "Cousin Harriet, here is the *Boston Evening Transcript*."

A phrasing like "evening quickens faintly in the street," quintessential early Eliot at his best, has nothing sensational about it; but it will slip into the memory almost subliminally. It is serious, precise, mysterious. And the sound resonances around it (the internal off-rhyming of "evening" and all the participles, for instance, and of "*Transcript*," "quickens," and "wakening") are only a few examples of the poem's virtuosity, devastatingly impressive to young poets-in-the-making who spoke it aloud. Our young ears were ravished by the strategically distributed consonance and assonance (*w*'s, *h*'s and long *e*'s in particular) and the remarkably varied series of five-stress lines—stretched to seven stresses in the antepenultimate and final lines that exquisitely act out the bored self-distancing affected at the end. It was not a matter of analyzing the prosody but of responding to the way it gave the little poem more dimensions than seemed probable. The comic side of the poem, the atmospheric accuracy of certain lines, the witty posturing at the close and the irreverence toward bourgeois certainties were all clear enough. The sound and rhythm, however, were absorbed more or less unconsciously.

If I hadn't lived in Boston, this poem might never have caught my attention. After all, the world of Cousin Harriet and the *Transcript*—the world of genteel Boston—was light years away from the somewhat bohemian immigrant Jewish circle of my parents, working people who were interested in ideas and art and world politics although they had little formal education. Among them were some Yiddish-speaking poets who in the course of their development had picked up a mixture of influences ranging from German Romanticism and French Symbolism through Russian Futurism to the cadences of Whitman. I listened to them recite their pieces, receiving what they had to offer as best I could. Would that I had learned much more from that breed—they were carriers of a cosmopolitan tradition of experiment and openness—already being rendered obsolescent by history. Oddly enough, given Eliot's second-rate politics and ignorant cracks about Jews, I was prepared for his sensibility by these men and women despite my inability to appreciate their art thoroughly. If their sense of humanity was larger and more adult than his, their wry mixture of strong feeling with a zest for the ridiculous had obvious affinities with his irony.

Of course, there's a strongly adolescent flavor to a great deal of Eliot's poetry, although at the same time a highly sophisticated mind and vision are at work. The adolescent element in Eliot (like the limbic system in the human brain) is a constant, underlying the complex overlay. It accounts for the dreary sexual and political infantilism in his mentality that made him, despite his infinitely superior genius, a child (sometimes ugly, sometimes dangerous) of American provincial prejudices.

Leaving aside the well-phrased sniggering in pieces like "Mr. Appollinax" ("Priapus in the shrubbery / Gaping at the lady in the swing") or the prose poem "Hysteria" ("I decided that if the shaking of her breasts could be stopped, some of the fragments of the afternoon might be collected, and I concentrated my attention with careful subtlety to this end"), Eliot's most striking early work is all in the adolescent keys of unresolved self-doubt, endlessly self-directed sensitivity and defensively cruel cool posturing. I hasten to add that I am not calling into question his poetic success, only pointing to an important element in what his poetry was successful in projecting—an actual inner state or quality of reverie, doubtless a reflex too of one type of cultivated American male psyche of Eliot's generation.

"The Love Song of J. Alfred Prufrock" is a perfect instance. Whatever else one may say about this first poem of Eliot's to command strong attention, it positively sweats panic at the challenge of adult sexuality and of living up to one's ideal of what it is to be manly in any sort of heroic model. Those challenges are the special monsters haunting adolescent male imagination, especially of the more introspective and introverted varieties. The furtive restlessness of the start, the fear of women's ridicule, the sensual longings, the forebodings of loneliness and eternal frustration, the painful self-mockery side by side with the persistent romanticism—these are the very stuff of that imagination. The age of the "I" of the poem, who is not in any case a sharply delineated dramatic character but rather a half-delineated one (the other half being the kind of floating sensibility both Eliot and Pound were to evolve a little further down the line), isn't specified. He may be an unusually self-conscious very young man, or perhaps he is older. It really doesn't matter. Adolescent readers took to him because he expressed their feelings while seeming to be someone other—the stuffily named and brought up "Prufrock" of the title. Fear of impotence, failure and isolation continue into adult life, of course, but they are the particular unwanted burden of the young.

"Prufrock" holds all this burden of vulnerability, and also the accompanying need to mask desire ("Is it perfume from a dress / That makes me so digress") and not give the game away to "the women" as they move about and chatter and seem so politely, unshakably self-contained. How old was Eliot, actually, when he wrote the poem—about 21 or 22? It is a poem whose essence is distilled from teen-age memories, felt as deeply private yet almost universally shared—"I have heard the mermaids singing, each to each. / I do not think that they will sing to me."

Exactly! And that is why we could recite the poem at the drop of a hint, and could absorb its music unthinkingly, so that it mingled with equally rueful tones and rhythms out of Edwin Arlington Robinson and Robert Frost in the great American symphony of unrealized grace and heroism. (Later a talented university classmate of mine, Isaac Rosenfeld, did a brilliantly funny translation into Yiddish, a parody that nevertheless struck just the right Eliotic note of stand-up comic self-demolition in the extended-adolescence mode.)

But the great lyrical triumph of the "Prufrock" volume was "Rhapsody on a Windy Night," in which many of the motifs of "Prufrock" reappear in altered context. "Rhapsody" offers the same murkily squalid context of seedy late-night streets, the same horror of sex (here focused in the figure of the prostitute who "hesitates toward you in the light of the door / Which opens on her like a grin" and again in the image of the moon as a crackbrained old whore), and, at the end of the poem, the same fear of waking into ordinary life. If "Prufrock" merged in my mind with poems like Robinson's "Eros Turannos" and Frost's "Reluctance," the music of "Rhapsody on a Windy Night" very largely displaced the others.

Eliot's narrow psychological base remained intact (the adolescent limbic system); yet it became identified with the harsh metropolitan awareness of Europe, specifically of the darker side of Paris, and beyond that with the sense of brute impersonality as the key to what memory means and to a pervasive gross atmosphere of madness. Adolescent terror is thus stretched beyond itself and assimilated to the gathering blackness of the West not long before World War I. This sense of dread imminence, not necessarily objectified as the definable pressure of a historical moment, is rhythmically mobilized in the irregularly patterned verse units that mark out a four-hour procession through city streets in a waking nightmare beginning at midnight. The succession of distorted, skeletal, mechanically grasping images, phallic gone sterile, adds up, as the slightly overexplicit ending explains, to a desperate vision of life's macabre essence. It is like the shock of death-realization in puberty.

Now, our own historical moment in the 30s was a reprise, with differences, of Eliot's around 1911. We were a generation that had grown up with the sense that we were doomed to have another such war—only worse, because Mussolini and, especially, Hitler were worse than their imperial predecessors, and because the weapons were bound to be worse. (We had no inkling how much worse, or that it could be our own side that would use the worst of all.) Our premonitions were basically our internalization of the past; and in its violent images and death-march sense of an irreversible destiny, Eliot's morbid vision of the inner reality of things confirmed what we felt in our bones, no matter how blithe or hopeful our essential personalities might be or how optimistic our surface attitudes concerning the possibility of preventing a new war.

All this happened without our needing to identify it consciously, and was felt independently of what our political views might be. For Eliot transmitted what W. H. Auden, in another, though related, context, was later to call "the unmentionable odor of death" of our century; he also transmitted a raspingly disturbed sense of a world out of kilter and out of control. The European generation of Auden and Bertolt Brecht did not question the pervasiveness of that traumatized awareness, although many in Eliot's own generation—and Eliot himself—resisted accepting it. Their religious inheritance and conservative ideas of social and political order (or a mystical neo-primitivism) helped them refuse the evidence of their deepest psychological perception.

Nevertheless, Eliot's most telling poetry before "Burnt Norton"—that is, his most telling poetry as it came to me in mid-adolescence—conveyed that perception incisively and beautifully and also insidiously. We have had no other poet, I believe, whose phrasing infects the reader's nervous system as Eliot's infected that of embryonic poets of immediately succeeding generations. William Butler Yeats remains our greatest modern poet, Ezra Pound our great embroiler and William Carlos Williams our great humanizer; but Eliot, while he was still enmeshed in unresolved youthful struggles of spirit, showed us a decisive image of ourselves in the mirror of a terrified age being quick-marched nowhere though still capable of making wonderful jokes about it all. The major work that made up this psychic mirror consisted of "Rhapsody on a Windy Night," *The Waste Land,* "The Hollow Men" and Ariel poems, "Sweeney Agonistes" and "Coriolan."

Years later—it must have been, say, 1978—I saw the film made by the Hebrew poet Haim Gouri and others: "The 81st Blow," the most effective of the various documentary films of the Holocaust. In one brief sequence, by no means the most dreadful, we see decently dressed men and women, German Jews, being hustled along Berlin streets, past familiar shops and other buildings, toward wherever they would be loaded onto vehicles bearing them to concentration camps. How unbelievable it must have seemed to them, there on the very streets they had known all their lives. They must have felt that it couldn't be true, that the nightmare must end at any moment. And at the same time they must have felt, too, if only unconsciously, that, being Jews, this was what they had always expected. How often through the centuries the barbarism of their neighbors had suddenly struck; and yet they were citizens, good Germans, a fair number of them war veterans, a fair number of them people who had shown good will and kindness to many other people. Rushed off to the camps, stripped of their clothes, beaten, raped, reduced to the most exposed condition, exterminated. All this was a matter of indifference to most of the world, as in the God-abandoned realm of "Rhapsody on a Windy Night" or "Fragment of an Agon" or the endless destruction of the cities by mindless hordes in "The Waste Land." In the early 30s all these events to come, and—yes—the dropping of the atomic bomb on Japanese cities, and other such enormities were prefigured, in those staggering works, for youngsters just coming of age. In this very curious and strange sense, Eliot's poems meant more to us than they did to their creator.

The New York Times Book Review (20 October 1985)

❧

Discovering E. P.

ELIOT'S poetry took on authority in the United States well before Pound's, although for a while, in their thirties, they were running a close race. Pound had a fast start with the Boston firm of Small, Maynard and Company, which printed his *Provença* in 1910 and his *Ripostes* in 1913, but the work in these volumes had little impact until included in the 1926 *Personae: The Collected Poems* (Liveright). A larger American splash came with Knopf's publication of his *Lustra* in 1917, three years before the same firm brought out Eliot's 1920 volume *Poems*. Then, in 1921, Boni and Liveright did Pound's *Poems 1918–21*, which included *Homage to Sextus Propertius, Hugh Selwyn Mauberley,* and versions of Cantos 4–7. The next year, though, they published *The Waste Land,* and Eliot became the undisputed champion of an experimental modernism rigorously attentive to what it could learn from tradition.

I may be overstating the case, but it is certainly striking to me, now, that I began to be familiar with Eliot's work in 1932, when I became fifteen—and that I remember particular poems of his with the exact original feeling of being taken by surprise—while Pound grew on me far more slowly. At the University of Chicago, where I was an undergraduate during 1934–37, a course on Eliot's poetry was being offered (although the young professor teaching the introduction-to-poetry course when I was a freshman confessed to me that he found Eliot's poetry too difficult and uncongenial for him to deal with). We weren't far from *Poetry* magazine (edited in those days by Morton Dauwen Zabel), of course, but by that time Pound's halcyon days of bullying Harriet Monroe were past, and in any case his contributions to magazines in the 1930s were pretty much limited to political and economic harangues. With people like Paul Goodman, Jean Garrigue, and Edouard Roditi on campus, and an active Poetry Club to which they and other bright and gifted young poets belonged, I am sure that Pound's name must have passed our lips. I remember reading the Propertius adaptations and *Mauberley* and *Personae* and *A Draft of XXX Cantos* in library or borrowed copies. But I can't remember any intense exchanges, in or out of classrooms, about Pound, although we "tired the sun with talking" about Eliot and Yeats and Auden and the vexed issue of whether, if one wrote a poem exactly, say, in the style of Donne or Keats, that would be a good thing.

We are talking of a period when the academic-literary world was almost as many light-years away from what was most importantly in the making as it is now. The really knowledgeable persons, whose work of the time we now take for granted and assume was the center of the literary universe, were part of a very tiny group indeed. A token of the times was Harry Hayden Clark's *Major American Poets,* published in 1936 by the American Book Company. Clark, the leading figure in the University of Wisconsin's formidable body of American literature scholars—mighty bibliographers and annotators all—limited himself to "the ten generally recognized major American poets" (Bryant, Whittier, Emerson, Poe, Longfellow, Lowell, Holmes, Dickinson, Lanier, and Whitman), "along with Freneau to illustrate the neglected but important early development of our poetry as inspired by scientific deism, and along with Robinson and Lindsay to represent two contrasting aspects of the modern temper in the East and the West, respectively."

Lucky that Walt and Emily got in with that bunch! To do Professor Clark credit, the Whitman selection is excellent, some eighty double-column pages including the whole of *Song of Myself* and the 1855 Preface—only five fewer pages than Whittier though almost 50 pages fewer than Longfellow and some 25 pages fewer than James Russell Lowell. Poor Emily (this was in the days before the Johnson edition, remember) had just over seven pages, ending appropriately with the poem (#569 in Johnson) that begins: "I reckon—when I count at all—." Her punctuation, of course, was still being "normalized," and there were other improvements. Lindsay and Robinson had about 20 pages each.

Essentially, anthologies rarely begin to catch up with contemporary masterpieces until very late. Matthiessen's great anthology of American poetry, still the best for its moment, would not be forthcoming until 1950. The other two most influential anthologies, Oscar Williams' *A Little Treasury of Modern Poetry* and the "Mid-Century Edition" of Louis Untermeyer's anthology of modern British and American poetry, appeared in 1946 and 1950 respectively. Even the sensitive, knowledgeable Matthiessen included only one complete canto (the admittedly splendid but very early Canto 2) and a passage from another (the "pull down thy vanity" passage in 81) with his otherwise fine Pound selection and, in his introduction, written shortly after *Pisan Cantos* had appeared in 1948, questioned whether *The Cantos* "will ever be more than a series of brilliant fragments." Nor, despite his accurately responsive representation of earlier Williams, did he include anything from the first three books of *Paterson,* published in 1946. Oscar Williams, who listed himself but not WCW as one of "the chief modern poets," limited the other Williams to two poems: "Tract" and "The Yachts." Both he and Untermeyer, like Matthiessen, scanted *The Cantos* and managed to have nothing from *Paterson*. But all three provided adequate, defensible selections by Eliot, perpetuating the assumption of his special place in the modern canon.

All this goes to explain why news of the mighty poetic explosions, revolutions, and lesser tumults was so slow in reaching so many of us who came of age during the Depression and World War II. I was barely in my twenties when, by one of life's little accidents, I was offered a job teaching at Michigan State College (now "University"). There I soon met the poet A. J. M. Smith, who not only had what struck me as perfect pitch in poetry—he was one of a handful of people I've known who could get the tonal quality and basic sense of a poem almost at once—but owned all the books. It was through his collection that I caught up with Pound and Williams and late Yeats: i.e., with most of their work that appeared before 1945. Smith considered himself a rigorous "classicist" and was something of a specialist in seventeenth-century verse, but actually he was head over heels in love with the real thing in whatever form. One of Canada's foremost poets, he was a grand friend to have in the poetically isolated world of Michigan State College of Agriculture and Applied Science. Full of dogmatic opinions he could be laughed out of at once, he possessed the indispensable double nature of the best literary minds: *videlicet*, he knew what a serious enterprise poetry is, and also he was never solemn about it. In the highest sense, and like Pound, he didn't give a damn.

My first-acquired copy of *Personae: The Collected Poems*, picked up during my Michigan State period, must be the 1938 New Directions impression from the original 1926 Liveright plates. It's so battered now, and filled with my innocent early notes and underlinings, that I can hardly bear to look at it, let alone touch it. Nevertheless, leafing through it and trying to recapture its first impact, I become aware once more of something barely noticeable: the process by which a poetic force insinuates itself ever so quietly. Take the arresting start of the first poem in the book, "A Tree," which no one ever mentions nowadays:

> I stood still and was a tree amid the wood,
> Knowing the truth of things unseen before,
> Of Daphne and the laurel bow . . .

—An abrupt quotation, I know, and yet the genius of Pound's metamorphic imagination is there in embryo, foreshadowing the miraculous annexation of Odysseus' persona in *The Cantos*, and the glorious proliferation of images of transformed being in Canto 2, and the mysterious extensions of identity in Cantos 47 and 74. The rest of the poem, without relinquishing its enchanted sense of physical rebirth in another form, lapses into pretty archaisms and imitation Yeats such as Eliot would never have allowed himself to publish—but the authority of experienced vision remains. Similarly, a single line in the early tribute to Browning called "Mesmerism"—"Here's to you. Old Hippety-Hop o' the accents"—stands out amidst all the forced phrasing startlingly and summons up that poet as a vital forerunner of the modern. It's a long way from there to the beginning of Canto 2, so brilliant in its linking of "Sordello" with the metamorphic imagination I've just noted and with the troubadour style:

Hang it all, Robert Browning,
there can be but the one "Sordello."
But Sordello, and my Sordello?
Lo Sordels si fo di Mantovano.

It took me a fairly long time to see how Pound's special poetic genius connects with this linkage. I didn't realize it fully until I came upon Browning's greatest lyrical masterpiece, "The Englishman in Italy," whose metrical energy and bounce contribute so exuberantly to its densely packed evocation of the rural Italian countryside and daily life and then, but in the key of awefilled revelatory encompassment, to the sudden repossession of the calmly radiant, myth-informed classical world from the vantage-point of a mountain height away from the teeming peasant-existence below. The same sort of thing happens in "Sordello" at the point where, after the opening thicket of language, the poem finds itself in another such realm. A comparable emergence occurs again and again in *The Cantos*—in Pound's manner, not Browning's, when the dynamics are working most beautifully. It seems to me a curious fact that, in seeing into Browning as he did, Pound could liberate one's understanding of that poet's true accomplishment and take the basic bearings of his own work. We don't usually speak of Guido, Dante, Shelley, and Browning in the same breath, but Pound unifies our sense of the welcome continuity of one transcendent tradition through his practice.

That's what he makes us conscious of, when we've lived with his writing enough to objectify what's going on. But he quickened my attention before I had much of a clue, just through a lively phrase of affectionate admiration like "old Hippety-Hop o' the accents" that made Pound and Browning seem fellow jackrabbits leaping and improvising and juxtaposing and diving out of sight and re-emerging somewhere else. The perception had to come through the poems, not as an abstraction but as sensed magnetic process one was invited to enter: "I stood still and was a tree amid the wood,/Knowing the truth of things unseen before." Turn a couple more pages of *Personae* and you're into "Marvoil," a Provençal poem (as it were) in Browningesque lingo, complete with screamers, but scrambled into free verse despite its ultimate pentametric base of reference. (Open to argument, I'll admit.) Also, the more lyrically and Platonically exalted side of the Provençal tradition, as it came down to us in English by way of Shelley and Rossetti, takes over toward the end. Any young poet could see in this spirited piece by the young Pound clues to aerating his own work: keeping it both colloquial and full of the music of feeling, improvising formally, slipping from one mood to another. At the end of Pound's life, he was still writing that way, as in the *sogenannter* Canto 116:

Came Neptunus
                    his mind leaping
                                        like dolphins . . .

This combining of opposites, these torques of style, are not merely a technical matter, it should go without saying. From the Provençal masters and from Browning, Pound learned to combine his more exalted lyricism with an earthiness that could be ribald: to let go both ways. That is, he took Swinburne-like risks of high-flown language such as most poets today no longer know how to use at all, and he also cultivated a grittier, hardboiled style—often in the same poem, as in his "Translations and Adaptations from Heine." Thus, his rendering of the romantic song of Princess Ilza stands side by side with the bittersweet satirical ironies elsewhere and with such tougherminded verses as:

> The mutilated choir boys
> When I begin to sing
> Complain about the awful noise
> And call my voice too thick a thing.
>
> When light their voices lift them up,
> Bright notes against the ear,
> Through trills and runs like crystal,
> Ring delicate and clear.
>
> They sing of Love that's grown desirous,
> Of Love, and joy that is Love's inmost part,
> And all the ladies swim through tears
> Toward such a work of art.

Early Pound has little of the irresistibly seductive intimacy of early Eliot—of such a line, say, as "When evening quickens faintly in the street" ("The *Boston Evening Transcript*"), which imprints itself quietly but decisively on the nervous system; or of a poem like "Rhapsody on a Windy Night," which opens out onto a shared world of private terror. Moreover, early Pound can be a slapdash mixture of very telling work and Wardour Street fake-archaic or simply awkward writing. But the reach is of a different sort, with a noble beauty as in "Ballatetta"—

> The broken sunlight for a healm she beareth
> Who hate my heart in jurisdiction—

or with rhetorical force rooted in relentless personal honesty, as in the surprising "In Exitum Cuiusdam," which picks up from a phrase of Yeats' in a totally different context—

> "Time's bitter flood"! Oh, that's all very well,
> But where's the old friend hasn't fallen off,
> Or slacked his hand-grip when you first gripped fame?
> I know your circle and can fairly tell
> What you have kept and what you've left behind:
> I know my circle and know very well
> How many faces I'd have out of mind.

At its best, there's a sense (as in the best cantos and canto-passages) of power beyond Eliot's, demanding total attention while it unfolds a vision at once intense and impersonal. We see this quality in early work like "The

Return" and "The Coming of War: Actaeon." These are both triumphs of poetic vision, but it is tragic vision in both instances, more pathos-laden in the former poem, more darkly fatalistic in the latter. Their impact on a young reader was staggering, especially as so many of the poems surrounding them seemed not so far beyond one's own ability. The Actaeon-poem in particular still makes me think of Yeats' phrase "high and solitary and most stern." It links the world of private terror (to recall the phrase with which I characterized Eliot's "Rhapsody on a Windy Night" a few sentences back) with that of myth and of the disastrous 1914–18 war that had broken out in Europe, but totally without self-pity or sentimentality. When I first read these poems I could see no connection with the mind that compromised itself politically, and apparently irrevocably, after they were written. And when, soon afterwards, I read *A Draft of XXX Cantos,* I felt those cantos as closer to the world of *The Red and the Black, The Sentimental Education, The Magic Mountain,* and *Man's Fate* than to anything like the Major Douglas/corporate-state/racist field of association.

It was through creating the poems I have mentioned that Pound confirmed for poetry in English the thrilling and dangerous implications of the new sense of the dynamics and crucial role of lyric poetry that has been evolving over the past hundred years and more. By thinking of politics as an aesthetic construct, Pound misled himself; but that's another matter, too sad, ugly, and familiar to be rehashed here. His essential magic, the lyrical energizing that enable one to jump out of the cage of identity and realize into states of being and feeling independent of one's own, was his great gift that magnetized a generation of young readers and poets. He brought us into a treacherous region to be wandering about in, one that he found inseparable from the poet's role. As his use of the Actaeon-figure in the early poem and again in *The Cantos* shows—and also, even more, his assumption of the Odysseus-model (of voyager into the unknown and into realms no calculation or dependence on the supposed laws of fatality can absolutely predict as of "the process")—the violation of taboos is inevitable for such wanderers. To enter another's soul is, as it were, to discover Artemis naked at her bath. As Pound's greatest work began showing us early on, the world of literally experienced exploration by the imagination is as perilous as human history itself.

Paideuma (Fall/Winter 1986)

Notes Toward an Unauthorized Autobiography

I

I'M seventy today! The Biblical prophecy's half right! From now on it's sheer gravy! I'm in position to bet against the odds.

As for the past, I agree: One ought to have learned *something*—not just that things do change and people do die. But what? How am I to sort things out when everything that comes to mind at once becomes, by that very token, important? (I.e., "important.")

Everything. My father bought me (age 3½–4½) a marvelous tricycle. Later, after my mother had borne me off elsewhere, I would spend my holidays with him; but the tricycle had disappeared, never again to be seen. Why?—seeing that he was a most indulgent father?

Everything: the first conscious sight and touch of snow; the smell of earth and grass when one's scarcely more than a few inches above the ground; finding a prize in a Crackerjack box for the first time, while watching an amateur production of *The Drunkard* (what a vile brute he was to his wife and children!) with my parents in Brentwood, Maryland, whence my mother and I departed, one strange and fatal day, not long afterward.

Was that departure a "good thing" for me? I'll confess I didn't think so then. Yet I had a happy childhood, or so it now seems despite what Hart Crane called "the curse of sundered parentage"; for indeed the separation remained a constant aching reality. I was five. I thought to persuade my parents it was only logical to come together again. And when my mother remarried, I tried to persuade my new stepfather that there was no reason why all four of us couldn't be loving inmates of the same household.

We were now in Woodbridge, Connecticut, just outside New Haven. Those were long country days after interminable travels and visits with friends, in one city after another. I entered first grade in a small, friendly school. I must have seemed strange: a curious little Jewish newcomer (the only non-Christian child there) who had been reading since the age of four and who loved games and running races and the tiny bottles of milk served at recess and the Eskimo Pies sometimes given us as well. Aching heart or not, how ready I was to be happy!

I'm curious (is it too self-indulgent?) about that little newcomer. Devoted to both parents as he was, and for good reason, he early grew accustomed to "seeing both sides" of things, not without guilt at "betraying" both at the same time. Did he have any sort of Yiddish accent in those days? I'm sure he must have done. His parents were left-wing *(Poale-)* Zionists, and saturated with a religious background both undogmatic and morally powerful; all decisions and relationships were deeply considered, however carefree and spontaneous they might seem. The father retreated into orthodoxy as he aged, especially after his late second marriage. The mother held to her vulnerable moral independence, shaken by her own daring, full of self-reproach and doubts yet staunchly her own person, anyone's equal, self-educating, too much given to sacrifice, with a genius for friendship and love.

Those two immigrants, with relatively little formal education, yet were possessed of knowledge and much-pondered memory and enlightened concern. The father, gentle, a bit passive, stubborn, fond, could not at last cope with the mother's more turbulent energy. But he retained, without insistence, his little son's loyalty despite the extroverted confidence, and kindness, of the stepfather. So of course the outsider, the stepfather anxious to show and receive affection, was only guardedly accepted. His keen mind and fiery hatred of oppression were striking and endearing but bordered on ideological intolerance. The boy, more like his own parents, learned much from this man and from the experiences of a company of sad dreamers unknown to most Americans.

To what avail? A child of loving parents divorced from one another—a boy, that is, with a natural father and a good stepfather who is nonetheless alien to him—is an exiled prince, honored within his generously large confinement. His circumstances are to him baffling, irrational. But he is a child, running, playing, falling asleep sometimes in his stepfather's arms, impressed by the man's certainties and bohemian flair yet holding himself apart. He learns the humanity of the unacceptable, if mainly to justify his beautiful mother. Later, whenever he hears any vehement dogmatic assertion, he is seized with annoyance. Sorrow seems natural; anger, merely chaotic.

Surely, on one's seventieth birthday, complacency is in order? Well—on one count perhaps. There was, after all, freedom from the ordinary tyranny of family, from the sense that there is only one way of life. And that freedom, despite necessary sorrow, has been a perpetual emotional gyroscope for me.

II

THE drama of ordinary life: I was born in Washington, D. C., and taken fairly quickly to nearby Mount Rainier and Brentwood, Maryland. In Brentwood I entered kindergarten and—to quote Hart Crane again—I "quickly fled." That is, I walked home at recess-time the same morning, satisfied I had experienced "school" for what it was worth and that was that. Some thirty-two years later, my younger son, Alan, was to go through the same thwarted realization, stopping on his midmorning return homeward to join a funeral throng outside a Catholic church. A good neighbor recognized him and led him home, whence his mother forthwith—amidst kisses and admonitions—drew him back to "shades of the prison house" to resume his education. So it was with me. Guided back to kindergarten by my mother, and carrying the congratulatory orange-tinted marshmallow bunny she had been saving to greet me with after my triumphant return at the end of the school day, I was then and there initiated into the larger madness of things. I couldn't even divide the bunny with my classmates. It simply disappeared into the world's storehouse of lost childhood possessions and hopes, like the tricycle, and the trip to the circus that never happened, and the restoration of the Eden I had shared with my parents.

A flurry of sorts in New York City, about which I remember nothing save a day (hour? minute?) in Washington Square Park, a scene held with such photographic brilliance and precision in memory that when I next saw it after more than a score of years I reentered that eternally fixed and prolonged childhood moment. The memory has the vividness of the powerful images or visions that have always appeared to me, intensely real and "recognized" in color, form, and detail, but that I can rarely trace to actual experience.

And then—the tranquility of Woodbridge: a pet turtle; fishing with a bent pin from the aforesaid small "wood bridge"; the dirt road rising into the hillside; West Rock, where "Judges' Cave" (hiding place of regicide judges protected and fed by local farmers) is still, I should hope, commemorated; the marsh at the foot of the hill where I first found water lilies; the small, hospitable, tomato-fragrant farms all along the road; the Italian farmers scattered here and there with their scrappy little sons who taught me that "Jew" was an insult and that the price of friendship was an obligatory fight. Thither we were brought after the long blurred interval by my stepfather. And there my half-brother Danny came into being, at first sickly but thereafter a sturdy, clever, endearing child.

Woodbridge I remember as an idyll, a time of special contentment. My stepfather, a house painter, worked in New Haven. Very early on, he began bringing me books (among them the entrancing one I knew simply as "the King Arthur stories"—probably Howard Pyle's version) from a library near the trolley line he rode to and from the city. Our grown-up friends were a volatile crew of laborers and their wives, intellectually and politically vivacious people and avid readers. Among them were Yiddish poets and an occasional artist. They were skilled workmen of one sort or another, and I would listen, enthralled by their passionate speech, to their discussions during their improvised "banquets." A group would suddenly arrive, laden with bags filled with corned beef, pickles, rye bread, and so on. There would be a noisy downing of tiny glasses of *schnapps* (one drink for each), accompanied by an exuberant "*l'chaim!*" and, perhaps, some woman's laughing shout: "Look! I'm getting drunk!" But for the rest of the evening it was simply tea and sandwiches and ardent talk. Often the visitors would bring their children, and we would alternate playing games with listening to our elders, sometimes asking questions or even offering a squeaky opinion that was invariably greeted with fond laughter and congratulations.

In the winter, if there was a sudden snow, I would trudge the half mile or so to the end of the trolley line to meet my stepfather and give him his galoshes. When we returned home, I would warm my feet in the huge woodstove provided by our landlord, Mr. Laudano, who dwelt downstairs. The house we'd lived in previously belonged to Mr. Pipi, whose name gave us a certain innocent pleasure. Like many other small landowners in that part of Woodbridge, he was a truck farmer who worked his land in the manner of the *Mezzogiorno*. But the dairy farmers thereabouts were of New England stock. For all I know, they didn't particularly care for immigrant newcomers; but when I carried a small milk-can to the Warners' house for fresh warm milk straight from the source, they were exceedingly welcoming.

Two or three years ago I revisited Woodbridge after doing some work at the Yale library—not unlike my stepfather, who was once employed painting some Yale buildings. Mr. Laudano's house, and the little wooden bridge, and the small farms along the road, and the dirt road itself were all gone: a world of organic soil for human continuities obliterated by an "industrial park." Only my childhood body-sense of the earth's contours there under the concrete made the little necropolis of memories at all familiar.

All over the country America's forgotten history lies buried in eternal anonymity under concrete resurfacings and the official memoirs and documents of important persons.

I could return in memory to Woodbridge and live there forever. It seems to me the matrix both of my dream-life and my education in the world's larger realities. My first fight, for example: over a difference of opinion. I had told some boys I was playing with that I'd been born in Washington, D.C., and that it was the capital of the United States. I was called a liar. *Hartford* was the capital. I admit that at the time I didn't yet know that Hartford existed, let alone that it was the capital of Connecticut. An infuriated little demon punched me on the ear—very painful; and as he seemed about to repeat the punch I imitated what he had done and gave him pause long enough for an older boy to step between us. From another playmate I learned that I was a dirty Jew, and that the Jews had killed Christ. I relayed the news to my mother, who seemed to have heard it already. She explained who Christ was supposed to have been and that he had been crucified, if we were to believe the New Testament, by Roman soldiers: the ancestors, as it were, of the modern Italians.

With the natural gracious impulse that has always been with me to clarify things I do not quite understand to people who probably know even less, I hastened to explain all this to the child who had first instructed me. The result was my second fight, which lasted longer and ended just as inconclusively. We then shook hands and more or less forgot the terms of the quarrel. That never happened in the Polish neighborhood we lived in later on for a while, in Passaic, New Jersey, where being Jewish was unalterably wicked and there were no handshakes after the almost daily fights thrust upon me. But in Woodbridge things were different. Italian children seemed less principled in their observance of anti-Semitic dogma.

Jobs became scarce in the New Haven area, and so we moved on after the fourth grade to Passaic, and thence to Newark, and thence to Boston, and thence to Cleveland, and thence to Chicago. We were certainly extremely poor. My mother occasionally took menial jobs; and I earned some money as a newsboy, and by hauling blocks of ice in my small wagon for the neighbors and delivering suits and dresses that had been cleaned and pressed or repaired by a tailor, or tutoring other children. Yet we never considered ourselves *needy*, or even insecure, but rather as persons of privilege in transit.

Like a tiny Tolstoy, I moved among varied social levels, observing and thinking all the time. No Russian aristocrats were among our acquaintances, but I did, for instance, get to know the family of a prosperous bootlegger whose son, Maxie, I tutored from time to time. They owned a huge house on the other side of town (though distances in Passaic were not great). It was full of shiny furniture, rich rugs, and gaudy lamps—and doubtless much else I was hardly equipped to notice. Our tenement flat had only the barest furnishings; Van Gogh's paintings of peasant interiors will give you the idea, except that the flat had bookcases and piles of newspapers in strategic places. And we had neither telephone nor radio anywhere we lived (strange even to imagine now) but never seemed to miss them. We didn't feel deprived, though. Maxie's house seemed to me a cluttered palace; and the meals his father and mother, who addressed me as "Einstein," forced upon me seemed wantonly sumptuous.

Summers and at Christmas break I would be put on a train to visit my father in Washington. *He* was hardly wealthy either, but he was neither bohemian nor proletarian. He boarded with friends in a middle-class home, with sturdy furnishings, a dining room, regular mealtimes, a radio *and* a telephone (of course), sets of *The Book of Knowledge* and *The Harvard Classics*, and separate rooms for their children. They went to bed at decent times, dressed nicely, and owned, respectively, a successful tailor shop and a successful beauty parlor. They never bought groceries on credit from a poor devil almost as strapped as his customers. They had *meat* whenever they wished. And suddenly I would be dropped into their midst from a world in which cream, or pot roast, or going to a movie was a very special treat. And they were generous folk, old family friends with the simple hospitality of another age. I was treated as a loved child along with their son and daughter, and lived in guilty "luxury" during these precious intervals with my father, a talented salesman with undeveloped musical gifts. He dreamt of setting up his own business and occasionally, in a small way, did so. He was made for high talk and good song, not the loneliness and hard, unrewarding work in which he was trapped.

It was the same when I'd spend a week or two with the families of my mother's sisters and brothers in Baltimore, or with those of my father's sister in nearby Maryland and brother in nearby Virginia. Affection was rampant, and with it pocket money and utterly unwonted lazy ease if I so chose. Then back to the freer, more astringent, intellectually more strenuous life of poverty-hidden *noblesse*. I grew used to the nomadic life, to meeting entirely new people every year or two as we moved along, and became restless if we lingered in any one city. In Passaic, great textile center wracked by the strikes of the twenties and befouled by the stench of the Botany woolen mills, I learned in school, alongside the transplanted peasant children destined to become millhands, how to work hand and machine looms. A smell like burning rubber often filled the air along the river; had I been just a little less sturdy, my life would have been full of terror because of the daily fights I have mentioned. Even so, I often had dreams of being in a jungle at the mercy of wild beasts. At the same time, I somehow relished being able to see how forms of life that touched me intimately, sometimes bitterly, and yet were not, ultimately, *my* life were nevertheless ineradicably real. Gaunt figures with hardened faces were everywhere in the slums of Passaic, of the same kind we can see in the neighborhood of the abandoned old Black Church in Dublin today.

And there were special joys. The bliss of roller-skating on city streets more or less free of heavy traffic, moving from comparatively rough surfaces that caused a thrilling, half painful vibration in one's feet and legs to the smoother ones that made skating seem a form of flying, pre-sexual ecstasy, like Willie Wordsworth's sensation in his stolen boat. The aroma of newly baked Polish rye bread, still hot and silkily doughy when you bought it in the bakery. The divine charlotte russes sold in the streets: a sort of shortcake topped with generously piled-up whipped cream, doubtless sufficiently bacteria-laden (though no one ever thought of it) to lay the city low overnight. The Yiddish school I attended two late afternoons a week, whose teachers, far superior to those in the public schools, were genuinely literate: writers and scholars and thinkers eking out a minimal income from their knowledge of the Yiddish of Sholem Aleichem and the poets. And of course it was in Passaic, too, that I became a friend to the beautiful and gifted Eva E., my first little innocent love. She was to die of tuberculosis at the age of seventeen or eighteen, when we were already out of touch because of my family's peregrinations—we had long since left New Jersey for Boston and then the Midwest. The charm of our walking and talking and reading together lingers, disappears, returns recurrently like a cherished yet elusive state of mind.

I had no other friend "like" Eva until I entered the world of more conscious love (if "conscious" ever fits the case). But in Newark, where I began high school, I discovered adolescent boon companions and had my first taste of Latin and of French, sweet studies that opened unsuspected worlds at the same time that reading ancient history was doing so as well. In early spring, though, we moved to Boston, where I went first to Dorchester High School for Boys, famous then for food-battles in the lunchroom and, with a few exceptions, a reciprocally bored faculty and student body. Hearing that Boys' Public Latin School was a superb and demanding place, I rode the trolley there one day and asked the headmaster if I might enroll. He quizzed me orally, then and there, on Latin and mathematics, and forthwith invited me to enter.

Boston Latin School stirred me awake in a new way. It was a brief sojourn, just one year, yet confirmed my interests mightily and made whatever difference a school can make. It was a wrench, despite my never-failing pleasure in discovering new cities, to have to leave the delights of having a reasonable number of truly bright and thoughtful friends, the prospect of a scholarship to Harvard, and the chastely warm exuberance of Irene L., who attended Girls' Public Latin School, a paradise just a short way off. Nevertheless, autumn found me beginning my senior year in Cleveland, then a beautiful and tranquil, tree-lined city. There, at the suggestion of teachers, I took a scholarship examination for the University of Chicago. This was a happy coincidence, for Chicago was the family's next place to alight in its migrations—and thus it came to pass that I went to the University of Chicago near the start of its much-publicized New Plan, for better or for worse.

And thus, too, endeth my account of earliest years, much condensed as may well be imagined. All the experiences I've been describing have in one way or another entered my poems or shaped (or distorted, or eroded, or reoriented) my thinking. It is that fact alone, it seems to me, that could conceivably justify the public sharing of private memory. That consideration aside, it strikes me that my somewhat chaotic life proves nothing much psychologically—that too much depends on the luck of the draw, on one's inner gyroscope, and on the unpredictable benefits of adversity ("and the like, and their opposites," as my old Latin grammar put it concerning verbs and compound-formations taking the dative of the indirect object).

III

CONCERNING the *Sturm und Drang* of college years and after, there are films and novels aplenty to fill in all possible details. For our purposes here, it's enough to offer just a very few details. The most important is that I met my future wife, Victoria, when we were students at the university, where she took a degree in sociology and then went on, after three or four years, to become a psychiatric social worker. I, meanwhile, studied English and American literature, earning B.A. and M.A. degrees at the same university and, after the war, my doctorate at New York University. The war years themselves I spent at Michigan State College (later Michigan State University), where I taught Army Air Force cadets and Army Specialized Training Program engineers, as well as the usual civilian classes. (I had volunteered for air combat intelligence service in the Navy, but my physical examination showed I would need some minor surgery before being accepted. The surgery took place, but the surgical wound did not heal in time for me to serve either as a naval officer or as an enlisted man in the Army.)

I have jumped ahead a bit. My prewar university years were of course in the time of the Depression. I had felt the vocation of a writer—a poet especially—since childhood. The vocation itself was my special secret privilege, for it made me sure of myself in some strange way, persisting independently of whatever circumstances I found myself in. Thornton Wilder encouraged me, during the brief time he taught creative writing in Chicago. But I didn't have the turn of ego or, I suppose, the confidence of social status and family money, that enabled my exact contemporary (and later, my friend) Robert Lowell to present himself to Allen Tate as an insistent disciple. The starting points, the life-involvements, the clarity about one's place and rights within the culture were simply very different. All this reveals itself to me in retrospect only, for it never occurred to me to think in terms of literary self-advancement. In truth, I had no inkling of such things but simply drifted. I was always absorbed in literature, and scholarships and fellowships came my way, and so I became a graduate student while writing my poetry. Unemployed except for tutoring, I applied to the Federal Writers Project and was accepted on the basis of a sheaf of poems. I hitchhiked to Michigan one day to visit a friend teaching at Michigan State College and shortly thereafter was offered an instructorship there by the chairman, whom we had visited and who engaged us in what seemed to me an unpleasantly abrasive conversation. (It turned out he "liked challenging young people.")

So it was that I floated into the worlds of scholarship and teaching. I found it easy to publish prose and found myself writing essays and reviews in *Poetry* and elsewhere but in the main kept my poems to myself during the war years and for a few years thereafter. I cannot quite understand why this should have been so. I should like to think that something like modesty was involved; for a long time I cherished the notion, without quite formulating it to myself, that I would publish poems only when they seemed to me to "make it new," in Pound's famous phrase. Meanwhile, sending them to magazines to "get published" seemed too much like the world's ordinary business, like taking time to get a haircut or to check a bank statement. It was only later, after we left the comparative isolation of East Lansing, Michigan, that I realized the subjective usefulness of publishing one's poems: namely, that doing so frees one's psyche of the particular pressures they embody—frees it for more such pressures, it's true, but yet is a disengagement from previous fixations of style and form and literal subject. In any event, I escaped both the advantages and the disadvantages of developing "in public."

Everyone's life had special complexities during the war years. The victims of the Nazis had the worst of it, suffering the unspeakable. And there were the innocents of all countries, the children and others, whose "incidental" killing and maiming and terror are so taken for granted that the word "atrocities" is rarely used for what happened to them. Nor is it used for what happens to men and women in combat: the "normal" casualties of "honorable" warfare. For the rest of us, in this country at least, our discomforts were negligible. And yet the war distorted our lives, and often made us mark time, too. Deprived of the "opportunity" for adventure abroad, even if in olive drab, I pursued my solitary writing like an addiction, and was also immersed in a merry-go-round teaching program as new groups of soldiers kept arriving on campus. As we had anticipated my going into the Navy or Army, Victoria had accepted a fellowship in social work at the University of Chicago and therefore lived in the city through much of 1943–44. We contrived to be with each other as often as possible. It was a long, slow train-ride from Lansing to Chicago, or vice versa, in those days, with the trains full of service men and women and war-brides and people who, like us, had become inter-urban commuters because of the war's contingencies. Life on the rail lines had a restless, nomadic flavor. Conversation sprang up easily; people told all; it was a kind of street-life on wheels. I was on my way to Chicago the day the news broke of Roosevelt's death. A conductor went through the cars making the mournful announcement. A sleeping woman just ahead of me woke with a start and cried to her seat-mate:

"Whuddee say?"

"The President died."

"Whuh President?"

"Roosevelt."

"Who's President now?"

"Truman."

"Is he a Democrat?"

Writing, teaching, commuting, I laid waste the hours. My one writer-companion in East Lansing was Art Smith—i.e., A. J. M. Smith, a Canadian poet of distinction who had studied seventeenth-century literature with the formidable Herbert Grierson in Edinburgh and was the first influential advocate of the new poetry in Canada. He affected a "classical" stance as perceived by Eliot, Tate, and others while in reality he took delight in anything, however anarchic or romantic, that had the spark of life in it. He had perfect pitch in poetry; that is, he caught the rhythmic life and basic sense of a poem as quickly as anyone I've ever known, picking up its tonalities at once. We concocted a plan for a wonderful anthology of international avant-garde literature so dazzling and original that only we and a few other radiantly anointed spirits could possibly teach from it, and sent it to the college textbook department at Macmillan. It was the mad autumn of 1944, when the war still had its final agonies to go through, and when nothing and anything seemed possible. Art and I planned to attend the Modern Language Association meeting in New York that December, and wrote Macmillan we'd be happy to discuss the book during our visit.

Macmillan's college advisor in literature then was Professor Oscar Cargill of New York University, a pioneer in American literature study (then still only a very small part of the scholarly scene). He was enthusiastic about the book—or so he said—but knew it could not hope for more than a very few adoptions. At the same time, though, he persuaded me that I should leave the Midwest and come to New York University as a teaching fellow to complete my doctorate. I could work with him and write my dissertation on living poets, and in general could be in my natural literary milieu.

Ergo, the end of the summer of 1945 saw us bidding farewell to our little patch of uneaten corn and tomatoes in the countryside a few miles from East Lansing and setting off in our 1937 Dodge with our books and records and not-yet-born first son, David. Life really does change. The war was over, and I had the old gay feeling of moving into the unknown again.

Yeats, in another context, used the phrase "Gratitude to Unknown Instructors" as the title of a poem. With any luck, one's life is brushed by the wings of good angels from time to time. Often we do not know who the good angel, making a decision or recommendation or inquiry somewhere away from us, may be. But there are the known ones, like Oscar, who flew overhead as we drove along the Pennsylvania Turnpike, making sure that our good old Dodge didn't break down and that we'd actually reach New York. Art Smith was another such, exchanging poems with me, recommending my work to a magazine or two, and—in particular—considering me a peer despite his greater age and established reputation. And a writer must feel fortunately indebted—as I do toward Sheldon Meyer of Oxford University Press and the late J.G. Chase of Macmillan—to editors who have shown confidence and given good counsel over the years. There are other men and women whom I should name, as well, simply because, sometimes quite unwittingly, they reinforced my self-regard when some confirmation was devoutly to be wished. God forbid, though, that I should give public credit for benign acts my benefactors may perhaps have grown to regret! Yet such people are there—offstage or on it—in the theater of every life that has known some gratification.

Human indebtedness, in any case, presses constantly, and mostly unconsciously, on all our souls. I am aware, in writing these pages, that as I do so I am accompanied by shadowy presences, seen in another dimension as with night-vision, many of whom I would not even recognize. But there are also many I *would* recognize, figures associated with pleasure or grief or humiliation the psyche can hardly cope with, some deeply involved with my life and others known only for a few passing moments. And there are scattered instances when one suddenly *saw* a hidden reality, had a fleeting insight, grasped the glory or horror lurking in existence, either through personal engagement or just as a casual observer. I do believe we are tremendously indebted to all that we experience, happy or sad. The revelatory moment, objectifying the subjective, is what makes us human; and art, especially the art of poetry, enables us to grasp and hold the moment and explore its resonances.

I am not speaking abstractly. The accidental death of my friend Thomas Riggs, Jr., over thirty years ago, a young man close to our whole family and with a promising literary career just opening for him, makes him no less vivid a figure in my psyche than he was the summer we spent together, with our two young wives and tiny David, writing our dissertations. We read poems aloud, talked, swam, drank, played tennis and poker, in the Riggses' country home. Our conversations, those rich days, Tom's face—all still here.

I was on leave from Michigan State when we went off to New York, but we never returned except as visitors. Life there had been limiting and isolated, as it must be in any setting removed from the many dimensions and challenges of a metropolis. And yet Victoria and I had been given a blessed opportunity to grow up together in a quieter world than Chicago's and to experience the kindly friendship of my new colleagues and their families, who showed extraordinary tolerance toward our naïve young ways and radical attitudes. We were, after all, children of the thirties as a later generation was of the sixties, although we didn't dramatize the fact through the way we dressed or through taking street-language for our very own. The Depression, the still-lingering disillusionment of intelligent elders with World War I, and the grimness of what the Axis was already doing made for a considerably different atmosphere from the one that produced hippies, flower-children, the Beats, and the demonstrations against the Vietnam War, although a tortuous psychological bond links the two eras.

Of course, the thought wouldn't have occurred to you that the Third Reich had anything to do with your own life had you been a boy or girl from, say, Holland, Michigan, scuffing the autumn leaves on your first day as a freshman at MSC the year we arrived (1939) as the youngest faculty couple in town. The "other world" of vicious history receded a little even for us. We assimilated a bit of what it was to be a Midwesterner in the rural sense, and found it pleasant, and learned a good deal from our faculty elders. When the war crashed in on Michigan with a vengeance—altering the character of the auto plants, bringing floods of black workers from the South and of women from their homes into the factories, and superimposing the map of the world on isolationist minds, a certain innocence disappeared pretty rapidly. And yet, for all that, the cultural isolationism remained fairly intact. I think it was reflected in a heartwarming experience I had when I returned to the campus to take part in a conference on modern literature a few years after leaving. To my amazement, the entire English Department came to meet me at the airport in Lansing; it was a community, a family, held together by alienation from surrounding indifference to the life of art and ideas, and I was a son who had gone forth into the much-mocked dream-world of New York and was returning to tell about his adventures. (And in fact the title of my paper was "Alienation of Sensibility and 'Modernity' in Literature.")

After two years in the city, I was offered an instructorship at New York University, and so the break became final. I was indeed writing my dissertation on contemporary poets. It was called "Chief Poets of the American Depression," and served me primarily as an extended exercise in exploring and evaluating poetry, and drawing relevant conclusions from the study inductively—"with my bare hands"—concerning work by living, uncanonized poets of substance. In the course of writing the dissertation, I came to develop fairly close friendships with the three poets on whom it centered, all of whom lived in or very near the city: Horace Gregory, Kenneth Fearing, and Muriel Rukeyser. They were all survivors of the literary and political battles of the thirties, increasingly neglected—though at the height of their productivity—in the postwar repressive backwash already well under way in the late forties. They were all hospitable, and very unalike: Gregory increasingly conservative, with an air of distinction well-earned but vulnerable; Fearing boisterously witty, alcoholic, and mordant in his dead-accurate, Flaubertian hostility to cruelty and cant; and Rukeyser a most generous-spirited and affectionate woman, half-mystic, half-scientist in her pursuit of correlations (as in her study of Willard Gibbs) of historical, literary, and scientific tendencies in America.

As in my earlier relations with my parents, I experienced a certain natural conflict between my affection for these people and my need to think quite independently about what I saw in their poetry. They were all the real thing, yet they—especially Gregory and Rukeyser—had certain weaknesses as well. Clearly, I had to avoid compromising, and therefore corrupting, my inner seismograph critically: a felony that might also, somehow, warp my own poetry in the process. What happens in this circumstance (as in personal relationships that demand choices) is a curious inner click of detachment, enhancing affection because it becomes more free but also clearing one's mind for greater objectivity.

We had come to New York on the strength of my fellowship, our savings from Victoria's work in a child guidance clinic in Lansing, and the royalties from a textbook I had helped write. We found a small, inexpensive apartment not far from Manhattan, in a corner of Brooklyn that soon became our son David's first address. It was a working-class neighborhood, largely Italian, close to Prospect Park in one direction and the East River in the other. At that time the *New York Herald-Tribune* was still flourishing, and its Sunday book-review section was edited by Irita Van Doren. I liked the tone of her section and one day, thinking of ways to make ends meet a bit more handily, telephoned her and asked about reviewing. She invited me to visit her office, gave me a sample review to write, and in short order I became, for a time—almost until the demise of the paper—her chief poetry reviewer. I then, luckily, had a similar experience with Robert Hatch, literary editor of the *New Republic*. Openness to young free-lancers in tough New York was something I hadn't really anticipated. But the result, for me, of these fine editors' accessibility was that I had my choice of the most interesting new books of poetry to read and think about and review for a number of years. My *New Republic* reviews, actually, were often essays. When the *New Republic* moved to Washington, Hatch did not go with it, nor did my columns. A couple of years later, however, he became literary editor of the *Nation* and asked me to be its poetry editor, and so we worked together for another five years or so, until the end of my first Guggenheim Fellowship year in London, in 1961.

IV

THUS it was that various life-contingencies gave me a reputation as critic and editor before my first book of poems, *Blue Boy on Skates*, appeared in 1964, and even before my poems began appearing from time to time in various magazines. In the early 1950s, too, Macmillan (at the indefatigable Oscar's suggestion) invited Art Smith and me to write a poetry textbook, with a format somewhat similar to that of the famous *Understanding Poetry* of Cleanth

Brooks and Robert Penn Warren: that is, combining our own commentary with a suitable anthology. I had, naturally, been immersed in modern and contemporary poetry in my teaching as well as my reviewing, and before that in the reading for my dissertation. So I was happy to turn my august attention again to the nature and varieties of poetry in general.

Arthur and I were thoroughly familiar with the approach embodied and popularized in the Brooks and Warren text. "New Criticism," often ignorantly dismissed nowadays, was more a tendency than a united movement with shared principles. People as different in all sorts of ways as I. A. Richards, John Crowe Ransom, Allen Tate, Kenneth Burke, William Empson, T. S. Eliot, and a host of others were simply carrying their thought to levels free of the kinds of facile impressionism and academic historicism that were dominant at the turn of the century. Of course, sensitive response to what one reads—too easily dismissed as "impressionism"—is necessary if criticism is to be of any use. And scholarly knowledge, when not trivialized by pedantry, is indispensable for obvious reasons. However, twentieth-century poetic criticism could hardly help venturing on new paths—partly under the influence of scientific method, partly out of curiosity about the light that modern developments in psychology, anthropology, politics, and art itself might shed on poetry, and mainly because of interest in objectifying poetic process and structure. Whatever its limitations, "New Criticism" was a reflex of all this.

We called our book *Exploring Poetry*. We wanted to humanize poetic analysis, using a "poet's poetics" (a phrase that occurred to me much later, however) to emphasize the elusive, living stuff of actual poems. The book took us only so far toward the liberation of criticism and teaching from classroom formulas of interpretation, especially the habit of seeing poems as subtle discourse rather than volatile expression. We ourselves were not entirely free of the spell of such terms as "irony," "ambiguity," and "voice": terms useful enough at times but too readily picked up by minds impervious to the evocative elements that constitute a poem. One can hardly say that the liberation we sought has finally been achieved in most discussion of poetry today—but that is quite another subject.

Written over thirty years ago, *Exploring Poetry* was for me just a start. Most of my teaching and criticism has had to do with actual poems: how they take on their specific organic life and what they teach us about themselves, not only as works of art but as expression responding to life-pressures. From these concerns came my books *Poetry and the Common Life* and *The Poet's Art* and also my efforts to understand the leading directions of twentieth-century poetry in four other books: *The Modern Poets: A Critical Introduction; The New Poets: American and British Poetry since World War II; Sailing into the Unknown: Yeats, Pound, and Eliot;* and *The Modern Poetic Sequence: The Genius of Modern Poetry* (a collaboration with Sally M. Gall). These are all forays in self-education, whatever else they may be—for, despite the mountains of critical and scholarly tomes in our libraries, the ones engaging individual works with both human companionability and artistic empathy are few and far between.

What I've just done, in the preceding paragraph, is to describe my attachment to inductive poetic theory without going into the detail that would show the revolutionary implications of such exploratory engagement. We have ancient enough precedent, at least as far back as Longinus' wonderful insights into Sappho's most famous poem. But Longinus only started the job.

Self-education has always been my instinctive critical purpose. It is inseparable from an almost helpless participation in any poem I read, as though I had merged with its author and were in some sense thinking my way into it once more. From one perspective, every poem is a draft that might have gone beyond its present point and might have been altered in some interesting way or other; and so we cannot respond fully to its quality, or respect its elastic integrity, without understanding the tentative nature of even the most accomplished writing. It's for this reason, I think, that I've never felt a conflict, except of time, between my vocations as poet and critic or teacher: that is, between writing poems and thinking, or talking, about them.

V

AS I write this account, my sixth book of verse, *As for Love: Poems and Translations,* waits at the publisher's, proofread and ready to appear fairly soon. These six books are my only "authorized autobiography"—if any phrase so long and heavy can do for what, Paul Verlaine wrote, verse should be:

> Let your verse be a winged living thing
> Fleeing, we feel, from a soul in flight
> Towards other skies, to other loves.
>
> Let your verse be sheer good luck
> Scattered in the crisp gusts of morning wind
> That arrive breathing mint or thyme . . .
>
> ("Art Poétique")

These lines, in my translation from the lovely original, may at first appear merely intangible romantic fantasy, but in fact they suggest an empirical reality. The essential, internal drift of our lives in action—no matter what wise characterizations of ourselves we may propose in sober prose—reveals itself only glancingly, in quick flashes of reverie or in the way insights and phrases emerge from the subconscious while a poem is in the making.

I had meant to quote passages from certain poems here as illustrations, poems somehow related to my wife and children and others, living and dead, close to my heart. But now, when I come to the point, I see that many of these poems are too intimate and elusive—too much already "fleeing from a soul in flight"—to be commented on readily once they intrude their intractable selves within this hitherto orderly account. They will not serve to show the external facts, for instance, about our children: David, Alan, and Laura, now grown up—a writer, a composer and pianist, and a doctor respectively, and two of them parents themselves. Rather, they "tell" of other things: a cold night in London when I thought one son was lost and I went searching for him through deserted streets and "met" an image of irrevocable loss, the sudden memory of my dead father, instead; a moment of intense love after reproaching another child; a dream in which "one of us" was about to die and I learned with elation that it was myself rather than anyone close to me; a remembered scene in which adult family-members and friends stood in silent wonder for a minute around a newborn grandchild:

> A sleeping infant, babe of the stars,
> holds a roomful of men and women in thrall:
> the distance, untouchable distance,
> and delicate persistence
> light years away, in the sway
> of the streaming hours.

The passage is part of a poem which begins with memories from my Woodbridge days and ends with the later discovery of the obliteration of my little world there and with images widening the scope beyond my own personal memory. The lines on the "sleeping infant" do not name our little grandchild who occasioned them, nor do they offer any other *fact*. They tell much, especially in the context of the poem, and yet I shall have to let them—and other passages in many other poems that "tell all" about me and my world—speak for themselves.

It is interesting, at any rate to me in my present mood, to think how everything in a life flows together, no matter how disparate one's experiences and activities. My career as a teacher, which began as an accident, is an instance. I never felt "academic," in the nasty sense in which many poets use the word, although there is hardly an American poet now alive who has not taught in the academy and very likely found a home in it. But still, I've had a full-fledged, very professional and devoted teaching career. I have "taught poetry" almost from the start, from undergraduate literary and creative-writing courses to advanced doctoral and post-doctoral seminars in every aspect of poetic theory; and I sometimes think that I've directed more dissertations on modern poetry than anyone else. The strange thing, to my mind, is that while the teaching has been so varied and has involved so many different subjects and such a wide variety of works, my plain orientation has always been the same: thinking about what happens in poems, from a poet's point of view.

That word "thinking" I mean literally, not just in the sense that someone in love "thinks" about the beloved—although that certainly (all ye shallowly "anti-romantic" poseurs take note) is very much part of the process. One must think about poetry both in relation to one's own practice and in response to the practice of others very unlike oneself. If the labor is one of love—and it is—perhaps we should use the word "passion" to get at what that means; for sweetness and bliss are not the only feelings involved. Rather, conflict, endurance, self-doubt, and fear or despair have also played their parts.

Put another way, the critic's labor is an effort to strengthen one's understanding of poetry as an art—but as an art with tremendous human bearing: one to be apprehended as simply and directly as possible, through a poem's movement of feeling, to start with; and always so to be apprehended despite the most sophisticated ramifications. As a teacher I have tried—for my own sake quite as much as theirs—to encourage a group of students at any given time with whom I would be able to discuss poems beyond the most elementary levels. This was my larger motive in founding the Poetics Concentration and Poetics Institute at New York University just as, more tangentially, it has been in my criticism as well.

For all this, I cannot say how much I've "finally" learned. But at least I know something about living within poetry as a natural human element and about surfacing to look at that life objectively from time to time. The poets I've loved being with most have taken their art seriously in a manner unfamiliar even to most knowledgeable readers. They have had something like mystical faith in the revelatory power of language, at whatever cost of dire recognitions. W. H. Auden—who would utter almost any half-truth that came into his mind at a given moment—said, notoriously, that "poetry makes nothing happen." But he went on, in the very same poem ("In Memory of W. B. Yeats"), to instruct Yeats's poetry in what, after all, it must make happen:

In the prison of his days
Teach the free man how to praise.

—Safe enough advice to give a body of poetry as sure to outlive its creator into the distant future as any body of poetry can be—and whose "praise" is often in the elegiac mode, or consists of defiant or "giddy" assertions in the teeth of dark knowledge. But one of the chief forms of affirmation, in a very special sense of that word, achieved in poetry is its implicit belief in the organic coherence of one's life: that the bits and fragments and accidents of relationship and situation scattered through the years constitute a whole that means something of great import. Wordsworth's *Prelude* is perhaps our most obvious example.

If I try to summon up representative instances from my own life, in addition to those in the earlier sections of this account, I turn most naturally (in part as a way of avoiding the overly confessional) to periods when I have lived or traveled abroad. In the 1960s, on Guggenheim fellowships and at other times as well, we spent two full years and parts of other years in London, and briefer periods in Paris, and I sometimes returned to both cities on my own for a month or so each time. During the same decade, I also found myself invited to Pakistan to organize a conference on the uses of criticism in a developing country. (I discovered this only on arrival. I had been under the impression that I was simply going to give a few lectures on Western poetry and criticism at the University of Karachi.) A couple of years later, I had a period of lecturing in Poland, Bulgaria, and Rumania, and more recently have had similar missions in France, Switzerland, and, most often, in Italy. Our son David lived for some years in Barcelona, absorbing Catalan life and literature, and we have visited him there. The most exotic single sojourn abroad, I suppose, was a period of some five weeks in China, where the Distinguished Scholar Exchange Program brought me in 1982, and where I lectured in various cities, talked with poets and other writers, and walked the streets as much as possible.

The subjective side of these and other such periods is crowded with disparate memories that yet "connect" with one another and compel my imagination. For one thing, the shock of British hospitality in the sixties was overwhelming in its geniality, so that I was almost an immediate participant in the world of the poets shortly after arrival. London seemed bent on depositing new friendships on our doorstep every other day, including lifelong ones like those with the Welsh-Jewish-English poet Dannie Abse and his scholar-wife, Joan, and Al Alvarez, advocate of a new style of English poetry that would have some bite to it (and who took me tearing about in his hair-raisingly fast sports cars as though we were acting out in the flesh the kind of daring we both called for in verse). People seemed to have plenty of time for conversation, from the cheerfully if vehemently argumentative Eric Mottram to poets like gently intense Jon Stallworthy or the highkeyed couple Sylvia Plath and Ted Hughes, who came walking across Hampstead Heath to visit. Neither resembled their later reputations, on short acquaintance at any rate. Sylvia Plath seemed a typical gifted young woman of her American generation, eager to excel in everything quickly, at once confiding and proud, perhaps somewhat angry. I never spoke to her alone, and had no warning of her problems or the drastic choice she constantly considered.

Other new friends or close acquaintances crowded into those years: the ebullient, irritable Peter Redgrove; the stubbornly rural Charles Tomlinson (of Brook Cottage, Ozleworth Bottom, Wotton-under-Edge, Gloucestershire) who was cultivating one of the most sophisticated, symbolism-&-American-experimentalist-influenced styles in Britain; the ex-South African deaf poet David Wright and his wife, Philippa Reid, an actress whom I met while coaching actors in reading Pound aloud for a program George Fraser and I prepared for the Mermaid Poetry Festival—where, in turn, I met Louis MacNeice, John Montague, and other Irish poets, etc., etc. Those years, too, brought me to Christopher Grieve (Hugh MacDiarmid), the great Scottish poet, whose *Collected Poems* I had edited as virtually my first act upon becoming Macmillan's poetry advisor in New York—a mild-mannered, gently agreeable man who apparently reserved his wrath for printed diatribes against chosen literary or political enemies—and with him Norman MacCaig and other poet friends of his in Edinburgh. There too lived one of the anathematized, the Concretist Ian Hamilton Finlay. In Ireland, we had been warmly received by the novelist Francis MacManus and his wife Joan (one of those immediately lifelong friendships that take us by utter surprise) and were soon introduced to the group that included the composer Seán Ó Riada, the publisher and theatrical producer Liam Miller, and the poets Thomas Kinsella and Austin Clarke. Suddenly I was "discovering" the new Irish poetry!

Along with this little flood of names and circumstances, came certain jolts of private observation: our children's school experiences (as, for instance, Alan's being taunted by classmates with a song about some British victory during the American Revolution); a visit with Robert Lowell during his sad time with his new family in Kent, when he precariously served us each an artichoke and we shared a sort of chummy, gossipy misery for some hours; conversations with Clarke in his crumbling house that he neglected because his mother's will stipulated that it go to the Church after his death (and also because, despite the fact that he was then Ireland's most distinguished poet, he eked out only the barest living from radio broadcasts and newspaper columns); a visit with Grieve and his wife Valda in their damp cottage in Lanarkshire, during which he amazed our American children by his unselfconscious avowal that he was a Communist (and amazed me by seeing no contradiction between that and his being a Scottish Nationalist—although I shouldn't have been amazed, since I knew his work and also something of modern history); a strange meeting, in his favorite pub on Harry Street in Dublin,

with Patrick Kavanagh, who in some way became the conscience of literary Ireland: a reminder of working-class and poor-farmer origins, of elitist pretensions, and of the humiliations of poverty and alcoholism and other seedier realities of Ireland.

I must stop myself before launching into a description of life in a whore-infested hotel where I'd often stay, near the Luxembourg Gardens in Paris—a place recommended by Ramon Guthrie for its cheapness and its relative cleanliness. There my friend Serge Fauchereau, the dynamic lover of everything experimental, exciting, or genuine in art, or the Irish poet Montague, who lived in Paris for many years with his first wife, would seek me out for boisterous discussions and forays. I shall head myself off from all that by recurring to our Chinese adventure and memories of Chinese poets weeping as they read me poems about humiliation and worse during the Cultural Revolution; of tiny dwellings open to the street in which so many people lived their stricter-than-Spartan lives; of dauntless survivors of more than one anti-intellectual campaign, in the wake of Japanese and Nationalist atrocities; of workers in their thousands cycling to work in the morning and home again in the evening, impassive multitudes whose masked expressions gave an oddly nightmarish impression (like the packed-in masses of New York subway riders during rush hours). And there was one poet—I am not at all sure what his whole oeuvre amounts to—who showed me a single poem recalling youthful days in Souzhow that magically, with painful nostalgia, opened his living sense of the past to me in such a way that it became mine too.

I have plucked this and that from here and there, have not mentioned the gaudily exotic wild birds flying freely in the great marketplace in Karachi, or the deliberately mutilated beggar-children in the same place, or the great scholar of classical Chinese poetry who showed such exquisite courtesy to me while excoriating with sharp wit certain local philistinisms in his country, or the long evening with poets and thinkers in Jerusalem that went on and on because, after our very grave discussion, as we were all leaving, I asked if there were any good Israeli jokes. What a foolish question—but what a glorious result! *(Do you know the story of . . . ?)* I have not mentioned my quixotic intellectual comrade-in-arms, Emile Capouya, critic, editor, and nonconforming thinker, who shared with me the launching of the Macmillan Paperback Poets: a score or so of new volumes before we were stopped. Nor have I mentioned other close friends or, certainly, any of my more ludicrous mistakes. Stay tuned, if you're still with me, for more news on some other station, at some other time.

Contemporary Authors Autobiography Series, Volume 6 (1987)

Afterthought, Plus a Few Notes

THE occasional annotations in the foregoing pages are the original ones. Like the essays and reviews they accompany, they reflect what I was aware of at the time of writing; to alter them now would be to alter the book's purpose as well. For the same reason, I have left unchanged certain terms in earlier pieces that were innocent courtesies of usage in their moment—before "he" fell deservedly from grace as shorthand for "he or she," and before new usages like "Ms." and "African-American" came into their own.

Such matters aside, a very few additional notes may be useful despite my reluctance to weigh down the book with unwelcome baggage:

page 10. *The Seventh Cross* (1942): a novel by Anna Seghers, translated from the German by James A. Galston.

page 27. Gregory's "essay on Landor": "On Walter Savage Landor and the Elegiac Tradition in English," in Horace Gregory, *The Shield of Achilles* (1943)

pages 66, 86. *The Collected Poems of W.B. Yeats* ("Definitive Edition"): The description "definitive edition" (first used in the 1956 New York version of the edition published in London in 1949) has been called sharply into question since these pieces—"Sources in Myth and Magic" and "Metamorphoses of Yeats"—were written. See *The Poems of W.B. Yeats* (1989), edited by Richard Finneran; and Finneran, *Editing Yeats's Poems: A Reconsideration* (1989). For a rival collection based largely on the "Definitive Edition," see *Yeats's Poems* (1989), edited by A. Norman Jeffares, and its "Appendix," by Warwick Gould, arguing the "Definitive" case. For a comparative discussion, see M.L. Rosenthal, "New Work with Yeats's Texts" in *Yeats: An Annual of Critical and Textual Studies*, 8 (1990).

page 93. "The four passages from *Paterson*": Originally printed together with the essay "Salvo for William Carlos Williams," two of these passages (beginning, respectively, "There is a woman in this town" and "or the Satyrs") appear in Part II of Williams's *Paterson*, Book V; the other two (beginning "Peter Brueghel, the elder" and "The measure intervenes") appear in Part III.

Books Reviewed or Otherwise Discussed

(SELECTED LIST)

Abse, Dannie, *White Coat, Purple Coat: Collected Poems 1948–1988* (London: Century Hutchinson, 1988; N.Y.: Persea, 1991)

Aiken, Conrad, *The Kid* (N.Y.: Duell, Sloan and Pearce, 1947)

Alvarez, A., ed., *The New Poetry* (London: Penguin, 1962)

Ammons, A.R., *Uplands* (N.Y.: Norton, 1970)

Auden, W.H., *The Age of Anxiety* (N.Y.: Random House, 1948)

———, *The Collected Poetry* (N.Y.: Random House, 1945)

———, ed., *The Criterion Book of Modern American Verse* (N.Y.: Criterion Books, 1956)

———, *Nones* (N.Y.: Random House, 1951)

———, *The Old Man's Road* (N.Y.: Voyages Press, 1957)

Bann, Stephen, *Ian Hamilton Finlay* (Edinburgh: Wild Hawthorn Press, 1972)

Baraka, Amiri (Leroi Jones), *Black Magic Poetry 1961–1967* (Indianapolis: Bobbs-Merrill, 1969)

———, *The Dead Lecturer* (N.Y.: Grove Press, 1964)

———, *Preface to a Twenty Volume Suicide Note* (N.Y.: Totem / Corinth Books, 1960)

Berryman, John, *Homage to Mistress Bradstreet* (N.Y.: Farrar, Straus and Cudahy, 1956)

———, *77 Dream Songs* (N.Y.: Farrar, Straus and Giroux, 1964)

Blackburn, Paul, *The Cities* (N.Y.: Grove Press, 1967)

Brecht, Bertolt, *Selected Poems*, tr. H.R. Hays (N.Y.: Reynal & Hitchcock, 1947)

Brooke, Rupert, *The Collected Poems* (N.Y.: John Lane, 1915)

Brooks, Gwendolyn, *In the Mecca* (N.Y.: Harper and Row, 1968)

Bunting, Basil, *Collected Poems* (N.Y.: Oxford University Press, 1978)

Carmi, T., in *Selected Poems of T. Carmi and Dan Pagis*, tr. Stephen Mitchell (London: Penguin, 1976)

———, ed. and tr., *The Penguin Book of Hebrew Verse* (N.Y.: Viking, 1981)

Carson, Ciarán, *The New Estate* (Winston-Salem, N.C.: Wake Forest University Press, 1976)

Catullus, *The Poems*, tr. Horace Gregory (N.Y.: Covici-Friede, 1931)

———, *The Complete Poetry*, tr. Frank Copley (Ann Arbor: University of Michigan Press, 1957)

Char, René, *Hypnos Waking* (N.Y.: Random House, 1956)

Ciardi, John, ed., *Mid-Century American Poets* (N.Y.: Twayne, 1950)

———, *Other Skies* (Boston: Little, Brown, 1947)

Clarke, Austin, *Selected Poems* (Winston-Salem, N.C.: Wake Forest University Press, 1976)

Connor, Tony, *Lodgers* (London: Oxford University Press, 1965)

———, *With Love Somehow* (London: Oxford University Press, 1962)

Creeley, Robert, *A Day Book* (N.Y.: Charles Scribner's Sons, 1972)

———, *Contexts of Poetry: Interviews 1961–1971* (Bolinas, Cal.: Four Seasons Foundation, 1973)

———, *Listen: A Play* (Los Angeles: Black Sparrow Press, 1972)

Cummings, E. E., *Collected Poems* (N. Y.: Harcourt Brace, 1938)
———, *95 Poems* (N. Y.: Harcourt, Brace, 1958)
———, *Xaipe* (N. Y.: Oxford University Press, 1950)
Davie Donald, *Events and Wisdoms* (London: Routledge and Kegan Paul, 1964)
———, *Ezra Pound: Poet as Sculptor* (N. Y.: Oxford University Press, 1964)
Dickinson, Emily, *The Manuscript Books*, ed. R. W. Franklin (Cambridge, Mass.: Harvard University Press, 1981)
———, *The Poems*, ed. T. H. Johnson (Cambridge, Mass.: Harvard University Press, 1955)
Duncan, Robert, *Letters* (Highlands, N. C.: Jonathan Williams, 1958)
———, *Roots and Branches* (N. Y.: Charles Scribner's Sons, 1964)
———, *Selected Poems* (San Francisco: City Lights, 1959)
Eliot, T. S., *Four Quartets* (N. Y.: Harcourt, Brace, 1943)
———, *The Waste Land*, ed. Valerie Eliot (N. Y.: Harcourt Brace Jovanovich, 1971)
Fearing, Kenneth, *Angel Arms* (N. Y.: Coward McCann, 1929)
———, *Dead Reckoning* (N. Y.: Random House, 1938)
———, *Poems* (N. Y.: Dynamo, 1935)
Feirstein, Frederick, *Survivors* (N. Y.: David Lewis, 1974)
Ferlinghetti, Lawrence, *A Coney Island of the Mind* (N. Y.: New Directions, 1958)
Fitts, Dudley, tr., *Poems from the Greek Anthology* (N. Y.: New Directions, 1956)
Foix, J. V., *When I Sleep, Then I See Clearly: Selected Poems*, tr. David H. Rosenthal (N. Y.: Persea, 1989)
Freeman, Joseph, ed., *Proletarian Literature of the United States* (N. Y.: International Publishers, 1935)
Frost, Robert, *In the Clearing* (N. Y.: Holt, Rinehart and Winston, 1962)
———, *The Poetry* (N. Y.: Holt, Rinehart and Winston, 1969)
Fuller, Roy, *Buff* (London: André Deutsch, 1965)
Gardner, Brian, ed., *Up the Line to Death* (London: Methuen, 1964)
Gardner, Helen, *The Composition of Four Quartets* (N. Y.: Oxford University Press, 1978)
Ginsberg, Allen, *Howl and Other Poems* (San Francisco: City Lights, 1956)
———, *Kaddish and Other Poems* (San Francisco: City Lights, 1961)
Gregory, Horace, *Collected Poems* (N. Y.: Holt, Rinehart and Winston, 1964)
——— (and Marya Zaturenska), *A History of American Poetry 1900–1940* (N. Y.: Harcourt, Brace, 1946)
———, tr., *The Poems of Catullus* [See Catullus.]
Gunn, Thom, *Selected Poems* (N. Y.: Farrar, Straus and Giroux, 1979)
Guthrie, Ramon, *Asbestos Phoenix* (N. Y.: Funk & Wagnalls, 1968)
———, *Maximum Security Ward and Other Poems* (N. Y.: Persea Books, 1984)
Hamilton, Ian, ed., *The Modern Poet* (London: MacDonald, 1968)
———, *The Visit* (London: Faber and Faber, 1970)
Hassall, Christopher, *Rupert Brooke: A Biography* (N. Y.: Harcourt, Brace & World, 1964)
Hoskins, Katherine, *Villa Narcisse* (N. Y.: Noonday Press, 1956)
Hughes, Ted, *Crow* (N. Y.: Harper & Row, 1971)
———, *Wodwo* (London: Faber and Faber, 1967)
Ignatow, David, *Selected Poems* (Middletown, Conn.: Wesleyan University Press, 1975)
Jarrell, Randall, *Blood for a Stranger* (N. Y.: Harcourt, Brace, 1942)
———, *The Complete Poems* (N. Y.: Farrar, Straus and Giroux, 1969)
———, *Little Friend, Little Friend* (N. Y.: Dial Press, 1945)
———, *Losses* (N. Y.: Harcourt, Brace, 1948)
———, *The Lost World* (N. Y.: Macmillan, 1965)
———, *Pictures from an Institution* (N. Y.: Knopf, 1954)
———, *A Sad Day at the Supermarket* (N. Y.: Atheneum, 1962)
———, *The Seven-League Crutches* (N. Y.: Harcourt, Brace, 1951)
———, *The Woman at the Washington Zoo* (N. Y.: Atheneum, 1960)
Johnston, John H., *English Poetry of the First World War* (Princeton, N. J.: Princeton University Press, 1964)

Jones, David, *The Anathémata* (N.Y.: Viking, 1965)
Kennedy, X.J., *Growing into Love* (Garden City, N.Y.: Doubleday, 1969)
Kinnell, Galway, *The Book of Nightmares* (Boston: Houghton Mifflin, 1971)
Kinsella, Thomas, *Notes from the Land of the Dead* (Dublin: The Cuala Press, 1971)
———, *Peppercanister Poems 1972–1978* (Winston-Salem, N.C.: Wake Forest University Press, 1979)
———, *Poems 1956–1973* (Winston-Salem, N.C.: Wake Forest University Press, 1979)
Kunitz, Stanley, *Selected Poems 1928–1958* (Boston: Little, Brown, 1958)
Laing, Dilys, *The Collected Poems* (Cleveland: The Press of Western Reserve University, 1967)
Layton, Irving, *A Laughter in the Mind* (Highlands, N.C.: Jonathan Williams, 1958)
Levertov, Denise, *O Taste and See* (N.Y.: New Directions, 1964)
Lewis, Cecil Day, *The Poetic Image* (N.Y.: Oxford University Press, 1947)
Lowell, Robert, *For the Union Dead* (N.Y.: Farrar, Straus and Giroux, 1964)
———, *Imitations* (N.Y.: Farrar, Straus and Cudahy, 1961)
———, *Life Studies* (N.Y.: Farrar, Straus and Giroux, 1960)
———, *Near the Ocean* (N.Y.: Farrar, Straus and Giroux, 1967)
———, co-ed., *Randall Jarrell, 1914–1965* (N.Y.: Noonday Press, 1967)
MacNeice, Louis, *The Burning Perch* (N.Y.: Oxford University Press, 1963)
Matthias, John, ed., *23 Modern British Poets* (Chicago: The Swallow Press, 1971)
Mayakovsky, Vladimir, *The Bedbug and Selected Poems*, ed. Patricia Blake (N.Y.: Meridian, 1960)
Middleton, Christopher, *Torse 3* (N.Y.: Harcourt, Brace, 1962)
Montague, John, *The Rough Field* (Winston-Salem, N.C.: Wake Forest University Press, 1979)
———, *Selected Poems* (Winston-Salem, N.C.: Wake Forest University Press, 1982)
Moore, John A., *Science as a Way of Knowing III—Genetics* (Washington: American Society of Zoologists, 1986)
Moore, Marianne, *Collected Poems* (N.Y.: Macmillan, 1951)
———, *The Complete Poems* (N.Y.: Macmillan / Viking, 1967)
———, *Like a Bulwark* (N.Y.: Viking, 1956)
Muir, Edwin, *One Foot in Eden* (N.Y.: Grove Press, 1956)
Neruda, Pablo, *The Heights of Macchu Picchu*, tr. Nathaniel Tarn (N.Y.: Farrar, Straus and Giroux, 1967)
———, *Residence on Earth*, tr. Donald D. Walsh (N.Y.: New Directions, 1973)
Olson, Charles, *In Cold Hell, in Thicket* (Ashland, Mass.: Origin Press, 1953)
———, *The Maximus Poems* (N.Y.: Jargon / Corinth, 1960)
Pagis, Dan [See T. Carmi.]
Parsons, I.M., ed., *Men Who March Away: Poems of the First World War* (London: Chatto and Windus, 1965)
Plath, Sylvia, *Ariel* (N.Y.: Harper and Row, 1966)
———, *The Colossus* (N.Y.: Knopf, 1960)
Plumly, Stanley, *In the Outer Dark* (Baton Rouge, La.: Louisiana State University Press, 1970)
Pound, Ezra, *The ABC of Reading* (N.Y.: New Directions, 1960)
———, *The Cantos* (N.Y.: New Directions, 1949)
———, *Literary Essays* (Norfolk, Conn.: New Directions, 1954)
———, *Personae: The Collected Poems* (N.Y.: New Directions, 1949)
Raine, Kathleen, *Defending Ancient Springs* (London: Oxford University Press, 1967)
Reznikoff, Charles, *By the Well of Living & Seeing* (Los Angeles: Black Sparrow Press, 1974)
Riding [Jackson], Laura, *The Poems* (N.Y.: Persea Books, 1980)
Robson, Jeremy, ed., *The Young British Poets* (London: Chatto and Windus, 1971)
Rosenthal, David, *Eyes on the Street* (N.Y.: Barlenmir House, 1977)
Rukeyser, Muriel, *Breaking Open* (N.Y.: Random House, 1973)
———, *Elegies* (N.Y.: New Directions, 1949)

———, *The Green Wave* (Garden City, N.Y.: Doubleday, 1948)
———, *The Life of Poetry* (N.Y.: A.A. Wyn, 1949)
———, *Orpheus* (San Francisco: Centaur Press, 1949)
———, *The Speed of Darkness* (N.Y.: Random House, 1968)
———, *Theory of Flight* (New Haven: Yale University Press, 1935)
———, *A Turning Wind* (N.Y.: Viking, 1939)
———, *U.S.1* (N.Y.: Covici Friede, 1938)
Schwartz, Delmore, *In Dreams Begin Responsibilities* (N.Y.: New Directions, 1938)
———, *Summer Knowledge* (Garden City, N.Y.: Doubleday, 1959)
Shapiro, Harvey, *Lauds* (N.Y.: Sun Publications, 1975)
Simpson, Louis, *People Live Here: Selected Poems 1949–1983* (Brockport, N.Y.: BOA Editions, 1983)
Sitwell, Edith, *The Canticle of the Rose* (N.Y.: Vanguard, 1949)
Smith, A.J.M., *The Classic Shade: Selected Poems* (Toronto: McClelland and Stewart, 1978)
Snodgrass, W.D., *Heart's Needle* (N.Y.: Knopf, 1959)
Stevens, Wallace, *The Auroras of Autumn* (N.Y.: Knopf, 1950)
———, *The Letters*, ed. Holly Stevens (N.Y.: Knopf, 1966)
———, *The Poem at the End of the Mind* (N.Y.: Knopf, 1971)
———, *Three Academic Pieces* (Cummington, Mass.: The Cummington Press, 1947)
Thomas, Dylan, *Collected Poems* (N.Y.: New Directions, 1953)
———, *The Notebooks*, ed. Ralph Maud (N.Y.: New Directions, 1967)
Tomlinson, Charles, *A Peopled Landscape* (London: Oxford University Press, 1963)
Vallejo, Cesar, *Human Poems [Poemas Humanos]*, tr. Clayton Eshleman (N.Y.: Grove Press, 1968)
Wain, John, *Wildtrack* (London: Macmillan, 1965)
Warren, Robert Penn, *Brother to Dragons* (N.Y.: Random House, 1953)
———, *Promises* (N.Y.: Random House, 1957)
———, *Selected Poems 1922–1943* (N.Y.: Harcourt, Brace, 1943)
———, *You, Emperors, and Others* (N.Y.: Random House, 1960)
Weiss, Theodore, *Fireweeds* (N.Y.: Macmillan, 1976)
Wilbur, Richard, *The Beautiful Changes* (N.Y.: Reynal and Hitchcock, 1947)
———, *Things of This World* (N.Y.: Harcourt, Brace, 1956)
Williams, William Carlos, *The Autobiography* (N.Y.: Random House, 1951)
———, *The Build-Up* (N.Y.: Random House, 1952)
———, *The Collected Earlier Poems* (Norfolk, Conn.: New Directions, 1951)
———, *The Collected Later Poems* (Norfolk, Conn.: New Directions, 1950)
———, *The Great American Novel* (Paris: Three Mountains Press, 1923)
———, *In the American Grain* (N.Y.: Albert and Charles Boni, 1925)
———, *In the Money* (Norfolk, Conn.: New Directions, 1940)
———, *Kora in Hell: Improvisations* (Boston: Four Seas, 1920)
———, *Many Loves and Other Plays* (Norfolk, Conn.: New Directions, 1961)
———, *Paterson* (N.Y.: New Directions, 1963)
———, *Selected Essays* (N.Y.: Random House, 1954)
———, *Spring and All* (Paris: Contact Publishing Co., 1923)
———, *White Mule* (Norfolk, Conn.: New Directions, 1937)
———, *The William Carlos Williams Reader*, ed. M.L. Rosenthal (N.Y.: New Directions, 1966)
Winters, Yvor, *Forms of Discovery* ([?]: Alan Swallow, 1967)
Yeats, William Butler, *The Collected Plays* (N.Y.: Macmillan, 1953)
———, *The Collected Poems* (N.Y.: Macmillan, 1950) [See also *The Poems: Revised*, ed. Richard J. Finneran (N.Y.: Macmillan, 1989)]
———, *The Variorum Edition of the Poems*, ed. Peter Allt and Russell K. Alspach (N.Y.: Macmillan, 1957)
———, *A Vision* (N.Y.: Macmillan, 1956)
Zukofsky, Louis, *Prepositions: The Collected Critical Essays* (London: Rapp & Carroll, 1967)
———, *"A": 1–12* (Ashland, Mass.: Origin Press, 1959)

Index